An Introduction to Early Childhood Special Education

Birth to Age Five

Linda L. Dunlap

Marist College

Upper Saddle River, New Jersey
Columbus, Ohio

Library of Congress Cataloging-in-Publication Data

Dunlap, Linda L.
    An introduction to early childhood special education : birth to age five / Linda L. Dunlap.
        p.   cm.
    Includes bibliographical references and index.
    ISBN-13: 978-0-205-48872-8 (pbk.)
    ISBN-10: 0-205-48872-2 (pbk.)
    1. Children with disabilities—Education (Early childhood)—United States.   2. Special education—
Law and legislation—United States.   I. Title.
    LC4019.3.D86   2009
    371.9'0472—dc22

                                                                                    2008009673

Executive Editor and Publisher: Virginia Lanigan
Series Editorial Assistant: Matthew Buchholz
Director of Marketing: Quinn Perkson
Marketing Manager: Kris Ellis-Levy
Production Editor: Annette Joseph
Editorial Production Service: Omegatype Typography, Inc.
Composition Buyer: Linda Cox
Manufacturing Buyer: Linda Morris
Interior Design: Omegatype Typography, Inc.
Cover Designer: Jenny Hart

This book was set in Sabon by Omegatype Typography, Inc. It was printed and bound by
R.R. Donnelley. The cover was printed by Phoenix Color.

Pearson Education Ltd.   Pearson Education Australia Pty. Limited
Pearson Education Singapore Pte. Ltd.   Pearson Education North Asia Ltd.
Pearson Education Canada, Ltd.   Pearson Educación de Mexico, S.A. de C.V.
Pearson Education–Japan   Pearson Education Malaysia Pte. Ltd.

Photo credits appear on p. 508, which constitutes an extension of the copyright page.

10 9 8 7 6 5 4 3

Merrill
is an imprint of

www.pearsonhighered.com

ISBN 13: 978-0-205-48872-8
ISBN 10: 0-205-48872-2

About the Author

Linda Dunlap is a full professor of psychology. She has taught psychology and education courses since receiving her Ph.D. from the University of Iowa in 1980. She served as a part-time faculty member at State University of New York at New Paltz, Dutchess Community College, and Ulster Community College in New York from 1980 to 1984. Since 1984 she has served as a full-time faculty member and chair of the psychology department (1984–2005) at Marist College in Poughkeepsie, New York. In addition, she served as a child development specialist for the Saint Francis Hospital Preschool Program in Poughkeepsie from 1986 to 1994. This program provides services for children 2 to 5 years old who have developmental delays. Dr. Dunlap served as a board member and executive officer for the Dutchess County Child Development Council. She frequently contributes to articles on child development, teacher education, and parenting issues for national newspapers and magazines. She has also served as a consultant for local school districts. Dr. Dunlap is married and has a son, Jason, and daughter, Jennifer.

BRIEF CONTENTS

CONTENTS

3   *Intervention Services*   54

4 *Parents and Professionals Working Together*   90

6 *Cognitive Abilities*   155

7 *Motor Abilities*   182

10 *Health Impairments*   *284*

11 *Adaptive Abilities*   *316*

12 *The Importance of Play*   352

13 *Behavior Management*   389

14 *Transitions: Preparing for the Next Step*   *416*

PREFACE

This book is unique because it focuses on the wide variety of professionals who work with young children who have developmental delays. Most special education texts briefly mention the wide variety of disciplines providing services to children with disabilities and focus primarily on types of developmental disabilities young children may experience and the role of the special education teacher. This book is also unique because it provides in-depth coverage of the history of early childhood education, special education, and litigation related to special education services and the importance of using unbiased, highly effective assessments; an overview and discussion of the application of major theories; and an extended discussion of health-related contributors to disabilities (e.g., HIV, alcohol, cocaine) related to early childhood development.

The field of early childhood special education has undergone major changes during the past two decades, resulting in an increase in the number of books on the topic. The language used to describe children with special needs has also changed. The term *handicap* has been replaced with *special need* and *developmental disability* or *delay*. Children are described as "children with disabilities" rather than "disabled children" to focus on the whole child rather than the disability. This book introduces the reader to the terminology needed to effectively interact with parents of children with developmental delays and with their service providers.

Children learn through play and must be provided with developmentally appropriate and safe environments, which enhance play opportunities and ensure ample interactions with adults and peers. Families of children with developmental delays naturally expect the children to receive the best services available. Each family has its own unique needs. This results in the need for a variety of services. Most parents want to be actively involved in their child's education, but many do not know how to contribute effectively. These issues provide the basis for this book.

Special education teachers and therapists are dedicated individuals who know a great deal about their disciplines. They readily acknowledge the need to work cooperatively with other professionals, but they often struggle to do so effectively. Many professionals have limited knowledge regarding the terminology associated with other disciplines and may have limited training focusing on early child development. This knowledge is crucial to providing optimal service for young children with developmental delays. This book discusses various professionals and the services they provide.

Day care providers and preschool teachers are likely to have children with developmental disabilities in their care. It is valuable for these individuals to become familiar with attributes associated with a variety of disabilities and early childhood special education services.

This book begins with an overview of the history of education and special education, focusing on the history of early childhood special education. Chapter 1 also provides an extensive discussion of federal laws related to special education. It summarizes key litigation related to special education.

Chapter 2 begins with a discussion of various measurement concepts. It continues with an overview of the assessment of infants, toddlers, and preschoolers. The need to use culturally sensitive instruments is emphasized. Several standardized tests used to evaluate young children are introduced.

Chapter 3 discusses the impact of nature and nurture on children's development. Theories related to early childhood development are presented and applied to early childhood intervention services. It is important to understand the theories and sequences of typical development to provide an effective and least restrictive environment for children with disabilities. The types of early intervention services and location of service delivery are also discussed. Key attributes of highly effective intervention programs are outlined.

Federal laws require professionals to collaborate in evaluation and service delivery. Most professionals acknowledge the importance of parents' involvement in children's education but are not trained in creating successful partnerships. Chapter 4 addresses the importance of collaborating with other professionals and developing effective parent–professional partnerships. This chapter discusses effective communication strategies and methods to deal with conflicts that naturally occur among adults working together to provide services for children with disabilities.

Chapters 5 through 11 further discuss major areas of development (communication, cognitive, motor, social-emotional, and adaptive skills as well as health status). Each chapter describes normal development, theories focusing on these areas, assessment methods used to help determine if developmental delays exist, and the types of services provided to enhance these areas of development. Each chapter demonstrates how various disciplines enhance the development of the whole child, including cognitive, speech and language, physical, and social-emotional areas.

Collaboration is most effective when special education teachers and therapists have a basic understanding of each other's disciplines. Chapters 5 through 9 describe the services and terminology of professionals who provide early intervention services for young children. Each chapter also provides practical suggestions for intervention strategies for children with specific needs. In addition to discussing health impairments young children may experience, Chapter 10 discusses AIDS, cocaine, and alcohol—contemporary factors that may place children at risk and create a need for early intervention services.

Chapter 12 discusses the value of play, art, and music activities for assessing children's abilities and for integrating intervention services into play and art activities. Chapter 13 describes behavior management techniques. Chapter 14 discusses the importance of designing effective transition plans and methods of helping children with developmental delays develop positive self-esteem. It also discusses likely future trends in the field of early childhood special education.

This book is based on the belief that all forms of early intervention must center on the philosophy that children must be valued and that all children can grow and learn. Each chapter begins with key points, provides a chapter summary, and includes review questions and suggested student activities. Throughout the book there are examples of services provided for young children with special needs.

I want to thank the earlier contributors to this book: Eileen Taylor Appleby, Allyson Burns, Susan M. Covel, Marjorie DelForno, Sherry Dingman, Melanie A. Gardner, Susan Karnes Hecht, Lorraine Hedrick, Nancy M. Pate, Kathleen Ryan, Melinda A. Sage, Mary Scalise-Annis, Linda G. Seto, Mary E. Thompson, Awilda Velez, and Suzanne J. Ward. I also wish to thank Jessica Forney, Beth Maffia, Cristina Mauro, and Laura Spallone for their contributions to this book, as well as the reviewers: Ann Bingham, University of Nevada; Rebecca J. Cook, Eastern Illinois University; and Megan Purcell, Eastern Kentucky University. This book would not have been completed without the many hours of work, technical assistance, patience, and support of Dr. Gregory L. Dunlap. All of these individuals helped me better understand the value of supportive collaboration.

History of Early Childhood Special Education

1

*"By the year 2000, all children in America will start school ready to learn. . . .
All children will have access to high-quality and developmentally
appropriate preschool programs that help prepare children for school."*

(National Education Goals Panel, Goal 1, 1997)

CHAPTER KEY POINTS

- The history of education, particularly special education, has had a major impact on the evolution of early childhood early intervention practices.

- Young children receiving early childhood special education services are classified as having a wide array of disabilities and come from increasingly diverse backgrounds.

- Many federal laws have affected early childhood special education services.

- Litigation related to special education has affected early childhood special education intervention practices.

This chapter provides an overview of the history of special education, meaning programs specially designed to meet the unique needs of children with disabilities. (In this text, *disability* will be used to refer to both delays and specific congenital and acquired conditions.) This overview is followed by a discussion of federal laws which, in part, determine the basic characteristics of early childhood special education programs today. In addition, this chapter briefly discusses litigation that has impacted the legislative history of, and practices related to, special education. This chapter concludes with a projection of future trends related to early childhood special education.

History of Education and Special Education

History of Education

The history of special education programming is clearly tied to the general history of education. American education history begins around 1635 with the founding of the first private and public schools (Koenig & Holbrook, 2000). Special education history formally began in France during the late 1700s with the story of Victor, a child believed to have grown up with wolves. **Jean-Marc Itard** developed and implemented an education program to teach Victor (the "wild boy of Aveyron") language and social skills (Aiello, 1976).

Later, a student of Itard, **Edouard Seguin,** who emphasized the importance of early childhood education, developed a procedure for the use of detailed assessment information to develop remediation plans for children with disabilities. Initially, these techniques were not viewed as useful. In fact, until the 1960s the preferred treatment for individuals with disabilities in the United States and elsewhere was institutionalization (Rury, 2002).

During the early 1800s, **Friedrich Froebel,** a highly respected German educator, introduced the concept of programs much like modern kindergartens. In 1860 the first public kindergarten program was established in the United States. Soon after, the **National Education Association (NEA)** recommended that kindergartens be integrated into public school programs. By the early 1900s, approximately 50% of U.S. kindergartens were operated by public schools. Initially, the impetus for the establishment of kindergarten programs was the potential benefits to poor children. Over time the focus increasingly was on early academic achievement and socio-emotional development for all children (Ballard, Ramirez, & Weintraub, 1982).

During the Depression many school districts discontinued their kindergarten programs. Following World War II, kindergarten programs once again grew in favor. By 2000, 88% of 5-year-olds in the United States were enrolled in a school-based kindergarten program. Currently, kindergarten programs are not mandated throughout the United States, although they are found in most school districts. An estimated 3 million U.S. children are enrolled in kindergarten. Increasing numbers of kindergarten programs have moved from half-day to full-day programs; as of 2006 an estimated 50% of kindergarten programs were full-day (Mulligan & Flanagan, 2006).

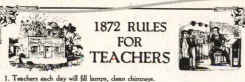

1872 RULES FOR TEACHERS

1. Teachers each day will fill lamps, clean chimneys.

2. Each teacher will bring a bucket of water and a scuttle of coal for the day's session.

3. Make your pens carefully. You may whittle nibs to the individual taste of the pupils.

4. Men teachers may take one evening each week for courting purposes, or two evenings a week if they go to church regularly.

5. After ten hours in school, the teachers may spend the remaining time reading the Bible or other good books.

6. Women teachers who marry or engage in unseemly conduct will be dismissed.

7. Every teacher should lay aside from each day pay a goodly sum of his earnings for his benefit during his declining years so that he will not become a burden on society.

8. Any teacher who smokes, uses liquor in any form, frequents pool or public halls, or gets shaved in a barber shop will give good reason to suspect his worth, intention, integrity and honesty.

9. The teacher who performs his labor faithfully and without fault for five years will be given an increase of twenty-five cents per week in his pay, providing the Board of Education approves.

OLDEST WOODEN SCHOOLHOUSE
St. Augustine, Florida

The roles of teachers and the rules regarding their behavior have changed a great deal.

The **Compulsory Attendance Act** of 1852, enacted by the state of Massachusetts, was the first general law focusing on children's quality of life. This act emphasized the importance of school attendance and resulted in increased public support for education. This law mandated that children ages 8 to 14 attend school at least 12 weeks each year, with at least 6 of those weeks being consecutive. This law did not apply to those who attended a private school for at least the same amount of time, had demonstrably already learned the subjects, lived in poverty, or had physical or mental disabilities. In 1873 the act was revised so that the upper age limit was reduced to 12 and the minimum annual attendance was increased to 20 weeks (Pulliam & Patten, 2006).

Special education, in particular, has changed a great deal during the past 100 years. In the late 1800s and early 1900s, children with developmental disabilities were often viewed as lost causes. During the early years of addressing special education needs, the use of stigmatizing terms such as *idiot, moron,* and *dummy* was common.

The United States has a long history of special education technology-related assistance. As far back as 1897, the U.S. Congress gave the American Printing House for the Blind a $10,000 grant to produce materials in **Braille** (a system of raised dots that blind people read by touch). Over time, commercial vendors have developed an increasing number of technology-related assistive devices. In 1996, of the 187,348 infants and toddlers receiving early intervention services, 13,525 had assistive technology devices as part of their services (U.S. Department of Education, 1997).

During the 1900s most U.S. states established at least one residential institution for individuals with disabilities; few special education classrooms were located within public schools, and in such cases children in special education classes usually were segregated from children in regular education classrooms. It was also common for special education classrooms to be located in substandard settings.

As discussed earlier, the concept of preschools or nursery schools (similar to modern kindergartens) was firmly established by the early 1900s. In England the **MacMillan sisters** established nursery schools (initially as health clinics) to provide for the emotional and physical well-being of poor children.

In Rome in 1907, **Maria Montessori** established an early education program, referred to as Casa dei Bambini (children's house) for poor children. Based on her experience as a physician and director of an institution for children with mental retardation, these programs were established after she developed an interest in the diseases of children and in the needs of those said to be uneducable. In the United States Montessori's methods did not attract interest until the 1960s and then were most popular with middle-class families.

During the 1920s, U.S. interest in nursery schools increased. U.S. nursery schools were, in part, based on the MacMillans' model, which emphasized the importance of parental involvement. By the 1930s there were more than 200 nursery schools in the United States, with approximately half being connected to colleges or universities and the other half being operated by private schools and welfare agencies. During the Depression the number of nursery schools increased due to the establishment of federal relief programs to subsidize unemployed teachers. Additionally, during World War II the need for women workers in support of the war effort led to the creation of additional nursery schools and day care centers for the children of working women. These centers were supported by the **Lanham Act of 1940,** which authorized federal grants or loans to public or private agencies for operation of public works, which were later interpreted to include child care facilities in war-impacted areas (Cohen, 1996).

In 1912 the **Children's Bureau** was established within the U.S. Department of Labor to address infant mortality, poor physical health among children, and exploitation of working children. Special attention was given to children with abnormal development or physical or mental illness and to preventing these disabilities. In 1921 the **Sheppard-Towner Act** increased public health nursing services and led to the creation of state maternal and child health centers. Services for the poor continued to receive more attention than those for individuals with disabilities.

In 1930 the **White House Conference on Child Health and Protection** recommended increased federal funds for programs focusing on "crippled children." In 1935, under **Title V,** the passage of the **Social Security Act** established the importance of the federal government's involvement in ensuring the well-being of children and mothers. Specifically, Part I of Title V authorized funds for states to develop programs to promote the health of mothers and children, with special emphasis on rural and low socioeconomic areas. Part II provided federal matching funds, in part, for the prevention of "crippling" diseases. Part III provided funds for state welfare agencies to develop programs for homeless, dependent, and neglected children.

The **Civil Rights movement** (1955–1965) and the 1954 *Brown v. Board of Education* decision helped ensure equal protection under the law for individuals from minority backgrounds. Subsequent laws would guarantee equal protection for those with disabilities. During this time, parents who had created special education advocacy groups in the 1930s began public advocacy for better educational opportunities for their children (Treanor, 1993).

During the 1950s an estimated 12% of U.S. children with disabilities received special education services. As late as 1962, only 16 states included children who were classified as **educable** (capable of being educated) under laws mandating school attendance up to a particular age (usually 6 to 16 years old). Typically, even children with only mild disabilities were not allowed to attend public schools.

In 1965 the **Medicaid** provision of the **Social Security Act, Title XIX,** focused on improving the quality of medical services for those living in poverty. An **Early and Periodic Screening, Diagnosis, and Treatment Program (EPSDT)** was developed to provide periodic medical, dental, vision, and developmental screening, diagnosis, and treatment of children younger than 21 years old whose families were eligible for Medicaid.

As recently as the early 1970s, U.S. children with severe disabilities did not receive a free public education (Gallagher, 1989). Typically, children with disabilities continued to be taught in separate classrooms or buildings. This often resulted in isolation and stigmatization. Usually, children with disabilities were not given opportunities to participate in many activities that occurred in regular classrooms, including art, music, and field trips.

In the United States the field of early childhood education has contributed greatly to current early childhood intervention service models. Initially, most early childhood programs were developed for poor children and provided some services to their parents. One of the earliest and best known of these programs was **Head Start** (Cahan, 1989).

Head Start was established in 1965 as a compensatory program for 4- and 5-year-old children in low-income families. It provided, and continues to provide, services focused on health, education, social services, and parental involvement. Head Start was expanded to serve infants and toddlers.

During the Kennedy Administration, the U.S. government became increasingly involved in providing services to children with disabilities. Advocates for children with disabilities called for the federal government to assume the primary role in providing leadership and funding to help ensure a **free appropriate public education** (**FAPE**) to all children with disabilities (Turnball & Turnball, 2000; Ballard et al., 1982). The U.S. Congress moved toward this goal in 1966, with the establishment of the **Bureau of Education for the Handicapped (BEH)** under **Title VI of the Elementary and Secondary Schools Act (ESEA)**. Following this act, a number of initiatives provided limited federal funds for services to children with disabilities. Additional legislative initiatives occurred during this time, including the 1968 **Handicapped Children's Early Education Assistance Act (P.L. 90-538)**. This act provided federal funds for demonstration (model) programs designed to educate infants and preschool-age children with disabilities. In addition, this law raised public awareness regarding the value of early childhood intervention. The U.S. Department of Education's **Office of Special Education and Rehabilitation Services** developed an early childhood branch promoting early childhood services.

As early childhood intervention programs steadily grew in number, the Bureau for the Education of the Handicapped recommended that these programs be integrated under a single federal law. The **Education of the Handicapped Act** (EHA, P.L. 91-230) resulted in 1970 (Martin, Martin, & Terman, 1996).

During the 1960s and 1970s, parents advocated laws requiring **local educational agencies (LEAs)** to offer special education services and funding for students with disabilities. Despite the passage of such laws in a number of states and the provision of limited federal funding through the EHA, many children with disabilities did not receive necessary services (Martin, Martin, & Terman, 1996). Although mandated in early laws, a FAPE was not being provided for many children with disabilities.

Prior to the 1970s, most children with disabilities were not educated within regular classrooms, and some states' laws continued to permit public schools to deny admission to children with disabilities. Litigation challenged these practices, and public schools gradually assumed the responsibility for providing education for children with disabilities, although services were typically provided in separate classrooms or buildings (Alexander & Alexander, 2001).

Two landmark federal court decisions, *Pennsylvania Association for Retarded Children v. Commonwealth of Pennsylvania* in 1971 and *Mills v. Board of Education of the District of Columbia* in 1972, clearly established that states and local school districts were required to provide appropriate educational experiences for students with disabilities. These rulings were based on the equal protection clause of the **Fourteenth Amendment** of the U.S. Constitution, which states, "No State shall make or enforce any law which shall abridge the privileges or immunities of citizens of the United States; nor shall any State deprive any person of life, liberty, or property, without due process of law . . ." (U.S. Department of Education, 1995). These decisions set the stage for additional special education laws. "States joined advocates in seeking the passage of federal legislation to provide consistency, federal leadership, and federal subsidy of the costs of special education" (Martin, Martin, & Terman, 1996, p. 29). These and other cases led to the **Education of All Handicapped Children Act (EAHCA, P.L. 94-142)**.

EAHCA was enacted to help ensure that all students with disabilities receive a FAPE and to provide funding to defray the cost of services (Martin, Martin, & Terman, 1996). The EAHCA required public schools to provide FAPE for students with a broad range of disabilities, including physical handicaps; mental retardation; speech, vision and language problems; emotional and behavioral problems; and various learning disorders. In addition, it mandated that states provide identification programs that locate and evaluate all children 3 to 5 years old with developmental disabilities or delays (Saranson, 1990).

The EAHCA also required **multi-factored evaluation** (**MFE**) to determine if children were eligible to receive free intervention services. It mandated that children be evaluated in all areas of development, including cognitive, speech and language, physical, social-emotional, and self-help skills. If significant delays were noted in any of these areas, which may negatively affect a child's ability to learn, special education services must be designed and put in place to meet the child's needs. Additionally, the EAHCA called for school districts to provide these programs within the **least restrictive environment** (**LRE**) possible. The EAHCA and its amendments continue to have a major impact on special education in the United States (U.S. Department of Education, 2002; Individuals with Disabilities Education Act, 2000). The law stipulated that services be provided in a way that would allow the child to maintain, as much as possible, a normal lifestyle. For example, whenever possible, children should be allowed to engage in the same types of activities (such as field trips) as those experienced by children without developmental disability or delay (Farran, 1990; Kirk, Gallagher, & Anastosiow, 2003). Although the LRE is not always a regular classroom, the law indicated that children should be segregated as little as possible (Ordover & Boundy, 1991).

Because free (no cost to parents) preschool programs are generally provided only to children who have developmental delays or are at risk of developing delays, such children often are educated in special early childhood programs. At the preschool level, including children with developmental disabilities or delays in regular education classrooms is most likely to occur when special education programs are located within buildings that also provide preschool programs for children who do not have developmental delays (Carta, Schwartz, Atwater, & McConnell, 1991; Shackelford, 1998).

Many preschool classrooms designed for children with developmental disabilities or delays remain segregated even when they are located in public school facilities. The idea of inclusion is slowly moving into the preschool special education system. Increasing numbers of special education programs are being designed to include child care centers, which provide day care and special and regular preschool programs within the same facility. In most cases, toddlers and preschoolers spend only a small portion of the day attending early childhood intervention programs. Therefore, there is generally sufficient time for most parents to create inclusion experiences for their own child—for example, attending a regular day care or preschool program in addition to the program for developmental disability or delay (Allen & Schwartz, 2001).

The EAHCA also guaranteed parents the right to due process, which provides for a judicial hearing if parents disagree with Committee on Preschool Special Education (CPSE) decisions regarding services provided to their child (Smith, Finn, & Dowdy, 1993). Due process ensures parents' right to be fully informed, fully participate in education decisions regarding their child, obtain mediation with an independent disinterested party, challenge the school district's decisions, appeal decisions before an impartial hearing officer, and have access to their child's school records.

The EAHCA also mandates that other services, including transportation, testing, diagnosis, and therapy, be provided as needed to children with disabilities. These services include "transportation and such developmental, corrective, and other supportive services as are required to assist a child with a disability to benefit from special education" (IDEA, §300.24, 1997). These types of services are referred to as related services. The Individuals with Disabilities Education Act (IDEA, P.L. 101-476) mandates that children be eligible to receive related services only after a full evaluation has determined that the child has a disability and it has been established that this disability warrants related services. For children younger than school age, this assessment must include evaluation of health, vision, hearing, social and emotional status, general intelligence, communicative status, and motor abilities [IDEA §300.532(g)]. If the child qualifies for special education services, particular necessary related services must be specified in the child's individualized education program (IEP) and must include a statement of the program modifications and profession that will be part of each child's service plan. The child should

1. advance toward annual goals,
2. be involved and progress in the general curriculum (as children do who do not have disabilities),
3. participate in extracurricular and other nonacademic activities, and
4. be educated and participate with other children with and without disabilities. [IDEA §300.347(a)(3)]

An IEP is developed based on assessment results. It specifies a child's needed related services, if any are deemed appropriate. An IEP specifies where and by whom related services will be delivered. It also must indicate when the services will begin, how often they will be provided, and their anticipated duration. Changes in the extent of related services cannot be made without convening an IEP meeting, although minor adjustments in schedule and services can occur without another meeting.

The **Handicapped Children's Protection Act of 1986 (HCPA**, P.L. 99-372) amended the EHA to authorize the award of reasonable attorneys' fees for those involved in due process lawsuits. The HCPA "provides for reasonable attorneys' fees and costs to parents and guardians who prevail in administrative hearings or court when there is a dispute with a school system concerning their child's right to a free appropriate special education and related services" [20 U.S.C. §1400; 34 C.F.R. §300.1].

In 1986 the U.S. government made a more specific commitment to providing early intervention services with the passage of the **Education of the Handicapped Act Amendments** (P.L. 99-457). Later renamed the Individuals with Disabilities Education Act (IDEA), this act amended the EAHCA and mandated comprehensive services for infants and toddlers (younger than 3 years old) who have developmental delays or are at risk of developmental delays, as well as for their families. This law was the first to focus on the needs of children with disabilities birth through 2 years old. The law was designed "to develop and implement a statewide, comprehensive, coordinated, multidisciplinary, interagency program of early intervention services for infants and toddlers with disabilities and their families" [20 U.S.C. §1431(b)(1)]. It focused on minimizing the potential for delays in children birth through preschool age and required that family members be allowed to participate in making decisions and receive direct services such as counseling (Salisbury & Vincent, 1990).

The intent of the law was to reduce educational costs once children reach school age. The law emphasized the development of methods by which states, local agencies, and service providers should identify and evaluate previously underrepresented populations (e.g., minority, low-income, inner-city, and rural populations).

The law specified that qualified personnel must provide referrals to determine eligibility for special education services within a "timely, comprehensive, multidisciplinary evaluation" [20 U.S.C. §1431(b)(1)]. It specified that it is appropriate to provide children and their parents with services and a multidisciplinary team. A parent or guardian must develop an **individualized family service plan (IFSP)**, which must be reviewed at least every six months and formally evaluated at least once a year.

Part C of the amendment indicated that states must ensure smooth and effective transitions and that an IEP must be developed and implemented before the child's third birthday. This provision ensured there would be no lapse in services if the child was eligible to continue receiving services under Part B. The law also required that a transition plan be developed if a child did not continue to be eligible for services.

The amendment also described due process, a legal concept ensuring that the family be notified and given an opportunity to be heard. It stated that when there is a plan to reduce or terminate services, families must be notified within a reasonable time frame and must receive a written explanation describing the new service plan or refusal to provide services, as well as a statement regarding the rights and procedures for challenging the decision in a hearing. Prior to such a hearing, parents are entitled to attempt to resolve the dispute through mediation. The law further indicates that when a hearing is necessary, a state hearing officer will hear testimony from both sides, consider assessment data and other reports, and provide a written decision. The entire process, including mediation, is mandated to occur within 30 days.

The federal **Family Support Act** (1988) and the **Child Care and Development Block Grant** (1991) emphasized the value of establishing early care and education programs. These programs authorized states to develop programs that would ensure child care, Head Start, and other children's services. Unfortunately, due to limited resources, program access was primarily confined to children of low-income families.

In 1990 the EHA was reauthorized as the IDEA, which resulted in services for millions of students previously denied access to FAPE. After passage of this law, most students with disabilities were in school, provided services within small classroom settings, and taught by specially trained teachers who focused on adapting instruction to each student's needs. Schools were required to provide any additional **related services** (services supplemental to the student's instructional program and necessary for the student to benefit from special education—e.g., physical therapy, transportation, and assistive devices) needed for students to reach their full potential. Students receiving special education services were increasingly being **mainstreamed** (taught, to the fullest extent possible, in regular classroom settings).

The IDEA changed the EAHCA's language, replacing the term *handicapped* with *children with disabilities*. In addition, it added autism and traumatic brain injury as classification categories.

The **IDEA Amendments of 1992** (P.L. 102-119) were the first amendments of IDEA. These amendments restructured IDEA into four parts:

Part A, General Provisions,

Part B, Assistance for Education of All Children with Disabilities,

Part C, Infants and Toddlers with Disabilities, and

Part D, National Activities to Improve the Education of Children with Disabilities.

The amendments focused on Part C. They designated federal assistance to states to establish early intervention services for infants and toddlers with disabilities (birth to 2 years old) and their families; indicated that funds were to be used to plan, develop, and implement state comprehensive, coordinated, interagency multidisciplinary systems related to providing early intervention services; and allowed states to designate funds for direct services not provided by other public or private sources or to expand or improve current services.

In 1997, the **IDEA Amendments of 1997** (P.L. 105-17) affected early child education (see Figure 1.1). The amendments strengthened parents' right to be involved in educational decisions affecting their children (see Figure 1.2), adopted a more

Young children often benefit from early intervention services.

outcome-based approach to assessment, and clarified that schools must educate children with disabilities in general education classrooms, the LRE. This process of accomplishing LRE is now referred to as **inclusion,** which means that all students in a school, regardless of their strengths or weaknesses in any area, are immersed, as much as possible, in the school community. Related services are provided at no cost to children and their families. State and local education agencies (LEAs) are responsible for the cost of these services.

The amendments also strengthened methods to ensure the provision of related services by establishing interagency agreements. These agreements establish a relationship between public agencies responsible for children's education and other noneducational public agencies within the state. The amendments require states to coordinate interagency agreements in a timely and appropriate fashion [§300.142(a)(4)].

Although IDEA 1997 does not require that related-services personnel attend IEP meetings, it does indicate that it would be appropriate and likely useful for these individuals to participate in developing IEPs. IDEA 1997 states, "Other individuals who have knowledge or special expertise regarding the child, including related services personnel as appropriate" may be members of a child's IEP team [§300.344(a)(6)]. Participation may include attending the IEP meeting or sending a written recommendation regarding related services. Additionally, states may legislate their own related services requirements, which may include services beyond those specified in IDEA 1997.

State Medicaid and other public insurers for children with developmental disabilities or delays are part of this agreement, which allows Medicaid to reimburse services provided within a school context. Although private insurance may be used

Figure 1.1   **Aspects of the Individuals with Disabilities Education Act (IDEA) Amendment of 1997 Relevant to Early Childhood Special Education**

- Individual Education Programs (IEPs) and access to general education curriculum: indicated that the IEP must focus on the student's ability to access and participate in general educational curriculum
- Involvement of the general education teacher: required that a general education teacher be a member of the IEP team
- Parental participation: clarified parental participation in the IEP and decision-making process
- Eligibility and evaluation: clarified assessment of children living in families who have limited English proficiency
- Attention-deficit/hyperactivity disorder (AD/HD): listed AD/HD as a separate disability category, making children with AD/HD eligible for services under the health-impairment category "Other."

to help pay for related services, parents cannot be required to enroll in public insurance plans before their children receive FAPE as defined by IDEA. In addition, the public agency cannot require parents to pay for services or even to pay deductibles or copayments. Also, the public agency cannot use children's benefits if this will deplete lifetime insurance coverage by increasing premiums or causing loss of insurance. LEAs may access parents' private insurance resources only with parents' written consent. This consent must be obtained each time the insurance is accessed. Parents can refuse to allow access to their private insurance. If parents do allow

Figure 1.2   **Aspects of IDEA 1997 That Strengthen the Role of Parents**

- Ensuring access to the general curriculum and reforms
- Focusing on teaching and learning while reducing unnecessary paperwork requirements
- Assisting educational agencies in addressing the costs of improving special education and related services to children with disabilities
- Giving increased attention to racial, ethnic, and linguistic diversity to prevent inappropriate identification and mislabeling
- Ensuring schools are safe and conducive to learning
- Encouraging parents and educators to work out their differences through nonadversarial means

access, the insurer cannot refuse to pay for related services, or delay payments; the school district is responsible for the cost of services.

In 2001 the **No Child Left Behind Act (NCLB, H.R.1**) was passed, resulting in greater educational accountability by states. NCLB required states to implement outcome assessment systems for all public schools and students. Although it did not include specific assessment requirements for children before third grade, early intervention often will be necessary to meet its third-grade requirements. NCLB also provided support for **Early Reading First**, which involves competitive grant funding for high-quality programs for young children, particularly those from low-income families. The act also emphasized the importance of employing highly qualified teachers. Although the law did not dictate this requirement for early childhood teachers, many states implemented it for teachers of young children. The **Early Childhood Educator Professional Development (ECEPD) Program** was a quality provision of NCLB, which provided competitive grants for schools to provide high-quality professional development for early childhood educators working with children birth through kindergarten from low-income families and high-need communities. Figure 1.3 lists activities funded through this program.

Present Status of Early Childhood Special Education

The **Individuals with Disabilities Education Improvement Act of 2004 (IDEA** 2004, **P.L. 108-446**), often referred to as IDEA '04, added several changes to IDEA 1997. As with passage of prior federal laws, these amendments have resulted in litigation, new laws, and further amendments relevant to early childhood special education (Gargiulo, 2003).

Amendments in IDEA 2004 affecting early intervention services included changes or clarifications regarding the complaint process, dispute resolution, consent for services, IEP content, IEP team member attendance, notice of procedural safeguards, requests for evaluation, time frame for evaluation, and transferring districts. In addition, the amendments called for employment of **highly qualified teachers** and prohibition of mandatory medications. Schools cannot make medication (such as that prescribed for children with ADHD) a prerequisite for attendance (Katsiyannis,

Figure 1.3   **Activities Funded through the Early Childhood Educator Professional Development Program**

- Application of recent research on language and literacy development and early childhood pedagogy
- Collaboration with parents to provide and support developmentally appropriate school readiness services
- Work with children who have limited English proficiency and/or special needs
- Selection and use of screening and diagnostic assessments designed to improve teaching and learning

Yell, & Bradley, 2001). IDEA 2004 and other laws will be discussed in greater detail later in this chapter.

IDEA 2004 provided critical changes to IDEA affecting children birth through school age with disabilities and their families. These changes concentrated on the IEP process, due process, and discipline provisions. A new section of the Act suggested that states minimize the number of rules, regulations, and policies to which school districts are subject. Figure 1.4 lists due process mandates of IDEA 2004.

According to IDEA 2004, parents of a child transitioning from Part C services (early childhood) to Part B services (school age) have the right to attend the initial IEP meeting to help ensure smooth transition of services. This provision does not require a Part C representative to attend, but it does encourage collaboration. In addition, it designates that when children transfer to another school district, the new school district must provide all services described in the IEP and provided at the time of the transfer, until a new IEP is implemented.

IDEA 2004 added several due process safeguards, including that parents must receive a notice of procedural safeguards once a year, at the time of initial referral, when they request an evaluation or copy of these safeguards, and when they file a due process complaint.

IDEA 2004 also mandates that parents have 2 years in which to exercise their due process rights after they know or should have known that an IDEA violation has occurred. The interpretation of the language "should have known" is critical. Parents who feel their child's educational rights have been compromised must file a complaint with the school district (and send a copy to the state) providing the child's name and contact information, describing the nature of the problem, providing supporting facts, and proposing a resolution. Further, school districts must file a response within 10 days unless the district notifies the state hearing officer within 15 days

Figure 1.4   **IDEA 2004 Due Process Requirements**

- Examination of records: Parents have the right to review all of their child's educational records.

- Evaluation: Parents have the right to obtain an independent evaluation of their child at their expense, or at the school's expense, when a hearing officer requires it.

- Prior notice: Schools must provide parents with written notice before changes are made to the child's identification, evaluation, or placement.

- Consent: Parents must give consent before evaluation of their child.

- Contents of notice: Parental notice must include an understandable description of proposed actions in writing or orally in the parent's native language.

- Impartial due process hearing, mediation, and resolution: Parents or schools can initiate a due process hearing, which first requires mediation or resolution of the dispute.

Source: IDEA 2004, Washington DC: U.S. Government Printing Office.

from the time the parents file a due process complaint notice. The state hearing officer has 5 more days in which to file a judgment.

In addition, the amendments mandate that parents go through a resolution session before due process. The school district convene a meeting within 15 days of receiving a parent's due process complaint. The school district has 30 days from the time the complaint is filed to resolve the complaint to the satisfaction of the parents, after which a due process hearing can occur. Additionally, the law indicates that parents may have to pay the school system's attorney fees if the due process hearing or court action is determined to be frivolous, unreasonable, or without foundation. The law also specifies qualification requirements for hearing officers.

To understand the present state of early childhood special education, it is useful to understand the characteristics of children and their families who are receiving early childhood intervention services. In 1988 an estimated 128,000 infants and toddlers received early intervention services. This number rose to 189,000 in 1998. In 2000 approximately 24 million children younger than 6 years old lived in the United States (U.S. Census Bureau, 2000). In 2000 approximately 231,000 children ages birth to 2 years received early intervention services under IDEA, Part C. This number represented approximately 2% of infants and toddlers. As of December 1, 2001, IDEA, Part C was serving 247,433 infants and toddlers. This number represents a 31% increase (from 189,462 to 247,433) from 1998 to 2001. See Figure 1.5 for

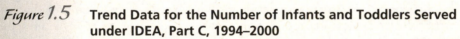

Figure 1.5   **Trend Data for the Number of Infants and Toddlers Served under IDEA, Part C, 1994–2000**

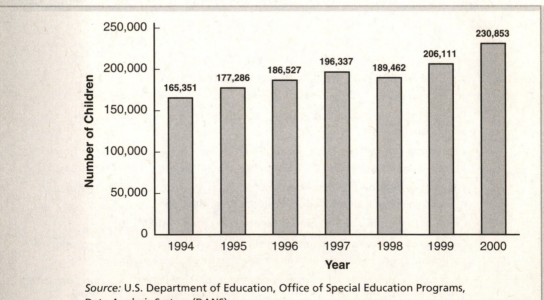

Source: U.S. Department of Education, Office of Special Education Programs, Data Analysis System (DANS).

trend data regarding the number of infants and toddlers served under IDEA, Part C, 1994–2000.

Of the infants and toddlers receiving services under IDEA, Part C as of 2001, approximately 65,000 remained eligible to continue receiving services under IDEA, Part B (services for 3- to 5-year-olds); 12,300 ineligible for Part B were referred to other programs not covered under IDEA; 6,750 ineligible for Part B received no referral to other programs; and for 12,660 eligibility for services was not determined.

During the 2000–2001 school year, approximately 600,000 children with disabilities ages 3 to 5 years received services under IDEA, Part B. This number represented approximately 5% of all preschool children. From 1992 to 2001, the number of 3-year-olds receiving services increased approximately 44%, the number of 4-year-olds increased approximately 38%, and the number of 5-year-olds increased approximately 22% (U.S. Department of Education, 2002). Refer to Figure 1.6 for numbers of preschoolers receiving services under IDEA for 1992–1993, 1996–1997, and 2000–2001.

Figure 1.6   **Numbers of Preschoolers Receiving Services under IDEA 1992–1993, 1996–1997, and 2000–2001**

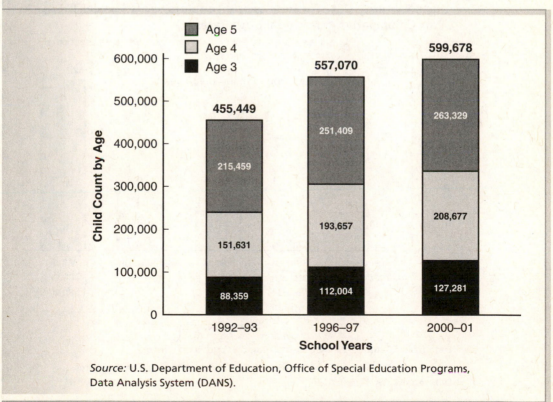

Source: U.S. Department of Education, Office of Special Education Programs, Data Analysis System (DANS).

Infants and toddlers ages birth to 2 years served under IDEA, Part C reflect the growing diversity of the United States. Most infants and toddlers receiving early intervention services are Caucasian. Hispanics constitute the next largest racial/ethnic group, followed by African Americans.

Currently, an estimated 21% of infants and toddlers (birth to age 3) receiving services are African American, and an estimated 53% are Caucasian. These numbers differ from the general population percentages: 14% African American and 61% Caucasian. Other ethnic groups served include Hispanic (18%), Asian/Pacific Islander (4%), and Native American (1%). Of those receiving services, African American children are younger (20.0 months) than Caucasian (21.7 months) and Hispanic (21.6 months) children when they first receive services. Figure 1.7 shows race/ethnicity data for infants and toddlers served under IDEA, Part C compared to national birthrates. Figure 1.8 shows race/ethnicity data for preschoolers served under IDEA, Part B compared to national birth rates (U.S. Department of Education, 2002).

In 2001, younger infants and toddlers were more likely to be classified as having a diagnosed condition or as being at risk (more likely than average to develop a disability) than older infants and toddlers. Three-month-olds were most likely to have a diagnosed condition, and 6-month-olds were most likely to be categorized as at risk.

Figure **1.7**　**Race/Ethnicity Data for Infants and Toddlers Served under IDEA, Part C Compared to National Birth Rates**

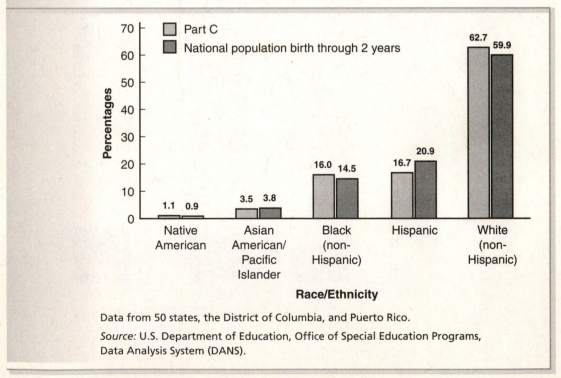

Data from 50 states, the District of Columbia, and Puerto Rico.

Source: U.S. Department of Education, Office of Special Education Programs, Data Analysis System (DANS).

Figure 1.8   **Race/Ethnicity Data for Preschoolers Served under IDEA, Part B Compared to National Birth Rates**

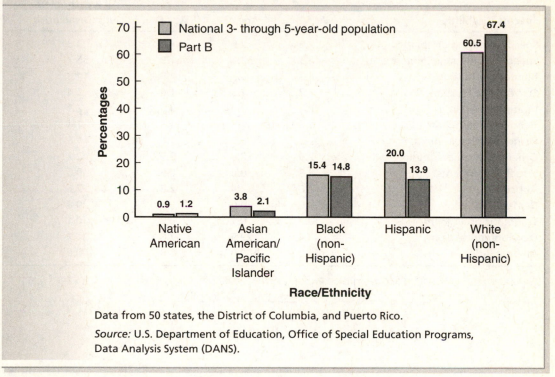

Data from 50 states, the District of Columbia, and Puerto Rico.

Source: U.S. Department of Education, Office of Special Education Programs, Data Analysis System (DANS).

Most infants and toddlers who entered into intervention services with a developmental delay were 27 months old or older (U.S. Department of Education, 2002).

There is a vast array of disabilities among young children. Infants and toddlers with disabilities are most likely to be classified as having prenatal/perinatal (during pregnancy/after birth) abnormalities or motor delays, whereas preschoolers with disabilities are most frequently classified as having speech or language delays. Males are more likely than females to receive early childhood intervention services, especially if they have developmental delays, although girls tend to enter intervention services earlier. Most children eligible for services are classified with developmental delays.

Children are most likely to begin services in their first or third year of life. Those with diagnosed or risk conditions are most likely to enter services before their first birthday. Those with developmental delays usually enter after their second birthday. Of infants who receive services, most have prenatal or perinatal abnormalities, followed by motor delays or impairments. Older children are more likely than younger children to have speech or communication impairments or delays (U.S. Department of Education, 2002). Table 1.1 lists the percentages of preschoolers, by age, receiving services during 2000–2001.

Table 1.1	Percentage of Preschoolers Receiving Services during 2000–2001		
Specific Disabilities	**Age 3**	**Age 4**	**Age 5**	**All Preschoolers with Disabilities**
Specific learning disabilities	2.6	2.9	4.1	3.3
Speech or language impairments	46.3	52.1	61.9	55.2
Mental retardation	4.1	3.7	4.8	4.3
Emotional disturbance	1.2	1.3	1.6	1.4
Multiple disabilities	2.4	2.0	2.0	2.1
Hearing impairments	1.6	1.3	1.3	1.4
Orthopedic impairments	2.3	1.7	1.6	1.8
Other health impairments	2.5	2.0	2.2	2.2
Visual impairments	0.8	0.6	0.5	0.6
Autism	2.6	2.4	2.8	2.6
Deaf-blindness	0.0	0.0	0.0	0.0
Traumatic brain injury	0.2	0.1	0.2	0.1
Developmental delay	33.4	29.9	17.0	24.9
All disabilities	100.0	100.0	100.0	100.0

Source: Washington, DC: U.S. Government Printing Office, 2006.

Families receiving early intervention services are more likely to be poor. Families whose incomes are below poverty level constitute approximately 27% of families receiving early intervention services, but only 21% of the general population. A higher percentage of children from families with low incomes are provided services than children from families who have higher incomes. In addition, families classified as ethnic minorities who are receiving services are more likely to be poor. (Approximately half of all African American families receiving services are classified as poor.)

Children who receive services at younger ages have mothers who have less education and income and who are less likely to be employed. Children receiving services who have diagnosed conditions tend to have mothers with higher educational levels. Those receiving services who are categorized as at risk are more likely to live in low-income families; live with someone other than their biological parents; have older employed mothers; and have mothers who received prenatal public assistance, receive food stamps, and live in public housing. In addition, children in foster care are significantly overrepresented among children who receive early childhood intervention services and they enter services earlier than other children (Ysseldyke, Algozzine, & Thurlow, 2000).

No single set of characteristics readily describes children and their families who are receiving early intervention services. Effective early intervention services must be provided in a wide variety of ways to meet the diversity of children's and families' needs. Box 1.1 presents a case study relevant to the history of early childhood special education.

Special education teachers who primarily serve students with disabilities ages 3 to 5 years classify themselves as Asian (2%), Black (5.8%), White (90%) and other (2%). The lack of diversity among teachers reflects the lack of diversity in college enrollment: 63.1% of White high school graduates were college students, whereas only 54.8% of Black graduates and 51.5% of Hispanic graduates were (U.S. Department of Labor, 2002).

The terms applied to individuals with disabilities have gone through many changes. The current preference is for **people first language,** which describes what a person *has,* not what they *are.* That is, a child is a child first. This philosophy leads to the preferred practice of saying "child with a disability" or "child with autism" rather than "disabled child" or "autistic child."

Use of the term *handicapped* has been considered inappropriate for some time. Most recently, use of the phrase *special needs* has been questioned. Some people consider it inappropriate to refer to someone as "special." Currently it is recommended that *special needs* be replaced with the terms *impairments, developmental delays,* or *disabilities.*

Box 1.1 *Aaron*

After learning that they would be having their first child, Elizabeth and John could not have been happier. Elizabeth, a healthy 23-year-old, anticipated an easy pregnancy and birth because her mother and three sisters had all experienced problem-free births for a total of 12 children.

As anticipated, Elizabeth felt wonderful throughout her pregnancy and went into labor one day after the due date. She was in labor ten hours, less than the average length of labor for first-borns. As delivery progressed, everything occurred as anticipated.

Elizabeth and John were thrilled to learn the sex of their new baby boy. They had hoped for a boy, because Elizabeth's three sisters had all had girls. However, their main desire was that their baby be healthy. Their baby, Aaron, weighed 7 pounds, 3 ounces and was 20 inches long—a normal weight and length. Elizabeth and John could not wait to begin caring for their newborn.

Soon after delivery, the doctor who had aided in the delivery entered the room with a pediatrician. As they gazed at Elizabeth holding Aaron and John standing beside them, the doctors looked concerned. John asked, "Is something wrong?"

After a pause, Dr. Gray said, "I'm afraid I have some sad news," and he told Elizabeth and John that Aaron had Down syndrome. Dr. Gray explained the characteristics associated with Down syndrome and the services that Aaron likely would require.

Imagine Aaron was born in the early 1900s. Now imagine he was born in 2006. Consider the difference in terms of Aaron's future and that of his parents.

Litigation Affecting Early Childhood Special Education

For more than 50 years, litigation and court decisions related to special education have clearly established that individuals with disabilities are protected by the same laws that guarantee equal protection under the law without discrimination based on disability. That is, individuals with disabilities are protected by the Fourteenth Amendment and the same ruling that guaranteed rights on the basis of race. Although many specific federal laws and federal and state litigations have challenged these rights, this guarantee remains.

The court decision regarding *Brown v. Board of Education* set the stage for litigation and federal laws related to special education. On May 17, 1954, the U.S. Supreme Court ruled that schools must provide students with equal protection under the law, without discrimination on the basis of race. This ruling provided the basis for laws that prevent discrimination based on disabilities. The Justices declared that "separate educational facilities are inherently unequal" and, as such, violate the Fourteenth Amendment, which guarantees all citizens "equal protection of the laws" and that exclusion "generates a feeling of inferiority as to their status in the community that may affect their hearts and minds in a way unlikely to ever be undone" [*Brown v. Board of Education*, 347 U.S. 483 (1954)].

Following this case, one of the first and most relevant cases was ruled on in 1963. **Roncker v. Walter** addressed the issue of bringing educational services to the child versus bringing the child to the services. The case was resolved in favor of integrated rather than segregated placement and established **the principle of portability:** "If a desirable service currently provided in a segregated setting can feasibly be delivered in an integrated setting, it would be inappropriate under P.L. 94-142 to provide the service in a segregated environment" [*Roncker v. Walter*, 700 F.2d 1058 (6th Cir.) at 1063, cert. denied, 464 U.S. 864 (1983)]. These questions were asked to determine whether mainstreaming should occur:

1. What in the segregated program makes it better than a mainstreaming program?
2. Can these things (e.g., modified curriculum, different teacher) be provided in the regular school environment?

The Court ruled that placement decisions must be made on an individual basis and that school districts that automatically place children in a predetermined type of school solely on the basis of their disability (e.g., mental retardation) rather than on the basis of the IEP violate federal laws.

It is not enough for a district to simply claim that a segregated program is superior. In a case where the segregated facility is considered superior, the court should determine whether the services which make the placement superior could be feasibly provided in a non-segregated setting (i.e. regular class). If they can, the placement in the segregated school would be inappropriate under the act (I.D.E.A.). [*Roncker v. Walter*, 700 F.2d 1058 (6th Cir.) at 1063, cert. denied, 464 U.S. 864 (1983)]

Perhaps the most far-reaching court ruling was *Mills v. Board of Education of the District of Columbia*. In 1972 the U.S. District Court established that school districts could not refuse to serve children with disabilities on the grounds that they had inadequate resources. The ruling indicated that the Fourteenth Amendment requires school districts to provide children with disabilities access to a free public education appropriate to their needs, regardless of the type of disability.

In addition, the ruling required districts to ensure full procedure protection, including notice of proposed changes in services and access to school records and a right to be heard and represented by legal counsel at a hearing. Further, school districts were constitutionally prohibited from planning special education programs in advance and offering them to students only as long as space was available. Chief Justice Earl Warren stated, "A sense of inferiority affects the motivation of the child to learn" [*Mills v. Board of Education, DC*, 348 F.Supp. 866 (D. DC 1972)].

The 1989 the ruling in *Daniel R. R. v. State Board of Education* declared that regular education placement is appropriate if a child with a disability can receive a satisfactory education, even if it is not the best academic setting for the child, because nonacademic benefits must be considered. The Court stated, "Academic achievement is not the only purpose of mainstreaming. Integrating a handicapped child into a nonhandicapped environment may be beneficial in and of itself . . . even if the child cannot flourish academically" [*Daniel R. R. v. State Board of Education,* 874 F.2d 1036 (5th Cir. 1989)]. The Court of Appeals developed a two-pronged test to determine if a district's actions are in compliance with the IDEA:

1. With the use of supplemental aids and services, can education be satisfactorily achieved in the regular classroom?
2. If it cannot, has the school mainstreamed the child to the maximum extent appropriate?

The Court stated, "The needs of the handicapped child and the needs of the nonhandicapped students in the pre-kindergarten class tip the balance in favor of placing Daniel in special education" [*Daniel R. R. v. State Board of Education*, 874 F.2d 1036 (5th Cir. 1989)].

The 2006 Supreme Court case *Arlington Central School District v. Murphy* addressed whether parents can seek reimbursement for experts or consultants. The New York Arlington Central School District argued that the IDEA's spending clause must be interpreted very narrowly; therefore, the U.S. Court of Appeals for the Second Circuit erred (1) in holding that the court was authorized to award expert fees to the parents of a child with a disability who is a prevailing party under the IDEA and (2) in awarding expert witness fees. The district contended, "Congress failed to provide in IDEA the 'explicit statutory authority' that would authorize payment of expert witness fees" (Petitioner's Brief, pages 18–19). The parents and respondents, Pearl and Theodore Murphy, argued that the IDEA's text confirms that expert costs may be recovered by prevailing parents. They argued that Congress used *costs* in its ordinary sense—to cover the expenses that parents incur in IDEA proceedings, including the costs of consultants and experts. The Supreme Court ruled 6 to 3 that the IDEA does not authorize parents who prevail in special education cases to seek reimbursement from school districts for fees paid to experts.

Conclusions

Educational practices have changed greatly over the past 4 centuries. These changes have laid the groundwork for the education of children with disabilities. Modern special education began with the 1972 *Mills v. Board of Education of the District of Columbia* Supreme Court ruling that guaranteed equal protection under the Fourteenth Amendment to students with disabilities, requiring that adequate alternative educational services be provided.

Soon after, in 1975, the EAHCA became law. It mandated that all students with disabilities receive FAPE and funding to help defray the costs of special education programs. The EAHCA also required public schools to provide FAPE for students with a broad range of disabilities and to do so in the LRE. The EAHCA set the stage for a wide range of federal laws guiding early childhood special education practices. Clearly, children with disabilities born in the 1600s faced very different futures than those born today.

CHAPTER SUMMARY

- Over the past 400 years, educational practices have significantly changed. The changes have impacted current special education laws and guided the development of early childhood and early intervention practices.

- Special education laws that focused on older children have had a major impact on services provided to young children.

- A diverse group of children currently receive early childhood special education services.

- Federal laws that have affected current early childhood special education practices reflect the belief that all children with disabilities have a right to FAPE, which must be provided without discrimination, as guaranteed by the Fourteenth Amendment.

- A variety of litigation that intensified in the early 1960s led to increased services for individuals with disabilities.

CHAPTER KEY TERMS

Jean-Marc Itard
Edouard Seguin
Friedrich Froebel
National Education Association (NEA)
Compulsory Attendance Act

Braille
MacMillan sisters
Maria Montessori
Lanham Act of 1940
Children's Bureau

Sheppard-Towner Act
White House Conference on Child Health
 and Protection
Title V
Social Security Act
Civil Rights movement
Brown v. Board of Education
educable
Medicaid
Social Security Act, Title XIX
Early and Periodic Screening, Diagnosis, and
 Treatment Program (EPSDT)
Head Start
free appropriate public education (FAPE)
Bureau of Education for the Handicapped (BEH)
Title VI of the Elementary and Secondary Schools
 Act (ESEA)
Handicapped Children's Early Education
 Assistance Act (P.L. 90-538)
Office of Special Education and Rehabilitation
 Services
Education of the Handicapped Act (EHA,
 P.L. 91-230)
local educational agency (LEA)
*Pennsylvania Association for Retarded Children v.
 Commonwealth of Pennsylvania*
*Mills v. Board of Education of the District
 of Columbia*
Fourteenth Amendment
Education of All Handicapped Children Act
 (EAHCA, P.L. 94-142)
multi-factored evaluation (MFE)

least restrictive environment (LRE)
due process
Committee on Preschool Special Education
 (CPSE)
Individuals with Disabilities Education Act
 (IDEA, P.L. 101-476)
individualized education program (IEP)
Handicapped Children's Protection Act of 1986
 (HCPA, P.L. 99-372)
Education of the Handicapped Act (EHA)
 Amendments (P.L. 99-457)
individualized family service plan (IFSP)
Family Support Act
Child Care and Development Block Grant
related services
mainstreaming
IDEA Amendments of 1992 (P.L. 102-119)
IDEA Amendments of 1997 (P.L. 105-17)
inclusion
No Child Left Behind Act (NCLB, H.R.1)
Early Reading First
Early Childhood Educator Professional
 Development (ECEPD) Program
Individuals with Disabilities Education
 Improvement Act of 2004 (IDEA 2004,
 P.L. 108-446)
highly qualified teachers
people first language
Roncker v. Walter
principle of portability
Daniel R. R. v. State Board of Education
Arlington Central School District v. Murphy

REVIEW QUESTIONS

1. In the early 1980s it was difficult for a child
 with disabilities to access equal and appropriate education. How has this situation changed
 over the years?

2. What federal laws have contributed to the increase in early intervention services since the
 1960s?

3. Which major areas are evaluated when a child
 is suspected of having a developmental delay?

4. What does "least restrictive environment" mean?

SUGGESTED STUDENT ACTIVITIES

1. Research the state requirements governing services for children with developmental delays in your state. Find out what services are available for families and children.

2. What additional federal laws do you think might enhance early intervention services?

3. Research changes or reauthorizations of the Individuals with Disabilities Education Improvement Act of 2004 (P.L. 108-446). What are the significant changes?

4. Contact an organization that advocates for early intervention. Find out what services they provide and which issues they are currently addressing.

The Assessment Process

CHAPTER KEY POINTS

- It is important to understand the meaning of various measurement concepts.

- Assessment of infants, toddlers, and preschoolers requires unique instruments and skills.

- Valid assessments are culturally sensitive.

- The assessment process has several steps.

- Federal laws mandate specific assessment procedures to determine if young children have developmental delays.

- Both developmental delay and disability are used to describe children's eligibility for early intervention.

- Many standardized tests appropriate for screenings and full evaluations are available.

- Research evaluating early intervention services indicates these services are effective.

Within the context of early childhood special education, assessment focuses on gathering and analyzing information primarily for diagnosis, placement, program development, therapy, service delivery, and instructional decisions (Schorr & Yankelovich, 2000; Shepard, Kagan, & Wurtz, 1998). The assessment process includes referral, screening, full evaluation, determination of eligibility for services, and guidance, monitoring, and evaluation of program planning.

Concerns about children's rate of development lead to referrals for evaluation. Understanding possible causes of delays and disabilities helps in determining whether children should be referred for assessment (Illingworth, 1987; Westling & Koorland, 1989). A screening determines if a full evaluation is warranted. To best understand the assessment process it is helpful to understand key concepts.

Research suggests that early intervention may help prevent or reduce the need for later special education services. In addition, research indicates that early intervention special education services have many short- and long-term benefits (American Psychological Association and National Council on Measurement in Education, 1999).

Assessment Concepts

Although often used interchangeably, the terms *test, measurement, evaluation,* and *assessment* differ in meaning (Gronlund, 2006). Assessment is the process of gathering information in order to make a decision. It is a critically important component of early childhood intervention. Effective early childhood intervention assessments consider children's ages as well as the nature of the developmental delays being assessed. Early childhood assessment offers a unique opportunity to facilitate parental participation in the intervention process (McLoughlin & Lewis, 1999). Major forms of assessment include observation, rating scales, checklists, interviews, and standardized tests.

Parents are typically most knowledgeable about their children. A comprehensive assessment process includes gathering information on a wide range of a child's abilities. Parents often have extensive information about their child's motivation, interactive abilities, learning styles, and tolerance for learning. Therefore, parental participation in assessment is essential and sets the stage for parents to continue to participate in all aspects of their children's early intervention process (Safran & Safran, 1996; Salvia & Ysseldyke, 1998).

With regard to early childhood intervention, assessment has three distinct purposes: screening, diagnosis (determining eligibility for services), and program planning. Screening involves attempting to identify children who have a developmental delay or disability. Diagnosis determines if a child should have a complete evaluation and if they are eligible for early childhood intervention services. Program planning addresses early intervention objectives, strategies, and outcomes. To understand the assessment process, it is necessary to understand various assessment terms and methods.

Test is the narrowest measurement term. A test is a method for observing a person's responses. A variety of tests are appropriate for assessing very young children, but no single test is appropriate for assessing all children. For example, a child living in a family whose members do not speak English would require a test appropriate for children who live in non-English-speaking families.

When used with children birth through kindergarten, a test includes the children's responses to stimuli or verbal requests. For example, an infant may have a rattle placed in their hand to determine whether they are capable of holding a rattle, or a 2-year-old might be asked to point to a cup. Test responses typically are observed behaviors following the presentation of specific stimuli or verbal responses to questions or statements. Also, a child's parents may be asked to respond to a questionnaire or participate in an interview. These tests are usually administered individually.

Tests are administered by a variety of professionals making up a transdisciplinary assessment team (Losardo & Notari-Syverson, 2001). Often a psychologist assesses a child's overall development. Other team members are likely to assess specific areas of development.

The terms *measurement, evaluation,* and *assessment* are frequently used interchangeably, although there are distinctions between them. **Measurement** involves assigning numbers or symbols to a person's characteristics based on predetermined guidelines (e.g., translating test results into scores).

The process of **evaluation** entails using what has been measured or otherwise assessed and determining how a score might be used or interpreted. It typically includes both qualitative and quantitative data and often includes judgments as to a behavior's desirability. Evaluations can be formal or informal.

To have value, all forms of assessment must be highly reliable. **Reliability** refers to the extent to which a measurement instrument yields consistent, stable, and uniform results over repeated observations. The most critical feature of an assessment method is **validity.** *Validity* refers to how accurately a measurement instrument measures what it is designed to measure.

Formal assessment involves planned, systematic assessments that lead to diagnosis, classification, opinion, or action. It is the process used to determine whether a child is eligible for services. For example, the assessment team may observe the child, ask the child to perform specific tasks, talk with the child and their parents, and use other methods to gather information. Federal laws mandate that assessments be performed in five areas: communication, cognitive, physical, social-emotional, and adaptive development. Each of these areas will be discussed in later chapters.

Naturalistic observation is commonly part of the assessment process. Typically it is systematic (formal assessment); the observer looks for and records data related to one or more behaviors. This type of assessment is often referred to as **performance-based assessment.** This form of observation involves gathering information by watching children, without interfering, while focusing on behaviors of interest as they normally occur. The frequency, duration, and intensity of one or more behaviors are noted. Sometimes behavior is audio- or videotaped. After data are collected, the child's behavior is compared to their previous behavior or to typical behavior of peers.

Informal assessment, often referred to as informal observation, is nonsystematic—brief and possibly unplanned assessment. Observation may include **anecdotal assessment** (based on casual observations), which involves recording information regarding behavior that appears to be significant (Diamond, 1993). Informal evaluations are used to help determine whether formal assessment is needed and what type of formal assessment may be appropriate. In combination with formal assessment measures, informal assessment aids in developing a diagnosis or classification (Gronlund, 2006). Current assessment trends include a focus on the use of informal assessments. Formal and informal evaluation may occur while children play. This type of assessment is referred to as **play-based assessment.**

Some observational data are collected through interviews of the child or their parents or through a parent's completion of a questionnaire in the form of a **rating scale** or **checklist**. A rating scale is a structured assessment instrument that involves asking a rater to respond to a set of descriptive words or phrases (typically three to seven choices) that indicate performance levels. For example, the rater might select from *always, sometimes,* or *never.* Another structured method, a checklist, asks the rater to select between only two choices indicating the presence or absence of a particular attribute. For example, a child might be asked to answer yes or no to the question "Can you tie your shoes?"

Developmental rating scales and checklists are designed to assess children's functioning in their daily lives. They examine four of the major domains required by the Individuals with Disabilities Education Act (IDEA): social-emotional development; motor development; language and communication; and adaptive behavior. One benefit of these measures is the partnership between the assessor and the **informant, the person providing information about the child.** Informants may be parents (working together or separately), grandparents, teachers, or other care providers. The assessment process may involve several informants providing information regarding a single child. Ratings provided by various observers in a variety of settings are helpful in determining the child's responses in a range of settings and in the presence of a variety of individuals. Although often useful, checklists, questionnaires, and rating scales typically have lower reliability and validity than standardized tests.

Many parents value the opportunity to participate in assessment of their child's strengths and weaknesses. Others find it overwhelming to be asked to answer questions about their child's development and family behaviors and needs. Parental cooperation is more likely if the assessor says something like, "We really need your help in gathering information about your child. Your knowledge can provide us with information that would be impossible to obtain without your help. The information that you provide will play a major role in developing an appropriate program for your child."

Assessment instruments include a variety of **standardized tests.** They are administered and scored under conditions that are standardized (identical or as identical as possible) for all individuals. To be useful, selected assessment instruments must match the intended outcomes of the assessment. In screening or other assessment, standardized psychological assessment in the form of intelligence and neuropsychological tests may be included along with other appropriate assessment (e.g., tests of hearing, vision, speech and language, or physical development). Some professionals believe that the natural behavior displayed by preschool-age children limits the usefulness of standardized evaluations, but others believe that a full evaluation should include standardized test data.

Standardized tests usually are **norm-referenced;** they evaluate an individual's performance as compared to that of others who took the same test (Hopkins, 1998; Kubiszyn & Borich, 1993). Norm-referenced tests compare a particular child's development to that of other children the same age. Most college students experienced this type of test when they took the Scholastic Aptitude Test or American College Test.

Other assessments are **criterion-referenced** (sometimes referred to as **domain-referenced**) scores/tests. These assessments compare a child's performance to a predetermined standard, often referred to as the **cut score** or **cutoff score**. Criterion-referenced tests help determine whether a child has acquired or mastered a particular behavior. A cut score (cutoff score) is a reference point used to divide a set of data into two or more classifications regarding which action should be taken—for example, qualifies/does not qualify for early intervention. Professionals such as lawyers, doctors, and teachers often are required to take licensing examinations; they pass or fail (obtain a license or do not).

Some parents resist having their child assessed. They are naturally reluctant to expose themselves to the possible risk of learning that their child has a developmental delay or disability. Parents may question whether they can emotionally cope with such news and provide the support their child will require. Additionally, they often fear that assessment will result in their child being labeled in a way that elicits negative reactions from teachers, peers, family members, care providers, and others.

At times, discrepancies between formal and informal testing indicate that a child has acquired certain knowledge or skills but for some reason is not using them in everyday functioning. Sometimes the opposite occurs: the child displays certain abilities in everyday activities but not during formal testing. Formal test scores indicate only how a particular child performed on a particular day on a particular test. It is crucial for assessors to understand that factors other than children's abilities affect how well they perform in formal testing.

Assessing Children Birth through Preschool

Assessment of infants, toddlers, and preschoolers requires special training and skills. Individuals who conduct assessments with this age group need training in (1) normal and atypical early childhood development, (2) methods, procedures, and assessment tools appropriate for very young children, (3) selection of appropriate techniques and assessment tools, (4) services available to children with disabilities and their families, and (5) legal and ethical issues related to assessment of very young children (Bracken, 2000; Sattler & Hoge, 2006).

Effective assessment requires **developmentally appropriate evaluation (DAE)** (Bricker, 2002). Although variations in rates of children's development are typical at all ages, significant variations are most likely among children birth through preschool (Greenwood, Luze, & Carta, 2002). For example, some children say their first word at a very young age (e.g., 7 months) or speak in two- or three-word phrases before the typical age. A child who begins to talk at an early age may not walk early and may even be slow to walk. This pattern would likely not result in concerns about rate of overall development.

When children display significant delays in development (there is limited agreement regarding "significant"), these delays may indicate the presence of a disability or may be due to natural variations among children. Early development is emergent; therefore, a child lacking a skill at a particular time may demonstrate the skill within a few weeks or months. This makes it difficult to determine what should be considered a significant level of developmental delay. The naturally wide variation within children's development may cause subtle delays to be overlooked, particularly when assessment covering all developmental areas has not occurred (Katz, 1997).

Family members and doctors are often reluctant to discuss potential concerns regarding a child's development, particularly when children are very young. There is a natural tendency to hope the child will outgrow the delay.

Assessing children, particularly very young children, is subject to many extraneous factors including the child's being tired or scared, noise distractions, and degree of rapport between the child and the examiner (Neisworth & Bagnato, 2000). An assessment approach that is highly engaging for one child may bore another. Because very young children have limited attention spans, it often is difficult to assess them. Children's temperamental differences are likely to affect the data's reliability. In addition, socioeconomic, ethnic, and cultural differences can create very different early learning environments. Culturally insensitive assessment tools cannot provide accurate information about children's strengths and weakness (McConnell, Priest, Davis, & McEvoy, 2002; Meisels & Atkins-Burnett, 2000; Shepard, Kagan, & Wurtz, 1998).

Typically a parent is present during, or participates in, the assessment. Children's behavior may vary depending on whether or not a parent is present. Children's responses also are affected by their rapport with the assessor and how competent this individual is at eliciting responses. In addition, children tend to display inconsistent behavior. For example, a child may speak at home but not talk when strangers are present. There are natural variations in expected behavior.

Because assessments are conducted to determine whether a child has a disability, it is logical that specific child attributes will require special testing accommodations. This includes accommodating a child's particular physical characteristics (e.g., visually impaired or wheelchair-bound), a child's cultural characteristics (e.g., not fluent in English), and parental characteristics (Shepard, Kagan, & Wurtz, 1998).

Federal Assessment Mandates

As discussed in Chapter 1, the Education of All Handicapped Children Act of 1975 (P.L. 94-142) was the first federal law to establish U.S. special educational policies. Many of its assessment mandates remain in effect today. Passage of IDEA 1997 (P.L. 105-17) brought major changes regarding appropriate methods for assessing children with disabilities. IDEA 1997 mandated that children who may have a disability receive a full formal evaluation to determine whether they have a disability. In addition, children determined to have a disability must be reevaluated at least every 3 years to determine if they continue to have a disability (DeMers & Fiorello, 1999).

Early childhood special education services covered under IDEA cannot be provided without a full, individual evaluation of the child. The child's parents must consent to the initial evaluation and all reevaluations. In rare cases, if a parent does not consent, a court may order an evaluation to determine whether a child has a disability and, if so, the educational needs of that child (Bagnato, Neisworth, & Munson, 1997; Bailey, 1996).

Figure 2.1   **IDEA 1997: Major Changes Regarding the Initial Assessment of a Child**

- The assessment team must examine existing evaluation data and use the data if appropriate.
- Parents must be allowed to provide information about their child during the evaluation and are to be involved in the decision-making process.
- The evaluation must provide information that can be used to determine whether a child has a disability and decision-making information to guide the planning of needed intervention services.
- A full reevaluation of all areas related to the child's disability must occur at least every 3 years.
- Reevaluation may occur more frequently than every 3 years if a parent or teacher requests a reevaluation.
- Reevaluations require parental consent; before the passage of IDEA 1997, parental consent was needed for only the initial evaluation.

IDEA mandates the use of appropriate, highly reliable and valid, efficient, economical, and nondiscriminatory evaluation practices. By law it is not appropriate to use only one procedure to determine whether a child has a disability or to plan education programs. That is, a variety of assessment tools and strategies to gather relevant information about the child must be used to document whether or not a child has a disability. Also, assessment must be multidisciplinary; the evaluation team must comprise qualified individuals with training and experience in different areas. Federal law also mandates that all assessments be administered in the child's native language. Figure 2.1 lists assessment requirements.

The most recent (2004) version of IDEA, the Disabilities Education Improvement Act (P.L. 108-446), includes additional assessment guidelines. This law emphasizes the need for nondiscriminatory evaluations. Assessment tools may not be racially or culturally biased.

Developmental Delay or Disability

A **developmental delay** is a lag in development that results in a child's functioning at a level below the norm for their age. A developmental delay may or may not indicate a long-term developmental disorder. The term *developmental delay* usually is used to identify infants and toddlers who would benefit from early intervention services but who are not being labeled with a specific disability.

A child may have developmental delays in one, a few, most, or all areas of development. Symptoms of specific disabilities are often difficult to evaluate in very young children. Although not all developmental delays lead to developmental disabilities, early intervention services may prevent a child with a developmental delay from developing a disability. Approximately 10% of all U.S. infants, toddlers, and preschool children are classified as developmentally delayed (UNICEF, 2005a; U.S. Department of Education, 2000; U.S. Department of Education, National Center for Education Statistics, 2003a; U.S. Department of Education, National Center for Education Statistics, 2003b). Many children who qualify for early intervention services do not receive them, partly because it is difficult to detect mild delays and children's disabilities widely differ in type and severity.

The term **developmental disability** usually refers to a more severe, chronic disability involving mental or physical impairments. This term is associated with long-term impairments, which are likely to continue indefinitely. It is applied to older children only if they show significant delays in three of the six major developmental domains (Pavri, 2000).

In the case of children younger than 9 years old, *developmental disability* refers to a substantial developmental delay or specific congenital or acquired condition. These individuals may be viewed as having a developmental disability without meeting traditional criteria if they are likely to meet the criteria later in life unless they receive appropriate services and supports earlier in life [Developmental Disabilities Assistance and Bill of Rights Act of 2000 (P.L. 106-402)]. Approximately 10 million U.S. citizens have developmental disabilities (e.g., mental retardation, cerebral palsy, autism, epilepsy, or Down syndrome). An estimated 12 to 16% of all U.S. children have disabilities. As indicated in Chapter 1, this textbook uses the term *disability* to refer to both delays and specific congenital and acquired conditions.

IDEA broadly describes who is eligible for services: individuals diagnosed with physical or mental conditions likely to result in developmental delay(s). States are not required to provide services to those considered at risk of developing delay, but they may do so at their discretion (Ramey, Campbell, & Blair, 1998).

Studies indicate that IQ as determined by cognitive tests taken before age 6 or 7 typically does not predict future academic or occupational attainment except with regard to individuals at the extreme ends of the distribution. Infants or toddlers who score very low on standardized tests are likely to experience future developmental delays. However, factors other than those measured by IQ tests impact a child's future. Wariness about the predictive validity of scores remains appropriate.

Children may become what they have been labeled. This phenomenon is called a **self-fulfilling prophecy.** Parents and professionals clearly do not want a label to prevent children from fulfilling their potential. On the other hand, ignoring low test scores or avoiding testing and assessment primarily out of fear of negative labeling may deny children valuable intervention services (Bredekamp & Copple, 1997).

Referral for Evaluation

The process of identifying a child with a disability and providing special education services involves several steps (Peck, Odom, & Bricker, 1993). The first step in the process of receiving early intervention services is a formal **referral**, which occurs when a parent or another individual suspects a child may have a developmental delay or disability. The child must first be referred to a department of health, a **Committee on Preschool Special Education (CPSE)**, or some other agency or program that handles early intervention referrals.

Once a referral has been made, the child's strengths and needs are assessed and evaluated to determine whether the child is eligible for services and what types of services the child may need. During the referral process, family members are informed of the potential benefits of early intervention, and an initial service coordinator is designated. This coordinator describes family rights and discusses the list of evaluations that may be administered (Buck, Polloway, Patton, & McConnell, 2002). Information about insurance (possibly including Medicaid) is collected along with other relevant information.

Although a child's parents or physician typically recognizes disabilities with clear medical bases soon after the child's birth or during their preschool years, subtle disabilities may remained undetected until the child enters elementary school. Figure 2.2 lists several potential warning signs of developmental delays.

Figure 2.2   **Warning Signs of Possible Developmental Delays**

Infants (0–2 years)

- Little or no interest in surroundings
- No or minimal eye contact or smiling
- No responsiveness to sound
- No babbling by 12 months old
- No walking by 15 months old
- No use of hands to manipulate and explore objects

Toddlers (2–3 years)

- Little or no interest in other children
- Limited or no use of words or gestures to communicate needs
- Repetitive, noncommunicative, or merely imitative speech
- Very repetitive, nonpurposeful play

Preschoolers (3–5 years)

- Speech that is very difficult to understand
- Little or no imaginary play
- Little or no interest in social interaction
- Difficulties with balance, running
- Difficulty using crayons or scissors, manipulating small objects

A child's pediatrician is the first professional with whom most families have regular contact. Most parents assume that their child's pediatrician has expertise in all areas of child development. Although many pediatricians have knowledge about all areas of development, their primary focus is on maintaining a patient's health and treating illness rather than on making referrals for developmental evaluations. When children are seen by a physician, they often are examined for only a few minutes and at a time when they are not feeling well. This is not the setting in which developmental delays are likely to be noted.

Parents should be made aware that their child may have a developmental delay unnoticed by the pediatrician. Teachers, day care providers, medical professionals, and parents or guardians of young children should not hesitate to request referrals for developmental evaluations simply because a pediatrician or other medical professional has not initiated the referral (Heisler, 1972).

Referrals are for the purpose of initiating a developmental **screening**, which determines whether further evaluation is warranted. The screening process may take as long as 2 hours. After the screening, if a developmental delay is suspected, a psychologist or other interdisciplinary team member selects or develops a test battery (set of assessment materials) that will be most useful during a full, in-depth evaluation.

Culturally Sensitive Assessment

Cultural variations must be considered when selecting assessment tools. The child's native language must be considered. Federal laws mandate that assessments be conducted in the child's native language. In the case of bilingual children, assessment should use both languages.

It is insufficient to consider a child's language when attempting to administer culturally appropriate assessments (i.e., **culturally sensitive assessments**) (Lynch & Hanson, 1996). Differences in cultural norms and values must also be considered. For example, cultures vary regarding expected levels of independence and sustained attention. Prior to making judgments regarding the meaning of assessment results, a person must consider cultural variations. For example, if children of a particular cultural group traditionally are spoon-fed through age 3, they are likely to score below the norm on assessments of self-feeding. This illustrates why no single test is appropriate for all children.

Some professionals develop assessments designed to reflect the norms of their community rather than national norms. They advocate conducting assessments in the child's dominant language and use trained test administrators who are very familiar with the family's culture, practices, and beliefs. Early childhood professionals from a variety of disciplines (e.g., speech pathology, occupational therapy, physical therapy, and special education) often conduct assessments focusing on specific components of development (e.g., speech and language, fine and gross motor, social-emotional, and cognitive). They may lose sight of the child's overall development. Their approach may also be in conflict with that of cultural groups who traditionally monitor a child's development using a more situational approach (e.g., examine how the child functions within their home and community) (Kagitcibasi, 1996).

Some professionals believe that the age norms assigned to developmental domains primarily reflect white, middle-class child rearing norms (e.g., Lynch & Hanson, 1992; Mangione, 1995). They argue that attainment of developmental milestones is directly influenced by child-rearing values and practices and that use of standard normative data may not be appropriate for all individuals (Harry, 1992). For example, some families do not encourage their child to independently spoon-feed or drink from a cup until shortly before the child attends public school at 5 or 6 years of age, even though 18 months is the age listed as the norm on most developmental checklists.

Professionals must measure all of a child's skills, not only those they value based on their own upbringing. Garcia Coll (1990) studied various developmental skills (e.g., tactile stimulation, verbal and nonverbal interaction, and feeding routines) in multicultural families (African American, Chinese American, Hopi, Mexican American, and Navajo). He reported that "minority infants are not only exposed to different patterns of affective and social interactions, but that their learning experiences might result in the acquisition of different modes of communication from those characterizing Anglo infants, different means of exploration of their environment, and the development of alternative cognitive skills" (p. 274).

Teachers and therapists must distinguish between a developmental or maturational lag and behaviors that have not been taught within certain cultures but can readily be learned once the child has the relevant opportunities (Dworkin, 1992; Glascoe, 1996). For example, when children do not self-spoon-feed, it is important to determine whether they have a motor or cognitive delay or simply have not learned the skill because they have not been given opportunities to do so.

In part, disability is a social and cultural construct (Danesco, 1997; Harry, 1992; McDermott & Varenne, 1996). Danesco found that many culturally diverse parents view their child's developmental level as temporary or able to be remedied. She also reported that it is not uncommon for parents to use a combination of home remedies or alternative practices in an attempt to help their child. In addition, families greatly vary regarding how much confidence they have in various professional, educational, and medical interventions as compared to alternative interventions. Because families have different views regarding what constitutes a delay or disability, labeling their children disabled often results in misunderstandings and mistrust between family members and professionals.

The influence of cultural factors on evaluation of possible developmental delays highlights the need for an array of assessment tools and an in-depth understanding of a child's culture. It is often helpful for test administrators to use interpreters and to provide print and audiovisual materials in the family's dominant language. They should also develop means of connecting parents to other parents within the same cultural group who are dealing with similar issues (Chen & McNamee, 2007; Maddox, 2003).

Screening

A **screening** is used to judge developmental progress to determine if a full assessment is necessary. The major goal of developmental screening is to reduce the time between assessment and the provision of intervention services. For screening to be optimally effective, it must be accurate, comprehensive, and cost-effective. Screening can include parent interviews, observations of the child, use of a specific instrument or checklist, or other methods. Due to wide variations in normal development and behavior during the early years, the skills of infants and young children can be very difficult to screen accurately. Parental involvement in the screening process often helps to diminish the difficulties (Meisels & Provence, 1989).

As indicated earlier, for a child to qualify for federally mandated early intervention services, the child's developmental level must be evaluated. The parents' written consent is required before an evaluation can be conducted. The evaluation should be conducted in the child's dominant language. The assessment must be performed by trained professionals such as a special education teacher, psychologist, and speech and language pathologist. There is no direct cost to families for a screening, an evaluation, or services funded, in whole or part, by the federal government (Bricker, 2002).

A screening is conducted to determine if the child might benefit from a full evaluation. For children younger than 5 years old, screenings are usually completed by a special education teacher or a speech and language pathologist. If a screening suggests a developmental delay, the child then undergoes more-extensive evaluation. Formal evaluation or testing is usually completed by a team of qualified professionals from several disciplines. They collaborate to determine the child's eligibility for early intervention services. Delays of more than 6 months in one or more areas of development usually indicate a need for further evaluation by appropriate specialists (Slentz & Bricker, 1992).

Gathering data in a way that leads to accurate conclusions is a vital aspect of evaluation. In some cases, informal observation of children suffices. In other cases, detailed data gathered from daily or hourly observations or standardized assessment instruments are needed (Bricker & Squires, 1989; Glascoe, Altemeier, & MacLean, 1989). A wide variety of developmental screening instruments may be used to help determine if children have developmental delays. These tests evaluate one or more areas of skills development, including adaptive (self-help), general cognitive (intellectual), gross and fine motor, and speech and language (Meisels, 1996; Nagle, 2000).

Developmental screening tests have inherent limitations. Even highly reliable and valid tests have limited ability to predict children's future abilities. Assessments may lead to over- or under-detection of disabilities. Under-detection results in children's not receiving potentially beneficial early intervention services and in increased cost of special education services later in life. Over-detection may lead to life-long labeling and unwarranted cost related to early intervention services.

Full Evaluation

Full developmental assessment typically includes evaluation of sensory (including sensory integration), cognitive (including neurological), fine- and gross-motor, and language development (Gibbs & Teti, 1990). Parents and professionals work together to accumulate useful information regarding children's current developmental levels and developmental history (Kamphaus, Petosky, & Rowe, 2000; Meisels & Fenichel, 1996; Rosetti, 1990). Team members include, but are not limited to, psychologists, social workers, early interventionists or special educators, occupational or physical therapists, and speech–language pathologists. Full assessments are provided at no cost to parents. Federal laws mandate the requirements for appropriate diagnostic instruments and procedures.

Full evaluations are also conducted with children who have been receiving intervention services and need reassessment to determine if they continue to qualify for services. Evaluations help determine why intervention plans or methods were or were not effective. For example, a particular behavioral plan may work with one child but not another. Evaluation should also include the various service delivery systems and their ability to continue to provide the needed services for the child and family. Additionally, because children "age out" of preschool services (no longer qualify because they are too old), it is important to determine if there are appropriate services available to the child and family during the child's transition to the next school situation. (See Chapter 14 for an in-depth discussion of transitions.)

Assessment of the Child

When assessment indicates the presence of a developmental delay or disability, early intervention services usually are recommended. Some parents are relieved to learn why their child is not progressing at a normal developmental rate. Others resist any label that indicates their child has a developmental delay or disability. Early intervention may result in fewer services being needed during school years. Before the assessment begins, a referral for evaluation must be made.

Assessment is a means of documenting a child's growth, and ongoing assessment is a necessary part of curriculum planning. Assessment allows those who provide services to determine a child's strengths and weaknesses (e.g., cognitive development) and determine where growth has occurred. Assessment helps teachers and parents create a child's individualized family service plan (IFSP) or individualized education program (IEP) for the coming year and guides the development of appropriate teaching strategies and learning environments. Special education teachers often use assessment information to develop classroom activities tailored to each child's needs.

As discussed earlier in this chapter, assessment of infants, toddlers, and preschoolers can be formal or informal. It can involve observation and formal questioning, such as is found on standardized tests. Some of the more common assessments methods are discussed below.

Diagnostic Assessment. Diagnostic assessment typically involves an in-depth analysis of a child's strengths and weaknesses in a particular area. The data may be collected in the child's natural environment or within a setting designed for testing. Diagnostic testing often is criterion-referenced: it determines whether a child's performance meets pre-established criteria or levels of mastery. This type of assessment often does not emphasize the child's relative standing but instead provides a measure of the level of progress toward mastery of developmentally appropriate skills (Smith, Finn, & Dowdy, 1993). This form of assessment aids teachers in designing individual instruction with a focus on specific skills. Although standardized criterion-referenced tests may be used, many criterion-referenced assessments are designed by the teacher or are built into the program (Slentz & Bricker, 1992).

Ecological Assessment.   **Ecological assessment** involves evaluating how children function within their various environments as well as the environments themselves. During an ecological assessment, parents may be asked how their child responds to various situations, and children may be observed interacting with peers, parents, and teachers in normal daily settings. Ecological assessment evaluates the child's past and current environments and predicts how the child may function in future environments (Karnes & Stayton, 1988). Ecological assessments are designed to provide information about the child's strengths within natural settings. Intervention methods can then be based on those strengths.

    Arena assessment is a form of ecological assessment often used by transdisciplinary teams (professionals from several disciplines working together during assessment). Typically, all team members, including parents and professionals, are available for the assessment session. During this session, one or more team members interact with the child while other team members observe. Usually, a team leader organizes the assessment process (Bagnato & Neisworth, 1999). Play-based assessment, another form of ecological assessment, is discussed in Chapter 12.

Assessment of the Family

As previously discussed, federal laws mandate that direct family services be provided to families of children with disabilities younger than 2 years old. For older children, it is typically useful to assess family needs, although funding for this process often is not available. When this is the case, informal methods may be used to obtain family needs information.

    Family assessment involves examining the strengths and capabilities of the family, the child care ability of the family's informal support system, and the resources available in the formal support system. Assessment of families' needs includes their self-identified resources, priorities, and concerns. These issues should be central in determining appropriate services for children and their families when full evaluations indicate that a child has a disability and qualifies for early childhood intervention services.

    Involving family members in the assessment of very young children is crucial and sets the stage for their long-term involvement in their child's education. Family members have intimate and unique perspectives regarding a child's development and needs. It is possible to involve parents at all stages of evaluation. They are key members of the assessment team.

    Open communication between parents and those conducting assessment is crucial. Parents have intense feelings for and close bonds with their children, for whom they are responsible. Because infants and toddlers are dependent on their parents and other family members, change is most readily accomplished through these relationships. Typically, family members are a child's most consistent and capable long-term care providers, teachers, and advocates.

Effective assessment requires collaboration among the service coordinator and other team members, including family members. They must work together to compile, evaluate, rank, and combine various factors found within the family's environment. This process is designed to help create possible solutions for the identified needs of the family. The needs noted by the service coordinator and family must be considered in relation to the assessments of needs made by other professionals (Moxley, 1989). Seligman and Darling (1989) developed the Parent Needs Survey (PNS), which professionals frequently use to assess the needs of families of young children with disabilities. Figure 2.3 lists the major areas of assessment on the PNS.

The parents of children with disabilities often receive a tremendous amount of information from the combined assessments of a team of professionals. Service coordinators and families must work together in an attempt to effectively use all of the information. Service coordinators evaluate assessment information at two levels: they assess the ability of families to understand the information provided by members of the service team, and they assess the capability of families to implement the recommendations from team members. While these two areas may seem similar, they are actually quite distinct.

Initial assessments of children with disabilities are geared toward discerning their needs and determining areas of delay. Assessment involves family interviews, case histories, observations, and use of various needs-assessment instruments. A team member (often a social worker) may also assess the cognitive strength and, perhaps more importantly, emotional strength and functioning of the family (Buckley, 1983).

A disability that emerges during the child's development generally evokes a wide range of emotional responses from family members (Hughes & Rycus, 1983). After first learning of a child's developmental delay, families respond with varying

---

Figure **2.3**   **The Six Major Areas of the Parent Needs Survey (PNS)**

1. Diagnosis, prognosis, and treatment
2. Medical, therapeutic, and educational services
3. Formal support from public and private agencies
4. Informal support from relatives, friends, neighbors, co-workers, and other parents who have children with special needs
5. Material support including financial support and access to resources
6. Competing family needs, including needs of other family members (usually parents and siblings) that may affect the family's ability to attend to the needs of the child with special needs

Source: Seligman & Darling (1989)

levels of mobilization and experience emotional and functional turmoil. It is vitally important for families and professionals to understand the emotional merry-go-round many families experience. Overwhelming amounts of insensitively transmitted information may devastate families (Rolland, 1994). It is important for service coordinators and families to assess the family's emotional ability to deal with this type of information. Parents may find the information confusing or contradictory. Families are capable of effectively dealing with unanticipated information, but to do so they may need the support of service coordinators.

Standardized Assessment of Infants through School Age

Many standardized tests are available for screening and full assessment. Tests frequently used for initial screening and in full evaluations are briefly discussed below. Tests designed to assess specific areas of development are discussed in later chapters. Several standardized tests are commonly used during the screening process. The first and most commonly administered assessment of infants is briefly described below.

In most hospitals, formal observation occurs shortly after birth. The Apgar scores are one of the best-known screening instruments for infants (Apgar, 1953). The Apgar test usually is given both 1 minute and 5 minutes after birth. If a baby has serious health problems or the first two scores are low, the test may also be given 10 minutes after birth and additional times. APGAR is an acronym for activity, pulse, grimace, appearance, and respiration. Table 2.1 illustrates Apgar scoring.

Table 2.1	Summary of Apgar Scores			
	Attribute	**0 Points**	**1 Point**	**2 Points**
A	Appearance (skin color)	Blue-gray, pale all over	Normal except for extremities	Normal over entire body
P	Pulse	Absent	Below 100 bpm	Above 100 bpm
G	Grimace (reflex irritability)	No response	Grimace	Sneeze, cough, pulling away
A	Activity (muscle tone)	Absent	Arms and legs flexed	Active movement
R	Respiration	Absent	Slow, irregular	Good rate, crying

Source: Apgar, 1953

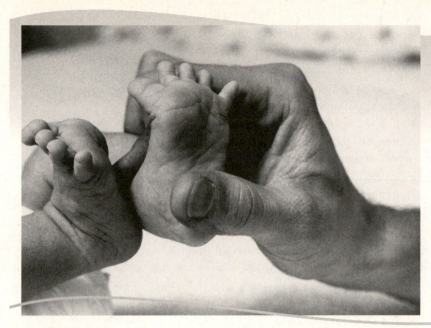

A newborn's health status is assessed using Apgar scoring.

Developing Early Intervention Plans

Once a full evaluation has been completed and a child has been found eligible to receive early intervention program (EIP) support, the next step is the development of an individualized family service plan (IFSP) for children birth to 3 years old or an individualized education program (IEP) for children 3 years and older.

During the initial service planning meeting, a multidisciplinary team (which must include the child's parents) reviews all data, results, and reports. The team then identifies the child's strengths and weakness and determines which support services will best meet the child's and family's needs.

IFSPs

Requirements for IFSPs are described in Part C of IDEA, which provides guidelines for the early intervention process for children with disabilities and their families. "Individualized" means that the plan is designed for a specific child. Inclusion of the term *family* emphasizes that the plan focuses on the family and the outcomes the family hopes to achieve for the child. *Service* refers to the intervention support and services that will be provided for the child and family (Zhang & Bennett, 2000).

An IFSP is a written document outlining early intervention services. Through the IFSP process, family members and service providers work as an interdisciplinary team to plan, implement, and evaluate services tailored to the family's and child's needs. When a child is deemed eligible for early intervention services, the assessment

Figure 2.4 **Development of an Effective Intervention Plan**

1. Identify family concerns, priorities, and resources.

2. Identify and analyze the family's and community's activity settings, which may provide opportunities for learning.

3. Conduct an assessment that focuses on the family's questions, concerns, and priorities and that includes information on the child's strengths, needs, and preferences with regard to activities, materials, and environments.

4. Collaboratively develop and review expected outcomes in relation to the family's concerns, priorities, and resources.

5. Using a transdisciplinary team model, assign intervention responsibilities to all team members and the family.

6. Plan implementation strategies. Identify which of the child's surroundings are likely to facilitate learning, and select strategies to bring about the desired outcomes.

process in preparation for developing an IFSP must be completed within 45 days of the referral to services, unless a parent requests a delay.

To develop the ISFP, a transdisciplinary team meets to discuss the plan. At this time the family identifies the outcomes they desire, early intervention services are specified, a written plan is developed, all team members agree to the plan, and an ongoing service coordinator is designated. Figure 2.4 lists steps for developing an effective intervention plan.

IDEA requires that the IFSP be evaluated and revised annually and that periodic reviews be conducted at least every 6 months (sooner if requested by the family). If a child is 2 years, 9 months or older when identified for early intervention services, the IFSP must include a transition plan. Otherwise, the IFSP must include such a plan before the child reaches 3 years of age.

IEPs

The IEP is a written statement describing the child's needs and the educational program designed to meet those needs. Children 3 to 21 years of age who receive special education services must have an IEP. When the school district receives a referral, the district has 90 days in which to complete a full evaluation, hold one or more mandatory meetings, determine what educational services will be offered, and send parents formal notification that tells them where the child will receive early intervention services (Clark, 2000; Gibb & Dykes, 2000; Siegel, 2004).

IDEA mandates that the IEP specify reasonable goals for each child eligible to receive special education services and specify the services that will be provided (Drasgow, Yell, & Robinson, 2001). Figure 2.5 lists information that must be included in each child's IEP.

Figure 2.5   **Information That Must Be Included within an IEP**

- The child's present levels of development
- Annual goals that can realistically be accomplished within a year
- Special education and related services that will be provided
- Level of participation with children who are not receiving services
- When services will begin, how often and where they will be provided, and how long they will last
- Transition goals and services (steps that may help the child adjust to and function in a new setting, procedures that may help program staff or other qualified personnel who will be providing services to the child facilitate a smooth transition)
- Methods that will be used to measure progress

The IFSP differs from the IEP in several ways (see Figure 2.6).

Figure 2.7 shows a sample IEP form.

Although IFSPs and IEPs are similar in content, they differ in focus. An IFSP relies on a family-centered, community-based orientation to service delivery, whereas an IEP typically uses a public school-based model of service delivery. Many states are increasingly integrating family- and community-centered models for early childhood intervention and preschool special education. IDEA regulations indicate that the U.S. Office of Special Education Programs supports this philosophy.

Figure 2.6   **Major Differences between an IFSP and an IEP**

Unlike an IEP, an IFSP

- includes outcomes targeted for the eligible child and family, not just for the child
- includes a focus on delivery of services within the child's "natural" environment, such as home and community settings including the park, a child-care facility, and gym classes
- focuses on creating opportunities for interventions within everyday routines and activities rather than only in formal environments
- integrates services into one plan provided in conjunction with multiple agencies
- designates a service coordinator to support development, implementation, and evaluation of the plan

Figure 2.7   **Sample IEP Form**

Child's name:_____

Service provider:_____ Meeting date:_____

Date of evaluation/report:_____

Mother's name:_____

Mother's address:_____

Mother's daytime telephone number:_____

Mother's evening telephone number:_____

Father's name:_____

Father's address:_____

Father's daytime telephone number:_____

Father's evening telephone number:_____

Purpose of meeting:_____Develop IEP_____Review IEP_____Develop Transition Plan

Child's present level of performance:_____

Child's placement status:_____

Cognitive: test name:_____

Verbal score:_____

Performance score:_____

Full-scale score:_____

Speech/language: test name:_____

Articulation skill:_____

Receptive language skills:_____

Expressive language skills:_____

Physical development: test name:_____

Fine motor:_____

Gross motor:_____

Vision:_____

Hearing:_____

Self-help skills: test name:_____

Eating:_____

Toileting:_____

Dressing:_____

Figure 2.7   **Continued**

Bathing:_____

Social/emotional: test name:_____

Relationship with peers:_____

Relationship with adults:_____

Self-concept/esteem:_____

Adjustment to school/community:_____

Attention span:_____

Primary classification:_____

Secondary classification:_____

Status:_____eligible_____ineligible_____exit (no longer available)

Service coordinator:_____

Team member name/role:_____

Team member name/role:_____

Team member name/role:_____

Team member name/role:_____

Team member name/role:_____

Placement location:_____

Program type:_____

Projected starting date:_____

Committee meeting date:_____

Review date:_____

Reevaluation date:_____

Note: Additional relevant goals and objectives for the child would also be stated on the IEP form.

Special education teachers are often responsible for developing IFSP or IEP goals and objectives for each child. Goals and objectives are written after the assessment team has completed the child's assessments and consulted with the child's parents. To develop an appropriate IEP or IFSP, the special education teacher must view the child as a child first and then consider the child's needs. This includes viewing each child as having the potential to grow and change rather than viewing the child as being limited to a certain level of development.

After the long-term goals have been established, the special education teacher breaks these goals into small, sequential steps to establish short-term objectives in a process similar to **task analysis.** This process involves sequencing tasks from easiest to most difficult. Generally, the skills needed to complete a task are more important than task completion. For example, the task of stringing beads is designed to enhance fine-motor skills, including using two hands together, grasping objects, and developing strategies for completing the task.

The local school district must approve an IFSP or IEP and place the child in the least restrictive program. If a child is not recommended for services, the family may be assisted in finding other programs or services that may benefit the child and family. If the parents do not agree with the recommendations in the IFSP/IEP or feel that the child should be eligible for services that are not being recommended, they have a legal right to due process. That is, the parents have the right to appeal the decision in a hearing before a judge (Wasik, Ramey, Bryant, & Sparling, 1990). In most states a wide variety of potential services are available to children and their parents through EIPs (Slentz & Bricker, 1992). IFSPs and IEPs must be reviewed every 6 months and updated at least once a year.

Monitoring Service Plans

Careful program monitoring advances the identification of additional needs as they arise and contributes to a smooth progression for the child and family (Moxley, 1989). Monitoring requires that all aspects of the service plan be recorded in detail, including who is responsible for effecting the plan, what implements are needed, and how soon the goals should be reached. Monitoring primarily involves evaluating the usefulness of the services.

As children move from early intervention services to public school kindergarten, assessment of school readiness is based on typical physical, social, emotional, and cognitive development. It is often difficult to accurately predict school readiness. This difficulty may lead to placing children in kindergarten programs who are not ready and discouraging placement for children who later are very successful in school. In addition, there are frequently concerns that test results are not equally valid for various groups. (Chapter 14 focuses on the transition from early intervention services to kindergarten programs or other appropriate placement.)

Moxley (1989) believes that the assessment process should include the family's evaluation of the service coordination. This evaluation should indicate the family's attitudes regarding service coordination as well as empower the family to be more than service consumers. This evaluation directly evaluates the worth, significance, and benefit of the service coordination for the family.

Service coordinators also monitor service plans by evaluating the productivity of the service plan, its bearing on the functioning of the child and family, the social network's ability to reinforce the family, and the capacity of the social service professionals to work with the family. Evaluation focuses on whether the plan achieves the desired outcomes (Moxley, 1989).

During the evaluation phase, outcomes related to intervention are examined. The service coordinator must determine whether projected goals are achieved. For example, a service coordinator may determine if the child is able to self-feed or if the

A teacher assesses a young child's progress.

home or service-providing facilities are wheelchair-accessible. These types of evaluations help determine whether service plans produce the desired results.

Effectiveness of Early Childhood Special Education Services

Research on the effectiveness of early childhood special education programs is limited. The cost- and outcome-effectiveness of an early childhood special education program strongly depends on how many disabilities a child has and of what type(s).

Research indicates that EIPs usually reduce the number of life-long special education services that an individual needs and the number of times that a child fails to move to the next grade level. In some cases they enable children to develop skills comparable to those of children who do not have a disability. Research further indicates that highly successful early childhood special education programs provide services as early as possible, involve parents in the child's services, and tailor services to the child's and family's needs (Guralnick, 1997; Smith, 1988; White, 1991).

Research has revealed that early childhood is a key period for brain development. Brain-development research suggests that newborns possess an innate ability and drive to learn through interactions with the environment (Gopnik, Meltzoff, & Kuhl, 1999). Neuroscience has shown that brain growth is greatest up to 3 years of age and that there are critical periods during which particular sensory, motor, and language capabilities must develop normally or permanently remain impaired. In addition, there is evidence that the first 3 years of life may be a critical period for mental health and social functioning. This suggests that children at risk will benefit from spending time with nurturing care providers and from receiving any needed services as early as possible (Gunnar, 1990).

Early identification of developmental delays and disabilities is crucial. Early intervention services have been shown to be beneficial and cost-effective (Dawson & Osterling, 1997). Emphasizing the importance of early intervention, Karnes and Lee (1978) have stated, "Only through early identification and appropriate programming can children develop their potential" (p. 1). Evidence regarding the long-term effectiveness of early intervention services varies. It appears that the more extensive studies report more significant positive long-term effects (The Office of Educational Research Improvement, 1990).

In the 1930s Howard Skeels and colleagues investigated the impact of the environment on young children who were labeled mentally retarded. He removed some "mentally retarded" children from an orphanage and placed them in an institution for adults who were classified as mentally retarded. These children received intensive attention from women who were labeled mentally deficient and from the institution's staff. After 2 years, the children showed significant increases in their intelligence scores. A follow-up study conducted 25 years later indicated long-term gains for these individuals. Overall they had a higher quality of life as indicated by indices such as marriage, educational level, and employment than individuals of the same age who had remained in the orphanage.

Research conducted by Samuel Kirk in the late 1950s also indicated the value of early childhood intervention. He studied 81 children classified as mentally retarded, 43 of whom received preschool experience. In general, the children with preschool experience showed IQ gains of between 10 and 30 points, whereas those without preschool experience showed IQ declines (Kirk, 1962, cited in Reynolds, 1998a, 1998b).

Another study by René Spitz in the 1950s compared infants raised in normal environments to those raised in sensory-deprived environments (sterile environments that do little more than meet an individual's basic physiological needs). The sensory-deprived infants showed substantial deterioration of physical health and mental capacity. A follow-up study of these same individuals at ages 10 to 14 indicated deficiencies across all developmental and behavioral domains in the individuals who had been sensory deprived.

The **Infant Health and Development Program** founded in 1985 examined whether EIPs prevented or mitigated adverse outcomes for low-birth-weight, premature infants. At age 3, infants who had participated in the program had significantly higher intelligence scores, more advanced cognitive development, and fewer behavioral problems than 3-year-olds who had not participated (Gross, Spiker, & Haynes, 1997).

Most studies examining the effectiveness of early childhood special education programs were conducted with poor children at risk for delayed development. During the 1960s, several studies—including the **Head Start** program—investigated the effects of early childhood intervention on children from low-income backgrounds. After a much-publicized study questioned the effectiveness of Head Start, a number of other studies applied more rigorous methodology to study the effects of early childhood intervention on preschool-age children. These studies documented that participation in well run or model programs resulted in increased IQ, enhanced socio-emotional development, and fewer future placements in special education classes (Barnett, 1993).

One of the most comprehensive studies examined the **Perry Preschool Project,** which served low-income children. This study evaluated individuals from childhood into adulthood and found significant differences between individuals who had been enrolled in the Perry Preschool Project and those, in the control group, who had not. Quality-of-life indicators suggested that program participation was highly beneficial. Other well-controlled studies have documented similar findings (Hebbeler et al., 2001).

Subsequent research has indicated that programs similar to the Perry Program also have economic benefits. Individuals who attended similar programs experienced fewer grade retentions, reduced need for special education services, enhanced productivity, lower welfare costs, increased financial earnings, and lower juvenile justice costs than individuals who did not attend. In addition, program participants proved more committed to schooling; more of them graduated from high school, attended postsecondary programs, and were employed. They also scored higher on reading, arithmetic, and language achievement tests, received approximately 50% fewer special education services, and engaged in fewer antisocial or delinquent behaviors in and out of school (Heckman & Masterove, 2004).

In the 1960s, Sandra Scarr-Salapetek and Margaret Williams investigated the effectiveness of specific treatment of at-risk infants who spend their first weeks of life in hospital intensive-care nurseries. They found that premature infants who received extra handling by nurses cried less than those who received minimal handling (the recommended treatment at the time) and showed better motor, auditory, and visual development (Scarr-Salapetek & Williams, 1973).

Infants with disabilities often are not identified as such at birth or during the newborn period. Research indicates that older infants and toddlers who have disabilities benefit from early intervention. Analysis of 32 infant and toddler intervention programs within the Handicapped Children's Early Education Programs network indicated that the programs enhanced children's development, particularly social-emotional development. Approximately 66% of program participants attended regular education classes when they entered school. In addition, the skills of program participants were superior to those of children with disabilities who had not participated in the programs (Hanson & Hanline, 1985). Many other studies have reported that the earlier the intervention, the more effective it is (Stock et al., 1976).

Research findings indicate that involving parents in EIPs enhances children's developmental gains and reduces future education costs. Parents who participate in these programs report more-positive parental feelings, increased self-esteem, and an enhanced sense of competency with regard to caring for their children as compared to parents who had young children with disabilities but who did not participate in these programs. Parental involvement has also been reported to enhance parents' abilities to implement the child's program at home, thereby reducing stress and facilitating the health of the family (Smith, 1988).

The **National Early Intervention Longitudinal Study** (NEILS, 2003) surveyed U.S. families of 3,338 infants and toddlers who received early intervention services. The NEILS described families' experiences with these services, including first concerns, diagnosis, the search for early intervention services, referral to services, and development of the required IFSP. Figure 2.8 summarizes key findings of the NEILS.

It is difficult to determine the exact cost-effectiveness of EIPs, although it is clear that delaying intervention results in more children's requiring more costly services later in life. Research indicates that there are substantial monetary benefits when intervention begins by age 2 years (e.g., Reynolds, Chang, & Temple, 1998; M. E. Wood, 1981).

In a longitudinal study, Schweinhart and Weikart (1980) reported that the annual $3,000 cost of a child's participation in the Perry Preschool Project was immediately recovered in savings in special education services.

M. E. Wood (1981) estimated the cost of services to children through age 18 years depending on whether the children began receiving services at birth, 2 years old, or 6 years old. The earlier intervention began, the less the total cost of special education services. Similarly, Colorado's statewide early intervention services have reportedly resulted in savings of $4.00 for every dollar spent within a 3-year period (Chambers, Parrish, Liebermann, & Woman, 1999).

Highly structured early childhood special education programs are reported to be more successful than less structured ones (Karoly et al., 1998). Highly structured programs frequently monitor and assess child and family behavioral objectives and utilize teacher behaviors and activities that have been shown to be highly effective.

Research findings help guide the design of EIPs. Specifically, they suggest that while it may be most useful to intervene before 3 years old, interventions after this

Figure 2.8   **Key NEILS Findings on Parents' Satisfaction with Their Child's Services**

- Approximately 86% of families discussed their concerns with a doctor or other medical professional, 64% indicated that this professional was very helpful, and 12% indicated that the professional was not at all helpful.

- Most parents indicated that it was relatively easy to find and secure services, but approximately 10% indicated that doing so required a lot of effort.

- Although an IFSP had recently been developed for their child, approximately 18% of parents were unaware of its existence.

- Approximately 81% of the parents who were aware of the IFSP reported that families and professionals worked together to develop the goals.

- Approximately 77% of parents reported that they were satisfied with their level of involvement in the ISFP process.

- An estimated 97% of parents felt that their child's services were somewhat or highly individualized.

- Approximately 76% of parents reported that they believed their child was receiving the right amount of therapy service.

- Most families felt that their interactions with professionals were very positive.

age also are very effective. Research further suggests that effects of early intervention are generally larger for children who are considered more disadvantaged, providing further rationale for developing additional programs for these children (Favazza, Phillipsen, & Kumar, 2000).

A longitudinal intervention study, the Infant Health and Development Program was a multi-site, randomized project involving low-birth-weight, premature infants. One group of infants were provided 3 years of home visits, child care, medical care, and access to parent groups. A second group of infants received only health-related services. At age 3, Group One infants scored higher than Group Two infants on tests of mental ability (Forness, 2001).

Many reviews of early childhood intervention literature cite scores of studies completed in recent years. While many of these studies have methodological limitations (e.g., lack of control groups or narrowly defined outcome measures), most researchers argue that early childhood intervention is effective (Barnett, 1993; Guralnick, 1997; Karoly, Greenwood, et al., 1998; Krauss, 1997; Lesar, Tivette, & Dunst, 1996, Moss, 1994).

Early intervention has been shown to result in parents' having more positive attitudes toward themselves and their children, improved information and skills for teaching their children, and more time for leisure and employment. These gains ultimately result in decreased dependence on social institutions, primarily due to parents' enhanced ability to meet their children's needs (Heckman & Masterove, 2004).

Fifty years of research indicates that early intervention increases a child's developmental gains, improves the family's functioning, and results in long-term benefits for society. Available data also indicate the long-term cost-effectiveness of early intervention. Although highly specialized, comprehensive early intervention services often are initially more costly than traditional school-age service-delivery models, overall they appear to save money over the long term, the entire period during which children qualify for special education services (Annie E. Casey Foundation, 1998).

It is clear that additional research needs to be conducted to help ensure the effectiveness of early childhood intervention services (Reynolds, 2000; Simeonsson et al., 1996). This topic will be further discussed in Chapter 14.

Conclusions

Federal laws mandate specific requirements for the assessment of children who are suspected of having developmental disabilities. Appropriate assessment includes formal and informal data collection and may included standardized assessments. All assessments must be culturally sensitive and unbiased. A referral must be made for the initial screening, which will determine if a full evaluation is warranted. Special skills and assessment tools are required to effectively assess infants, toddlers, and preschoolers due to their unique characteristics.

Although research regarding the effectiveness of early intervention services is limited, the studies that do exist indicate positive, cost-effective outcomes (Gilliam & Zigler, 2001). Research must be ongoing to reveal specific program attributes that result in the most positive outcomes for children and their families.

CHAPTER SUMMARY

- It is important to understand the meanings of various assessment terms, including *test, formal assessment, informal assessment, evaluation, assessment, norm-referenced,* and *criterion-referenced.*

- Special methods of assessment are often required because infants, toddlers, and preschoolers have limited attention spans and lack highly developed verbal skills.

- IDEA mandates specific assessment procedures including use of appropriate, highly reliable and valid, efficient, economical, varied, and nondiscriminatory evaluation practices.

- Assessments are useful in determining whether a child has a developmental delay or more serious disability. The term *disability* is appropriate for referring to children who require special education services.

- Valid assessments are culturally sensitive and are administered, in whole or part, in the child's primary language. Parental assessments should be administered in the parent's native language.

- Mandated assessment requires referral for assessment, screening, and full evaluation, as well as guidelines for reassessment.

- Professionals may administer a variety of standardized tests during screenings and full evaluations.

- Assessment of the usefulness of early intervention services indicates that these programs are effective, although there clearly is a need for additional research to clarify the qualities of effective programs.

CHAPTER KEY TERMS

assessment
test
measurement
evaluation
reliability
validity
formal assessment
naturalistic observation
performance-based assessment
informal assessment
anecdotal assessment
play-based assessment
rating scale
checklist
informant
standardized test
norm-referenced
criterion-referenced
domain-referenced
cut score

cutoff score
developmentally appropriate evaluation (DAE)
developmental delay
developmental disability
self-fulfilling prophecy
referral
Committee on Preschool Special Education (CPSE)
culturally sensitive assessment
screening
developmental assessment
full evaluation
diagnostic assessment
ecological assessment
arena assessment
family assessment
Parent Needs Survey (PNS)
Apgar scores
early intervention program (EIP)
individualized family service plan (IFSP)
individualized education program (IEP)

task analysis
Infant Health and Development Program
Head Start

Perry Preschool Project
National Early Intervention Longitudinal Study
(NEILS)

REVIEW QUESTIONS

1. What are the two key components of highly effective assessments?

2. What are similarities and differences of norm-referenced, criterion-referenced, and domain-referenced assessments?

3. What are similarities and differences of formal and informal assessment, naturalistic observation, performance-based assessment, anecdotal assessment, play-based assessment, rating scales, and checklists?

4. What are the characteristics of each of the mandated steps in the assessment process?

5. What types of attributes do standardized tests for young children typically assess?

6. What have research findings suggested about the effectiveness of EIPs?

SUGGESTED STUDENT ACTIVITIES

1. Interview a psychologist who participates in the assessment of young children with developmental delays. Ask about types of assessment instruments used to assess these children. Also ask about difficulties involved in assessing young children with developmental delays.

2. Compile a checklist for parents to use in evaluating whether a young child has a disability or is at risk of developing one.

3. Research current recommendations regarding developmentally appropriate, culturally sensitive assessments.

4. Write a statement that is designed to be read by parents and that describes each step of the assessment process.

Intervention Services 3

CHAPTER KEY POINTS

- Nature and nurture affect children's development.
- Knowledge of developmental theories aids in development of appropriate services.
- Services are provided in a variety of locations.
- Service delivery involves the collaboration of professionals and family members.
- Effective intervention programs have several key attributes.

Early identification of children with disabilities is crucial. It may help prevent developmental delays from becoming more serious or leading to additional problems (Blackman, 2002; Odom & McEvoy, 1990). Families of children with disabilities usually accept services and often are relieved to learn that services are available (Harris, 1983). Early intervention programs (EIPs) are designed to meet the child's and family's needs for information, services, and training (Bagnato & Neisworth, 1991; Brazelton & Greenspan, 2000; Meisels & Shonkoff, 1990).

Early childhood is an important time for all children. For children with disabilities, the first few years of life are critical because the earlier a child is identified as having a disability, the greater the likelihood that they will benefit from intervention strategies. In addition, early identification provides family members with formal and informal support during the intervention process (Bartel & Guskin, 1980; Scott, Hollomon, Claussen & Katz, 1998; Scott-Little, Kagan, & Clifford, 2003). When early intervention services are provided, schools and communities typically have decreased cost of services because children provided early intervention services arrive at school more prepared to learn.

Early childhood intervention services focus on the enhancement of children's abilities and support of their families (Lerner, Mardell-Czudnowski, & Goldenberg, 1987; Paasche, Gorrill, & Strom, 2003). Families with young children with disabilities experience complex demands and benefit from carefully designed, comprehensive, well-coordinated intervention programs. Services that are flexible, responsive, and family-centered help ensure an optimal start for young children with disabilities (Odom, 2002).

Nature and Nurture

Development begins at the moment of conception. Changes in all areas of development occur throughout life. However, during the first few years of life the amount of growth is tremendous (Nilsson, 1990). The first few years are critical for development, in part because brain growth is greatest during the first 3 years of life. Theorists continue to debate regarding what specific factors contribute to development and the level at which **genetic** and **environmental factors** influence various aspects of development and behavior (Greenough, 1991; Plomin & McClearn, 1993).

Genetic endowment, often referred to as **nature** or **heredity,** is believed to play an important role in development. Genetic endowment has to do with the genetic code for development received from parents at conception. Hereditary information signals the body to grow and is known to contribute to characteristics such as eye color. It also contributes to the development of many skills such as musical aptitude (Scarr & Kidd, 1983). Some theorists argue that children's development is based primarily on a genetically determined sequence of events, which automatically unfolds as children mature (Loehlin, 1992). Those theorists, often referred to as **nativists,** believe that heredity is the primary determinant of behavior and each child has an inborn clock guiding growth and maturation (attainment of functional capacity).

Theorists who believe that the environment (**nurture**) has a major influence on development are called **environmentalists.** Many early theorists believed that children are passively influenced by their environment. Currently, most theorists believe that children actively interact with their environment, influencing that environment and being influenced by it. Environmental influences include events that children experience in their homes, communities, and schools. Environmentalists believe that parents, siblings, teachers, friends, and society create events that help guide development (Plomin, 1989).

Research indicates that a combination of genetic and environmental factors influences development. Currently, most educators and psychologists believe that both the environment and heredity contribute to development. Individuals who hold this view are **interactionists.** They argue that, although genetic information influences development, the environment affects whether development reaches full potential. That is, they believe that development results from the dynamic interplay of nature (inborn tendencies, genetically directed) and nurture (environmental influences, learned behaviors). For example, most theorists would agree that heredity plays a major role in determining a person's height, but if a child is undernourished, the child is not likely to grow to full stature. Most educators and psychologists believe that heredity and environment contribute to all major areas of development (i.e., cognitive, language, motor, and social-emotional) (Kuhn, 1992; Smith & Luckasson, 1995).

Brain-development research elucidates how nature and nurture work together to shape human development and why EIPs usually have significant positive effects on children's development (Bruer, 1999). At birth the brain's neurons are relatively isolated from one another. Although the number of neurons remains the same, during the first 3 years of life neurons become increasingly interconnected through **synapses,** specialized junctions at which nervous-system cells signal to one another. Synapses are crucial for all types of sensory input and motor activities.

As children age, their synapses become more complex. Synapse development continues until about age 10. Between birth and age 3, the brain creates more synapses than are needed. Synapses that are used regularly become a permanent part of the brain; others are eliminated. Therefore, frequent social and learning opportunities can increase the number of permanent synapses (Wachs, 2000). In contrast, lack of environmental stimulation places a child at risk for developmental disabilities. Figure 3.1 lists environmental factors that may place a child at risk.

Developmental Theories

As discussed above, child development theories can be classified as either biologically or environmentally based. The **transactional developmental theory** combines these two views by emphasizing the interaction of biology and environment. It suggests that the interaction between the child and the environment is a continual process and that biology and environment are intertwined and cannot be clearly separated. The transactional theory emphasizes that the environment can be used to modify a child's biological limitations and a deficient environment may result in negative impacts on a child's development. This theory emphasizes children's relationships with their care providers and has greatly impacted the development of early intervention strategies (Shonkoff & Phillips, 2000).

Figure 3.1   **Environmental Factors That May Contribute to Childhood Disabilities**

- Living in a family at a lower socioeconomic level
- Living in a family of non-mainstream cultural background
- Living in a family classified as dysfunctional
- Having been born to a teenage mother or a mother more than 40 years old
- Growing up in a home in which English is not the primary spoken language
- Being prenatally exposed to viruses, drugs, or alcohol
- Being born into a family with one or more other children who have developmental delays
- Being born to a mother who was malnourished during pregnancy
- Being born to a mother who has diabetes, a thyroid disorder, syphilis, or a viral infection

Although children with developmental delays often do not progress in one or more areas of development at the same rate that is typical for most children the same age, generally they do acquire skills in the same order. Therefore, an understanding of typical patterns of development is useful when designing or providing services for children with disabilities.

Studying children and evaluating rates of development fall within the scope of the field of child development. Child development is a field of study dedicated to understanding all aspects of human growth and change from conception through adolescence (Berk, 1994). Child development is part of the broader study of human development, which involves changes experienced throughout a lifetime. Professionals who focus on human development are often referred to as **developmentalists** or **child developmental specialists** (Bertenthal & Campos, 1987).

Developmentalists focus on describing, explaining, and predicting how individuals at different stages typically think, feel, and behave (Horowitz, 1990). They often summarize sequences and rates of development in charts, called **developmental charts,** that indicate **universal norms** (Thelen, 1989).

Universal norms suggest that development unfolds through a series of sequences or patterns and within a typical period of time for most children. They provide an estimate as to when a certain level of development will be reached. Use of universal norms is referred to as the **normative approach.** Most children begin sitting, standing, walking, and talking at about the same age. In most cases, **milestones** (significant developmental events or accomplishments) that occur at an early age provide a foundation for more complex skills that will develop later in life (Thelen & Adolph, 1992).

Children with disabilities typically do not progress in one or more major areas of development at the rate indicated by universal norms. Concerns about children's rates of development occur when skills are significantly delayed in one or more areas. There is no agreement regarding criteria for determining whether a child has significantly delayed rates of development. Children frequently are classified as having a developmental delay when they acquire skills several months later than is typical for their age. Even when rate of acquisition of skills is slower than is typical, developmental charts are useful for tracking and providing support for the acquisition of skills (Lewis & Miller, 1990).

A variety of theories focusing on one or more areas of development have attempted to explain how and why development occurs and to predict development. Understanding various theories helps guide individuals who work with children in determining what intervention strategies are likely to help maximize development. Developmental theories can be classified as either **organismic** or **mechanistic** and either **continuous** or **discontinuous** (Berk, 1994).

Theorists with an organismic orientation view children as active participants in their own development. Cognitive theories, including the theory of **Jean Piaget** (1950), have an organismic theoretical orientation. Organismic theorists believe there are certain structures within children that underlie their development and that development is affected by experiences (Ginsburg & Opper, 1988; Thomas, 1990). Organismic theorists also view children as active and purposeful participants within their environment. Children are seen as determining their own learning, although environments that support growth must be made available. That is, organismic theories suggest that the environment supports, rather than causes, development (Flavell, 1992).

In contrast, mechanistic theorists view children as passive recipients of environmental stimuli. That is, the environment determines growth and development. One mechanistic theory, behaviorism, proposes that patterns of rewards and punishments control children's behavior (Horowitz, 1992).

Theories are also classified on the basis of whether development is viewed as being continuous or discontinuous. Theorists who view development as continuous believe that children perceive events in similar but less complex ways than adults. They focus on the fact that children have less information available to them than adults do because they have had fewer experiences. Over time, children acquire an increasing amount of information and number of abilities through experiences (Flavell, 1992). For example, children and adults can remember events. The number of events (stimuli) that can be remembered varies by age, with children typically remembering fewer stimuli than adults. That is, changes in development are **quantitative,** a matter of number or amount.

Other theorists view development as a discontinuous process. That is, development is believed to progress through distinctly different stages, as in Piaget's theory. In other words, children think and feel differently than adults; new ways of thinking and behaving emerge at different stages. Discontinuous theories support the idea that change is not only quantitative but also **qualitative** (pertaining to the *way* information is processed). The discontinuous perspective suggests it is necessary to accomplish the milestones of prior stages before moving on to more complex stages of development. It also suggests that change may be sudden rather than gradual, at certain points in time (McHale & Lerner, 1990). In addition, the discontinuous perspective stresses that stages of development are in the same sequence for all children. Rates of moving through stages vary from child to child, but all children go through the same sequence of developmental stages (Berk, 2005).

Most developmental theories focus on one or more of the major domains of development (communication, cognitive, motor, social-emotional, and adaptive). In most cases, no single theory encompasses all five domains. A discussion of several of the major developmental theories that are particularly relevant to early childhood development is found below.

Maria Montessori

Maria Montessori, an Italian physician, greatly influenced education in the early 1900s and again in the 1960s (Chen, Krechevsky, & Viens, 1998). Her experiences working with children living in institutions for the mentally retarded led her to conclude that children learned most effectively from adults who focused on children's natural tendencies and interests (Wentworth, 1998). Montessori theorized that children's development moves through **sensitive periods,** genetically preprogrammed blocks of time during which children most readily master certain tasks (Kuhl, 1984). Currently there are many Montessori-based schools throughout the world.

Montessori believed that children benefit from having many opportunities to explore nature, engage in gardening, and interact with nonhuman animals. She believed these activities naturally stimulate children's powers of observation and joy of learning (Korfmacher & Spicer, 2002). She did not approve of forced memorization but encouraged independent mastery corresponding to each child's needs. Montessori felt that children benefit from free choice and time to fully investigate a particular task or topic. She did not believe the use of rewards and punishment was appropriate because their frequent use results in children's becoming overly anxious.

Jean Piaget

Piaget's stage theory focused on understanding the development of children's cognitive skills. His theory supports the organismic perspective and views development as discontinuous. Piaget believed that between birth and adolescence children progress through four distinct stages of development: **sensorimotor, preoperational, concrete,** and **formal operational**.

Piaget (1950) described infants and toddlers as acquiring information through their various senses, including sight, sound, and touch. He labeled this first stage the sensorimotor stage, and it applies to children birth to 2 years. He viewed information processing in young children as initially limited to the use of their senses and physical movement, rather than involving thinking independent of sensory input. As language is acquired during the sensorimotor stage, children move from being primarily dependent on physical movements to increasingly interacting with their environment in mental ways.

During the sensorimotor stage the ability to imitate appears. Toddlers' competence increases as they develop the ability to imitate others. **Object permanence** (the understanding that objects continue to exist when out of view) gradually develops. For example, children at 4 months of age do not look for an object placed out of sight. Two-year-olds search for objects placed out of sight because they know those objects continue to exist even though they cannot see them.

Most children 2–6 years old are classified as being at the preoperational stage. There are two substages of preoperational thought: symbolic function and intuitive thought. The first substage, **symbolic function,** occurs between the ages of 2 and 4. During this time, children acquire the ability to mentally represent what is not actually present, but these representations often are not completely real or logical (Piaget, 1971). **Animism,** the belief that objects have the characteristics of animate beings (e.g., the chair's leg hurts if it is kicked), and **artification,** the belief that all things are human-made (e.g., people with big bulldozers dug the ocean and piled the dirt to make mountains), are characteristic of preoperational thought.

The second substage of Piaget's preoperational thought is **intuitive thought.** In this stage, children 4 to 7 years of age become insightful thinkers. They want to know the answers to all kinds of questions, including "Why?" and "Where?" They are more confident about their knowledge and understanding. They also begin to develop **metacognition** (an awareness of how they gained their knowledge) and **metamemory** (an awareness of how they remember things).

During the preoperational stage, children tend to focus on one characteristic of someone or something while ignoring other aspects. They display **centration,** an inability to consider multiple characteristics, and base a decision or judgment on one characteristic (Piaget, 1971). According to Piaget, even though internalized thinking skills have developed, a preschool child's thinking is often rigid and illogical at this stage. Thinking is strongly influenced by how a particular object looks at a particular moment. For example, a piece of clay may appear big when rolled into a ball. The same amount of clay may be seen as small when flattened into a pancake.

Children at the preoperational stage also lack **reversibility,** the ability to mentally move through a series of steps and then reverse direction to move back to the starting point. In addition, they gradually begin to use symbols and develop concepts and ways of classifying objects. The classification system often is incomplete.

Another characteristic of children at the preoperational level is that they are egocentric. Piaget used the term *egocentrism* to describe preschoolers' self-centered view of the world. **Egocentrism** refers to children's inability to consider other people's perspectives that may be different from their own. This lack of awareness of other perspectives leaves children to focus on their own perspectives rather than to consider the perspectives or needs of others. For example, imagine a 3-year-old facing the teacher and showing the teacher a picture. The child is likely to hold the picture facing themselves rather than the teacher. In this case, it is not that the child refuses to recognize another's perspective or is selfish or inconsiderate; rather the child is unable to consider another's perspective. Children at the preoperational level believe others perceive, think, and feel the same way that they do (Piaget, 1952).

Some researchers (Gelman, 1972; Wooley & Wellman, 1990) have suggested that Piaget underestimated the cognitive abilities of infants and preschoolers. These researchers have demonstrated that, when materials and language are less confusing, children often are able to perform more-complex tasks and demonstrate more-mature reasoning than Piaget's research indicated. For example, when young children are told, "Remember to hold the picture so I can see it," they are more likely to accommodate another's perspective, rather than respond in an egocentric fashion by holding the picture toward themselves so that the adult cannot see it.

Frequently, adults expect young children to think in ways that are much more typical of older children. Piaget describes two later stages of thinking skills not acquired until the school-age years. The concrete operational stage spans ages 6 to 11 years, and the formal operational stage spans the ages of 11 years and above. Reasoning at these stages is governed by the principles of logic, but it is not until the formal stage of development that children are able to think abstractly and use deductive and inductive methods of reasoning.

Piaget's theory set the stage for the belief that children are active learners and, therefore, should be provided with opportunities for **self-discovery learning** and direct contact with the environment. Piaget believed that the environments with which children interact should include areas designed to stimulate thinking skills. Piaget's theory does not support attempts to accelerate development but supports creating environments that provide each child opportunities to build on their own current level of reasoning. The ability to reason affects the way children store and remember events.

Lev Vygotsky

Lev Vygotsky rejected the assumptions of theorists, such as Piaget, who argued it was possible to separate learning from its social context. He argued that cognitive and language development is a product of social interactions (Vygotsky, 1978). Vygotsky emphasized the importance of interactions between children and their care providers and teachers (Bodrova & Leong, 2001; Bodrova, Leong, Norford, & Paynter, 2006).

Vygotsky proposed a **zone of proximal development (ZPD)**, which he defined as an area of development in which a child cannot accomplish a task independently but can do so with the assistance of an adult or more capable peer. He believed that effective instruction occurs within the zone lying just beyond the skills already mastered by the child. Vygostky also referred to methods that support children's learning within the ZPD as forms of **scaffolding** (Bodrova, Leong, Paynter, & Hughes, 2002; Wood, Bruner & Ross, 1976).

When applied to young children with disabilities, Vygotsky's approach clearly focuses on the need to understand each child's development in all domains and to provide support (scaffolding) specific to each child's needs. This approach clearly supports the idea of developing individualized family service plans (IFSPs) and individualized education programs (IEPs), which focus on each child's unique needs (McGonigel, Kaufmann, & Johnson, 1991).

Howard Gardner

According to the **multiple intelligences** theory of **Howard Gardner**, each of us possesses at least eight intelligences (ways to learn or be smart): **verbal/linguistic, logical/mathematical, visual/spatial, musical/rhythmic, bodily/kinesthetic, naturalistic, interpersonal,** and **intrapersonal.** Gardner's theory suggests that educators should teach and assess their students using all of these intelligences. Although a child may have stronger and weaker intelligences, each child can learn and should be encouraged to do so through use of the eight intelligences. Children benefit when adults allow them to access their strong intelligences (Gardner, 1973). Children also benefit when adults help them enhance less strong intelligences.

Often, adult–child teaching and learning interactions focus almost solely on verbal skills. Additionally, formal curricula typically focus on verbal and mathematical intelligences. Gardner emphasizes that learning is most effective when there are ample opportunities to use other intelligences. For example, children who have communication delays benefit from opportunities to learn using nonverbal intelligences rather than focusing primarily on use of verbal skills. It logically follows that children who have motor delays benefit from learning opportunities that do not focus solely on bodily/kinesthetic skills.

Most young children are naturally drawn to and positively respond without inhibitions to music. Use of the musical intelligence is often very beneficial for learning in all subject areas as well as enhancing the development of other intelligences. For example, singing incorporates speech and language skills. Often, children who have communication delays can sing a song even if they are unable to speak fluently. Using musical instruments involves use of bodily/kinesthetic and visual/spatial intelligences. In addition, singing and playing instruments involve noting patterns and counting rhythms, which are forms of logical-mathematical intelligence. Successfully producing music with others requires teamwork, sensitivity to others' needs, and respectfulness, which are all related to interpersonal intelligence. Music can excite and calm emotions and encourages self-reflection and self-expression, all of which are related to intrapersonal intelligence. This, in turn, often enhances a sense of belongingness, self-esteem, and confidence. Naturalistic intelligence is embedded in musical compositions that evoke ocean waves, storms, pastoral scenes, moonlight, sunshine, or other natural phenomena.

Developmentally appropriate practices (DAPs) acknowledge that young children readily learn when they are free to move about and explore their environments using all their intelligences (Jipson, 1991; Kostelnick, 1992; Odom, 1994). Fortunately, teachers of young children frequently use a variety of intelligences to enhance children's learning.

Behaviorist Perspectives

Behaviorists view behavior from a mechanistic and continuous perspective. They claim that all aspects of development can be explained through behaviorist principles.

Behaviorist **B. F. Skinner** formally described **operant conditioning**, the use of **reinforcement** or **punishment** to elicit a particular behavior. Reinforcement increases the likelihood of the behavior it follows (Berk, 1994; Skinner, 1957). Consider a situation in which a parent praises a child for fitting a piece into a puzzle. Praise would be considered a **reinforcer** if it increased the child's attempts to fit pieces into puzzles.

In contrast, punishment decreases the likelihood that the behavior it follows will reoccur. For example, a parent may take a toy away from a child (punishment) because the child grabbed it from another child. If the parent consistently takes toys away when the child grabs a toy, and over time the child becomes less likely to grab toys, then the action of taking the toy away from the child would be considered a form of punishment. The impact of reinforcement and punishment can be used to explain the development of a wide variety of behaviors.

Another major behaviorist perspective is based on **Ivan Pavlov's** theory of **classical conditioning,** in which an originally neutral stimulus (a stimulus that does not initially elicit a particular response) becomes associated with a positive or negative stimulus that results in a particular response. For example, if each time a child receives a painful shot, the nurse giving the shot wears a white coat, the child may learn to be afraid of people wearing white coats. In this example, the neutral stimulus, the nurse's white coat did not naturally cause a child to be fearful but became a negative stimulus because the child learned to associate pain with white coats. The child is likely to cry when seeing medical personnel in white coats and also anyone else wearing a white coat (generalization of the response). The classical conditioning perspective is easily applied to how fears and other emotions are acquired.

Information Processing

Information processing theories (also referred to as cognitive theories) focus on **perception, attention, reasoning,** and **memory** (Fry & Hale, 1996). According to these theories, information is processed in stages that include encoding, storage, and retrieval.

Perception.   Perception, awareness of stimuli (events), is the first level of cognition. Perception involves the ability to make sense of information provided to the brain from the sense organs for seeing, tasting, touching, hearing, smelling, and physical movement of one's own body. Everyone processes and interprets sensory information differently. Therefore, each person experiences unique reactions to the environment based on varying perceptions (Gibson & Spelke, 1983). Knowledge about early perceptual abilities is used to develop environments that enhance learning. Perceptual abilities allow children to learn from active exploration of their environment.

Infants are born with perceptual abilities that allow them to begin learning immediately. Initially, newborns respond **reflexively** (automatically) to certain stimulation (Berk, 1994). For example, they close their eyes in response to intense light. Another inborn tendency is to turn the head toward a source of light. Turning toward stimuli increases the number of experiences for newborns. Most newborn reflexes fade between 2 months and 1 year of age as the brain matures.

Attention.   For children to learn, they must be able to focus their attention on the most relevant information and learn to ignore less relevant information. **Selective attention** is the ability to focus on specific stimuli over a period of time. Typically, even young children without developmental disabilities have difficulty focusing on details, are easily distracted, and do not engage in one activity for long periods of time (Stodolsky, 1974). As those children mature, however, they gradually become more purposeful in their activities.

Children with learning disabilities who have sensory impairments or who are classified as having attention deficit hyperactivity disorder (ADHD) are often unable to focus or retain attention on specific stimuli. Children classified as ADHD typically have significantly shorter attention spans than most children their age (Stodolsky, 1974; Wellman, Somerville, & Haake, 1979). The ability to attend allows for the next crucial step in cognition, which includes reasoning about events.

Reasoning.   The ability to reason is another important aspect of cognitive development. As mentioned earlier in this chapter, different theories convey different perspectives about cognitive skills acquisition. Explanations of how children solve problems (reason) are of particular interest to theorists. Initially, infants and toddlers use their senses to physically explore the environment. While exploring the environment, children discover ways to solve problems (Aslin, 1987b). For example, while an infant is investigating a toy piano, they are likely to touch one of the piano keys and cause the piano to sound. In this example, the child discovers that touching a key produces sound and may perceive this event as reinforcing.

The thinking processes of preschool-age children are not typically governed by logical qualities (Gelman, 1972). Children may solve many problems correctly, but they often use intuition rather than logic. At times they can solve problems without being able to explain why the solution is correct. Children appear to use rules to govern their behavior, but they often do not use rules consistently (Piaget, 1965). This type of reasoning is demonstrated when children use limited and changing rules to group objects. For example, when a child is asked to group objects that go together, a brush may go with a doll in one case. In this case, the brush was grouped with the doll because the child learned that it can be used on the doll's hair. In another case, a brush may be classified with a hammer. This time, the brush and hammer were seen as types of tools.

Young children's reasoning abilities are limited, but young children consistently follow the principle of looking for simple and direct causes (Piaget, 1965). Preschoolers also tend to use **transductive reasoning,** which is reasoning from one instance to another. This type of reasoning is less complex than **inductive reasoning,** reasoning from single instances to generalizations, and less complex than **deductive reasoning,** reasoning from general instances to particular ones. Inductive and deductive reasoning do not develop until children are school age or older.

Often, the tendency to look for simple and direct causes results in children's attributing human qualities to non-living objects—animism. For example, a 4-year-old may believe that a stone feels pain when someone kicks it and that their father hangs the sun in the sky every morning before he goes to work. This type of immature reasoning limits the ability of young children to process certain types of information.

Memory.   Another important area related to cognitive development is memory ability. The memory processes include the ability to store and retrieve information (Schneider & Pressley, 1989). Memory is complex and depends on the processes of attention and perception. Potential information, which is perceived and remembered only momentarily, is constantly presented inside and outside of the body. Information from stimuli that is in the **sensory memory** (momentary memory) is ignored, forgotten, or stored in **short-term memory.** Short-term memory storage lasts less than 60 seconds and allows for storage of about seven items, give or take two, for adults and fewer for children (e.g., 2-year-olds typically can remember only two items) (Lipsitt, 1990). Information is generally not placed into short-term memory unless it is interesting or important and the individual is purposely attentive.

Long-term memory potentially stores information permanently and is limitless in capacity. Information is stored in long-term memory after being processed by short-term memory. Intent to remember is aided by **rehearsal** (repetition) and other methods. Information from short-term memory is most effectively transferred into long-term memory using some form of memory enhancement techniques (DeLoache & Todd, 1988).

Most preschoolers do not spontaneously rehearse information to aid memory. Presenting information repeatedly, providing rehearsal strategies, and encouraging rehearsal may help children to remember certain information. For example, a child may be able to remember a telephone number after being encouraged to repeat it many times (Lange & Pierce, 1992).

Children's rehearsal strategies are limited and often ineffective when they are very young (Carr & Schneider, 1991). This limits the amount of material stored in long-term memory and how easily the stored material may be retrieved. **Constructivists,** such as Piaget, suggest that much of the information encountered by children is selected and interpreted on the basis of already existing knowledge.

Abraham Maslow

Intervention programs for young children vary greatly but nearly always involve a combination of education and care. **Abraham Maslow** has postulated a **hierarchy of needs,** an order of needs that must be met to ensure development of potential. According to Maslow, the basic needs of physical safety, emotional security, and sense of belonging and self-esteem must be met before higher levels of intellectual skills can develop (Thiele & Hamilton, 1991).

These needs are often depicted within a pyramid consisting of five (sometimes seven) levels. The four lower levels are grouped together as **deficiency needs** while the top level is termed **"growth needs"** (cognitive, aesthetic, self-actualization) and is associated with psychological needs. Maslow believed that deficiency needs must be met (at an adequate level) before learning, a growth need, can optimally occur. For example, children who are hungry, cold, or fearful are likely to have difficulty focusing on and benefiting from learning activities. According to Maslow, all individuals have vast potential, but at times their potential is blocked by unmet needs. He believed that everyone should be provided with supportive environments that allow them to move toward self-actualization. Figure 3.2 shows Maslow's hierarchy of needs.

The first needs that must be met are **physiological needs,** including food, water, and sleep. These needs help maintain the human body. **Safety needs** are next in the hierarchy and include being free from harm (being hurt by others' or one's own behaviors). When children feel unsafe, growth is likely to be slowed until they feel comfortable in their learning environment. This dilemma suggests that it is crucial

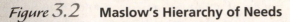

Figure 3.2 **Maslow's Hierarchy of Needs**

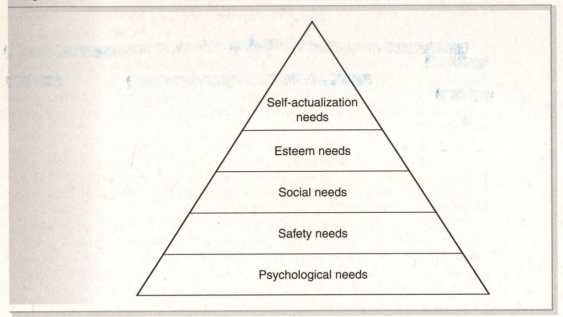

that adults who interact with young children develop effective behavior management techniques and ensure that the environment is pleasant and unthreatening.

Love and belongingness needs have to do with the human need to affiliate with others and to feel accepted by them. When adults are empathetic, provide one-on-one time, and support peer-group interactions, children are more likely to develop a sense of belonging. This need suggests that children with disabilities are likely to benefit when they are fully integrated with children who do not have disabilities.

Esteem needs involve the feeling of self-worth. Children are more likely to develop self-esteem when others focus on and build on their strengths rather than their weaknesses. Self-esteem is also enhanced when adults are quick to notice and provide support for children experiencing difficulties. Children need to be respected, have self-respect, and respect others. They need to gain recognition and engage in activities that provide a sense of contribution and self-importance. If these are not provided, children are likely to have low self-esteem. (Refer to Chapter 14 for a discussion of the development and support of self-esteem needs.)

With regard to meeting children's **cognitive needs**, Maslow believed that children benefit from being allowed to explore their environment through a guided self-discovery process. He also emphasized the value of creating an aesthetically pleasing environment, which is clean, appealing, organized, and interesting. According to Maslow, to maximize children's learning, adults must consider the hierarchical order of human needs. When this occurs, children are most likely to continue movement toward their highest level of potential (self-actualization).

Urie Bronfenbrenner

Urie Bronfenbrenner (1979) suggested that an individual develops within a context or ecology. His **ecological systems theory** (also referred to as **bioecological systems theory**) emphasized that a child's own biological makeup is the primary environment affecting development. He further suggested that each person is significantly affected by interactions among overlapping ecosystems, with the person being the center of this system. Bronfenbrenner hypothesized that development occurs through increasingly complex reciprocal interactions between the individual and the environment.

For children, the **microsystem** includes family members, peers, care providers, classrooms, and neighborhoods. Interactions among the microsystems take place within the **mesosystem.** For example, parents and teachers coordinate efforts to educate the child. The mesosytem involves linkages between microsystems, which indirectly, rather than directly affect the person. The **exosystem** surrounds the microsystem and includes external networks, such as local educational, medical, employment, and communications systems, which influence the microsystems. The **macrosystem** influences all other systems and includes cultural values, political philosophies, economic patterns, and social conditions. These systems make up the social context of human development.

To best meet the needs of children with disabilities and their families, one must consider each of the systems described by Bronfenbrenner. Refer to Figure 3.3 for a representation of Bronfenbrenner's theory.

Clearly, knowledge about various theories has been and should be used to guide the development of the basic philosophy of early childhood special education programs. It is important to understand the underlying philosophies that guide the development of these programs.

Philosophy of Early Childhood Special Education

The philosophy of most early childhood special education programs is to acknowledge each child's present level of development, create developmentally appropriate practices (DAPs), and help each child move to a greater level of competency (Kostelnick, 1992; Walsh, 1991). For example, if children enrolled in a special education program are functioning at a 2-year-old level even though they are 4 years old, activities provided should be appropriate for children at a 2-year-old level. In addition, effective programs recognize the value of including children's families in all aspects of program planning and delivery (Brown, 1993; Bruder, 1993; Groark, Mehaffie, McCall, & Greenberg, 2007).

Children receiving early childhood intervention services may have a disability in one or more areas of development, or one type of delay may cause delays in other areas (e.g., language delays often affect social and cognitive skills areas) (Graham & Bryant, 1993; Bailey & Wolery, 1984). Therefore, activities and therapies must be developed with a focus on each child's specific area(s) of need and provided in the least restrictive environment (LRE) (Mahoney, Robinson, & Powell, 1992; Carta, Schwartz, Atwater, & McConnell, 1991; Norris, 1991; Brown, 1982). The LRE may be found within a variety of settings, depending on the child's specific needs.

Figure 3.3   **Urie Bronfenbrenner's Theory**

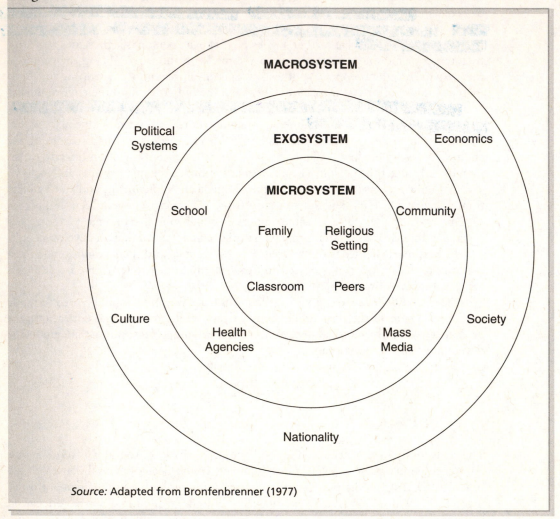

Source: Adapted from Bronfenbrenner (1977)

Settings of Early Childhood Special Education Services

Home-Based Settings

In some cases, children are provided early intervention services primarily at home (Schweinhart et al., 2005). This is especially likely in the case of children who are younger than 2 years old, are severely physically impaired, or have multiple disabilities. **Home-based programs** recognize that the child is a member of a family and community and that services must be provided within the child's primary environment and focus on the strengths and priorities of the parents and other community care providers (Gargiulo, 1985). In some cases, home-based services are provided at a doctor's office, clinic, or hospital (Association for the Care of Children's Health, 1984; Gomby, Culross, & Behrman, 1999).

Many home-based services emphasize having professional staff teach parents how to most effectively meet their children's needs. In addition, home-based programs are child-oriented and emphasize having professionals provide direct intervention services. In home-based programs, children may receive some services at their regular day care or preschool program (Wasik, Ramey, Bryant, & Sparling, 1990).

Based on federal laws, early intervention services must be family-systems oriented. This orientation is child- and family-centered. The entire family system is provided intervention services. IFSPs for each child are developed based on the needs of each child and family within a family ecology context. In all types of EIPs, it is necessary to help the child adapt to thrive within various environments and to modify environments to fit the child's needs, creating ecological congruence (a good fit).

Day Care and Preschool-Based Settings

When children receive services within a day care or preschool environment, they benefit from interactions with other children. They learn through observing and modeling the behavior of peers and adults. Children who have developmental delays benefit from opportunities to interact with children who do not have delays (Johnson, Pugach, & Devlin, 1990). They need opportunities to gain confidence in their abilities and strengths within the context of the real world (typical daily settings) and through interactions with a variety of people. When services are provided in a setting with children who have special needs and those who do not, the setting is referred to as an **inclusion classroom** (Cavallaro & Hney, 1999).

Center-Based Settings

In **center-based programs,** children may receive therapy intervention within the classroom or may be pulled out for therapy outside of the classroom. When services are provided within classrooms designed specifically for children with disabilities, these classrooms are referred to as **self-contained classrooms.** Self-contained classrooms typically include a special education teacher who provides most of the daily instruction to students who are segregated in a special class. It has been determined that a self-contained classroom provides the LRE for children receiving services in this type of setting. Children with moderate to severe delays often learn most effectively in self-contained classrooms, although the ultimate goal is to integrate these children into regular classes.

Therapy is often provided within the context of classroom activities (Johnson et al., 1990). For example, occupational therapy goals may be practiced while the child is playing at a sensory table physically exploring different materials such as sand or rice. Speech therapy can occur during an informal child–adult interaction, such as during play or other activities. Services may also be provided when a child is temporarily pulled from the classroom for therapy within another building.

Children learn from each other while playing with clay at a center-based program.

All children need a chance to acquire basic problem-solving skills, tools for effective communication, a capacity to persist at tasks, and a positive attitude about the process of learning. Research indicates that a center-based program is effective, in part, because learning often is maximized when children interact with one another (Dunst, Snyder, & Mankinen, 1989).

In all forms of service delivery, parents remain primary contributors to their child's education. Parents need opportunities to meet and interact with other parents who have children with disabilities. Programs designed to meet the needs of children with developmental delays should provide the help needed to create these opportunities (Guralnick, 2001).

In 2000, 71.8% of infants and toddlers with developmental delays were being served primarily in their homes, and 10.9% were being served in center-based programs. Between 1996 and 2000, the percentage being served primarily in center-based programs decreased by more than 50% while the percentage being served primarily in the home increased by more than 15%.

Team Members and Collaboration

For the education of children with disabilities to be effective, many individuals must collaborate. Team members working within an EIP should have an understanding of typical and atypical development, knowledge about family support, competency in child and family assessment, the ability to conduct program evaluations, and knowledge about proper professional conduct (Bailey, McWilliams, & Simeonsson, 1991;

Lowenthal, 1992; U.S. Department of Labor, 2002). It is important that team members have

- training and experience related to early childhood,
- a professional license or certification in a specific discipline, and
- the ability to work effectively as a member of a team.

Some team members were described in Chapter 2, and several other team members are discussed in detail in subsequent chapters. Team members commonly include social workers, parents, special education teachers, speech and language pathologists, teachers of the deaf and hearing-impaired, audiologists, and occupational and physical therapists. In addition to these individuals, several other individuals may provide services in early education programs for children with disabilities. The following sections describe the roles of various service providers.

Special Education Teachers

Training for the **special education teacher** typically involves course work in several areas, including specific disabilities, human development, curriculum strategies, measurement and evaluation, reading and mathematics instructional methods, behavior management techniques, and prescriptive teaching techniques (suggestions for intervention). Although some programs focus on working with young children, in some cases course work in early childhood special education is offered as electives rather than required courses. Special education teachers have a bachelor's or master's degree in special education. Depending on state certification requirements, teachers may be allowed to teach in programs from preschool and kindergarten through 12th grade or only at certain designated grade levels.

Odom and McEvoy (1990) argue that college and university programs should require course work in general and special early childhood education for certification as an early childhood special education teacher. Some states do require this specialized level of training, but others do not (Association of Teacher Educators & National Association for the Education of Young Children, 1991; Burton, Hains, Hanline, McLean, & McCormick, 1992).

Special education teachers should remain up to date on research in education and related fields. Up-to-date information is useful for optimal understanding of specific disabilities, as well as learning about new and effective teaching strategies. It is important for teachers to remain open to new opinions and ideas and to be willing to try new approaches. As an advocate for children and parents, the special education teacher should share new information with parents and other staff members. Therefore, developing effective communication strategies is crucial (Accarpo, O'Connor-Leppert, Lipkin, & Rogers, 2005; Bruder, Klosowski, & Daguio, 1989; Edyburn, Higgins, & Boone, 2005; Wolock, 1990).

The responsibilities of special education teachers described below are specifically geared toward early childhood special education teachers, but they also apply to special educators who work with older children. The examples provided concentrate on teachers working with children in group settings, but they are relevant to teachers working in individual home settings or clinics as well.

Using Knowledge about Typical Rates of Development.   It is essential for the special education teacher to have a thorough understanding of the typical stages of child development. The special education teacher uses this knowledge when doing assessments, determining curriculum, and establishing appropriate expectations for each child. Possessing knowledge about typical stages of development helps teachers understand the sequence of steps necessary to reach the desired educational outcomes for a particular child.

Being aware of education practices for typically developing children is also relevant when creating the LRE for children. Children must learn to function in a variety of environments. It is important to know what types of expectations are common in regular preschool and early elementary programs.

Service Coordination.   Within a preschool setting, the special education teacher is typically responsible for coordinating each child's overall education program and may be thought of as the umbrella that covers all areas of development. As service coordinator, the special education teacher often schedules services provided by other team members and arranges meetings at which professionals and parents work together to plan and implement programs designed to meet a child's needs. Service coordination is discussed in greater detail in Chapter 4.

Developing and Implementing an IFSP or IEP.   Special education teachers are often responsible for developing the IFSP or IEP goals and objectives for each child. These goals and objectives are written once the team has completed the child's assessment and has consulted with the child's parents and relevant professionals. To develop appropriate IFSPs or IEPs, the special education teacher must view the child as a child first and then consider the child's needs. This includes viewing each child as having the potential to grow and change rather than viewing the child as being limited to a certain level of development.

After the long-term goals have been established, the special education teacher breaks these goals into small, sequential steps to establish short-term objectives in a process referred to as task analysis. This process involves sequencing tasks from the easiest to the most difficult. Generally, the skills needed to complete a task are more important than task completion itself.

Early Childhood Teachers

Early childhood teachers should possess the knowledge, skills, and abilities to work sensitively with young children and their parents, as well as others whose interactions may affect these children. They must be able to adjust to the wide variety of children's interests and needs in a diverse society. The highly qualified teacher is a licensed or certified professional.

Early childhood teachers have an associate's, bachelor's, or master's degree in education, day care services, or early childhood. They have received training on the typical stages of development and regular early childhood curriculum. This training helps them be well prepared to help create and maintain federally mandated LREs, which include children with disabilities in as many typical daily activities as possible.

Because some special education teachers do not receive special training for teaching children younger than school age (5 years old), early childhood teachers often help fill knowledge gaps (Deiner, 1993). Early childhood educators often work as coteachers with a special educator or other staff members, such as a speech or language pathologist, teacher of the deaf or hearing-impaired, or occupational or physical therapist. These individuals may not have specific training that focuses on children birth through school age.

Early childhood educators are involved in the planning, organizing, and implementing of activities designed to enhance development in all areas for preschool and school-age children. They often supervise assistants and provide care and guidance to preschool children. They are employed in child care centers, kindergartens, nursery schools, and early childhood special education centers.

Teacher Assistants

Teacher assistants often function much as teachers do and may be referred to as teachers, although they typically are not certified as teachers or therapists. They may have a 2-year degree in child care or early childhood education, but this degree often is not required. Teacher assistants often supervise many of the classroom activities, but they typically do not conduct formal assessments and are not responsible for writing IFSP or IEP reports. Often, though, they attend meetings for planning the child's goals. They are a vital part of service delivery (Pickett & Gerlach, 2003; Pickett, Gerlach, Morgan, Likens, & Wallace, 2007).

Day Care Providers

Many young children are cared for during part of the day by adults other than their parents. Day care providers are sometimes extended-family members, but often they are not. In either case, day care providers frequently spend more time with children when they are awake than any other person. Therefore, they should be members of a child's service team.

Team Collaboration

Typically, a single individual cannot provide all the services that a child with developmental delays requires. Team members bring varied expertise and philosophies, which, when combined, allow for the development and fulfillment of the most effective educational plans. Although involving a variety of professionals makes the process more complex and difficult to coordinate, typically the more professionals represented on a team, the more complete the services (Montie, Xiang, & Schweinhart, 2006). Chapter 4 provides an extended discussion of team collaboration.

To develop an overall philosophy on how best to provide services to each child, it is often necessary for staff members to modify or compromise their personal philosophies to best meet a child's needs (Karnes & Stayton, 1988). Individual team members may need to relinquish their professional turf to develop a true respect for all areas of expertise, including that of colleagues and parents, which results in the most effective team possible. In addition, all team members must maintain the highest ethical standards. In 1993 the **Council for Exceptional Children (CEC)** developed a *Code of Ethics and Standards for Educators,* which provides guidelines for all individuals who work with children (cited in Salisbury & Vincent, 1990). Figure 3.4 summarizes this code.

It is crucial that no member of an early intervention team attempt to take over a parent's responsibilities. It is imperative that they not undermine the role of a parent because the parent is an integral part of planning and implementing the child's educational plan. Families must be allowed and encouraged to develop their own competencies and learn to be as self-sufficient as possible (Slentz & Bricker, 1992). Team members should not act as experts in areas outside their expertise. For example, families should be referred to psychologists or social workers when counseling is needed rather than receive counseling from a teacher.

When parents and children receive intervention services, professionals must recognize the parents' role as services recipients and as members of the team planning the child's services. In addition, parents may serve in other capacities such as school or program board members, advocates and lobbyists, classroom therapy aides, fundraisers, or events organizers. They can help write or produce newsletters, build equipment, perform clerical or office work, and so on. Typically, parents who become actively involved improve their parenting skills, feel more confident, become more accepting of their child's developmental level, and become better advocates for their child (Goodman, 1992).

Infants and young children with disabilities benefit from the combined expertise of a variety of professionals who provide specialized services. The coordination of

---

Figure 3.4   **Summary of the CEC *Code of Ethics and Standards for Educators***

- Provide opportunities for children to realize their educational and quality-of-life potential.
- Promote and maintain a high level of professional competence.
- Engage in professional activities designed to support children with disabilities, their families, and your colleagues.
- Make objective judgments.
- Continually advance your knowledge and skills.
- Work within your profession's standards and policies.
- Know, adhere to, and improve laws, regulations, and policies related to special education services.
- Behave ethically and legally, and abide by professional standards.

Source: Adapted from Council for Exceptional Children (1993, § 3, Part 2, p. 4). Adopted by the CEC's Delegate Assembly in 1983.

people and services is often complex. Typically, service providers represent different professional disciplines and philosophical models. Each discipline has it own training requirements (some require undergraduate degrees while others require graduate degrees), licensing and certification requirements (such as specialization with young children), and treatment modality. Each has its own professional organization (e.g., National Association for the Education of Young Children), which may or may not focus on the entire life span.

To comply with federal laws and improve the efficiency of the individuals providing early childhood intervention, services must be delivered through a team approach. A group of people can be a highly effective team only when their purpose and function are derived from an agreed-on philosophy and shared goals. The three service-delivery models for young children with disabilities are multidisciplinary (involving multiple disciplines), interdisciplinary (involving multiple individuals from the same discipline), and transdisciplinary (involving two or more people, including family members, working together to better understand and more effectively and efficiently address the needs of the child and family). Chapter 4 provides a more extensive discussion of each of these team approaches.

Attributes of Intervention Programs

The **National Association for the Education of Young Children (NAEYC)** has provided guidelines for early childhood programs for all young children, with and without developmental delays. The guidelines remind educators and parents that their most important responsibilities are to keep children safe and healthy and to provide a nurturing, responsive setting for all children. These responsibilities include recognizing and respecting the uniqueness of each child. NAEYC also emphasizes the belief that family members should play a major role in a child's development. Its guidelines clearly support the mandates of federal laws that specifically relate to early childhood special education intervention services.

Although programs for young children vary greatly, all should involve a combination of education and care (Bailey, Hebbeler, Scarborough, Spiker, Malik, 2004; Baker & Brightman, 2004). As Abraham Maslow's hierarchy of needs suggests, the basic needs of physical safety, emotional security, and sense of belonging and self-esteem all need to be met before higher levels of intellectual skills may be developed. In addition, nurturing and educating children involve simultaneous commitments to language, cognitive, social, emotional, and physical growth (Council for Exceptional Children, 2003).

Developmentally Appropriate Intervention Strategies

DAPs are organized and designed on the basis of a child's age and developmental level. People providing services to young children with disabilities develop these strategies within a child's IFSP/IEP as a foundation and individualize them to meet the child's unique needs. That is, the child should not be expected to adjust to a preconceived curricular content; instead the curriculum should be adapted to meet the child's needs.

First and foremost, a DAP ensures that children's biological needs are met, including their need to feel physically and psychologically safe and secure. Once children's basic needs are ensured, they are naturally open to learning. They learn best while engaging in daily activities and through play. A DAP provides support for children to develop the skills needed to communicate well, interact effectively with others, develop positive and caring relationships with others, analyze situations and solve problems, and assess information through various modalities. Figure 3.5 lists NAEYC's guidelines for DAPs.

Responding to Diversity

Children who receive early childhood special education services and their families reflect U.S. cultural and linguistic diversity. DAPs mandate cultural sensitivity, based on an interactive and experiential philosophy. In addition, in order to provide for each child's unique needs, knowledge about the child's social and cultural background is crucial. Diversity refers to more than race/ethnic origin. It includes gender, religion, socioeconomic status, and family characteristics (dual-parent, single-parent, extended, grandparent-headed, foster, with employed/unemployed parent(s), large/small, with homosexual parent, etc.) (Benner, 1998; Currie, 1998).

Increasingly, early childhood special education services provide support for children with disabilities who have diverse family backgrounds. This diversity creates many challenges and opportunities for service providers. For services to be optimally successful, service providers must become knowledgeable about and responsive to children's increasingly diverse needs (National Association for the Education of Young Children [NAEYC], 2005).

Figure 3.5   **NAEYC Guidelines for DAPs**

- Curriculum that reflects the program's philosophy, goals, and objectives
- Predictable yet flexible daily schedule that is sensitive to children's individual needs
- Orderly, safe, and healthy learning environment
- Effective behavior management and transition techniques
- Curriculum that incorporates active, senses-based indoor and outdoor exploration, primarily during play
- Self-directed hands-on learning balanced with teacher-directed instruction
- Frequent interactions between children and their teachers and peers
- Daily activities that ensure movement and quiet activities
- Ongoing assessment that guides program services
- Program staff who work as a team

Source: Adapted from NAEYC (2005).

In 2004, U.S. Census data indicated that ethnic minorities constitute more than 25% of the U.S. population. Projections of U.S. ethnic composition in 2050 indicate the following changes: the Asian American population will increase 3–8%, the Hispanic American population will increase 10–25%; the African American population will increase 13–14%; and Caucasians will decrease approximately 14%. If these predictions are accurate, Caucasians will constitute less than 50% of the total U.S. population in 2050. Currently, approximately 20% of all U.S. children live in households in which English is not the primary language spoken (NAEYC, 2005). Therefore, educators must increasingly prepare themselves to help children acquire language and other skills in their first and second language.

Values and beliefs regarding appropriate social interactions often vary greatly across cultures. For example, some cultures discourage calling attention to oneself or behaving competitively, whereas other cultures highly value these behaviors. Variations in eye contact, adult–child interactions, parenting methods, reaction time before responding, willingness to ask for help, degree of self-disclosure, and so on require educators to adjust their interactions to cultural expectations. Acknowledging and validating cultural differences, and using communication methods familiar to individuals of various cultures, allows children and their families to feel more comfortable and therefore be more open to educational opportunities (Gonzalez-Mena, 1998).

Staff members must also avoid assuming that common customs exist across various cultural groups. For example, different cultural groups celebrate different holidays; some do not believe in celebrating holidays or birthdays. Therefore, class activities based on certain holidays may not be appropriate for some families. Making Mother's or Father's Day cards is not be an appropriate activity for all children, because not all children have both a mother and a father.

Additionally, staff must avoid assuming that children and family members have common knowledge across various cultures (Irvine, 2003). For example, a child who lives on a farm is likely to have greater knowledge about crops than a child who lives in an urban setting. Children who live in Florida are likely to know more about beaches and sea life than about mountain habitats and species.

Within a classroom setting, teachers should select materials that reflect cultural differences in a nonstereotypical way. Visual images should accurately reflect variety within racial and ethnic groups. That is, not everyone within a given cultural group looks alike or behaves in exactly the same way; there is great variety within each cultural group. Images of various cultural groups should reflect the differences within various subcultural groups. Ideally, various groups are presented in a balanced fashion, with images of different individuals within various groups being presented. These individuals should be shown engaging in a wide variety of activities at home, at play, and at work rather than as dependent or passive (Klein & Chen, 2000).

Images with printed words should reflect languages spoken by the families of children in the classroom. Books should include pictures of various cultures, family arrangements, and people with disabilities. Learning materials should accommodate children with disabilities. Activities should reflect various cultures. For example, cooking activities should regularly include foods from a wide variety of cultures. Music should also routinely include songs, dances, and movements of various cultures. Cultural activities should occur regularly, rather than merely on special occasions, and they should be connected to daily activities through hands-on experiences.

In addition, because family members are children's primary educators, family members should be encouraged to continue to use their home language so that their children will learn the family language. To do otherwise would make the transition between home and school more difficult. The NAEYC position on the need to support use of children's home language is clarified in the following statement: "For the optimal development and learning of all children, educators must accept the legitimacy of children's home language, respect (hold in high regard) and value (esteem, appreciate) the home culture, and promote and encourage the active involvement and support of all families, including extended and nontraditional family units" (p. 1). Figure 3.6 lists NAEYC's recommendations for creating a culturally responsive learning environment.

Educators should continually learn about various cultures. Children's family members and staff members from diverse backgrounds should be viewed as excellent resources for educators who are developing culturally appropriate activities. In addition, educators should be provided ongoing professional development focused on cultural issues.

Educators must not assume that hardship or minority status creates a negative destiny for children. For example, educators must not assume that a child who lives in poverty, is homeless, lives in a non–English-speaking family, or lives in a minority family is destined to fall behind in skills as compared to children who do not share these circumstances. That is, educators must have high expectations for success for all children, regardless of their backgrounds. All children can learn and must be appropriately supported as they move toward their full potential (Zhang & Bennett, 2000).

Figure 3.6   **NAEYC's Recommendations for Creating a Culturally Responsive Learning Environment**

- Children are cognitively, linguistically, and emotionally connected to their home language and culture and are allowed and encouraged to demonstrate their skills through many modalities.
- Children's family members are actively encouraged and provided with the skills to be actively involved in a child's education.
- Educators obtain professional preparation related to cultural diversity, and teachers from diverse backgrounds are recruited and supported.
- Children learn English while their home language is respected.

Source: Adapted from NAEYC (2005).

Least Restrictive Environment

To best serve children with developmental delays, developmentally appropriate strategies must be used in combination with age-appropriate placements. Age-appropriate placements occur when children with disabilities receive services within environments with peers of similar ages who do not have disabilities. As discussed in Chapter 1, age-appropriate placements are consistent with federal laws, which mandate that children be educated in the LRE—integrated to the fullest extent possible. Mainstreaming and partial and full inclusion are forms of integration.

Mainstreaming involves placing children with special needs services within a special education classroom for part of the day and within regular education settings for the remainder of the day. In contrast, inclusion involves keeping children with and without developmental disabilities in the same classroom throughout the day. When attending an inclusion program, a child with developmental delays may be taken to another room to receive therapy services for a limited portion of the day.

Inclusion involves more than merely integrating children with disabilities into the same physical space as classmates who do not have disabilities. It requires that children with disabilities have consistent opportunities to interact with other children and participate in the same activities as their peers. Inclusive placements allow educators, parents, and children with disabilities to better understand typical expectations with regard to other children. Inclusion is valuable for children with and without developmental delays. It provides them with the experience of interacting with many types of people within a variety of environments. Children and adults are typically more comfortable and positive toward individuals with developmental delays after participating in integration/inclusion experiences (Carta, 1994).

Full inclusion does not provide the LRE for all children (Baker, Wang, & Walberg, 1995). Proponents of inclusion as part of a continuum believe that educators must make inclusion work for children for whom it is appropriate, but it is a mistake to have only one type of placement. One size does not fit all (Fuchs & Fuchs, 1994–1995; O'Neil, 1994–1995; Shanker, 1994).

Inclusive settings allow services to be provided in natural environments (homes, schools, playgrounds, etc.). This is not always the most effective service delivery method. That is, in some cases, full inclusion does not provide the LRE, and services are best provided in noninclusive settings (Guralnick, 2001).

Many factors influence determination of the best setting for service delivery for infants, toddlers, and young children with disabilities. There is no single best setting. Determination of which setting best meets each child's unique needs includes considerations regarding location of intervention programs, space allocations, children's specific needs, transportation resources, and family preferences. If a child requires a wide variety of services, services may be provided in multiple locations and settings, which are likely to change as the child's and family's needs change.

Research focusing on childhood integration indicates that an increasing number of early childhood programs are modifying philosophies and curricula to incorporate education practices effective for children with and without developmental disabilities (Odom & McEvoy, 1988; Peck, Odom, & Bricker, 1993; Wolery et al., 1993). Professionals and parents involved in these integrated programs perceive many benefits (e.g. children develop a greater understanding of individual differences) and report that classroom activities are relatively easily adapted to the needs of children with and without developmental delays.

Some problems still hinder the success of integration in early childhood education programs. These problems include teachers' being inadequately prepared to work with children who have disabilities, teachers' having too few opportunities to consult with other professionals, inappropriately large child–teacher ratios, and a lack of adequate funding.

Collaborative communication between professionals is essential for creating successful integrated classrooms. When working in integrated classrooms, special education teachers must use their knowledge of typical development and regular education practices to establish appropriate curriculum practices for all children. They must also develop an understanding and respect for regular and special early childhood education programs, as discussed later in this chapter.

Many educators involved in inclusive programs report that classroom activities are relatively easy to adapt to meet the needs of all children. However, in some cases teachers' lacking adequate early childhood special education preparation and consultation opportunities with other professionals, inappropriately large child–teacher ratios, and a lack of adequate funding limit the effectiveness of inclusion programs. Effective communication and collaboration between professionals and family members is essential for creating successful inclusion classrooms.

Effective Interaction with Parents

Effective early childhood programs enhance parents' competency and confidence. These programs acknowledge that parents of all economic levels and family backgrounds share common concerns but that each family also has individual needs that must be met. Meeting these needs may require individual or group counseling. Early childhood programs should include counseling services or, if they do not, offer assistance in finding appropriate counseling services (Deiner, 1993).

As previously discussed in this chapter, staff members must develop cultural sensitivity, which includes becoming aware of communication styles, values, and customs of families with different cultural and linguistic backgrounds. Service providers need to understand that children and their families may have had experiences that can lead to aloofness and skepticism regarding the usefulness of services (Bornstein, 1992). Service providers should openly share their philosophies with family members but must not attempt to change the family's value system. Chapter 4 provides further discussion of the importance of parental involvement.

Programming for Varying Needs

Ideally, an early childhood program serves children with a broad range of disabilities rather than only those within a narrow range of classifications, such as children with ADHD or autism (Bailey & McWilliams, 1990). Typically, when children with varying disabilities are learning together, a wider range of activities are provided. Also, staff members are less inclined to develop a rigid format regarding how to care for a particular type of child and instead become accustomed to adjusting the curriculum to meet the wide variety of needs (Bailey & Wolery, 1984).

Ideally, a center-based program provides contact between children without disabilities and their families and children with disabilities and their families. Special education programs must strive for a careful balance between accepting children as they are (not thinking of them as broken and in need of fixing) and helping them learn to fit in. The desire to ensure that children are happy and well adjusted is appropriate, but the goal should not be achieved by attempting to fashion the child into a likeness of the ideal child. It would be unreasonable to expect a 4-year-old with severe disabilities to have the skills of a typical 4-year-old. If a child can perform only at the cognitive level of a 2-year-old, it is likely that this child will also behave similarly to a typical 2-year-old both emotionally and socially. Therefore, the child's needs must be met at this level in an attempt to move development forward at the rate most appropriate for the child.

Recognizing Each Child's Individuality

As discussed above, service providers must view each child as a unique individual; they must recognize varying levels of abilities across all areas of development. Adults should expect different abilities and learning styles from different children, accept them, and use the current levels of abilities to design appropriate learning experiences. Not all children should be expected to perform or enjoy the same activities. Activities should be designed that help develop a child's self-esteem and positive feelings toward learning.

Children should not be required to participate in all activities in order to obtain adult approval or extrinsic rewards or to avoid punishment. Again, it is important to respect individual needs and preferences. Children with disabilities frequently require that the pace of the curriculum be modified. Teachers often worry that these children will fall further behind if instruction is not designed to push the child. In fact, it is more likely they will fall further behind if they are forced to deal with material they are not yet developmentally ready to process. They may also come to dislike those who attempt to support their development or develop a self-handicapping strategy (a pessimistic outlook that becomes an excuse for anticipated failure), which is demonstrated when a child says, "I can't do anything well," and ultimately completely resists learning.

Adults should avoid presenting activities to a child when the child is not ready to grasp them. Children may become discouraged and avoid certain activities when they experience excessive failure. They may interpret frequent failure as their being unable to learn, and they are more likely to be unsuccessful when they believe that they lack competency or when adults send them messages that suggest they are unlikely to succeed. Too frequently, activities, materials, books, and stories used in preschool classrooms have themes that are too complex or boring for children at a particular developmental level.

Individual goals and objectives must be determined for each child who is classified as having a disability, and they must be stated within the child's IFSP or IEP. Goals and objectives are most useful when they are stated in terms of behaviors that adults believe would be desirable for the child to achieve. IFSP or IEP objectives are often stated with more specificity than objectives set for children who do not have special needs. An objective such as "Jill will be able to catch, unassisted, a 6-inch ball thrown from 3 feet away, on four of five trials" indicates what the child should be doing rather than how the child will be taught. When objectives are stated in this manner (in behavioral terms), adults know what to teach but are not limited as to how they should teach, and they know when the objective has been achieved. There needs to be a middle ground between helping the child fit into the environment and modifying the environment to fit the child. For example, conformity and self-expression are both desirable outcomes.

Children as Active Participants in Learning

Children should engage in **active learning,** or **self-directed learning,** rather than passively be lectured or watch others' behaviors. For example, young children may be actively involved in learning by making and building things. At the same time, they are likely to benefit from opportunities to observe and experience events around them. They also often benefit from opportunities to talk about what they see and draw pictures representing their experiences or act out experiences through dramatic play. Young children also benefit from interactions with adults and other children, as they explore materials and their surroundings.

The younger children are, the more informal the learning environment should be (Kamii & DeVries, 1997). Children need ample time for informal play during which materials, props, and equipment are readily available for them to play with spontaneously. Children need opportunities to work together—for example, by jointly making things or pursuing topics or projects (Kohlberg, 1969). Teachers and parents should encourage children to maintain an interest in learning. The desire to learn is present at birth, but there are many obstacles to maintaining and strengthening this disposition, particularly for children with disabilities (Johnson-Martin, Jens, & Attermeier, 1986).

When children learn concepts through observation and interaction with other people, the learning is more meaningful, useful, and likely to be retained. Children should have opportunities to discover or invent solutions to concrete problems rather than simply encouraged to memorize rote information. Activity-based instruction provides meaningful discovery and hands-on activities, such as measuring the ingredients for cookies, working with wood and tools, sorting objects, playing with gears and wheels, and working with clay (Malone & Stoneman, 1990). Chapter 11 provides a detailed discussion regarding the value of play for enhancing children's learning.

There should be a balance between teacher-guided learning and less structured learning, frequently called **discovery learning,** and between opportunities for quiet and more-active periods. A rigid daily schedule should not interfere with children's spontaneous activities. Generally, it is inadvisable to remove a child for therapy during an activity in which the child is fully engaged, at snack time, or right before a positively anticipated activity. Whenever possible, movement to individual therapy should occur during a natural transition time between activities (Salisbury & Vincent, 1990).

Service delivery should occur in a setting in which the child can have fun and learn. Ideally, certain areas of the classroom are designed for specific activities. Most

Children enjoy actively playing together.

preschool classrooms have three to four major areas. Refer to Chapter 11 for a discussion of the major areas typically found within a preschool setting.

Development of Attitudes and Emotions

Clearly, early special education is focused on helping children acquire knowledge, skills, habits, and tendencies that will enable them to respond to the world in positive and effective ways. These skills include healthy attitudes. Specific attributes that children should maintain or acquire include curiosity, creativity, and cooperation, as well as being friendly, helpful, hardworking, and resourceful. These characteristics are most readily acquired by being around people who have these qualities and model them to children. Children are most likely to acquire and demonstrate these dispositions when they are aware that adults value them.

Early childhood education also contributes to emotional development. Feelings of confidence, competence, and security often develop through school experiences. In addition, children learn to like and dislike certain things. They also develop fears and learn to avoid certain situations, as well as learn to control their feelings. Children's feelings of belonging, acceptance, or rejection are important for life-long growth and development. Children should be supported to develop these skills.

Providing Experience with Pre-Academic Activities

An effective early childhood program avoids pressuring children to learn many academic skills or acquire many specific pieces of knowledge (e.g., memorize the alphabet). Such skills are unlikely to be useful, if, during the process of acquiring them, the child's desire to use them diminishes. Educators should help children acquire skills and strengthen their desire to use these newly learned skills. Generally, the best way to do this is to employ a wide variety of enjoyable teaching methods that emphasize language and cognitive skills.

Children receive services designed to enhance the development of many types of skills. These skills develop only when they become meaningful to children. For example, children are often provided many opportunities to discover or observe how reading and writing are useful before they are instructed in letter names, sounds, and word identification. Meaningful experiences include listening to and reading stories and poems, taking field trips, seeing classroom charts and other print material, participating in dramatic play and other experiences requiring communication, and experimenting with writing by drawing and copying. Academic instruction in reading and writing stresses isolated skills such as recognizing single letters, reciting the alphabet, or coloring within the lines. These activities are not meaningful or useful for most young children (Mahoney, O'Sullivan, & Fors, 1989). Refer to Chapter 5 for an in-depth discussion of communication skills and to Chapter 6 for a more detailed discussion of the development of cognitive skills.

Providing Activities That Enhance Physical Development

In addition to opportunities to develop cognitive, communication, and social skills, children should have daily opportunities to use their muscles. Children learn as they move. Running, jumping, and balancing enhance large-muscle abilities (gross-motor skills). Ideally, children spend a great deal of time outdoors engaged in activities that allow and encourage freedom of movement. Outdoor time also provides an appropriate setting for children to be loud and spontaneous in their verbal expressions. Outdoor time should not be viewed as interfering with real instructional time or be seen as a recess from learning; rather, it is an excellent time for learning in all developmental areas.

Children also need daily small-muscle (fine-motor) activities, such as playing with puzzles, art supplies, and peg-boards. Fine-motor activities should not be limited to writing with pencils or coloring within the lines. In fact, in most cases these are not the most appropriate activities for young children with or without disabilities. (See Chapter 7 for a discussion of motor development.)

Children also need a chance to experience music and art on a regular basis. They should be allowed to experiment and explore during these activities. Art and music should not be considered extra activities or used just as special treats. Music should include movement, and art should include imaginative creation, not merely replicating a model. Children are naturally creative and should be encouraged to use their creativity. Music and arts support not only muscle development but also the development of language and cognitive skills. Often, preschool children who hesitate to carry on a conversation or answer questions can sing the words to a song. In addition, some children who hesitate to participate in other activities readily participate in art or music. Chapter 12 provides a more detailed discussion of the value of using music and art as learning experiences.

Play-Oriented Service Delivery

Opportunities to watch and play with others are particularly important during infancy and the preschool years. Young children's play involves exploring the environment. During play most children enjoy interacting with others (Howes & Matheson, 1992). Adults might tickle children, play peek-a-boo with them, shake a rattle, or demonstrate how to make a toy piano produce sounds. As children mature, their play becomes more active and often is self-initiated.

Play is the major activity of 2- to 6-year-olds. During the preschool years, play time allows children to learn to share, lead, follow, and solve problems. For example, when children experience aggression during play, they learn about bullies, self-protection, the need to consider others' feelings, and how to say, "I'm sorry" (Black, 1992).

Children also learn about themselves through play. They learn what they like to do, with whom they like to play, and what skills they have and have not mastered (Brownell & Brown, 1992). Play is one way for children to express their emotions, build relationships, and develop imagination (Connolly, Doyle, & Reznick, 1988). Play not only provides a mechanism for cognitive growth but also provides opportunities for children to develop friendships. Chapter 12 provides a more detailed discussion of the importance of children's play.

Curriculum Development

An effective curriculum focuses on and, whenever possible, integrates the development of communication, cognitive, motor, social-emotional, and adaptive skills; it is modified to meet each child's individual needs. In addition, it incorporates effective teaching approaches that are developmentally, linguistically, and culturally appropriate. The curriculum must ensure children's physical and emotional safety and meet their aesthetic needs (i.e., create mental and physical sensations and be artistically and culturally appealing).

An early childhood special education curriculum should be relevant to children's everyday needs. That is, the curriculum should support and aid children's daily interactions with people and things. It should build on what children already know by reviewing skills and building new concepts and skills. As these new concepts and skills develop, the curriculum should provide guided practice to help ensure that they are maintained and generalized to a variety of settings. Effective curricula support children's home culture and language while supporting children's interactions in a variety of settings. Additionally, curriculum goals must be attainable by those for whom the curriculum is designed.

Daily Schedules

Most children are most comfortable when daily routines are consistent. Over time, children learn to expect certain things to occur at specific times and in a particular order, and they feel most comfortable when they do. A daily schedule is also valuable because it helps teachers and therapists avoid wasting time deciding what should occur next and making less than maximally effective learning plans. The schedule, however, should be flexible enough to allow service providers to seize the moment and capitalize on unexpected educational opportunities. For example, schedules should be modified to allow children to interact with unexpected visitors, gaze at a rarely occurring rainbow, read a second book, or watch a fire truck outside the window.

Children should not constantly be hurried to complete one task in order to move on to another. A schedule that too rigidly allocates a specific amount of time for each activity is likely to result in fragmentation (not enough time to fully engage in an activity) and frustration for the child. When children find an activity very engaging, teachers should increase the amount of time allotted for the activity, even when this results in inadequate time for something else that was planned. If a planned activity is scheduled to take 30 minutes but children are not successfully engaged in the activity for that amount of time, the activity should be abandoned or the allocated time shortened. Children need opportunities to engage in activities that interest them, require sustained effort, and extend over time (Lee, O'Shea, & Dykes, 1987).

Each day's schedule should include time for free play, which allows children to select from several activities provided by the teaching staff. These activities can include puzzles laid out on tables, easels and paint, a sensory table, and dress-up clothes. Ideally, available activities vary from day to day.

In addition, time should be allocated for small- and large-group activities. There also should be fine- and gross-motor activities, as well as opportunities for art and music activities. Some children with disabilities cannot spend an extended amount of time in structured activities. Therefore, the amount of time children are encouraged to pursue a particular task will vary depending on each individual child. As the year progresses, expectations regarding the length of time that children can attend to activities is likely to increase for each child. Figure 3.7 provides an example of a daily classroom schedule.

Cleaning up materials should be a cooperative-learning opportunity. Such opportunities often occur during transition periods. Some children have great difficulty with transitions. They may not want to change activities because they are not ready to, or they may not want to clean up materials. It is often useful to provide children with advance notice that a transition will soon occur. This notification may be accomplished by ringing a bell or dimming the lights and announcing, "In 5 minutes,

Figure 3.7   **Sample Daily Classroom Schedule**

- 8:30–9:00   —   Free play with at least three activity options
- 9:00–9:15   —   Review of the previous day's activities in a large group or circle
- 9:15–10:10   —   Outdoor play activities
- 10:10–10:30 —   Snacking in groups of 3 to 5 students
- 10:30–10:50 —   Small-group activities such as art or cooking activities
- 10:50–11:00   —   Review of the day's activities in a large or small group, followed by dismissal

we'll be cleaning up so we can go outside." It is often useful to explain to children that the reason they should help clean up materials is that they will then be allowed to engage in another enjoyable activity.

Conclusions

Research indicates that the earlier intervention occurs, the better the outcome. That is, early intervention provides a foundation for later learning. It also provides support for children and their families that may help prevent or lessen the impact of other types of problems. In most cases, early intervention also helps family members adjust to a child's needs by providing training in specific methods of working with the child.

Ideally, early intervention service personnel focus on guiding young children rather than leading them. In fact, whenever possible, children should be encouraged to do the leading. Early childhood education programs must give children and their parents a sense of hope and warmth. Rather than viewing children and families as victims, service providers should see them as capable of making decisions and creating their own solutions to problems. Early childhood programs are most successful when children and their families deserve most of the credit for meeting the child's special needs.

CHAPTER SUMMARY

- Nature and nurture affect children's development in positive and negative ways and may put them at risk for later developmental difficulties.

- Knowledge about continuous versus discontinuous theories, and organismic versus mechanistic theories, can guide the development of appropriate services.

- Services are provided in a variety of locations including homes, clinics, doctors' offices, hospitals, day care centers, preschools, and intervention programs.

- Service delivery involves the collaboration of professionals and family members.

- There are several key attributes of effective intervention programs, including the use of DAPs designed to meet each child's individual needs in culturally sensitive, inclusive, and play-oriented ways.

CHAPTER KEY TERMS

genetic factor
environmental factor
genetic endowment
nature
heredity

nurture
environmentalist
interactionist
synapse
transactional developmental theory

developmentalist
child developmental specialist
developmental chart
universal norm
normative approach
milestone
organismic theory
mechanistic theory
continuous theory
discontinuous theory
Jean Piaget
quantitative change
qualitative change
Maria Montessori
sensitive period
sensorimotor stage
preoperational stage
concrete operational stage
formal operational stage
object permanence
symbolic function
animism
artification
intuitive thought
metacognition
metamemory
centration
reversibility
egocentrism
self-discovery learning
Lev Vygotsky
zone of proximal development (ZPD)
scaffolding
multiple intelligences
Howard Gardner
verbal/linguistic intelligence
logical/mathematical intelligence
visual/spatial intelligence
musical/rhythmic intelligence
bodily/kinesthetic intelligence
naturalistic intelligence
interpersonal intelligence
intrapersonal intelligence
developmentally appropriate practice (DAP)
behaviorist
B. F. Skinner
operant conditioning
reinforcement
punishment

reinforcer
Ivan Pavlov
classical conditioning
information processing theory
perception
attention
reasoning
memory
reflexively
selective attention
transductive reasoning
inductive reasoning
deductive reasoning
sensory memory
short-term memory
long-term memory
rehearsal
constructivist
Abraham Maslow
hierarchy of needs
deficiency needs
growth needs
physiological needs
safety needs
love and belongingness needs
esteem needs
cognitive needs
Urie Bronfenbrenner
ecological systems theory
bioecological systems theory
microsystem
mesosystem
exosystem
macrosystem
home-based program
center-based program
self-contained classroom
special education teacher
service coordinator
early childhood teacher
teacher assistant
day care provider
Council for Exceptional Children (CEC)
Code of Ethics and Standards for Educators
National Association for the Education of Young
   Children (NAEYC)
active learning
self-directed learning
discovery learning

REVIEW QUESTIONS

1. Why is it useful to know about the typical rates of development when developing and providing services for young children with developmental delays?

2. Why is knowledge of major developmental theories important for the development of early childhood special education programs?

3. What are the major duties of special education teachers, early childhood teachers, teacher aids, and day care providers?

4. What are key attributes of highly effective staff collaboration?

5. What are key attributes of highly effective EIPs?

SUGGESTED STUDENT ACTIVITIES

1. Visit a preschool classroom that includes children with developmental delays. Describe the ages and developmental delays of the children who attend. Ask the staff to explain the rationale for the classroom daily schedule and activities.

2. Learn about EIPs in your community. Describe the basic philosophy of one or more of these programs. Describe characteristics of these programs as they relate to information within this chapter.

3. With a group of your peers, discuss potential pros and cons of using full inclusion in early childhood special education programs.

Parents and Professionals Working Together

CHAPTER KEY POINTS

- Cooperative partnerships benefit children with disabilities and their families.

- There are many aspects to effective communication.

- It is important for all team members to be well prepared to help ensure optimally effective meetings.

- Service coordination is crucial for meeting children's and families' needs.

- Various team methods may be used to provide services for children and their families.

- Intervention service can be direct or indirect.

Parents (or other primary care providers) and professionals must effectively collaborate to help ensure that young children with disabilities receive appropriate services (Decker & Decker, 2003; McConkey, 1985; Shea & Bauer, 1991). Although professionals know a great deal about intervention services geared toward specific disabilities, parents typically know their children best. Parents are children's first and primary teachers. In most cases, they provide the most effective and economical support for children's growth and development. When parents and professionals combine their knowledge of services and the child, a plan of action can be developed that supports the child's overall growth and development (Dettmer, 2002; Wikler, Wasow, & Hatfield, 1983). Professionals have information and resources useful to parents while parents have specific knowledge of their child that professionals can use to guide their decision making (Kratochvil & Devereux, 1988).

Parental involvement was a mandated feature when Head Start was first established in 1966. In 1968 the federally supported **Handicapped Children's Early Education Program (HCEEP),** renamed the **Early Education Program for Children with Disabilities (EEPCD)** in 1990, extended the role of parents. In 1975 the Education of All Handicapped Children Act (EAHCA, P.L. 94-142) mandated parental participation in the writing, approval, and evaluation of each child's early intervention plans (individualized family service plans [IFSPs] or individualized education programs [IEPs]).

The Collaboration Process

Early childhood intervention services and programs differ from services for school-age children. Children receiving early childhood services are often more diverse in family background and disabilities than older children. They require highly flexible intervention schedules and service delivery approaches. Family members typically play a more active role in early childhood intervention, so there is an increased need for team-based models of service delivery (Friend, 2000).

Three Key Characteristics of Early Childhood Special Education

Every child is a member of a family or other group of people who live together. The adults in a child's family are responsible for caregiving, supporting the child's development, and enhancing the quality of the child's life. This means that the family must be viewed as the primary stable factor in the child's life and, therefore, should be the focus of service delivery. It is necessary for early childhood interventionists to acknowledge, understand, and respect the individual families they serve. Staff members must honor family members' decisions regarding children's early childhood intervention programs (Turnbull, Turbiville, & Turnbull, 2000).

Parents of young children with disabilities cannot understand their role or be prepared to parent prior to experiencing parenting a child with a disability. They gradually come to understand the unique challenges of parenting a child with a disability. Parents often find it difficult to keep up with the many visits to doctors, clinics, and hospitals. They need time to adapt to their parenting roles. Most parents report added stress after the birth of a child; parents with infants who have a disability have more than typical levels of stress, pressure, and responsibility. This can lead to parents' feeling overwhelmed.

Initially, parents benefit from help in finding and accessing support networks. These networks are formal (e.g., assistance with finances, finding doctors, and using equipment) or informal (e.g., connecting with other parents). The family's needs must be individually met. Rather than being exclusively on the child's development, the focus initially must be on helping the family adapt.

This type of approach is often referred to as **family-centered care,** which focuses on the care of children with disabilities and their care-giving families. The philosophy of family-centered care is based on the belief that the family is central to each child's life and has the greatest impact on the child's development.

To work effectively with infants and young children with disabilities, early childhood interventionists must become aware of each care-giving family's priorities, concerns, and resources. Professionals must effectively communicate with the family to establish program goals for the child and family and to design optimal intervention plans. The effectiveness of a family-centered approach hinges on the relationship between early childhood interventionists and family members. Mutual trust and respect is crucial.

Early childhood interventionists must be knowledgeable about and sensitive to the cultural background of all families. As discussed in earlier chapters, the families of infants and toddlers in the early childhood intervention system represent many cultural backgrounds, including various languages, communication styles, religious beliefs, values, customs, food preferences, and taboos. All cultural factors potentially affect the family's perception of disabilities (Decker & Decker, 2003; Kalyanpur & Harry, 1999; Pengra, 2000).

Professionals who help provide early childhood intervention services must develop the ability to understand the similarities and differences between their own cultural beliefs and values and those of the families with whom they work. Just as there is no typical child who receives services, there is no typical family. Due to the wide variety of family backgrounds, a wide variety of methods must be used to work with families. For example, services most effective for a 20-year-old father who dropped out of high school, lives in poverty, and is the sole guardian of a deaf infant likely will differ from the most effective services for an upper-income family, in which the mother is a well-educated homemaker and the father is traditionally employed.

Parent–Professional Collaboration

Parents and other primary child care providers play a key role in early intervention for children. Without the active involvement of parents, the effects of early intervention cannot be as positive. Unless parents learn how to work effectively with their child, the gains that are accomplished while the child is in an early intervention program are less likely to be maintained outside of the program activities.

Parents can contribute valuable information about their child and about the family unit. They know many things about their child that others initially are unlikely to know, including their child's strengths and weakness, likes and dislikes, and medical history. In addition, parents often play important roles in the programs in which their children are enrolled—for example, by serving as voluntary aides, preparing materials and newsletters, raising funds, and providing support to other parents.

When parents and professionals work together in a cooperative rather than adversarial manner to address the individual needs of children, children benefit. Professionals must take the responsibility for determining how best to develop this cooperative partnership (Mittler, 1979). It is often difficult for parents to feel part of the team when they are surrounded by professionals, each with distinct opinions, expertise, vocabulary (professional jargon), and suggestions. Effective partnerships do not magically develop; they require ongoing communication, conflict resolution, and mutual respect (Batshaw, 1991).

All individuals working on a team must feel they are an important part of the team. Each member must view the others as equal partners. The shared goal should be to remain focused on finding the most effective method of providing services for the child (McConkey, 1985). Box 4.1 describes a scenario that illustrates the importance of developing highly effective partnerships between parents and professionals.

Changing Perceptions

Parents and professionals have a very significant similarity: they are people first. (Recall that the same is true of children; they are children first.) Although this fact is obvious, perceptions often change when people play various roles. Because parents typically know their children best, professionals must carefully consider parents' perceptions of their children. Parents are often the first to sense that their child has a developmental delay in some area (McConkey, 1985). When parents first bring their child to a professional for help, their hope is often that the professional can fix their child's problem (Mittler, 1979).

Generally, professionals in the field of special education are very caring individuals who sincerely want to help children and their families (Leviton, Mueller, & Kauffman, 1992). And they typically provide useful suggestions, guidance, support, and opinions for the parents. Yet, frequently professionals may lead parents to believe that professionals have all the answers and always know what is best for children (Tizard, Mortimore, & Burchell, 1988). Professionals, however, are responsible for ensuring that parents understand that professionals do not have all the answers.

Professionals are responsible for providing a variety of information and at a level that enables parents to readily understand. Ideally, parents take an active role in their child's educational process. Their role is crucial because they are generally the most influential people in the child's life (Davie, Butler, & Goldstein, 1972). Professionals will come and go, but in most cases parents are parents throughout life.

Professionals must make sure that parents know their own feelings and ideas are important. Professionals should allow and encourage parents to be advocates for their children (Brudoff & Orenstein, 1984). They should also assist parents in understanding that parents are ultimately responsible for their child. Federal laws guarantee parents the right to be a part of the educational decision-making process. If parents do not fully participate, it is more likely that their child will get lost in the educational system and, therefore, not receive optimally appropriate services.

Box 4.1 Keisha: One Family's Story

The importance of parent–professional partnerships became very real for my husband and me as we spent most of our time for 3 ½ months in a neonatal unit with Keisha.

Before Keisha was born, our obstetrician spent 7 hours telling us that he thought my pregnancy would end in a miscarriage. He told us there was very little chance that our baby would be able to survive outside the womb because she would be born too prematurely. Much to the surprise of the doctor, Keisha was born alive. Fortunately, she was born just as a medical emergency team arrived at the hospital to transport another sick infant to Albany Medical Center, in Albany, New York.

The transport team was asked to provide assistance to Keisha because she was fighting to stay alive. While the arrangements were being made for Keisha's transport, I was being consoled by a nurse who thought Keisha would not survive. She explained that it was good to begin the mourning process and eventually get on with my life. I held my baby and was shocked to find she was still fighting for life. I gratefully signed a permission form allowing the transport team to administer an experimental drug that might help Keisha breathe more easily.

The team explained that Keisha had a little less than a 50% chance of survival. With teary eyes and shaking hands, I signed a paper directing the team not to take extraordinary measures to keep Keisha alive. I looked down into a special incubator that would take her in a helicopter to Albany Medical Center. That day ended my partnership with the doctor who had delivered.

The next morning I began a new chapter in my life. I had no idea what was in store for my daughter or what it would be like to sit with my husband at the hospital day after day, wanting Keisha to live. This experience taught me a great deal about partnerships.

My husband and I were treated with great consideration when we arrived at Albany Medical Center. The medical staff explained what was being done for our baby and what we could expect to happen next. The nurse who helped during transport brought me to see Keisha. She showed me how I could safely touch her. As the tears of joy rolled down my cheeks, she hugged me and said, "Crying is allowed." Each day nurses, residents, and doctors helped my husband and me become as involved as possible in the care of our baby. Most importantly, they told us to talk to, sing to, and touch our baby. They taught us how to greet her "with open arms."

As any parent who has been through the neonatal unit knows all too well, at times things do not go smoothly. The neonatal unit staff reminded my husband and me that for each step forward we should expect two steps backward. These backward steps were very difficult. During one of these steps, the primary doctor at the medical center pulled my husband and me aside and told us how important we were to the team. He said, "You may not have the medical background or the expertise to understand why certain procedures are done, but you hold a very important key. You know your baby. For over a month, you have sat by your child's side. You know what she likes and what upsets her. You know the body positions in which she functions the best." As it turned out, avoiding body positions that upset our baby and using the positions that she preferred made a positive difference in Keisha's oxygen levels, which were key to her continued development.

Box 4.1   **Continued**

The doctor also told us that he had cited us as an example to the resident physicians of how to work with parents. He explained, "The resident doctors must understand how important parents are in the process. They need to listen to parents. If they do not, they may miss vital pieces of information."

The doctor's words have stayed with me, and I often reflect on them as I work as a teacher with families of children who have special needs. Parents are a vital part of a team. They hold a very important key because they know their child best. (Keisha's story will continue later in this chapter.)

Program staff should realize that when parents do not actively participate in their children's education, it often is because they cannot. Sometimes parents are too overloaded with work to attend meetings or events, although they desperately wish they could. Professionals, on the other hand, often find it frustrating when parents do not fully participate in their child's education (Glidden, 1993). Sometimes, suggestions sent home are not followed, and meetings are cancelled. Even if these events occur, professionals must avoid viewing parents as uncaring. Some professionals interpret a lack of parental involvement to mean that family members do not care

It is important for teachers to maintain contact with parents, including by calling home to discuss a child's progress.

about the child. This conclusion usually is inaccurate. Many parents have an excessive number of demands placed on their time; asking them to do one more thing, such as attend a workshop or do a special homework assignment, is enough to upset the delicate balance in their lives (Turnbull & Turnbull, 1990).

Professionals may tend to focus primarily on the child's needs rather than on the needs of the whole family. This may be due to the fact that they are trained to assist in a child's development. In contrast, they may have received little or no training in effectively interacting and working with parents or in working on collaborative teams. They are likely to become frustrated when parental involvement is not at the level that they believe is appropriate. Instead of becoming frustrated or developing a negative attitude toward the parents, professionals must realize that if a parent is not as involved as the professional would like, it is most likely due to the fact that the parent simply cannot give more time at this particular time. Professionals must accept the level at which parents become involved. Staff members must focus on the individual needs of each family and avoid placing demands on parents that are likely to add stress to a stressful life. Logically, parents who are overstressed cannot effectively help their child (McConnell et al., 1998; Mittler, 1979).

Parents naturally focus on the needs of their own children rather than those of other children with whom professionals work (Mahoney & Filer, 1996; Hanson & Hanline, 1990; Mittler, 1979). A professional, however, must be concerned about all the children who receive their services. This focus often conflicts with the parents' focus, which is on their individual child (Shea & Bauer, 1991; Turnbull & Turnbull, 1990).

"The squeaky wheel gets the grease" is often true for parents who attempt to acquire services for their child. Parents who make demands (advocate) on behalf of a child generally do receive more attention from professional team members (Vaughn, Bos, Harrell, & Lasky, 1988). Professionals often tell parents they must be an advocate for their child, yet a parent who argues or pleads for a child's perceived needs frequently is labeled as a difficult or overly demanding parent. Most parents do not want to create tension or be perceived as difficult or unreasonable; most do not intend to make unreasonable demands (Bailey, Palsha, & Simeonsson, 1991). When professional staff imply that parents' advocacy is not valued, parents may be reluctant to continue in their advocacy role (McWilliam, Snyder, Harbin, Porter, & Munn, 2000; Turnbull, Turbivill, & Turnbull, 2000).

Many parents benefit from guidance on how to be assertive without appearing unreasonable (Bailey & Simeonsson, 1988a). Learning and, more importantly, using effective communication skills, such as reflective listening (restating a speaker's comments), providing feedback to the speaker, and being assertive but not aggressive, assists parents in effectively navigating the educational system. Parent programs focused on effective communication methods are often a valuable and necessary addition to early childhood special education programs. Reading books or attending workshops or college classes focused on developing communication skills is often worthwhile for parents and professionals.

Assertive parents, who are active participants in their children's education, are the reason that many children receive required services. That is, when therapy services are in short supply, it is usually the assertive parent, with an understanding of the laws that pertain to special education, who secures services for their child (Dunst,

Trivette, & Deal, 1988). Professionals need to acknowledge that when parents complain about or question the services being offered, parents usually do so because they believe that doing so is in their child's best interest. Parents who are actively involved in their children's educational programs must be encouraged to continue being actively involved (Bailey, 2001; Bailey, Scarborough, & Hebbeler, 2003; Mittler, 1979).

"People unfold as they have been folded." This statement was shared at a professional workshop. Every person has a unique set of life experiences. These experiences influence how people deal with difficulties and challenges presented to them. Professionals must remember that parents deal with a child with a disability in their own unique way. Dealing with people's folds (individual differences) builds character, may provide a person with something to hide behind, or can lead to a better understanding of the situation. A child with a disability is just one of a parent's folds. It is not the professional's job to try to smooth out or eliminate all of the folds in a parent's life. Ideally, professionals provide support while allowing time for parents to unfold themselves at a rate appropriate for their unique needs (Buscaglia, 1975; Dunst, 2002). Box 4.2 describes a scenario in which the perceptions of one mother changed as she experienced the role of teacher at two similar meetings.

Professionals must recognize that parents who have children with very similar disabilities often have nothing more in common than parents whose children do not have disabilities (Westling & Koorland, 1989). For example, one parent may appear to quickly accept their child's disability and readily become involved in the child's education while another parent may appear to be so overwhelmed with a normal response of sadness and fear about the additional challenges that they assume their child is destined to face that this parent initially struggles to face each new day.

Box 4.2 *Attending a Meeting in the Role of Parent*

I have attended many school district Committee on Preschool Special Education (CPSE) and Committee for Special Education (CSE) meetings. At one CPSE meeting, I sat on one side of the table as a teacher. I was there to discuss a student's progress and give recommendations for classroom placement that would best match the child's developmental level and educational goals for the following year. The meeting went smoothly, and the parent was very happy with the recommendations.

The next meeting was about my daughter, Keisha, so I sat on the other side of the table as a parent. In my professional role, I knew this was a very straightforward meeting. As I sat there knowing all of Keisha's struggles and achievements during the past year, my emotions took over; I suddenly became very choked up and had difficulty talking. The chairperson joked a bit and said, "What happened to you?" What did happen? The committee members were telling me that Keisha was making great progress and they were going to continue with the support he needed. In the role of parent, I was unable to separate the educational assessment and planning from the personal struggles and emotions.

The goal should be to help parents reach an adaptation phase where they are fully aware of their child's needs and learn to compensate for these needs while enhancing their child's development. A sense of frustration or sadness may remain, but this should be considered normal as long as parents do not allow such feelings to interfere with their effort to assess services designed to enhance their child's development.

A parent's primary role is to love and encourage their child and to create a caring and safe environment (Darling, 1983). Sometimes professionals appear to feel that they need to help parents learn to accept their child's disability. The professional might tell parents that they are in denial or that to help their child they must first accept that the child has a disability. It is often not helpful for parents to hear what they likely already know.

Parents must be allowed to love their child while hating that their child has a disability. Again, it is not the professional's responsibility to make parents accept a child's disability (Batshaw, 1991). Rather than telling parents how to feel, professionals should provide encouragement and specific information on how parents may assist their child (Brinkerhoff & Vincent, 1987). Parents do not benefit from being lectured or having their hopes and dreams dashed by being told that their child's ability will be limited to a certain level.

Professionals often spend much of their personal time thinking about the children in their care and preparing materials or plans designed to help children and their families. Doing so contributes to professional burnout (Gargiulo, 1985). Burnout does not necessarily cause professionals to leave and abandon their careers, but it contributes to a loss of energy—energy required to be effective on the job. Professionals must remember that they are entitled to personal time and cannot eliminate all of the problems that children and their families experience. This lesson is often very difficult, but is one that all professionals who wish to remain effective must learn (Buscaglia, 1975).

Effective Communication

Communication between professionals and parents is vital for successful programs to be implemented for children with disabilities. Effective communication is also vital for the development of successful partnerships. The power of effective communication cannot be underestimated. Several components of effective **verbal** and **nonverbal communication** are discussed below (Kaessler, 2006).

Most individuals use a variety of verbal and nonverbal forms of communication. Verbal communication includes spoken, written, and sign language. Nonverbal communication includes clothing, physical distance, eye contact, facial expressions, and gestures (DePaulo, Rosenthal, Green, & Rosenkrantz, 1982).

Verbal Communication

The words used during speech are important, but the context and the way they are spoken or written often is even more important. Parents and professionals benefit when they reflect on the words selected, as well as the tone in which they are presented. This is especially important when sharing information with team members

Figure 4.1   **Summary of Communication Styles**

Styles that provide little information

- Superficial—playful, sociable, happy-go-lucky
- Commanding—accusing, dictating, manipulating, blaming

Styles that provide more information

- Knowledge-based—information and elaboration at the listener's intellectual level
- Caring—showing concern, sharing, displaying feeling, open, authentic

who were not present at a meeting. Words are easily repeated, but if the tone is changed, the meaning is often changed. Tone of voice is very important and affects how messages are interpreted. Communication between parents and professionals is generally most effective when the caring style is used. Figure 4.1 lists several verbal communication styles that people often use.

This father feels welcome and valued at this early intervention program.

Written communication plays an important role in most early childhood special education programs. Because of the need to document services provided to children with disabilities, all communication that occurs should be documented. It is important to remember that although written communication has its purpose, it is not always the best way to develop or maintain ongoing communication between parents and professionals. When the most important thing becomes what is written down about the child, meaningful information often is lost. It is very difficult to get a full picture of children by relying solely on what is written about them.

The major limitation to written communication is that it lacks the information included in body language and tone of voice. For this reason, written communication sometimes is misinterpreted. When written communication is required, it must be carefully written. For example, faulty communication may occur when classroom staff write home to parents or when parents write to staff. The words may be clear, but the message may not be clear because written words often leave out feelings. They may be perceived as uncaring or misleading.

Written notes may be confusing or misleading because they lack sufficient detail. In most cases, written notes should be followed by telephone or face-to-face conversations to clarify their meaning. For instance, consider the following situation. Joey's special education teacher sent this note home to his parents: "Joey did not eat his snack." The words are clear, but the message is not. Was the teacher indicating that Joey was being disobedient? Did the teacher think that Joey was sick? Was the teacher concerned because Joey does not try different types of food? The message was unclear, in part, because it was unclear whether the teacher thought Joey's behavior was typical of him.

Language barriers also may lead to misunderstandings. Written information should be in the parents' primary language. During meetings with parents, it may be necessary to have a translator present. If a translator is necessary, professionals should look at the parents while talking rather than at the translator.

Different cultural groups invest particular words and behaviors with different meanings. For example, the term *advocate* may have positive meaning for some people and may be seen by others as a form of aggression. Members of some cultural groups look directly at a speaker; others consider looking at a speaker to be impolite. It is important for all team members to consider potential cultural differences in modes of communication and in the meanings associated with various words and phrases (Hanson, Lynch, & Wayman, 1990; Vincent, 1992).

Nonverbal Communication

To help ensure effective communication, professionals and parents must be conscious of the nonverbal messages they are sending. One example of nonverbal communication in a school setting is the clothing worn during a meeting. A person's choice of clothing is frequently interpreted as an indicator of the importance the person places on the meeting or their level of respect toward those with whom they are meeting. For example, preschool staff members often wear comfortable but neat clothing while at work. Those who work directly with young children know that their clothes are likely to get dirty during art activities, science and cooking projects, outdoor play, snack time, and so on.

When meetings occur at the preschool site during the day, attire usually remains casual. When professionals meet with parents after regular school hours or during the day at school district special education meetings, they usually dress in less casual attire. This does not mean that business attire is necessary for meetings between parents and professionals, but attention to mode of dress and grooming is often viewed by various attendees as very important (Deutch, 1973).

Eye contact, facial expressions, the physical space between people, and gestures send important messages. Placing hands in a pocket, looking down, or otherwise avoiding eye contact can suggest insecurity or dislike. Turning away, so that the back is partially toward others, may suggest a lack of interest or a desire to end the conversation (Aiello, 1987). In most cultures, leaning toward the speaker indicates interest. Sitting unusually far from a person may suggest annoyance, anxiety, or disinterest.

For example, friends generally stand closer together than do strangers or people who dislike each other. Therefore, distance may send intended or unintended messages. Facial expressions also send many messages. For many people, squinting or frowning indicates uncertainty or disagreement, whereas smiling indicates comfort, happiness, or relief (DePaulo et al., 1982).

Some researchers report that body language sends a more powerful message than words alone. If this is true, professionals and parents must reflect on the messages they may be sending when they communicate with each other. In addition, when meetings between parents and professionals are spent shuffling papers and body language is ignored, communication is unnecessarily diminished (DiMatteo, Friedman, & Taranta, 1979).

Listening

The quality of friendships, cohesiveness of family relationships, and effectiveness at work depends, in large measure, on a person's ability to listen. Research suggests as much as 75% of spoken communication is ignored, misunderstood, or quickly forgotten (Hamlin, 1988). Well-developed listening skills are necessary for effective parent–professional partnerships. Listening involves more than just hearing words. Listening is an activity involving the ears, eyes, mind, and heart. True listening is an active process in which few people have been adequately trained.

Active listening involves attending to, observing, and interpreting nonverbal cues; inviting a speaker to continue speaking; and reflective listening. A good listener is actively attentive to the speaker. For most people, attentiveness involves directing eyes and body toward the speaker. Positioning oneself at a comfortable distance from the speaker, maintaining an open posture (i.e., appearing interested and positive), and leaning slightly toward the speaker typically sends the nonverbal message that the listener is interested in the speaker's words. To ensure the most effective communication possible, the listener must concentrate on the factual information and feelings being expressed to determine what the speaker is trying to convey. To facilitate concentration, noise from environmental factors, such as radios, televisions, and telephones, should be reduced as much as possible (Shields, 1987).

Consider the following example. A mother who walks into a classroom with her head down and slumps into a seat for a meeting with the classroom teacher may do so for a variety of reasons. The mother may be expressing disinterest, tiredness, or sadness. It is likely that this mother would benefit from having someone respond to her needs. A comment made by the teacher such as "You seem down today" or "It doesn't look like you're having a good day" may serve as an invitation to this mother to freely discuss her feelings. Expressing herself likely will help her move on to other issues that should be discussed (Bailey & Simeonsson, 1988b).

Effective listeners use words and phrases that encourage a speaker to continue to share thoughts and feelings. Remarks such as "Go on," "Tell me more," and "Really?" convey to the speaker that what has been said is important and encourages the speaker to continue sharing information. However, such comments become routine or seem insincere if overused.

Active listening also involves responding to the speaker reflectively. An effective listener restates what has been said, and then clarifies the content and expressed feelings of the message. When reflective listening is effective, the speaker is assured that the listener heard and understands what was said (Hamlin, 1988). Active listening lets others know that their thoughts and feelings have been recognized. The benefits of active listening are numerous. It promotes a relationship of understanding and trust. It clarifies what is being said. Active listening also facilitates problem-solving (Apple & Hecht, 1982).

Communication skills are vital to any partnership (Bailey, 1987). It is important for parents and professionals to develop highly effective listening skills. There are many books and videotapes available to assist people in developing good communication skills. Community colleges, universities, parent organizations, and adult education programs in local school districts often offer courses designed to enhance communication skills. Clearly, it is often worthwhile for parents and professionals to learn more about effective communication.

Preparing for a Meeting

Meetings to discuss services for children with disabilities often require a great deal of planning (Bailey, 1987). When parents participate in meetings to discuss their child, they are at risk of being overwhelmed by several different professionals giving opinions and recommendations. Parents are likely to feel more comfortable participating in a meeting if they have adequately prepared for the meeting.

Preparing for a meeting requires that parents and professionals spend ample time thinking about and writing down questions, concerns, feelings, and expectations to be discussed at the meeting. Before the meeting, parents and professionals should also generate meeting goals. Goals must be realistic and listed in order of importance. Possible barriers to achievement of these goals should also be listed. Lists of goals and barriers to meeting the child's needs should be brought to the meeting, and team members should state the items on the lists, read them aloud, or provide them in writing (McConkey, 1985).

During the meeting, parents should listen carefully and repeat what they believe each professional said. Professionals should also respond to parents' contributions in this fashion. This process assists in clarifying concerns, opinions, and goals (Mittler, 1979).

Some parents bring an advocate, a friend, or another family member with them to meetings with professionals. This person helps the parent gain information by asking questions or expressing concerns the parent has difficulty conveying. The advocate may also take notes for the parent during the meeting.

Soon after the meeting, parents and professionals should write down what was discussed, while the meeting is still fresh in their memories. However, excessive note-taking during a meeting should be avoided because it limits the note-taker's ability to listen to the speaker and to observe nonverbal messages. A summary of the meeting should include information on the frequency and types of services a child will be receiving, where the services will be provided, when they will begin, and who will be providing each service (Marshall & Herbert, 1981). Parents may also want to include a statement of their own responsibilities.

Usually, the service coordinator or another primary service provider sends parents minutes from the meeting. When parents receive the meeting minutes, they should compare them to their own meeting notes. At the meeting the parents should be told that if there is any discrepancy or misunderstanding regarding the meeting minutes, they should call or write the service coordinator to express their concerns. If necessary, another meeting should be scheduled to address the parents' concerns (Masterson, Swirbul, & Noble, 1990).

Parents should be encouraged to keep a **home file** that includes all correspondence with agencies providing services for the child. Many parents keep notebooks with dividers for each area of development in which their child receives reports (e.g., cognitive or special education, speech, physical therapy, occupational therapy, and counseling). Organizing the file so that each new report is placed on top, so that the most current information is readily available, is often very useful.

The following example illustrates the usefulness of keeping a home file. When a family moved to another state and went to meet with the Committee on Preschool Special Education (CPSE) of their new school district, the family was prepared to provide all the information that the school district had requested. The family brought a notebook containing several years of documentation on their child's strengths, needs, and progress. At the conclusion of the meeting, the CPSE chairperson stated that services would begin at an earlier date than would have been possible if the parents had not provided such complete information (Tizard et al., 1988).

Role of the Service Coordinator

As discussed in Chapter 1, the EAHCA amendments of 1986, now referred to as the Individuals with Disabilities Education Act (IDEA), directs that services be provided to all children with special needs who are younger than 5 years old. Federal laws stress that all services are to be family-centered and community-based. An essential aspect of children's service plans is coordination of services (Able-Boone, Sandall, Stevens, & Frederick, 1992; Berman & Shaw, 1996).

In the past, service coordination often was referred to as case management, case coordination, or service management. Kirst-Ashman and Hull (1993) emphasize that it is important to note that it is not the family being managed but the services received by the family. This helps explain why case management came to be called service coordination in the 1991 reauthorization of IDEA (P.L. 102-119). Part H of the 1986 EAHCA amendments allows professionals from any of 14 disciplines to serve as service coordinators, including social workers, psychologists, occupational therapists, and special education teachers.

An IFSP must include "the name of the case manager from the profession most immediately relevant to the infant's or toddler's or family's needs who will be responsible for the implementation of the plan and coordination with other agencies and persons" (100 Stat. 1150). The law is not specific regarding the standards for determining "the profession most immediately relevant" (Woody, Woody, & Greenberg, 1991). In addition to engaging in assessment, planning, and intervention, the service coordinator monitors the service plan. Three aspects of monitoring are confirming that agreed-on services are being provided, analyzing the level of success of the service delivery systems, and evaluating the level of commitment of social network members.

It is essential that service coordinators have good organizational skills. They will often need to monitor many services provided by many different individuals. To be most constructive, the service coordinator must understand and value the expertise of the other team members, including family members. In addition, well-developed organizational skills help guarantee that details of the intervention plan are conveyed to all parties.

The importance of attention to detail may be seen in the following example. A service team agrees that a child should be assisted in learning how to get dressed. After several weeks the child is no closer to meeting this goal and often seems confused by the task. In this case the service delivery providers are not completing the service plan, and the child's status is problematic. It would be appropriate for any member of the team to contact the service coordinator about this difficulty because the service coordinator should have an overview of all aspects of the case. The service coordinator may suggest that the team meet or may suggest a possible solution. For example, it might be determined that the service plan was not specific enough. That is, the plan did not state which items of clothing would go on first. If this were the case, the plan would need to be modified. The service coordinator would direct this modification process.

Service coordinators are often responsible for scheduling and leading meetings and for generating the reports for team meetings. The most efficient way to monitor the service plan is for each member of the team to prepare a written report that is shared at the team meeting. It is often problematic and less productive when service coordinators lead the team meetings and also are responsible for writing the entire report, because it may be difficult for service coordinators to state specific objectives for areas in which they are not experts.

When each team member prepares their own written report, there generally is more time for productive discussions, which are likely to lead to well-considered recommendations. As discussed in Chapter 3, special education teachers often serve as services coordinators. Although many other team members might serve as the service coordinator, social workers are more likely than others to serve in this role (Dane, 1985; Moore, 1990).

The Social Worker as Service Coordinator

The primary role of the service coordinator is to assist the family in identifying and accessing appropriate services (DiMichele, 1993). The service coordinator may or may not be involved in providing direct services. Service coordination is one of many types of professional social work activities. A service coordinator is sometimes referred to as a case manager or case coordinator. They organize, coordinate, and sustain a network of formal and informal support systems and activities designed to enhance the functioning of people with special needs (Appleby, 1994).

Social workers often serve in the role of service coordinator for young children and their families. This is likely due to their profession's emphasis on client empowerment; an ability to perceive the interrelatedness of the individual, family, and community; and counseling skills (Fiene & Taylor, 1991). Service coordination is within the knowledge and skill base of all four practice levels of social work as designated by the National Association of Social Workers (NASW). A social worker has a bachelor's or higher degree.

Major Tasks of the Service Coordinator

The purpose of service coordination is to increase the family's knowledge of and ability to use social services and supports. Very young children with disabilities often require services from many parts of the care system, including medical care, rehabilitative services, financial assistance, special equipment, educational planning, and family counseling. When services are not coordinated, their effectiveness may be compromised. Gaining access to and coordinating these services may become an overwhelming task (Dennis, Williams, Giangreco, & Cloninger, 1993; Freedman & Clarke, 1991; Hanson & Lynch, 1992). Figure 4.2 lists the varied tasks performed by the services coordinator.

Most families are not well prepared to manage the wide array of social services. The initial purpose of service coordination is to help ensure that the child's and family's needs are identified and services are obtained. Additionally, these services must be coordinated, sustained, and updated (DuBois & Miley, 1992). This description suggests that the service coordinator works to enhance the competency of the family. The service coordinator performs four major tasks: assessing needs, planning and coordinating services, providing direct and indirect intervention, and monitoring and evaluating the service plan. The first task of the service coordinator, assessment of needs, is crucial and directly affects the remaining three tasks.

Figure 4.2   **The Service Coordinator's Activities**

- Coordinating services
- Serving as parents' single point of contact for information
- Assisting parents in gaining access to early intervention services
- Facilitating timely service delivery
- Seeking appropriate services and service locations
- Coordinating performance of assessments
- Facilitating and participating in the development, review, and evaluation of the IFSP
- Notifying parents and the local school district of any upcoming transition plans

Assessment of Needs.   According to Kirst-Ashman and Hull (1993), "Assessment refers to defining issues and gathering relevant information about a problem so that decisions can be made about what to do to solve it" (p. 25). In actuality, many types of assessment take place simultaneously on several different levels. Assessments generally are conducted by at least several professionals who are working with the child, including service coordinators; teachers; speech and language pathologists; psychologists; medical personnel; and occupational, physical, music, and art therapists. The role of the service coordinator is to facilitate interactions among all members of the assessment team. In addition, the service coordinator often directly assesses the family's needs, support networks, and social services.

Special education laws indicate that assessment should identify families' resources, priorities, and concerns. Assessments focus on the immediate and long-term developmental needs of the child and may also include assessment of the needs of the child's family.

As discussed in previous chapters, federal laws mandate that direct family services be provided for families of children 2 years or younger who have disabilities. To provide appropriate services, professionals must assess a family's needs. This assessment involves examining the family's strengths and skills, child care, informal support systems, and formal resources.

The assessment process requires collaboration of the service coordinator and other team members, including family members. Team members must work together to compile, evaluate, rank, and synthesize the family-needs assessment data. Family needs must be identified, and possible solutions to problems must be suggested (Moxley, 1989). As discussed in Chapter 2, Seligman and Darling (1989) developed the Parent Needs Survey (PNS). This assessment is frequently used by professionals to assess the needs of families of young children with disabilities. The combined assessments of entire teams of professionals often provide the parents of children with disabilities with a tremendous amount of information. Parents may find this information to be confusing or even contradictory. Service coordinators help other team members, particularly family members, effectively integrate all of the information. Service coordinators evaluate this information at two main levels. They assess the ability of families to understand the information provided by members of the service team, and they assess the ability of families to implement the team members' recommendations. While these two assessments may seem similar, they are actually quite distinct (Davis, 1987).

Initial assessments of children with disabilities are geared at determining areas of delay. As emphasized in Chapter 2, assessment involves family interviews, case histories, and observations in addition to the use of various needs-assessment instruments. Assessment may also include an evaluation of the cognitive and emotional strength and functioning of the family (Buckley, 1983).

When children are diagnosed as having a disability, this often evokes a wide range of emotional responses from family members (Hughes & Rycus, 1983). After first learning of their children's special needs, families respond with varying levels of mobilization while experiencing emotional and functional turmoil. It is vitally important for families and professionals to understand the emotional merry-go-round that many families experience. Overwhelming amounts of insensitively transmitted information may lead to a sense of despair (Rolland, 1994).

Featherstone (1981) describes being on this merry-go-round while receiving information about her son during the first year of his life:

> The doctor who had delivered Jody called to say that routine examination revealed a placenta infected with a disease called toxoplasmosis. . . . Over the next year we learned that Jody was blind, hydrocephalic, retarded, and that he suffered from cerebral palsy and from seizures. . . . Each week after that first telephone call brought new calamities. . . . We were almost numb with the pain. (p. 4)

It is important for service coordinators and families to assess families' emotional ability to deal with this type of information. Families are capable of effectively dealing with unanticipated information, but the support of service coordinators helps them do so most effectively.

Professionals sometimes behave as if delivery of the content of the material is more important than considering how well families will be able to deal with the information. When this happens, conflict may arise between families and professionals. Therefore, assessments of the emotional strength and functioning of the family are crucial. Once they are completed, family members are generally better prepared to identify potential difficulties in handling certain kinds of information. Being able to identify the family's emotional status is an important strength of a service coordinator.

Service coordinators often assist families in identifying the types of information they are best and least able to manage. It is often useful for families to identify past crises and feelings associated with those events so that the service coordinator can better analyze how the families cope with stress. Consider the following example. At age 4, Jesse was diagnosed as having fragile-X syndrome (FXS), the most common inherited cause of mental impairment and the most common known cause of autism. Family members became quite distraught when they received information about Jesse's cognitive delays. Because of the family's reaction, it initially was more crucial for the service coordinator to prepare the family to manage the information than it was to share specific information with the family. The service coordinator began interactions with the family by discussing the meaning and importance of cognitive development, its relation to developmental disabilities, and general information about FXS.

The service coordinator became aware that Jesse's father had very high expectations for himself, his employees, and his three sons. Although Jesse's father acknowledged his son's diagnosis, initially he was not prepared to accept the ramifications of the diagnosis. The service coordinator discussed the importance of having appropriate expectations regarding Jesse's development. The service coordinator also provided the family with a description of services available to Jesse and family members. After a few days the father began requesting additional information and clearly acknowledged the ramifications of the diagnosis. In fact, he became a very effective advocate for his son.

The second level of assessment performed by service coordinators involves assessing the ability of a family to implement recommendations from various professionals. Consider the following. A team of service providers recommended that the parents of a 4-year-old with communication delays spend a minimum of 30 minutes each day reading to their child from books sent home by the speech and language pathologists. This recommendation was made without knowing that the parents spoke Italian and could not read English. Clearly, the family could not implement the recommendation.

A family's ability to implement intervention recommendations is often directly related to its skill levels and emotional strengths. If a family is not cognitively or emotionally able to handle certain issues, it may be put under additional stress by being asked to implement treatment recommendations. Also, if specific skills are not developed within the family, it may not be able to meet a child's needs until it acquires the necessary skills. When children with disabilities are involved, families frequently must be taught many new skills, including how to dispense medication, deal with assistive equipment, and implement complex behavioral regimens.

Social Networks.   Before needed support networks can be developed, assessment of available **social networks** should occur. After assessing the support networks, service coordinators often assist in designing additional support systems, which integrate skills development and involvement of preexisting support systems. One aspect of a support system is the social network (Brill, 1976). Social networks include the individuals and institutions with which families connect and maintain relationships.

Social networks are particularly important for the families of children with disabilities because the support and influence of these networks often sustain the family as they cope with the demands of daily living with a child who has a disability. Social networks serve to help strengthen the family's individuality, provide dependable communication and feedback regarding the child's development, provide emotional support and assistance with specific tasks, and direct families toward valuable resources (Bishop, Rounds, & Weil, 1993).

Research confirms the beneficial effects of social networks on families' abilities to cope with the demands of dealing with the needs of children with disabilities (Moxley, 1989). For example, Biale (1989) found adjustments to the birth of such a child were more positive when families consistently used network resources, especially extended family networks. Helping family members gain support through their social network provides an important supplement to service available through **formal support systems.**

Informal support systems include the nuclear and extended families, neighbors, friends, and work colleagues. The service coordinator and family members work together to assess the accessibility of social-network members and the degree of informal support available. The assessment centers on the number, proximity, and capabilities of the individuals in the social network, how often they have contact with the family, and the significance of the relationship with the family (Dudley, 1987).

To identify individuals who would be most supportive to the family, Moxley (1989) developed an interview system designed to explore the range of social relationships available. He recommended asking clients to list individuals with whom they have been in contact during the past year and to indicate how they are related to those individuals, based on six categories: household members, primary kin, extended kin, work colleagues, neighbors, and informal acquaintances within the community. Service coordinators can use this system or a similar one to help families identify support networks.

An example of the importance of assessing social networks involves a young couple whose son needed to be physically active or stimulated for as much of the day as possible. Providing physical stimulation and movement was not a problem when the child was in school, but it was on weekends and holidays. The family needed a large support system of individuals who lived nearby, had the time to help, and were physically able to help. The couple had a positive relationship with their parents, but their parents were elderly and lived several hundred miles away. The couple needed to enlist friends and neighbors to become part of their support network. The service coordinator's role was to guide the couple in recognizing and planning their need for support.

It is valuable to assess the support network system before attempting to provide families with services, which they may not be able to readily use (Early & Poertner, 1993). For example, families may not be able to fully utilize services (e.g., attend parent training sessions or workshops) because of the lack of adequate child care. Appropriate child care may be needed on a regular basis, on specific occasions, or during emergencies. Although adequate child care is often hard to find for any family, adequate child care for children with disabilities is often even more difficult to obtain. The specific needs of some children with disabilities require that all care providers receive specific training on proper care (e.g., some children require ongoing connection to oxygen tanks or have catheters that must be maintained). In many cases, family members cannot attend parenting classes or receive counseling services until appropriate child care is found.

Social Services.   Even though services provided by professionals may not be the first choice for families of children with disabilities (i.e., they wish to personally provide for all of their children's needs), typically, at some point, various professionals become a part of the process. Most service coordinators and social service agencies have lists of resources available to families of children with disabilities. These lists typically include information about mental health, medical care, transportation, day care, legal help, and respite services (temporary relief from caring for the child). However, providing families with lists of services that contain addresses, telephone numbers, contacts, eligibility requirements, and fees may not be enough. Service coordinators also need to evaluate the adequacy of available services.

Planning Services.   In addition to assessing service needs, the service coordinator ensures the development of a comprehensive service plan, which includes professional involvement and maximum family participation. Federal laws mandate that assessment be multidisciplinary. Therefore, teamwork is generally considered the best model to use in developing a comprehensive service plan. The team approach is characterized by several professionals with various areas of expertise sharing their perspectives and suggesting treatments or services for children and, in some cases, for the children's families.

Types of Teams

One of three types of team approaches typically is utilized: **multidisciplinary, interdisciplinary,** or **transdisciplinary.** Family members, social workers, psychologists, physicians, speech and language pathologists, audiologists, nurses, teachers, day care providers, and occupational, physical, art, and music therapists may all be team members (Dettmer, 2002; Filer & Mahoney, 1996; Goldberg, 1997).

Multidisciplinary Teams.   In the case of a multidisciplinary team, the professionals act as consultants, but they may or may not provide hands-on treatment themselves. Each professional is responsible for assessment of the child and family needs related to their area of expertise. One individual, often the service coordinator, is then responsible for summarizing the information. Using the multidisciplinary team model, those who participate in assessment may have difficulty reaching consensus about appropriate services, because they may not meet together. At times, assessment results and recommendations do not match and may even contradict each other, because reaching consensus is not the focus of multidisciplinary teams.

Interdisciplinary Teams.   In contrast, an interdisciplinary team consists of professionals who work directly with the child and family. Interdisciplinary teams typically place greater emphasis on communication among team members. Each member of the team may complete assessments independently or in collaboration and then meet with other team members to discuss their findings and recommendations. Once team members have provided one another with feedback, final recommendations are developed through consensus. Each child's IFSP or IEP integrates team members' recommendations.

Transdisciplinary Teams.   A transdisciplinary team includes parents and various professionals who assess the child's and family's needs and plan and provide early intervention services. Team members teach one another about their areas of expertise and may assess a child or interview the family together.

For example, a speech and language pathologist, a special education teacher, and occupational and physical therapists might all observe the child at the same time, recording their own observations, which focus on skills specifically related to their own area of expertise, as one of them takes the child through a set of predetermined tasks. Using a transdisciplinary team approach, one member of the team usually is designated the team leader for a particular child and family. This method requires a major commitment of time and coordination of schedules.

The transdisciplinary approach originally was conceived as a framework to aid professionals in sharing important information and skills with primary caregivers. This approach integrates a child's developmental needs across the major developmental domains. The transdisciplinary approach involves a greater degree of collaboration than other service models and, therefore, may be difficult to implement. It has been identified as ideal for the design and delivery of services for infants and young children with disabilities receiving early childhood intervention.

A transdisciplinary approach requires team members to share roles and systematically cross discipline boundaries. The primary purpose of the approach is to pool and integrate the expertise of team members such that efficient and comprehensive assessment and intervention services are provided. The communication style with this type of team involves continuous give and take among all members, including parents, on a regular, planned basis. Using this team model requires professionals from different disciplines and parents to teach, learn, and work together to accomplish a common set of intervention goals for a child and their family. Role differentiation by discipline is defined by the needs of the situation, as opposed to discipline-specific characteristics. Assessment, intervention, and evaluation are carried out jointly by designated team members. Other characteristics of the transdisciplinary approach include coordinated team effort and staff development designed to help ensure continuous skill development among all team members.

The transdisciplinary approach involves implementation of the child's program by one or more professionals, with ongoing assistance provided by team members from other various disciplines. In most early childhood intervention programs, the classroom teacher and assistants assume the primary service delivery role. Most often this role is assumed by a special education teacher who provides services on a regular basis or serves as the primary teacher, within a center-based program or within a preschool or day care setting.

Related-services support staff, most commonly therapists, often serve as consultants to the teachers. In this way the child's therapy, as well as other needs, is integrated into the daily routine of the classroom. This strategy facilitates the delivery of appropriate services across developmental domains, as opposed to having individual curricula designed for speech, cognitive, fine-motor, gross-motor, social-emotional, and adaptive skills. In addition to providing services embedded within the curriculum, therapists often provide direct services to children to ensure that they maintain direct contact with the child. Therapy may be provided directly by the therapist during classroom activities, and it may be augmented with additional one-on-one therapy outside of the classroom or may be provided in a designated therapy room.

Although collaborative, transdisciplinary service delivery teams appear simple in concept, implementation of this approach is often more difficult than implementation of more familiar, structured, discipline-specific intervention structures. In particular, the time commitment and flexibility required to implement a transdisciplinary collaborative team model effectively may be difficult to attain. Regardless of the type of team approach, service coordinators are needed to ensure continuity and feedback and to establish a system of accountability to guarantee appropriate services.

Roles of Team Members

Kirst-Ashman and Hull (1993) have identified time, leadership, and communication as factors contributing to team building. They have stated that the team leader should be qualified and experienced in working with teams. Additionally, team members need to familiarize themselves with the terminology of other disciplines and communicate in a jargon-free manner. Often this is difficult because one of the attributes of a profession is its symbols (language). Family members are usually the least likely to understand professional jargon and acronyms; they should be encouraged to ask for clarification. The service coordinator must be prepared to translate and interpret professional jargon and encourage other professionals to avoid excessive use of jargon.

Major Team Goals.   The goal of team collaboration is to formulate an organized evaluation and develop a service plan for the child. When children are younger than 3 years old, this plan also includes determining and implementing appropriate services for the child's family. The success of the plan depends, in part, on the communication level of all the participants. While professionals such as educators, psychologists, social workers, and therapists often have training and experience working in teams (although formal training in this area is often lacking or insufficient), this may be a new experience for family members. An important aspect of the service coordinator's role is to assist the family members to understand their roles as part of the team and to participate as effective members of the team. Duwa, Wells, and Lalinde (1993) list delineation of roles, respect, and effective communication as the factors that they believe contribute to an effective team approach.

Parental Involvement.   One of the six major principles of EAHCA addressed parental participation (Turnbull, 1983). It mandated that parents have access to information, be provided due process, and be encouraged to participate in public hearings, advisory panels, and advocacy groups. EAHCA also mandated that parents be members of the committee that develops their child's IFSP or IEP (Bishop et al., 1993; Cone, Delawyer, & Wolfe, 1985). The service coordinator is responsible for ensuring that appropriate procedures for developing an IFSP or IEP are followed and that services listed on the IFSP or IEP are provided.

Duwa et al. (1993) have cautioned that family involvement should not be considered synonymous with family-centered programming. They have stated that family-centered programming includes family members as decision, policy, and program participants and recipients of support, whereas family involvement entails that parents help their children but not receive services themselves. The service coordinator must ensure that families are allowed and encouraged to participate in planning services.

Sheehan (1988) reviewed research on parental involvement in early childhood assessment and planning of services and found that parents' evaluations of their children's accomplishments differed from other team members' assessments. That is, parents tended to rate their children's accomplishments at a higher level than other team members did and test scores indicated. In addition, parents frequently reported dissatisfaction with the parent–professional relationships, stating that they felt blamed, suspected, ignored, and patronized by professionals while being viewed as uncooperative and angry (Smith, 1992). More-recent surveys discussed in Chapter 2 suggest that parents' level of satisfaction regarding various aspects of early interventions services, including their level of satisfaction with parent–professional relationships, has steadily increased.

Duwa et al. (1993) have cautioned that families should not be criticized, put at a disadvantage, or glorified as exemplary based on the extent to which they participate in the decision-making process. Again, it is the service coordinator's responsibility to ensure that families receive the services they need and be allowed to participate at the level ensured by federal laws.

It is critical to determine the type of parent–professional relationships that best serve children's needs. Mulliken (1983) asserts that a team approach, with parents as full members, is most beneficial for children because parents generally know a great deal about their children.

Types of Intervention Services

In addition to assessment and planning services, the service coordinator typically provides intervention services for the family. These services include direct and indirect intervention. **Direct intervention services** include teaching parents effective communication skills, suggesting ways to solve problems, and providing family counseling. **Indirect intervention services** include the service coordinator's acting as a broker who locates services and as an advocate who helps the family acquire needed services.

Direct Intervention

Service coordinators directly intervene to help families strengthen their self-care skills and capacities. Summers et al. (1990) reported that families often need assistance in developing the skills needed to work with professionals and service delivery systems. Modeling and coaching are often helpful techniques for teaching family members new skills, demonstrating problem solving, and developing an inventory of responses that may be used in difficult situations.

Effective modeling requires that service coordinators call parents' attention to the behavior they are modeling for them and explain why the modeled behavior may be useful. In some cases, modeling behavior through role play is very helpful. Coaching involves service coordinators' encouraging family members to share their concerns or observations with other team members. It also may involve providing opportunities to practice methods of sharing these concerns (Kirst-Ashman & Hull, 1993).

Shy or reticent family members may benefit from help in learning how to participate or ask for clarification at team meetings. Using role playing and coaching may help them become more assertive. For example, a service coordinator might ask a parent to participate in a role play in which the service coordinator takes the role of special education teacher. During this role play, the service coordinator, in the role of special education teacher, would create a variety of scenarios allowing the parents to practice responding to these situations. After each scenario, the service coordinator and parent would discuss the interactions and note effective and ineffective strategies. When parents use effective strategies, the service coordinator should acknowledge this.

Families with young children who have disabilities are often reluctant or too inexperienced to share their thoughts, experiences, and observations of their children with professionals. In many cases, family members must interact with many different types of professionals throughout the child's educational experience and beyond.

There is a strong possibility that less assertive parents will quickly become frustrated and even angry because they believe their perspective is not being considered. It is nearly impossible for professionals to meet parents' needs if those needs have not been effectively communicated. For this reason, it is important for parents to learn to represent themselves and their perspectives clearly and in a timely manner. Coaching and modeling are often effective strategies for developing this skill.

The need for parents to learn to speak out is demonstrated in the following situation. A group of preschool personnel speculated as to why a child arrived at school acting very tired. The staff discussion took place in the presence of the child's mother. The staff spoke about the child's seizure-medication regime, speculated about bedtime routines at home, and expressed concern about the effects of the child's long bus ride to school. The mother, a shy young woman, became agitated while listening to the staff talk about her child, but she said nothing. Several days later the service coordinator shared the mother's feelings with the staff and went on to explain that the child typically slept only 4 hours each night, often waking up and screaming for more than an hour. The mother, feeling responsible, guilty, and exhausted, did not share this behavior with the staff. After the service coordinator provided her with opportunities to practice communication skills through the use of modeling and coaching, the mother was able to describe her child's behavior to the team and participate in formulating treatment recommendations. Much of a service coordinator's direct work with families centers on very specific situations such as this one.

The service coordinator is often involved in providing counseling services to families of children with disabilities. Parents' emotional needs must be met before they can optimally meet the needs of their children. Children may also require counseling services, which may be provided in the form of play therapy. Social workers and school or counseling psychologists often provide this type of child counseling therapy, which involves using toys to reenact situations or express feelings. Chapter 12 provides a discussion of the use of play therapy.

Indirect Intervention

Indirect services encompass the service coordinator's two roles of broker and advocate. Very few individual programs are capable of meeting all needs of the child with disabilities and their family. The broker links families with a variety of useful resources (Kirst-Ashman & Hull, 1993). The long-term goal of the broker is to help enable families to deal with systems on their own once the connections have been established (Popple & Leighninger, 1993).

The Service Coordinator's Role as Broker.   An example of the role of the service coordinator as a **broker** involves finding a pediatric dentist who is trained and able to treat children with disabilities. The service coordinator needs to model and coach the family with regard to methods for finding an appropriate dentist. If the service coordinator initially contacts the dentist on behalf of the family, the family should be informed about all the steps taken to find the dentist and establish a union between needs and services. This will help the family to meet subsequent needs without the assistance of the service coordinator. It is often best if family members observe the process. For example, the service coordinator could invite the parents to sit and listen as the service coordinator talks with the dentist.

Another example of indirect services involves finding additional support networks. Families may require help finding support groups, such as those that may be found during interactions with other parents who have children with disabilities. Families of children with disabilities often experience similar circumstances and feelings while having many unique needs. The value of parent groups in providing support and education is somewhat neglected in the literature. Even though parent groups have received limited attention, research has suggested a number of important aspects of parent-support groups for families of children with disabilities.

Daniels (1982) studied parent groups to learn about parents' self-identified needs, Collins and Collins (1990) began parent support groups at parents' requests, and Alexander and Tompkins-McGill (1987) initiated parent groups to encourage leadership.

When providing suggestions to professionals who work with families who have children with disabilities, Alexander and Tompkins-McGill (1987) recommend bringing together families with children who have similar diagnoses so that they can share information and lend support to each other. Ferris and Marshall (1987) reported on a family-support project in which a crisis group for families provided an effective emotional outlet and allowed families to identify with other families and discern their own feelings.

Friesen (1989) reported that about half of the respondents to a national survey of parents who had children with serious emotional disorders and who were attending support groups with other parents of children with disabilities found this involvement helpful. In another study involving families of young children with disabilities, Petr and Barney (1993) reported that parents cited the need for emotional support as their most crucial need. The authors of this study further reported, "The most reliable and inspirational source of support was other parents of children with similar disabilities" (p. 250).

Professionals should be aware of and direct family members to family support groups. Many community newspapers periodically publish a comprehensive list of support groups. In addition, local United Way offices, mental health associations, and departments of social services, among others, often provide listings of support groups. If appropriate parent support groups are not available, the service coordinator should consider helping to organize such groups. Increasingly, parents and professionals are finding that meeting online is a practical alternative to meeting in person.

The Service Coordinator's Role as Advocate.   Additionally, the service coordinator's role of **advocate** helps to ensure that service providers are responsive to the family's needs (Morales & Sheafor, 1992). For example, a pediatric dentist might be found, but the dentist might initially refuse to take the child's case for any number of reasons. An advocate could speak on behalf of the family while modeling advocacy and assertion skills that the family members will need to access services for themselves in the future. This advocacy process lays the groundwork for children with disabilities and their families to learn to self-advocate later in life. Families unable to self-advocate are less likely to teach their children to advocate for themselves.

Monitoring Service Plans

In addition to engaging in assessment, planning, and intervention, the service coordinator monitors the service plan. Three aspects of monitoring include confirming that agreed-on services are being provided, analyzing the level of success of the service delivery systems, and evaluating the level of commitment of social network members.

Careful program monitoring tends to advance the identification of additional needs as they arise and contributes to a smooth progression for the child and family (Moxley, 1989). Monitoring requires that all aspects of the service plan be recorded in detail, including who is responsible for effecting the plan, what implements are needed, and how soon the goals should be reached. Monitoring primarily involves service delivery and evaluating the usefulness of the services.

Service coordinators also monitor service plans by evaluating the productivity of the service plan, its bearing on the functioning of the child and family, the social network's ability to reinforce the family, and the capacity of the social service professionals to work with the family. Evaluation focuses on whether the plan achieves the desired outcome (Moxley, 1989).

Assessment of outcomes related to the child includes determining if the child has positive social relationships and acquires and uses knowledge and skills. Additionally, assessment of outcomes specifically related to the family should occur. These outcomes include the family's understanding of their child's disabilities, strengths and weaknesses, and needs, and the family's knowledge of their rights, level of self-advocacy, involvement in their child's education, support systems, and ability to access desired and appropriate services, programs, and activities.

During the evaluation phase, outcomes related to intervention are examined. The service coordinator needs to make certain that the projected goals are achieved. For example, it may be important to determine if the child can self-feed or if the home or service-providing facilities are wheelchair-accessible. These types of evaluations help in determining whether service plans are producing the desired results.

As discussed in Chapter 2, a vital aspect of evaluation is deciding how best to gather data to draw accurate conclusions. In some cases, informal observations of children are sufficient. In other cases, detailed data gathered from daily or hourly observations or standardized assessment instruments are needed. It is also valuable to attempt to determine why plans or methods of intervention were or were not effective.

Moxley (1989) developed a helpful introduction and questionnaire for securing professional reaction to the service plan and its effectiveness. The results of questionnaires may be summarized at or before a team meeting. Questionnaires provide necessary evaluations of the service plans. Moxley believes that the assessment process should include the family's evaluation of the service coordination. This evaluation should indicate the attitudes of the family regarding service coordination as well as empower the family. The family directly evaluates the worth, significance, and benefit to them of the service coordination.

Conclusions

Children with disabilities and their parents have broken through many societal barriers. An increasing number of day care and preschool settings are including children with disabilities in their classrooms, allowing children with and without developmental delays to learn together using the inclusion model. Professionals, parents, and children are working through differences that initially appear very great. They are finding common ground that will help them feel accepted and worthwhile.

To ensure that their common goal is reached, parents and professionals must work in successful collaboration. The world is full of possibilities for children with disabilities. Many of these possibilities came about because of the collaboration of parents and professionals. The service coordinator is responsible for ensuring that this collaboration is effective and leads to development and delivery of appropriate services for children and their families.

Although children with disabilities and their families frequently require special education services for extended periods of time, a highly effective service coordinator will ultimately impart service coordination skills to the families. After all, where will the children learn service coordination skills so that they ultimately can become self-sufficient if they do not learn them from their families? These skills are crucial because children with disabilities strive for independence, and a significant aspect of that independence is the ability to advocate for oneself.

CHAPTER SUMMARY

- A cooperative partnership between professionals and parents is necessary to provide highly effective services to children with disabilities.

- The two major types of communication are nonverbal and verbal. Listening is a critical requirement for effective communication.

- Preparing for a meeting involves writing down questions, concerns, feelings, expectations, and realistic goals and may include information compiled in a parent's home file.

- The purpose of service coordination is to foster a family's knowledge and abilities regarding how to effectively use social services and supports and how to develop self-reliance skills.

Service coordination includes coordination of services for children and their families.

- Assessment activities of the service coordinator include defining issues, gathering information from other professionals, and working with children and their families to determine types of services needed.

- Direct intervention involves working with families to strengthen their ability to help themselves. Indirect intervention involves gaining access to other services that may be needed by families.

- Service coordinators monitor and evaluate service plans to ensure that the plans are being followed and that children are achieving set goals.

CHAPTER KEY TERMS

Handicapped Children's Early Education Program (HCEEP)

Early Education Program for Children with Disabilities (EEPCD)

family-centered care

verbal communication

nonverbal communication

active listening

home file

service coordination

social worker

National Association of Social Workers (NASW)

Parent Needs Survey (PNS)

social network

formal support system

informal support system

multidisciplinary team

interdisciplinary team

transdisciplinary team

direct intervention services

indirect intervention services

broker

advocate

REVIEW QUESTIONS

1. How might assertiveness training benefit parents with children in need of services?

2. What are the key characteristic of effective communication between parents and teachers?

3. How might nonverbal cues help and hinder communication? What are the characteristics of active listening skills and why is it crucial for these skills to be developed?

4. What are the three "faces" of conflict, and why is conflict resolution between parents and professionals crucial?

5. What are the major tasks of service coordinators? Why are these tasks important?

6. Why are social networks important? Why are different types of networks needed?

7. What are direct and indirect interventions? Why are both important?

SUGGESTED STUDENT ACTIVITIES

1. Form groups of three. Have one person in each group tell a story while a second group member actively listens. The third member of the group will try to list all of the active listening skills and nonverbal communication displayed. How would this list be different if the storyteller were purposefully outwardly aggressive, silly, or passive?

2. Write a vague or ambiguous note from a teacher to parents. Also write a clear note asking a parent to meet with staff members to discuss their child's current level of development.

3. In pairs or groups, have one person display body language that represents a particular feeling while the other person or group members

try to guess the feeling. Discuss what you learned from participating in this activity, relating your discussion to team collaboration and parent–teacher relationships.

4. With a partner, role-play effective and ineffective meetings between a parent and professional.

5. Contact a social worker, and discuss the role of the service coordinator and the services that this person provides.

6. Imagine that you are a service coordinator who is assisting a deaf child and their family. Specifically, what types of tasks would you have to perform to help this child get appropriate education? What sorts of services would be helpful to the family?

7. What are direct and indirect interventions? Why are both important?

Communication Abilities 5

CHAPTER KEY POINTS

- Speech and language delays are the most common developmental delays in children younger than 5 years old.

- Several theories attempt to explain why language development occurs.

- Understanding typical stages of communication development helps ensure appropriate assessment and intervention service planning.

- Several potential factors contribute to the occurrence of language disabilities.

- Referrals for speech and language evaluations are made by a variety of individuals.

- Speech and language evaluation often includes informal and formal assessment.

- Early intervention is crucial for children with communication delays.

- Speech–language pathologists play a major role in assessment and therapy related to communication disorders.

- Speech and language therapy may be conducted in individual or group sessions in a variety of settings.

Communication delays are the most common disabilities before school age (age upon entering kindergarten). Children with **communication disorders or delays** have deficits in their ability to exchange information with others (Boone, 1987; Lue, 2001). Language acquisition is one of the key developmental milestones in infants' and toddlers' development. Communication delays often negatively affect the development of cognitive and social skills (Nicoladis, Mayberry, & Genessee, 1999; Owens, Metz, & Haas, 2000).

By conservative estimates, 3 to 10% of children age 2 to 3 years old may have a communication delay (Bowerman, 1985). It is estimated that children with communication disorders make up 25 to 50% or more of young children eligible for early intervention programs (Butler, 1991; Goodman, 1992). Approximately 2% of school-age students are classified as having a communication disorder as their primary disability. An additional 15% are considered to have a communication disability as a secondary disability (e.g., Down syndrome is the primary disability and language disability is a secondary disability). Two-thirds of school-age children who have a communication disability are boys. Approximately 5% of school-age children with a communication disability receive direct services from a speech and language pathologist. It is estimated that communication disorders (including speech, language, and hearing disorders) affect 1 in 10 people in the United States.

"My child isn't talking," parents are likely to say when they first become concerned that their child may have a speech or language delay. Most parents are keenly aware of their child's communication abilities, because communication is the basis for interaction between parents and child. Parents typically bond with children by communicating nonverbally and verbally. Verbal communication skills are a tangible way for parents to measure the development of their child's skills and compare the child to others the same age (Acredolo, Goodwyn, Horobin, & Emmons, 1999; Bernstein & Tiegerman, 1989).

When parents suspect that their child is not communicating as much or as well as most children their age, it is appropriate for the parents to consult a speech and language pathologist. This specialist is frequently referred to as a speech therapist, but that term is misleading because **speech** refers to the sounds produced when talking, whereas communication involves many more components. Speech and language pathology is the study of normal, delayed (late), and disordered (different) communication (Koniditsiotis & Hunter, 1993; Kripke, 2004).

Theories Related to Communication Skills Development

Communication skills acquisition is likely determined by the interaction of biological, cognitive, psychological, and cultural factors (Bates, 1993; Bates, O'Connell, & Shore, 1987). **Nativists** and **empiricists** provide the two major perspectives regarding language acquisition. Nativists suggest that language acquisition is primarily based on innate mechanisms, which act as blueprints that guide development. In contrast, empiricists believe that language is primarily acquired through learning opportunities (Nelson, 1973).

Nativists

In part, nativists' belief that language acquisition is based on an innate mechanism has to do with the rapidness of language development (most children can engage in relatively complex conversations by age 3) and the consistency with which the stages of language development occur across cultures. Nativists recognize that imitation and reinforcement play a role in language acquisition, but they believe that these are guided by an innate predisposition. They believe there is a **critical period** (absolutely necessary time), or **sensitive period** (time when certain experiences are crucial for later development), for language development. Nativists find support for their theory in the fact that language appears to occur naturally, requiring little effort. Case studies indicate that children who are not exposed to language before their early teens will not fully acquire grammar and syntax.

One of the best-known nativists, **Noam Chomsky,** proposed the existence of a **language acquisition device (LAD)** that includes universal grammar rules (basic rules underlying all human languages). Chomsky argued that the LAD is a biologically based, innate tool designed for language acquisition, which is initiated by verbal environmental experiences. Chomsky cited the nearly identical stages of language development across most languages as evidence supporting the existence of a LAD.

Evidence of a LAD is seen when children who live in English-speaking families use *-ed* to indicate the past tense of irregular verbs. For example, they might say, "He runned," instead of "He ran." This is an example of **overregularization** (Marcus et al., 1992). The tendency to apply regular rules of grammar in situations that do not follow the rules is found in nearly every language. Because adults do not typically say "runned," it is unlikely that children learn to say "runned" based on imitation or reinforcement (Cromer, 1991; Harris, 1998).

Empiricists

Empiricists believe that language is acquired through imitation, especially of parents. They emphasize that infants learn to say words that others have repeatedly said and coaxed the child to say. For example, a father coaxes his child by saying, "Say 'Daddy.' Come on. Say 'Daddy, Daddy, Daddy.'" As a result, "Daddy" is likely to be one of the child's first words.

Behaviorists such as B. F. Skinner (1957) believe that language is also acquired through operant conditioning (use of reinforcement and punishment). For example, once a child says "Daddy," a father is likely to be very excited. He may jump around laughing and give the child hugs and kisses. Most infants find this type of behavior enjoyable and reinforcing, so it increases the likelihood of their saying "Daddy" in the future. Although children need to develop oral-motor skills (muscular control of the mouth etc.), which will allow them to speak, behaviorists view language development as primarily the result of experiences rather than an innate acquisition device.

Behaviorists have difficulty explaining why 2-year-old children often say things like "I goed to the store" when they have heard others correctly say, "I went to the store." Behaviorism has difficulty explaining that, although adults correct only the most obvious grammatical mistakes that children make, over time children learn rules in a stage-like order. In addition, this theory cannot readily explain the tendency for children to use telegraphic speech (which sounds like a telegram, shows correct word order, makes sense, but usually contains only key nouns and verbs) because this speech pattern is not typically modeled. For example, a child might say, "Go car?" instead of "Are we going in the car?"

Constructivists

Constructivists emphasize that children's early language is based on expressing concepts already meaningful to them. Children are seen as active learners. According to this perspective, language acquisition is based on cognitive and emotional development and social interactions. Social and cultural environments are viewed as fundamental to language development. Constructivists emphasize that the child's purposeful behavior and interactions with others promote language learning. The role of adults is to adapt to the child's responses by providing an environment supportive of each child's needs and level of development.

Interactionists

Most developmentalists have an interactionist perspective. **Interactionists** believe that both innate and environmental influences play key roles in language development. They believe that children must be allowed time for their innate abilities to mature and must be provided opportunities to observe and imitate language. In addition, they acknowledge that reinforcement and punishment influence rate and quality of language development.

Typical Speech and Language Development

A crucial aspect of communication is the reciprocal interaction of young children with others. Forms of communication vary with children's age and developmental status. During the first year of life, communication focuses on hearing, physical contact, body movements, gestures, facial expressions, and vocalization. During the second year of life, most children speak individual words. After this time, children who have typical language development rapidly increase their vocabulary and begin using two-word combinations. During the third year, typical language development includes a rapid increase in vocabulary as well as the use of increasingly complex language (Kuczak, 1986).

Infants without hearing disabilities are prewired to respond to human voices. As general cognitive abilities develop during the first year of life, so do language abilities. The ability to understand language (**receptive language**) precedes the development of speech (**expressive language**) (Reznick & Goldfield, 1992). For example, at about 6 months of age, most children respond to their own names. They turn and look at a person who says their name. At about 9 months, most children appropriately respond to words such as "come" and "up."

Newborns reflexively yawn, grunt, burp, and sigh. Crying is a precursor to speech acquisition. Initially **undifferentiated,** soon after birth, cries begin to sound different depending on a child's reason for crying. Over time, different needs are signaled by **differentiated crying.** This development suggests that infants learn which sounds are most likely to prompt others to help them resolve certain needs such as cessation of pain, hunger, or fatigue. As infants gradually gain control of breathing and coordination of muscles, they become capable of producing specific sounds (Oller & Eiler, 1988).

As children begin to increase the number of their vocalizations, adult modeling of language becomes increasingly important. Parents and other caregivers demonstrate **semantics** (the meaning of words), **syntax** (the rules of sentence construction), and **phonology** (language sounds). They also model the rules of conversational speech, called **pragmatics,** which include taking turns speaking during a conversation (Kaiser & Warren, 1988). Adults also provide reinforcement by responding to a child after the child vocalizes (Norman & McCormick, 1993).

Adults frequently use **motherese/fatherese/parentese,** also referred to as **child-directed speech.** Such speech is simpler, shorter, and slower than regular adult speech. Vowels and pitch variations are exaggerated, and sentence structure tends to be repetitive. As a child matures and begins saying words, adults often expand on the child's vocalizations. For example, **expansion** is demonstrated when a child says, "Go car?" and the mother responds, "Yes, Daddy went in the car." Parentese and expansion seem to enhance language development (Leonard, 1986).

Most infants begin to coo between 1 and 3 months of age. **Cooing** involves repeated, song-like vowel prolongation such as "oooooh" or "aaaaah." Typically, infants coo more when others interact with them. Between 3 and 4 months of age, most infants add consonant sounds to their speech. They begin to babble at 4–6 months old. **Babbling** consists of consonant and vowel sounds. When babbling, infants combine these consonant and vowel sounds into sequences such as "mamama," "bababa," and "dadada" (Berk, 2006). Infants babble in reaction to stimuli (individuals, objects) and, gradually, to express needs. Cooing and babbling during interactions with others allow infants to gradually develop a sense of the importance of give-and-take language interactions (Apel & Masterson, 2001).

Typically, babbling becomes more melodic when an infant is 9–12 months old. **Intonation** (rise and fall of the voice's pitch) starts to sound more like adult patterns. When a child coos or babbles and an adult is present, the adult usually responds to the child in some way. For example, after a child babbles, "Nananana," the adult may turn toward the child, imitate the child, or respond in some other way. Adults' responding to children in this manner usually reinforces vocalization. That is, children are more likely to engage in further cooing or babbling if an adult has responded (Fey, 1986).

Most children use gestures before they say their first words (Goldin-Meadow, 1998; Goodwyn & Acredolo, 1998; Messinger & Fogel, 1998). The most common gestures include giving (holding an object toward another person), pushing away, raising the arms (indicating "Pick me up"), showing, reaching, waving, pointing, shaking the head "no," and nodding "yes." Most children give objects, show objects, and wave by 10 to 11 months. By 1 year of age, most children show at least six of the listed gestures, which are typically acquired and displayed in the order indicated (Gopnik & Meltzoff, 1986).

When children first begin to say words (at 12–20 months), they are content words (nouns, verbs, adjectives, and prepositions that refer to concrete things, qualities, actions, and individuals rather than abstract concepts such as love and sadness. Common first words include *Mama, Dada, book, car, up*, and *down*. Early speech usually is not articulated clearly. For example, "book" may sound like "boo" or "ook." At early stages of speech acquisition, children often drop consonants or consonant clusters from the beginning or end of a word.

Sometimes a single word may represent an entire thought. "Boo" may mean "Read me a book" and "Juice!" may mean "I want a drink of juice!" Such a one-word sentence is called a **holophrase** (Bloom & Lahey, 1978; Yoder & Warren, 1993).

Vocal symbols (words) serve as a method by which children store their experiences in short- and long-term memory. Initially, children often **overextend** words—apply them to an overly broad set of stimuli. For example, they might refer to all drinks as "juice." They also **underextend** words—apply them to an overly narrow set of stimuli, as when a child applies the word *dog* only to one particular dog (Carroll, 1986).

Children's use of art, language, and other symbols to represent objects, individuals, and events demonstrates **symbolic thinking.** The ability to think symbolically is directly related to language development (Gopnik & Meltzoff, 1986). Symbolic thought is evident in preschoolers' dreams, imagery, and play. This type of thought allows children to start fantasizing and create novel images by manipulating symbols in complex and personal ways. The ability to use symbolic thinking depends on prior development of cognitive abilities that allow a child to think about, organize, and process information internally (Norman & McCormick, 1993).

Most toddlers (1–2 years old) remember the names of several objects. They are likely to imitate other's speech. They point to toys, pictures in a book, or parts of the body when they are named by others. Gradually they name objects themselves. Initially, children comprehend more language than they can produce (Blank, Rose, & Berlin, 1978). For example, they may be able to respond appropriately to an adult's saying, "Give me your shoes," yet be unable to produce that sentence. Children without developmental disabilities begin speaking single words before they are 2 years old.

After age 2, most children start to use two-word phrases such as "Go car" and "My ball." These phrases tend to be **telegraphic speech** that includes core words (key verbs and nouns) but omits less important words (Goldfield & Reznick, 1990). For example, a toddler is likely to say, "More juice," rather than "I want more juice." By age 3 toddlers typically have acquired a vocabulary of 25 to 300 words. However, speech varies widely among toddlers. A small proportion of toddlers appear to be very reluctant to speak (they are **selectively mute**), but once they do speak, they typically display rapid vocabulary growth (Warren & Kaiser, 1988).

Wide variations in the number of words produced by children when they are speaking are common even for children of the same age. One method that **psycholinguists** (psychologists who study language development) use to measure children's language development is **mean length of utterance (MLU)**. Typically, MLU gradually increases with age. The average sentence length for a child 2 years old is two words. Children typically use sentences about three to six words in length by 3 to 4 years old (Hoffang, 1989).

Children 2 to 4 years old develop language skills consisting of communicative and noncommunicative language. Communicative language is children's ability to tell others what and how they themselves are thinking. **Noncommunicative language** consists of **repetition, monologue,** and **collective monologue.** Repetition is shown when children repeat what others say (Berko, 1989). This is frequently observed when children have older siblings or are in a preschool or day care setting. Children often repeat someone else's statement, acting as if it is their own.

Children's language is referred to as a monologue (or **self-talk**) when they talk out loud to themselves. Children often use this type of noncommunicative language while playing alone (Berk, 1992). A collective monologue occurs when children sit together and talk, but not to each other. This type of language may help guide problem solving. For example, a child may think aloud and say, "My tower is tall. I'd better be careful, or it'll fall down." When preschoolers think aloud in monologues, they are often guiding their own thoughts and actions by communicating with themselves. For example, a 4-year-old might say while putting toys away, "This goes over here." A child who talks out loud may also be engaging in positive self-talk such as "I can do this." Children who use this type of self-talk are more likely to have positive self-esteem than children who use negative self-talk such as "I can't do this."

Children often control their impulses through **inner speech,** cautioning themselves as their parents would. This type of speech may be seen when a child tries to stay out of the cookie jar by saying, "Wait until after dinner!" Inner speech helps direct children's thinking as they mature. During early childhood, inner speech begins as a whisper or mutter to oneself. As the child matures, self-talk (a form of inner speech) becomes silent talking, talking inside the head (Green, 1976). Inner speech, however, does not disappear altogether. Most people use it from time to time, saying things like "I can't believe I did that," "I can't believe how that person is driving," or "I need to be more careful!"

By 3 or 4 years old, most children have a rapidly increasing vocabulary. At this time, children's language typically includes the basic rules of speech and grammar, the set of rules that govern how words are used, combined, and altered (Bernstein & Teigerman, 1989). English-speaking children use simple sentences with subject-verb-object word order. Children at 3½ years have typically learned the basic rules of grammar so well that they frequently over-apply the rules (i.e., they overregularize) (Behren, 1988). For example, a child is likely to say, "The childs goed to the store." Although this sentence is not grammatically correct, it indicates that the child understands that plurals typically are formed by adding *s* and past tense is formed by adding *ed*.

In most cases, throughout the preschool years, children's communication skills continue to become more effective. Children tell others what they want and may use language to manipulate how others perceive a situation. Preschoolers, though, frequently cannot describe important features of objects. For example, a 3½-year-old may attempt to ask an adult to take a truck down from the closet shelf. If the shelf has several trucks on it, the child may have difficulty clearly communicating the specific desired truck (Acredolo, Goodwyn, Horobin, & Emmons, 1999; Apel & Masterson, 2001; Peccei, 1994).

As discussed in Chapter 3, teachers and other professionals often use developmental charts to compare a child's development to the average development of other children the same age. Table 5.1 provides a very general list of language-development milestones that normally occur between birth and 5 years. The ages represent averages based on developmental information found in a wide variety of literature and other resources. The table is presented with the caution that children who develop normally vary greatly in their maturation patterns and timetables (Greene, 1975). No single skill should form the basis of any important decisions concerning assessment or treatment. Rather, all areas of development must be considered (B. S. Wood, 1981).

Causes of Speech and Language Delays and Disabilities

Not all children develop communication skills at the typical rate. In most cases, the causes of speech and language impairments are unknown. Causes may be **organic** (having a physical cause) or **functional** (not having a physical cause). Children with other developmental disabilities (e.g., hearing loss, oral-motor feeding problems, mental retardation, cerebral palsy, autism spectrum disorders, or Down syndrome) often have accompanying speech and language disabilities. Other conditions that affect children's communication abilities include attention deficit hyperactive disorder; cleft lip or palate; ear infection; dental abnormalities; lack of adequate prenatal care; prenatal exposure to viruses, drugs, or alcohol; premature birth; prolonged illness; hospitalization; physical neglect or abuse; and malnutrition (Toppelberg & Shapiro, 2000). In addition, lack of high-quality speech models (frequent opportunities to hear fluent speech) contributes to delays in the acquisition of speech and language abilities (Roseberry-McKibbin & Hegde, 2000).

Brain or Neurological Abnormality or Damage

Speech requires the ability of the brain to coordinate neuromuscular signals to the lungs, mouth, and larynx (upper portion of the trachea, which contains the vocal cords); hearing adequate to receive input (sound); and satisfactory ability to comprehend and use signals. The auditory cortex areas of the brain are responsible for recognizing and receiving sounds. Language comprehension cannot occur without correct auditory input. Abnormal brain development or damage due to accident or illness also contributes to language delays.

Table 5.1   Overview of Speech and Language Development

Average Age	Receptive/Comprehension Skills	Expressive Skills
0–3 months	• shows a startle response to noise • makes eye contact • attends to voice	• initially undifferentiated cries • differentiated cries for various needs
2–8 months	• localizes voice • responds to name • responds to "No"	• cooing and vowel sounds ("oohs" and "ahhhs") • vocalization after hearing speech • gurgles, laughing sounds, grunts • first babbling, consonant/vowel combinations (e.g., "bababa," "dadada," "gagaga") • use of intonation
12 months	• follows simple directions • responds to name and "No" • understands many words, begins to associate words with actions	• first words • one-word sentences (holophrases) • gesturing and babbling • word imitation • playing of peek-a-boo
18 months	• retrieves a requested object	• 20 words
24 months	• points to several body parts • answers yes/no questions • distinguishes among pronouns	• 150 words on average • word combinations, two-word utterances • first appearance of early grammatical features • imitation of environmental sounds • referring to self by name • first use of yes/no questions • relates experiences to words • takes turns speaking • verbalizes needs • correctly produces h, m, n, p, w sounds
30 months	• follows two-part directions • understands big, little, in, on, one • understands a few color names	• 350 words • begins to use personal pronouns • begins to use wh- questions • recites songs and rhymes
36 months	• identifies objects by their function • understands long or complex sentences • answers questions about the functions of objects	• 700 words • begins complex sentence development, three-to-four-word sentences • makes up stories

Table 5.1	Continued	

Average Age	Receptive/Comprehension Skills	Expressive Skills
		• talks about experiences • asks many questions • names a few colors • rote counting • tells own gender • states own full name • uses past and present tense • uses private speech • overextends grammatical rules • recites simple rhymes • correctly produces *b, d, f, h, k, y* sounds
48 months	• follows three-part directions • understands time concepts	• 1,500 words • average sentence length of five words • links phrases into causal relationships ("The baby is crying because his mommy left") • counts to five • uses verbs and plural nouns
60 months	• understands common opposites • retains information in sequence	• 2,000 to 3,000 words • defines words • tells attributes of an object • tells sequences of events • asks what words mean • defines simple words • counts to 10 • uses grammatically correct sentences • recites familiar stories by memory • correctly produces *l, r, ng, ph, t*

The left hemisphere of the cortex primarily controls language activities; the right hemisphere has less impact. Damage to **Broca's area** (the left frontal lobe) often results in speech difficulties (Broca's aphasia). Although their speech is slow and words are not properly formed, people with Broca's aphasia generally can understand language.

Damage to **Wernicke's area** (the left temporal lobe) results in poor speech comprehension and limited short-term memory, which is needed for speech recognition and production. This pathology is called Wernicke's aphasia. Speech production remains fluent, but speech often contains nonsense words, and speech comprehension is limited.

Damage to or abnormal development of the **arcuate fasciculus** (the neural pathway that connects the posterior cortex with the frontal cortex and that is thought to connect Broca's area to Wernicke's area) generally results in conduction aphasia. This results in an inability to repeat words spoken by another person.

Difficulty in controlling muscles directly affects speech. The area of the brain that controls the muscles of the face and mouth is located near Broca's area. Children who have motoric problems (e.g., cerebral palsy or brain damage) frequently have difficulty producing intelligible words. Other communication disorders occur due to oral-motor difficulties (e.g., apraxia or dysarthia), aphasias, traumatic brain injuries, and stuttering.

Communication Disability or Cultural Difference?

Language delays are sometimes attributed to cultural differences. In these cases, delays are not based on language disorders but are influenced by the styles of communication to which the child is exposed. Cultural variations in styles of communication include degree of eye contact, physical space between speakers, use of gestures and facial expressions, and amount and rate of speech (Goldin-Meadow, 1998; Lahey, 1988). It is often difficult for teachers to tell if children from various cultures have a disability or problems resulting from acculturation and language learning.

It is natural for children who learn English as a second language to intermix two languages in the same sentence or paragraph. When this occurs, this is not considered a language disorder. Children who speak English as a second language or speak another dialect do not have a communication disorder simply because of their different dialect or language. In addition, for a communication disorder to be diagnosed, symptoms of the disorder must be present in English and in the child's native language/dialect. In addition, if the child has not been regularly exposed to English, such as when English is not the primary language or not spoken in the home, it may be difficult to determine if a language disability is present.

For children from a bilingual or multilingual home, the early expression of language is likely to vary as compared to children raised in a monolingual environment. In most bilingual homes, children initially access one language when selecting words. Between the ages of 2 and 3 years, both languages develop, although development may be more complex in one than the other. After the age of 3 years, children typically use the appropriate syntax and grammar to express themselves in each language (Laing & Kamhi, 2003; Paradis, 2005; Zevin, 1998).

Indicators of Speech and Language Delays

Children with communication disabilities display a wide array of symptoms, including difficulty following directions, attending to a conversation, pronouncing words, perceiving what was said, expressing oneself, or being understood. Language problems include difficulty expressing ideas coherently, learning new vocabulary, understanding questions, following directions, recalling information, understanding and remembering things, learning the alphabet, and identifying sounds that correspond to letters. Speech difficulties include being unintelligible (often as a result of a motor problem or deficient learning environments); sounding hoarse, breathy, or harsh; and dysfluency (lack of smooth flow of speech—stuttering) (Tabors, 1997).

The first indicators of possible speech or language delays are typically noted during the first year of life. At this age, infants who are described as quiet, who make few vocal sounds other than crying, and who appear to be content to be left alone (receive few verbal interactions) are more likely to be delayed in speech and language skills (Fahey & Reid, 2000; Shames, Wiig, & Secord, 1994).

The age at which children begin to speak may also be an indicator of language delays. Most children use one or more words within a few weeks of their first birthday. They often use two-word phrases around 8 to 24 months. Children who do not say single words by 18 months or are not using two-word phrases by 30 months are likely to be classified as speech- or language-delayed. Between about 42 and 50 months, most children begin to experiment with and practice their language skills. They ask many questions and attempt to gain attention by using their verbal skills. If children do not use language in this way, they may have a speech or language delay (McReynolds, 1986).

Among children younger than 5 years old, those with speech and language disabilities constitute the largest group receiving early intervention services (Nelson, 1993, 1998). The pattern changes once children reach school age. Then children with speech and language delays or disorders make up the second largest group of children receiving special education services from birth through high school. The most common communication disorders involve articulation (speech sound production). Between 5 and 15% of all children birth to 20 years of age demonstrate an articulation problem. Once children enter school, language delays are often more specifically classified as some form of learning disability.

Children learn to produce sounds found within the language of their culture, and these sounds have varying degrees of production difficulty (Stoel-Gammon, 1991). For example, sounds requiring the letters S, R, and L are often difficult for a preschool-age child to pronounce. A child, for instance, may say "thoup" for "soup." Articulation problems are typically the easiest problems to correct in young children (Creaghead, Newman, & Secord, 1989).

Other children speak clearly but have difficulty understanding and effectively using words and sentences. They have language disorders rather than speech disorders. Typically, language disorders are more difficult to modify and may require longer and more intense therapy (Conti-Ramsden & Botting, 2001).

Although some speech and language patterns are viewed as baby talk and part of a young child's normal development, they become problems when they are not outgrown. That is, delays in speech and language or in initial speech patterns may become a disorder that can result in learning difficulties.

Teachers, pediatricians, and speech and language pathologists are often asked, "Should my child be evaluated?" Suspected delays in any area of speech and language development are a legitimate basis for assessment. Most children whose parents ask, "Should my child be evaluated?" benefit from having communication skills evaluated. Parents who show concern about language development may unintentionally change the nature of their interactions with the child; for example, they may talk less with the child or frequently correct the child's speech. Therefore, a formal speech and language evaluation is often valuable because a child's motivation to talk may be decreased when an adult pays more attention to the details of sound and grammar than to the topic of conversation (Cheng, 1989).

Even if a child is found to be developing within normal ranges, a parent's feeling that their child is okay is often a beneficial assessment outcome (Wetherby et al., 2002). Concerned parents should be wary of taking advice from well-intentioned friend, or even professionals in fields unrelated to child development, who say things such as, "Don't worry. My child started out the same way, and he's fine now," or, "It's just a stage. He'll grow out of it." Many children do not "grow out of it" without help. In fact, valuable time is lost when speech and language intervention is postponed (Cowley, 2003; Fey, 1986).

In most cases if an 18-month-old does not seem to understand specific words such as their own name, names of common objects, or simple commands such as "Come here," the child should be referred for a speech and language evaluation. A 2-year-old who speaks only a few words, does not use two-word sentences, or seems to have poor comprehension should also be referred for an evaluation (Bloom & Lahey, 1978). Children who are at-risk or high-risk, including those who spent time in neonatal intensive care units, should be tested early and at regular intervals. Other risk factors include diagnosed medical conditions. Children with no high-risk features should be evaluated if their speech and language is not similar to that of other children of the same age. Table 5.2 provides a list of behaviors by various ages that may indicate a child has a speech or language delay.

Role of the Speech–Language Pathologist

Speech and language pathologists are typically trained at the bachelor's or master's level (Wilcox, 1989). For example, in New York State, therapists with a bachelor's degree are qualified to practice in schools, but therapists require a master's degree to practice in most other settings or to have a private practice. In most states, speech and language pathologists with a bachelor's degree are required to complete a master's degree to be permanently certified or licensed. Both types of degrees entail a specified amount of student teaching, called a clinical practicum (American Speech-Language-Hearing Association, 2001; Kerrin, 1996; Leeper & Gotthoffer, 2000).

Speech and language pathologists at the master's level may also hold a Certificate of Clinical Competence from the American Speech-Language-Hearing Association. Speech and language pathologists evaluate and provide therapy for several areas of communication skills discussed later in this chapter.

Speech and Language Evaluation

Referral and Screening

A variety of individuals and agencies can provide information about obtaining speech and language evaluations. Early identification of and intervention for communication disorders is important for young children with significant communication disorders

Table 5.2	*Indicators of Possible Communication Delays by Age*

0–3 months	• lack of responsiveness, awareness of sound, or environment • undifferentiated crying (same cry for tired, hungry, in pain) • sucking or swallowing difficulties
3–6 months	• does not turn toward sound • limited attention • easily overstimulated • lack of awareness of people and objects
6–9 months	• does not appear to enjoy social interaction • lack of eye contact, reciprocal eye gaze and social games, vocal turn-taking • limited or no babbling
9–12 months	• readily upset by sounds • does not clearly request object of attention • limited babbling • lack of responses indicating comprehension of words or gestures
12–18 months	• lack of gestures • does not persist in attempts to communicate • understands fewer than 50 words or phrases without gesture or context clues • says fewer than 10 words • lack of growth in vocabulary from 12 to 18 months
18–24 months	• use of gestures without verbalization • says fewer than 50 words • no two-word combinations • limited consonant production • largely unintelligible speech • regresses in language development, stops talking, or begins to inappropriately echo phrases
24–36 months	• words limited to single syllables, lacking final consonants • few or no multi-word utterances • does not demand a response from listeners • asks no questions • poor speech intelligibility • frequent tantrums when not understood

Source: Adapted from New York State Department of Health (2002).

(McLean & Cripe, 1997). Assessing speech and language development in children younger than 3 years old is particularly challenging because there is considerable variability in development and the distinction between typical and delayed language is not clear-cut. To help ensure the most accurate assessment, all professionals involved in evaluation of communication disorders should have considerable experience working with infants and young children (Law, Boyle, Harris, Harkness, & Nye, 1998).

As discussed in Chapter 2, the setting of the assessment must be appropriate to the developmental stage of the child and be comfortable for both parent and child. Assessment materials and strategies should reflect developmentally appropriate practice. Assessments may be formal or informal and may include standardized tests; direct observation of play or interaction with care providers; reports by parents, teachers, or physicians; and analysis of spontaneous speech samples. Several assessment sessions and ongoing evaluation often are needed to obtain adequate information to make accurate diagnoses.

The Role of Parents in Identification and Assessment.

As emphasized throughout this book, parents play an important role in helping to monitor the development and health of their child. Parents will be involved in all forms of assessment of young children. Parents and other care providers (e.g., grandparents, babysitters, neighbors, and family day care providers) often are a valuable source of information about a child's development. Information provided by the parents and other care providers aids in early identification of possible problems. Information provided by the parents should be seen as crucial to an adequate assessment of the child's communication.

Parents are often present during the assessment sessions. Observation of child–parent interactions is a crucial component of assessment. Parents also help professionals make decisions about assessment and treatment goals for their children. Learning about language acquisition stages helps parents to provide the most useful assessment information and optimize their interactions with their children.

The Assessment Team.

When communication delays are a concern, the assessment team may include one or more of the following professionals: a speech and language pathologist, **audiologist** (specialist in testing hearing), psychologist, neurologist (physician who diagnoses and treats disorders of the nervous system), **otolaryngologist** (physician who specializes in treatment of the ears, nose, and throat), pediatrician, nurse, and social worker. Communication delays may be due to a variety of causes; therefore, each professional is potentially crucial to the evaluation.

Cultural Considerations and Linguistic Variation.

As discussed earlier, communication occurs within a cultural context. It is often difficult to provide an accurate assessment of young children from a bilingual/multilingual home. Professionals must make sure they understand typical language development with regard to each child's language and cultural environment. They must determine whether any apparent language delay is a difference resulting from the influence of learning a second language or a true disorder. This distinction is often difficult.

Appropriate assessment of a child's communication development must include consideration of the languages and dialects spoken within the child's home and the culture of the child's family. While a variety of standardized tests are available for Spanish speakers, there are fewer tests available for other languages. Ideally, professionals screening and evaluating children's communication abilities will be fluent in the child's primary language or be accompanied by an interpreter and will be familiar with the family's culture, values, beliefs, and communication style.

Standardized Screening Tests.   There are several standardized screening tests and questionnaires for communication disorders. Screening instruments may also be used in conducting periodic monitoring of the child's progress and assessing intervention outcomes. Ideal screening tests are inexpensive, simple to administer, and highly accurate. Typically, even easy-to-administer screening instruments require that a highly qualified professional (one knowledgeable about communication disorders in young children) interpret the results and present the findings to the parents. Screening for communication disorders may include open-ended questions, formal and informal checklists, formal standardized screening tests, and observation of parent–child communicative interactions in a naturalistic setting (Pickstone, Hannon, & Fox, 2002).

Checklists such as the Children's Communication Checklist-2, Language Development Survey (LDS), Ages and Stages Questionnaire (ASQ), MacArthur Communicative Development Inventory (CDI), and Vineland Adaptive Behavior Scales (VABS) involve parents' responding to lists of questions about their child's communication abilities. Some of the common standardized tests that rely on direct observation of children by professionals include the Early Language Milestone (ELM)

A speech and language pathologist assesses a young child's verbal skills.

Scale, Receptive-Expressive Emergent Language Scale, Third Edition (REEL-3), and Clinical Linguistic Auditory Milestone Scale (CLAMS), which combines historical information from parents and direct observation of the child.

Although there are many language and communication screening tests available, these are the most commonly used tests:

- Peabody Picture Vocabulary Test, Third Edition (PPVT-III)—assesses verbal abilities in children 2½ years and older.
- Screening Kit of Language Development (SKOLD)—assesses language development in children 2 years, 6 months old to 4 years, 11 months old.
- Test of Early Language Development, Third Edition (TELD-3)—screens language development in children 2–7 years old.
- Clinical Evaluation of Language Fundamentals-4 Screening Test—assesses language disorders in children 3 to 6 years old.
- Kindergarten Language Screening Test (KLST-2)—assesses language skills in children 4 to 6 years old.

If a screening instrument suggests a possible communication disorder, more in-depth assessment is needed to determine whether a disorder exists and to establish a diagnosis. It is also appropriate to assess the child for other developmental or medical problems, which may have contributed to the problem. Not all children with communication disorders can be identified early because the time of onset and severity of symptoms vary from child to child. Therefore, it is useful for screenings to be repeated at various age levels when concerns for communication disorders persist or become apparent. In the case of some children who have a communication disorder, the disorder will not be detected during screening. Conversely, some children who display a possible communication disorder during the screening process will not have a communication disorder.

Full Evaluation

Full evaluation helps determine if a communication disorder is present, establish a specific diagnosis, assess the severity and specific attributes of the communication disorder, determine if intervention is appropriate, aid in planning intervention strategies and selecting treatment, and establish a baseline for measuring progress and determining the effectiveness of intervention programs. Full communication assessments may include standardized tests of expressive and receptive language, samples of spontaneous speech collected in a natural context, and observations of communicative interactions.

As discussed earlier, evaluation of children with disabilities often involves a team of specialists who collaboratively complete evaluations. A comprehensive speech and language evaluation begins with gathering case history information and conducting a personal interview with the parents and child before completing a formal or informal assessment. Case history data include information about the child's birth, the child's medical and developmental histories, family members' health and developmental histories, previous assessment or treatment of the child, summary of treatment gains, and reasons for the evaluation referral. This information may be acquired during the interview or from a written questionnaire or checklist completed by the child's primary care provider. This information is crucial for forming an accurate picture of a child's speech and language development (Fey, 1986).

If a written questionnaire is not provided in advance of the evaluation, it may be helpful for a parent to summarize a child's developmental milestones or provide this information in writing—for example, by bringing a baby's record book in which milestones have been noted. Sometimes it is very difficult for parents to recall information accurately during the interview, particularly if the child is one of several children in the family. Also, parents often experience anxiety during the evaluation, which may limit their ability to remember specific information.

Typically, after the case history has been obtained, an assessment of the child's speech and language is completed. Formal, standardized tests that provide normative data often are used during the assessment. Some formal tests include specific tasks the child is asked to perform. Other formal assessments are scales that the clinician fills out based on observations of the child. Many speech and language standardized tests are available for use with preschoolers (Koniditsiotis & Hunter, 1993).

Some young children have great difficulty participating in formal testing for a variety of reasons. For example, the test materials or tasks may not interest them, or they may not have the attention span necessary to complete the test. In such cases, the evaluator must rely primarily on informal measures, observation, and interviews. Informal assessment lends itself to a more natural play-type environment. Informal information is usually considered as useful as, and sometimes more useful than, information gathered from formal tests. It is important to remember that the evaluator is interpreting data, and comparing the child's skills to established developmental stages, even when using informal measurements; that is, there is some subjectivity involved (Lahey, 1988).

The evaluator may request that the parent and child separate for a short time during certain parts of the evaluation. The parent is often asked to assist by communicating to the child "It is okay" and indicating that they will return after a short time. If the parent remains present during formal testing, it is important that they not coach the child, repeat the clinician's questions, or provide feedback, even nonverbal, regarding the appropriateness of a response.

Depending on where the evaluation takes place, a hearing screening or full audiological evaluation may be part of the assessment process. Because hearing is usually a primary method of learning language, it is important to rule out the possibility of a hearing loss for any child demonstrating speech or language delays. This is especially true when there is a history of frequent or severe ear infections.

A hearing screening assesses whether a child responds to certain sound frequencies (high and low pitches) that are presented at a quiet but audible level. This may be accomplished using an instrument called an **audiometer,** which has earphones, or with an **audioscope,** which looks like a physician's otoscope (ear scope) but also produces beeps when placed in the ear. Other screening methods are also available. A screening may be performed by a speech pathologist, audiologist, nurse, or other professional. The screening provides information only as to whether a sound is heard.

Frequently it is difficult to conduct hearing screening with very young children because they have difficulty following directions regarding how they are to respond to the sounds they hear. If this is the case, a full hearing evaluation may be recommended because the required information could not be gathered with a quick screening. If a screening is completed and the child appears unable to hear sounds, a full hearing evaluation should be done (Lahey, 1988). Hearing assessments and impairments are discussed in greater detail in Chapter 9.

Sharing Assessment Results with Parents

After the speech and language assessment has been completed, the evaluator presents the parent(s) with diagnostic information and makes recommendations based on that information. In a written evaluation, usually following the assessment, the clinician is likely to use a variety of technical terms. These terms are important because they are an accurate, standard means of communication between professionals (as between the evaluator and the treating therapist). Parents should be provided with clear explanations of all technical terms (Tannock & Girolametto, 1992). They also should be told the strengths and limitations of the assessment measures. In addition, they should be provided with information as to how the child's level of communication skills may affect other developmental areas and answers to other questions they may have. See Figure 5.1 for a list of questions that parents often ask and that the therapist should be prepared to answer.

Assessing the Need for Augmentative Communication

If a speech and language disability is detected, it is often necessary to assess the need for an **augmentative communication** method, especially when speech is not an effective mode of communication for the child. There are many augmentative communication methods, including **sign language, eye-gaze boards, communication boards,**

Figure 5.1 **Questions That Parents Ask and That the Therapist Should Be Prepared to Answer**

- Why does my child have this delay?
- What specific communication areas are affected? How do they relate to one another and to other areas of development? What are my child's strengths and areas of need?
- How delayed is my child? What are typical speech and language abilities for children this age?
- What do ratings such as "mild," "moderate," and "severe" mean?
- Does my child need speech and language therapy? If so, what type, how often, and for how long? What are some different treatment options or resources?
- Are there any specific strategies that should be used with my child at home?
- What will be the long-term result of therapy?

high-tech devices, and **facilitated communication (FC).** Augmentative devices are often useful for severe **dysarthria** (lack of coordination or spasticity of the muscles used for speaking as a result of emotional stress, brain injury, or paralysis). They are also useful for children with **apraxia** (inability to make a voluntary movement in spite of being able to demonstrate normal muscle function) and oral-motor dysfunction, neuromotor disorders such as cerebral palsy, autism, or severe neurodegenerative disorders (deterioration of certain nerve cells) and for children dependent on ventilators. Use of augmentative communication systems does not preclude the development of spoken language and often facilitates the development of speech. Often, augmentative communication systems (including sign language) are used transitionally or temporarily.

Assessment of augmentative needs is typically conducted by a multidisciplinary team that may include a speech language pathologist, physical therapist, occupational therapist, and audiologist. These professionals assess the child's positioning needs (sitting, lying down, etc.), fine- and gross-motor capabilities, vision and hearing status, level of cognitive skills, and receptive language as well as the family's multicultural needs and the setting for use (home, child care, etc.).

Types of Speech and Language Delays and Disabilities

The two main categories of communication disorders are speech disorders and language disorders. Speech disorders are related to **voice** (quality, pitch, loudness, resonance, duration), **articulation** (speech sounds), and **fluency** (rate and rhythm of flow). These skills are all related to production of language. Language disorders are related to comprehension or use of spoken or written words. These skills are related to the reception of language. As discussed earlier, the ability to understand language (receptive skills) develops earlier than the ability to speak (expressive skills).

When a young child's communication skills are evaluated, the areas discussed below are evaluated because they are considered important components of communication. These areas include general behavior and the ability to pay attention, prelinguistic skills, general receptive language (i.e., voice, fluency, articulation), general expressive language, oral-motor skills, hearing, play skills, and problem-solving skills.

General Behavior and Ability to Pay Attention

When evaluating communication skills, it is important to consider a child's general demeanor and activity level. The speech and language pathologist notes how a child reacts to new people and situations and may encourage a brief separation from the parent during the evaluation. The child's ability to make or maintain eye contact with others is also observed. When given appropriate toys and materials, most children exhibit curiosity and interest in touching and playing with them. The child's ability to pay attention to age-appropriate activities is noted, as are the levels of activity, distractibility, impulsiveness, and perseverance. The child's frustration level when faced with a challenging task is also evaluated (Creaghead, Newman, & Secord, 1989).

Prelinguistic Skills

During the first year of life, a child usually masters a number of skills prerequisite for language development. These skills are considered when assessing very young children or those who exhibit significant language delays. **Prelinguistic skills** (also called presymbolic) are listed in Figure 5.2.

A child who has a severe language delay but talks is often found to have inconsistent prelinguistic skills (Owens, 1982). Missing links in the full set of prelinguistic skills may underlie difficulties with more complex language skills (Cantwell & Baker, 1987).

Receptive Language Skills

Receptive language refers to language comprehension. There are a number of aspects of receptive language, including the following:

- Understanding vocabulary (words).
- Understanding sentences and grammatical structures.
- Following directions.
- Understanding concepts (e.g., prepositions, sizes, colors, numbers).
- Understanding questions (e.g., "What?" "Where?" "Who?").

Children may demonstrate much better skills in some of these areas than in others. They may be able to speak relatively well yet have receptive language deficits.

Expressive Language Skills

Expressive language refers to the language that a child produces. Expressive language development may be delayed or not occur at all. Possible causes for language disabilities include hearing loss, mental retardation, autism, illness, abnormal brain development or brain injury, emotional disturbance, and environmental deprivation.

Figure 5.2   **Prelinguistic Skills**

- The ability to pay attention to visual and auditory information
- The ability to imitate gestures and sounds
- The development of object permanence (understanding that an object still exists even when it is removed from sight)
- The ability to take turns
- The ability to understand that objects have intended purposes (understanding of cause-and-effect relationships)
- The use of basic communicative gestures and the ability to associate a heard word with its meaning

A commonly accepted model of expressive language consists of three parts (Bloom & Lahey, 1978):

- Expressive vocabulary—number and types of words a child has acquired.
- Syntax—word and sentence formation (rules for ordering of words).
- Pragmatic development—the ability to use language socially (to interact and accomplish an objective).

All of these parts working together constitute expressive language. Many children who have a language delay or language disorder exhibit a large disparity between their receptive and expressive language skills (Nelson, 1991).

Articulation Skills

Articulation is the production of speech sounds. This requires using muscles and other body structures to shape sounds from exhaled air. Some children can understand and produce language but cannot speak clearly. Most phonological disorders have no physically identifiable cause, although some physical causes include neurological and neuromuscular causes, cleft palate, abnormal dental formation, hearing loss, tumors, and brain damage. In most cases, expressive language disabilities are related to the lack of opportunity to learn appropriate speech patterns, due to the absence of a good model to imitate. When articulation is assessed, the therapist evaluates the following:

- Whether a child uses the oral structures (muscles, teeth, and tongue) to produce sounds correctly.
- How a child uses sounds to create meaning.

For children with severe articulation disorders, assessment is complex and detailed. Some basic elements that are evaluated include how individual sounds are produced in words and continuous speech, the child's overall speech intelligibility (clarity), and the child's ability to correctly imitate sounds that the child produces incorrectly when speaking. An ability to imitate sounds not spontaneously produced correctly may decrease the likelihood of the need for direct treatment (Mannix, 1987). Certain error patterns (e.g., difficulty clearly pronouncing "s" or "th" sounds) are normal in development and must be considered within the context of a child's age and language level. By the time children enter kindergarten, their speech should be easy to understand. Figure 5.3 lists the four major types of articulation errors.

Figure 5.3 **Types of Articulation Errors**

- Distortion: unfamiliar sound production
- Substitution: incorrect sound is used within a word
- Omission: sound is omitted within a word
- Addition: sound is added within a word

Voice

The physical health of the **voice,** as well as how it is used to communicate, is within the realm of speech and language pathology. Some aspects of the voice that are assessed formally and informally are the pitch (high or low frequency), volume (loud or soft), and quality (e.g., hoarse or nasal) (Moore, 1986). Speech and language pathologists often recommend that a child be evaluated by an ear, nose, and throat doctor if any aspect of the voice suggests a possible physical problem. This evaluation should be done before providing voice therapy (Lindfors, 1987). The most common causes of voice disorders are vocal abuse, larynx trauma due to accidents or medical procedures, malformation of the larynx, and tumors.

Fluency

Fluency problems, often referred to as **stuttering** or **dysfluency**, are interruptions in the flow of speech. Stuttering affects four times as many males as females. An estimated 20% of all children display dysfluencies at a level that leads their parents to express concern. There are several possible causes of dysfluency. It should be noted, though, that children who have dsyfluencies are no more likely to have psychological or emotional problems than children and adults who do not, and there is no evidence that emotional trauma causes stuttering.

Dysfluency includes pauses, prolonged sounds, or repetition of sounds and words. In cases of severe dysfluency, secondary characteristics such as jerking motions or blinking may be present. It is important to note that a certain level of mild dysfluency is normal for many young children and occasionally even older children. Children whose level of dysfluency interferes with their ability to communicate or the willingness of others to interact with them often benefit from speech therapy services. A speech and language therapist assesses dysfluency to determine whether it is a developmental stage or a true disorder (Owens, 1991). If stuttering persists longer than three to six months or is particularly severe, seeking the services of a speech and language pathologist who specializes in stuttering is often useful.

Oral-Motor Skills

Oral-motor skills relate to the development of the mouth and surrounding area in terms of its structure and functionality. Weaknesses in this area may affect articulation development. An important part of assessing oral-motor skills is determining if a child has any difficulty eating, drinking, or swallowing. The speech and language pathologist often provides intervention related to oral-motor and feeding skills in conjunction with other professionals, such as an occupational therapist (Mannix, 1987).

Hearing

For most children, hearing is a primary means of learning to communicate. For this reason, when speech and language development is delayed or disordered, it is essential to find out if the child is hearing adequately (Oyler, Crowe, & Haas, 1987). Assessment may take the form of a screening or full hearing evaluation. If a hearing impairment is found, the speech and language pathologist often works with an audiologist or teacher of the deaf and hearing-impaired to provide intervention services. Chapter 9 provides a more detailed discussion of children with hearing loss.

Play Skills

Children progress through developmental stages of play. Each of these stages of play relates to speech-and-language and cognitive milestones. A variety of play experiences must take place for language to develop, especially as the child uses more symbolism (Cheng, 1989). It is important for the speech–language pathologist to engage or observe children during play activities to best understand their level of speech and language development. Chapter 12 provides an extensive discussion of the importance of play.

Problem-Solving Skills

Language assessment also includes consideration of how a child uses language to perform thinking and reasoning tasks appropriate to the child's age. In younger children, these skills are manifested in abilities such as matching or naming. As children become older, they should be able to analyze things that they encounter in more complex ways. They should become able to use language to perform more difficult tasks such as explaining and predicting events (Blank, Rose, & Berlin, 1978).

Importance of Early Intervention

The ability to communicate is integral to all aspects of development and has a long-term impact on socialization and learning. Through the years, increasing emphasis has been placed on the value of special education early intervention. The benefits for the child are clear: the sooner developmental problems are identified, the sooner they may be addressed. Early intervention may result in more-effective and shorter treatment (Theler & Ulrich, 1991). Many parents hope that their child will no longer have a delay by the time the child reaches school age (5 years old). This does not always occur. Many children who receive early intervention services continue to need treatment during or even beyond the elementary school years. Starting early, however, may help children reach their maximum potential and prevent the need for more-intensive services (Paul-Brown & Caperton, 2001).

If developmental problems have a neurological basis, early intervention can take advantage of the immature brain's relative plasticity (flexibility) to develop compensatory strategies for learning and communicating. Early intervention also benefits parents. They receive support and education through the often difficult process of accepting a child's disability, which may allow them to become more effective in providing for their child's needs. Early intervention is also cost-effective because it has the potential to shorten treatment time and the intensity of required services (Warren & Reichle, 1992).

Young children with communication delays typically have a **developmental language delay (DLD)**. DLD is characterized by expressive delays (delays in speaking). Children with DLD display normal age-appropriate visual language skills, including recognizing parents and objects and responding to facial expressions and requests accompanied by a gesture. In addition, children with DLD typically have normal or nearly normal comprehension (receptive language, or understanding of others' speech) and auditory receptive skills (e.g., turning toward sounds, following one- or two-step commands without a gesture, and pointing to named body parts and objects). In most cases, early intervention (speech therapy) enhances speech, and results in age-appropriate speech levels by the time children begin school.

Children with expressive delays may simply be late talkers for no specific reason (referred to as "constitutional delays"). These children develop normal speech and language skills as they age, without any treatment. Unfortunately, it is very difficult to differentiate between children whose speech will improve without intervention and children who need intervention services.

Speech and Language Therapy

Many communication problems can be improved by therapy. Some problems may never be entirely eliminated, but children can learn new strategies to overcome their difficulties (e.g., attention deficit or stuttering). Some children overcome their deficits (e.g., mild language delays) as they grow older while others may compensate by communicating through electronic means (e.g., an augmentative communication device or hearing aid).

Speech and language therapy occurs within a wide variety of settings, ranging from an individual session in a clinic or child's home to a group session in a classroom. The evaluator who is making recommendations typically outlines possible approaches and discusses the benefits and disadvantages of each to enable a parent to participate in the decision-making progress (Nelson, 1989).

During individual treatment a child receives a therapist's undivided attention. Therapy is specifically geared to the objectives set for that child. Individual treatment may take place in a clinic, home, preschool, day care center, or school. During individual treatment at preschool, day care, or school, the child may be taken to a separate room or area, or the therapist may go with the child to regular classroom activities, using those activities as a vehicle for treatment. The choice of therapy setting often depends on the particular goal being addressed.

For example, a child might need to learn how to produce a particular speech sound such as an "s." Initially, the therapist might use some structured activities such as sitting at a table with a mirror and showing the child where to place their tongue to produce the sound. The child might then practice using the new sound by working with pictures or objects, using a computer, or playing games. Once the child has mastered the new sound through these methods, the therapist may accompany the child in group activities to monitor and encourage generalization (Langdon, 1989). The therapist is also likely to discuss ways that teachers and parents can help the child practice this new sound throughout the day.

Some goals require interacting with other children. For example, if a child needs to learn how to ask for a turn, individual treatment might take place in settings that require sharing materials or equipment, such as a child-directed play period (when children have freedom to select an activity) or playground (McMorrow, Foxx, Faw, & Bittle, 1986). The choice of individual treatment settings also is affected by the age and attention span of the child. For example, a very young child, or a child with a limited attention span, might be unable to work one-on-one for speech therapy but be able to work for 30 minutes if the therapy is incorporated into classroom activities (Westby, 1980).

Group treatment includes structured group activities and informal interaction with a therapist. It may be provided in a clinic, day care, or preschool setting where individual treatment also occurs. Group treatment in a preschool may consist of language groups. In these groups, activities are focused on a limited number of objectives appropriate for all the children within the group. For example, the therapist plans a cooking activity, making each child's goal to verbalize a request to have a turn in each step of the process (Girolametto, 1988). This method helps children learn the functional value of language in a highly motivating setting.

The therapist may also lead general class activities, emphasizing individual objectives during interaction with each child. For example, at snack time each child might be required to ask for a snack using the most complex sentence structure feasible for that child. The required response may vary widely among children. One child may provide a one-word request; another may provide a full-sentence request. In this way a group activity takes advantage of more-natural settings and peer interactions. There are more opportunities for generalization of new skills during interactions with a variety of people in a variety of situations. Group treatment often results in a high success rate in meeting many kinds of speech and language goals, even those traditionally addressed in structured individual settings. Working in groups encourages conversations as well (Wilcox, Kouri, & Caswell, 1991).

Conversations are more likely to occur in small groups of three to four children than in larger groups (MacDonald, 1985). Many teachers attempt large-group conversations when the entire group is brought together, including groups of 12 to 20 children (as during circle time). If a teacher is spending a great deal of time reminding children that it is not their turn to speak because someone else is speaking, the group is probably too large for useful two-way conversation (Kaiser & Warren, 1988).

Conversations are most likely to occur when the topic is of real interest to a child and more likely to be prolonged when adults respond to a child rather than ask questions. Often, when an adult asks a child a question, the child interprets the situation as a need to figure out the right answer. In this case the question becomes a test rather than a method of prolonging conversation. Children generally respond well to comments such as, "I never heard that before," "That's really a funny

A teacher engages young children in conversation during a routine activity.

story," or "That's very interesting." In general, the younger the child, the more the teacher should use small groups and one-to-one conversations and avoid many one-way conversations with the entire class (Nelson, 1989).

Research suggests that more statements and requests are made by one child to another when there is no adult in the immediate area (Westby, 1980). On the other hand, more responses to direct questions occur during playtime when an adult is present. The presence of an adult increases the number of verbalizations by children during more-structured group activities. Different types of conversations occur with adults present. Therefore, children need opportunities to play with other children when adults are nearby as well as when adults are not in close proximity (Wilcox et al., 1991).

Early childhood is a critical period for developing communication competence. This competence includes self-expression, communicating with others, and verbal reasoning (Girolametto, 1988). The development of communicative competence requires children to be engaged in conversation and not simply be passively exposed to language, as when they watch television or hear a story read.

Roles of Team Members

Increasingly, a great deal of speech and language treatment is provided within the context of collaboration between the therapist and the classroom teacher (Roulstone, Peters, Glogowska, & Enderby, 2003; Wilcox, 1989). Collaboration means that lessons and activities are jointly planned and executed to fulfill both professionals' objectives. The therapist may use classroom activities as a vehicle for treatment so that speech and language learning may be more relevant to a child's typical routines. An example of a typical collaborative activity is the use of an obstacle course, which requires a child to perform a variety of fine- and gross-motor tasks (such as playing with peg-boards or jumping). While the child performs these tasks, opportunities arise for teaching the appropriate vocabulary and concepts, such as *jump, push, in, around,* and *next.*

Preschool classrooms that promote the development of speech and language skills include interesting materials and activities. Situations that are visually stimulating tend to elicit labeling and questioning by the child. Children communicate more about things that interest them. To maintain interest, it is often necessary to vary the environment frequently and include new activities or materials. One way to do this is to rotate materials, putting some things away and reintroducing them later (McKnight-Taylor, 1989).

In most cases it is desirable to have materials located where children have easy access to them. Placing some items out of reach of children but in their view encourages them to communicate by requesting the object. During snack time, children may initially be given very small portions, so they will need to communicate that they want more. Providing more than one type of snack item encourages children to choose and communicate the choice. Situations that require children to request assistance, such as help removing the lid of a modeling clay container, also encourage communication.

Children typically are encouraged to communicate when teachers or parents say or do silly things. For example, an adult who puts a coat on upside down and then struggles to use the zipper is likely to encourage children to communicate that the adult is doing something wrong. For example, if the temperature outside is very cold and a teacher says, "I think it would be a good day to go swimming at the beach," children will be motivated to use some form of communication to let the teacher know that this is a silly idea.

Language should be a natural part of a daily routine, and adults should provide a language-rich environment that includes naming familiar objects, reading books, singing songs, and including children in conversations (McCormick & Schiefelbusch, 1990). **Cloze activities,** in which a key word is left out of a common song, story, or nursery rhyme and children are encouraged to fill in the missing word, are excellent language-enhancement activities. Adults can encourage children to problem-solve by saying something such as "I can't find your shoe. What should we do?" This method also helps encourage speech and language skill. When reading books, asking a child to predict what will happen next also is useful.

Children who have fluency problems (e.g., frequently stutter) benefit when others speak in a relaxed, unhurried way and frequently pause. Being told to "slow down" is likely to increase dysfluency. Commenting on children's actions, rather than asking children many questions, allows children to more freely express themselves. Children find it easier to talk when there are few interruptions and they have the listener's attention.

Augmentative Communication

Some children are initially unable to use speech to communicate. In these cases, therapy may include teaching the child sign language for words important to the individual (e.g., *stop, yes, no, more,* and *mine*) or using a communication board as a temporary means of communicating. Children with severe disabilities who are nonverbal may need to use one of these systems on a long-term basis. Using alternative communication systems (e.g., sign language or communication boards) provides such children a means to communicate when they are unable to produce words and reduces their frustration. Some parents respond negatively to the idea of their child's using alternative communication systems because the parents understand that the speech-and-language goal is learning to speak. However, using other types of communication is only one step in the communication process. Using symbols other than spoken words often helps a child learn to speak (Schlosser & Lloyd, 1991).

Augmentative and alternative communication (AAC) refers to the use of a technological device or system in addition to or in lieu of verbal communication. AAC includes gestural systems (i.e., sign language), low-tech visual systems (e.g., eye-gaze boards), and high-tech computerized devices (e.g., voice or visual output systems).

Sign Language.   Sign language is a gestural system widely used within the deaf community. Sign language includes **American Sign Language (ASL)** and **Signing Exact English (SEE).** ASL is a visual-gestural language. SEE uses additional signs for word endings (e.g., to indicate verb tenses) and basically follows the exact pattern of spoken English.

Many people worry that teaching infants to sign will lead to delays in speech. When infants use gestures before saying the corresponding word, they are indicating that they understand the meaning of the word. This is a major step in learning to speak because they are demonstrating that they understand the concept the gesture stands for and understand that the sounds that others make are equivalent to the sign. Researchers have found that use of sign language does not delay verbal development; rather, it often enhances speech development (Goodwyn, Acredolo, & Brown, 2000).

Eye-Gaze Boards.   Eye-gaze boards are often useful for children who do not use speech. Children communicate using these boards by looking at the objects on the board. The boards can be made in a variety of ways. Board pictures often include photographs of people, objects, and activities whose names children would say if they were able to use words.

A specific type of eye-gaze board is the **Picture Exchange Communication System (PECS).** This system initially uses pictures and later adds word phrases or sentences to allow children to make choices and communicate needs. PECS can readily be used at home or to label objects (e.g., boxes and toy containers). Pictures of tangible things (i.e., individuals and objects) are often presented first, followed by abstract concepts (e.g., feelings) and line drawings. Picture size varies depending on the needs of the child, and pictures can be mounted on a variety of surfaces.

PECS is an augmentative communication system designed to help children acquire functional communication. It is appropriate for children who do not speak or who have very limited speech, have articulation or motor planning difficulties, or show a lack of initiative in communication. Children and adults typically find PECS easy to understand. Children using PECS typically appear highly motivated to use the system. PECS materials are inexpensive, easy to prepare, and portable (e.g., handdrawn pictures, photographs, magazine cut-outs). They can be used with a wide variety of communicative partners (e.g., parents, day care providers, teachers, or therapists) (Tincani, 2004).

Typically, there are six phases of PECS, although the child may work on two or more phases simultaneously. Phase I involves determining what children are highly motivated to request. During this phase, an adult draws a child's attention to an object that the child likes. When the child reaches for this object, the adult says, "What do you want?" while physically guiding the child to pick up a picture of the item and then hand it to the adult. Next, the adult gives the child the desired object while verbally indicating, "Oh, you want the _____ [name of the object]." This process continues until the child can independently select and give the adult the card corresponding to the desired object.

Phase II begins once the child can independently and consistently select a single picture in exchange for the desired object. The child is then encouraged to generalize the acquired skill. As the child requests items or activities, they are gradually required to move a longer distance to access a communication partner or picture. The child is also required to make requests in a variety of settings and with a variety of communication partners. Although only one card is available, the number of potential vocabulary symbols increases over time.

Phase III requires the child to discriminate between a number of pictures (initially just two, with more being added over time) when requesting items or activities. The child is initially asked, "What do you want?" Over time this prompt is diminished as the child begins to make spontaneous choices.

Phase IV involves teaching the child to use sentence strips to make longer and/or more-complex requests. For example, the child can combine a picture signifying "I want" with a picture of the requested item or activity. The two pictures are attached to a sentence strip, and the entire strip is then given to the communication partner in order to gain access to the pictured item or activity.

Phases V and VI occur simultaneously. In Phase V the child extends the sentence structure by adding adjectives and other words to refine requests. In Phase VI the child uses pictures to make comments about the environment (e.g., "I am cold," "I smell spaghetti," or "I hear birds").

Communication Boards.   Communication boards, which are similar to eye-gaze boards, are often used for children with mental or physical disabilities that prevent the effective use of sign language or speech (Love, 1992). Communication boards contain the vocabulary that the child needs to use to answer questions, make requests, direct the actions of others, direct a sequence of events, or make choices. Typically, the child communicates by pointing to objects on the communication board. Communication boards may be handmade or expensive computerized devices. In many cases the less expensive boards are very effective because they can easily be individualized for each child and several duplicates can be developed for placement at different locations.

A communication board may have pictures (e.g., of a glass or food) and the words *yes* and *no*. It may contain miniature toy objects, photographs, or words. The purpose of the board is to allow the child to communicate by pointing to the objects on the board. The child learns that the objects, pictures, or words represent things or individuals in the environment. They provide the child with a step toward more-sophisticated forms of communication, including speech.

High-Tech Devices.   **High-tech AAC devices** include anything from a single switch to a complex computerized device. An AAC team of specialists, which may include a speech and language pathologist, occupational therapist, physical therapist, and rehabilitation engineer, evaluate children's needs for AAC devices. They determine needs through an extensive evaluation and often try out several devices and access methods with each child.

Facilitated Communication.   A controversial form of communication is facilitated communication (FC). When this method is used, a facilitator supports the child's hand and arm, allowing the child to communicate by typing on a keyboard. This support is highly individualized, based on specific needs. Some individuals receive strong backward pressure on their hand or a light touch on the shoulder after each key stroke. Others independently type with one or both hands. The goal of FC is for individuals to achieve independent expression, often a combination of typing and speech. FC using alphabet symbols is rarely used with children younger than school age because being required to read and write is not developmentally appropriate for preschool children. FC's effectiveness is debated by researchers (Biklen, 1992).

Parents' Role

Regardless of the setting for treatment, parents can enhance the effectiveness of therapy in a variety of ways. Regardless of their age or disability, children are typically sensitive to their parents' feelings and reactions; they may understand more than their parents realize. Parents need to communicate to their children, verbally and nonverbally, that therapy is a positive experience. When a parent smiles as they separate from their child who is about to receive therapy, they communicate that therapy is a positive experience (Davis, Stroud, & Green, 1988).

While parents should ask questions and honestly state concerns about their child's therapy, some comments are best saved for private discussion, when the child is not present. Parents should try to avoid scheduling treatment at a time of day when the child usually is tired. Parents and classroom staff should support the therapist by following through with homework (practice that is needed at home and school) or record keeping. If these tasks are stressful to the child or appear to make the child unhappy, the therapist should be informed.

Parents should follow through on therapy suggestions because in most cases they spend more time with their child than therapists or teachers do. Initially, it may seem overwhelming to parents to try to remember certain methods of talking or working with their child. It may be helpful for parents to set aside a particular time during the day to practice therapy skills with the child. In this way parents may experience opportunities to feel good about helping their child, as well as develop new habits that may gradually become more natural and easier to use. Parents should remain open to receiving training on how to work most effectively with their child (Tannock & Girolametto, 1992). Figure 5.4 offers general suggestions that parents and teachers may find helpful for enhancing young children's speech and language development. Figure 5.5 (on p. 152) contains information about things that may discourage language development.

Conclusions

Communication difficulties are often parents' first clues that their child has a developmental delay. When communication problems are suspected, a speech and language pathologist should be consulted. A comprehensive speech and language evaluation assesses a variety of areas and may lead to a recommendation for speech and language treatment. Early intervention is important because it may result in more-effective or shorter treatment (Roberts et al., 1989).

Figure 5.4   **Methods Likely to Encourage Speech and Language Development**

- Make talking and conversation a positive experience.
- Talk, talk, and talk to the child about what they and others are doing.
- Name objects, and give information about these objects (such as their function and characteristics).
- Encourage conversation by making sure that the child receives a turn in family and group conversations (such as at the dinner table).
- Play pretend and guessing games.
- Sing songs, and use nursery rhymes.
- Sort and classify things in the child's environment.
- Be attentive and interested when the child speaks. Periodically confirm that the child's message has been understood, by paraphrasing its essential elements to the child.
- Try to expand on the child's spontaneous utterances by repeating the child's words in the same order or with added information. For example, if the child says "Ball," you might say, "Ball" (direct imitation), "A ball" (expanding grammar), or "Big ball" (adding information).
- Encourage the child to ask questions to obtain additional information.
- Encourage the child to imitate non-speech sounds such as mechanical noises or the sounds of nonhuman animals.
- Use sound-making and voice-activated toys.
- Encourage games that strengthen the muscles of the mouth such as blowing bubbles or playing musical instruments that require blowing.
- Read, read, and read to the child. Read everything, not just books: signs, packages, labels. The importance of reading to a child cannot be overemphasized. Talk about stories and pictures while explaining new vocabulary. Encourage the child to fill in words or phrases when you stop reading and predict what will happen next. Let the child retell the story in their own words or take a turn reading to you. Use picture stories without words to help the child learn to use their imagination.
- Provide new and interesting experiences such as field trips and cooking.

One of the most supportive things a parent or other care provider can do for a child with a speech and language delay or disorder is to accept the child at their developmental level and provide language stimulation appropriate to that level. The effectiveness of therapy is enhanced when parents communicate to the child a positive attitude toward the people and activities involved in therapy and when an honest exchange is maintained between a parent and therapist.

Figure 5.5   **Methods That Discourage Language Development**

- Correcting speech or language errors by telling the child "No," implying that the child did something wrong, or insisting that the child repeat a correct model.
- Discussing any suspected speech or language problems in front of the child.
- Withholding favorite things to make the child speak.
- Placing unreasonable demands on the child such as insisting that they speak or perform in front of others.
- Interrupting the child.
- Allowing others to tease or make fun of the child.

Language is a tool that every child needs to acquire. Without this tool, countless other skills may not emerge. The child who receives speech and language treatment is not only learning how to communicate with others but is also placing a key piece into the complicated developmental puzzle.

CHAPTER SUMMARY

- Speech and language delays are the most common developmental delays in children younger than 5 years old and make up 25 to 50% of young children eligible for intervention services.

- Nativists, empiricists, constructivists, and interactionists provide the major perspectives regarding language acquisition.

- Comparing a child's development to typical rates of development is crucial for diagnosing and providing therapy.

- Brain or neurological abnormality or damage and culture experiences may contribute to the occurrence of language disabilities.

- Referrals for speech and language evaluations are made by a variety of individuals, but usually are initiated by parents, physicians, day care providers, or preschool staff.

- Speech and language evaluation often includes informal and formal assessment and often includes parents' responses to questionnaires, case histories, standardized tests, and observations of the child.

- Early intervention is crucial because language development affects the development of cognitive and social-emotional skills.

- Speech-language pathologists play a major role in assessment and therapy related to communication disorders while working with other key team members, including parents. Assessment evaluates children's ability to pay attention, prelinguistic, receptive language, expressive language and articulation, oral-motor skills, voice, fluency, hearing, play skills, and problem-solving skills.

- Speech and language therapy may be conducted in individual or group sessions at the child's home or in a clinic, therapy room, or classroom and is typically most effective when integrated into normal daily activities. Other staff members and parents play major roles in speech and language therapy.

CHAPTER KEY TERMS

communication disorders/delays
speech
nativist
empiricist
critical period
sensitive period
Noam Chomsky
language acquisition device (LAD)
overregularization
behaviorist
constructivist
interactionist
receptive language
expressive language
undifferentiated crying
differentiated crying
semantics
syntax
phonology
pragmatics
motherese/fatherese/parentese
child-directed speech
expansion
cooing
babbling
intonation
holophrase
overextend
underextend
symbolic thinking
telegraphic speech
selectively mute
psycholinguist
mean length of utterance (MLU)
noncommunicative language
repetition
monologue

collective monologue
self-talk
inner speech
organic
functional
Broca's area
Wernicke's area
arcuate fasciculus
speech and language pathologist
audiologist
otolaryngologist
audiometer
audioscope
augmentative communication
sign language
eye-gaze board
communication board
high-tech device
facilitated communication (FC)
dysarthria
apraxia
voice
articulation
fluency
prelinguistic skills
stuttering
dysfluency
oral-motor skills
developmental language delay (DLD)
cloze activity
augmentative and alternative communication (AAC)
American Sign Language (ASL)
Signing Exact English (SEE)
Picture Exchange Communication System (PECS)
high-tech AAC devices

REVIEW QUESTIONS

1. What are prelinguistic skills, and when do they typically develop? Provide examples.

2. What is the difference between receptive and expressive language skills? Why is it useful to understand this difference?

3. What methods may enhance young children's language development? Provide specific examples of the use of some of these methods, and describe why these methods are useful.

4. What is the purpose of using parentese? Describe the elements of this method of speaking to young children. Discuss how each element may aid in the development of speech and language skills.

5. Is there a connection between lack of paralinguistic skills and delayed language development? If so, what are the implications of this connection?

6. What are some possible signs of communication delays? Comment on the importance of having a child evaluated if their care providers are concerned about the rate of development.

7. What is the parent's role in the child's speech and language therapy?

8. What methods may be useful for enhancing communication skills within a classroom setting? Provide examples of each.

SUGGESTED STUDENT ACTIVITIES

1. Research common standardized assessment tools used in the assessment of children with speech and language delays. Are they the same across age groups?

2. Observe an early intervention classroom and determine how speech and language development is encouraged.

3. Interview a speech and language pathologist. Ask about common language impairments and the best ways to treat them.

4. In small groups, brainstorm about warning signs of speech and language delays in children. Consider paralinguistic skills.

5. Imagine you are a parent of a child in therapy for speech delays. How might you practice therapeutic skills at home?

Cognitive Abilities 6

CHAPTER KEY POINTS

- Cognitive development affects all areas of development.

- Understanding key concepts related to cognitive development and typical cognitive development is useful when working with children who have cognitive delays.

- Many factors contribute to cognitive disabilities.

- There are several key indicators of possible cognitive delays.

- Screening and full assessment must occur to determine if a child has a cognitive delay.

- Special education teachers play a crucial role in providing early childhood special education services.

- Many categories of disabilities include cognitive delays.

- There are several important guidelines for working with young children who have cognitive delays.

Cognitive development focuses on thinking skills, including learning, understanding, problem-solving, reasoning, and remembering. Development of cognitive skills directly relates to development of other skills, including communication, motor, social-emotional, and adaptive skills.

Cognitive disabilities result in the inability to develop thinking skills at a typical rate of development. Cognitive disabilities are observed in most children who receive early intervention services or receive services in elementary or secondary schools. Cognitive disabilities are sometimes referred to as **mental retardation** (Crane, 2002; Denning, Chamberlain, & Polloway, 2000; Kaufman, 1999). A discussion of use of the term *mental retardation* occurs later in this chapter.

Children who are cognitively delayed often have delayed speech and language development. They tend to develop speech at a slower rate, have difficulty understanding symbolic concepts, and have inadequate syntactic structure and vocabulary as well as articulation problems (Deiner, 1993). Specifically, speech patterns of preschoolers with moderate to severe cognitive delays are often limited to single words. They are likely to have difficulty responding to verbal requests and to avoid eye contact. They are also likely to appear to ignore others who attempt to interact with them. Preschoolers with cognitive delays often have delayed motor abilities, including difficulty with balance and coordination. These children also are more likely to have hearing and visual impairments and may be more susceptible to infections (Loraas, 2002).

Additionally, children with cognitive delays often have difficulty applying what they learn in one situation to another situation (**generalizing**). They are also less likely to acquire information through **incidental learning.** This type of learning involves gaining skills as a result of participating in activities and experiences not specifically geared toward teaching that skill. For example, children learn about colors when adults say things such as "Let's find a blue shirt to match your blue pants." Children with cognitive delays often need more-direct and more-repetitive instruction and do not learn as readily from incidental experiences (Polloway & Patton, 1993). They may also have difficulty selecting and focusing on tasks. For example, many of these children have difficulty selecting a toy with which to play and are likely to play with any one toy for a very limited amount of time before moving on to a new toy.

Most children with cognitive delays need only limited or intermittent support for regular daily functioning. These children are classified as mildly delayed and constitute about 89% of all individuals classified as cognitively delayed. Relatively few children experience cognitive delays at a level such that they need extensive or regular daily aid at home and school (Smith, Finn, & Dowdy, 1993).

Concepts and Theories Related to Cognitive Development

Most theorists acknowledge that cognitive skills are acquired through the interplay of neurological structures, which include the brain and nervous system, as well as cultural–environmental influences. This combination results in each child's development being unique (Ginsburg & Opper, 1988). Similarities, however, do exist among children, so it is possible to predict the typical sequence of development. (Refer to Chapter 3 for a more detailed discussion of several theories related to early childhood development.)

As discussed in Chapter 3, **basic cognitive processes** include **perception, attention, reasoning,** and **memory.** These form the foundation on which other cognitive skills grow (Kuhn, 1999). Deficits in any of these areas may contribute to cognitive delays, as well as delays in other areas of development.

Typical Cognitive Development

Infants have a tremendous capacity to learn about their world through touch, hearing, sight, taste, and smell. Infants progress from gaining knowledge only through immediate sensory experiences to mentally experimenting with their environments. Cognitive development involves learning that one is separate from the environment, followed by learning about people and objects within the environment. During early childhood the brain develops faster than any other part of the body. It attains approximately 90% of its adult weight by 5 years of age.

One of the most important concepts to develop is the principle of cause and effect. Between 4 and 5 months, infants initially make this connection by accident, while noticing the effects of their actions (e.g., noticing that wiggling and kicking makes the mobile swing). Over time, infants intentionally modify their movements in an attempt to influence their environments. Increasingly, they use mental representation and symbols, such as words, to figure things out. Initially, though, children's ideas about the world are often illogical and limited by the inability to consider other points of view (**egocentrism**) (Carroll, 2003).

During the first few months of life, infants react as if things existed only when they see them. After about 4 months, infants learn that objects and people continue to exist even when they are out of sight (**object permanence**). At this point the learning process has become more thoughtful. Language comprehension is increasing, and the infant begins to form mental images of things, actions, and concepts (Clark, 2006).

Over time, toddlers begin to solve problems by performing mental trial-and-error instead of relying on physically manipulating objects. As memory and intellectual abilities develop, children begin to understand simple time concepts (Lipsitt, 1990; Luciana & Nelson, 1998). Additionally, toddlers begin to understand the relationships between objects and to recognize the purpose of numbers in counting objects. During this time, children appear to believe that all events are the result of something they have done.

Toddlers typically view things in absolute and simple terms. They often confuse fantasy with reality. They interpret language literally. For example, comments that adults consider funny or playful, such as "If you eat any more, you may explode," may actually cause a toddler to panic because the child does not understand that the adult is joking. Three-year-olds typically spend most of their day questioning what happens around them. For example, they will ask, "Why do I have to... ?" They are likely to pay close attention to the answers to their questions when the answers are simple and direct.

In-depth explanations or reasoning about the purpose of rules is generally not useful because young children are not prepared for complex reasons and are not interested in detailed explanations. When adults attempt to engage children in complex conversations, the children are likely to appear to stare into space or turn their attention to more interesting activities. Simply telling young children to do something "because it's good for you" or "so you don't get hurt" often will make more sense to them than a detailed explanation would.

Responses to children's more abstract "Why?" questions are more complex because there may be hundreds of such questions each day and because adults often do not know the correct answer. If the question is "Why is the sky blue?" or "How does a television work?" it is often best if adults respond with something like "I don't know" (if they don't know) or invite children to join the adult in researching the question further by finding a book about the sun or about television. Children benefit from having their questions responded to in meaningful, honest ways. Responding in this way allows increased knowledge, feeds curiosity, and encourages children to reason more effectively.

When children 3 years old and younger are faced with specific learning challenges, their reasoning often focuses on one aspect (**centration**). They have difficulty viewing issues from various perspectives and solving problems that require them to simultaneously consider more than one factor or perspective. For example, if one of two identical cups of liquid is poured into a short, wide container and the other is poured into a tall, thin container, young children typically state that the tall container holds more water than the short container. This response occurs even after they initially state that the two cups hold equal amounts of liquid. They typically focus on one aspect of the cup, either height or width. When they say the taller cup has more water, they are focusing on the greater height of the taller cup and not considering the greater width of the shorter cup. They lack **conservation** abilities and use of **reversibility** (understanding that something that is done can be undone). It is not until approximately age 7 that most children understand that they need to consider multiple aspects of a problem before arriving at their answer—for example, the answer that the two cups have the same amount of liquid because no liquid was added or removed.

When children are around 3 years of age, their sense of time becomes more meaningful. As they become increasingly familiar with their daily routine, they use this routine to gauge time and understand others' schedules. For example, they learn that the mail comes most days after lunch and that the garbage truck picks up garbage only on the first day after the weekend. They gradually come to understand that certain special events, such as holidays and birthdays, occur infrequently but that there is a Monday every week (Flavell, Miller, & Miller, 2001).

By age 4, children begin to explore many basic concepts that will be taught in greater detail in school. For example, they begin to understand that each day has a morning, afternoon, and evening. By the time they enter kindergarten, many children know some days of the week and that each day is measured in hours and minutes. They also begin to understand counting, the alphabet, size relationships (big versus small), and the names of several geometric shapes. Children should not be pressured to learn these things because pressure often results in their resisting learning when they enter kindergarten. This is discussed in greater detail in Chapter 14.

Preschoolers generally have a great interest in the world around them and seem to make daily developmental gains. They want to directly experience things and try them out for themselves by touching, tasting, smelling, and listening. Most preschoolers are eager to learn new things. Preschoolers learn from their play, and by experiencing and doing. Through play and real-life experiences, they develop skills, use language, and struggle to gain inner control. The value of play will be discussed in greater detail in Chapter 12.

Factors That Contribute to Cognitive Disabilities

Cognitive disabilities can be caused by any condition that impairs development of the brain before birth, during birth, or during the childhood years. Those with cognitive delays have notably lower than average intellectual functioning as defined by the **intelligence quotient (IQ)**. An estimated 2.5 to 3% of the general population (translating to 6.2 to 7.5 million people) have cognitive delays (Arc, 2002).

Hundreds of potential causes of cognitive delays have been discovered, but in approximately one-third of cases the causes remain unknown. According to the *Diagnostic and Statistical Manual of Mental Disorders, IV-TR* (American Psychiatric Association, 2000), approximately 5% of cases of mental retardation are attributed to heredity. Abnormal embryonic development accounts for approximately 30% of cases of mental retardation; approximately 10% of the cases are caused by difficulties during pregnancy or at birth. General medical conditions (such as infections or trauma) account for approximately 5% of cognitive delays. An estimated 15 to 20% of cognitive delays are attributed to environmental influences (such as lack of positive nurturing and social or language stimulation) (Polloway & Smith, 2001; Wesson & Maino, 1995).

Genetic Conditions

Some cognitive delays have been linked to abnormal genes inherited from parents, errors when genes combine, infections, exposure to radiation, or other factors occurring during pregnancy. The most common genetic conditions are **Down syndrome, fragile X syndrome,** and **Rett syndrome** (Bailey, Skinner, Hatton, & Roberts, 2000). Genetic errors of metabolism, such as **phenylketonuria (PKU)** may result in cognitive delays. More than 100 chromosomal abnormalities have been related to cognitive delays (Walzer, 1985).

Problems during Pregnancy

Cognitive delays may occur when prenatal development is abnormal. For example, there may be abnormal cell division during prenatal development. A pregnant woman who drinks alcohol, smokes, uses drugs, or experiences illness (e.g., rubella) during pregnancy may have a baby with cognitive delays. (The potential effects of drugs and alcohol are discussed in depth in Chapter 10.) Malnutrition, glandular disorders, diabetes, meningitis, cytomegalovirus, and many other illnesses of the mother during pregnancy may result in a child's being born with cognitive delays. Physical malformations of the brain and HIV infection originating during prenatal development may also result in cognitive delays. The potential effects of HIV/AIDS are further discussed in Chapter 10.

Birth Complications

Complications during labor and birth contribute to cognitive and other delays. **Birth trauma** can involve any part of the mother's or child's body. Birth trauma is estimated to result in long-term negative effects in 2–7 of every 1,000 live births (approximately 0.5%). The most severe forms of birth trauma typically involve injury to the child's brain or nervous system. In approximately 80% of children with developmental delays there is a history of traumatic birth (Burack, Hodapp, & Zigler, 1998).

Mild, moderate, or severe damage to the brain caused by low oxygen supply (hypoxia or anoxia) during labor may cause permanent injury and a variety of neurological problems. Conditions that contribute to low oxygen supply include maternal eclampsia (pregnancy-induced hypertension), placental problems (e.g., premature separation from the uterus), umbilical problems (e.g., knotted umbilical cord), hemorrhage (fetal or maternal bleeding), infection (e.g., chorioamnionitis, a serious infection), and fetal problems (e.g., heart abnormalities).

Prematurity.   Every day, 1 in 8 infants born in the United States is premature (Martin et al., 2006). **Premature birth** can happen to any pregnant woman, and the causes are frequently unknown. Preterm birth contributes to several long-term disabilities, including mental retardation, cerebral palsy, vision and hearing problems, and chronic lung disease.

Approximately 61% of premature infants experience low achievement or need special education services once they reach school age, as compared to 23% of full-term children. Premature infants score lower than full-term children on intelligence and achievement tests and receive lower ratings from parents and teachers on measures of social and behavioral functioning. Premature infants require more educational support than full-term infants and are held back a grade and diagnosed with learning disabilities more frequently (Martin et al., 2006).

Low Birth Weight.   **Low birth weight** often occurs when children are born prematurely. In addition, full-term babies may be born with low birth weights. *Low birth weight* is the term used for children born weighing less than 2,500 grams, or 5 pounds, 8 ounces; *very low birth weight* is the term used for children weighing less than 1,500 grams, or 3 pounds, 5 ounces. Although many infants with low birth weights function normally during childhood and beyond, they are more likely than children with normal birth weight to experience health and developmental problems. Low-birth-weight infants who do not suffer from motor disabilities at birth remain at risk for subtle social, behavioral, or cognitive developmental delays, which often go undetected until children begin school. Low birth weight is strongly correlated with living in poverty (Blanc & Wardlaw, 2005).

Environmental Conditions

Diseases such as whooping cough, measles, encephalitis, and meningitis may result in brain damage. Cognitive delays also may be caused by extreme malnutrition, inadequate medical care, or exposure to poisons, including lead or mercury. Accidents such as a blow to the head or near drowning also contribute to children's cognitive delays (Bergland & Hoffbauer, 1996).

Social Conditions

Social and family interactions have major impacts on cognitive development. Children deprived of appropriate stimulation during critical periods of brain development are more likely to have cognitive delays. Deprivation may be due to neglect or abuse, parental skill level, cultural norms, or decreased opportunities. Limited stimulation may result in irreversible damage and is a potential cause of mental retardation. In addition, being born to older or very young mothers, into poverty, or to a family with a low education level increases the likelihood of cognitive delays, as does being the youngest child in a large family. Children from minority groups are more likely to live in poverty and are, therefore, more likely to have cognitive delays.

Indicators of Cognitive Delays

About 87% of individuals with cognitive delays have mild delays (i.e., they are a little slower than average in learning new information and skills and can live independently during adulthood). When very young, children with mild cognitive delays may not have obvious delays and often are not classified as having a cognitive delay until they reach school age (Beirne-Smith, Patton, & Kim, 2006; Thomas et al., 1997). The remaining 13% of individuals with cognitive delays have considerably more difficulty in school, at home, and in the community. A person with more severe retardation will need more intensive support their entire life. Figure 6.1 lists early indicators of possible cognitive delays.

Assessment of Cognitive Delays

Early detection of cognitive disabilities and appropriate intervention can significantly improve functioning and reduce the need for lifelong intervention. Although routine infant developmental screening is widely recommended, there are currently no national data tracking the state of this practice and how it is integrated into primary care.

Cognitive delays are diagnosed by evaluating the ability of a person to learn, think, solve problems, and make sense of the world (intellectual functioning, IQ) and their ability to perform skills required for independent living (adaptive behavior or

Figure 6.1   **Early Indicators of Possible Cognitive Delays**

- Very irritable or passive
- Difficult to feed
- Abnormally high-pitched cry
- Unable to visually track objects
- Abnormal muscle tone (very floppy or spastic)
- Slow to reach developmental milestones
- Not smiling by 2 months
- Little recognition of parents after 4 months of age
- Not babbling by 6 months
- Not sitting unsupported by 7 months
- Not saying single words by 18 months
- Not walking by 18 months

adaptive functioning). Intellectual functioning, or IQ, is often measured by some form of intelligence test. An average IQ score is 100. Individuals scoring below 70–75 are typically classified as having cognitive delays (frequently referred to as "mental retardation"). Adaptive behavior is assessed by evaluating what an individual can do in comparison to other people the same age. Commonly assessed skills include daily living skills (e.g., getting dressed, going to the bathroom, and feeding one's self), communication skills (e.g., understanding what is said and being able to communicate effectively), and social skills (e.g., interacting with peers, family members, and others).

Screening

The Individuals with Disabilities Education Act (IDEA) Amendments of 1990 to 1997 require that individual states establish programs to identify and assist children at risk for developmental delays. The Centers for Disease Control and Prevention (CDC) has recommended the development of community-based programs within primary care settings and other settings to screen children early to identify developmental disabilities to help ensure that children with these conditions receive appropriate care. To accomplish this, the CDC has recommended that knowledge and skills in developmental screening should be incorporated into professional health care training. The agency also has recommended that raising awareness about the need for and benefits of developmental screening must be prioritized.

Newborn screening includes identification of biochemical or other inherited conditions that may result in cognitive delays, other disabilities, health problems, or death. Infants are screened for various conditions by conducting tests on blood collected from a heel stick onto filter paper. In addition, health status is assessed using observational methods. The Apgar test, discussed in Chapter 2, is one of the most common tests used at birth.

Full Assessment

There are many appropriate standardized tests available to assess cognitive development in children birth to school age. Because level of cognitive development affects all areas of development, these tests often assess all or several major areas of development.

Types of Cognitive Delays

Mental Retardation

The category *mental retardation* replaced terms such as *feebleminded, idiot,* and *moron* approximately 50 years ago. Currently the use of this label is criticized; some individuals propose that the terms *intellectually impaired* or *educationally disabled* replace *mentally retarded.* Most states still use *mental retardation* or a similar term as a disability category. Although definitions of *mental retardation* have somewhat changed over the past 50 years, all have focused on limited intellectual ability and difficulty in coping (i.e., difficulty adapting to the demands of everyday activities) (American Association on Mental Retardation, 2002; Davis, Stroud, & Green, 1988; Minnes, 1998; Wehman, McLaughlin, & Wehman, 2005).

   Mental retardation refers to a wide range of abilities from mild to severe limitations. IDEA's definition of *mental retardation* is "significantly subaverage general intellectual functioning, existing concurrently with deficits in adaptive behavior and manifested during the developmental period, that adversely affects a child's educational performance" [34 *Code of Federal Regulations* §300.7(c)(6)]. The **American Association on Intellectual and Developmental Disabilities [AAIDD]** (previously the **American Association on Mental Retardation [AAMR]**) defines *mental retardation* as "a disability characterized by significant limitations both in intellectual functioning and in adaptive behavior as expressed in conceptual, social, and practical adaptive skills" (AAMR, 2006). According to this new definition, an individual is considered to have mental retardation if their intellectual functioning level (IQ) is below 70–75, significant limitations exist in two or more adaptive skill areas, and the condition is present from childhood (defined as age 18 years or less) (AAMR, 2006). The AAMR/AAIDD classification system focuses on the individual's capabilities rather than limitations. The categories describe the level of support required: intermittent, limited, extensive, or pervasive (Luckasson, 2002; Pader, 1981; Polloway, 1997; Wehmeyer & Patton, 2000).

   Children's strengths and weaknesses may be determined by formal testing, observations, interviewing key people in the child's life, interviewing the child, and interacting with the child in their daily life. In addition, an interdisciplinary team determines needed supports (i.e., intermittent, limited, extensive, or pervasive). *Intermittent support* refers to support needed occasionally, not on a continuous daily basis. *Limited support* refers to the need for regular support in one or more areas. *Extensive support* refers to the need for daily support across some but not all areas. *Pervasive support* refers to constant support across all areas and may include life-sustaining measures (i.e., feeding) (Krauss & Selzer, 1998; Shapiro, Blacher, & Lopez, 1998).

Intelligence tests are designed to assess mental capability, which includes the ability to reason, plan, solve problems, think abstractly, comprehend complex ideas, learn quickly, and learn from experience. Intelligence is represented by IQ scores obtained from standardized tests administered by a trained professional (e.g., the Wechsler Intelligence Scale for Children and the Stanford-Binet test). Typically, the degree of intellectual disability is reflected in an IQ significantly below average. IQ tests assign an approximate numerical value to intelligence; individuals with average ability score from about 90 to 110. Those with mental retardation score below 70–75. Table 6.1 shows definitions for various degrees of mental retardation based on IQ. Figure 6.2 shows limitations in adaptive behaviors found in children with mental retardation.

Although the effect of mental retardation varies greatly among people, approximately 85% of those classified as mentally retarded are classified as being mildly affected; they are a little slower than average in learning new information and skills. In children this level of mental retardation often is not readily apparent and may not be detected until school age. As adults, most individuals with mild delays lead independent lives. Those with IQs from 50 to 75 typically acquire academic skills at the 6th-grade level. They can become fairly self-sufficient (AAMR, 2006).

Approximately 10% of individuals with mental retardation have moderate mental retardation (an IQ between 40 and 50). Despite some cognitive limitations,

A special education teacher assesses a young child's cognitive skills.

Table 6.1	Degrees of Mental Retardation	
Classification	**Approximate IQ**	**Percentage of the Population**
Average	85–115	68
Borderline	70–84	14
Mild	50–69	2
Moderate	35–49	0.13
Severe	20–34	< 0.10
Profound	below 20	< 0.10

with early intervention, a functional education, and appropriate supports as adults, these individuals can comfortably live in the community when they are provided with daily living support. They can complete work and self-care tasks with moderate supervision. Typically they acquire communication skills in childhood and are able to live and function successfully within the community in a supervised environment such as a group home (AAMR, 2006).

Approximately 3% of those classified as mentally retarded are severely retarded (IQ scores of 25–40). These individuals typically master very basic self-care and social skills and acquire some communication skills. They need nearly constant supervision and often live in a group home (AAMR, 2006).

Approximately 1% of individuals classified as mentally retarded are classified as profoundly retarded (i.e., IQ scores below 25). Their development is often limited to the infant or toddler level. Their retardation is often due to a neurological disorder. They need constant and intensive care (AAMR, 2006).

It is often difficult to accurately assess children's IQ when they are younger than 4 or 5 years old. The classification "mentally retarded," therefore, is generally not used to classify children younger than 4, although children severely or profoundly disabled may be classified at this age. Additionally, preschool-aged children may be classified as mentally retarded if they are severely delayed in acquisition of skills such as walking or speaking their first

Figure 6.2 **Mental Retardation and Adaptive Functioning**

Limitations in two or more of the following skill areas:

- communication
- self-care
- home living
- social/interpersonal skills
- use of community resources
- self-direction
- functional academic skills
- work
- leisure
- health
- safety

words (Beirne-Smith, Patton, & Ittenbach, 1994). For example, a 3-year-old might be classified as mentally retarded if they are unable to perform skills that most 1-year-olds can perform. Guidelines listed in the Education of the Handicapped Act (EHA) Amendments of 1986 indicate that the classification "developmental delay," rather than "mental retardation," is generally most appropriate for preschoolers.

Down Syndrome

Down syndrome is the leading cause of mental retardation. It is a genetic abnormality caused by triplicate material of chromosome 21. Routine health maintenance is important because infants and children with Down syndrome are more likely to have respiratory infections, otitis media, thyroid disease, congenital cataracts, leukemoid reactions, dental problems, gastrointestinal defects, heart defects (40 to 60% of all children with Down syndrome), and feeding difficulties. Motor, language, social, and adaptive skills are often delayed. There is a wide variation in mental abilities, behavior, and developmental progress in individuals with Down syndrome. Level of retardation ranges from mild to severe, with the majority functioning in the mild-to-moderate range (Pueschel, 2001).

Physical expression of the syndrome is widely variable as well. Hypotonia (decreased or low muscle tone) is often one of the first characteristics of Down syndrome that is noticed. Surgical techniques, early therapy to minimize developmental delays, and health supervision allow for enhanced functioning.

Learning Disabilities

Another class of cognitive delays is **learning disabilities (LDs)**. Children classified as learning disabled have achievement levels below their measured level of aptitude. Preschool children usually are not classified as learning disabled because it is very difficult to accurately assess their aptitudes. During the first few years of life, children display tremendous variations in growth and maturation. This limits accuracy in assessing IQ (Cravioto & DeLicardie, 1975; Lerner, 2000; Lyon et al., 2001). Children diagnosed with brain injuries may be classified as learning disabled before they enter elementary school.

The classification **"developmental learning disability"** is more frequently used with preschool children. Children with developmental LDs have difficulty acquiring the skills prerequisite for later academic tasks. Figure 6.3 lists early warning signs for learning disabilities.

Learning disabilities frequently accompany conditions such as perceptual disabilities, brain injury, neurological impairments, minimal brain dysfunction, dyslexia, and developmental aphasia. Children who have learning problems that are primarily the result of visual, hearing, or motor delays; mental retardation; emotional disturbance; or environmental, cultural, or economic disadvantage are not classified as learning disabled (Bender, 1992).

Prenatal exposure to alcohol and cigarettes and traumas during birth are potential causes of LDs. LDs have also been linked to postnatal events such as high fevers, meningitis, and head traumas. In some cases, LDs are believed to be linked to genetic

Figure 6.3   **Early Warning Signs of Learning Disabilities**

- Short attention span (e.g., at 5 years of age, child cannot sit long enough to listen to a short story)
- Easily distracted
- Poor listening skills
- Difficulty following directions
- Appears not to try (e.g., seems lazy or defiant)
- Immature speech and language
- Awkward or clumsy in movement (e.g., cannot fasten a button, hop, etc.)
- Exhibits immature behavior for age
- Generally disorganized
- Difficulty with paper and pencil tasks
- Unable to put words into sentences by 2½ years
- Use of speech that cannot be understood 50% or more of the time

abnormalities. Children with LDs are more likely than children without LDs to have family members with LDs.

Traumatic Brain Injury

Traumatic brain injury (TBI) is often cited as a cause of cognitive delays (Savage, 1988). TBI may also lead to other classifications, including health-impaired, mentally retarded, or emotionally disturbed. TBI is not degenerative or congenital. It is caused by an external physical force such as might occur in a car accident or from physical abuse. It may be temporary or permanent. Long-term effects of TBI may include reduced stamina, seizures, headaches, excessive levels of activity, and a sense of helplessness or apathy. TBI may also affect hearing and vision, memory, attention, IQ, reasoning, problem solving, word retrieval, motor speech, language comprehension and acquisition, and concept acquisition (Bigge, 1991).

Multiple Disabilities

IDEA defines multiple disabilities as "concomitant [simultaneous] impairments (such as mental retardation-blindness, mental retardation-orthopedic impairment, etc.), the combination of which causes such severe educational needs that they cannot be accommodated in a special education program solely for one of the impairments." The term does not include deafness-blindness, which is listed as a separate category.

An estimated 120,000 students (approximately 2% of all students receiving special education services) are currently classified as having multiple disabilities.

Children with multiple disabilities have two or more disabilities resulting in multisensory or motor deficiencies and developmental delays in the cognitive, social-emotional, or motor areas that interfere with learning. Those with severe or multiple disabilities exhibit a range of characteristics including limited speech, communication, and basic physical mobility; a tendency to forget skills through disuse; difficulty generalizing skills from one situation to another; a need for support to perform life activities; and various medical problems.

Evaluation of children with multiple disabilities is complex and often involves many different types of specialists. Approximately 2% of all children receiving special education services are classified as multiply disabled (U.S. Department of Education, 1995). Multiple disabilities causing educational problems so severe that a child cannot be accommodated in special education based on the limitations caused by a single impairment are referred to as **"concomitant impairments."** Children with multiple disabilities may suffer the most from the negative reactions of others.

In the past, students with severe or multiple disabilities were typically denied access to public schools. Since passage of the EHA (P.L. 94-142), now the IDEA, public schools have provided services for many children with severe or multiple disabilities. When children are born with severe or multiple disabilities, educational services are typically begun during infancy. At that time, and continuing throughout life, services focus on increasing the level of independence and adaptive skills (discussed in detail in Chapter 11).

Effective educational programs for children with severe or multiple handicaps incorporate a variety of components to meet the wide variety of individual needs. For these individuals, related services and the use of the multidisciplinary approach are crucial. Typically, speech and language therapists, physical and occupational therapists, and medical specialists need to work closely with classroom teachers and parents to help ensure effective intervention programs. Individuals with severe or multiple handicaps frequently have difficulty with skill generalization. Therefore, related services are often most effective when they are provided during the natural routine in the day care center, school, and community rather than as isolated therapy.

Classroom arrangements and adaptive aids (e.g., wheelchairs, typewriters, headsticks (head gear), clamps, modified handles on cups and silverware, communication board) must be provided in ways that do not interfere with children's needs for medications, special diets, or other special equipment. Computers are increasingly being used to aid communication and mobility and are being integrated into equipment design.

Professional Guidelines for Early Intervention

Providing services to help individuals with cognitive delays has led to a new understanding of how we define mental retardation. After the initial diagnosis of cognitive disability is made, the focus should be on determining children's strengths and weaknesses. In addition, it is important to determine the level of support that the child and family will need in a variety of settings over time (Parrette & Brotherson, 1996). Several early childhood organizations have suggested central components that are useful for enhancing young children's development in all areas.

In 1987 the National Association for the Education of Young Children (NAEYC) and the National Association of Early Childhood Specialists in State Departments of Education published a joint position statement regarding appropriate early childhood curriculum and assessment practices (cited in Bredekamp, 1987). Some educators advocated using these guidelines when teaching children with and without disabilities. Other educators have suggested that developmentally appropriate practices are usually suitable guidelines for children with early developmental delays but that some adaptations also are needed (Wolery & Bredekamp, 1994). The Division for Early Childhood of the Council for Exceptional Children stresses the belief that child-directed activities are the hallmark of all early childhood programs (Odom, 1994). Carta (1994) has suggested that the appropriateness of any practice may be determined only by evaluating its fit to each child. Wolery and Bredekamp have further suggested that evaluation of the appropriateness of any early childhood practice should result in affirmative responses to a number of specific questions.

Regular early childhood practices are often the starting point for developing curricula for all young children. These practices include enhancing a child's overall development, independence, creativity, self-esteem, and positive socialization through play. These basic practices are the base from which the special education teacher and other early intervention specialists may make adaptations to successfully teach children with disabilities (Wolery, Doyle, Gast, Ault, & Simpson, 1993; Wolery, Strain, & Bailey, 1992).

Classrooms for Toddlers

Classrooms for toddlers are set up to allow them to explore freely and interact with their environment. Toddlers learn primarily through their senses and physical movement (Rogers, 1991). Therefore, toddlers should have many opportunities for a variety of tactile, movement, and music experiences on a daily basis. Activities should be memorable and relevant to their lives. For example, rather than simply reading a book about fire stations, children benefit from being taken on a field trip to visit a fire station in their neighborhood. If a field trip is not feasible, local fire companies are often willing to bring a truck and equipment to the children.

Group activities must be limited in duration because most toddlers and even older children with disabilities have a limited attention span. They should not be expected to pay attention to any one activity for more than a few minutes. Activities should be presented in a variety of ways including one-to-one with the teacher and in small and large groups.

Classrooms for Preschoolers

A typical preschool classroom for 3-, 4-, and 5-year-olds includes several learning centers. These may feature blocks, books, easels for painting and drawing, and manipulatives. Most activities are open-ended (having no particular goal) rather than goal-directed. Activities must be presented at a developmentally appropriate level. There should be an area for gross-motor activities within each classroom. (Refer to Chapter 12 for further discussion of classroom setup and play materials.)

Developing and Implementing Curricula

Special education teachers are often responsible for establishing classroom lesson plans. It is often helpful if teachers create annual, monthly, weekly, and daily activity plans. Ideally, special education teachers ask other team members, including parents, to collaborate in developing lessons. Plans must be related to a child's goals and objectives. Parents and other team members benefit from receiving outlines of lesson plans so that they have the opportunity to use similar activities when interacting with a child. Special education teachers are usually responsible for preparing materials to be used during the day's activities and developing alternate plans if the planned activities are ineffective on a given day (Kamii & DeVries, 1997; Wolery & Bredekamp, 1994).

Ideally, curriculum plans include exposure to books on a daily basis. Books should be read to children, but children should also be able to look at books independently. Children begin to connect spoken and written words through exposure to books and other printed materials. Charts, lists, labels, and the child's comments written on paper encourage preliteracy (pre-reading and -writing skills).

As children mature and their play skills increase, the number of play choices provided also may be increased. It is important to note that while a special needs class may have fewer play choices available, the activities made available typically remain child-directed. For example, if the teacher's lesson plan calls for making masks and the children start making hats, teachers should be prepared to adjust their plans. Children are frequently more interested in their own ideas, and it is important to encourage their own expansion of an activity. Along with flexibility in activities, teachers must allow sufficient time for children to complete activities without their feeling rushed. There should be some teacher-directed activities as well because children must begin to learn that by school-age teachers will expect them to complete certain tasks in specific ways (Carta, 1994).

Daily classroom activities must include using self-help skills. Everyday activities such as snack time, using the toilet, washing hands, and putting on outer wear provide opportunities to practice self-help skills. It may take a little longer for children to attempt or complete these tasks independently, but performing these independently may build confidence in addition to specific skills.

It may be difficult to find the balance between providing children with appropriate support and encouraging independence. Most young children struggle between the desire to be independent and the need for adult assistance and reassurance. For example, children may want to be able to put on a coat without help but not want other children to laugh at them if they cannot (Cook, Tessier, & Klein, 1992; Haywood, Brooks, & Burns, 1990).

Use of Themes for Activities

Preschool teachers often plan classroom activities around themes, including seasons of the year, types of vehicles, and holidays. With regard to holidays, teachers must be particularly sensitive to differing cultural and religious orientations. Holiday themes provide an excellent opportunity for children to learn about other cultures and religious beliefs. Teachers must realize, though, that some families do not celebrate holidays, so the teachers must be creative in planning alternative activities for those children (Wolery, Strain, & Bailey, 1992).

Using themes helps provide a starting point or focus for activities, but children should not be limited to a certain theme during their play. For example, if the classroom theme is "going to the beach," one child might pretend to be swimming while the theme might remind another child of snow. The teacher's role is to facilitate play by asking questions, making suggestions, and describing events in meaningful and interesting ways, whether or not they relate to the theme.

Choosing Behavior Management Techniques

Choosing behavior management techniques is often the responsibility of the special education teacher. When choosing behavior management techniques, it is essential to focus on the goal of assisting children to develop appropriate social skills. For some children with disabilities, a greater variety of behavior management techniques must be used. When implementing a behavior management technique, it is important to try different strategies until one is successful, but avoid shifting strategies too quickly. In addition, a child must be allowed to start each day with a clean slate. Once an incident is over, it is over and must not be harped on (Graves & Strubank, 1991).

As part of selecting appropriate behavior management techniques, teachers should create a positive environment by using affirmative and specific terms when communicating with children. It is important to tell children what they should do rather than what they should not do. For example, telling a child, "I like the way you shared your cookies with your friend," is better than saying, "I don't like it when you don't share." Stating expectations in a positive way takes practice, but the more this approach is used, the more spontaneous it becomes (Graves & Strubank, 1991).

Betz (1994) has discussed the importance of using positive behavior management techniques with young children and stated, "Discipline is not a separate entity from the educational process as a whole. If a goal is to help children develop an internal control and a sense of social values, discipline must be seen as an ongoing, year-long project, one that never ends and is a vital part of the process of growing up" (p. 10). Positive behavior management techniques often used with young children include employing logical consequences (consequences that fit the behavior, such as having the child pick up toys after playing) and redirection strategies (focusing the child on desirable activities). These techniques are discussed in more detail in Chapter 13.

Helping Children Learn Problem-Solving Skills

In addition to using appropriate discipline techniques, creating a positive learning environment includes helping children develop skills to solve problems. The goal is to have children stop and think about what is happening and why and then attempt to discover solutions independently. Problem-solving skills encompass all aspects of children's daily interactions and include cognitive and social skills.

Problem-solving skills may be enhanced by teachers asking children guiding questions or making comments that encourage them to analyze a situation. Ideally, teachers encourage children to ask for help in solving problems before children become overly frustrated. For example, a teacher might say, "What can you do about your problem?" or "What do you think will happen if . . . ?" During the early phases of children's learning to solve their own problems, adults may suggest possible solutions. When adults provide possible solutions, children should be encouraged to provide suggestions, too. However, adults must gradually encourage children to generate their own solutions.

This technique may be used with toddlers as well as older children. For example, a child who cannot get out of a chair while sitting at a table but has not reached the point of becoming overly frustrated (i.e., has not begun to cry) should be allowed to try to figure out a solution. The teacher might approach the child and comment, "It looks like you are stuck in the chair. What can you do about it?" Even if the child simply uses a gesture indicating that they want to get out of the chair or says, "Help me," the child is beginning to use problem-solving methods. If adults consistently use this approach, children gradually use this technique on their own.

This method may also be used during conflicts between children. Consider the following example of conflict resolution using problem-solving techniques. Two children are playing in the sand table and both want the same shovel. The teacher approaches the sand table because the children are in a physical struggle over the shovel. Although it may appear obvious, the first thing the teacher might say is "Do you have a problem?" The teacher should take possession of the shovel so that the children are more likely to focus their attention on the conversation with the teacher. Ideally, the teacher avoids asking children what happened or who was at fault. Young children tend to find it very hard to take another person's perspective (they show egocentrism), so such questioning is usually unsuccessful. Next, the teacher might summarize the apparent problem by saying, "It looks like you both want the shovel." To encourage the children to solve the problem, the teacher might add, "How can you solve this problem?" It is likely that both children will respond, "Give me the shovel." At this point the teacher might be tempted to ask who had it first but should not. It is important for the teacher to realize that each child is likely to think they had it first. The teacher may attempt to validate their feelings by saying, "I know you both really want the shovel, but we have only one." Ideally, the teacher asks the children for suggestions as to how to resolve the conflict. After the children have been given time to suggest solutions, the teacher might suggest trying one of the solutions or say something such as, "One of you may use the shovel for 5 minutes. Then the other may have a turn." The teacher should restate the solution to ensure that the children have heard and understood it. The teacher must monitor the interaction to ensure that the children follow the agreed-on solution. Ideally, the teacher also helps the child waiting to use the shovel become involved in another activity until their turn.

If the teacher were to intervene by taking the shovel away from the children, the teacher would not be helping the children learn problem-solving skills. In addition, both children would probably be angry or upset, and the same or a similar incident would be more likely to occur in the future. The children also would not have received instructions on how to cope with the conflict. In some cases a toy must be removed from a play area to resolve or help prevent conflicts. This should occur only after attempts to get the children to resolve the conflict have been unsuccessful or if they continue to fight over using the toy.

Young children or children with disabilities frequently are unable to provide suggestions for solutions, but in most cases they can learn to use words rather than physical force when there is a conflict. Most children, even those with limited language skills, can learn to say, "No!" As a child's language develops, the teacher may help the child learn more-complex communication strategies. The ultimate goal is for children to stop and think and then use words to solve conflicts rather than physical, aggressive behavior or crying.

Problem-solving skills are also necessary during interactions among children. Some children with developmental delays have difficulty developing and maintaining the positive social skills necessary to interact with and learn from their more socially competent peers (Goldstein, 1993; Kohler & Strain, 1993). It is often helpful for teachers to model appropriate social problem-solving skills, mediate interactions, and sequentially guide children through various steps of social interactions to help ensure that children experience successful interactions. The goal is for the teacher to gradually reduce the level of intervention.

Providing Choices

Providing children with choices also promotes a healthy emotional environment because choices give children some level of control over the environment. Choices must be appropriate for each child's developmental level; generally, the younger the child, the fewer the choices provided. Too many choices may overwhelm young children or those who have developmental delays. Choices may be as simple as asking a child, "Do you want to wear your blue or your red shirt?" or "Do you want juice or milk?" When adults provide children with choices, they must be willing to accept the children's choices. There may be times when a child is too upset to choose. When this occurs, an adult could comment, "I can see you are not ready to decide. I will decide for you." Once the adult has made the decision, it must be acted on.

Another modification that may be needed for children with disabilities is limiting the choices of activities or play materials rather than allowing freedom to use everything in the classroom. This modification may be necessary because too many choices can be overstimulating or overwhelming for some children. For example, children with a limited attention span frequently move from one activity to another without truly exploring any of them. When choices are limited, these children are more likely to attend to each activity longer or more thoroughly explore a particular toy, which is likely to enhance learning.

Encouraging Active Exploration

Children learn through play involving exploration of materials and the environment. One of the most important responsibilities of a teacher is to create and maintain an

A teacher encourages young children while they play with puzzles.

environment where children may freely play (Bredekamp, 1987; Rogers 1991). (Chapter 12 provides a detailed discussion of play.)

For some children who have special needs, self-initiated exploratory play does not spontaneously occur. If this is the case, teacher intervention is necessary. To assist children in developing play skills, a teacher may use **hand-over-hand assistance,** which involves taking a child's hands and guiding the child through certain actions, or modeling. Hand-over-hand assistance is frequently useful for children who have motor-skills difficulties.

Hand-over-hand assistance also provides information about appropriate ways to use classroom tools such as crayons or paintbrushes. Using this method helps children with a short attention span stay focused on an activity. This type of assistance provides a touch of encouragement, telling the child, "Let's try this together."

Children with disabilities may need direct instruction and individual practice before they attempt a particular play activity independently. Prescriptive teaching is a method of working individually with a child on skills development with a clearly defined goal in a sequential manner. Prescriptive teaching is used to enhance play skills by developing a particular skill, such as teaching a child how to string beads using task analysis. After a particular skill is developed, the goal is to have the child use the new skill and generalize it during more spontaneous play.

Providing Engaging, Stimulating Environments

Most children benefit from a colorful, stimulating environment such as one with many pictures on the walls, items hanging from the ceiling, and a wide variety of activities. However, some children with disabilities are easily distracted by visual stimuli and do not learn well in such visually stimulating environments. These children require less visual stimulation to focus and learn. The teacher may accommodate the educational requirements of these children by carefully determining where wall hangings such as artwork, posters, and signs are placed and deciding whether props (items for children to look at or hold) enhance or distract from learning.

For example, limiting irrelevant stimuli during large-group activities may help children who are easily distracted better attend to these activities. For these children, large-group activities are frequently most effectively presented in a section of the room where the floor is carpeted in a neutral color and where no objects hang from the ceiling or on the walls. To the observer, this may seem overly plain, but some children benefit from this type of environment because they more easily focus on relevant stimuli.

On the other hand, some children require visual and tactile aids to encourage them to focus their attention on an activity. For example, while singing "The Itsy-Bitsy Spider," children who have difficulty attending who are given pipe-cleaner spiders as props may be able to focus on the activity. These children may not focus on the activity without the props. Props may also help children focus on other types of activities such as listening to a story. Some children benefit from holding objects because the objects keep their hands busy. When their hands are busy, their eyes focus on the activity; when their hands are not busy, their eyes constantly scan the environment.

Creating and Promoting a Supportive Classroom Environment

Another important role of the special education teacher is to create a classroom environment in which children are respected and guided in a supportive, positive manner. This type of orientation helps children strengthen their confidence and contributes to the development of positive self-esteem.

Adult–child interactions often foster positive self-esteem when adults express respect for, acceptance of, and support for children. Powell (1991) lists attributes of positive interaction styles that may be used with children, including providing enjoyable activities, encouraging social interaction with peers, encouraging child-initiated activities, sharing control with children, approaching children at their level of understanding, and encouraging children to experience success by providing activities that are not too easy or difficult.

Powell (1991) describes how adults may provide a give-and-take interaction with children: "Adults follow the child's lead when talking with a child or entering his or her play activities. Conversations between adults and children are reciprocal exchanges: the adult does not dominate the exchange by asking didactic questions" (p. 102). See Chapter 14 for further discussion of the importance of helping the child develop positive self-esteem.

Creating a Language-Rich Environment

In most preschool classrooms the flow of conversation and nonverbal communication is unending. Children are involved in self-talk and conversations with peers and teachers. (See Chapter 5 for discussions of self-talk and other forms of communication.) In most preschool environments, teachers follow children's conversation leads rather than initiate most conversations. Regular preschool teachers typically do not modify their language but talk in extended and relatively complex sentences.

When working with children with disabilities, adults frequently initiate language. For example, in a classroom for children with disabilities there is often less child-initiated language and more teacher-initiated language during play. This imbalance exists because children who qualify for placement in the special needs preschool class often have language delays. During play a teacher may initiate more play interactions and language with a child.

A teacher may also use grammatically incomplete sentences (telegraphic speech). For example, a teacher may say, "Open juice?" instead of "Do you want me to open your juice?" Although it is important to provide a model for correct language usage, a teacher may use a language stimulation strategy called parallel talk. This language pattern is a level of speech designed to match the child's present language ability or be one step above it rather than at a more complex adult level.

For example, if a child is at the two-word sentence stage, the teacher would make two- or three-word statements because five- to seven-word statements might be too complex for the child. Special education teachers are also likely to expand on a child's speech. For example, if a child says, "More cookies," the teacher might slightly expand this statement by saying, "Want more cookies." If the child says, "Want more cookies," the teacher might expand by saying, "Want more cookies, please," and then "I want more cookies, please."

Another difference that may be found in the special education preschool classroom is that teacher interactions may include the use of sign language or communication boards (cards or boards with letters, words, symbols, or pictures mounted on them). Sign language and communication boards allow children to express their needs using physical movement. This may ease their frustration at being unable to express needs through verbalization. For some children, using a communication board or sign language assists in the acquisition of verbal communication skills. See Chapter 5 for a discussion of the use of communication boards and sign language.

In contrast, when working with some children who have special needs, a teacher may not respond to some forms of nonverbal communication, including gesturing, pointing, or sign language. To an observer the teacher may seem unaware or even unresponsive. In most cases, though, teachers are aware of the nonverbal cues the children make but are trying to encourage the children to use words to communicate rather than rely solely on nonverbal communication.

For example, during snack time a child might be asked, "Do you want another cookie?" and the child might nod or sign, "Yes." The teacher might ignore this response if they know the child can respond by using words. In this case the teacher might prompt the child by saying, "Use your words to tell me what you want. Do you want another cookie?" and might not give the child a cookie until the child says, "Yes" or gives some other developmentally appropriate verbal response.

Process versus Product

Ideally, goals and activities for young children remain focused on the process of doing rather than completing an activity. At times, adults become too focused on the child's creating a particular object or doing something the correct way. The process of manipulating objects is generally more important than what is made. Children should, therefore, be provided with many open-ended activities that provide materials for manipulating and exploring, rather than for creating a specific object. Open-ended activities allow the child to explore materials in a personally relevant manner.

Some children with disabilities have limited attending skills and may require special strategies to help them stay focused on activities. For these children, the special education teacher may establish specific expectations. In such cases it might appear that the focus is on creating a product when, in fact, the focus is on improving attending skills. For example, a child might be told, "I want you to complete this puzzle before you leave." In this case the goal in requiring the child to finish the puzzle is to enhance attending skills. This goal is important because a limited attention span often affects other areas of development, such as cognitive or social skills. Figure 6.4 outlines a process of working with children who have limited attention spans.

Children with limited attention spans may exhibit behavior that diminishes their own exploration of materials and distracts others. A special chair called a **Rifton chair** helps some children more effectively focus on large-group and tabletop activities. This chair has a solid back and sides, wide legs, and often a seat belt to help support children with postural difficulties. It also appears that the chair

Figure 6.4   **Methods for Effective Interactions with Children Who Have Limited Attention Spans**

When encouraging children with a limited attention span to continue to work at a specific task, it may be helpful to

- use physical touch,
- establish eye contact by having the child look directly at the speaker's face,
- provide verbal reminders,
- use verbal prompts for each step of an activity,
- have the child repeat each verbal prompt before they are told the next step in a set of directions,
- hold the object of discussion directly in front of the child while talking about the object,
- be in close proximity to the child when communicating with them,
- get down to the child's physical height to communicate, and
- use songs or other music, rather than conversation, to communicate.

provides some children with a sense of security that may help them focus on activities for a longer period of time. The seat belt serves as a reminder to continue with a task. It does not serve as a restraint because most children can easily unfasten the belt. Rifton chairs are also more stable than ordinary chairs and help prevent children from rocking back and forth and tipping over. Figure 6.5 provides additional tips for working with young children.

Working with Family Members

One of the most important roles of the special education teacher and other team members is to help parents understand how important they are to their child's education. In addition, special education teachers often coordinate the efforts of parents and professionals working together to design and implement programs for children with disabilities. Special education teachers must maintain ongoing communication with parents to ensure that parents know their contributions are being considered. A journal sent back and forth between home and school each day is one effective way of maintaining contact with parents.

Teaching staff can visit the child's home, and family members can observe class activities, to further promote contact between staff and family members. Such visits also allow parents and teachers to directly observe methods of interacting with the child. Regular communication also includes informal and formal meetings, classroom

Figure 6.5 **Tips for Teachers**

- Learn as much as you can about cognitive delays.
- Recognize that you can make an enormous difference in children's lives.
- Find out what each child's strengths and interests are, and emphasize them.
- Create many opportunities for success.
- Become familiar with each child's individualized family service plan (IFSP) or individualized education program (IEP).
- Consult with other specialists as necessary.
- Be as concrete as possible. Demonstrate what you mean. For example, rather than just relating information verbally, show a picture; rather than just showing a picture, provide the student with hands-on materials and experiences.
- Break long or new tasks into small steps, demonstrate the steps, and have the child complete each step while you provide assistance as necessary.
- Provide immediate feedback.
- Work with the child's family and other team members to create and implement an educational plan tailored to meet the child's needs.
- Frequently communicate with family members.

visits, telephone calls, and written communication. Programs are most effective when parents are encouraged to initiate communication rather than just be passive recipients of information (Carta, 1994).

Because special education teachers are frequently responsible for coordinating the variety of therapy services that a child may receive, they often become the primary contact person for family members. Early intervention services are typically designed to support children who are at risk of developmental delays or have special needs and their families. Special education teachers are often responsible for ensuring that services are provided to parents, including training, support, and information. These services usually help develop positive parent–child relationships, an essential part of the foundation for the child's development.

Conclusions

Typically, children who have cognitive delays also have delays in other developmental areas. Knowledge of theories, typical rates of development, and indicators of possible cognitive delays guide assessment and intervention services. Therefore, screenings and full assessments typically evaluate most, if not all, major developmental domains (i.e., cognitive, speech and language, motor, social-emotional, and adaptive). Special education teachers play a key role in the assessment of and services provided for young children with cognitive delays.

There are many possible causes of cognitive delays and many types of disabilities that include cognitive delays. The three most common causes of cognitive delays are Down syndrome, prenatal exposure to alcohol, and fragile X syndrome.

There are several specific recommendations regarding working with young children with cognitive and other delays. Those working with young children who have disabilities should have knowledge about curriculum development; behavior management techniques; methods for working effectively with family members; lesson planning; creating engaging, supportive, and language-rich environments; and methods to encourage young children to solve problems, make choices, and feel confident enough to actively explore their environments.

CHAPTER SUMMARY

- Cognitive development affects all areas of development, including language, motor, social-emotional, and adaptive skills.

- When one works with children who have cognitive delays, it is useful to understand key concepts related to cognitive development—including perception, attention, reasoning, and memory—and key aspects of developmental theories related to typical cognitive development.

- Many factors may contribute to cognitive disabilities, including genetic abnormalities, problems during pregnancy or birth, environmental conditions, and social experiences.

- There are several key indicators of possible cognitive delays; cognitive delays often are not detected until children reach school age.

- Screening and full assessment must occur to determine if a child has a cognitive delay. Many standardized instruments may be used as part of the assessment process.

- The special education teacher plays a crucial role in providing early childhood special education services. Typically, they play a key role in the assessment and education of children who have cognitive delays.

- Down syndrome, fetal alcohol syndrome, fetal alcohol spectrum disorder, fragile X syndrome, TBI, cocaine exposure, and HIV/AIDS are among the causes of cognitive delays.

- Guidelines for working with young children who have cognitive delays include recommendations for curriculum development; classroom management; working with children's family members; lesson plan development; helping children learn to solve problems and make choices; encouraging children to actively explore their environments; developing engaging, stimulating, supportive, language-rich environments; and focusing on the process of learning rather than the products.

CHAPTER KEY TERMS

cognitive development
cognitive disability
mental retardation
generalizing
incidental learning
basic cognitive process
perception
attention
reasoning
memory
egocentrism
object permanence
centration
conservation
reversibilitiy
intelligence quotient (IQ)
Down syndrome

fragile X syndrome
Rett Syndrome
phenylketonuria (PKU)
birth trauma
premature birth
low birth weight
American Association on Intellectual and
    Developmental Disabilities (AAIDD)
American Association on Mental Retardation
    (AAMR)
intelligence test
learning disability (LD)
developmental learning disability
concomitant impairment
hand-over-hand assistance
Rifton chair

REVIEW QUESTIONS

1. Why do some people feel that the category "mental retardation" should be replaced with other less stigmatizing terms? What are your feelings about this matter?

2. What are the major characteristics of children affected by the three major causes of cognitive delays?

3. What are the major categories of causes of cognitive delays? Briefly describe each.

4. How can service providers go about providing engaging, stimulating, supportive, and language-rich environments?

SUGGESTED STUDENT ACTIVITIES

1. Develop the components of an individualized family service plan (IFSP) for a 2-year-old with Down syndrome.

2. Explain how you would help preschoolers learn to recognize letters, and the sounds associated with each letter, using the good practices discussed in Chapter 6.

3. Research current intervention methods used for young children with TBIs. Analyze how things have changed. What are some projected future intervention methods?

4. Give a specific example of focusing on the process rather than the product when helping young children learn to solve an eight-piece puzzle.

5. Develop a pamphlet for parents with children who have Down syndrome. Include incident rates, agencies, and other helpful information.

Motor Abilities

CHAPTER KEY POINTS

- Knowledge about the typical rates of fine- and gross-motor development is crucial when working with young children with motor delays.

- Physical therapists and occupational therapists play crucial roles in the assessment of motor delays.

- Several disabilities have motor delays as their primary characteristic, and other disabilities have motor delays as a secondary characteristic.

- Physical therapy focuses on large-motor skills.

- Occupational therapy focuses on fine-motor skills.

During infancy and early childhood, **motor development** includes the increased ability to control inborn primitive reflexes and to engage in purposeful activity. **Gross-motor skills** involve movements of the head, body, legs, arms, and large muscles. **Fine-motor skills** involve the use of the small muscles of the body, especially in eye–hand coordination tasks. Motor skills affect cognitive, language, and social development, in part because motor development expands experiences. They are directly linked to performance of various adaptive skills.

A **physical therapist (PT)** evaluates the range of motion of joints, muscle strength and development, and the functional level of the child. PTs evaluate gross-motor development and design appropriate treatment and activity programs. An **occupational therapist (OTR)** focuses on fine-motor and eye–hand coordination and on general development. OTRs often assist children and their families in the development of daily living (adaptive) skills and focus on hand strength and use of arms and hands. These professionals, and the therapy services that they provide, will be discussed in greater depth later in this chapter. Providing early intervention for young children with motor delays often helps prevent delays from persisting or becoming more severe (Sander, 2002).

Theories and Concepts

Motor abilities are genetically preprogrammed and greatly influenced by brain development. At birth the brain centers that control and coordinate voluntary movements are not well developed. Motor development matures in a head-to-toe (**cephalocaudal**) sequence. That is, brain areas controlling movement of the head and neck muscles mature earlier than those controlling arm, leg, and trunk muscles. Motor development also progresses in an inward-to-outward (**proximodistal**) sequence, meaning that the development of the brain areas controlling movement of the center of the body, such as the spinal cord, occurs before that of the brain areas controlling arm and leg muscles (Mathew & Cook, 1990). Children's physical development progresses at a rapid rate during the first few years of life (Berk, 2005).

Along with genetic influences, the environment influences gross-motor development (Thelen, 1989). For example, toddlers who have frequent ear infections may have difficulty maintaining their balance while learning to walk. Children who have limited opportunities to climb stairs may not master climbing stairs as quickly as those who do have these experiences. Research indicates that once children have these experiences, they often quickly acquire the skills typical of children their age (Illingworth, 1987). Several theories help explain motor development.

Behaviorism

Behaviorists emphasize feedback and reinforcement schedules when explaining the development of motor skills. They emphasize that long-term development and retention of motor skills often depends on regular practice. The behaviorist perspective also emphasizes the value of repetition once task mastery is achieved (i.e., encouraging overtraining) and retraining to help enhance prior learning. Additionally, enhanced quantity and quality of feedback improves learning and retention of sensory-motor skills during training (Huitt & Hummel, 2006).

Information Processing

Information processing theory emphasizes the importance of selective attention in determining motor behavior and feedback when modifying motor behavior. This perspective suggests that learning motor skills is facilitated by slowing the rate at which information is presented and reducing the amount of information. In addition, information processing theorists emphasize the value of prompting and guidance while a child learns motor skills, in contrast to letting the child rely on trial-and-error or self-discovery strategies. Mental rehearsal, especially involving imagery, is also believed to facilitate motor abilities (Huitt, 2003).

Other Theories

Among others, **Albert Bandura** and **Lev Vygotsky** emphasized that many forms of sensory-motor behavior are learned by imitation, especially complex movements. Theories focusing on individual differences, such as **Howard Gardner's** theory of multiple intelligences, have identified various sensory-motor abilities. For example, the core elements of Gardner's bodily-kinesthetic intelligence (body smartness) are control of one's bodily motions and the ability to skillfully handle objects. This intelligence also includes a sense of timing and the goal of a physical action (Gardner, 1999).

Jean Piaget

As discussed in earlier chapters, **Jean Piaget** noted that children initially learn about their environment almost exclusively through physical exploration. Later development also involves learning through physical interactions. The level of cognitive development directly affects motor development. The reverse is true as well: motor development directly contributes to acquisition of cognitive and social-emotional skills (Piaget, 1980).

Arnold Gesell

Arnold Gesell believed that motor development results from neuromuscular maturation in infants' brains, muscles, and growing bodies. The maturational theory is based on the idea that human development is the result of the unfolding of the individual's genetic inheritance (Berk, 1992).

Gesell's earliest work focused on cataloging motor milestones. These normative descriptions of milestones are widely published in books, journals, and newspaper columns. For example, Gesell identified 22 stages in the development of crawling, beginning when infants lift their heads from a prone position and ending when they can crawl smoothly on their hands and feet. He identified stages of motor development in all major areas, as well as language, cognitive, and social-emotional development, during the early years. This work led to the development of the **Development Schedules,** a set of four timetables devised to evaluate the physical, emotional, and behavioral development of infants, toddlers, and preschoolers. Pediatricians, child psychologists, and other professionals use these schedules to evaluate young children's development. The schedules will be discussed in more detail later in this chapter.

Typical Motor Development

Infants develop motor abilities in the same order and, in most cases, at approximately the same age. Many developmental milestones during infancy are motor in nature. As already mentioned, motor skills are divided into gross- and fine-motor skills. Gross-motor skills involve large muscles, and fine-motor skills involve refined movements. Fine-motor skills are lacking at birth, but precursors are present in the form of reflexes (e.g., the grasping reflex). In most cases, fine-motor movements require coordination of gross-motor muscles. During the first few months of life, small and large muscles begin to work together. For example, infants begin using a deliberate reach to grab objects and can transfer toys from one hand to the other (Bigge, 1991).

At birth, babies are not very muscular. Peak muscle growth is not reached until adolescence. Good nutrition during the early years of development is particularly important because muscles, bones, and the brain grow the most during this period (Keogh & Sugden, 1985).

During infancy, neck and back muscles strengthen, allowing the head to become more mobile and hand and arm movements to become more controlled (Harrison & Kositsky, 1983). Starting at about 2 years of age, the rate of physical developmental change gradually slows. This slowing is particularly true in the area of weight gain, which is usually greatest during the first 2 years.

At about 2 years, children begin to lose their babyish appearance. Their overall body proportions begin to resemble those of an adult. At birth, babies' heads constitute about 25% of total body length and about 33% of body weight, compared to 15% of length and 10% of weight during adulthood. By the time children are 6 years old, about one-half as much body fat remains as was present at 1 year. For example, babies' waists are generally about the same size as their hips. By age 6, children's waists are usually narrower than their shoulders and hips (Berk, 1992).

Gross-Motor Development

Gross-motor development refers to children's learning to move their large muscles. The sequence of gross-motor skills development is similar for all children, but the rate of growth may vary greatly. Gross-motor skills include learning to crawl, stand, jump, walk, and run. These types of skills develop as young bodies become less top-heavy and centers of gravity shift downward toward the trunk. Newborns can move their arms, legs, and heads and use their mouth muscles for sucking. Gradually, head movement becomes more mobile and controlled as the neck and back muscles strengthen. Infants' hands and arms gradually come under voluntary control (Fraser & Hensinger, 1983; Hagerman, 1999).

As body proportions change, balance greatly improves, aiding children in successfully completing tasks that involve large-muscle groups. Learning to walk is one of the most significant gross-motor accomplishments of infancy. Initially, children walk with a very wide-footed stance, and their arms are held out as if they were walking on a tightrope. Gradually, children stand and walk with their feet closer together and bring their hands closer to their bodies (Connor, Williamson, & Siepp, 1978).

Fine-Motor Development

In contrast to gross-motor development, fine-motor development involves small-muscle groups and includes movements such as reaching, grasping, waving, and writing. Similarly to gross-motor development, fine-motor development drastically improves during early childhood (McHale & Lerner, 1990). During infancy, children develop the ability to grasp and manipulate objects (Bigge & Burton, 1989). During the preschool years (2 to 5 years old), fine-motor development includes the ability to complete puzzles, build structures out of small blocks, color, cut with scissors, and paste. These skills develop as a result of increased muscle control of the hands and fingers. During the preschool years, fine-motor skills progressively improve in two areas: the ability to care for one's own bodies and the ability to draw and write (Rogers, 1982).

In caring for their bodies during the preschool years, children begin to become more self-sufficient at dressing and feeding themselves. Preschoolers enjoy a new sense of independence because they can care for themselves. The typical 3-year-old can independently take care of toilet needs. Most 4- and 5-year-olds can dress and undress with minimal adult aid. When children are tired or in a hurry, though, they may need help. For example, their shirts may be inside out or their buttons may be unfastened. One of the most challenging self-help tasks for preschoolers is tying shoelaces and jacket hoods. This task is usually mastered by 6-year-olds. The ability to tie shoes requires a longer attention span, greater memory (cognitive) skills, and more advanced sequencing skills to coordinate the detailed hand movements (motor skills) needed to complete the task (Espenschade & Eckert, 1980). Chapter 11 provides an extended discussion of adaptive skills.

Assessment of Motor Delays

Limited head control, inability to reach and grasp, and too loose or rigid muscle tone are indicators of motor delays in young children. As with other areas of development, there are two major steps in the assessment of motor development. The first step is a brief and relatively informal assessment of motor development involving physical and occupational therapy screenings. The second step, called a full formal assessment, occurs only if screening indicates the likelihood of a motor delay. This assessment is more detailed (Tingey-Michaelis, 1983).

Teachers may be the first to notice motor delays in children enrolled in a day care facility or preschool program. If a teacher suspects a child may have a motor delay, the teacher should inform a parent and make a referral for the child to have a physical or occupational therapy screening (Bleck & Nagel, 1982). When parents are the first to suspect motor delays, they often talk with a pediatrician and discuss their concerns with those who care for their child. If the pediatrician also believes the child's motor development is delayed, they may recommend that an assessment be completed (Wermer, 1987).

Consider the following example. A bus driver reported that 2-year-old Katie took a very long time getting on and off the bus. Based on this report to Katie's teacher, combined with the teacher's belief that Katie's motor development appeared to be delayed, a PT was asked to conduct an initial physical therapy screening. The results of the screening indicated that Katie might have motor delays. The PT followed up with a full physical therapy assessment. This evaluation helped explain why Katie was having difficulty getting on and off the bus.

It was determined that Katie had low muscle tone, including limited strength in her legs and difficulty balancing on either leg. Using movement patterns within the normal sequence of development, such as kneeling and half kneeling, the therapist worked on strengthening Katie's hip muscles. As hip muscle strength increased, the therapist added standing activities such as placing one foot on a block and the other foot on the floor while playing at a table. Practice stepping onto objects of different height while balancing helped prepare Katie for climbing stairs and getting on and off the school bus.

All of these intervention strategies could be done in Katie's home; at a clinic, regular day care facility, or preschool; or within a special program for children with developmental delays. Most of the intervention strategies could be integrated into daily activities.

Gross-Motor Assessment

Physical Therapists. PTs are health professionals whose goal is to help people develop total body muscle control. PTs receive training in evaluating and treating posture and movement disorders. They have a bachelor's degree, master's degree, or Doctor of Physical Therapy (Fostig & Maslow, 1970). A PT may also be certified in neurodevelopmental treatment techniques (NDT). This certification requires training specifically in physical therapy for children (Stern & Gorga, 1990; Zaichkowsky, Zaichkowsky, & Martinek, 1980).

PTs provide services to help prevent or minimize a disability, relieve pain, develop and improve motor function, control postural difficulties, and establish and maintain maximum physical performance (Johnston & Magrab, 1976). They also evaluate the physical environment and assess gross-motor skills.

Physical therapists make recommendations for moving a child from one area to another and selecting appropriate adaptive equipment. They also provide movement therapy (exercise). Within an educational environment, physical therapy services are directed at helping children with disabilities obtain maximal physical independence in all education-related activities (Snell, 1987). Many school districts and preschool programs use PTs as consultants to work with children with gross-motor delays. However, PTs may also have private practices. PTs are frequently employed by a hospital or rehabilitation center.

PTs may also recommend the best handling procedures for transfers such as moving children from wheelchairs to toilets and for positioning devices such as braces designed to improve posture (Maddox, 1987). For example, some children cannot stand on their own and require special support devices such as braces, shoe molds, or walkers to help them stand and, in some cases, move about the school environment independently.

In other cases, children benefit from special chairs designed to support their trunk, which may help to improve the use of their hands. These chairs provide needed support so that children do not have to use their hands to support their body weight (Campbell, Green, & Carlson, 1977).

Within a school or home, PTs also analyze physical environments to help ensure independent mobility and safety for children with disabilities. For example, small curbs may become major obstacles to children in wheelchairs. To evaluate the physical environment and make recommendations for modifications, PTs observe how children move within their normal environments during indoor and outdoor play. During these observations, PTs focus on large-muscle movements such as climbing, jumping, running, balancing, and catching and throwing balls (Bobath & Bobath 1975). In some cases physical therapy may be needed; however, before physical therapy can be provided, children must be assessed.

Physical Therapy Screening.   A physical therapy screening is a relatively simple procedure. The purpose of a screening is to determine if full physical therapy evaluation is warranted. During the screening the therapist receives information from parents, day care providers, preschool teachers, and others regarding the child's physical skills. PTs may also directly observe the child at home or in a classroom to determine the level of gross-motor development. Box 7.1 describes Billy, a child with delays in gross-motor development. Children such as Billy should be referred for a physical therapy screening.

During screening and full assessments, PTs observe how children move from one area to another. For example, a PT might observe how children navigate around furniture and interact with other children in the process of getting ready to go home. This type of observation provides information about children's level of awareness of their body in space. The therapist also observes the postures that children assume during play and other activities to gain insight into their muscular strengths and weaknesses (Hale, 1979). This evaluation is particularly important because children must coordinate their large muscles to maintain various body positions, as well as coordinate the use of their hands, eyes, tongues, and feet during different tasks.

PTs also watch for signs of fatigue. Children with weak muscles use more energy to accomplish the same tasks than do their peers with stronger muscles. The extra energy needed to accomplish motor tasks may limit children's attention span or use of cognitive skills. Fatigue may be indicated when children have shortness of breath after minimal physical activity. Some children have spurts of energy followed by frequent rest; this pattern also indicates muscle weaknesses. Other children cannot focus on tasks as the day progresses, which may indicate that they are excessively tired because of weak muscle development (Batshaw & Perret, 1986).

During a gross-motor screening, the therapist asks a child to attempt a set of gross-motor tasks. This may be done with one child alone or during group gross-motor activities, such as playing outdoors or indoors on climbing and riding equipment, dancing to music, or any other activity that involves whole body movement.

Box 7.1 *Billy*

Once in the classroom, Billy begins the process of removing his jacket and placing it and his backpack in his cubby. While putting his things away, Billy knocks several other children's belongings onto the floor. After taking longer than all the other children to put his belongings into the cubby, Billy awkwardly walks toward the play area, stepping on coats and bags that he knocked down. One of the children yells at Billy, telling him not to walk on the coats. Billy does not seem aware that he is walking on these objects.

Billy approaches the other children, who are engaged in an art activity at a large table. He stands beside a vacant chair, but it is too close to the table for him to sit in it. Billy tries to sit down without moving the chair by putting his foot in front of the chair and wedging his body between the table and chair. After this fails, Billy struggles but manages to pull the chair awkwardly away from the table. He sits in the chair, which is now misaligned with the table. Billy asks the teacher for some crayons. After handing Billy a box of crayons, the teacher moves Billy's chair into a position more aligned with the table. Billy begins the art activity that most of his classmates have nearly completed.

As the art activity concludes, Billy abandons his barely started project and attempts to get up from the chair. He frantically moves about in every direction, appearing not to have a plan for getting up from the chair. He finally pushes away from the table, knocking the chair over backward. Billy walks over to the area where a group activity (circle time) has already begun. As he joins the class seated on a rug, he plops onto the floor and immediately moves into a W-sitting position (knees together and feet out to the side).

During the 10-minute group activity, Billy frequently changes positions. He moves from the W position to leaning forward on his hands, to lying back on the floor, to leaning against the wall or the teacher, who is sitting next to him. He does not stay in any one position for more than a minute. When the teacher asks him a question, Billy is in the middle of changing positions and does not answer. Another adult helps move Billy into an appropriate sitting position, with his legs crossed in front of him. The teacher repeats the question. This time Billy responds enthusiastically and appropriately.

As circle time ends, the teacher announces that it is free-play time (when children choose where they want to play). During free play, Billy quickly moves from playing with a toy train to blocks, to cars and trucks. He lies on the floor instead of sitting upright to play with each of the toys. He does not play with any one type of toy for more than 2 or 3 minutes. Billy begins wandering around the classroom.

Billy notices another child building a house with blocks. Billy tells this child that he wants to help. He takes a block and tries to add it to the roof of the house. During the attempt, he accidentally knocks over most of the building. The other child cries and says, "I don't want to play with Billy!" This appears to upset Billy, who hides his face.

The teacher approaches the children and asks Billy to help rebuild the house. Billy tries to fix the house with the teacher's assistance. Again he accidentally knocks over several blocks. This scenario is typical of the rest of Billy's day. By the time the bus arrives two hours after Billy began his morning at school, he is exhausted and lying on the floor.

Is Billy a bad child who gets into a lot of mischief? Does he need some kind of behavior modification program? Is he lazy? Is he just careless? The following information suggests why Billy may have the difficulties described above and how he may be helped.

continued

Box 7.1   **Continued**

Billy appears to have significant gross-motor difficulties that interfere with his ability to pay attention and to learn and use social skills. These gross-motor delays are likely to lead to negative self-esteem.

Not all children who qualify for physical therapy have all or even many of the characteristics that Billy exhibited. Some children have only one or two of the gross-motor difficulties described in Billy's case. Any motor difficulty that interferes with a child's educational experiences should be assessed to determine if physical therapy services are needed.

During the screening process, most PTs also request information from the child's parents regarding motor difficulties the child may have at home (Baker, Banfied, Killburn, & Shufflebarger, 1991). PTs provide professional expertise to help understand children, but children's parents often know their children better than anyone else does. To fully understand a child's abilities, therapists often ask parents to describe any physical limitations or difficulties the child displays when with the parents. Therapists may ask, "Does your child like the merry-go-round at the playground?" to learn how a child copes with various physical activities (McWilliams & Sekerak, 1995).

PTs may also ask parents to indicate concerns they have regarding their child's physical development. Parents may notice that their child falls more often than most children the same age or is more fearful of certain physical activities, such as climbing up a ladder to a slide. Open communication between parents and the therapist is essential for gaining a total picture of the child's needs and strengths, as well as for developing an appropriate physical therapy intervention plan (Williamson, 1987).

Circle time, when a group of children at a preschool or day care center sit on the floor or in chairs in a circle, is often an excellent time to observe a child. Circle-time activities generally require that trunk muscles actively function to ensure an upright posture. For children whose muscles are sluggish, the effects of this weakness are often observed as they sit during circle time (Bigge, 1991).

For example, during circle time some children slump forward, which results in rounding of their backs. They may lean forward with their hands on the floor or with their elbows on their knees and their hands supporting their head. These postures are part of the normal developmental sequence as children gain strength in their back and stomach muscles. These children should not be judged as being lazy or inattentive (Anderson, Bale, Blackman, & Murphy, 1986).

Therapists may also observe children sitting in a W position (with knees together and feet out to the side). Children assume this position because it widens the base of support and decreases trunk movement and energy output. W sitting may indicate a gross-motor delay. This position is believed to be detrimental to the development of good hip alignment and should be discouraged. Children should be asked to sit in a different way such as cross-legged or with their legs straight out in front of their bodies. Children with poor hip alignment are more likely to develop walking patterns in which their feet turn inward. An unusual pattern may interfere with balance as well as the ability to perform other motor tasks (Tyler & Mira, 1993).

Children who have low muscle tone in the trunk region often compensate by positioning themselves against a wall, leaning against another person, or leaning on their own arms. These positions result in additional support for maintaining an upright position. Children who sit away from a group of children and lean against a wall may be viewed as loners when instead they may be leaning because of weak muscles. Leaning against an adult may be misinterpreted as a sign of attachment or affection (Schleickorn, 1993).

During free play, children with gross-motor delays often lie on the floor rather than sit upright to play with objects. Children with gross-motor delays may sit on the floor and play in a W-sitting position, move to lying on the stomach, or use side-sitting throughout the free play time. When children with motor delays move to more upright positions such as kneeling or standing, they frequently lean heavily with the body or arms on a support surface such as a table (March of Dimes, 1992). Leaning on furniture may also be observed as these children attempt to step over objects on the floor.

Children with low muscle tone tend to lock their joints to help them control their movement (Robinson, 1973). For example, when children are in standing positions, the knees may be held rigid, and they might even appear to be knock-kneed. The arches in their feet may be collapsed. For these children, movements requiring more-complex skills, such as jumping, often look rigid or awkward.

When children with low muscle tone bounce a ball or draw a circle with one hand, the other hand may move in the same manner. While children concentrate on such activities, extraneous movements of the mouth, lips, or tongue may also occur (Hirst, 1989).

Children with gross-motor delays may appear to be in perpetual motion and unable to stay at any activity more than a few moments. These children's movement transitions are often quick and impulsive-looking. This may be because children with atypical muscle tone have difficulty moving their muscles gradually (smoothly). They may also have problems moving one part of their body in isolation from the other parts, which may lead to their bumping into things or losing balance (Blackman, 1984).

Motor delays often affect children's social interactions and play skills (Bartel & Guskin, 1980). For example, children who adapt to motor delays by playing on the floor rather than sitting or standing at an activity may not have an appropriate level of eye contact with their peers or with adults. Children who are constantly in motion may also be shunned by other children because active children often end up physically stepping on friends or toys during play time. Ultimately, extremely active children may develop negative self-esteem and withdraw. These children may also be inappropriately labeled as having attention deficit hyperactivity disorder (Michaud, 2004).

In addition, some children with gross-motor delays may act silly or intentionally misbehave to divert attention from their awkwardness during gross-motor tasks. For example, children who think they cannot perform a motor task may deliberately fall on the floor, anticipating that other classmates will laugh. This allows children with gross-motor delays to be viewed as silly or funny instead of clumsy (Baker & Brightman, 1989).

While all behavior problems do not indicate a need for physical therapy, it is important to determine whether there is a behavioral or motor problem (Anastasion, 1978). If children have had a significant motor delay, they may need physical therapy to be successful and develop positive self-esteem. Self-esteem is often less positive for children who are uncoordinated (Thompson, Rubin, & Bilenker, 1983). Knowing that there is an underlying physical cause for lack of coordination often helps parents and teachers be more responsive and have more patience with the child.

Safety is often a concern for children with gross-motor delays. Children with poor balance and coordination often trip over things, bump into other children or objects, or fall. Many children with developmental delays have decreased mobility in their ankles, which may cause them to trip and fall because their ankles do not quickly adjust to changes in walking surfaces (Bricker & Bricker, 1976). These children may have difficulty lifting their toes off the floor because their legs swing while they walk, which may result in their tripping over their own feet. For these children, falling may occur even more frequently outdoors because of varying terrains that constantly require motor adjustment (Adelson & Fraiberg, 1975).

Poor motor coordination may cause preschool-age children to lag behind other children or have difficulty moving through a crowd. Some children may also have difficulty standing behind the children in front of them on a line. This may become a safety concern during a fire drill or other situations when it is important to leave an area quickly and in an orderly way.

Toddlers or preschoolers who are very insecure about their ability to balance or who lack appropriate muscle strength may feel uncomfortable on stairs and choose to crawl up or down (Hanson, 1984). Such crawling often results in the children's lagging behind their peers' development. However, children who have difficulty maneuvering on stairs are typically noticed relatively quickly and often referred for a physical therapy screening (Orelove & Sosbey, 1987).

Children who have trouble with motor planning (automatically starting, performing, and completing a series of movements to achieve a desired outcome) may have trouble with something as simple as sitting in a chair without falling off, putting on a coat, or smoothly moving from being on the floor to standing up (Ayers, 1972). They may have difficulty planning movements needed to perform everyday activities. Children with motor planning difficulties may have trouble playing safely on outdoor equipment. These children are often described as awkward or uncoordinated (Orelove & Sosbey, 1987).

Uncoordinated children typically have more bumps and bruises because of a decreased awareness of their body in space (Mulligan-Ault, Guess, Smith, & Thompson, 1988). In other words, these children often have slower balance responses that may contribute to an increased number of bumps and scrapes. Children with motor delays frequently do not demonstrate good judgment when it comes to potential dangers on the playground (Goldfarb, Brotherson, Summers, & Turnbull, 1986). For example, these children may climb too high on the playground equipment and be unable to get down without assistance.

Physical Therapy Full Formal Assessment. If information collected during the physical therapy screening indicates possible gross-motor delays, the PT will request a full physical therapy evaluation. The referral for a full physical therapy evaluation includes the reason for the referral, the child's background history, and general observations including the child's responses to movement activities within the home or classroom (Bricker & Bricker, 1976). Parental permission must be obtained before a formal physical therapy evaluation can be conducted (Berger & Fowlkes, 1980).

Adding to information obtained during the screening, PTs assess a child's muscle tone and joint ranges. To accomplish this, the PT guides the movement of the child's joints through their normal ranges to evaluate muscle response (Johnston & Magrab, 1976). Muscle tone may be too high or too low. High-tone muscles feel rigid and low-tone muscles feel loose when the extremities and trunk are moved. Tight joints may indicate a need for stretching exercises. Overly loose joints may indicate a need for exercises designed to strengthen the muscles around or near the joint (Zaichowsky et al., 1980).

Further assessment includes having children move through a developmental sequence during play (Eastman & Safron, 1986). The developmental sequence involves placing the child in several positions, including supine (lying on the back), prone (lying on the stomach), rolling, sitting, quadruped (on hands and knees), crawling, kneeling, half kneeling, transitional from floor to standing and then to walking, and running.

During the progression through these developmental sequences, PTs analyze children's quality of movement and their patterns of transition within a sequence. In the case of children who walk fairly well, other more advanced motor skills may be evaluated, including stair climbing, jumping, throwing and catching a ball, and balancing (Johnston & Magrab, 1976).

Sometimes children's motor delays are obvious, as in Billy's case (see Box 7.1). Children who cannot participate in motor activities in which their peers engage may have a motor delay. For example, some children can ride a tricycle by pushing the pedals whereas others the same age can move the tricycle only by pushing off the floor with their feet (Campbell, 1987a).

In other cases, behavior indicating a delay in gross-motor skills may be more subtle (Johnston & Magrab, 1976). For example, children may kick or push over a balance beam because they know they cannot walk across it. In addition to other general assessment discussed in Chapter 2, the Test of Gross Motor Development, Second Edition (TGMD-2) is a standardized test commonly used during the assessment of motor development in children 3 years and older. Figure 7.1 lists behaviors that children may manifest that may indicate gross-motor delays.

Billy, the child discussed in Box 7.1, has many of the characteristics listed in Figure 7.1. These delays are likely to interfere with future gross-motor, fine-motor, cognitive, adaptive, and social-emotional development.

Sometimes, however, children's motor delays are inaccurately evaluated as behavioral problems. Children may be described as having behavioral problems when, in fact, they do not have the physical control needed to do what is asked (Campbell, 1978b). These children may be aware of their own limitations and use inappropriate

Figure 7.1   **Behavior That May Indicate Gross-Motor Delays**

Significant gross-motor delays may be found in children 2 years and older who

- frequently trip, fall, or bump into things or other people;
- have balance problems;
- need extra support to maintain basic positions;
- frequently avoid gross-motor activities;
- tire easily;
- seem fearful of or avoid playground equipment or certain types of gross-motor equipment, such as a slide;
- frequently lag behind other children during transitional activities;
- use age-inappropriate movement patterns, such as a four-year-old's always walking on tiptoes; or
- act silly or misbehave when requested to participate in a gross-motor activity.

behavior to divert attention from their inability to perform a gross-motor task (Fiorentino, 1972). For example, a child may run around the room to avoid activities they find difficult, such as throwing and catching a ball.

The PT develops a summary statement of all observations, including the effects of motor delays on classroom and at-home functioning, social interactions, and, when appropriate, level of self-esteem. Most agencies and schools require standardized assessment and scoring using developmental motor scales as additional evidence of the need for physical therapy intervention (Berger & Fowlkes, 1980).

As with other types of delay, if it is determined that a child has a significant gross-motor development delay, physical therapy may be provided. Evaluations and recommendations the PTs make are typically presented to a Committee on Preschool Special Education (CPSE), department of health, or other designated agency (agencies responsible for approving children to receive agency-funded therapy services vary from state to state). Following approval for physical therapy treatment, the child's physician must write a prescription authorizing physical therapy. Although evaluations may be performed without a doctor's prescription, in most states therapy cannot occur without a prescription (Dubowitz, 1990).

Fine-Motor Assessment

Before, during, or shortly after a child's birth, it may be determined that the child has a physical delay that requires an OTR's services. In other cases, it is not until a child is a toddler or attending a day care or preschool program that motor delays are detected. If a child is already enrolled in a preschool program, referrals for OTR services are usually generated by the child's teacher or other professionals working closely with the child on a regular basis. If a child is not enrolled in a preschool program, referral sources include pediatricians, public health nurses, other health professionals, or the parents, as in the case of PT referrals.

A screening is usually requested by teachers or other professionals working with the child or by parents concerned about the child's ability to function in daily activities. Potential areas of concern include social and play skills, activities of daily living such as eating and washing hands, or preacademic skills such as prewriting (tracing shapes and letters) and reading readiness.

Occupational Therapists. There are two types of occupational therapy professionals. A registered OTR has a minimum of a bachelor's degree and has 6 to 9 months of field work in occupational therapy; they may also have a master's or doctorate in occupational therapy or a related field. A **certified occupational therapy assistant (COTA)** has an associate's degree and field work in occupational therapy. OTRs and COTAs are required to pass a national registration exam to practice occupational therapy, and most states now require licensing as well. Some states further require licensed therapists to periodically take courses and attend seminars on occupational therapy to continue to qualify for licensing. This chapter refers to all people providing occupational therapy as OTRs.

Occupational Therapy Screening. The screening assesses whether a full, in-depth occupational therapy evaluation is warranted (Rogers, 1982). If a full evaluation is deemed necessary, the school district's CPSE is petitioned for approval. If the evaluation is approved, an OTR conducts it and generates specific goals for areas in which delays are detected. These recommendations are then taken back to the CPSE for approval before treatment begins. Once committee approval is obtained, it is usually the parent's responsibility to obtain a written prescription from a doctor for specific occupational therapy services. OTRs practicing in New York state or any of many other states are required by law to have a written medical prescription before treating any child.

Occupational Therapy Full Assessment. The stated occupational therapy goals and objectives determined during the initial evaluation become part of the child's individualized family service plan (for children less than 3 years old) or individualized education program (for children 3–5 years old). Annual reassessment will occur to evaluate changes in the child's growth and development. Any changes in, additions of, or deletions of goals are made at the time of the annual evaluation (Malina, 1980; McEwen, 2000). As discussed throughout this book, parental input is an important part of this process.

There are many ways an OTR can assess a child's level of performance. As in the case of physical therapy evaluations, one of the primary sources of information is clinical observations. Clinical observations are objective observations of children in their typical environment (home or school) while engaged in daily activities. Through these observations information is gathered on muscle tone, range of motion, and social and play skills. Often, OTRs and PTs exchange and compare information obtained during observations. Information gathered from the child's teachers and parents is also used in the evaluation process. In addition, OTRs may use formal evaluation tools.

Motor Disabilities

Although assessment of motor abilities often leads to children's qualifying for intervention services targeted at enhancing motor abilities, several disabilities include motor delays as the primary area of impairment—for example, cerebral palsy, muscular dystrophy, multiple sclerosis, spina bifida, and amputations. In addition, other disabilities have motor delays as a secondary condition.

Cerebral Palsy

Cerebral palsy (CP) is a lifelong, irreparable, nonprogressive disorder, resulting from brain damage, that affects movement and coordination (Bleck, 1987). *Cerebral* refers to the brain while *palsy* refers to movement or posture disorder. Brain damage may occur before, during, or after birth (Russman & Gage, 1989).

Anoxia, lack of oxygen to the brain before or during birth, is one of the most common causes of cerebral palsy. Low-birth-weight infants are more than 200 times more susceptible to cerebral palsy than children who did not have low birth weights. Childhood diseases such as meningitis, encephalitis, or influenza may also result in cerebral palsy. Head injuries resulting from accidents, child abuse, or poisoning (e.g., from lead or carbon monoxide) may also result in cerebral palsy. In about 25% of all cases of cerebral palsy, the causes are unknown (Pellegrino, 2002).

CP may affect different groups of muscles. In **diplegia CP** only the legs are affected. In **hemiplegia CP** one side of the body is affected. In **quadriplegia CP** all four extremities are affected; facial and torso muscles may be affected as well. The degree of muscle involvement varies from mild (very little effect) to severe (almost total incapacity). Children with cerebral palsy often have associated disabilities that affect vision, hearing, speech, perception, or behavior (Pellegrino, 2002).

Children with **spastic CP** can move the affected muscles voluntarily, but the movement is slow, stiff, and erratic (jerky). This form of CP accounts for approximately 80% of all CP cases. It is characterized by one or more tight muscle groups that limit movement. Children with spastic CP often have difficulty moving from one position to another, as well as difficulty holding or letting go of objects. In addition, facial expressions are often affected.

Children with **athetosis CP** constitute about 10% of CP cases. They walk in a lurching, nonrhythmical manner; have difficulty controlling their posture (due to low muscle tone); and appear to move constantly. They may squirm or grimace as they try to accomplish voluntary muscular activities. Athetosis CP involuntary movements may interfere with activities requiring coordinated movements, including speaking, feeding, reaching, and grasping. Also common is involuntary grimacing and tongue thrusting, which can result in swallowing problems, drooling, and slurred speech. Involuntary movements associated with this form of CP are likely to increase during periods of emotional stress and diminish during sleep.

About 10% of children with cerebral palsy have what is known as **mixed-type CP.** Spasticity is the first noticeable attribute of this form of CP. In the case of children with mixed-type CP, involuntary movements typically increase between 9 months and 3 years of age. The most common mixed form includes spasticity and athetoid movements, but other combinations occur.

Children who have **ataxic CP** have low muscle tone and poor coordination. They appear unsteady and shaky (tremor-like) and have an impaired sense of balance and depth perception. Children with ataxic CP walk by placing their feet unusually far apart, high step, and are prone to falling. About 5 to 10% of the children diagnosed with CP have ataxic CP.

Therapy for children with CP typically involves a team that includes an OTR, PT, and speech–language pathologist. Early and ongoing treatment reduces the effects of CP. Special equipment such as braces, splints, and adaptive toys are often required for children with CP. Box 7.2 provides a brief story of a young child who was diagnosed with cerebral palsy.

Muscular Dystrophy

Muscular dystrophy (MD) is a class of diseases involving the voluntary muscles. Muscular dystrophy is an incurable, usually painless, progressive disease. It results in gradual muscle deterioration, leading to the need for a wheelchair. The small muscles of the hand are usually the last to deteriorate.

The most common form is **Duchene's MD** (sometimes referred to as **"pseudo-hypertrophic MD"** or **"childhood MD"**). Onset usually occurs between 2 and 6 years old. This form of MD affects only males. Most children with Duchene's MD die between 10 and 15 years after onset. Early signs of Duchene's MD include a waddle-like walk, swayback, difficulty climbing stairs and getting up from the floor, and calf-muscle enlargement (Dubowitz, 1978). This is the only form of MD affecting children. Other forms are found in male and female adolescents and adults.

Therapy for MD involves occupational and physical therapy activities, including strengthening muscles and doing breathing exercises to help keep the lungs healthy. Sometimes slings, braces, or other special devices are used. Very young children usually have a limited number of symptoms, although they are likely to have

Box 7.2 *Milena*

Milena was born 7 weeks early. Everyone, including the doctors, initially believed that she was surprisingly healthy for so premature a baby. Two days later, just as everyone was confident that Milena would be going home in a couple of weeks, she stopped breathing. She was quickly resuscitated. The doctors were unable to determine why Milena had stopped breathing, and they detected no other problems. Milena went home after 3 weeks in the hospital. Her mother noted that she had trouble sucking her bottle and drooled excessively. At six months, Milena had not rolled over and could not sit well even when supported. In response to the concerns of Milena's mother, the pediatrician referred Milena to a developmental specialist, who informed Milena's parents that Milena had CP.

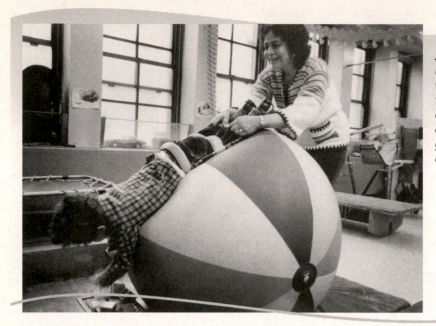

A physical therapist uses a therapy ball with a young child to provide exercise designed to enhance gross-motor development.

difficulty climbing stairs. When symptoms are noted, these children often benefit from special exercises.

Multiple Sclerosis

Multiple sclerosis (MS) is a rare degenerative nervous-system disease leading to the loss of myelin, which covers the nerves. It is mentioned here because MS is often confused with MD. The cause of MS is unknown. It is not infectious, and the course of the disease is unpredictable. It leads to muscle weakness, loss of coordination, and visual impairment and may affect intellectual functioning. This disease rarely occurs in children (Pratt & Allen, 1989).

Spina Bifida

Another type of physical disability is **spina bifida** (**SB,** cleft spine), a condition in which the spine has not completely closed and which causes some nerves to protrude. SB is the most common permanently disabling birth defect (Williamson, 1987). This condition usually occurs in the lower part of the spine. Below this point on the spine, children are partially or completely paralyzed. The child may not have bowel or bladder control. Infants with spina bifida may also have hydrocephalus, too much fluid around the brain (Brooke, 1991; Lutkenhoff, 1999).

Types of spina bifida range from mild to severe. **SB occulta** includes an opening in one or more vertebrae without obvious spinal cord damage. **Meningocele** occurs when the spinal cord's protective covering (meninges) protrudes through the opening in the vertebrae; it is characterized by an intact spinal cord. Typically, this form of SB can be repaired with little or no nerve damage.

Myelomeningocele is the most severe form of SB in which a portion of the spinal cord protrudes through the back. The spinal sacs may be covered with skin, or nerves may be exposed. Approximately 70 to 90% of children born with myelomeningocele have hydrocephalus. Fluid in the brain can be relieved with the surgical placement of a shunt (drain). Without this procedure the pressure buildup can cause brain damage, seizures, or blindness. These children often have learning difficulties, including difficulty paying attention and expressing and understanding language.

SB is a very serious condition usually discovered at birth. Typically, the infant undergoes surgery to close the lesion. If the hydrocephalus does not spontaneously stop, an operation is performed to shunt the excess fluid away from the brain to other parts of the body. If the shunt stops working, the child may become lethargic, complain of headaches, and vomit. This situation requires immediate medical attention.

As mentioned above, because children with SB may have muscle weakness or paralysis below the affected area of the spine and lack bowel or bladder control, they often need a **prosthesis** to walk. Prostheses include braces, crutches, walkers, and wheelchairs. To avoid pressure sores, children with SB should be prompted to change positions frequently while sitting. They may learn to use the upper parts of their body quite well. They may become independent in self-help skills, wheelchair skills, and other activities with the help of an OTR/PT (Williamson, 1987).

Amputations

Amputations, acquired and congenital, are another cause of physical disability. Of the acquired amputations, almost 70% result from some type of injury; the remaining result from disease. Congenital amputation includes complete or partial absence of one or more limbs. Children born without an arm or a leg typically are fitted with a prosthesis when they are between 3 and 6 months old (Hale, 1979).

Parents and teachers of children with amputations may need to help children adapt to various activities and environments. For example, therapy for a child who has lost a leg begins with activities designed to enhance balance and then progresses to walking and developing endurance. After the child learns to move well indoors, the child receives training for participating in outdoor activities such as going to a playground.

Most children can learn to control a prosthesis (artificial limb) by 4 or 5 years of age. Children who must concentrate on controlling a prosthesis are likely to tire quickly. Children who have an amputation often need occupational or physical therapy to help them learn to use the artificial limb (Tingey-Michaelis, 1983).

Rett Syndrome

Rett syndrome (RS) is a rare neurodevelopmental genetic disorder resulting in developmental arrest or lack of brain maturation. It is seen almost exclusively in females and occurs in all racial and ethnic groups. Children with RS are healthy at birth and appear to have normal development during early infancy. The age at which RS begins usually is 6–18 months. The severity of different symptoms varies.

A period of regression follows onset of this disorder. The child loses communication skills and purposeful use of their hands. The head does not continue at a normal rate of growth. Children with RS often display stereotyped hand movements and gait disturbances. They also frequently display disorganized breathing patterns and seizures. There are often periods when the child will continually grow. Over time, motor problems often increase while eye gaze, seizures, and irregular breathing may improve. A child with RS may have difficulty crawling or walking. They are likely to survive into adulthood if serious illnesses and other complications do not occur. RS is often misdiagnosed as autism, cerebral palsy, or nonspecific developmental delay (Kerr & Ravine, 2003).

Physical Therapy

For young children with developmental disabilities, physical therapy focuses on maintaining and improving the use of bones, joints, muscles, and nerves. Treatment is provided by a trained PT.

Blueprints for Gross-Motor Development

Early motor development lays the foundation for development of later motor skills, as well as skills in other areas (Bayley, 1935). There are no specific ages at which motor milestones must occur. Charts listing the ages at which developmental milestones are typically achieved, such as those provided in Chapter 2, provide guidelines for understanding the sequences and typical rates of motor development (Johnston & Magrab, 1976). These charts are often referred to as **blueprints for gross-motor development.**

If children cannot perform a particular motor skill within the prescribed age range, that alone does not suggest a significant motor delay. Other factors must be taken into account, including overall motor development, ability to function in daily activities, muscle tone, motivation, and whether the delay affects cognitive, language, or social-emotional development (Zaichkowsky et al.,1980). It is difficult to determine whether children younger than 3 years old have significant gross-motor delays because children's rates of motor development vary greatly. For example, children usually walk at about 12 months old, but a normal range for learning how to walk is 7–18 months old (Berger & Fowlkes, 1980).

Motor delays do not necessarily qualify preschool-age children for access to free physical therapy through a public school or clinic. It must be documented that the motor delay or disorder interferes with learning or that the child's physical safety is at risk. Children who do not exhibit gross-motor skills typical of their age but who function well within a day care setting and at home are not likely to qualify for funding of the therapy (Casto & Mastropieri, 1986).

Common Parental Concerns about Physical Therapy

Many parents are concerned when they are told that their child should receive physical therapy because they believe the therapy is painful. When therapy is done correctly, it does not cause excessive pain. Children may resist therapy because it often makes them tired, just as exercise makes many people tired. Therapists must determine children's tolerance of therapy and work within that limit. PTs work toward increasing a child's ability to endure exercises by lengthening the duration of the therapy. They also vary activities to maintain children's interest (Brooke, 1991).

Most children are eager to participate in individual therapy because they receive the therapist's undivided attention. They also enjoy participating because equipment and activities used during physical therapy are often novel and attractive. Within the classroom, children generally welcome therapists because therapists help them feel more confident while participating in activities (Fraser & Hensinger, 1983).

Parents may be concerned that the child is getting either too much or too little therapy. When children receive therapy paid for by the parents, parents may negotiate a change in the frequency of therapy with the therapist. When children receive therapy paid for by public funding, parents must discuss changes in the frequency of services with the therapist and classroom teacher. Typically, the CPSE in the school district in which the child resides must meet to discuss and authorize schedule changes (Orelove & Sosbey, 1987).

Parents may be concerned that a stigma will be attached to a child receiving therapy. Children often are sensitive to the attitudes of those around them. If peers, teachers, or parents have a negative view of therapy, children are more likely to develop a negative attitude. To help children avoid feeling that they are being singled out, therapists may work with two or more children who have gross-motor delays at the same time (i.e., use small-group therapy). It is important for parents to realize that it is generally more stigmatizing to appear clumsy than to receive therapy (Fraser & Hensinger, 1983).

Physical Therapy Models

Developmental Model. The **developmental model** provides therapy by teaching children skills in the order in which they appear in the normal developmental sequence. This is also called a **bottom-up model** because it moves a child from low-level skills to more-complex ones (Casto & Mastropieri, 1986).

For example, an 18-month-old whose gross-motor development is at a 3-month-old level would be taught skills in the same sequence in which babies normally acquire them, starting at the 3-month level. For instance, the sequence of therapy might move from holding up the head to rolling from stomach to back and back to stomach. The bottom-up model stresses the need to master earlier developmental stages before attempting motor skills found later in the developmental sequence (Bayley, 1935).

The goal of this developmental approach is to let children catch up to the point at which they no longer have significant gross-motor delays. When a PT uses this model, their primary role is to move each child step by step through the normal developmental sequence of gross-motor skills acquisition. This model may be helpful for children whose development is 3 to 12 months delayed or who are less than 3 or 4 years old. In the case of children who have severe gross-motor delays, this is generally not the most effective model for therapy (Jaeger, 1987).

Top-Down Model.   Typically, moving through the normal sequence of skills acquisition is not the best therapeutic method for children who are no longer infants or toddlers because they do not have time to practice all the skills found in the normal developmental sequence. It is unlikely that these children will catch up using the bottom-up model. Children who have severe or profound motor delays appear to benefit most from using the **top-down model.** This model focuses on developing the basic functional (adaptive) motor skills (movements needed to engage in day-to-day activities) needed for adult life (Hale, 1979).

Research by the Kern County School District indicated that by age 7 or 8 years, children with severe gross-motor delays typically begin a gradual regression on developmental scales. As children's bodies become larger, gravity becomes the enemy. Proper positioning becomes harder, and children often are left in one place because it becomes increasingly difficult to move them around. For instance, bathing and eating require one-on-one assistance (Perske, Clifton, McClean, & Stein, 1986). If children are not toilet-trained by 7 years, attempts to do so are often abandoned. These goals, however, do not need to be abandoned when implementing the top-down model (Snow & Hooper, 1994).

Top-down therapy combines natural body movements with an instructional process. It does not focus on normal skills in a set developmental sequence. The focus is on the child's using normal life activities to systematically acquire motor skills (Lifchez & Winslow, 1979). For example, if the goal is to have the child learn to hold a cup, this skill would be developed *without* the child's first having less complex skills found at earlier stages of development. In the top-down method, the steps needed to hold a cup would be broken down by completing a task analysis. Each step would be taught until mastered, and the child would be moved through the steps until the target goal of independently holding and drinking from a cup was reached (Gold, 1976).

PTs frequently provide consultation to other team members, including parents, to help the team develop a top-down plan designed to let children practice skills while engaged in other educational and leisure activities (Williamson, 1987). PTs typically consult with children's parents and teachers regarding goals that they believe will be useful for each child. Teachers and parents are then instructed on how to integrate activities and appropriate body positioning into daily routines to help children meet specific goals (Finnie, 1975).

For therapy to be effective, and for the child to become more independent, the child must practice skills every day, and these practice sessions must be integrated into daily activities. Appropriate movement, rather than static positioning, is crucial for improving bone and muscle health and developing independent skills. Merely placing children in good static (fixed, without movement) positions does not teach them how to move. Also, using substitutes for motor skills, such as adaptive equipment, does not teach motor skills (Casto & Mastropieri, 1986). To move children toward greater independence, therapy plans must include gradual reductions of physical aid provided to the children. Children should be given only as much help as they absolutely need to accomplish movement (Cartwright, 1981).

Using a top-down model, a set of skills such as sitting, standing, and walking may be taught simultaneously. In this case, goals for standing correctly might be introduced before sitting skills are mastered. In contrast, the developmental model would require that sitting skills be mastered before standing skills were introduced. The top-down approach is based on the assumption that most people can learn to sit, stand, and walk when given enough physical assistance and that children can improve their motor skills if they are taught and practiced systematically (Jaeger, 1987). With the top-down model the question is not "Can they learn?" but "How long will it take them to learn?"

Physical Therapy Services

Recommendations for physical therapy treatment may include direct treatment on an individual basis, ongoing monitoring of the child's gross-motor skills when delays are minimal, consultation with the teaching staff to encourage carry-over of the physical therapy goals, and gross-motor therapy intervention with groups of children (Baker & Brightman, 2004). Practicing gross-motor skills is important for building endurance and confidence regarding activities involving specific gross-motor skills. Group therapy activities are particularly effective for this purpose (American Physical Therapy Association, 1996).

The goal of physical therapy is for children to generalize motor skills performed during therapy to various situations and environments (Crump, 1987). Called home plans, plans that suggest physical therapy activities to integrate into daily activities at home are crucial to meet the goal of generalizing motor skills. PTs show parents how to integrate therapy activities safely so that parents do not injure the child (Thompson et al., 1983). Once children begin receiving physical therapy, it is important for parents and therapists to maintain regular communication to exchange information about the child's progress. It is useful to determine whether the child is using newly acquired skills within the home and school environments and allow parents to ask questions about therapy goals and activities (Tingey-Michaelis, 1983).

When children receive physical therapy in school, at a day care program, or in a clinic, it is often helpful for parents to occasionally observe the therapy sessions. These observations allow parents to see what occurs during therapy. During the sessions, PTs may show parents activities and exercises that should be practiced at home and how to best use toys or other equipment (Berger & Fowlkes, 1980). Children need many opportunities to practice various types of skills and patient, supportive adults who give them practice time.

Physical therapy requires a major commitment of time and may be exhausting to therapists, parents, and children. However, the effort is warranted because physical therapy often results in less energy being needed for daily-living activities (e.g., dressing the child) once children are physically more independent. Moving children from little or no self-care to independent self-care results in less time being spent on custodial care (Lifchez & Winslow, 1979).

Parents and professionals work together to develop a plan that helps children develop gross-motor skills. Goals should be set that are appropriate to the child's developmental level. After goals are established, task analysis is used to break skills to be acquired into small incremental steps (Davis & Broadhead, 2007). These steps are gradually introduced and focused on until mastered. Once skills have been well established, it is necessary to develop a maintenance plan and help children generalize skills learned during therapy to new and varied situations.

In some cases the focus of therapy may not be on developing skills but on changing muscle tone. Children with high muscle tone have difficulty consciously making their muscles relax. When they get excited or exert effort, muscles become tenser. In this case exercises designed to help children relax may decrease muscle tension. Children engaged in enjoyable activities gradually become more relaxed as they experience success. Children with low muscle tone become stronger with practice that occurs in routine daily activities. Exercise helps postpone deformities, and proper positioning slows deterioration of the skeletal system, but neither leads to skills development (Beller, 1979).

Most children love to explore their environment because exploration helps satisfy their natural curiosity. Much of what they learn is acquired through movement. Movement is required for nearly all forms of work and play (Bigge, 1991; Pauls & Reed, 2003).

Parents, day care providers, and preschool staff must make sure that all children have daily opportunities for gross-motor activities (Dubowitz, 1990). This is especially true for children with gross-motor delays. Providing time for gross-motor movement helps children with motor delays develop new skills and helps those without motor delays to continue to develop age-appropriate skills. Gross-motor activities also provide children with a positive outlet for their seemingly boundless energy.

Early intervention is often valuable for children with motor delays. A mild delay may turn into a more severe delay without appropriate intervention (Orelove & Sosbey, 1987). Early intervention also allows PTs to help children more comfortably progress through the development of normal movement patterns before the children develop bad habits (Blackman, 1984).

Typically, the earlier children receive intervention, the more positive the outcome for their life-long motor development (Baker & Brightman, 1989). As children grow, gaps between their rate of development and typical rates often increase, making it less likely that they will attain average levels of development. When children have positive experiences with therapy at a young age, they are more likely to be willing to continue therapy, if necessary, as they get older (Bartel & Guskin, 1980).

Children who receive physical therapy as very young children often perceive therapy as a normal activity. In addition, unlike school-age children, preschool-age peers typically do not question why other children receive physical therapy or react in a judgmental fashion. However, if peers do react negatively—for example, by saying, "What's wrong with you?"—children in therapy may feel less positive about themselves (Bartel & Guskin, 1980).

Providing Physical Support during Therapy. PTs help improve the sitting posture of preschoolers by physically supporting children who sit on their laps or on the floor. PTs help teachers and parents learn where to place their hands to best support children (i.e., which location most encourages development of muscle tone). Providing too much support discourages muscle development, while providing too little may result in children's avoiding or not participating in activities they find challenging (Wolff, 1979).

Some children benefit from additional chair support. For example, a **Rifton chair,** which has a solid back and sides and widely spaced legs that prevent rocking the chair, may provide support that allows children to focus more readily on tasks. A Velcro® seat belt may be used for preschoolers who need to sit in this type of chair, to help support their hips. Feet should be placed flat on the floor to provide additional support. Therapists should advise parents and teachers about the correct size chair for the child (Seamon & Depauw, 1989).

Chair height should allow children to place their feet flat on the floor with their knees below hip level. If a chair of proper height is unavailable, a step should be placed in front of the chair at the level at which the feet are flat on the step. Proper sitting position is crucial for learning because the less energy that children use to maintain a position, the more energy they have left to focus on the activity (Tansley, 1986). Children with gross-motor delays often sit on a chair while playing at a table even if the table is at standing height. These children should be encouraged to stand for as long as possible at the table to enhance their muscle strength.

It is important, though, to set realistic expectations to avoid frustrating or overtiring children who have gross-motor delays. Expectations vary from child to child, depending on the current level of functioning. One child may be able to walk on a balance beam independently, another may need a hand held, and another may merely want someone close by for additional help if needed. It is important to acknowledge that children may be successful at different levels.

Activities should be geared to each child's developmental level. For example, most 4-year-olds can hop on one foot. If a 4-year-old cannot, the child should be offered activities that develop prerequisite skills, such as balancing and strength, that are needed for hopping. If a 4-year-old is unable to perform motor skills typically mastered by 4-year-olds, the teacher should provide tasks appropriate for that child.

Adults need to closely monitor children's movement and serve as spotters, watching the children as they play. To further protect children with motor delays, people must evaluate and maintain the environment to ensure safety. Furniture may need to be moved, and extra supervision may be required to help ensure that children can safely maneuver in their environment.

Physical Therapy during Daily Activities.   Physical therapy activities may readily be integrated into classroom and home routines (Jaeger, 1987). Turning activities into game-like events helps increase the likelihood that activities are attractive to children. For instance, most children enjoy climbing on large equipment and playing with things such as a bright, sturdy very large (more than 3 feet in diameter) therapy ball, often used as therapy equipment. Pretending to go on a camping trip would encourage children to climb over, under, and through various pieces of equipment; they would be working on balance and coordination while having fun.

Occupational Therapy

Once a child has been identified as needing early intervention services, occupational therapy may be one of the services provided. An OTR working in an early intervention program delivers services geared toward children's reaching normal motor developmental milestones with maximum focus on fine-motor development (American Occupational Therapy Association, 2000).

As the importance of occupational therapy has become more widely recognized, its role has been clarified. In 1986 the American Occupational Therapy Association adopted this definition, which nonmedical professionals can understand: "Occupational therapy is the therapeutic use of self-care, work, and play activities to increase independent function, enhance development, and prevent disability. It may include adaptation of task or environment to achieve maximum independence and to enhance the quality of life" (Pratt & Allen, 1989, p. 2).

Developmental Areas Addressed by Occupational Therapy

After being told that their child needs occupational therapy, parents often think, "But my child doesn't need a job." The word *occupation* misleads many people. However, in its broadest sense *occupation* includes all areas of daily activity, such as bathing, dressing, learning, and working.

OTRs work with a wide variety of populations, including children, the elderly, the developmentally disabled, and the mentally ill. Typically, OTRs who work with children younger than school-age use play as the principal teaching strategy. Children who have physical limitations or motor delays that require adaptive equipment often receive therapy services from OTRs as well as PTs (Bailey & Wolery, 1984). Locations at which OTRs may provide therapy to such children include schools, nursing homes, day treatment centers, hospitals, and private practices. Occupational therapy is holistic therapy that focuses on treating the entire person, including their physical, social, and emotional needs (Lerner, Mardell-Czudnowski, & Goldenberg, 1987; Walker & Ludwig, 2004).

When working with children in a preschool setting, OTRs generally work on a team with other professionals. The team may include teachers, PTs, social workers, speech and language pathologists, and psychologists. Team members work together to address areas of delay as determined through a formal evaluation of the child (Connolly & Russell, 1978).

Occupational Therapy Intervention Services

As mentioned earlier, occupational therapy intervention is applied to a wide variety of populations and in various settings. Within the pediatric framework, OTRs are involved with children birth through 21 years old. Pediatric intervention is broken down into three phases: infants (birth to 2 years), preschoolers (2–5 years), and school-age children (5 years and older).

Controversy surrounds early intervention for infants. It is unclear whether children younger than 1 year experience direct, lasting positive effects from occupational therapy. However, the law currently mandates early intervention for all children birth to 2 years old who qualify for services. As stated by Hopkins and Smith (1991), "Statistics have shown that while 1 to 2% of neonates are classified with developmental disabilities, the number of children with identified problems increases to 8 to 9% by school age and 11 to 12% if estimates of preschoolers with significant developmental problems are included" (p. 99).

The main goal of occupational therapy is to enhance a child's daily experiences. This goal is accomplished through direct treatment, fabrication of equipment as needed (such as hand-splinting), and environmental adaptation if necessary. OTRs focus on enhancing a child's ability to be independent (Fredrick & Fletcher, 1985).

A main area of emphasis of occupational therapy for children is upper-extremity functional skills, such as the ability to hold a rattle or bang two blocks together (Trombly, 1983). Enhancement of a child's ability to interact with the environment is included in the treatment of upper-extremity skills. Postural stability and control, such as the ability to remain upright when sitting, is an upper-extremity skill that may be strengthened during therapy. Upper-extremity skills therapy also includes independence in self-care skills, such as bringing objects to the mouth to self-feed (Morris, 1977).

At birth, children have several primitive reflexes that dominate upper-extremity movement. These obligatory (involuntary) movements control a child's movement and block the ability to move voluntarily. Between the ages of 4 and 6 months, these primitive reflexes begin to become integrated, or nonobligatory (voluntary). At this point children typically begin to develop purposeful body movements, such as rolling from side to side, reaching, grasping, and releasing objects (Copeland, 1982).

In most cases, inborn reflexes such as sucking or grasping gradually disappear from a child's repertoire. If these primitive reflex patterns do not become integrated at an early age, the child's pediatrician or another professional may recommend therapeutic intervention (Levy, 1974). Occupational therapy intervention focuses on helping a child to move through specific motor developmental stages, as well as assisting in educating family members about methods to enhance a child's development through proper positioning and play activities at home (Jaeger, 1987, 1989).

When children mature and begin to learn by exploring their environment, other aspects of development may be assessed (Jensen, 2000). For example, the refinement of **prehension** (grasping) and manipulation skills can be monitored. These skills include bilateral manipulation skills; the ability to meticulously use two hands together develops and ultimately enables children to perform functional skills such as passing a toy back and forth between two hands and more-complex skills such as tying shoes. The preferred use of a dominant hand begins to emerge between 2 and 3 years of age.

Specific Goals of Occupational Therapy

OTRs provide therapy in a number of areas, including development of upper-extremity proximal stability, visual perception, cognitive-adaptive skills, sensory integration, and self-care skills (Bundy, 1991). OTRs also help evaluate, design, and fabricate assistive equipment; determine appropriate seating and positioning;

and evaluate the environment to determine any need for modifications (Frostig & Maslow, 1970).

Upper-Extremity Proximal Stability. **Upper-extremity proximal stability** refers to the stability (firmness) of a child's body from the trunk and shoulders (the proximal area) to the arms and hands (the distal area). Proximal stability is believed to be the foundation on which hand skills develop. Proximal stability assists children in sitting upright, which allows them to participate in tabletop activities (Frostig & Maslow, 1970).

Because of the importance of proximal stability, the OTR often places children on therapy equipment such as bolsters or scooter boards to enhance proximal stability. Working the trunk and upper body through exercises and activities is thought to promote proximal stability and distal hand skills (use of fingers for fine-motor manipulation), which are needed for nearly all areas of educational and daily life (Larsen & Hammill, 1975).

Visual-Perceptual Motor Skills. **Visual-perceptual motor skills** are another area of emphasis in occupational therapy. These skills relate to children's physical responses to visual stimulation. These skills are later used in skills such as reading from left to right or copying from a blackboard. During occupational therapy treatment, OTRs introduce activities that begin to challenge a child's visual-perceptual performance skills. They often do this by breaking tasks into small steps and guiding children to increasingly complex steps. Activities such as finding hidden pictures (which involves distinguishing between figure and ground), bingo and lotto (which entail visual scanning), concentration or memory card games (which involve visual memory and matching), stringing beads, sewing cards, and block design replication (which entails perception of visual-spatial relations) address different aspects of visual-perceptual motor skills. Figure 7.2 provides an example of a task broken down into sequential steps.

Cognitive-Adaptive Skills. **Cognitive-adaptive skills** are another area of focus in occupational therapy. These skills include a child's ability to cognitively, emotionally, and physically interact with others and adapt to different environmental situations such as going to a new classroom, adjusting to rearrangement of the classroom, or adjusting to new teachers.

OTRs work with family members and teaching staff to assess skills acquisition and formulate and present activities designed to enhance growth and development in this area. Some of the assessed elements of cognitive-adaptive skills include how children interact with peers and adults in one-to-one and group situations, whether they play or sit with peers or prefer to play alone, how they respond to reinforcement or discipline, and how well they solve problems and adapt to new people and situations. For a more in-depth discussion of social skills, refer to Chapter 8. For more on behavior management, see Chapter 13.

Sensory-Integration Skills. Another area of development that an OTR addresses is **sensory-integration skills.** A child engages in sensory integration when they incorporate sensory information into purposeful, successful interaction with the

Figure 7.2 **Breaking a Task into Steps**

Goal: The child will independently string four beads.

1. The child visually notices the string and beads.
2. The child maintains the posture needed to complete the task (e.g., sits in a chair or on the floor).
3. The child extends one arm and reaches for the string.
4. The child picks up the string using a pincer grasp.
5. The child extends their other arm and picks up a bead.
6. The child positions the bead so that the hole is in the proper position.
7. The child uses the hand holding the string to push the string through the hole.
8. The child grabs the string, passes it through the hole using the pincer grasp, and pulls the string through.
9. The child repeats the process for the remaining beads.

environment. Sensory information is interpreted by all of the senses, including touch (the tactile system), sight (the visual system), hearing (the auditory system), smell (the olfactory system), and balance or equilibrium (the vestibular system) (Ayers, 1972). Chapter 9 provides a more in-depth discussion of sensory integration.

Self-Care Skills. Another area of occupational therapy intervention is **self-care skills,** such as eating, getting dressed, using the toilet, and bathing. These will be discussed in Chapter 11.

Use of Adaptive Equipment. The OTR observes a child's environment to assess the need for **adaptive equipment.** This includes anything that may be used to enhance the child's ability to be independent (Fredrick & Fletcher, 1985). Adaptive equipment is sought only after it is determined that the child cannot perform tasks without such equipment.

The main focus and goal in using adaptive equipment is to help a child function within the environment. The next section describes some types of adaptive equipment. Because equipment is available for numerous skill areas, it is impossible to list all relevant equipment that is commercially available or has been developed by therapists.

Many forms of technology are available for children with disabilities who have a limited ability to independently access their environment. For a child with decreased upper-extremity skills, battery-operated toys can be adapted to allow for single-switch activation. OTRs often incorporate the use of switches in their treatment sessions. Switches enable a child with physical disabilities to activate battery-operated objects such as equipment, toys, or radios (Esposito & Campbell, 1993; McMurray, 1986; Mistrett, Raimondi, & Barnett, 1990).

Play at a sensory table helps enhance a child's sensory integration skills.

Many types of switches are available from commercial manufacturers. Also, many types may be fabricated by family members or therapists for use with toys. Switch activation has opened up a new world for children with special needs. They now have the opportunity to develop more independence in play activities, access computer programs, and activate a speech communication system. All of these opportunities allow children with disabilities to expand their knowledge, skills, and interaction with others and the environment. In the case of children who have severe physical disabilities, special switches are often used to control power wheelchairs that may allow independence in mobility (Landecker, 1980). Parental input regarding a child's ability to function at home with various switches may provide the therapist with the information needed for recommending the appropriate switches (Bleck & Nagel, 1982).

To help children learn to dress independently, adapting the environment may be as simple as changing the type of clothing that they wear. For instance, buttons and zippers may be particularly challenging for the child; therefore, clothes with elastic waistbands, slightly oversized clothes, front rather than back openings, or pullover shirts with loosely woven neck openings may be recommended. Velcro® closures are particularly useful for facilitating independent dressing. Equipment that may help encourage independent dressing includes button hooks, long-handled extenders, and shoehorns (Bleck, 1987).

Bathing a child is often a concern for parents and caregivers. An OTR may recommend that a bathtub be equipped with a nonslip surface or mats inside and out to help prevent falls. Grab-bars secured to the walls may also be recommended for children who require assistance moving in and out of the bathtub (Lazzaro, 1993). Other pieces of equipment may include long-handled sponges, bath mitts (useful for children with limited grasp ability), and handheld shower extensions (Butera & Haywood, 1992).

Using the toilet may also require adaptive equipment. Many different types of toilet seats are available. Children who have poor balance and trunk control may require a seat with handlebars on both sides to help keep them from falling. The height of a toilet seat may need to be modified for a child in a wheelchair. Such issues are best addressed by having the OTR visit the home or classroom. That way the OTR can better determine the most useful adaptive equipment, demonstrate how to use the equipment, and provide information on how to aid a child without injuring the child or oneself (Cannings & Finkel, 1993).

Frequently the OTR needs to recommend adaptive equipment to assist with eating. Many factors may interfere with a child's self-feeding. The type of adaptive equipment that a therapist chooses depends on the nature of the child's problem. For example, a suspension sling, or mobile arm support, may be used to assist arm placement during mealtime. Various types of splints may be used to correct the positions of the hands or arms. Universal cuffs (straps to help secure objects) or utensils with built-up or modified handles may accommodate a weak or absent grasp. Extended handles and swivel spoons may be used for children with limited motion ability in the arms and hands. A nonslip placemat, a plate guard, and scoop dishes often assist children to eat and decrease the amount of spilled food.

These aids also enhance children's ability to feed themselves with only one hand (Carney, 1983). Children who are severely physically disabled may use battery-powered self-feeding devices. Again, the OTR may assist in choosing feeding equipment that may be needed to enhance a child's ability to become more independent, and in teaching the proper use of that equipment.

The terms **orthotics** and **splints** are often used interchangeably, especially in reference to the upper-body extremities. While the professional responsible for fabricating children's splints may vary among facilities, OTRs are typically responsible for recommendations regarding upper-extremity splinting. Many splints can be custom-designed, constructed, fitted, and applied within 1 to 2 hours (Meisels & Shonkoff, 1990).

Other Environmental Modifications. An OTR may recommend ways to adapt the environment to the child's needs. For example, the OTR may recommend accessible bathrooms, drinking fountains, and play materials that encourage independence. An OTR may analyze rooms to determine if they are set up in a way that allows free movement of children who are in wheelchairs or have braces. The OTR should make certain that shelves are strong enough for children with limited muscle strength to lean against or use to pull themselves up. The OTR should help select developmentally appropriate toys and other equipment designed to encourage exploration and learning (Ysseldyke, Algozzine, & Thorlow, 2000).

Importance of Seating and Positioning. The proper seating and positioning of children are of prime importance and may have a major effect on how well they interact with their environment. Bergen (1990) suggests that proper seating and positioning can provide several benefits to children with physical disabilities.

The optimum seating positions for children are straight trunk (back); hips, knees, and ankles flexed to 90 degrees; legs separated; and feet supported, not dangling. It is important that the parent or other caregiver and the therapist work together to develop an appropriate seating system. Physical therapists and speech and language pathologists may also be involved in the process because proper positioning affects children's speech development (Male, 1994).

Funding for assistive equipment is often a critical issue. Families may have insurance that provides coverage for purchased or rented equipment. Funding may also be available through the child's school or the agency providing services for the child. There may also be special funding programs available that a social worker or other personnel could help identify (Male, 1994).

Once a decision has been made regarding a proper seating system, the OTR usually writes a letter of justification, which is sent to the funding source. This letter states why the child needs a particular seating system. Seating systems include wheelchairs, other types of chairs or support systems, and positioning aids.

Conclusions

With regard to children with motor disabilities, PTs and OTRs are often an integral part of a service team in an educational setting. Often, PTs and OTRs collaborate. While some overlap among professionals is desirable, each discipline plays a critical role in the overall treatment of such children.

Physical therapy is a valuable service, especially at the preschool level. Gross-motor delays may be prevented or modified. Physical delays often affect children's cognitive and social skills and attention span. These delays may contribute to negative self-esteem and limit children's abilities to function safely within their environment. Early identification and remediation of motor delays is important. PTs, teachers, and parents must work together to identify, evaluate, and provide services for children.

Like PTs, OTRs are concerned with sensorimotor development, but they focus more on fine-motor rather than gross-motor development. OTRs work with children in a holistic way to enhance function and independence while promoting a positive sense of self through purposeful activity and environmental adaption.

Increasingly, OTRs who work with young children are working side-by-side with teachers in the classroom or with parents at home rather than working one-on-one with a child in a therapy room. This method allows parents and staff to learn how to provide activities that enhance motor development. The goal is to integrate therapy into the child's daily routine. This often is done through play. OTRs should be involved in ongoing staff training in the area of fine-motor skills development.

The OTR is sensitive to each child's cognitive-skills level and introduces only those activities that are likely to provide the child with a feeling of success while challenging them so that their overall development is enhanced. The OTR may also offer suggestions for carry-over (generalization) of these skills by the classroom staff, other therapists, and parents. Carry-over is critical for acquiring these skills because repetition helps increase the likelihood of skills acquisition and because the OTR is with a child for only a limited time.

CHAPTER SUMMARY

- Knowledge about typical rates of fine- and gross-motor development is used to evaluate children who may have motor delays and to monitor their development.

- PTs and OTRs play key roles in the assessment of motor delays. They assess children's level of functioning by observing the child in typical daily activities and by using standardized formal assessment instruments.

- A number of disabilities have motor delays as their primary characteristic—for example, cerebral palsy, MD, MS, spina bifida, amputation, and Rett syndrome.

- Physical therapy focuses on large-motor skills. The goal of physical therapy is for children to generalize motor skills acquired during therapy to everyday situations.

- Occupational therapy focuses on fine-motor skills, including restoring, reinforcing, and enhancing motor performance while focusing on upper-extremity proximal stability, visual-perceptual motor skills, cognitive-adaptive skills, sensory-integration skills, self-care skills, and the development and use of adaptive and assistive equipment.

CHAPTER KEY TERMS

motor development
gross-motor skills
fine-motor skills
physical therapist (PT)
occupational therapist (OTR)
cephalocaudal
proximodistal
behaviorist
information processing
Albert Bandura
Lev Vygotsky
Howard Gardner
Jean Piaget
Arnold Gesell
Developmental Schedules
certified occupational therapy assistant (COTA)
cerebral palsy (CP)
diplegia CP
hemiplegia CP
quadriplegia CP
spastic CP
athetosis CP
mixed-type CP
ataxic CP
muscular dystrophy (MD)

Duchene's MD
pseudohypertrophic MD
childhood MD
multiple sclerosis (MS)
spina bifida (SB)
spina bifida occulta
meningocele
myelomeningocele
prosthesis
amputation
Rett syndrome (RS)
blueprint for gross-motor development
developmental model
bottom-up model
top-down model
Rifton chair
prehension
upper-extremity proximal stability
visual-perceptual motor skills
cognitive-adaptive skills
sensory-integration skills
self-care skills
adaptive equipment
orthotic
splint

REVIEW QUESTIONS

1. How do PTs and OTRs assess motor development in young children?

2. What types of behavior indicate that children may have motor delays? What information do PTs and OTRs collect during screenings and full formal assessments?

3. Why do PTs and OTRs often provide therapy within the young child's normal daily environment?

4. What types of assistive equipment may OTRs recommend?

5. How might a PT or OTR alleviate concerns that parents may have about their child's receiving physical therapy?

SUGGESTED STUDENT ACTIVITIES

1. Visit a local early childhood special education program, and observe an OTR and/or PT providing therapy services.

2. Review the formal assessment instruments listed in this chapter. Describe their purpose, strengths, and weaknesses.

3. Observe an OTR fabricate a piece of assistive equipment. Ask how it would be used, and have the OTR describe how the child and parents would be trained for its proper use.

4. Observe a young child with motor delays, and analyze the environment. Determine what environmental adaption(s) may aid the child.

5. Using Billy's case (Box 7.1), develop a list of recommendations for Billy's teachers and parents.

6. Create a motor activity based on an age-appropriate story book and designed to enhance the motor abilities of 5-year-olds.

Social-Emotional Abilities 8

CHAPTER KEY POINTS

- Social-emotional development affects all other areas of development.

- Several theoretical positions help describe social-emotional development.

- Knowledge about typical social-emotional development is crucial for the development of effective intervention services.

- Biological and environmental factors contribute to social-emotional disabilities.

- When social-emotional disabilities are suspected, prompt referral for evaluation is recommended.

- Formal and informal evaluation methods are used to assess social-emotional development.

- Several types of social-emotional disabilities may occur during early childhood.

- Early intervention designed to meet the needs of children with social-emotional development is useful for young children.

The **social-emotional development** of young children is related to their abilities to experience, regulate, and express emotions; form secure relationships; and explore and learn within the context of family, community, and cultural expectations (Davidson, Jackson, & Kalin, 2000; Wicks-Nelson & Israel, 1991). As children grow older, their social development includes knowledge of social rules and standards and emotional development, including feelings about self and others. This development includes a range of positive and negative emotions and the ability to control and regulate feelings in culturally appropriate ways. Self-worth, self-confidence, and self-regulation are important features of social-emotional development (Whitman, 1990). Healthy social-emotional development is crucial for success in school and life.

The newborn brain is designed to integrate environmental experiences, including social experiences. Inborn capacities often are not maintained when specific environmental experiences are lacking. That is, early social experiences are crucial. Even newborns experience intense feelings and are active participants in their environment. Differentiation and complexity of young children's emotional and social development rapidly increase over a short period of time. Children's development reflects their inborn individual differences as well as attributes of their environments.

Mental health difficulties are linked to environmental stressors as well as biological predispositions. Stigmas regarding mental health problems contribute to the lack of implementation of prevention programs, early identification, and adequate intervention services for young children. Early intervention is crucial because it is estimated that young children who display severe behavioral and emotional problems have a 50% greater chance of mental health problems during adolescence and adulthood.

At the Surgeon General's Conference on Children's Mental Health in 2000, the Surgeon General, Dr. David Satcher, emphasized the importance of children's mental health: "Mental Health is a critical component of children's learning and general health. Fostering social and emotional health in children as a part of healthy child development must, therefore, be a national priority. Both the promotion of mental health in children and the treatment of mental disorders should be major public health goals" (U.S. Public Health Service, 2000).

Theories Related to Social–Emotional Development

Several theories help describe young children's social and emotional development. Various theories focus on specific aspects of social-emotional development. Theories not discussed in previous chapters will be discussed below, and some theories previously discussed are expanded on in terms of social-emotional development.

Behaviorist Theory

As discussed in Chapter 3, **behaviorists** focus on **classical conditioning** to explain how humans develop responses to certain stimuli that are not naturally occurring. For example, when we touch a hot stove (or anything else that is hot), a reflex automatically pulls our hand back due to the heat, not the image of the stove. The response (pulling one's hand away) does not have to be learned; it is a survival instinct. After being burned, some people pull their hand back even if the stove is not turned on. That is, they associate the image of the stove (initially a **neutral stimulus** that did not naturally result in pulling one's hand away) with heat, so that the stove becomes a conditioned stimulus.

In a well-known experiment using Little Albert, **John B. Watson** noted that emotions, particularly emotions related to fear and safety, often develop after a previously neutral experience (e.g., looking out a window) is associated with a negative one (e.g., nearly falling out of the window), thereby creating conditioned fear. One or more instances of negative association may lead to the development of fears or safety concerns (Frolov, 1937).

Watson believed that care providers become **conditioned reinforcers**. He believed attachment is learned through conditioning when care providers meet infants' physical needs. Over time the infant associates care providers with having needs met and then generalizes these feelings into feelings of attachment, security, and so on when care providers are present (Speltz, DeKlyen, & Greenberg, 1999; Vondra, Shaw, Swearingen, Cohen, & Owens, 2001).

B. F. Skinner argued that certain behaviors can be increased by following them with reinforcement (e.g., food, praise, special privileges, or a new toy). Behaviors can also be decreased through the use of punishment (e.g., withdrawal of privileges, scolding, or taking away desired objects). According to Skinner's theory of **operant conditioning**, children acquire a variety of behaviors through interactions with their care providers. For example, infants whose mothers provide them with food and other comforts learn to smile and look at their mothers.

Social Learning Theory

Social learning theory incorporates cognitive and behavioral theories. The social learning theory of **Albert Bandura** emphasizes the importance of observing and modeling others' behaviors, attitudes, and emotional reactions (Grusec, 1992). Bandura argued that most human behavior is learned observationally through modeling. Social learning theory has been extensively applied to the understanding of aggression and psychological disorders. According to Bandura, the basic processes underlying observational learning are

1. attention (e.g., distinctiveness, complexity, prevalence, value) and observer characteristics (e.g., sensory capacities, arousal level, perceptual set, past reinforcement);
2. retention, including symbolic coding, cognitive organization, symbolic rehearsal, and motor rehearsal;
3. motor reproduction, including physical capabilities, self-observation, and accuracy of feedback; and
4. motivation, including external, vicarious, and internal (self-) reinforcement.

Psychoanalytic Theory

The **psychoanalytic theory** of **Sigmund Freud** focuses on five **psychosexual stages** of development and three major components of the personality. The first three stages are relevant to early childhood.

The first stage is the **oral stage**, during which pleasure centers on activities involving the mouth. According to Freud, children are born totally governed by the **id**, which is totally subconscious. The id requires **immediate gratification**, satisfaction of survival needs. The id follows the **pleasure principle**; it desires whatever feels good without considering the reality of the situation (e.g., others' needs or limitations of the environment). For example, when a child is hungry, the id wants food; therefore, the child cries.

The **anal stage** begins at about 18 months and focuses on bowel control. During this period the **ego** develops, although the id remains active and important throughout life. The ego is a more rational component of the personality. The ego—one's sense of self—is governed by the **reality principle** (the understanding that society expects certain types of behavior and that one must consider others' needs and the limitations of the environment). The ego recognizes the value and necessity of **delayed gratification**. The development of the ego corresponds with adults' making demands on children (i.e., expecting certain types of behavior and not others). As the ego develops, children learn that they will not always immediately receive exactly what they want but can nevertheless remain safe and adequately satisfied. The ego meets the id's needs while taking the reality of the situation into account.

According to Freud, during the third stage, the **phallic stage**, children 3 to 6 years old derive pleasure from stimulation of the genitals. During this stage, children learn to identify with their same-sex parent. The **superego** develops during this stage. It guides societal moral development and ethical restraints. Freud believed that the superego develops from the ego. It begins to develop during the third year of life but is not fully developed until adolescence or beyond. Freud believed that the superego controls and regulates impulses and helps the individual achieve structure and stability. It assists people in developing positive self-esteem and becoming law-abiding members of society (Jones, 1981).

Psychosocial Theory

Erik Erikson's psychosocial theory of social-emotional development encompasses the entire life cycle and recognizes the impact of society, history, and culture on personality. Erikson viewed the first stage of development as the foundation for all others; he suggested that it is difficult to advance through later stages if the challenges of the first stage are not resolved. The first three stages are relevant for children 6 years old and younger.

According to Erikson, the issue of **trust versus mistrust** is crucial from birth to approximately 18 months. An infant needs a consistent environment with warm, dependable care providers. When there is inconsistent care or rejection, children are likely to develop a sense of mistrust—the feeling that others will not provide for their needs—which may result in later adjustment problems (Erikson, 1950).

The second psychosocial stage, **autonomy versus shame and doubt,** affects children from 18 months to approximately 36 months. During this stage, children often have difficulty controlling their will (as evidenced by tantrums, stubbornness, or negativism) and accomplishing tasks independently. Well-adjusted children emerge from this stage with a sense of control; they feel proud of their abilities rather than ashamed or doubtful. Too much pressure or control from others may result in children's feeling shame or doubt. An appropriate level of adult support helps children develop a sense of control and positive self-esteem.

From approximately 3 to 6 years of age, children experience the stage of **initiative versus guilt**. Erikson referred to this age as the play age. The primary task during this stage is to develop a sense of competence, purpose, and initiative. Children who are given opportunities to participate in meaningful activities are more likely to develop positive self-esteem and a willingness to pursue activities. When children are not encouraged to make decisions (e.g., when decisions are made without their input or things are done for them that they could do themselves), they tend to feel guilty when they attempt to take the initiative and may look to others to solve their problems and provide for their needs. During this stage, healthy development involves learning through play and cooperation (leading and following). When children are filled with guilt, they are likely to become fearful and overly dependent on others, less likely to make friends, and have delayed development of play skills and imagination. Table 8.1 summarizes the first three stages in Erikson's theory.

Theories Related to Emotional Development

Emotions reflect tendencies present in infancy that continue throughout life. Emotions help define individuality according to their degree of consistency, sensitivity, and responsiveness. In this sense, emotional responses define **temperament** (Kagan, Reznic, & Snidman, 1990; Pedlow, Sanson, Prior, & Oberklaid, 1993; Strayer, 1986). Emotions motivate infants to approach or withdraw from situations and to maintain or terminate stimulation. Infants' emotions communicate needs to care providers as well as communicate feeling.

Infants do not have the full repertoire of emotions at birth. At birth, infants are believed to experience only simple emotions, including distress, contentment, and

Table 8.1	*Erik Erikson's Postulated Stages of Early Childhood*

Stage	Age	Summary
Trust vs. mistrust	0–18 months	Infants develop trusting, loving relationships or sense of mistrust.
Autonomy vs. shame and doubt	18–36 months	Development of physical skills and competencies allows a level of autonomy, whereas lack of competencies leads to shame and doubt.
Initiative vs. guilt	3–6 years	Successes lead to more initiative whereas failures lead to guilt feelings.

Source: From Coles (2001).

interest. Between 2 and 4 months children begin to display happiness, as evidenced in infants' smiles.

During the middle of the infant's first year, others' emotional expressions take on new meaning. The infant engages in **social referencing,** searching out the emotional expressions of significant others, as a guide to behavior. For example, when an infant's mother smiles at a person unknown to the infant, the infant is more likely to engage with that individual; if, instead, the mother looks frightened, the infant is likely to withdraw. Emotions (e.g., interest, surprise, and pleasure) also guide infants' tendencies to explore and learn about the environment.

One limit of young children's emotional understanding is their inability to grasp complex emotions such as gratitude, envy, and pity. They are also unable to make sense of a situation with conflicting cues (e.g., someone laughs after something sad or scary has occurred).

Repeated interactions allow care providers to appropriately adjust their own emotions and actions in relation to children's emotions. Care providers help infants regulate their emotional states (e.g., calm their cries by feeding or comforting them). Repeated experiences with emotionally available care providers help children learn about emotional regulation and how emotions are communicated. During the second year empathy, pride, and shame typically develop.

During the preschool years, most children begin to control their emotional outbursts in accordance with others' reactions. They use strategies to control their emotional response (e.g., cover their ears or eyes). Over time, children observe how adults handle their own feelings. Children often imitate adults' strategies to regulate their own emotions.

Children are born with only two fears: of falling and of loud noises. As a child grows, different fears may be noticed at different times. Having a bad experience or seeing someone else react in a fearful way often contributes to childhood fears. Children's maturity level and emotional susceptibility also affect the types of fears they display.

Theories Related to Children's Temperaments

A number of theorists believe that children are born with a particular temperament, a particular style of interacting with individuals, places, and things. Stella Chess and Alexander Thomas (1986) have identified nine temperament characteristics that are present at birth and influence development throughout life. Studies have demonstrated a connection between temperament traits and level of health and development (Chess & Thomas, 1986). The nine temperament characteristics are listed in Figure 8.1.

The nine temperament traits combine to form three basic temperaments. Approximately 65% of children fit one of three patterns: **easy** (40%), **difficult** (10%), or **slow-to-warm-up** (15%). The other 35% of children display a combination of these patterns (Kagan, 1991a, 1991b). Characteristics of these three types of temperaments are briefly described in Figure 8.2.

Infants classified as having easy temperaments typically respond well to various child-rearing styles, whereas infants classified as difficult often have adjustment problems no matter how their parents interact with them (Bagnato, Neisworth, Salvia, &

Figure 8.1 **Temperament Traits**

- *Activity:* movement and relaxation styles
- *Rhythmicity:* regularity of eating and sleeping habits
- *Approach/withdrawal:* reaction to strangers
- *Adaptability:* need for routines and reaction to transitions
- *Intensity:* level of reaction to situations
- *Mood:* positive or negative outlook
- *Persistence and attention span:* degree and length of perseverance
- *Distractibility:* ability to focus on tasks
- *Sensory threshold:* responsiveness to stimuli

Source: From Chess & Thomas (1986).

Hunt, 1999). Typically, infants classified as slow-to-warm-up take longer to adjust to social situations and initially have a negative orientation to new situations. Adults are affected by children's personalities; infants' temperaments often affect the type of care they receive. Temperament style is related to the development of attachments.

Theories Related to Development of Attachments

Attachment refers to the affectional bond that forms between the infant and individuals who provide consistent care and interactions. Infants' innate tendency to seek and maintain physical proximity with others helps protect them from harm (Gunnar, Brodersen, Nachmias, Buss, & Rigatuso, 1996). The development of

Figure 8.2 **Temperament Types**

- *Easy or flexible*—generally calm, happy, regular in sleeping and eating habits, adaptable, and not easily upset
- *Difficult*—often fussy, irregular in feeding and sleeping habits, fearful of new people and situations, easily upset by noise and commotion, high-strung, and intense in their reactions
- *Slow-to-warm-up*—relatively inactive and fussy, tending to withdraw or react negatively to new situations, although reactions typically become more positive

Source: From Kagan & Snidmar (2004).

attachments clearly ties to Erikson's focus on the development of a sense of trust, which is the primary developmental outcome of the first years of life. Most children become securely attached to nurturing care providers. Over time, most children attach to a variety of people.

Attachment begins and typically grows as the parent and child strengthen their love for each other by synchronizing their communication through touching, smiling, and playing (often referred to as the "dance" between children and their care providers). Primary attachment (attachment to one person) is usually established by 7–8 months of age (Ainsworth, Blehar, Waters, & Wall, 1978). Unfortunately, insecure attachments do occur.

According to **John Bowlby** (1980), primarily during the first 2 years of life the quality of attachment evolves over time as infants interact with their care providers. The quality of attachments is determined by the interaction between children and their care providers and brain development. Bowlby believed that early attachments form the basis for subsequent social relationships. Table 8.2 briefly describes Bowlby's stages of attachment.

Secure attachment occurs when infants can consistently rely on care providers to be available and nurturing. When infants are securely attached, they use care providers as a secure base from which to explore. Securely attached children are likely to protest separation from those to whom they are attached, although they usually can be calmed within a reasonable amount of time (Bowlby, 1980).

Table 8.2 Bowlby's Phases of Attachment Development

Stage	Phase	Approximate Age	Behavior
1	Asocial (preattachment)	0–3 months	Infant enjoys social interactions and smiles at others.
2	Indiscriminate attachments	3–6 months	Infant responds differently to familiar and unfamiliar individuals and prefers familiar individuals.
3	Specific attachments	6–8 months	Infant exhibits a preference for one primary care provider, develops a fear of strangers, and displays anxiety upon separation from the primary attachment figure.
4	Multiple attachments	1 year	Infant's preference for the primary attachment figure diminishes. Multiple attachments begin to develop.

Source: Adapted from Bowlby (1980).

Infants who have incompetent, uncaring, or inconsistent care providers often display **insecure attachment** behavior. Insecure attachment ranges from ignoring the caregiver to excessive expressions of distress and may even lead to disorientation.

When developmental delays or mental or physical conditions alter a child's ability to attach, care providers face many challenges in developing secure attachments and often must give more effort to helping the child develop a sense of security. For example, infants who have disabilities (e.g., are deaf or blind) might not smile, coo and babble, clap hands, or sit on the floor and play. Children who have disabilities may not provide clear messages about their needs. When parents have difficulty understanding babies' cues, or the baby does not respond as expected, the dance synchrony (coordination between infant and care provider) is disrupted.

Children who are not securely attached often ignore their mothers while playing. They may act distressed when their mothers leave but not seek contact with their mothers when they return or find comfort in that return. When their mothers return, they are likely to turn their bodies away from their mothers and avoid eye contact or reach out and cling to their mothers but soon angrily push them away.

Understanding the attachment process is important because early experiences have a direct effect on later development. The label *attachment disorder* is assigned to older children and adults who do not form close relationships with others and who often display aggressive, disruptive behavior (Shelton et al., 2000).

Typical Social–Emotional Development

Children's social-emotional development parallels, complements, and interacts with other areas of development. Soon after birth, infants develop a sense of who they like and can trust, generally enjoy being with people, and express positive and negative feelings. As the frontal cortex of the brain increases its activity, infants become more effective at regulating their own comfort level and soothing themselves. Infants have their own preferences regarding types and levels of sensory stimulation (Greenspan, 1999).

Most newborns respond reflexively to physical stimulation. For example, when newborns' cheeks are stroked from the corner of the mouth toward the ear, they turn toward the stroking hand. They grasp a finger placed in their palm. Infants also respond positively to seeing a human face, hearing a person's voice, and being held (McHale & Lerner, 1990).

During the first 6 months of life, most infants begin smiling and laughing when others are in view. Over time they smile more at familiar people. Most children without hearing disabilities stop crying when someone begins speaking (Grusec, 1988).

Nine-month-olds tend to respond positively when someone speaks to them and appear to understand much of what is said. They may continue an activity they have lost interest in after receiving encouragement to continue (Gunnar, 1990).

By age 1, interactions include give-and-take and play is more people-oriented. One-year-olds prefer being with familiar individuals. They show fear, anger, and jealousy and develop a sense of humor (Harris, 1989). They display awareness of others' feelings and needs and often appear to want to please others. One-year-olds are more willing to cooperate but demand considerable autonomy.

At 12–18 months, infants begin to control their own behavior. Even when toddlers know that hitting is unacceptable, they often appear to be unable to control their impulse to hit, particularly when they are tired, hungry, or upset.

Gradually, young children learn adults' expectations for behavior. They display modesty, guilt, shame, and sympathy. Empathy for those in distress, cooperation, and helping others increase during the preschool years (Zahn-Waxler, Radke-Yarrow, & King, 1979). For example, 2- and 3-year-olds give gifts and often share their toys. Initially, gift-giving is used to initiate social contact. Over time children demonstrate growing generosity, cooperation, empathy, and helpfulness (Eisenberg & Miller, 1987).

During the preschool years, social-emotional development becomes increasingly complex and less predictable (Klimes-Dougan & Kistner, 1990). Typically, more fears develop. Four-year-olds' mixture of self-reliance and assertiveness may result in aggressiveness or bossiness. Four-year-olds often want to choose clothes and food. Five-year-olds typically are more culturally conforming and begin to display manners. Emotions now include pride, self-satisfaction, and persistence. Six-year-olds tend to be lively, energetic, and enthusiastic. They may become frustrated, angry, or quarrelsome when struggling to successfully engage in various tasks. They frequently display jealousy, and they may refuse to cooperate.

Social and emotional milestones are more difficult to specify than signs of physical and cognitive development. Distinguishing between typical and atypical social-emotional development is difficult, in part, because an estimated 40% of preschoolers engage in one or more antisocial behaviors daily. Additionally, there are wide variations across cultural groups with regard to what is considered normal (Walker et al., 1998; Willoughby, Kupersmidt, & Bryant, 2001).

Causes of Social–Emotional Disabilities

As with other areas of development, biological factors, family relationships, experiences, and social environment all can contribute to social-emotional disorders. It is often difficult, if not impossible, to determine the cause of most early childhood social-emotional disabilities.

Biological Influences

Continuous interaction between biology and experience shapes human development. Children are born with powerful inborn tendencies, which work for and against them. Genetic inheritance, biochemical abnormalities, and neurological abnormalities are biological factors that may contribute to social-emotional disorders. Children are more likely to display behavioral disorders that other family members also exhibit. This fact suggests that heredity affects these behavioral disorders. For example, children of depressed or schizophrenic parents are more likely to have social-emotional developmental problems. Also, one-fourth to one-third of biological parents of children with attention deficit hyperactivity disorder (ADHD) have or had ADHD themselves. Biological parents who have one child with ADHD have approximately a 33% chance of having another child with ADHD. When a child is born with a genetic predisposition to mental health problems, it is critically important that the environment support and guide the child in a positive, healthy direction (McGoey, Eckert, & Dupaul, 2002).

As discussed, children are born with a particular temperament; they show biologically based differences. Children with difficult temperaments have a greater likelihood of social-emotional problems. In contrast, children with easy temperaments tend to have positive social-emotional development, even when reared in a family categorized as dysfunctional.

Environmental Influences

Many young children live within settings that create environmental risks. Risk factors including poverty, parental substance abuse, unusually low or high maternal age, homelessness, parental mental health issues, child abuse or neglect, family violence, out-of-home placement, aggression, antisocial behavior, intense marital conflict, and ineffective parenting are linked to behavior problems in some children (Sherburne, Utley, McConnell, & Gannon, 1988). For example, ADHD has been linked to environmental toxicity including prenatal lead exposure, parental use of alcohol or tobacco, severe marital discord, maternal mental disorder, large family size, parental criminality, and foster care placement. In addition, children born preterm are 4 to 6 times more likely to be diagnosed with ADHD. Premature births contribute to neurological abnormalities, which are linked to social-emotional disabilities (Zito et al., 2000).

Quality of family interactions has a major impact on children's social-emotional development. Parenting style and social factors such as parent education level, family income level, family cohesion, mother's age, and marriage status are associated with social-emotional development.

Families of children with serious behavioral problems frequently report the presence of major stressors in their lives. Parents who abuse alcohol or other drugs are more likely to treat their children aggressively; such treatment increases the likelihood of behavioral problems. Children who are victims of sexual abuse and exposure to violence are particularly prone to emotional disturbances. Inconsistent or ineffective discipline techniques are also related to behavioral disorders (Sameroff, Seifer, & Zax, 1982).

In addition, culture influences every aspect of human development, including how infant mental health is understood, adults' expectations regarding young children's development, and child-rearing practices used to promote young children's mental health. Children first explore their world within the context of family and cultural community. They gradually learn to adapt to the varied demands of families and others (Merrell, 1999; Sattker, 2001; Shapiro & Kratochwill, 2000).

Assessment of Social-Emotional Disabilities

Referral

As with other developmental domains, a referral is required to conduct an assessment of the social-emotional domain (Gartin & Murdick, 2001; Inman, Buck, & Burke, 1998; Nielson & McEvoy, 2003; Zero to Three, 2005). Parents and child care providers are typically the first to notice social-emotional difficulties. The duration and intensity of troublesome behaviors and the age of the child must be considered in determining whether a referral for assessment is warranted. In addition, care providers should evaluate whether other factors—such as allergies, hearing problems, a change in medication, or stress—are contributing to social-emotional problems.

Infants who are unresponsive to their environment (e.g., do not show emotions such as pleasure or fear, look at or reach for objects, or respond to environmental changes such as in sound or light), are overresponsive (e.g., easily cry or are startled), or have unexplained weight loss or inadequate growth should be referred for an evaluation. Toddlers and preschoolers who continually engage in self-stimulating behavior (e.g., twist their hair or rock back and forth) to the exclusion of normal activities, are self-abusive (e.g., bang their heads, bite themselves, or hit themselves), do not form affectionate relationships with care providers, or repeatedly hit, bite, kick, or attempt to injure others should be evaluated (American Academy of Pediatrics, 2002a).

Figure 8.3 lists behaviors that may indicate mental health problems in young children. Figure 8.4 indicates questions that are useful when analyzing social-emotional development.

Emotional and behavioral disorders are often difficult to identify. There is no single measure or test used to classify children as emotionally or behaviorally disabled. The classification often involves subjective judgments. It is difficult to determine which preschool-age children need intervention because, from time to time, nearly all children display behavior atypical of children their age. In addition, cultural standards vary regarding what types of behavior are appropriate (DeGangi, 2000; Kauffman, 1993; Rogoff & Morelli, 1989).

Some children have transient behavioral disabilities, behavior patterns that come and go. These behaviors are related to children's reactions to their environment. For example, they may be anxious, have trouble sleeping, be tense, or seem depressed or have physical problems such as skin reactions, stomach pains, or respiratory disorders. Many things could contribute to these behaviors, including the child's being separated from a parent, moving to a new house, attending a new day care facility, experiencing the birth of a sibling, or experiencing the death of a family member or close friend. In some cases a much less significant event may hold great importance for a child and may lead to temporary behavior disabilities. For example, children often become depressed or angry after their favorite toy is misplaced (Ewing Marion Kauffman Foundation, 2002). When there are concerns about a child's emotional development, a referral should be made to a mental health professional—a psychiatrist, social worker, or psychologist.

Role of Psychologists and Other Professionals

Frequently, parents and children are referred to a **psychologist** for a general developmental evaluation focused on social-emotional development. Typically, a psychologist has a master's or doctoral degree in counseling, clinical psychology, or school psychology. Often they specialized in child or adolescent psychology. In most states they are either licensed or certified. Those who have a master's degree are sometimes

Figure 8.3   Behaviors That May Indicate Emotional or Mental Health Problems in Young Children

Infants and Toddlers

- Displays very little emotion.
- Does not show interest in sights, sounds, or touch.
- Rejects or avoids being touched or held or playing with others.
- Is unusually difficult to soothe or console.
- Is unable to comfort or calm self.
- Is extremely fearful or on guard.
- Does not turn to familiar adults for comfort or help.
- Exhibits sudden behavior changes.

Preschool Children

- Cannot play with others or objects.
- Lacks language and other forms of communication.
- Frequently fights with others.
- Is very sad.
- Is unusually fearful.
- Shows inappropriate responses to situations (e.g., laughs instead of cries).
- Is withdrawn.
- Is extremely active.
- Experiences a loss of earlier skills (e.g., toilet, language, motor).
- Shows sudden behavior changes.
- Is very accident-prone.
- Is destructive of self or others.

Figure 8.4   Questions to Consider When Assessing Young Children's Mental Health

- How severe is the behavior?
- How many weeks or months has the behavior been occurring?
- How long does the behavior last (e.g., minutes, hours)?
- How does the behavior compare with that of other children of the same age?
- Are there events at home or the child care facility that make the behavior better or worse?

supervised by a psychologist who has a doctorate. Psychologists may work within an early intervention program full-time or provide part-time consultation.

In most early childhood programs, psychologists focus on assessing children's intellectual level, psychological and emotional status, and level of adaptability. Psychologists often administer standardized assessment instruments (tests) and evaluate concept development as well as verbal, perceptual, social-emotional, self-help, and motor skills. Psychologists may classify or diagnose the child based on the results of a formal assessment and observation. For example, the evaluation may include classifying a child as having a pervasive developmental disorder.

In addition, psychologists evaluate the emotional needs of the child and family members to determine whether psychological support services are needed. These judgments are frequently made, in part, by interviewing the parents and observing the child. The data may be combined with data that a social worker or other staff members provide. The psychologist may provide counseling for the child and family members or provide referrals for counseling services.

Counseling may be provided for the child in the form of play therapy. Play therapy involves using puppets or toys to help children deal with traumas such as abuse or the death of a family member. This type of therapy is often inappropriate for preschool children because it requires verbal comprehension and symbolic play skills. Many preschool children with disabilities have delayed verbal skills, which further limit the usefulness of play therapy. A more extended discussion of play therapy is provided in Chapter 12.

In some cases a **developmental psychologist** (also referred to as a "developmentalist") may be a team member in a program designed to provide services to a child with disabilities. A developmental psychologist has a master's or doctoral degree in psychology or education and focuses on child development or education/special education. Often this person is not licensed as a counselor or certified to administer formal psychological evaluations.

Developmental psychologists focus on the developmental stages of childhood, learning theories, and methods of instruction. They may interact directly with children, teachers, or therapists within the classroom to help determine appropriate developmental goals and intervention strategies. They may be asked to help solve behavior management problems or determine the types of instructional methods that may be used to meet each child's needs. For example, a developmental psychologist may help a child with a high level of separation anxiety adjust to being away from their parent during their first few days of attending a new class.

Developmental psychologists often consult with other service providers regarding methods of interacting with children and their families to achieve a desired educational goal. They may participate in designing and implementing evaluation instruments used to assess the effectiveness of various types of intervention as well as assess overall program effectiveness. They may also provide in-service training (lectures or workshops) to staff and parents on a variety of topics, including discipline, appropriate expectations, and transitions to other programs.

A **child psychiatrist** may also be part of the evaluation and service team. This professional has a medical degree and psychiatric training (regarding social, emotional, and behavioral concerns), has been trained and certified to work with children, and can prescribe medication. A **developmental pediatrician,** a pediatrician with specialized training in children's development, may also be a member of the team.

Screening

Children with social-emotional disorders exhibit one or more of the following characteristics over an extended period and in various environments:

- Difficulty developing or maintaining relationships with peers or teachers.
- Inappropriate behavior or feelings.
- General unhappiness or depression.
- Physical symptoms or fears related to personal or school problems.

Typically, when one or more of these signs are present, a developmental screening should occur to determine if more extensive assessment is warranted. Several screening instruments assess all major areas of development, including social-emotional development (Feil, Severson, & Walker, 1998; Feil, Walker, Severson, & Ball, 2000; Forness et al., 2000; Squires, 2000). The goal in assessing and providing services to a young child should include helping families to acknowledge their own stresses and strengths.

Full Assessment

As with other areas of delays, when screening indicates that a child may have a social-emotional delay, a full assessment is warranted. A complete evaluation typically involves interviewing the parent(s) about the child's developmental history, direct observation of family functioning and interaction patterns, direct observation of affective expression, and use of one or more standardized tests.

Assessments of children's emotional development should be conducted by practitioners who are trained and experienced in this area. Social interactions are often assessed through the use of rating scales, in which case the rater makes judgments about the quantity or quality of behaviors.

Whereas standardized tests evaluate general social-emotional development, other assessments focus on specific areas of social-emotional development, including pervasive developmental disorder (PDD), ADHD, and depression.

Connor's Rating Scales (CRS-R) assess ADHD and other related problems (e.g., conduct, cognitive, family, emotional, anger-control, and anxiety problems) in children 3–17 years old (Miller & Sperry, 1987). There are two versions (short and long) for parents, teachers, and child. On average they take 20 minutes to complete. The longer version closely corresponds to the criteria for ADHD found in the *Diagnostic and Statistical Manual of Mental Disorders-IV* (DSM-IV) (U.S. Department of Education, 2003a). Figure 8.5 lists the CRS-R's areas of focus.

A number of standardized tests are designed to evaluate autism spectrum disorders, including the Asperger Syndrome Diagnostic Scale (ASDS), Autism and Communication Disabilities, the Autism Behavior Checklist (ABC), the Autism

Figure 8.5 **Connor's Rating Scales (CRS-R): Areas of Focus**

- Oppositional
- Cognitive problems/inattention
- Hyperactivity
- Anxious-Shy
- Perfectionism
- Social problems
- Psychosomatic
- ADHD index
- Restless-Impulsive
- Emotional Lability

Adapted from Connors (1989).

Diagnostic Interview, Revised (ADI-R), the Autism Diagnostic Observation Schedule (ADOS), the Autism Screening Instrument for Educational Planning, 2nd edition (ASIEP-2), the Checklist for Autism in Toddlers (CHAT), the Childhood Autism Rating Scale (CARS), the Diagnostic Checklist for Behavior-Disturbed Children (Form E-2), the Gilliam Autism Rating Scale (GARS), the Prelinguistic Autism Diagnostic Observation Schedule (PL-ADOS), the Social Communication Questionnaire (SCQ), and Social Responsiveness Scales (SRS).

There are a number of standardized assessments designed to assess ADHD, including the Attention Deficit Disorder Evaluation Scale, 3rd edition (ADDES-3), Attention Deficit-Hyperactivity Disorder Test (ADHDT), Brown Attention-Deficit Disorder Scales: Children and Adolescent Version (Brown ADD), and Early Childhood Attention Deficit Disorder Evaluation Scales (ECADDES) (Neisworth, Bagnato, Salvia, & Hunt, 1999).

Types of Social–Emotional Disabilities

Although early identification of young children with social-emotional disorders is often helpful, the use of clinical mental health diagnosis is often avoided to prevent labeling young children and running the chance of creating a self-fulfilling prophecy (Coleman & Webber, 2002; Tomlin & Viehweg, 2003).

Children's emotional difficulties can be serious and long-lasting and lead to negative outcomes, including limited academic achievement, failure to earn a high school diploma, substance abuse, delinquency, limited vocational success, inability to live independently, health problems, and suicide. A disproportionate number of children who live in low-income families experience emotional problems. Also, a disproportionate number of children who live in low-income families or racial/ethnic-minority families do not receive appropriate services for their emotional problems.

The terms *emotional problem* and *behavioral problems* typically are used to acknowledge the existence of a problem requiring intervention. Social-emotional disorders include behavior that is disruptive to self or others (Thomas & Clark, 1998). Children with social-emotional disorders tend to have poor impulse control and more frequently become angry. The category "emotional disturbance" (ED) is often used to describe school-age children. To be labeled ED, a child must display characteristics over an extended period that adversely affect educational performance and that cannot be explained by cultural, intellectual, sensory, or other health factors—for example, difficulty building or maintaining interpersonal relationships, pervasive unhappiness, physical symptoms or fears, and inappropriate feelings or behaviors. The Council for Exceptional Children uses the term **emotional/behavioral disorder (EBD)** to classify these children. Fortunately, very few children classified with social-emotional delays are classified as **seriously emotionally disturbed (SED)** (U.S. Department of Education, 1995).

Many young children, including children with disabilities, engage in behaviors that adults view as disruptive. There is considerable variation from individual to individual regarding what is considered disruptive. Different families, cultural groups, and communities define inappropriate behavior differently. In most cases, disruptive behavior is short-term and decreases with age and use of appropriate guidance strategies (U.S. Public Health Service, 2000).

Often, the disruptive behaviors of most concern are those most likely to result in injury to oneself or others, cause damage to the physical environment, interfere with the acquisition of new skills, or socially isolate those who display them. From time to time, all young children display challenging behavior. Fortunately, most children outgrow most of these behaviors before they become a serious problem.

In the case of some children, disruptive behaviors are intense, occur more frequently, and interfere with their ability to learn and form positive relationships. Such children may have mental health conditions or social and emotional disturbances.

Children with behavioral disorders often have lower self-esteem than other children. Signs of negative self-esteem include indecisiveness, lack of self-reliance, and not being able to accept being wrong. Children with negative self-esteem frequently do not attempt activities until they receive specific instructions on how to complete the task. They may blame themselves for mishaps or disappointments and may be shy and hesitant in new situations. They may think that they cannot handle problem-solving situations (Patterson, Kupersmidt, & Griesler, 1990). Methods that support the development of self-esteem are discussed in depth in Chapter 14.

Frequently, children with behavioral disorders also manifest speech delays, which can be directly attributed to their behavioral disorders. For example, stress related to negative behavior patterns may lead children to develop articulation problems or excessive stuttering (dysfluency). More-extreme language problems may surface, including echolalia (repeating another person's words) or bizarre speech (making up words or jumbling the words in a sentence). These language problems interfere with effective communication, creating further difficulty for these children. In some cases children may behave inappropriately to gain attention.

The most common early childhood psychiatric disorders include ADHD, oppositional defiant disorders, conduct disorders, PDD, and mood disorders (e.g., anxiety and depression). An estimated 12 million U.S. children suffer from some type of mental disorder, and fewer than 1 in 5 of these children are viewed as receiving appropriate treatment (Parr, Ward, & Inman, 2003).

Attention Deficit Hyperactivity Disorder

The Centers for Disease Control estimates that 4.4 million U.S. children 4–17 years old have been diagnosed with **attention deficit hyperactivity disorder (ADHD)** by a health care professional. Depending on the classification criteria used, 3–20% of U.S. children are classified as having ADHD. It is estimated that ADHD is diagnosed 6 to 9 times more often in boys than in girls (Connor, 2002; Kauffman, 1989; Jacob, O'Leary, & Rosenbald, 1978).

In 2003, 2.5 million U.S. youth were reported to be receiving medication for ADHD. An estimated 66% of children with ADHD have one or more coexisting conditions, the most common of which are disruptive behavior (oppositional defiant and conduct disorders), mood and anxiety disorders (including depression and bipolar disorders), tics and Tourette's syndrome, and learning disabilities. Children with ADHD commonly have serious, persistent difficulties with attention span, impulse control, and hyperactivity (not always present). Children with ADHD frequently display cognitive delays (American Academy of Pediatrics, 2000; National Institutes of Health, 2000).

According to the DSM-IV, for a child to be classified as having ADHD, they must have displayed at least 8 of the 14 characteristics listed in Figure 8.6 for at least 6 months by the age of 7 years. The most frequently cited indicators of ADHD in preschool children are excessive activity, such as frequently shifting from one activity to another, and talking when they are expected to be quiet. About half of all ADHD cases are diagnosed before the child is 4 years old (Resnick, 2000).

Children with ADHD often have problems with organization and following rules and are easily distracted. However, some children with ADHD are quiet and passive but have problems with organization and attentiveness. This type of ADHD likely is underdiagnosed because teachers and parents do not find it disruptive, although it interferes with children's ability to learn. ADHD has negative effects on a child's life at home, in school, and within the community. Most children with ADHD have difficulty with academic activities and in interactions with peers and family members (Hoagwood, Kelleher, Feil, & Comer, 2000; Lougy, Derive, & Rosenthal, 2007; Root & Resnick, 2003; Whalen, 2001).

Oppositional Defiant Disorder

Children with **oppositional defiant disorder (ODD)** tend to be noncompliant and angry. ODD typically includes a pattern of arguing with others; losing one's temper; refusing to follow rules; blaming others; deliberately annoying others; and being angry, resentful, spiteful, and vindictive. Children with ODD frequently test limits (Lavigne et al., 2001). For a child to be classified as having ODD, the behavior must exist for at least 6 months, and at least five of the behaviors listed in Figure 8.7 (p. 234) must consistently occur.

Conduct Disorders

Conduct disorders (CDs) are marked by intense and consistent hitting, temper tantrums, disobedience, defiance, destruction of property, lack of cooperation, resistance

Figure 8.6 Outline of the Definition of ADHD Found in DSM-IV

(A) Either (1) or (2):

(1) Six or more of the following symptoms have persisted for at least 6 months to a degree that is maladaptive and inconsistent with developmental level.

Inattention

- Fails to pay close attention to details or makes careless mistakes.
- Has difficulty sustaining attention during activities.
- Does not seem to listen when directly spoken to.
- Does not follow through on instructions (not due to oppositional behavior or failure to understand instructions).
- Has difficulty organizing activities.
- Avoids, dislikes, or is reluctant to engage in tasks that require sustained mental effort.
- Loses things necessary for activities (e.g., toys).
- Is easily distracted by extraneous stimuli.
- Is forgetful during daily activities.

(2) Six or more of the following symptoms have persisted for at least 6 months to a degree that is maladaptive and inconsistent with developmental level.

Hyperactivity

- Fidgets with hands or feet or squirms in seat.
- Leaves seat when remaining seated is expected.
- Runs about or climbs excessively in inappropriate situations.
- Has difficulty playing quietly.
- Is on the go; acts as if driven by a motor.
- Talks excessively.

Impulsivity

- Blurts out answers before questions have been completed.
- Has difficulty awaiting turn.
- Interrupts or intrudes on others.

(B) Some hyperactive-impulsive or inattentive symptoms that cause impairment were present before age 7 years.

(C) Some impairment from the symptoms is present in two or more settings (e.g., at school and home).

(D) There is evidence of clinically significant impairment of functioning.

(E) Symptoms do not occur exclusively during the course of a pervasive developmental disorder, schizophrenia, or other psychotic disorder and are not better accounted for by another mental disorder (e.g., mood disorder, anxiety disorder, dissociative disorder, or personality disorder).

Source: Adapted from American Psychiatric Association (1994).

Figure 8.7   Attributes of Children with Oppositional Defiant Disorder (ODD)

- Readily lose their tempers.
- Frequently argue with adults.
- Actively defy or refuse adult requests or rules.
- Deliberately behave in ways that annoy other people.
- Blame others for their own mistakes.
- Are easily upset by others.
- Are angry and resentful.
- Are vindictive.
- Use obscene language.

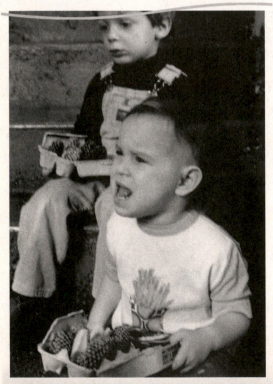

Some children have difficulty maintaining control of their anger and need help to do so.

to new experiences or people, being inconsiderate or disruptive, interrupting, being negative, seeking undue attention, lying, stealing, running away, and physical aggression. Approximately 4–10% of children classified as having a behavioral disorder are considered to have CD. Boys are approximately 8 times more likely than girls to be classified as having CD (Brandenburg, Friedman, & Silver, 1990). Behaviors used to classify CD fall into four major categories: 1) aggression toward humans and other animals, 2) destruction of property, 3) lying and theft, and 4) serious violations of rules.

Many factors are likely to contribute to a child's developing CD—including brain damage, child abuse, school failure, and negative family or school experiences. Children's CD behavior often elicits negative reactions from others, which result in more-intense CD behavior. Without treatment, individuals with CD often are unable to adapt to life's later demands and have problems with relationships and employment. They are likely to break laws or behave antisocially.

Pervasive Developmental Disorder

Another form of behavioral disorder is **pervasive developmental disorder (PDD)**, also referred to as "**autism spectrum disorder (ASD).**" The term *PDD* was first used in the 1980s to describe a class of disorders characterized by impairments in social interaction, imagination, and communication skills and by repetitive body movements. Some parents report symptoms as early as infancy, with the typical age of onset being younger than 3 years (Chakrabarti & Fombonne, 2001; DeMyer, 1979; Fitzgerald, 2004; Gillberg & Coleman, 2000; Matson, Mayville, & Laud, 2003; Wing & Potter, 2002).

The DSM-IV lists five disorders under the category PDD: **autism, Rett syndrome (RS)**, fragile X syndrome, childhood disintegrative disorder (CDD), **Asperger's syndrome (AS),** and pervasive developmental disorder not otherwise specified (PDDNOS). Children with PDD vary widely in abilities, intelligence, and behaviors (Massey & Wheeler, 2000; Powers, 2000). Some children with PDD do not speak; others speak in limited phrases or use unusual conversation patterns; still others display relatively normal language development. Children with PDD generally display repetitive play and limited social skills. Unusual responses to sensory input (e.g., loud noise and bright lights) are also common (Greenspan & Weider, 1999; McConnell & Ryser, 2006).

Autism.   Autism (a developmental brain disorder characterized by impaired social interaction and communication skills as well as a limited range of activities and interests) is the most common and most studied PDD. Although the U.S. Department of Education recognized autism as a separate category in 1990, psychologists and many medical professionals continue to view autism as a behavioral disorder. Autism affects verbal and nonverbal communication and social interactions. It is generally manifested within the first 3 years of life and is found at all intellectual levels. It is estimated that 0.2% of children have autism; the rate of occurrence among boys is three times the rate among girls. Children with autism often engage in repetitive activities (e.g., staring or excessive blinking) and movements (e.g., spinning wheels on a toy or flapping their hands), resist changes in routines, and have unusual responses to sensory stimuli (Cohen & Donnellen, 1987).

About half of all children classified as autistic do not speak. Those who do speak are more likely to use immature speech patterns, have limited understanding of ideas, and frequently use words in ways that do not accord with their accepted meanings. Autistic children often relate to people and objects in unusual ways. They may act as if they cannot hear; resist learning; show a lack of fear of real dangers; react negatively to changes in routine; be unreceptive to physical affection; avoid eye contact; sustain repetitive action patterns such as rocking, head banging, or hand twisting; and bite, scratch, or hit themselves (Sturmy & Fitzer, 2007; Batshaw & Perret, 1986).

Asperger's Syndrome.   AS is a milder variant of PDD. Children with AS are characterized by social isolation, communication (verbal and nonverbal) and transition difficulties, and eccentric behavior (e.g., obsessive routines; preoccupation with unusual objects; and acute sensitivity to sounds, tastes, smells, and sights). Their language productions tend to be grammatical, although inflection and articulation are often unusual and speech tends to be repetitive. Children with AS tend to be physically clumsy, and their interests often are limited and unusual for their age. They usually fall within the normal IQ range, and many individuals with AS exhibit exceptional skill or talent in a specific area. Children with AS exhibit a variety of characteristics, and the disorder can range from mild to severe (Griswold, Barnhill, & Myles, 2002; Myles & Simpson, 2003).

Childhood Disintegrative Disorder. **Childhood disintegrative disorder (CDD),** also known as **Heller's syndrome,** is another form of PDD that occurs in 3- and 4-year-olds who have developed normally to age 2. CDD occurs more frequently in boys than in girls. This disorder is characterized by severe regression in language (communication) skills, social behavior, and all developmental motor skills. Children with CDD have seemingly normal development for approximately the first 2 years of life, followed by several months of deterioration in intellectual, social, and language functioning. Although the cause of CDD is unknown, it has been linked to neurological problems, EEG abnormalities, and seizures. CDD is rare but probably underdiagnosed. It often is initially misdiagnosed as autism.

Rett Syndrome. RS is a unique neurodevelopmental PDD that begins to manifest during infancy or early childhood and is found almost exclusively in females. RS is found in all racial and ethnic groups. This disorder is caused by a mutation in a gene on the X chromosome. The mutated gene is responsible for regulating the activity of other genes and contributes to abnormal brain maturation due to abnormal synapse development. This deviation occurs at the end of the mother's pregnancy or within the first few months of the child's life, during the critical phases of synapse development.

Children with RS appear to develop normally until 6–18 months. Then skills slow down or stagnate. A period of regression follows, resulting in loss of communication skills and purposeful use of hands and abnormal rate of head growth. This is followed by stereotyped hand movements and gait disturbances. In addition, while the child is awake, disorganized breathing and seizures may occur. RS may be accompanied by irritability, including relentless crying. Over time, motor problems may increase while eye gaze improves and seizures and irregular breathing diminish. The inability to regulate motor movements (e.g., fine- and gross-motor skills, eye gaze, and speech) is the most serious attribute of RS. Unlike children with autism, those with RS almost always prefer people to objects and enjoy affection. Autistic-like features, seen at an early age, disappear.

Pervasive Developmental Disorder Not Otherwise Specified. The classification **"pervasive developmental disorder not otherwise specified" (PDDNOS),** also referred to as **"atypical personality development," "atypical PDD,"** and **"atypical autism,"** is applied to children who experience impaired social interaction, impaired communication, or stereotyped behavior patterns or interest but who do not meet the criteria for autism or other specified forms of PDD.

Mood Disorders

Reactive Attachment Disorder. **Reactive attachment disorder (RAD)** is a mood disorder displayed before age 5 characterized by an inability to form healthy social relationships with care providers (i.e., failure to initiate or respond to others). RAD is associated with an inability to form attachments, a lack of cause-and-effect thinking, and poor impulse control (e.g., frequent aggressiveness). The two major forms of RAD are **inhibited type,** characterized by a failure to initiate or respond to social interactions in a developmentally appropriate way, and **disinhibited type,** characterized by indiscriminate sociability or lack of selectivity in the choice of attachment figures.

Children with RAD often lack remorse. They appear to need to be in control rather than allow themselves to be guided by care providers. RAD is believed to occur due to neglect of infants' emotional needs related to parental isolation, lack of parenting skills, lack of consistent contact, and teen parents. Physical and emotional milestones of children with RAD vary significantly from expected developmental norms. Symptoms of RAD include intense watchfulness, resistance to comfort, a mixture of approach and avoidance, dullness, listlessness, and apathy. Some children appear joyless. Older infants show minimal curiosity about their surroundings and little exploratory behavior. They may show delayed responsiveness to a stimulus that normally elicits fright or withdrawal in other children.

Depression. Even very young children can have difficulty coping with difficult situations. **Depression** affects as many as 1 in every 33 children. Although recognizing childhood depression is often difficult, symptoms of depression include sadness, helplessness, fatigue, and low self-esteem. Very young children are typically not formally diagnosed as depressed (American Academy of Child and Adolescent Psychiatry, 2008).

Anxiety Disorders. **Anxiety disorders** are another form of behavioral disorder. Children with an anxiety disorder may be anxious, fearful, tense, timid, bashful, withdrawn, depressed, sad, disturbed, reluctant to participate in activities, easily brought to tears, secretive, and unresponsive to peers or adults. Inadequate or immature behavior includes overdependency on others and delays in developing self-help skills and interpersonal relationships. Other inappropriate behavior patterns associated with anxiety disorders include disregard of the consequences of one's actions, self-destructiveness, compulsive behavior, and perseveration.

Neuroses. Children classified with a **neurosis** appear to have inner conflicts and, therefore, often have difficulty interacting positively with other people and appear anxious. Their anxieties may be exhibited in the form of a **phobia,** an irrational, persistent, overwhelming fear. Phobias include fear of objects or situations that present no actual danger or fear out of proportion to the actual danger. There are many different phobias, including fear of high places, water, nonhuman animals, solitude, thunder, or darkness. It is not unusual for children to have mild fears, but phobias are unusual and are rarely used to classify children before school age (Quay & Werry, 1986).

Children with a neurosis tend to react to stressful situations with more than typical sadness. The child may appear to be dejected and discouraged for relatively long periods. Other forms of neurosis include compulsive (uncontrollable urges or actions) or obsessive (persistent intrusions of unwanted thoughts) behavior. For example, a child may continually think about a fire that nearly got out of control or engage in behavior they do not want to engage in, such as constantly checking for smoke.

Psychoses.   Rarely preschool-age children are classified as having a **psychotic disorder,** characterized by loss of contact with reality. Children with a psychotic disorder cannot handle typical daily demands of childhood. Most children who are psychotic are labeled schizophrenic. These children misinterpret reality and sometimes have delusions (false, fixed ideas) or hallucinations (false sensory impressions). They withdraw from others, regress to immature behavior, or act in some unusual way.

Intervention Services for Social-Emotional Problems

Young children are full of energy and need to explore their environment and begin defining themselves as separate people. One major task is for them to learn to behave appropriately with limited or no direct guidance. A care provider must try to balance a young child's need for independence with their need for guidance and safe boundaries. Even with appropriate guidance, most young children sometimes display inappropriate behavior (Heffron, 2000; Knitzer, 2000).

Chapter 12 discusses the importance of play and how to use play to enhance the development of children with disabilities, including social-emotional delays. Chapter 13 provides an extended discussion of behavior management techniques, including those appropriate for children with social-emotional disabilities. The section that follows discusses methods not focused on in those chapters.

Strategies for Prevention of Challenging Behaviors

Adults support children's emotional development and mental health by surrounding children with nurturing relationships. Happy, caring adults who provide stable, safe environments while having appropriate expectations enhance children's mental health. Adults who comfort and reassure children when they are scared, angry, or hurt also support social-emotional development (Serna, Nielsen, Lambros, & Forness, 2000).

As discussed in previous chapters, an effective classroom environment begins with a well-organized and engaging classroom that includes developmentally appropriate practices, activities, and materials. Children who are provided with interesting activities and materials appropriate for their developmental levels are less likely to engage in challenging behaviors. In contrast, when activities and materials are too difficult or too easy, challenging behavior is more likely to occur.

When children have social-emotional disabilities, intervention services take many forms and are generally most effective when specifically designed for each child. Intervention services may include psychotherapy, cognitive-behavior therapy, behavioral management training, parent education, social skills training, family support services, and pharmaceuticals. In addressing challenging behaviors in young children, it is useful to analyze the arrangement of the classroom environment, scheduling, and rules and routines. Additional strategies may be required for some social-emotional difficulties.

There is no one agreed-on strategy for dealing with social-emotional disorders. Several helpful methods of behavior management applicable to all children with and without social-emotional disorders are discussed in Chapter 13. Clearly, adults must remain patient and positive when interacting with children.

Designing effective classroom environments includes structuring the physical arrangement of the classroom to increase appropriate behaviors, such as engagement, and decrease challenging behaviors. Strategies for structuring the physical classroom include arranging it to ensure visual monitoring of children, arranging activity centers to support children's appropriate behaviors (e.g., limiting the number of children in a center) and smooth transitions between activities (e.g., organizing the location of materials on shelves), and arranging materials in the classroom to promote engagement, mastery, and independence. Young children need constant supervision. Lack of sufficient supervision often leads to conflict.

Increasing the accessibility, appropriateness, and availability of toys and materials often decreases challenging behaviors. For example, too few toys often leads to frustration and conflict between children (Killen & Turiel, 1991). In addition, attending to details such as the lighting, temperature, and noise levels can reduce the probability that children will engage in problem behaviors due to sensitivity to these environmental factors (e.g., as seen in children with autism). For example, some children easily become agitated by overstimulation (e.g., the room's being too noisy or cluttered). And children who are physically uncomfortable (e.g., too cold or hot) are more likely to experience social conflicts.

Consideration of the classroom's interpersonal climate is necessary to ensure an effective classroom environment. When teachers notice and acknowledge children's appropriate behavior and provide assistance when children need help (before the children become overly frustrated), children are less likely to engage in challenging behaviors. Highly effective environments prioritize catching children being good and acknowledging their appropriate behavior.

Daily schedules help provide predictability, which gives children a sense of security, which helps prevent challenging behavior. Schedules must be flexible enough to adapt to unexpected events. Young children often benefit from the use of photographic or picture schedules that provide concrete visual cues of the scheduled activities and routines. In addition, when organizing a daily schedule, teachers must remember to include transition times between activities and schedule more-challenging activities (e.g., those that require extended time sitting quietly) for times when the children are most alert and attentive.

Additionally, it may be useful to develop a schedule within activities as well as across activities. For instance, if the activity has several components, it may be useful to communicate what will come first, next, and so forth by showing children a sequence of visual cues (e.g., photographs or line drawings) that represent the activity's components. Again, this will communicate to the child what they can expect.

Embedding choices within the schedule, so that children have an opportunity to decide between one activity and another (e.g., blocks center or dress-up center) increases the rate of child engagement and decreases the likelihood of challenging behaviors. Choices also provide children with a sense of control and competency.

Developing classroom rules and routines provides structure for everyone in the classroom, including the adults. A routine could include a song, rhyme, game, kinesthetic movement, or any other activity that is used in a predictable, repeated pattern to communicate values, foster community, or remind children of behavioral expectations.

Rules provide children with the structure for evaluating which behaviors are appropriate and inappropriate in the classroom. For younger children, routines provide verbal and nonverbal cues and prompts that help them learn appropriate behaviors. For example, a bell that signals the end of playtime provides children with a cue about a schedule change and allows them to initiate the change without verbal prompting from the teacher. Routines provide stability and consistency and communicate values such as friendship, caring, or responsibility.

In addition, routines ease transitions, reducing the occurrence of challenging behavior that often occurs when children move from one activity to another. A fun routine may ease transitions and serve as a rule reminder when children are going to a place where they need to be quiet, such as the library, or when they are starting a quiet activity, such as naptime. For example, the teacher might say to the class, "Zip it, lock it, and put it into your pocket." In response, the children would zip an imaginary zipper over their lips, act as if they were turning a key at the end of the zipper, and put the imaginary key into their pocket.

When implementing rules and routines, teachers typically need to teach them to the children using small steps paired with positive, specific feedback and repeated over time until all of the children understand and are able to engage in the appropriate behaviors. Additionally, participating in developing classroom rules helps children remember the rules. When children understand what is expected and are given the opportunity and support to engage in appropriate behaviors, they are more likely to choose such behaviors and less likely to engage in challenging behaviors.

Some challenging behaviors are eliminated or diminished when adults modify their behaviors. For example, children often react to adults' lack of attention or setting unrealistic expectations by misbehaving. Therefore, modifying adult behavior to ensure that children are frequently acknowledged and that expectations are developmentally appropriate may prevent children's needing to display challenging behavior. Preventing disruptive behavior is generally easier and more effective than trying to modify behavior after disruptive behavior has been displayed.

When children are encouraged to interact in positive ways, disruptive behaviors diminish. They benefit when curriculum is designed to enhance prosocial behavior (behavior that assists another person). To behave prosocially, children must be able to consider others' perspectives (be non-egocentric) and have empathy (feel concern about another's distress). Various curricula have been developed to promote positive behaviors. Two of these programs are discussed below.

Specific Interventions for Disruptive Behavior

Applied Behavior Analysis.   Applied behavior analysis (ABA) is a therapeutic intervention often used with children who have PDD or other social-emotional problems. ABA involves systematic environmental modifications for the purpose of producing socially significant improvements and emphasizes skill development through the use of positive reinforcement.

ABA requires assessment of each child's current skills and deficits. These are assessed through observation focusing on exactly what the child does, when certain behaviors occur and at what rate, and what happens before and after particular behaviors. Once individual strengths and weaknesses have been determined, selection of behaviors to be modified occurs. This is followed by the development of instructional objectives, teaching methods, a time schedule, and skill sequences. One of the most crucial aspects of ABA is determining what reinforcers are motivating for each child.

Most ABA programs combine discrete-trial procedures (discussed below) with a variety of other ABA methods (e.g., child-initiated instructional sequences, incidental teaching procedures, task analysis, and chaining). Parents are trained to implement the procedures in a variety of settings outside of formal treatment sessions (e.g., home, playground, and community settings).

ABA emphasizes that maladaptive behaviors (e.g., stereotypic behavior, self-injury, and aggressive and disruptive behavior) should not be reinforced (i.e., they should be ignored) and appropriate alternative behaviors should be taught and reinforced. ABA task analysis breaks desired behaviors into small, sequential (simple to complex) component skills. Throughout the normal daily routine, the child is provided with repeated opportunities to learn and practice skills through ABA activities.

Learners' progress is measured frequently, using the direct observational measurement method. Progress is graphed and reviewed to help ensure that learning errors are noted and intervention methods are adjusted if progress is unsatisfactory.

Discrete trial training (DTT) is a specific type of ABA. A teacher using DTT sequentially presents a discriminative stimulus (an instruction) and provides consequences for a correct or incorrect response. DTT provides a clear message as to what is expected and immediately indicates the appropriateness of each response. When one-on-one instruction is used, DTT often results in rapid, efficient learning but with limited generalization. DTT consists of three distinct components, outlined in Figure 8.8.

Figure 8.8   **Parts of Discrete Trial Training (DTT)**

1. *Instruction* (discriminative stimulus) that is short and easy to understand (e.g., "Pick up the spoon").
2. *Child's response*
3. *Consequence* that is a reinforcing stimulus (e.g., a privilege, praise, affection, attention, a preferred activity).

Pivotal response teaching (PRT) is a method based on the principles of ABA. PRT uses naturalistic motivational procedures to increase the occurrence of desired behaviors in children with social-emotional disabilities (usually autism). PRT typically focuses on communication and play behaviors. The primary strategy of PRT is to determine pivotal behaviors that produce simultaneous changes in other behaviors and are therefore important in a wide area of functioning. PRT is based on the premise that changes in pivotal behaviors will positively affect many other behaviors. For example, learning to spontaneously ask questions allows children to interact with a variety of individuals.

Incidental teaching is a naturalistic strategy focusing on assessment of the child's interests and includes child-direct and child-focused instruction. Incidental teaching provides children with opportunities to explore whatever interests them. Teachers focus on children's interests to determine what skills will be taught. Incidental teaching focuses on the development of social and communication skills by transforming children's interests and attention into opportunities for learning. It uses natural settings and emphasizes maintenance of skills, generalization of skills, and learning through interactions with peers who do not have developmental delays.

Activity-based instruction is instruction that is embedded within an activity (i.e., the natural environment) and is characterized by teachers' sharing control with children. Activity-based instruction encourages generalization of skills during daily activities. This strategy uses highly motivating activities and focuses on mastery of various prerequisite skills.

Functional Routines and Environmental Structure.   **Functional routines** are routines that are meaningful to the child and family and that occur naturally within home or school settings. Instruction during natural routines is planned and systematic and

Activity-based instruction is useful for enhancing a wide variety of skills.

practiced during a variety of activities in varied settings. Skills taught include social interactions and adaptive skills. The steps in teaching functional routines include

- identifying skills to be developed,
- identifying routines/activities and settings in which skills can be taught,
- creating a teaching plan (e.g., developing objectives; developing teaching strategies; and determining where teaching will occur, who will be teaching, and what materials will be needed),
- breaking skills into small steps,
- determining prompts,
- determining the teacher's response to correct and incorrect performance, and
- determining methods of ongoing assessment.

Instruction using functional routines often involves a variety of behavioral teaching techniques including more physical interaction with children, less verbal prompting, shaping/successive approximations, and errorless learning (making children successful by using appropriate prompts, and frequent use of rewards early on). Developmentally appropriate teaching is also important in teaching functional routines. Ultimately, skills are expanded to encourage more independence and enable children to learn more complex skills.

Pharmaceutical Intervention.   **Pharmaceutical intervention** may be part of a behavior treatment plan, especially for children with ADHD, depression, anxiety disorders, neuroses, or psychotic disorders. A variety of psychotropic drugs have been demonstrated to be helpful in treating early childhood psychiatric disorders. Only a few drugs have been tested for safety and effectiveness in preschool and younger children.

Research indicates that for children with ADHD or other emotional disorders, a combination of medication and behavioral therapy typically is most effective. Use of pharmaceuticals requires ongoing monitoring of the medication's effects and effectiveness. Stimulants seem to be the most effective ADHD medications.

Methods for Extending Attention Spans.   Most preschool children have very short attention spans, and many children with social-emotional problems have even more-limited attention spans. This negative attribute affects children's ability to benefit from various intervention methods because children forget things quickly and quickly lose interest in activities that they initially viewed as being highly motivating. Teachers need to develop many ways to keep children engaged in activities, because children are likely to need a change every 5 to 10 minutes. Children benefit from having high-movement activities interspersed with quiet ones. This alternation helps children avoid becoming overly tired or overly excited. Activities that are playful and involve physical movement are typically most fun and engaging.

Conclusions

Although it is crucial not to label a child as having a social-emotional disability when the child's behavior does not warrant such a label, it is also crucial not to ignore social-emotional disabilities. Social-emotional development affects all other areas of development. Therefore, a failure to note a delay may result in delays in other areas of development.

Knowledge about various theories, development of attachment, self-esteem, self-concept, morality, prosocial behavior, typical social-emotional development, and possible causes of delays guides intervention strategies for children with social-emotional disabilities.

As with other areas of development, prompt referrals for screening and when warranted, full assessment, are crucial if social-emotional delays are suspected. Individualized behavioral intervention designed to meet the needs of children with social-emotional disabilities is crucial. When behavioral intervention is insufficient, pharmaceutical intervention may also be beneficial.

CHAPTER SUMMARY

- During the early childhood years, social-emotional development includes the ability to experience, regulate, and express emotions; form close, secure interpersonal relationships; behave according to social rules and standards; and develop self-worth, self-confidence and self-regulation.

- Behaviorists, psychoanalysts, cognitivists, and those who study the role of heredity help explain social-emotional development, why difficulties occur, and methods to enhance social-emotional development.

- Because brain development is so rapid during early childhood, knowledge about typical social-emotional development is crucial. Healthy social-emotional development is essential for success in school and in life (Dawson, Ashman, & Carver, 2000).

- Biological predispositions and environmental factors—including poverty, premature birth, environmental toxins, parental substance abuse, maternal age, homelessness, parental mental

health issues, child abuse or neglect, family violence, out-of-home placement, aggression, antisocial behavior, intense marital conflict, and ineffective parenting—may lead to social-emotional disabilities (Shaw, Bell, & Gilliom, 2000).

- When social-emotional disabilities are suspected, prompt referral for evaluation is warranted; therefore, knowledge of signs indicating possible social-emotional difficulties is crucial.

- Formal and informal evaluations are used to assess social-emotional development. A wide variety of standardized instruments are available for screening and full evaluations.

- Several types of social-emotional disabilities may occur during early childhood.

- Early intervention designed to meet the needs of children with social-emotional delays is crucial. Intervention methods include a variety of psychological therapies and may include use of pharmaceuticals.

CHAPTER KEY TERMS

social-emotional development
behaviorist
classical conditioning

neutral stimulus
John B. Watson
conditioned reinforcer

B. F. Skinner
operant conditioning
social learning theory
Albert Bandura
psychoanalytic theory
Sigmund Freud
psychosexual stages
oral stage
id
immediate gratification
pleasure principle
anal stage
ego
reality principle
delayed gratification
phallic stage
superego
Erik Erikson
psychosocial theory
trust versus mistrust
autonomy versus shame and doubt
initiative versus guilt
emotion
temperament
social referencing
easy temperament
difficult temperament
slow-to-warm-up temperament
attachment
John Bowlby
secure attachment
insecure attachment
psychologist
developmental psychologist
child psychiatrist

developmental pediatrician
Connor's Rating Scales (CRS-R)
emotional/behavioral disorder (EBD)
seriously emotionally disturbed (SED)
attention deficit hyperactivity disorder (ADHD)
oppositional defiant disorder (ODD)
conduct disorder (CD)
pervasive developmental disorder (PDD)
autism spectrum disorder (ASD)
autism
Rett syndrome (RS)
Apserger's syndrome (AS)
childhood disintegrative disorder (CDD)
Heller's syndrome
pervasive developmental disorder not otherwise
    specified (PDDNOS)
atypical personality development
atypical PDD
atypical autism
reactive attachment disorder (RAD)
inhibited type
disinhibited type
depression
anxiety disorder
neurosis
phobia
psychotic disorder
applied behavioral analysis (ABA)
discrete trial training (DTT)
pivotal response teaching (PRT)
incidental teaching
activity-based instruction
functional routine
pharmaceutical intervention

REVIEW QUESTIONS

1. What are the key areas of social-emotional development during early childhood?

2. How do the key aspects of behaviorism and psychoanalytic theory relate to the social-emotional development of young children?

3. How do inborn temperamental differences, development of self-concept and self-esteem, and moral understanding relate to children's social-emotional development?

4. What factors may contribute to social-emotional disabilities in young children?

5. What are some signs of possible social-emotional disabilities in young children?

6. What are the distinguishing features of various social-emotional disabilities that may occur during early childhood?

7. What are some methods of intervention for children with social-emotional disabilities?

SUGGESTED STUDENT ACTIVITIES

1. Research one type of early childhood social-emotional disability discussed in this chapter to determine current estimates regarding prevalence of this disability, intervention methods, and intervention outcomes.

2. Write a position paper about the value and potential problems of mandating early childhood assessment of social-emotional development.

3. List attributes of yours that may positively affect your ability to work with young children with social-emotional disabilities. Also list attributes that may interfere with your work. Indicate how you will compensate for these attributes.

Sensory Abilities 9

CHAPTER KEY POINTS

- Relatively few young children have serious sensory impairments.

- Sensory development includes hearing; vision; and introceptive, vestibular, and proprioceptive abilities.

- Sensory impairment has a variety of causes.

- Audiologists, otolaryngologists, and teachers of the deaf and hearing-impaired play key roles in the assessment of hearing loss and treatment.

- A wide variety of tests are used to assess hearing loss.

- Hearing delays include congenital, prelingual, postlingual, and adventitious deafness.

- Hearing impairments affect other areas of development.

- A variety of communication and intervention methods are useful for those with hearing impairments.
- Visual impairments include being partially sighted or blind.
- Ophthalmologists and optometrists play key roles in the assessment and treatment of visual impairments.
- Visual impairments affect other areas of development.
- A variety of methods and services are appropriate for children with visual impairments.

Children's sensory abilities affect their well-being and future development. Fortunately, most children do not have significant **sensory impairments**. When sensory delays exist, they usually are visual or auditory (U.S. Department of Education, 2006). Sensory impairments include the inability to sense, understand, or process perceptual information. They limit the amount of information available to the brain, and the lack of information contributes to delays in intellectual functioning (Aslin & Smith, 1988).

Research indicates that young children eligible for early intervention services are more likely to have vision impairment or hearing loss than those without disabilities. An estimated 70% of children with visual impairments have an additional disability. Approximately 75% of children with Down syndrome have hearing loss, and more than 35% of children with hearing loss have an additional disability (American Academy of Pediatrics, 1999).

Sensory Development

In a normally functioning system, the brain processes information from our senses (Bornstein, 1992; Dunn, 1999). Our senses include, but are not limited to, vision, hearing, touching, tasting, and smelling. Sight and hearing often are referred to as the **distance senses** because they provide information about what is occurring in our surroundings. Smell provides some distance information as well. Touch, taste, smell, and the balance senses are referred to as the **close senses** because they provide information about what is within arm's reach. Other important but less commonly discussed senses include **interoception** (the sensory system of the internal organs, including heart rate, hunger, digestion, state of arousal, and mood), the **vestibular** system (which provides information about movement, gravity, and balance, received primarily through the inner ear), and **proprioception** (receiving information about body position through the muscles, ligaments, joints, and so on; senses of well-being; and homeostasis, or balance).

Large amounts of sensory information constantly enter our brains. The brain must organize and integrate all of the sensations. The various sensory systems are closely related and must coordinate for proper functioning and motor planning. **Sensory integration (SI)** is the organization, or interconnection, of these systems

(Bundy, 1991; Bundy, Lane, Murray, 2002; Miller & Lane, 2000). When sensory systems function correctly, the brain can accurately interpret the information. There are critical (absolutely necessary) and sensitive (very important) stages of development in which the brain needs the stimulation in order for brain cells to learn how to accurately process sensory information. An imperfection in the coordination of sensory systems is a **sensory integration dysfunction (SID)** (Ayres, 2005).

At birth most babies use their senses of taste, hearing, sight, touch, and smell. For example, most infants can recognize familiar faces and perceive objects within 8–10 inches of their eyes. At birth hearing is well developed; babies are often soothed by lullabies and white noise. They can recognize familiar scents (including human scents). Infants also learn about the world through touch and their mouths. Initially, infants rely primarily on touch, taste, and smell, but they also gain information from sight and hearing. Over time they develop visual and auditory skills that enable them to acquire higher-quality information and interpret it more usefully.

Perceptual abilities allow children to learn from active exploration of their environment. In addition to supporting intellectual development, perceptual abilities allow children to recognize familiar people; this recognition contributes to the trust that emerges and motivates the child to communicate with others. Children who have a visual or hearing impairment can learn to communicate and trust others by using alternative sensory information.

Hearing

Hearing begins when sound enters the external (outer) ear and travels into the ear canal, causing the eardrum to vibrate. On the other side of the eardrum is a small space called the middle ear. Three tiny bones within the middle ear move in a chain reaction when the eardrum vibrates. These bones connect with the third part of the ear, the inner ear. The inner ear includes the cochlea, semicircular canals, and auditory nerve. The cochlea and semicircular canals are filled with a water-like fluid. This is where nerve impulses are stimulated. The nerves then carry sound to the brain. Hearing loss can result from a disruption in the transmission of sound anywhere within the system. Refer to Figure 9.1 for a diagram of the ear.

The ability to hear begins prior to birth and is nearly fully developed at birth, although adults can hear very quiet sounds that infants do not appear to hear. Infants are most receptive to sounds at normal speech range and appear to hear very high- or low-pitched sounds less well. Newborns listen longer to the human voice than to any other sound, prefer music to noise, listen longer to sounds that vary than those that stay the same, prefer female to male voices, and frequently cry when they hear high-pitched, loud sounds.

Newborns react to voices (turn their eyes and head toward the source of the sound), even when they cannot see the speaker. They recognize the voices of primary care providers prior to recognizing their faces. By 8–10 months, infants pay more attention to speech sounds of their native language than to other speech sounds (Elbers & Ton, 1985). For example, babies whose parents speak English focus on sounds used in English and begin to ignore sounds unique to other languages (e.g., the trilled *r*'s of French). Until approximately 8 months of age, infants can distinguish

Figure 9.1   **Diagram of the Ear**

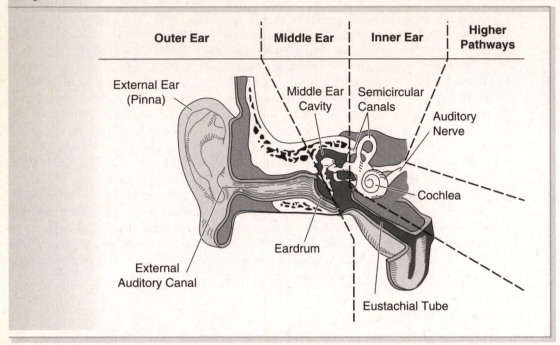

among phonemes of other languages not present in their own. Infants also develop sensitivity to prosody (intonation, pitch, rate, loudness, rhythm, etc.).

At 7–10 months of age, infants react to sounds they cannot see produced (e.g., familiar footsteps or voices, a dog's barking, a telephone is ringing, or their own name). Also at this age, babies emit different responses to different sounds. For example, they are likely to babble speech-like sounds when they hear voices and cry in response to thunder or other loud noises. At 11–15 months of age, toddlers begin to point to or find familiar objects or individuals when asked things such as "Where is mommy?" or "Find the ball." Most toddlers enjoy listening to certain sounds and attempt to imitate them.

Vision

The sense of sight is a primary learning avenue for most children. More than 98% of all infants are born with normal, healthy seeing organs. Vision guides the developing child's motor milestones and takes a lead role in all other developmental domains. Vision includes interpreting color, light, movement, locations, body language, facial expressions, and possible danger.

The visual system comprises an ocular system (the eyes and eye muscles) connected to a perceptual system, the brain. Vision requires the coordination of the eyes and the brain. If either system is dysfunctional, the visual system cannot provide adequate visual information. Visual acuity depends on the functioning of the optical components of the eye (e.g., lens and retina) and brain. Even though the eye's optics quickly mature, infants cannot see as well as adults because the brain areas responsible for vision require further maturation. Figure 9.2 provides a diagram of the human eye.

Initially, newborns cannot focus well. At birth **acuity** is 6 times worse than in normal adults. At birth, vision is unclear partly because the **ciliary muscles** have not fully matured. Even when infants focus correctly, vision may remain blurry because the **fovea** (responsible for detail and color vision) is immature. Infants focus at all distances, but initially they do not have good control of their ciliary muscles. They may focus too close (in front of the object) or too far (behind the object). At around 2 months of age, infants begin to focus images onto their retina, although images still are unclear.

From birth to full maturity of the visual system, the eye triples in size, with most of this growth being completed by age 3. Newborns have poor visual fixation ability, very limited ability to discriminate color, limited visual fields, and an estimated visual acuity of somewhere between 20/200 and 20/400. During the first month of life,

Figure 9.2   **Diagram of the Eye**

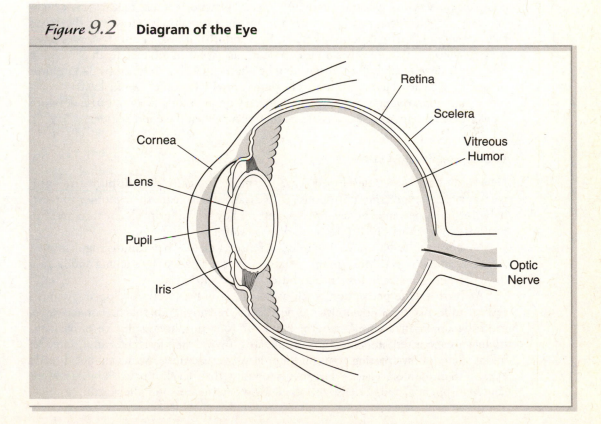

babies have an estimated visual acuity of about 20/120, equivalent to the ability to read only the big *E* on an eye chart. Visual acuity gradually improves and is similar to adults' acuity by 1 year of age (Aslin, 1987a).

Infants perceive movement before they see objects clearly. Most full-term babies can perceive facial expressions within a week of birth. Color vision and depth perception are not fully developed at birth but nearly fully mature during the first year. Babies may exhibit eyes turned in, turned out, or not working as a team when muscles on one side of the eye pull more than those on the other side. These conditions are forms of strabismus.

Newborns gaze longer at patterns than at solid forms and prefer to look at human faces rather than other objects. When looking at a human face, a newborn first focuses on the hairline or edge of the face. By 2 months of age, infants begin to focus more on facial features (e.g., eyes and mouth). At approximately 4–5 months old, infants distinguish between familiar and unfamiliar faces.

Vision soon becomes one of the infant's major sources of information. Infants can perceive color. As young as 2 weeks, they can distinguish red from green. Their color vision is not as well developed as adults' because the receptors and nerves in the eye that are most sensitive to color (in the fovea) are not mature. Infants cannot distinguish subtle color differences (e.g., between red and reddish-orange).

Infants attend more to high-contrast (e.g., black and white) and moderately complex objects and can track moving objects. Newborns most readily track high-contrast, large objects moving neither too fast nor too slowly. However, their eyes follow these objects with jerky motions. By 3 months of age, infants follow a slow-moving object with relatively smooth eye motions. At birth, infants' depth perception is not fully developed, but it is believed to be relatively well developed by 3–5 months of age, the age at which most infants begin to crawl (Gibson & Walk, 1960).

Visual impairments present at birth or early on are more likely to cause developmental delays than are visual problems that occur when the child is older.

Touch, Smell, and Taste

Newborns have a well-developed sense of smell. Typically they display a relaxed, pleasant facial expression in response to pleasant smells (e.g., their mother's breast, baby formula, perfume, honey, or chocolate). They frown, grimace, or turn away in response to noxious smells (e.g., ammonia or sulfur).

Newborns also have a well-developed sense of taste. They can distinguish salty, sour, bitter, and sweet. Most infants react to sweet substances by sucking and licking their lips and grimace in response to bitter or sour substances.

At birth **tactile perception**, such as touch, is not as well developed. At birth several inborn reflexes demonstrate newborns' sensitivity to touch. For example, touching an infant's cheek, mouth, hand, or foot produces reflexive movement. Infants are more responsive to air puffs directed toward their eyes than adults are. An infant's nervous system can transmit pain. However, because infants cannot directly express their comfort levels, it is difficult to know their level of pain. Pain cries (sudden, high-pitched, and not easily soothed away) are heard soon after birth.

In most cases, tactile interactions provide a sense of security. But some babies are overly sensitive to touch (e.g., move a great deal or atypically, such as by pulling away). These infants do not appear to find touch comforting and do not react positively to rocking and hugging (Aslin, 1987b).

Auditory Disabilities

"Your child has a hearing loss." Those words may cause any number of reactions ranging from shock and disbelief, to denial or anger, to sadness and confusion. Many images appear in the minds of parents when they hear that their child has a hearing impairment. Concern about their child's future and education contribute to the stress with which family members must cope. Each year 24,000 U.S. children are born with hearing loss (Hayes & Northern, 1996). Most of these children are born to parents with normal hearing.

Audiologists

Audiologists provide and coordinate services for children with auditory disabilities. They typically have a master's degree in audiology and are certified. They evaluate the level of auditory functioning. If a child has a hearing loss at a particular frequency, audiologists provide information about the types of sounds that may be difficult for the child to hear. They also recommend specific types of amplification or assistive devices to enhance the child's hearing.

Causes of Hearing Loss

Understanding the causes of hearing loss helps in preventing and detecting losses and in providing appropriate intervention services. Possible causes of **sensorineural hearing loss** (dysfunction of the neural elements involved in conducting or interpreting nerve impulses originating in the cochlea) include a family history of congenital sensorineural hearing loss and complications during pregnancy, including Rh-blood-type incompatibility or intrauterine infection (such as rubella, herpes, cytomegalovirus, or syphilis). Birth complications, including premature delivery with a birth weight of less than 1,500 grams (3 pounds) also are related to sensorineural hearing losses (Chase, Hall, & Werkhaven, 1996).

In addition, syndromes associated with hearing loss may be present at birth, such as **Alport syndrome** (a genetic condition characterized by the progressive loss of kidney function and hearing), **Pendred syndrome 9** (a disease characterized by congenital deafness), **Usher's syndrome** (a genetic disorder characterized by a hearing impairment and an eye disorder), **Waardenburg's syndrome** (a genetic disorder associated with hearing loss and changes in skin and hair pigmentation), and fetal alcohol syndrome (FAS). Prolonged high fever; childhood diseases such as measles, mumps, or chicken pox; viral infection, including meningitis or encephalitis; drugs; physical damage to the head or ear; and exposure to a prolonged or sudden intense noise are all known to contribute to sensorineural hearing loss in children (Green, 1976).

Possible causes of **conductive hearing loss** (blockage or other structural abnormality of the ear that prevents sound waves from reaching the inner ear) include wax or a foreign object that is blocking the ear canal, a tear or hole in the eardrum, fluid or infection in the middle ear, loud noises, maternal rubella during pregnancy, meningitis, congenital malformations such as sealed ear canal, and bony overgrowth called otosclerosis (Green, 1976).

Not all hearing losses are present at birth. Causes of hearing loss later in childhood include genetic factors, illness, and trauma (Hall, Oyer, & Hass, 2001). Figure 9.3 summarizes known risk factors associated with hearing loss (Arnos, Israel, Devlin, & Wilson, 1996).

Assessments for Hearing Loss

Referral.   It is crucial that hearing loss be identified as early as possible. The first 3 years of life are a critical time for speech and language development (Goldberg, 1993). Too often, children are not identified as having a hearing loss until after the age of 3. Even when parents suspect their child has a hearing loss, well-intentioned individuals often tell them, "Your child will probably outgrow these delays." Because

---

Figure 9.3   **Risk Factors for Hearing Problems in Young Children**

- Genetic or congenital factors
- Family history of hereditary childhood sensorineural hearing loss
- Congenital infections known to be associated with hearing loss
- Craniofacial anomalies
- Low birth weight
- Low Apgar scores (0–4 at one minute or 0–6 at 5 minutes)
- Hyperbilirubinemia (excessive bilirubin in the blood, characterized by jaundice) requiring exchange transfusion
- Ototoxic (damaging to the auditory system) medications
- Bacterial meningitis
- Mechanical ventilation (respirator) for 5 days or longer
- Recurrent or chronic otitis media (ear infections)
- Maternal infections during pregnancy, including rubella (German measles), syphilis, or herpes
- Abnormality in appearance of the ears, face, mouth, or throat (e.g., cleft palate)
- Use of certain intravenous antibiotics and diuretics after birth
- Head trauma with a skull fracture or loss of consciousness
- Recurrence or persistence of fluid behind the eardrum for at least 3 months

of this tendency, a national panel of experts on hearing loss who are supported by the National Institutes of Health has recommended that all infants be screened for hearing impairments.

Pediatricians are usually the first professionals parents interact with when a child's hearing loss is suspected. They check for earwax blocking the ear canals, middle ear fluid or infection, and a problem with the eardrum. If necessary, pediatricians remove wax and treat ear infections with antibiotics. If there is no fluid in the ear canal or other obvious signs of conductive hearing loss and the child still appears to be having difficulty hearing, the child is often referred to an **ear, nose, and throat specialist (ENT)**, also called an **otolaryngologist** or **otologist**. ENTs examine a child's ears, nose, and throat and often refer the child for an audiological examination to determine if there is a hearing loss and, if so, to what degree (Northern, & Downs, 1984).

Because hearing loss occurs in varying degrees, it may be difficult to identify a child with a hearing loss.

Screening.   As mentioned earlier, the Individuals with Disabilities Education Act (IDEA) requires states to develop and implement a statewide system of early intervention services for infants and toddlers with disabilities. These disabilities include auditory disabilities identified using at-risk criteria and appropriate audiologic screening techniques.

It is becoming common to give newborns hearing screenings before they leave the hospital or maternity center (Goldberg, 1993). Screening procedures for newborns and infants are designed to detect permanent or fluctuating, bilateral or unilateral, and sensory or conductive hearing loss. When newborn screening does not occur, the average age of detection of significant hearing loss is approximately 14 months (Task Force on Newborn and Infant Hearing, 1999). Currently, 44 states and the District of Columbia have **Early Hearing Detection and Intervention (EHDI)** laws or voluntary compliance programs, resulting in 95% of U.S. newborns' receiving hearing screenings.

Typically, an audiologist certified by the American Speech-Language-Hearing Association (ASHA), and state licensed where applicable, oversees hearing screening programs. The screening of newborns and infants involves use of noninvasive physiological measures, including **otoacoustic emissions (OAEs)** or **auditory brainstem response (ABR)**. These tests can be completed while the infant is resting quietly.

OAEs are inaudible vibrations that come from the cochlea when audible vibrations stimulate the cochlea. During an OAE test, the cochlea's outer hair cells vibrate, and this produces an inaudible vibration that bounces back into the middle ear. This vibration can be measured with a small probe inserted into the ear canal.

OAE screenings include **tympanometry, acoustic reflex**, and **static acoustic impedance**. Tympanometry introduces air pressure into the ear canal, resulting in vibration of the eardrum. The mobility of the eardrum is then measured. Tympanograms (graphs) show eardrum movement as normal or abnormal. Acoustic reflex is contraction of the ear muscle in response to loud sounds. The test assesses the loudness level at which the reflex occurs or determines the absence of the reflex, leading to diagnostic information. Static acoustic measures estimate the volume of air in the ear canal. This test is useful in identifying a perforated eardrum and determining whether ear tubes are clear.

ABR is sometimes used to screen infants' hearing. ABR involves placing electrodes on the head to record brain-wave activity in response to sound. ABR can detect damage to the cochlea, auditory nerve, and auditory pathways in the brainstem.

Typically, **visual reinforcement audiometry (VRA)** is the preferred auditory screening method for children between 6 months and 2 years of age. Use of VRA involves teaching the child to look toward a sound source by providing reinforcement (e.g., presenting a toy that moves) after the child looks toward the sound source.

Conditioned play audiometry (CPA) is often used to assess the hearing of children between 2 and 3 years of age. Children are taught to wait, listen, and respond to an activity (e.g., putting a block in a box, placing pegs in a hole, or putting a ring on a cone) each time they hear a sound.

The most accurate auditory assessment occurs when earphones are used. Earphones allow each ear to independently obtain information. When children refuse to use earphones or earphone placement is not possible, sounds can be presented through speakers inside a sound booth. This method (sound field screening) does not provide ear-specific information; therefore, hearing loss in only one ear may not be detected.

Comprehensive Assessment. When auditory screening indicates a possible hearing loss, a full auditory assessment is warranted. Accurately assessing children's auditory abilities requires gaining information about the child's history of otitis media (ear infections and fluid within the middle ear), auditory behaviors (reacting to and recognizing sounds), parents' general concerns about hearing and communication, and risk factors for hearing loss.

In addition to collecting this historical data, evaluators use various tests in combination with observation of the child's general awareness of sound (e.g., the mother's voice, environmental sounds, and music) to determine a general level of auditory responsiveness. This is often referred to as an **unconditioned behavioral response procedure**.

Audiologists measure the amount of a person's hearing loss by looking at two dimensions of sound: loudness, measured in **decibels (dB)**, and pitch, measured in Hertz (Hz). These two dimensions are plotted on a chart called an **audiogram**. Audiologists describe a hearing loss as mild, moderate, severe, or profound (Herer & Reilly, 1999; Pappas, 1985). Table 9.1 shows the generally accepted categories of hearing loss.

The numbers provided by an audiogram indicate how loud a sound must be before a person can hear it. For example, if Victoria has moderate hearing loss, a sound must be louder than 50 dB before she can hear it. Figure 9.4 shows Victoria's audiogram. The audiogram

Table *9.1*	*Degrees of Hearing Loss*
Decibel Range	**Diagnosis**
0–15 dB	Normal hearing
15–30 dB	Mild hearing loss
30–60 dB	Moderate hearing loss
60–90 dB	Severe hearing loss
90+ dB	Profound hearing loss

Figure 9.4   **Victoria's Audiogram**

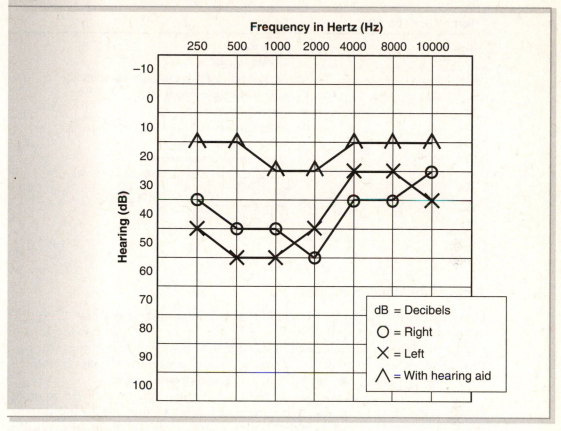

indicates hearing loss at all frequencies in both ears. For comparison, Table 9.2 shows the decibel levels of some common sounds.

Loudness and pitch are two important factors in sound. Clarity, another important factor, is harder to identify. Sounds may sometimes be distorted with a hearing loss, resulting in a loss of clarity and causing one sound to be mistaken for another. For example, the word "share" may sound like "chair." When children experience frequent distortions in everyday conversation, the hearing loss may adversely affect their daily functioning. To determine whether a child has a hearing loss, several different types of hearing tests may be conducted (Pappas, 1985).

As part of full auditory assessments, VRA, **conditioned orienting response (COR)**, and CPA are often used to determine threshold sensitivity in infants beginning at about 6 months of age (developmental age).

An audiologist tests the child's hearing and middle ear functioning and reports the findings to the referring physician. If hearing aids are recommended, approval from a physician is typically required (Bess, 1988).

Table 9.2	Decibel Levels of Some Common Sounds

Hearing Level (in dB)	Sounds
10–25	Whisper
40	Library sounds
25–50	Normal conversation, living room sounds
60	Crying baby, air conditioner
70	Vacuum cleaner
80	Ringing telephone, barking dog
90	Lawn mower, hair dryer
100	Electric razor, snowmobile
110	Power saw, jet engine, helicopter
120	Stereo
130	Rock concert
140	Jet engine (nearby)

Types of Auditory Disabilities

Degrees of hearing loss vary from mild to profound, including deafness. Categories of hearing loss include conductive (caused by diseases or obstructions in the outer or middle ear), sensorineural (caused by damage to sensory hair cells of the inner ear), **mixed** (caused by a combination of conductive and sensorineural factors), and **central** (caused by damage to the nerves of the central nervous system).

When sound cannot pass through the outer or middle ear, the problem is considered a conductive hearing loss. When the transmission of sound is disrupted somewhere in the inner ear, such as in the cochlea or auditory nerve, the problem is called a sensorineural hearing loss. When there is a conductive and sensorineural problem, it is called a mixed loss. Both ears may have a similar loss, or one ear may be more affected (Kaderavek & Pakulski, 2002).

Potential Effects of Auditory Disabilities

Many factors influence how well a person copes with a hearing loss. The degree of hearing loss determines how the hearing loss affects other areas, including speech and language, cognitive, and social-emotional development (Green, 1976; Moores, 2001). Having both ears, rather than just one, functioning below normal standards also affects the ability to cope with a hearing loss. In addition, the age of onset of a hearing loss affects development. Hearing loss at birth, called **congenital hearing loss**, typically has a greater negative effect on development than does a hearing loss that occurs after a child has developed speech and language at approximately age 3.

When deafness is **prelingual**—that is, occurs before a child develops speech—it often has serious consequences of speech and language development. Children who never hear language sounds have more difficulty acquiring speech and language skills than a child who had some hearing before the age of 2. **Postlingual deafness** (sometimes referred to as **"adventitious deafness"**) occurs after a child has acquired some language skills and typically has a less negative effect on language development (Lane, 1988).

The age at which hearing loss is identified also is important (Bess, 1988; Naiman & Schein, 1978). Early amplification with hearing aids and early intervention by specialists, such as a **teacher of the deaf/hearing-impaired** or a speech and language pathologist, may have a major effect on a child's development. Consistently wearing a hearing aid typically reduces the outcomes associated with the hearing impairment, including negative effects on speech and language, cognitive, and social-emotional skills (Northern & Downs, 1984).

The level of a child's innate intelligence also affects the influence of a hearing loss. Hearing loss affects intellectually gifted children less negatively than mentally retarded children. If a hearing impairment is a child's only developmental disability, this loss typically has less effect on development (McArthur, 1982).

The way in which a child's family reacts to the hearing loss may have a major effect on the child's development. Family members must reach a level of acceptance that allows them to commit to the development of the whole child rather than focusing on the disability (McArthur, 1982). Careful coordination of the type of communication method used at home with the language used at school may lessen the negative effect of a hearing loss (Gatty, 1996; Ling, 1989).

Children with hearing impairments should be encouraged to use the language skills they have rather than be allowed to not try to communicate. Because communication is often more difficult for them, use of language must be encouraged rather than expected. Children who are hearing-impaired are less likely to use language spontaneously but can use language when others encourage them to do so.

If a child has a profound hearing loss not identified and treated until after the child's third birthday, the effect is often significant. The most obvious effect of a hearing loss is difficulty in communicating (Boothroyd, 1978). Loss of hearing within two octaves of the normal range of human speech has a more negative effect on speech and language development than hearing losses at higher or lower frequencies.

Language Development.   Young children with and without impaired hearing begin to babble at approximately the same age. Over time, if they do not hear their own and others' voices, they stop babbling. This interrupts a critical period of speech practice. If babies do not continue to babble, the voice begins to lose its prosody (Stoel-Gammon & Otomo, 1986). In addition, the less babies babble, the less attention they receive. This results in fewer episodes of verbal communication, which decreases the opportunities for babies to develop language (Calvert, 1984).

By the time babies with hearing impairments reach their first birthday, they usually are already delayed in the development of receptive language (the ability to understand language). Without early intervention the gap usually widens (Schildroth & Hotto, 1991; Schildroth, Rawlings, & Allen, 1989; Stewart & Kluwin, 2001). Language is everywhere, but children who are hearing-impaired have limited access to it. They are likely to miss out on everyday conversations, questions from siblings, and responses made by parents and other adults.

Children with Down syndrome often have visual disabilities and cognitive delays.

Speech Development.   Children with severe or profound hearing loss often develop unique voice patterns (Bess, 1988). Their voices are sometimes too loud or soft. Their voices may lack prosody and sound monotonous or too high-pitched. Such children often do not support longer sentences with proper breathing and have incorrect patterns of syllable stress and phrasing. They may make numerous articulation errors. For example, the word "baby" may sound like "maybe," or the word "school" like "cool."

With early amplification through hearing aids and with intensive speech training, many of these speech patterns may be prevented or corrected. If, however, the hearing loss is identified after a child is 6–12 months old, years of speech therapy are often needed. About 25% of children with profound hearing loss and 45% of children classified as deaf have unintelligible speech, even with extensive speech therapy.

Cognitive Development.   Hearing loss does not determine a child's intelligence or achievement. However, language deprivation may contribute to a delay in the development of a child's knowledge base. Language aids in understanding and organizing information. Language facilitates many cognitive skills, such as storing and remembering information, discussing how things are similar or different, classifying things, defining and describing, reasoning, inventing, and solving problems. Language comprehension greatly affects academic achievement. If language is delayed, cognitive skills such as pre-reading abilities may also be delayed (Martin, 1987b; Moores, 2001).

Social-Emotional Development.   Because communication with family members and friends is often less frequent in children with hearing impairments, social interactions are limited in quantity and quality (limited to simpler concepts and vocabulary). Insufficient communication can result in feelings of isolation and inadequacy (Anita & Kreimeyer, 1992; Lee & Antia, 1992).

Until they develop more socially acceptable ways to communicate, young children with hearing impairments often express their needs and desires in physical ways, such as by grabbing or pushing, or by having temper tantrums. Once they learn the power of language, they learn the value of positive interactions, which allow friendships to develop. For most children, verbal negotiating and reasoning skills are gradually developed during the preschool years. Children with hearing impairments are at greater risk of negative self-esteem (Ling, 1984).

Hearing Impairment Intervention Services

Once a child's hearing loss has been identified, several important educational decisions must be made. It is critical for parents and preschool teachers to understand the special needs of a young child with a hearing loss so that appropriate interventions are made available to the child (Lowenbraun, 1988). Several key professionals are involved in providing services, including audiologists, special education teachers, speech and language pathologists, and teachers of the hearing-impaired and deaf.

Teachers specializing in hearing impairments typically have a teaching degree and a master's degree in education of the hearing-impaired and deaf. They know sign language and have knowledge regarding assessment and auditory equipment. Although the rate of hearing impairments remains low, too few teachers specialize in this area.

The auditory-oral method encourages children to make use of the hearing they have (**residual hearing**) and use hearing aids or cochlear implants (Craig, 1992; Geers & Tobey, 1992). Speech reading, sometimes called lip reading, is used to supplement residual hearing. In this method children learn to listen and speak but do not learn sign language (described below).

The **auditory-verbal** method focuses on encouraging children to fully use their residual hearing, either via hearing aids or a cochlear implant. Using this method, therapists work with children one-on-one to help them learn to focus on listening skills. Therapists also work with parents and other care providers to help them develop the skills they need to help children use their auditory abilities. This approach does not encourage speech reading, and sign language is not taught.

The **auditory-oral** approach is based on the philosophy that acquiring competence in receptive and expressive spoken language is an appropriate goal for most children with hearing impairments. This method emphasizes immersion within environments in which people exclusively use spoken language. The auditory-oral approach requires parental involvement, appropriate amplification, speech training, and language instruction.

Use of **cued speech** focuses on teaching children to visually process spoken language. Children are instructed to focus on mouth movements. This focus is combined with eight hand shapes (cues) that represent groups of consonants and four positions around the face that represent vowel sounds. Some sounds look alike on the lips (e.g., "b" and "p"), and others cannot be seen on the lips (e.g., "k"). The hand cues help children determine which sounds are being voiced.

There are two basic types of sign language. **Signing Exact English (SEE)** is an artificial language that follows the grammatical structure of English. **American Sign Language (ASL) (manual communication)** is a language system with its own strict linguistic rules. In ASL, hand signs represent letters, words, and phrases. ASL is often taught as the child's first or only language. If taught, spoken English is presented as a second language.

Total communication entails using any and all means available to the hearing-impaired learner to understand the message. This method includes using sign language, hearing aids or other sound amplification methods, speech reading, visuals, and natural gestures.

Assistive Technology

An **assistive listening device (ALD)** is a device used in day-to-day communication. An ALD can be used with or without hearing aids to overcome the negative effects of distance, background noise, or poor room acoustics. For those fitted with hearing aids, other ALDs can make hearing easier (less stressful and tiring) in many communication situations. ALDs are used to maximize children's hearing and learning capabilities. A certified audiologist is responsible for evaluating, selecting, procuring, and monitoring ALDs and for instructing teachers and students in their use (Bloom, 1996).

Hearing Aids.   **Hearing aids** are the most frequently used assistive devices for children with hearing impairments. Early hearing-aid technology involved vacuum tubes and large, heavy batteries. Today microchips and digitized sound are used in hearing-aid design.

Conventional analog hearing aids are designed with a particular frequency response based on an individual's audiogram. An audiologist's prescription for a hearing aid indicates to manufacturers what settings to install. This type of aid amplifies all sounds (speech and noise) in the same way. This technology is the least expensive and is appropriate for many different, but not all, types of hearing loss.

Analog programmable hearing aids have a microchip, which is programmed for different listening environments (quiet conversation, noisy situations, large areas, etc.). An audiologist uses a computer to program the hearing aid for different listening situations based on an individual's hearing loss profile, speech understanding, and range of tolerance for louder sounds. Some aids are capable of storing several programs, which adjust as the listening environment changes. These aids allow the individual to modify the settings of the hearing aid by pushing a button on it or by using a remote control to switch channels. The audiologist can reprogram these aids if hearing or hearing needs change. These aids are more expensive than conventional analog hearing aids but have a longer life and provide better hearing in a wider variety of settings.

Digital programmable hearing aids have all the features of analog programmable aids, but they convert sound waves into digital signals. In this type of hearing aid, a computer chip analyzes auditory signals to determine if the sound is speech or noise and automatically modifies the sound input to provide a clear, amplified, relatively distortion-free signal. Digital processing allows for optimal adjustments to each person's hearing loss pattern.

Hearing aids sold through mail-order catalogs or at local department stores are not effective for most children. An audiologist should guide the selection and proper fitting of hearing aids. Children may qualify for public assistance to pay for a hearing aid if insurance does not cover the cost.

Other Technology.   Another form of technological intervention is a wireless **frequency modulated auditory trainer.** It is most often used in educational settings (VanTasell, Mallinger, & Crump, 1986). Some parents find this technology useful at home with a child who is hearing-impaired. A personal frequency-modulation (FM) system is like a miniature radio station operating on a special frequency assigned by the Federal Communications Commission. It consists of two parts: a transmitter (microphone) worn by a teacher or other adult and a receiver worn by the hearing-impaired child. It functions like a hearing aid but adds two benefits: (1) the listener can receive sound signals from up to about 20 feet so the speaker can move around the classroom, and (2) the listener receives a strong auditory signal directly from the teacher that overrides most background noise in a classroom. In some situations an FM trainer may be more useful than a hearing aid because personal hearing aids cannot compensate for a noisy environment (Ross, 1981). FM trainers allow children to hear the teacher's voice at an appropriate, constant intensity, regardless of the distance between the child and the teacher and regardless of background noise.

Infrared systems transmit sound by sending infrared light waves to an individual receiver. These systems are often used in the home. For example, when the family is watching television, the volume can be set at a comfortable level for family members and the individual with hearing loss can use an infrared system to increase volume to an individual set of head phones.

Induction loop systems involve placing a thin wire around a listening area. This wire is connected to a special amplifier and microphone(s). As speech signals are amplified and circulated through the loop wire, a magnetic energy field is detected and amplified by the telecoil or telephone switch circuitry. This process creates a high-quality amplified reproduction of the original speech signal. This method results in enhanced speech intelligibility as well as reduction of background noise. Typically, induction loop wires are permanently installed (e.g., under carpet). They are connected to a speaker's microphone, or a wire loop is laid on the floor around the speaker.

One-to-one communicators are used when an individual needs to easily hear one person. This system involves giving the person a microphone to speak into. The sound is then amplified and delivered directly into an individual's hearing aid or headset, allowing the individual to adjust the volume to the most comfortable level.

Another technological intervention is a **cochlear implant**. This is a medical intervention that must be combined with educational interventions to succeed. It is also the last option after all other attempts to improve auditory functioning have failed. This device is designed to provide sound stimulation to profoundly deaf children and adults. Typically, it is available only to patients for whom hearing aids or vibrotactile aids have been of no benefit. It requires major surgery and a long period of auditory rehabilitation (learning or relearning how to process sound) with trained professionals. A cochlear implant is not a cure for deafness. It does not fully restore hearing, but it does provide increased sensitivity to sound for most patients. Even with intensive auditory training, most patients still have some level of hearing impairment.

There are many other ALDs, including amplifying devices for cordless, cell, digital, and wired phones; amplified answering machines, paging systems, computers, and wake-up alarms; and so on. **Visual systems** (e.g., flashing lights) can be used alone or in combination with listening devices and hearing aids. In addition, a wide variety of **alerting devices** signal when a sound has occurred—sounds such as a doorbell, knock, fire alarm, baby's crying, or clock alarm.

Exposure to a Language-Rich Environment

Much information comes from having a simple conversation and hearing books read. Children with hearing loss frequently do not have the benefit of experiencing conversations and other common parent–child interactions. For example, parents of hearing-impaired children may believe that their children do not benefit from having books read to them. Lack of experiences such as these can result in a gap between the cognitive abilities of children who are hearing-impaired and those who are not (Luterman, 1970). Rather than decreasing language-rich experiences, adults should increase communication with hearing-impaired children, including by frequently reading to them. In addition, adults should increase the knowledge base of hearing-impaired children by providing them with firsthand and hands-on experiences such as a trip to a farm, a train ride, and family discussions (Calvert, 1984).

Parents and teachers must use a variety of methods to increase concept development for children with hearing impairments (Ross, 1981). Hearing-impaired children must have information presented in ways other than verbal instruction. They acquire a great deal of information when visual images (pictures) and concrete props (actual objects) are used. For example, when attempting to teach a hearing-impaired child the word *apple,* showing a real apple or pictures of apples of various colors, shapes, and sizes while presenting the word helps the child acquire the concept "apple." Firsthand experiences are often the most meaningful for children, particularly for hearing-impaired children (Ross, 1982).

Parents and teachers need to provide opportunities for hearing-impaired children to think things through. For example, allowing a child to bring snow inside to discover what happens may help when explaining melting. Adults also need to resist doing things for children who are hearing-impaired that they can do for themselves. Children learn about sorting and classifying when allowed and encouraged to help put away their toys. They learn much more about the world and how things work when adults allow them to experience life firsthand (Gatty, 1992). It may be quicker for a teacher or parent to take control and put a coat on a child rather than to try to communicate to the child, "It is time to put on your coat," but it does not teach the child how to communicate.

Program Placement

A child with significant hearing loss is eligible for team evaluation. An assessment team meets with the child's parents and evaluates the child's degree of hearing loss and level of development in all major areas. After the evaluation has been completed, the team makes recommendations for specific early intervention services. These services may include home visits by a specialist, a specialist's coming to the child's day care or nursery school site, or a center-based preschool program for children with disabilities. Federal law mandates that the team find the least restrictive environment (LRE), an environment in which services are appropriately provided but which is as much like a typical learning environment as possible. Federal law further requires that the child's progress and program be evaluated annually.

Once the type of hearing loss is determined and appropriate medical interventions have been implemented (e.g., treatment for ear infection or removal of ear wax), the team develops educational interventions. The team members consider many factors, including the degree of hearing loss, age of the child, and existence of other disabilities. A recommendation is made regarding the types of early intervention services appropriate for a particular child and how those services are to be provided (Ling, 1984).

A child with a mild hearing loss and no other disability can usually function well with minimal intervention. Intervention techniques might include teaching parents or care providers how to face the child when talking, keep background noise to a minimum during conversations with the child, and maintain a hearing aid if one is prescribed. Regular preschool education is often appropriate for a child with mild or moderate hearing loss (Moores, 1985). Most children with mild hearing loss have difficulty hearing whispers or other faint sounds. They may need speech therapy to learn to discriminate between and produce certain sounds. Children with mild hearing loss may benefit from sitting near to the person speaking and having adequate lighting for lip reading. They may also need some form of sound amplification, such as a hearing aid or frequency modulated auditory trainer (Moores, 1985).

Typically, children with moderate hearing loss have difficulty with loud and soft speech and telephone conversations. They frequently have more difficulty understanding the speech of unfamiliar people than that of familiar people. These children generally function well in a regular education classroom with extra adult support as well as some form of amplification. They typically need speech and language therapy on a regular basis (Diefendorf, 1996; Quigley & Paul, 1990).

Children with more severe hearing loss generally require intensive speech and language training. Specialists help to maximize the development of the children's residual hearing. These children have difficulty identifying many consonant sounds. They hear only shouts, loud noises, or amplified speech. They typically have difficulty with speech unless they receive ongoing speech therapy. Children with severe hearing impairments frequently attend special classes.

Teaching children who have severe hearing impairments and their peers how to communicate with each other is also critical. The team of professionals and parents must decide as early as possible about the type of communication system to be used. This depends on the child's degree of hearing loss, age, and ability levels and on the parents' preferences. Once the decision regarding the method of communication has been made, all participants must make every effort to provide a unified program. Several different types of communication systems may be used (Bess, 1988; Luterman, 1970).

Total communication, a system in which all means of communication are used, might be chosen as the method of communication with a particular child. The child's family should then take every opportunity to learn and use sign language. When total communication is used, teachers should use sign language throughout the day in the classroom. Children who are not hearing-impaired should also be given an opportunity to learn sign language. It would be ideal if all the children could sign, but sometimes it is more realistic to teach basic sign language to one or two interested peers. Most preschool-age children are fascinated by sign language and learn it very quickly (Quigley & Paul, 1990).

In addition to using sign language, a child should wear hearing aids throughout the day. At school, a child's ability to hear speech should be amplified. However, hearing aids amplify all nearby sounds along with the speaker's voice, and many noise sources are found in a preschool setting. Therefore, many professionals strongly recommend a frequency modulated auditory trainer. The auditory trainer allows a teacher freedom of movement in the classroom and helps ensure that their voice carries over the classroom noise (Ross, 1981).

Preschool options for a child with hearing loss include attending regular nursery schools, preschool programs designed for children who have speech and language delays or are hearing-impaired, and schools for deaf children. There has been a major change of focus regarding the placement of children with disabilities. Most states are moving toward inclusion, placing a child with a disability in the same classroom as children without disabilities. Federal laws mandate that each child be educated in the LRE. This environment or placement option may be different for each child, depending on many factors such as the child's ability to comprehend language (Gatty, 1992).

Children who are hearing-impaired may benefit from inclusion, but several issues must be addressed throughout the school year to ensure that inclusion remains the best option. Figure 9.5 lists questions that should be asked to help determine the LRE.

A preschool class in a program designed specifically for the hearing-impaired is another placement option. This type of class might be provided within a facility with only hearing-impaired students of different ages or be located in a program in which some of the classes are for children with and without hearing impairments. In a program designed especially for children who are hearing-impaired, a teacher of the deaf typically establishes the main educational program. The teacher provides coordinated programs designed to ensure that each child who is hearing-impaired receives consistent language instruction throughout the school day. In addition, a speech and language pathologist provides speech and listening instruction that is integrated into classroom activities throughout each school day (Stewart, 1990).

Figure 9.5 **Questions That Should Be Asked to Help Determine Whether an LRE Exists**

- Does the child have access to instruction in sign language if needed?
- Is the teacher prepared for a child who is hearing-impaired to be in the class?
- Is the teacher making the appropriate adaptations to the daily program to accommodate the child's needs?
- Is the teacher using a frequency modulated auditory trainer? If so, is it being used properly?
- Is the hearing-impaired child progressing in speech, language, and cognitive skills?
- Is the child making friends?

Preschool programs that provide special services for children with communication disorders offer children with hearing loss the time to interact with children without hearing impairments. In this case, children who are hearing-impaired are in an inclusion setting while benefiting from a specially trained team, including a special education teacher, speech and language pathologist, and teacher of the deaf. Children who are not hearing-impaired also benefit from placements that incorporate inclusion because they learn how to interact with peers who are hearing-impaired.

In most cases, children with hearing impairments may be educated in regular preschool classes or in classes that focus on speech and language impairments. In some cases, however, preschoolers who have hearing impairments may attend a school for the deaf. Most deaf children do not attend these schools until they reach school age (usually age 5).

To attend a school for the deaf, a child must have profound hearing loss in both ears. Profound hearing loss, or deafness, is a low-incident (less than .01%) communication disorder. Schools for the deaf provide a peer group with similar needs. Deaf children often feel isolated when placed in the hearing world. A few schools for the deaf still use an oral-aural teaching method (the emphasis is on using cued speech methods to teach children to use spoken language for communication, and sign language is not used), but most schools for the deaf now use a total-communication approach (Evans & Falk, 1986).

There has been a movement toward the use of ASL, which does not use the voice for instruction, partly because many believe that this approach best preserves deaf culture (Lane, 1988). Philosophical differences regarding how best to communicate with and educate children who are deaf often cause great controversy among professionals in the field. Many people believe it is not reasonable to expect children who are deaf to learn two languages, oral and signing. In addition, people who are deaf believe that forcing children who are deaf to learn how to speak suggests that the children are not acceptable unless they can speak. Other individuals believe we should help children learn to speak the oral language of their community so that they are as assimilated as possible.

Visual Disabilities

Vision loss refers to eyesight that cannot be corrected to a normal level. Type and degree of vision loss varies greatly among children and may be caused by a variety of factors. Ideally, children's vision is assessed within 3 months of birth, between 6 and 12 months of age, and again at 3 and 5 years.

Risk Factors Associated with Vision Disabilities

Vision loss occurs due to eye damage, incorrect eye shape, or brain abnormalities. Some infants are born blind, although vision loss can occur at any time of life. Children's visual impairments are predominantly associated with genetic (53%) and prenatal (34%) factors (Lueck, Chen, & Kekelis, 1997).

Other risk factors include prenatal exposure to certain maternal infections (e.g., toxoplasmosis, syphilis, rubella, cytomegalovirus, herpes, HIV, and chicken pox), prematurity, hypoxia, and abnormal prenatal brain development (Teplin, 1995). Visual impairments may also result from accidents or illnesses. Prenatal exposure to drugs and diseases increases the likelihood of the child's being born with or developing a visual impairment. A recent analysis of data indicates that vitamin A deficiency is the leading cause of childhood blindness (Harvey, 1975; Huebner, Merk-Adams, Styker, & Wolffe, 2004). Diagnoses associated with vision problems include head trauma, cerebral palsy, specific syndromes (e.g., Down, fetal alcohol, trisomy 13, and Usher's), bacterial meningitis, and neurodegenerative disorders (e.g., neurofibromatosis and Tay-Sachs disease). In addition, nearsightedness or farsightedness in an infant's developing eye can cause the brain to favor seeing through one eye, suppressing vision in the other eye and leading to permanent vision impairment.

Warning Signs of Vision Problems

Indicators of vision problems include a drooping eyelid that covers the pupil; abnormal eye shape or structure; absence of a clear, dark pupil; persistent redness in the conjunctiva (normally white); watery or crusty eyes; pupils that look gray; or cross-eyedness. Other indicators include jerky eye movements (nystagmus), an absence of the eyes' moving together, or a sustained eye turn after the infant is 4–6 months old. Other indicators of possible visual impairment include lack of eye contact, visual fixation, lack of visual tracking of objects by 3 months of age, and an absence of accurate reaching for objects by 6 months old (Desrochers, 1999).

Depending on the type and degree of visual impairment, some children also display a preference for brightly colored or black-and-white objects. Some children pay more attention when objects are presented at particular distances or positions. Others are overly sensitive to bright light, which causes them to squint or close their eyes. They may have an unusual gaze or head position when looking at someone or something. Young children with visual impairment often have more difficulty discriminating, recognizing, and understanding pictures and letters.

Children who complain about scratchy eyes, itchy eyes, or headaches; rub their eyes excessively; or sit or move unusually close to objects may have a visual impairment. Children with visual impairments frequently exhibit stereotypical or odd movements of their hands. Those who are socially immature, overly self-conscious, withdrawn, overly passive, or overly dependent may be so due to a visual impairment. Figure 9.6 lists risk factors associated with visual impairments.

Assessment

Referral.   Children displaying one or more of the attributes listed above should be referred for an eye examination. If the child's parent(s) or pediatrician or optometrist (an eye specialist who is not a medical doctor and cannot treat diseases) believes the child may have a vision problem, the child typically is referred to a **pediatric eye doctor (ophthalmologist)**, a medical doctor specializing in eye disorders.

Screening.   Children often receive routine visual evaluations by pediatricians or optometrists. Although **optometrists** are not medical doctors and cannot treat diseases, they can measure vision and prescribe corrective lenses. Optometrists make referrals to ophthalmologists when a pathology is suspected.

Figure 9.6   **Indicators of Possible Vision Impairments**

- Rubs eyes frequently.
- Turns, tilts, or holds head in a strained or unusual position when trying to look at an object.
- Has difficulty finding or picking up small objects dropped on the floor (after the age of 12 months).
- Has difficulty focusing or making eye contact.
- Closes one eye when trying to look at distant objects.
- Eyes appear to be crossed or turned.
- Brings objects very close to eyes to examine.
- One or both eyes appear abnormal in size or coloring.
- Squints.
- Complains that things are blurry or hard to see.
- Holds objects close to eyes in order to see.
- Blinks more than is usual.
- Becomes agitated when doing close-up work (e.g., looking at books).
- One or both eyes are watery.
- One or both eyelids look red-rimmed, crusted, or swollen.

Optometrists typically evaluate visual acuity, refraction, motility, alignment, binocularity, and overall eye health. Assessments of visual acuity and refraction are largely intended to measure for nearsightedness or farsightedness. Following the assessment, the optometrist shares vision test results with the child's parents and, on request, will send a vision report to the child's pediatrician, family physician, or other appropriate specialist.

Full Assessment.   Vision assessment evaluates various visual skills, consistency, endurance, and the ability to generalize visual skills. Typically, family and child health histories are compiled before the assessment of a child's visual abilities. Information about health problems or disabilities that commonly include visual disabilities or that may limit the ability to effectively evaluate vision—for example, albinism, cerebral palsy, seizure disorder, and hearing loss—enhances the efficiency and accuracy of visual assessments. If medications are taken, it is important to obtain information of them because many have side effects. For example, anticonvulsant medications may influence the child's level of alertness and ocular and auditory functioning.

Traditional eye charts with letters or symbols cannot be used with infants and very young children. Therefore, assessment of infant visual acuity includes tests to ensure that the infant can fix their eyes on an object and follow it. Test materials such as pictures or gray cards with stripes of various sizes may be used to determine which objects the baby prefers to look at and at what distances. Lenses and a small hand-held light can be used to assess how the eye responds to particular targets. In addition, photographic testing is used to analyze the pupil reflex.

During the assessment process, parents provide an invaluable interpretation of their child's intent and communicative responses (e.g., changes in breathing or muscle tone). In addition, parents often hold their baby on their laps or on a lap pillow and may assist the examiner by holding objects designed to attract the baby's attention.

Testing materials should be objects common within the child's world and should be culturally and therapeutically appropriate. Both real-life items and toys are used during vision assessment. Assessment materials that might be needed in addition to actual testing items include an adaptive seating device for a child who has a physical disability. Other assistive technology materials may also be required.

As part of a vision assessment, an **ocular motility/alignment/binocular potential test** may be conducted. It assesses the child's ability to move, align, and jointly focus their eyes and can determine the presence of **strabismus** (the eyes aim at different places). Strabismus can lead to **amblyopia** (lazy eye) and ocular diseases. Vision assessment also evaluates eye coordination, the ability of both eyes to work together to create one three-dimensional image in the brain.

Pen lights often are used to gauge eye alignment while infants are shown finger puppets or toys. Red/green glasses (3-D) are used to assess an infant's depth perception. In addition, the eye's external structure (eyelids, tear ducts, etc.) is evaluated. Pupil function also is evaluated. The inner eye is examined through dilated pupils, allowing detection of ocular diseases such as retinoblastoma (the seventh most common pediatric cancer).

Visual acuity alone provides limited information about how much a person's vision loss will affect their life. Therefore, it is essential to assess how well a person uses the vision they have. A person's functional vision can be evaluated by observing them in different settings to see how they use their vision.

A **functional vision assessment (FVA)** is a major feature of the vision evaluation process. The goal of an FVA is to determine what and how the child sees, and what can be done to best facilitate visual learning. This information can be used to individually tailor educational programming, including selection of assistive devices.

Parent information and participation during FVA are crucial and involve collecting functional vision observations (information about children's use of vision during daily activities). FVAs typically occur over several sessions and in more than one environment.

Types of Visual Impairments

Children are classified as visually impaired when even with correction the visual disability adversely affects development. Normal visual field is about 160–170 degrees horizontally. The classification "visually impaired" includes children who have **low vision** (visual acuity between 20/70 and 20/400 or a visual field of 20 degrees or less) or are **partial sighted** or **legally blind** (visual acuity worse than 20/400 with the best possible correction or a visual field of 20 degrees or less) (Bower, 1977; Frailberg, 1977).

Children with visual impairments constitute less than 0.5% of all children receiving special education services (Bambring & Troster, 1992; Barraga & Erin, 1992). The prevalence of visual impairments increases with age. It is estimated that 4 of every 10,000 children are visually impaired. About 1% of children with visual impairments are classified as having severe visual impairment. Visual impairment is more prevalent in children from culturally and linguistically diverse backgrounds. In these cases poor nutrition and infection are believed to contribute to the higher rate of visual impairment (Thompson & Kaufman, 2003).

Children born with visual impairments are referred to as "blind" or "congenitally visually impaired," depending on their level of visual impairment. Children who develop visual problems after birth are referred to as **adventitiously visually impaired**. Unlike children who are born blind, children who lose their sight after age 2 generally retain some memory of visual experiences. The later sight loss occurs, the more visual memory of prior images remains. Visual memory appears to enhance development of concepts and other areas of learning.

Individuals with vision impairments cannot be corrected to a normal level. Vision impairment may be a lack of visual acuity (the eye does not clearly see objects) or loss of visual field (the eye cannot see as wide an area as is usual unless the eyes are moved or the head is turned). Approximately 66% of children with vision impairment also have one or more other developmental disabilities (e.g., mental retardation, cerebral palsy, hearing loss, or epilepsy). Children with more severe vision impairment are more likely to have additional disabilities than children with milder vision impairment (Sackes & Silberman, 1998).

Impact of Visual Impairments

Because vision is the primary organizational and integrative sense for children without vision impairments, the remaining senses are more important for the child with a visual impairment. Concepts about the world are built on perceptions (from various senses) of objects and events. In most cases, vision is an important source of distance information. Although hearing does provide some information about distance, it does not provide information as reliable as the information that vision provides.

Development in all areas—including cognitive, social-emotional, communicative, motor, and self-help skills—is often impacted when children have visual impairments. Because an estimated 85% of all early learning is visual, a blind or visually impaired child is at risk for developmental delays. No other sense naturally stimulates curiosity, integrates information, and invites exploration as efficiently and fully as vision does. Therefore, effective, intensive intervention for children with visual impairment is crucial, particularly during the early years. When a child is born with or acquires vision impairment, the family is challenged to understand the visual diagnosis, the impact of vision loss on development, and the need to bring the world to the child.

As discussed earlier in this book, mutual eye gaze facilitates attachment between infants and their parents. Eye gaze stimulates brain development in infants. Most young infants and their caregivers spend time gazing at, smiling at, and imitating each other. Over time, eye gaze helps establish joint references to objects of interest. When children's vision is impaired, attachment to and communication with parents is more challenging (Holbrook, 1996; Lewis & Allman, 2000).

Teachers of Children with Visual Impairments

Certification requirements for teachers of children with visual disabilities vary across states (some states have no specific certification). Traditionally, too few individuals have been qualified to work with children with visual impairments.

Typically, vision specialists are knowledgeable about methods of adapting the environment, toys, and other learning materials to make them accessible to children with visual impairments. They also are knowledgeable about methods to compensate for vision loss (e.g., to accomplish tasks using touch rather than vision and to learn to use all senses as effectively as possible). They often provide ongoing instruction in daily living skills. For young children, this instruction typically occurs during incidental learning activities using hands-on, step-by-step instruction to guide them to function optimally and independently during typical daily activities (e.g., self-care skills).

Intervention Services

Intervention and educational services for children with visual impairments are provided in a variety of settings, including the home, child care centers, community-based preschools, specialized classes, residential schools for the blind, or some combination of such settings (Amerson, 1999; Miller-Wood, Efron, & Wood, 1990). The effect of visual problems on a child's development depends on severity, type of loss, age at which the condition appears, and overall functioning level of the child (Hagood, 1997; Palazesi, 1986).

Children with visual impairments require specific interventions designed to promote optimal use of any level of vision and all senses. Early intervention services include use of environmental adaptations and optical devices. Professionals must collaborate with families to facilitate their understanding of each child's unique strengths and challenges to help ensure the creation of optimal learning environments (American Foundation for the Blind, 1998).

Teachers of children with visual disabilities assess each child's abilities, preferences, and needs, as well as family concerns and priorities. They adapt the learning environment to help ensure it is accessible and allows optimal use of all senses. Each child has a unique learning style, which requires their teachers to determine individual preferences for types and sequences of sensory information, motivating materials and interactions, pacing and cueing needs, general temperament, level of motivation, and so on.

Cognitive Development.   Effective cognitive development opportunities for children with visual impairments are experience-based (Larsen & Hammill, 1975). Experiences must be designed to teach concepts and problem-solving skills typically acquired primarily through vision through the use of other senses. Ideally, cognitive activities include activities that help prepare young children for Braille and printed-word experiences.

When vision is impaired, it is more difficult for children to acquire detailed, integrated information about individuals, objects, and the environment. Often, systematic learning does not occur incidentally or spontaneously for children with vision impairments.

Between ages 4 and 6 months, most children start to reach for or bat at the objects placed in front of them. Initially, reaching toward these objects occurs by chance. Over time, reaching becomes increasingly deliberate as children's vision and depth perception mature.

For children with vision impairments, this natural progression regarding manipulation of objects is often delayed. At first, these children may hesitate to touch objects. They need gentle encouragement to do so. Their hands need to be guided toward objects and to explore the objects. Young children with visual impairments need to develop a refined ability to use their hands for touch to learn about the world and develop functional skills. Initially, tactual exploration is the primary learning modality for young children with visual impairments.

When infants are on the floor or in the crib, it is often helpful to place items that make music or noise close to their bodies. Touching the item then provides immediate feedback. That is, auditory learning is paired with tactual learning, increasing the amount of information available. Placing visually high-contrast items or items with relatively bright lights in front of infants also enhances visual experience for many who have visual impairments. Between 6 and 8 months most children roll over and begin to crawl, so infants with visual impairments benefit from being provided with toys that can be accessed by rolling over or crawling a short distance.

Typically, from 8 to 12 months, children crawl and begin to pull themselves up to a standing position and walk. Children with visual impairments frequently benefit from being encouraged to continue crawling rather than engage in early walking. Continuing to crawl provides more eye–hand coordination experiences. Since children with visual impairments have limited depth perception, crawling remains a safer mode of movement during these months.

Children with visual impairments are less likely to ask questions because most questions young children ask are initially based on visual experiences. Therefore, adults need to anticipate what children may not understand and actively encourage them to ask questions. This helps children to learn through tactile or verbal activities. During routine daily activities, children with visual

A teacher of the deaf helps a young child learn how to use an augmentative hearing device.

impairment benefit when adults verbally describe the sequence of events. For example, during a class cooking activity a teacher might say, "Now I am taking an egg from the egg carton. Now I am cracking the egg on the side of the bowl. Do you hear the crack? Oh dear, my hands got sticky when I broke the egg. I will use the paper towel to wipe my hands."

Children with visual impairments are prone to become frustrated, abandon activities, or want adults to do things for them. Adults should avoid the tendency to solve children's problems for them and complete tasks that they can accomplish independently. These children often need extended time to figure out solutions or complete tasks. They also often need additional verbal encouragement to persevere at tasks they find frustrating.

Speech and Language Development.   Early intervention for infants with visual impairments and their families focuses on helping care providers learn to accurately interpret infants' communicative cues while also helping them learn to use communication cues (e.g., listening, turn taking, and nonverbal communication) that are not dependent on vision. This is crucial because children with visual impairments typically use language as a primary means of learning.

Frequent conversations with young children with visual impairments help develop cognitive and language skills. As discussed above, adults should describe what they are doing as well as what happens as a result of their actions. Children benefit from adults' naming and describing objects and actions. They further benefit when these objects are placed in their hands as the objects are named. This process enhances language and cognitive development by making the experiences more meaningful. During these experiences, children need extra time and frequent repetition to absorb information. Because it is difficult to learn while someone is talking, children benefit from stopping an activity to actively listen (Beukelman & Mirenda, 1998).

Motor Development.   The initial experiences of infants with visual impairments are with the things that they touch (e.g., a blanket, lotion, the touch of their care providers). As infants gain more head, trunk, and arm coordination, they initiate movements that allow them to make contact with what is close to their body. For an infant or young child with a visual impairment, feedback from vision may not be a motivator or reinforcement to move. Because an estimated 85% of early learning is visual, children with a visual impairment must learn differently and require various teaching strategies, activities, and environments.

Physical and occupational therapists (OTRs) are specifically trained in motor development and often guide educational plans to help enhance children's motor development. One of the specific focuses of occupational therapy is visual skills, therefore OTRs are frequently key team members. All individuals who work with children with visual impairments use methods to facilitate gross- and fine-motor development (as well as the development of physical control and stamina).

To help children learn to reach for an object, it is often useful to securely suspend objects with interesting and varied sounds and textures within reach so that accidental swipes will ultimately result in contact with those objects. In addition, it is useful to gently guide infants' hands toward the objects to let them know of the objects' presence.

At about 3 to 4 months, most infants begin to roll from stomach to back. Children who are visually impaired may need to be encouraged to roll over by tucking their bent arm under their chest while assisting with roll-over and following with verbal praise. Children can be encouraged to roll from back to stomach (typically at 5 to 6 months) by extending one of the child's arms up next to his or her head and gently rolling his or her head over one arm (toward the floor) while lifting the same-side leg (knee bent and crossing over the other leg). This should be followed by gently pressing the child's knee to the floor. The hip should follow, and the baby can be assisted to roll onto his or her stomach. This sequence should be followed by verbal praise for completing the sequence.

To encourage midline (in the middle of the body rather than off to the left or right) hand use, it is useful to play games such as patty cake and place infants' hands on care providers' faces during conversations. For children who have some vision, it is helpful to present objects with high contrast (e.g., black and white). Midline hand skills are essential to the development of tactual kinesthetic perception, which increases children's awareness of and attention to the differences in texture, form, and shape that ultimately are necessary for Braille reading and other activities. Highly effective play activities encourage the use of both hands to perform tasks such as scooping and filling containers with substances of different textures, squeezing sponges at bath time, or playing with toys with movable parts.

To encourage children with visual impairments to stand (10–11 months) and then walk (11–12 months), it is appropriate to guide infants to a standing position next to a couch or soft chair while placing toys within reach on the couch or chair. This encourages children to play with the toys while standing. Time standing should be limited to only a few minutes initially and gradually increased over time. Children often need assistance to sit down from this position. After ample practice with this activity, a child can be placed in a standing position, with his or her back against the wall, and then offered a hand or finger as he or she is encouraged to take forward steps.

Social Development.   Impaired vision makes the development of attachment and meaningful social relationships more difficult. Instead of smiling, cooing, and reaching for care providers who approach the crib, infants with visual impairment are likely to become very still as they listen for voices and movements. While approaching these infants, adults can speak softly to provide an alternative sensory cue that may result in smiles and coos. Teachers of the visually impaired often help care providers to interpret their infants' social cues and to help their infants learn to adapt to the environment, so that infants receive sensory information as effectively as possible.

To enhance social interactions in young children with visual impairments, it is often helpful to provide extra touching and conversation to compensate for lack of eye contact and facial expression information. Most young children observe and imitate many aspects of social interactions (e.g., waving goodbye, shaking the head "no," and nodding "yes"). For children with visual impairments, these aspects must be physically demonstrated through touch and sound.

Assistive Technology. When visual impairments are accompanied by other disabilities, professionals with expertise in other areas, such as augmentative communication or assistive technology, are often crucial. Teachers of the visually impaired often provide Braille (both literary and Nemeth code), live readers, recordings, slate and stylus, tactile graphics, tactile formats, computers, and low-vision optical and video aids. These assistive devices enable children who are partially sighted, low-vision, or blind to participate in many typical daily activities in which they could not participate without these devices.

Sensory Integration Disorders

In the 1960s, OTR A. Jean Ayres introduced an emphasis on the importance of sensory integration (SI). SI is the involuntary process by which the brain assembles a picture of the environment using information from all of the senses (Lane, Miller, & Hanft, 2000). It helps protect individuals from overstimulation by ignoring some information and reacting to other information, and it aids in learning from environmental experiences. SI occurs automatically and without effort in most children, but for some children the process is not effective.

SI disorder (SID) is a neurological disorder resulting from the brain's inability to appropriately or efficiently integrate sensory information. There are two types of SID: too much sensory input, resulting in brain overload, and too little sensory input, resulting in sensory deprivation and need for additional sensory information.

Children with SID often are unable to focus on learning activities and exhibit behavioral problems resulting from their frustration and their inability to screen out unnecessary sensory input. They may seem silly or immature, stare into space, or flap their hands. They may become very frightened by loud sounds or appear to find them painful. Other children with SID may become uncomfortable with the lack of noise when the room is quiet because this creates a form of sensory deprivation. These children are likely to create their own stimulation by humming, kicking things, and so on.

Children who are underreactive to visual stimuli may move their hands in front of their faces or hold objects unusually close to their eyes. In contrast, children who are overly sensitive to visual input might be frightened in a crowded mall or become either withdrawn or hyperactive in a room with bright lights and an abundance of color or movement. Children with SID may have difficulty responding appropriately to others' facial expressions, due to their inability to properly organize visual input. A highly decorated classroom may overstimulate children with SID.

Assessment

Typically a qualified OTR or physical therapist conduct evaluations of SID. Such evaluation may include standardized testing and structured observations of responses to sensory stimulation, posture, balance, coordination, and eye movements. The therapist analyzes test results and other assessment data, including information from care providers, and then makes recommendations regarding appropriate treatment.

Types of Sensory Integration Disorders

Children with SID may be hyper-responsive (overreactive) or hypo-responsive (underreactive) to movement. Hyper-responsiveness to movement may contribute to children's experiencing motion sickness in the car or on an amusement park ride, being afraid of heights, or disliking being upside down (gravitational insecurity). They may avoid crawling because they do not like to put their heads down.

Hypo-responsiveness to movement may result in children's appearing to always be in motion (e.g., spinning, swinging, rocking, flapping hands, and fidgeting). In addition, many children with SID are labeled as having attention deficit hyperactivity disorder (ADHD), autism, or, after they enter school, a learning disability. They are likely to have poor balance and may have difficulty moving about the room (e.g., they may bump into walls or trip over chairs). They may enjoy and be able to hang upside down or spin without becoming dizzy. These children are likely to misinterpret arm reach, with the result that they hit someone or something as they reach for objects.

Problems with the proprioceptive system (which monitors internal body changes brought on by movement) can be the main contributor to difficulties with motor planning (the ability to determine how to effectively move about). For example, when crawling under a table, a child with SID is likely to bend too low or not enough. Daily tasks such as dressing, tying shoes, and eating are likely to be very challenging.

Some individuals with SID are unusually sensitive to smells. For example, children may find the smell of play dough, markers, perfume, cleansers, and foods distressing. Others are underreactive to smells, so they hold things extremely close to their nose.

Children with SID may react violently to warm or cold surfaces or to any type of physical touch. They are more likely to not put on a coat or gloves on cold days or to wear a heavy coat on a hot day. Children who are underreactive to touch may be unaware of having an injury because they do not experience painful sensations. Children who are overreactive may strongly dislike getting dirty or being touched by unfamiliar objects, or they may have an intense need to touch everything or most things.

There are three main sensory processing disorders: **sensory modulation disorder (SMD)**, **sensory discrimination disorder (SDD)**, and **sensory-based motor disorder (SBMD)**.

Sensory Modulation Disorders.   There are various SMDs based on particular senses. SMDs include **sensory over-responsivity (SOR)**, **sensory under-responsivity (SUR)**, and **sensory seeking/craving (SS)**.

Tactile modulation is sensitivity to touch. It is an essential system because most people thrive on touch. Researchers report that children who lack adequate levels of human tactile contact may fail to thrive and even die. Children whose bodies do not appropriately interpret touch or who have tactile difficulties often perceive their world as unpleasant or threatening.

Children with **auditory modulation** difficulties may be extremely loud because they cannot distinguish between loud and soft voices. They may perceive a normal speaking voice as yelling.

Problems with **olfactory and gustatory modulation,** sensitivity to tastes and smells, result in children's having unusual responses to smells or tastes. Children with this disorder are likely to be finicky eaters and to react in exaggerated ways to various odors, including common scents.

Children with **visual modulation** disorders are likely to react intensely to light, color, or complex images. They often are very sensitive to visual changes in their environment. Children with these disorders are likely to hold their heads in unusual ways when required to focus on visual stimuli.

Vestibular-proprioceptive modulation problems relate to balance, movement, and body position. Children with these problems are likely to misinterpret where their bodies are in space and appear clumsy. They are often unaware of their own strength, the size of their bodies, or the amount of space that their bodies use.

Sensory Discrimination Disorder.   Another form of SID is sensory discrimination difficulty. Sensory discrimination is the ability to recognize differences in sensory stimuli (e.g., recognizing cold or hot, close or far). Children with discrimination difficulties often need assistance in appropriately interpreting sensory input.

Children with **tactile discrimination disorders** struggle to make sense of their own touch and that of others. They have difficulty identifying where they are being touched or if touch is friendly or dangerous. Children with this disorder are likely to behave aggressively toward others without provocation. Children with tactile discrimination difficulties often have limited fine-motor skills and struggle with coordinating their hands to perform daily tasks (e.g., button, zip, cut, write, buckle, or tie). Therefore, they are likely to avoid self-care activities (e.g., brushing their teeth or combing their hair).

Children with **auditory discrimination disorders** have difficulty interpreting sounds. They have difficulty interpreting whether a sound is close or far and may not be able to block out background noise. They are more likely to be perceived as being off task and not listening, paying attention, or following directions. Adults are likely to become frustrated with these children because they find it necessary to repeat statements several times to elicit responses.

Children with **visual discrimination disorders** are likely to experience the most difficulties because visual information plays a central role in how we feel, relate to others, and understand the world. Children who have visual discrimination difficulties frequently engage in behaviors that are confusing to themselves and others. For example, a child may have normal eyesight but be unable to see correctly. They are likely to have difficulty identifying numbers, letters, faces, or how visual stimuli relate to one another. This contributes to later difficulty learning to read and write.

Children with **vestibular-proprioceptive disorders** have problems with balance, movement, and body positioning. They are likely to be viewed as clumsy, accident prone, or careless. They may fall out of their chairs for no apparent reason, lose their balance, walk into walls, trip over their own feet, or run into others when walking. They are likely to depend on touch or vision to help them determine their position in space. They frequently invade others' personal space.

Sensory-Based Motor Disorders.   Another form of sensory integration difficulties is sensory-based motor disorders (SBMDs). Children with this type of SID have either postural disorders or **dyspraxia,** difficulty planning, sequencing, carrying out, and remembering motor movements. A child with dyspraxia typically has difficulty establishing routines, interpreting a procedure, or creating a pattern for going from point A to point B.

Intervention Services

Currently, pharmaceutical intervention has limited or no positive effects for children with SID. However, they often benefit from a therapeutic sensory program, which focuses on their difficulties processing sensations. Children who receive treatment at an early age often learn to successfully manage their disorder. The primary therapy goal is for them to interact with their environment more adaptively and successfully.

Traditional Intervention.   Therapy for SID is usually provided by OTRs and physical therapists during play sensory and motor activities. Therapy usually focuses on the senses of touch, movement, and body position, or some combination of these senses. The goal of **sensory integration therapy** (SIT) is to help children effectively process sensory information and have a more organized response to sensory stimuli. SIT, also referred to as a **sensory diet,** involves a planned, scheduled activity program designed to meet the specific needs of each child's nervous system and interests. A sensory diet stimulates the near senses (tactile, vestibular, and proprioceptive) through a combination of alerting, organizing, and calming techniques.

Nontraditional Intervention.   Currently, alternative SIT methods are used to complement conventional methods. For example, some OTRs use **therapeutic body brushing** with children who overreact to tactile stimulation. A non-scratching surgical brush is used to make firm, brisk movements over most of the body, focusing on the arms, legs, hands, back, and soles of the feet. Deep joint compression and massage typically follow brushing therapy. In most cases, OTRs teach these techniques to parents, who then provide this therapy for 3–5 minutes 6 to 8 times a day. This form of therapy is gradually reduced as the child begins to respond more naturally to touch.

The use of **cerebral electrical stimulation** (CES) has been found to help children with conditions such as moderate to severe autistic spectrum disorders, learning disabilities, and SID. CES is a modification of **transcutaneous electrical nerve stimulation** (TENS) technology, which is used to treat adults with various pain problems, including arthritis and carpal tunnel syndrome. CES entails applying low electrical stimulation to the scalp or ears, to improve brain activity. CES typically is administered for 10 minutes at a time, twice a day.

Specific Intervention Strategies

A child with tactile defensiveness, who has a hard time concentrating or who needs to touch most things, may benefit from carrying a stimulating object in a pocket (e.g., a small textured ball, a key ring, or something that vibrates). Also, children who do not like being touched often find firm pressure more tolerable than lighter touch. Sometimes, allowing children with SID to look away while listening may be useful due to their difficulty attempting to do two things at once (listen and look). Preparing children for upcoming sensory experiences that they may find uncomfortable is likely to help them prepare for and cope with the experience.

Children underresponsive to touch often benefit from being provided with a wide variety of tactile experiences, such as vibrations, stroking with a small soft-bristle (baby) brush, and rubbing. They benefit from activities such as playing with shaving cream, play dough, Silly Putty, corn starch mixed with water, rice, beans, and finger paints. They should be encouraged to use scissors, construction toys, markers, and chalk.

Children overresponsive to touch often avoid touch and prefer solitary play. They may struggle when picked up or cuddled. They may show aversion to play dough, finger paints, and glue. They benefit from gradual introduction to such contact. Sometimes firm touch preceding light touch makes light touch more tolerable. Anticipated touch is typically less aversive than unexpected touch, and self-applied touch is more easily tolerated than touch by others.

Children with overly responsive tactile systems often benefit from calming activities (e.g., dim lighting, soft music, slow rocking, deep pressure, being wrapped in a blanket, or being allowed to suck on something). Their environments need to be modified through the reduction of stimuli.

Conclusions

Fortunately, most children do not experience sensory disorders that result in a major negative effect on their development. The most common sensory disabilities are hearing impairments, followed by visual impairments. Disabilities range from mild to severe. SIDs are far more common in young children. These disorders affect all sensory functions. Children range from high sensitivity to extremely low sensitivity to various sensory input and may have difficulty integrating the various inputs from all senses. Young children with sensory disorders benefit from early intervention programs designed to help them make maximum use of their sensory abilities and use various assistive devices.

CHAPTER SUMMARY

- Relatively few young children have serious sensory impairments, but a variety of effective intervention services are available for those who do.

- Sensory development includes auditory, visual, introceptive, vestibular, and proprioceptive abilities as well as SI abilities.

- There are a variety of causes of sensory impairments, including neurological and genetic abnormalities, illness, various syndromes, and injury. Audiologists, otolaryngologists, and teachers of the deaf and hearing-impaired play key roles in the assessment of hearing loss using a wide variety of assessment devices.

- A wide variety of means are used to assess hearing loss, including OAEs, ABR, typanometry, acoustic reflex, static acoustic impedance, VRA, CPA, unconditioned behavioral response, and conditioned orienting response.

- Auditory disabilities vary from mild to profound and are categorized as sensorineural, mixed, or central hearing loss.

- Hearing impairments affect other areas of development, including language, speech, cognitive, and social-emotional development.

- A variety of communication methods and interventions are useful for those with hearing impairments, including auditory-oral, auditory-verbal, cued speech, SEE, ASL, total communication, assistive listening devices, hearing aids, and other technologies.

- Visual impairments include partial sight and blindness.

- Ophthalmologists, optometrists, and teachers trained to work with children with visual impairments play key roles in the assessment and treatment of visual impairments.

- Visual impairments affect other areas of development, including motor, cognitive, social-emotional, and adaptive skills.

- A variety of methods and services are appropriate for children with visual impairments, including language-rich environments, flexible placements, assistive technology, training of staff, and parental support.

- SI and sensory-based motor disorders, including dyspraxia, also affect young children. These children often benefit from early childhood special education services.

CHAPTER KEY TERMS

sensory impairments
distance sense
close sense
interoception
vestibular
proprioceptive
sensory integration (SI)
sensory integration dysfunction (SID)
acuity
ciliary muscles
fovea
tactile perception
audiologist
sensorineural hearing loss
Alport syndrome
Pendred syndrome 9
Usher's syndrome
Waardenburg's syndrome

conductive hearing loss
ear, nose, and throat specialist (ENT)
otolaryngologist
otologist
Early Hearing Detection and Intervention (EHDI)
otoacoustic emission (OAE)
auditory brainstem response (ABR)
tympanometry
acoustic reflex
static acoustic impedance
visual reinforcement audiometry (VRA)
conditioned play audiometry (CPA)
unconditioned behavioral response procedure
decibels (dB)
audiogram
conditioned orienting response (COR)
mixed hearing loss

central hearing loss
congenital hearing loss
prelingual deafness
postlingual deafness
adventitious deafness
teacher of the deaf/hearing-impaired
residual hearing
auditory-verbal
auditory-oral
cued speech
Signed Exact English (SEE)
American Sign Language (ASL)
manual communication
total communication
assistive listening device (ALD)
hearing aid
conventional analog hearing aid
analog programmable hearing aid
digital programmable hearing aid
frequency modulated auditory trainer
infrared system
induction loop system
one-to-one communicator
cochlear implant
visual system
alerting device
pediatric eye doctor
ophthalmologist
optometrist

Ocular motility/alignment/binocular potential test
strabismus
amblyopia
functional vision assessment (FVA)
low vision
partial sighted
legally blind
adventitiously visually impaired
sensory modulation disorder (SMD)
sensory discrimination disorder (SDD)
sensory-based motor disorder (SBMD)
sensory over-responsivity (SOR)
sensory under-responsivity (SUR)
sensory seeking/craving (SS)
tactile modulation
auditory modulation
olfactory and gustatory modulation
visual modulation
vestibular-proprioceptive modulation
tactile discrimination disorder
auditory discrimination disorder
visual discrimination disorder
vestibular-proprioceptive disorder
dyspraxia
sensory integration therapy (SIT)
sensory diet
therapeutic body brushing
cerebral electrical stimulation (CES)
transcutaneous electric nerve stimulation (TENS)

REVIEW QUESTIONS

1. What are the different types of hearing and vision screenings and tests for young children?

2. In what ways might hearing and visual impairments affect other areas of development.

3. How does a cochlear implant differ from a hearing aid and other assistive devices? What are the advantages and disadvantages of each?

4. What are the various types of sensory integration disabilities and how might they affect development?

5. Describe traditional and less traditional sensory integration therapy techniques.

SUGGESTED STUDENT ACTIVITIES

1. Contact your local school district or your state or local health department to find out how to obtain hearing screenings/evaluations and intervention services through your state's Early Intervention Program.

2. If your state has not passed universal newborn and infant hearing screening legislation (find out here: www.asha.org/about/legislation-advocacy/state/issues), write a letter to your legislators explaining why it is important, or organize a grassroots campaign for action.

3. Volunteer at a summer camp or classroom for children with hearing impairment.

4. Find out what early intervention services your state offers for children with hearing and vision impairments.

5. Learn more about the rate of various sensory integration disabilities.

Health Impairments 10

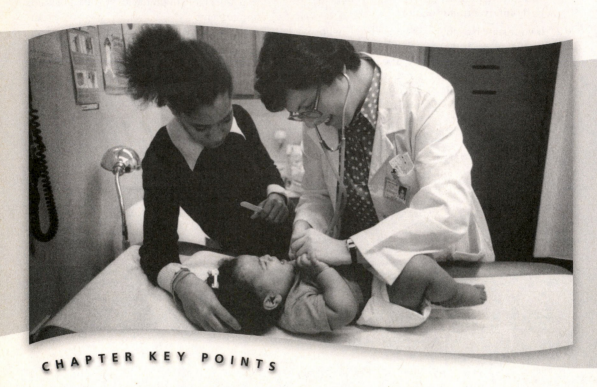

CHAPTER KEY POINTS

- A wide variety of health impairments may affect young children.

- Health impairments include exposure to alcohol, cocaine, and pediatric AIDS, either prenatally or postnatally.

- Services for children with health impairments are provided for under the Individuals with Disabilities Education Act (IDEA).

- Society bears many costs as a result of prenatal exposure to alcohol, cocaine, and HIV/AIDS.

Fortunately, only a small percentage of children have chronic health problems (DeAngelis & Zylke, 2006; van Dyck, Kogan, McPherson, Weissman, & Newacheck, 2004). Sadly, many children are affected by controllable environmental factors that include substance abuse (e.g., cocaine, alcohol). Although some of these factors are increasing, the number of U.S. cases of **pediatric human immunodeficiency virus (HIV)/acquired immunodeficiency syndrome (AIDS)** has begun to decrease (Jansson & Velez, 1999). IDEA lists **"other health impairments (OHI)"** as one of the 13 categories of disabilities that qualify for early intervention services. Knowledge about health impairments and environmental influences helps service providers meet the needs of children with health impairments and their families.

Children with OHI have limited strength, vitality, or alertness due to **chronic** (long-lasting) or **acute** (rapid-onset) **health problems** that interfere with development. They constitute about 1% of all children who receive special education services (U.S. Department of Education, 2006). The list of chronic or acute health problems included in the IDEA definition is not exhaustive. Children with attention deficit hyperactivity disorder (ADHD) may be classified as eligible for services under the OHI category in instances in which the ADHD results in limited alertness that adversely affects the child's educational performance and, therefore, creates a need for special education and related services.

Children with OHI often require accommodations, adaptations, and modifications in their educational program. In addition to specialized instruction, they may need related services such as specialized transportation, assistive technology devices and services, school health services, parent education and training, and counseling. Some children require major modification of their school day, including rest periods, a shortened school day, or flexible scheduling and services delivery.

Health impairments include, but are not limited to, **asthma, allergies, ADHD** (discussed in Chapter 8), **diabetes, epilepsy, cystic fibrosis, heart condition, hemophilia, lead poisoning** (discussed in Chapter 8), **leukemia and other cancers, nephritis, rheumatic fever, sickle cell anemia, tuberculosis (TB), prenatal drug exposure, cytomegalovirus (CMV)**, and HIV/AIDS (Haslam & Valletutti, 2004; Ondersma, Simpson, Brestan, & Ward, 2000; Sokol, Delaney-Black, & Nordstrom, 2003). Many health impairments do not interfere with learning ability, but some have a major effect (National Institute of Child Health and Human Development, 1990).

Children with health impairments may experience chronic fatigue or seizures. They may miss school due to illness, medical appointments, or special medical treatments. They are often viewed as fragile, and adults frequently hesitate to place developmentally appropriate demands on them (Brown, 1993). For example, asthma frequently causes coughing, shortness of breath, and wheezing. Some children with severe asthma cannot participate in school activities requiring physical exertion, such as field trips. Others can participate, but adults may hesitate to let them because of their health condition.

Children with health impairments may require special methods of teaching, therapy, and equipment. For example, a child with severe allergies or asthma may be given more indoor than outdoor opportunities for physical movement and require a nurse to be on staff to administer medicines. Medications designed to help control symptoms related to various health impairments can cause troublesome side effects, including headaches, tremors, stomach aches, lethargy, and reduced ability to concentrate.

Asthma and allergies may be aggravated by environmental conditions such as the presence of nonhuman animals, chalk, molds, plants, soap, clay, dyes in paint, chemicals, and foods. A child may be unable to attend school unless modifications eliminate many of the substances to which the child is allergic. Individuals who interact with children who have health impairments should obtain as much information as possible about the child's specific health needs (American Academy of Allergy, Asthma, and Immunology, 2004).

Health Care Professionals

A variety of health care professionals participate in planning and providing services for children with OHI. Those health care professionals who are most likely to be involved and who have not been discussed in earlier chapters are described below.

Nurses

Nurses who work with children who have special needs may be **licensed practical nurses (LPNs),** with a 2-year degree or **registered nurses (RNs)** with a 4-year degree. Although many nurses lack formal training in the specific needs of the developmentally disabled, most nursing degree programs require course work in developmental psychology. In addition, some nurses complete a master's degree in education; such nurses often are referred to as **"nurse-educators."**

Nurses often serve as consultants rather than full-time members of service teams providing early childhood special education programming. In this capacity they focus on the health of the child and the child's family. They conduct basic health screening related to each child's disability and provide instruction to staff and parents regarding methods to adequately care for each child's health, including how to use assisted ventilation (e.g., oxygen therapy), catheters (e.g., for elimination of body waste), and feeding tubes; administer medication; and deal with seizures or other medical emergencies.

Nurses frequently teach children, program staff, and parents about proper hygiene techniques such as methods of bathing and brushing teeth. They may help develop preventive health care plans by teaching parents and staff about ways to reduce the spread of infection and sickness. In addition, they often make referrals to other health care providers.

Pediatricians

Pediatricians are licensed physicians who specialize in the medical care of children. In some cases a medical doctor who is a family practitioner, general practitioner, or internist may be a child's primary physician. Pediatricians sometimes serve as part-time staff in early intervention programs, but parents usually choose their child's pediatrician (Heisler, 1972). Pediatricians play a crucial role because their referral is often required for a child to receive assessments such as a neurological or audiological (hearing) evaluation, occupational or physical therapy, or a prescription for assistive devices.

Pediatricians focus on children's health, including assisting family members to meet a child's health needs or help a child regain health after an illness. Pediatricians conduct health evaluations and provide information about how a physical condition may affect the child's rate of development. They also provide information about the benefits and side effects of prescribed medications. Because some medical conditions require restrictions of diet or activities, pediatricians recommend specific diets and appropriate activities. With the parents' approval, pediatricians may also assist other service team members regarding how to provide for a child's health needs and request information from school staff members about the child's health status.

Nutritionists

Within early childhood special education programs, **nutritionists** often help assess and implement plans to meet young children's nutritional needs. A nutritionist's primary goal is to maximize children's health and nutritional status. Nutritionists also provide general nutritional information to parents and staff. A nurse may fill this role, but most nurses have not received specific training in young children's nutritional needs. Nutritionists may work with other staff members regarding feeding problems or help find ways to facilitate the use of oral feeding mechanisms (e.g., food tubes). They also help plan diets for children with metabolic disorders (e.g., hormonal or blood sugar imbalances), severe allergies, diabetes, or other medical conditions.

Assessment of Health Impairments

Licensed physicians are required to document an OHI by conducting a thorough physical evaluation. Physicians provide a written statement describing the OHI, activity limitations, and dietary needs.

The next section describes some of the many health impairments that may negatively affect children's development. It is important to note that different illnesses or diseases can have similar symptoms, and certain symptoms can occur when there is no illness or disease. For example, a child who has been jogging may experience leg cramps, flushed face, and rapid pulse. These reactions are also symptoms of a diabetic coma (Batshaw, 1991).

Types of Health Impairments

Epilepsy

Epilepsy is a health impairment that entails recurrent seizures or convulsions. It is the most common neurological impairment of school-age children. Different types of seizures may occur, and some are more likely to occur when the child has a high fever.

Major seizures are referred to as **grand mal.** They may cause children to fall, lose consciousness, become stiff, drool, urinate, or have bowel movements. Breathing may be irregular, causing a pale or bluish skin color. Seizures generally last only a few minutes, although they may last much longer. After this type of seizure, children are often confused or complain of a headache and want to sleep. Parents should be notified when such seizures occur and should have their child seen by a physician as soon as possible.

Minor seizures are referred to as **petit mal.** They include staring spells lasting a few seconds. During this type of seizure, eyes blink rhythmically and the child responds as if the seizure never occurred. Such seizures may occur relatively frequently and give the appearance that the child is momentarily day dreaming.

In most cases, both types of seizures may be fully or partially controlled with anticonvulsant medication (Appleton, Nicolson, Smith, Chadwick, & Mackenzie, 2006).

Cystic Fibrosis

Cystic fibrosis, a genetic disorder, primarily affects the lungs and digestive tract. Children with cystic fibrosis often live to early adulthood, although the disease is eventually fatal. Most preschool children with cystic fibrosis appear normal except for a slight cough, although a more severely affected child may cough regularly, breathe hard, and tire easily.

Children with cystic fibrosis frequently have thin arms and legs, a barrel chest, and a protruding abdomen. They often eat more than expected and are more susceptible than other children to bacterial infections, such as those seen in certain types of pneumonia and bronchitis. Their cough is not contagious, but they are very susceptible to other children's infections. Children with cystic fibrosis take antibiotics, vitamins, pancreatic enzymes before each meal, intermittent aerosol therapy to aid breathing, and receive physical therapy. Most children with this disease can engage in typical daily activities but may need time to rest if they become fatigued (Cunningham & Taussig, 2003).

Cancer

Fortunately, the rates of all forms of cancer during infancy and preschool years are low. In the United States, leukemia accounts for about 25% of all childhood cancers and affects an estimated 2,200 children each year. It most commonly occurs in children ages 2 to 8 and has a peak incidence at age 4. Leukemia can be classified as acute (rapidly developing) or chronic (slowly developing). Approximately 98% of all childhood leukemia cases are acute. Leukemia causes large numbers of abnormal white blood cells to be produced in the bone marrow. Due to their defective nature, these cells do not perform their role of protecting the body against disease. Leukemia ultimately interferes with the body's production of red blood cells and platelets, resulting in **anemia** (low count of red cells) and bleeding problems. Fortunately, treatment can cure most children with leukemia.

Second to medical care, emotional support is the greatest need of families and children who experience cancer. Families often react with shock, disbelief, denial, and fear. Children who have cancer frequently miss school because of numerous trips to doctors and hospitals. They may receive painful medical treatments that have negative side effects, including loss of speech or motor abilities, which may require speech and language, occupational, or physical therapy (Ries et al., 1999; Spinelli, 2004).

Heart Defects

Congenital heart defects are a major cause of death in early infancy. Fortunately, surgery can correct or mitigate many heart defects. Heart defects frequently occur in children with other conditions, such as Down syndrome or congenital rubella syndrome. Often, heart defects are abnormal openings between the two sides of the heart that result in poorly oxygenated blood's mixing with freshly oxygenated blood. This requires the heart to work harder to provide sufficient freshly oxygenated blood to the body. Some heart defects are due to narrowing of major blood vessels.

Children with cardiac problems tend to have poor weight gain, irregular breathing patterns, unusual fatigue, and a bluish tinge to the skin, especially around the lips, fingers, and toes. Most children with heart disease lead relatively normal lives (Swanson, 2000).

Diabetes

Diabetes is an inability to use the body's sugar. It is controllable but not curable. Control is achieved by receiving insulin, eating the right foods, and exercising. Treatment includes eliminating foods high in sugar or starch, such as cakes, candies, sugar-coated cereals, cookies, jellies, syrups, puddings, and sodas. Fortunately, very few young children have diabetes, but those who do need appropriate substitutes for many of the refreshments served at preschools and events such as parties. They may also need to eat at specific times of the day.

Two serious situations associated with diabetes are **insulin reaction** and **diabetic coma**. An insulin reaction is due to inadequate blood sugar. A diabetic coma occurs when there is too much sugar. Service providers should watch for signs of undiagnosed diabetes, including extreme thirst, frequent urination, and excessive appetite without weight gain. More-severe symptoms include nausea, vomiting, abdominal pain, and apathy. A diabetic coma may occur if the child does not receive insulin or has a resistance to insulin. Stresses on the body such as infection, injury, diarrhea, or emotional upset may contribute to a diabetic coma (Watkins, 2002). Figure 10.1 lists early warning signs of insulin reactions and diabetic coma.

Hemophilia

Hemophilia is a bleeding disorder that usually affects males and occurs because the body lacks sufficient clotting factors (a substance that stops bleeding). It is incurable but may be controlled by replacing the clotting factors. Children with hemophilia bleed a great deal even after only minor abrasions or cuts. They are prone to internal bleeding, including in the brain. Symptoms of bleeding in the brain include severe headaches or mental confusion. In the most severe cases, such bleeding can be fatal. Children with hemophilia should be encouraged to play in grassy rather than hard-surface areas, avoid contact sports, and not have access to toys with sharp edges (Willett, 2001).

Figure 10.1 **Early Warning Signs of Insulin Reaction and Diabetic Coma**

Insulin Reaction	*Diabetic Coma*
dizziness	extreme thirst
shakiness	dry tongue
trembling	fruity odor to the breath
nervousness	deep and labored breathing
hunger	loss of appetite
excessive perspiration	blurring of vision
nausea	cramps in the legs or stomach
headache	flushed face
fatigue	dry skin
drowsiness	rapid pulse

Asthma

Asthma is one of the most common children's chronic health impairments and the leading cause of school absences. It results in difficulty breathing due to narrowing of the bronchial tubes. Asthma attacks may be physically painful and frightening. They usually occur after children come into contact with substances to which they are allergic, are exposed to cold air, or experience a stressful event. Fortunately, relatively few preschool children have severe asthma attacks (Farber & Boyette, 2001).

The percentage of U.S. children with asthma was approximately 3.6% in 1980, 7.5% in 1995, and 8.7% (6.3 million) in 2001. As of 2004 an estimated 4 million U.S. children under 18 years old had had an asthma attack within the past 12 months, and many others had undiagnosed asthma. The reason for the increase in asthma rates is unclear but is likely related to indoor and outdoor air quality (e.g., exposure to dust mites, cockroaches, pesticides, tobacco smoke, ozone, and soot).

Cytomegalovirus

CMV is a form of herpes, a venereal disease, which may lead to brain damage, blindness, and hearing loss. An estimated 1% of all fetuses contract this disease, and 10–15% of this 1% develop CMV. To help prevent the spread of this disease, child care providers should frequently wash their hands, dispose of diapers in sanitary ways, and keep toys and play areas clean (Children's Hospital of St. Paul, 1984; Levine, 1992).

Nephritis

Nephritis is a noninfectious inflammatory disease that includes hypertension, decreased kidney function, hematuria (blood in the urine), and edema (excessive accumulation of fluids). Primary nephritis involves the kidneys and secondary nephritis involves the kidneys and other organs.

The term *tubulointerstitial nephritis* (TIN) is applied to a group of unrelated inflammatory disorders that initially affect primarily the testes and kidneys. Most cases of acute TIN in children are viral or medication-related.

The prevalence of nephritis within the pediatric population is unknown, but it is more frequent among males, and affected children usually are older than 2 years. Although children can die from complications of severe hypertension or kidney failure, in the United States a fatal outcome is rare (Greenberg, 2004).

Rheumatic Fever

Rheumatic fever is a rare illness that may occur after a strep throat infection. Symptoms include arthritis, cardiac inflammation, rash, abnormal movements, and subcutaneous nodules (knot-like growths below the skin). It is most likely to occur in children 5 to 15 years of age and rarely is diagnosed in children younger than 4 years.

Sickle Cell Anemia

Sickle cell anemia is an inherited blood disorder found primarily in African American newborns. Sickle syndromes also occur in individuals from India, the Middle East, and the Mediterranean. Sickle cell anemia is a chronic illness that can become life-threatening at any time. Infections are the leading cause of death in children ages 1 to 3 years old who have this illness. Approximately 50% of U.S. individuals with sickle cell survive into their 50s.

Infants with sickle cell are likely to have painful swelling of their hands and feet. As the child ages, the pain often begins to affect the hip, knee, chest wall, back joints, and other parts of the body. Abdominal pain often occurs as well. Blood trapped in the spleen can result in an unusual lack of skin color, fatigue, and left-sided abdominal pain. Individuals with sickle cell may have gait disturbances, hemiparesis, paresthesia, aphasia, altered consciousness, or seizures. Infants and children are susceptible to anemia and jaundice. Young children with sickle cell anemia often are irritable or fussy and may experience feeding problems. As children with sickle cell grow older, they may develop abnormally angled fingers and toes and enlarged, malformed, and frozen joints, particularly at the knees and ankles (American Academy of Pediatrics, 2002b).

Tuberculosis

Between 1992 and 2004 the rate of TB among children 14 and younger decreased more than 51%. In 2004 in the United States, 961 children 14 and younger (1.6 per 100,000) had TB. Among U.S. children younger than 5 years, native Hawaiians and other Pacific Islanders had the highest TB rate (18.4 per 100,000), followed by Hispanics (6.7 per 100,000), Asians (6.2 per 100,000), Native Americans (5.2 per 100,000), African Americans (5.1 per 100,000), and whites (0.4 per 100,000). In 2004 three states (California, New York, and Florida) accounted for over 42% of new TB cases in children 14 and younger. Risk of TB increases when children live with someone who has active TB or is at high risk for contracting TB (e.g., has

Figure 10.2 **Medical Complications That May Occur during Children's First Month of Life**

- Hypoglycemia—low blood sugar
- Hypocalcaemia—low blood calcium
- Hyperbilirubinemia—a jaundice/yellow color due to abnormal blood pigments
- Respiratory distress syndrome—breathing difficulties that may be caused by immaturity of the lungs or infections; lack of adequate oxygen may damage vital organs, especially the brain, heart, and kidneys
- Traumatic disorders—injuries to the head, spine, hands, feet, or legs
- Brain infections such as meningitis or encephalitis—caused by viruses or bacteria
- Degenerative diseases—conditions that cause gradual deterioration of the nervous system
- Metabolic and generic disorders—disorders (usually inherited) that affect the brain because the child's body either does not make or destroys some substances it needs
- Brain tumors—growths on or within the brain
- Drug-induced delays—delays caused by prenatal exposure to prescription drugs, sedatives, vitamins, alcohol, or illegal drugs
- Seizure disorders—disorders that might indicate epilepsy or other brain diseases
- Battered child syndrome—injuries due to neglect or abuse

HIV infection). Medically underserved or low-income children, children living with individuals who immigrated to the United States within the past 5 years from countries with a high incidence of TB, or children in contact with someone who has been in prison are at greater risk (Blumberg, Leonard, & Jasmer, 2005).

Children with TB are likely to have a cough, fever, night sweats, swollen glands, decreased appetite and activity, weight loss, and difficulty breathing. TB can also result in meningitis and infections of the ears, kidneys, bones, and joints.

Many other health impairments not covered in this chapter may affect development. Figure 10.2 lists other medical complications that may occur during the first month of life.

Prenatal Causes of Health Impairments

Children who were exposed to alcohol, HIV, cocaine, or other illegal drugs intrauterine tend to have parents of low socioeconomic status. Many of these parents are members of minorities (Messinger, Bauer, Das, Seifer & Lester, 2004; Singer et al., 2002).

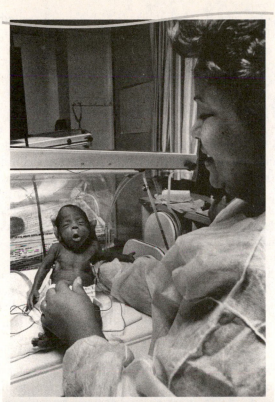

There are many reasons why a newborn has health problems and may be at risk of developmental delays.

Methamphetamine

Currently, children are being born to mothers addicted to **methamphetamine.** Methamphetamine may be snorted, smoked, or injected. As estimated by the 2005 National Survey on Drug Use and Health, more than 10 million Americans 12 years or older have used methamphetamine at least once in their lives for nonmedical reasons. This number translates to more than 4% of the U.S. population in that age group.

It is difficult to determine the direct effects of methamphetamine because most users also abuse alcohol, marijuana, and tobacco. Most babies born to methamphetamine-addicted mothers initially seem normal, but they are prone to sleep disturbance, tremors, muscle stiffness, and trouble grasping objects. They are at risk of having a stroke before they are born. Some babies suffer serious brain damage, others experience long-lasting developmental problems (e.g., ADHD), and others experience no serious health consequences. Thousands of children have been removed from the homes of their methamphetamine-abusing parents. With treatment most infants exposed to methamphetamine experience healthy development.

Alcohol

Alcohol, a legal and socially acceptable drug, takes its toll across all socioeconomic classes and ethnic groups. About 6 million women in the U.S. are alcoholics or alcohol abusers—far more than those who use cocaine (Richardson, 1998; Sood et al., 2001). Children prenatally exposed to alcohol are placed at developmental risk (Abel, 1999; Barth, 2001; Belcher et al., 2005; Mayfield & Chapman, 1998; McConnell et al., 2002). Prenatal exposure to alcohol is a leading cause of preventable birth defects. The damage is irreversible.

Prenatal exposure to alcohol results in a variety of disorders called **fetal alcohol spectrum disorders (FASD).** The most severe effects of drinking during pregnancy are referred to as **"fetal alcohol syndrome (FAS)."** FAS is a lifelong condition and one of the leading known preventable causes of mental retardation and birth defects (Anderson, 1982; Astley & Clarren, 2005; Duckworth & Norton, 2000; Harwood & Kleinfeld, 2002; Hoyme et al., 2005; Streissguth, Clarren, & Jones, 1985; Stoler & Holmes, 2004).

The three subcategories of FASD are **fetal alcohol effects (FAE), alcohol-related neurodevelopmental disorder (ARND),** and **alcohol-related birth defects (ARBD).** Children with FAE were prenatally exposed to alcohol but do not have all of the typical diagnostic features of FAS. In 1996 the Institute of Medicine replaced *FAE* with the terms *ARND* and *ARBD*. Children with ARND are likely to have functional and mental problems, including behavioral and cognitive problems. Children with ARBD are prone to heart, kidney, bone, and hearing problems. All FASD are 100% preventable. The children of women who do not drink during pregnancy are not at risk.

The term *FAS* was first used in 1973 to describe a collection of mental, physical, and behavioral characteristics of children born to mothers who consumed alcohol during their pregnancies (Jones, Smith, Ulleland, & Streissguth, 1973). According to most studies, the probability that the child of an alcoholic mother will be born with FAS is 2–8%. Today about 1 or 2 of every 1,000 infants born in the United States suffers from FAS. Other FASD are believed to occur approximately three times as often as FAS (Zuckerman & Bresnahan, 1991).

These statistics likely underestimate the incidence of FASD. Untrained observers may notice the unusual facial features of children with FAS, but they either do not correctly diagnosis the condition or do not record their observations. One investigation using the medical records of infants born to alcohol users revealed a 100% failure rate in diagnosing FAS, even though the features of FAS were present (Clarren & Smith, 1978).

About 25% of U.S. women report drinking during the first few months of pregnancy. Another 6% report drinking an average of two or more alcoholic beverages daily throughout their pregnancy. A concerted effort has been made to warn women of the dangers of drinking while pregnant. However, these warnings may not be presented in the settings in which they would be most effective.

A survey of New Jersey physicians revealed a reluctance to discuss alcohol consumption with pregnant patients (Ebrahim, Diekman, Decoufle, Tully, & Floyd, 1999). This reluctance was related to the physicians' own use of alcohol, lack of training in discussing the problem, poor awareness of the problem, denial that FAS occurs in private practice, disinterest, time limitations, fear of offending the patient, and the belief that patients will not be honest about their alcohol consumption if the issue is raised (Donovan, 1991).

Regardless of her drinking history, a woman who abstains from alcohol throughout her pregnancy is not likely to give birth to a child with FASD. However, recent investigations have revealed that alcohol consumption by fathers before conception may influence fetal development. Male alcoholics may have toxins in their semen that may cause abnormal development of their child. Paternal alcoholism has been linked to low birth weight and may result in the father's transmitting damaged genetic material to his offspring (Anderson, 1982). Table 10.1 lists categories of FASD.

A diagnosis of FAS requires that at least these three symptoms be present in the child: central nervous system dysfunction, growth retardation, and facial abnormality (Clarren & Smith, 1978; Cooper, 1987; Overholser, 1990). The related syndrome, FAE, may occur if the developing fetus is exposed to intermittent use or lower levels of alcohol. FAE manifests as learning or behavioral problems but does not cause structural abnormalities. Although FAE may be related to developmental delays, FAS is believed to create far more serious problems.

Table 10.1	Categories of Fetal Alcohol Spectrum Disorders (FASD)
Disorder	**Symptoms**
Fetal Alcohol Syndrome (FAS)	Small head/body, abnormal facial characteristics, brain damage
Fetal Alcohol Effects (FAE), approximately 10% of all FASD	Behavior disorders, attention deficits
Alcohol-Related Birth Defects (ARBD)	Heart defects, sight/hearing problems, joint anomalies, and other problems
Alcohol-Related Neurodevelopmental Disorders (ARND)	Attention deficits, behavior disorders, obsessive/compulsive disorder, and other problems

In FAS and FAE parts of the body and brain fail to develop normally because of prenatal exposure to alcohol. Like other drugs, alcohol is not easily eliminated by the body systems of a fetus. The alcohol consumed by a pregnant woman crosses the placenta and enters the body of her developing offspring within minutes, where it will remain in trace amounts up to 24 hours (American Academy of Pediatrics, 1993).

The cells of the developing brain begin to form during the first few weeks of pregnancy, and the brain continues to develop throughout pregnancy. Therefore, exposure to alcohol may affect the developing brain at any time during prenatal development. Infants with FAS tend to have very low birth weight and a small head circumference for their gestational age. These children are sometimes diagnosed with "failure to thrive" and may remain significantly below the norm in height and weight throughout their lives (Jones, Smith, Ulleland, & Streissguth, 1973).

Many children with FAS have below-average cognitive functioning because of brain damage. The degree of physical manifestations of the syndrome highly correlates with the severity of brain damage. That is, children with more severe physical abnormalities generally function at lower cognitive levels than children with less severe physical abnormalities (Streissguth, Clarren, & Jones, 1985). Children with FAS frequently lag behind other children of the same age in social and motor skills because of delayed mental development. See Table 10.2 for a list of characteristics associated with FAS. The next section focuses on the effect of another drug, cocaine.

Cocaine

Children are affected by the actions of the adults in their lives (Berger & Waldfogel, 2000). All too often children are the victims of adult **cocaine** use (Craig, 1993; Eyler, Behnke, Conlon, Woos, & Wobie, 1998). To understand the effects of cocaine use, it is helpful to consider the types of individuals likely to use cocaine, the rate of use, and the effects of use on children's development. Although this chapter does not

Table 10.2 *Attributes Associated with Fetal Alcohol Syndrome (FAS)*	
Central nervous system	Mental retardation, difficulty understanding abstract concepts, difficulty understanding cause and effect, difficulty with generalizations, easily distracted, difficulty perceiving social cues, motor-skills delays, hyperactivity
Retarded growth	Low birth weight, small head size, small brain mass, below-normal height and weight
Facial abnormalities	Short eye slits, droopy eyelids, widely spaced eyes, small upturned nose, flattened mid-face, small chin and jaw, malformed ears, lack of indentation in the upper lip, thin lips, cleft lip or palate
Other physical characteristics	Abnormalities of fingers and toes (small, bent, or joined), abnormal palm creases, hip dislocations at birth, clubfoot, heart and kidney defects, genital abnormalities, unusual skin pigmentation, strawberry birthmarks, excessive hair on body areas other than head

specifically address the influences of other types of illegal drugs, many of the outcomes associated with cocaine use are relevant to understanding the outcomes of using other drugs (Beckwith, Crawford, Moore, & Howard, 1995).

Before the mid-1980s, cocaine use was limited to individuals who could afford a very expensive high. Cocaine is now mass-marketed in the cheaper form of **crack,** which is smoked. Crack users now include many women of child-bearing age. Published estimates of the number of crack- or cocaine-exposed infants born each year in the United States range from 30,000 to 100,000, or 2–3% of all newborns (Gomby & Shiono, 1991). Since the mid-1980s an estimated one million children have been born in the United States after fetal cocaine exposure (Kilbride, Castor, Hoffman, & Fuger, 2000; Lester, LaGasse, & Seifer, 1998).

According to a 2003 Centers for Disease Control (CDC) study, approximately 3% of pregnant women use illicit drugs (e.g., marijuana, cocaine, ecstasy, other amphetamines, or heroin). Illegal drugs create risks for pregnant women and their unborn babies. These drugs may cause a baby to be born too small or have withdrawal symptoms, birth defects, or learning and behavioral problems. Because many pregnant women who use illicit drugs also use alcohol and tobacco (which also pose risks to unborn babies), it often is impossible to know the extent to which infant health problems are caused by a specific illicit drug or other negative environmental conditions.

Cocaine Use.   Whether snorted, taken intravenously, or smoked, cocaine creates a feeling of euphoria that has been called "the 30-minute thrill of a lifetime" (Craig,

1993). The short-lived high of cocaine is often followed by an uncomfortable rebound effect. Users tend to turn to other drugs such as alcohol to deal with the discomfort.

Injecting cocaine or smoking crack cocaine causes the drug to reach the brain rapidly. This creates an ecstatic rush that may lead to physical effects similar to those experienced during an anxiety attack. These effects include increased blood pressure, racing or irregular heartbeat, anxiety or paranoia, nausea, headache, and rapid, shallow breathing (Chasnoff, Landress, & Barrett, 1990).

Chronic users may reach a state in which they engage in meaningless, repetitive activities; experience insomnia and hallucinations; lose their appetite; and even deplete the brain's supply of the chemical messenger dopamine. This chemical is believed to affect many brain areas, including those that contribute to feelings of pleasure (Chasnoff, Bussey, Savich, & Stack, 1986).

Chronic cocaine users often crash into a depressed state a couple of hours after using the drug. This state is the opposite of the pleasant, aroused state first produced by the drug (Kalat, 1995). Over time, users may come to see the drug as the solution to all of their problems because cocaine initially alleviates their depression. This makes it difficult to persuade them to seek help for their addiction.

To obtain cocaine, female users frequently become involved in prostitution, exchanging sexual favors for cocaine, or begin selling drugs. One survey of pregnant substance abusers found that 36% of these women exchanged sex for drugs or for the money to buy drugs (National Institute on Drug Abuse, 1990). Women involved in this lifestyle are poorly prepared for motherhood.

Direct Impact of Prenatal Exposure to Cocaine.   Premature delivery, intrauterine growth retardation, and oxygen deprivation are associated with cocaine use, placing children at developmental risk. The experience of living with a mother who uses cocaine also places children at risk. The long-term developmental outcome for "crack babies" is under investigation; the data are far from complete (Litt & McNeil, 1997). The first generation of children prenatally exposed to cocaine is still growing up. It is simply too soon to know the full range of outcomes.

Prenatal cocaine exposure is associated with impaired fetal growth and smaller-than-normal head circumference at birth. Small head circumference may be due to smaller-than-normal brain mass, which is associated with higher risk of learning disabilities. Impaired growth and smaller-than-normal head size are thought to be caused by cocaine's constricting blood vessels in the placenta, the organ that provides nutrition and oxygen to the developing fetus (Gomby & Shiono, 1991). Chronic prenatal exposure to cocaine may also alter the functioning of the chemical messenger systems in parts of the developing brain that regulate orientation to stimuli (Chavkin & Kandall, 1990).

Pregnant cocaine users may experience premature, very rapid labor. Rapid deliveries are stressful, typically increase fetal heart rates, and may even tear the placenta from the uterine wall. Cocaine crosses the placenta and accumulates in the body of the developing fetus. It takes longer for the drug to be eliminated from the still-developing fetal system than from the mother's system. Children may be born addicted to cocaine and, if so, will suffer withdrawal effects.

In 1989, 4.5% of all babies born in New York City tested positive for drug exposure (Kim, Sugai, & Kim, 1999). About a third of babies prenatally exposed to drugs go directly from the hospital into foster care (Krauss et al., 2000). The vast majority of them go home, many to live with parents who use drugs. These children may enter the foster care system at a later date after falling victim to physical abuse or neglect. Or they may enter the foster care system because they are abandoned (Groze, Haines-Simeon, & Barth, 1994; Groze, Haines-Simeon, & McMillen, 1992).

Popular media have painted a gloomy picture of the plight of babies exposed to crack (Mayes, Granger, Bornstein, & Zuckerman, 1992). These infants have been portrayed as severely, irrevocably brain-damaged. They often are seen as damaged to the point at which they never will become functional members of society. Current scientific evidence does not support this media image (Mayes et al., 1992). Sensationalizing the plight of babies exposed to crack can harm these children. Misconceptions about their development make it more difficult to find foster care and other services for them (Waller, 1993). Unfortunately, even the scientific community does not seem to be immune to self-fulfilling prophecies about children prenatally exposed to cocaine. Evidence suggests that scientific articles on the effects of cocaine exposure are more likely to be accepted for publication if they report adverse effects. Studies that failed to find negative effects have been rejected for publication even when they were scientifically sound (Mayes et al., 1992).

Focusing on the potential biological damage of intrauterine cocaine exposure may divert our focus from the environmental impact this drug has on children. Many high-risk premature or chronically ill newborns develop into healthy toddlers. There is ample reason to discard a deterministic position (i.e., the belief that prenatal exposure to cocaine inevitably causes developmental delays). Additionally, the effectiveness of early intervention has been repeatedly documented (Gallagher, 1989; Klein, 1988). We should not concede defeat for this group of children simply because their mothers exposed them to cocaine in the womb, nor should we ignore cocaine's ongoing effects on their lives.

Studies have reported that children prenatally exposed to drugs may differ from their peers in several ways. As infants they seem more likely to be insecurely attached to their primary caregiver. As toddlers they are more likely to be restless and aggressive and to have less mature play skills. As preschoolers, they typically require more adult direction to cooperate and are less attentive and more restless than their peers. They also appear to struggle more with tasks that require self-organization (Beckwith, Crawford, Moore, & Howard, 1995).

One study found that prenatal cocaine exposure is related to less positive home environments, smaller-than-normal head size, and reduced perseverance (the ability to attend to a task for extended periods of time). Together, these three factors accounted for about half of the variation between the Stanford-Binet Intelligence Test scores of children who had been prenatally exposed to cocaine and the scores of those who had not. Level of perseverance during testing had the greatest influence on intelligence quotient (IQ) scores. Reduced perseverance was associated with lower IQ scores and had twice as much effect as the two other factors (Azuma & Chasnoff, 1993).

To date, no studies have been published that followed children prenatally exposed to cocaine from birth to elementary school. Early reports have linked cocaine exposure to moderate-to-severe developmental delays across developmental domains (Mayes, 1992). More-recent studies report mild or no impairments to overall developmental functioning (Mayes & Bornstein, 1995; Scherling, 1994; Zuckerman & Frank, 1992).

Indirect Impact of Cocaine Use on Children. Before a particular developmental outcome is attributed to cocaine exposure, it is necessary to rule out the effects of other variables known to place children at risk. Determining the specific effects of cocaine requires ruling out the effects of exposure to multiple drugs, premature delivery, poor prenatal care, and socioeconomic status. It would be very difficult to distinguish the impact of these other variables from that of prenatal exposure to cocaine without a very large number of subjects.

Studies investigating the effects of cocaine exposure on children have been based on relatively few subjects. A review of primary literature published between 1982 and 1989 indicates that research was limited to six geographical areas. In addition, the investigators were from only 10 academic institutions, all affiliated with clinical services (Lindenberg, Alexander, Gendrop, Nencioli, & Williams, 1991). These findings suggest that much of the existing scientific literature on intrauterine cocaine exposure is primarily a set of reports on the same groups of children. Many of these children were born to urban minority women receiving public assistance. Therefore, these children are likely to be at risk for developmental delays for multiple reasons. Most likely, they are not a representative sample of all children prenatally exposed to cocaine.

The timing, quantity, and duration of exposure to cocaine almost certainly play major roles with regard to any effects that exposure has on the developing brain. It may take years to disentangle any chemical effects unique to cocaine because this thread is one part of a web of cocaine's effects on the child's family and community. In addition, family drug abuse intensifies developmental risks associated with poverty, violence, abandonment, homelessness, multiple short-term foster care placements, and inadequate parenting (Chasnoff, 1988).

The crack epidemic has transformed some neighborhoods into war zones. Abusers are often short-tempered. When these individuals are involved in minor family arguments, these arguments are more likely to explode into violence. This violence is often directed toward the children in the household. Parental substance abuse, including of alcohol and cocaine, plays a role in about 70% of all child-abuse fatalities. In the case of victims younger than a year, substance abuse is involved in 90% of child-abuse fatalities (Groze et al., 1994).

Cocaine has another effect on children: children as young as 4 years old are being recruited to serve as lookouts and drug carriers. Dealers eventually introduce many of these children to the drug's euphoria. The caregivers of these children may look the other way because the children earn money. For intervention efforts to be most effective, they must address the environmental, as well as intrauterine, effects of cocaine (Oro & Dixon, 1987).

In many cases the mother's addiction impairs her ability to bond with her newborn. She may be insensitive to her child's needs and responses. Addiction may also drastically affect her ability to care for the child. For example, if the mother has gone without sleep, she is more likely to be irritable or aggressive toward her child. If she lacks an appetite (a typical side effect of cocaine), she may not think her child is hungry either and may fail to feed the child.

Many of the reported effects of cocaine exposure may result from a breakdown in communication between a mother who uses cocaine and her offspring. Human infants are helpless at birth. Their survival depends on communicating their needs to adults who care for them. Infants typically use the full range of emotional signals at their disposal, from cries to chuckles, to communicate how they feel and what they need. Under normal circumstances, a mother uses these messages to guide her actions to help the infant achieve goals. Normally, caregivers bring desired objects closer and provide comfort when infants signal distress. However, mothers addicted to drugs do not seem to respond appropriately to their infants' signals (Tronick, 1989).

Attentive, perceptive caregivers are crucial for all infants (Kinnison, Cates, & Baker, 1999). Perhaps they are even more crucial for infants whose developing brains have been exposed to cocaine. Women addicted to cocaine may be psychologically or physically unable to read their infant's messages. Studies of mothers who used cocaine report lack of back-and-forth interactions between these mothers and their infants. These studies also reveal a lack of mutual enjoyment in the relationships. Additionally, these mothers demonstrated less social initiative and resourcefulness in their relationship with their infants than did mothers who did not use drugs. Infants of mothers who used drugs showed fewer positive responses such as smiling, laughing, and prolonged eye contact than did infants with mothers who did not use drugs.

Infants who chronically fail to obtain adult help in modifying their emotional states have only limited resources on which to fall back. Babies have very few patterns of responses at their disposal for regulating their emotions. When confronted by a stimulus that causes strong emotions, infants can only turn away to escape. Continual use of this strategy can lead to problems interacting with objects and individuals. Mothers who use cocaine are more likely to have infants who use this strategy (Azuma & Chasnoff, 1993).

A preschooler who has difficulty playing in unstructured environments may have been an infant who learned to turn away from overly exciting objects. Habits formed in infancy may interfere with the exploratory behavior a toddler needs for normal cognitive development. Children who rarely succeed in engaging their mothers in emotional communication may come to view themselves as ineffective and other people as unreliable (Tronick, 1989).

Children born to mothers who repeatedly use cocaine have difficulty organizing their experiences, understanding cause-and-effect relationships, and controlling mood swings. These difficulties might not be caused by the intrauterine cocaine exposure. They may be caused by interacting with a mother addicted to cocaine. The effects of a mother who is physically or psychologically unable to provide critical learning experiences may be far more enduring than any direct damage from the drug. See Table 10.3 for a list of possible effects of exposure to cocaine.

Early intervention has been show to aid cognitive and language development in children prenatally exposed to cocaine. In addition, it reduces behavior problems (Claussen, Scott, Mundy, & Katz, 2004; Butz et al., 2001).

Table 10.3	*Possible Effects of Cocaine Exposure*
Effects on the mother	Increased blood pressure; irregular heartbeat; anxiety and paranoia; nausea and headaches; rapid, shallow breathing; insomnia and hallucinations; loss of appetite
Effects on the infant	Increased risk of spontaneous abortion, oxygen deprivation during gestation, premature birth, growth retardation, small head circumference, hypersensitivity to stimuli, irritability, withdrawal from stimuli
Effects on the child	Impulsiveness, mood instability, difficulty with concentration, lack of perseverance, difficulty with peer interactions, difficulty engaging in unstructured play, lower intelligence test scores

Studies published in the 1980s that investigated the effects of intrauterine exposure to cocaine should be considered in light of the magnitude of the overlap between maternal cocaine use and HIV infection. Women who use drugs may expose their unborn children to a far more serious risk than cocaine. By using needles to get high or by exchanging sex for drugs, women may expose themselves to HIV. The next section describes factors associated with HIV/AIDS.

Pediatric HIV/AIDS

HIV may lead to pediatric acquired AIDS, a chronic childhood illness alternating between periods of progression and periods of stability (UNICEF, 2005b; Lockhart & Wodarski, 1989; Rubin, 1984). When people are intoxicated on cocaine or alcohol, they are more likely to engage in unprotected sexual intercourse. Unprotected sex with multiple partners may be deadly because it facilitates the spread of HIV, which causes AIDS. The picture of the HIV/AIDS epidemic is filled with drug users who share infected needles or have sex with multiple partners in exchange for crack (*New Picture,* 1995). Children born with HIV or following intrauterine exposure to cocaine tend to have parents of low socioeconomic status and often belong to minorities.

During the first decade of the HIV epidemic, most women diagnosed with AIDS had become infected through intravenous drug use. In the 1980s a team of investigators found that 98% of mothers who had children with pediatric AIDS said that they had used drugs during their pregnancy (Rubinstein, 1986).

Pregnant cocaine users were 4½ times more likely than non-users to have a sexually transmitted disease (New York State Department of Health, 1990). Most of the children diagnosed with pediatric AIDS during the 1980s were born to such women (Childhood AIDS, 1991). The rate of HIV among injecting drug users continues to rise, but the overall pattern of the epidemic may be changing.

In 1992, heterosexual contact overtook injecting drugs as the major risk factor for HIV infection for U.S. women. A slow, steady rise in heterosexual transmission of HIV has already become apparent in poverty-stricken urban neighborhoods. An increase in HIV outside urban areas has also been documented. Some scientists believe this reflects the early stages of an epidemic among heterosexuals. About a quarter of all new HIV infections are now acquired through heterosexual contact. Between 70 and 80% of those infected through heterosexual contact are women who had sexual contact with men who inject drugs (Childhood AIDS, 1991).

In 1993 more than 75% of new HIV cases among women and 84% among children occurred in minority populations, particularly within African American and Latino communities. From 1984 through 1992, the estimated number of children diagnosed each year with perinatally acquired AIDS increased, then declined 43% from 1993 to 1996. The declines were similar by race/ethnicity, regions of the United States, and in urban and rural areas. A major factor in the decline is an increase in treatment before, during, and after pregnancy. It is expected that the perinatal transmission rate will continue to decline with increased use of aggressive treatments and obstetric procedures, such as elective cesarean section. The perinatal HIV transmission rate has sharply dropped from 10.9% in 1997 to 2.8% in 2004.

HIV may be the most serious epidemic ever to confront humans. HIV poses a serious threat to most sexually active adults and to infants born to infected mothers (Anderson & May, 1992). Every pregnant woman who becomes infected with the virus risks transmitting it to her unborn child. Medical authorities believe that counseling and voluntary testing should be routine for all women of child-bearing age with any identifiable risk of HIV infection. Unfortunately, the vast majority of women with HIV are unaware of their health status. Therefore, it is unlikely that they suspect their future children are at risk (Cohen, 1992).

About 25% of children born to women with HIV contract the virus from their mother, either across the placenta or while passing through the birth canal. Aggressive treatment of infected pregnant women with the drug **zidovudine/azidothymidine (AZT)** is believed to substantially reduce the infant's chances of infection (Connor et al., 1994). AZT interferes with the virus's self-replication.

Many state health departments have gone beyond the CDC's recommendations and suggested that women with HIV not give birth. The conveyed view is that children infected with HIV should not be born. To date, there is no way to predict whether a woman with HIV will transmit the virus to her unborn child, but the odds are that she will not. HIV is one of many conditions that can be passed from mother to fetus. Some less stigmatized conditions (such as birth defects linked to maternal diabetes) are more likely to affect the unborn child and are costly to society.

In some cases, women with HIV calculate the costs and benefits associated with reproduction. They evaluate the risk of transmitting the virus to an unborn child against other risks and alternatives. The odds that the baby will be born HIV-free are better than 75%. Women infected with HIV who choose to have children do not intend to cause harm. Usually they intend to bring good into their world (Levine & Dubler, 1990).

Women do not need to be injecting drugs to be exposed to HIV. They may simply live in a poverty-stricken neighborhood with a high infection rate. Poverty and geography often place women in the path of the HIV epidemic because their neighborhoods have been overcome by the cocaine economy.

Children who are infected or orphaned by HIV, are prenatally exposed to drugs, or grow up in families where parents abuse drugs must be provided with appropriate intervention services. These children should be viewed as the innocent victims of their environments. Children do not choose the families into which they are born. To avoid further victimization, prejudices about these children must be discarded.

In 2002, 158 new U.S. cases of pediatric AIDS were reported. In approximately 88% of these cases, the child was infected before or during birth. Since 1993 the number of new cases of perinatally transmitted AIDS has substantially declined. A major factor in this decline is the increased use of treatments before, during, and after pregnancy, which helps reduce HIV transmission.

Direct Impact of HIV on Children.   HIV destroys cells that play a crucial role in the immune system (Levin, Driscoll, & Fleischman, 1991). The incubation period for the virus is generally much shorter in children than in adults. Life-threatening infections and central nervous system damage may appear in children within months rather than years, as is the case for most adults.

Clinical symptoms of pediatric HIV include failure to thrive (failure to develop at the expected rate), recurrent bacterial infections, chronic or recurrent diarrhea, disease of the lymph nodes (lymphadenopathy), rare varieties of chronic pneumonia, viral infections, enlargement of the liver and spleen, and developmental delays. It is of paramount importance that people who work with children, especially in areas of high infection rates, be alert to symptoms of the illnesses afflicting children with HIV. Prolonging the lives of children with pediatric AIDS requires aggressive medical intervention against a host of pathogens that may invade their bodies (Childhood AIDS, 1991; Rudigier, Crocker, & Cohen, 1990).

The course of the illness in a given child depends on a number of factors, including the stage of immune system development at the time of exposure and the general status of the child's immune system. For example, if a mother's prenatal diet is low in protein or B vitamins, a child's immune system may be compromised even before exposure to the virus. The human immune system begins developing before the 12th week of fetal life and remains immature for some months after birth. Maternal antibodies cross the placenta and also are present in a mother's milk to provide immunities to her developing child (Heagarty, 1993).

Infants born to mothers with HIV may test positive for the presence of HIV antibodies because their mother's antibodies crossed the placenta. This does not mean that all infants who test positive for HIV antibodies at birth have the virus. The child's own immune system becomes mature enough to manufacture antibodies in response to the presence of the virus after about 15 months. At this time an HIV antibody test may detect whether a child has contracted the virus (Childhood AIDS, 1991). Figure 10.3 provides an overview of potential outcomes for infants born to women with HIV.

The first diagnosed U.S. cases of pediatric AIDS were infants. This fact fostered the perception that children infected with HIV always die of AIDS within a year or

Figure 10.3   **Overview of Potential Outcomes for Infants Born to Women with HIV**

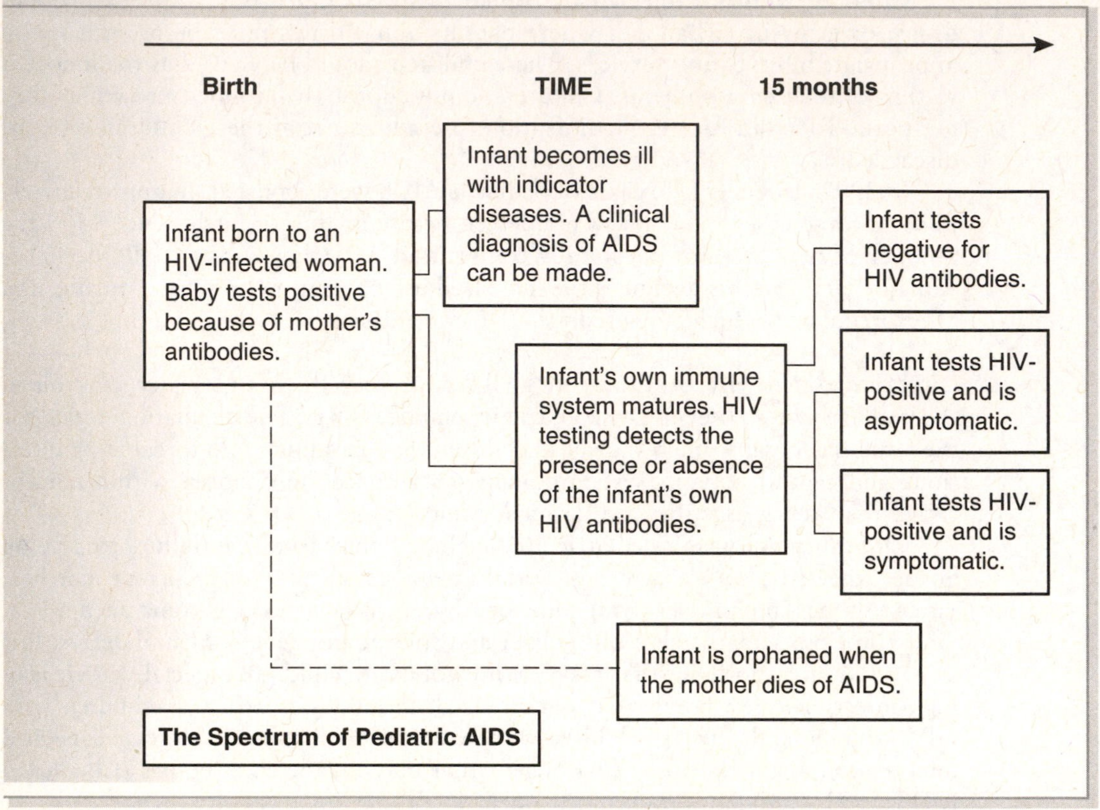

The Spectrum of Pediatric AIDS

two of birth. The prognosis is poor for infants who develop an HIV-related illness before their first birthday (Lockhart & Wodarski, 1989). Infants infected before birth may be born small for their gestational age and may not thrive after birth (Czarniecki & Dillman, 1992; Dokecki, Baumeister, & Kupstas, 1989). Many infected children are unlikely to be tested for the presence of HIV antibodies until they come down with an illness recognized as being related to HIV infection.

Based on more information, experts now estimate that 20 to 27% of children born to women with HIV develop AIDS by their 10th birthday. The median age of diagnosis for pediatric AIDS was about 5 years in the mid-1990s, which means that about half of infected children begin kindergarten before they are diagnosed with AIDS (De Gruttola, Ming Tu, & Pagano, 1992).

In 1987 the CDC developed a classification system for children affected by HIV (Czarniecki & Dillman, 1992). Some infants are born with full-blown AIDS and will die before their first birthday. Children older than 15 months born to women with HIV are classified as of "indeterminate infection" status if they show no symptoms of HIV infection. Children older than 15 months who test positive for HIV antibodies but do not show clinical symptoms of AIDS are classified as asymptomatic, although they may have abnormal immune-system functioning at times.

The CDC collects statistics on AIDS cases and establishes the criteria that physicians use for reporting AIDS cases. These criteria are modified as more is discovered about the illness. Physicians diagnose pediatric AIDS when a child develops an **opportunistic infection** that signals a breakdown of the immune system (immunodeficiency), fails to thrive, or has a progressive infection of the brain (encephalopathy) because of the virus (Roth, 1992).

Opportunistic infections account for most AIDS-related deaths. These infections do not ordinarily occur in people with properly functioning immune systems. Opportunistic infections may be caused by bacteria that normally live in soil, water, organic matter, plants, and nonhuman animals. Recurrent bacterial infections are often the first indication of HIV infection in children. They may include chronic and severe ear infections (otitis media), inflamed sinuses (sinusitis), inflammation of the digestive tract (gastroenteritis), and inflammation of the linings of the central nervous system (meningitis). Many children with HIV infections come down with a rare form of pneumonia caused by a protozoan (Scherer, 1991).

Children with HIV have a difficult time fighting off viral infections and should avoid close contact with people with contagious illnesses, including colds and flu. People who work with such children should receive a flu shot each year, keep their own immunizations up to date, and be vaccinated against hepatitis B. These precautionary measures help keep providers from transmitting illnesses that may be life-threatening to children with compromised immune systems. The herpes simplex virus, which causes boils, cold sores, and fever blisters, is life-threatening to children with HIV. It is very important to avoid exposing these children to people with those conditions.

A nurse interacts with two young children with health impairments.

Common childhood viral illnesses such as chicken pox and measles may kill children with HIV. Medical treatment within 72 hours of exposure to these illnesses may prevent children with HIV from becoming critically ill (Czarniecki & Dillman, 1992). It is, therefore, extremely important that day care providers and preschool personnel inform all parents about any chance of exposure to these common illnesses. Parents need to be afforded the opportunity to protect their children by seeking prompt medical care (Crocker, 1989).

Childhood immunizations may not afford the normal measure of protection for children with HIV. Their immune systems may not be capable of mounting a defensive response or producing antibodies. If a child has a weakened immune system, a vaccine made from a live virus may cause the disease it was intended to prevent. Live, oral polio vaccines given to household members pose a threat to someone with HIV. A child with HIV may contract a life-threatening case of polio from a household member who received the live-virus vaccine (New York State Department of Health, 1990).

The central nervous system is a primary site of HIV infection for children. Current data suggest that 80 to 90% of children with HIV will suffer some degree of central nervous system impairment over the course of their illness, from strokes, tumors, meningitis, encephalitis, or some combination of these. HIV is already one of the most common infectious causes of mental retardation and encephalopathy in children under the age of 13 (Armstrong, Seidel, & Swales, 1993). Unfortunately, powerful drugs used to treat opportunistic infections in people with HIV may have major side effects, including neurological symptoms that may mimic developmental problems (Scherer, 1991).

Children with HIV are now surviving longer because of advances in medical treatments for opportunistic infections. However, many children with AIDS who do not suffer an early death suffer some degree of brain damage. HIV leaves the brain vulnerable to opportunistic infections, and the virus itself may invade the brain. Nutritional deficiencies, shortage of oxygen in the blood, and drug side effects may also affect central nervous system functioning in these children. Treatment with AZT appears to provide some relief from cognitive symptoms (Wilfert, 1994).

Pediatric HIV infection of the central nervous system may include global developmental delays, abnormal motor functioning, cognitive disorders, sensory impairments, and impaired brain growth (Diamond, 1989). Two patterns of central nervous system involvement have been identified among children with AIDS (Fletcher et al., 1991).

One pattern of central nervous system involvement occurs in about 25% of all children with HIV, and the damage appears to be limited to certain areas of the brain. This form is known as a static pattern of infection. If abilities associated with the affected parts of the brain have already developed, effects will be negligible. Deficits may also be masked until a later developmental stage and not be noticed until a function fails to emerge on time (Armstrong et al., 1993). For example, if the affected area of the brain controls the ability to walk, no impact will be noticed until the child should be walking.

Children with a static pattern of infection may not achieve expected developmental milestones such as walking or talking. Additionally, their rate of development is likely to be slower than that of healthy children of similar ages. It is very unlikely that children with the static pattern of HIV will lose previously attained abilities in other functional areas. Unfortunately, this pattern of infection is often characterized by severely delayed cognitive functioning. Affected children may have difficulties thinking and reasoning. Motor abnormalities, which vary in severity, frequently accompany these cognitive deficits (Armstrong et al., 1993).

The more common pattern is progressive infection of the central nervous system, caused by a primary and persistent infection of the brain resulting from HIV. It resembles the AIDS-related dementia found in adults. Children with this pattern not only fail to achieve developmental milestones; they also deteriorate in functioning over time (Armstrong et al., 1993).

The infection progresses differently in different children. Some children experience a relentless deterioration in functioning whereas others experience times of relative stability between periods of deterioration. Ultimately, progressive infection results in cognitive and motor abnormalities, which are typically much more severe than those seen in the static pattern. Most children with HIV experience a progressive pattern of infection of the central nervous system.

A few children with HIV suffer only minimal functional problems. These children may show selective impairment of perceptual/visual integration and poor visual organization on measures such as the Kaufman-ABC test (Diamond, 1989). Some seem to have attributes associated with ADHD and a few may display autistic-like withdrawal (Levenson & Mellins, 1992; Levin et al., 1991).

Indirect Impact of HIV on Children.   Children with HIV face developmental risks apart from the risks caused by pathogens that invade their bodies. Children with this chronic illness must endure frequent and sometimes painful medical treatment, disruption of their daily routine for periods of hospitalization, and side effects from medication. Adults need to be alert for signs of pain in children who may not be able to explain how they feel. Inattention to their pain may lead to suffering and delay treatments for life-threatening infections.

The emotional impact of the infection may be as severe as the developmental delays it inflicts. Children with HIV may be placed in isolation wards while hospitalized and examined by gowned medical personnel. Even their family members may appear to be fearful when around them. Normal socialization experiences may be lacking. The children may develop negative self-esteem, loss of emotion, depression, and defense mechanisms for dealing with the situation. Children may interpret pain as punishment, attribute illness to family interactions, or blame themselves or other family members for their illness (Wiener, Moss, Davidson, & Fair, 1993).

Children with HIV also face risk factors inherent in their home environments. They may suffer from adjustment difficulties as they go in and out of the hospital or are moved from household to household. Intervention efforts for these children must take into account all of the neurological, medical, and social factors that may contribute to their developmental status. Figure 10.4 lists characteristics commonly found in infants and young children infected with AIDS.

Millions of children not infected with HIV will be affected by the HIV epidemic. By the year 2000, more than 125,000 U.S. children were orphaned by this epidemic. An estimated 40% of infected adults suffered from an AIDS-related dementia, which includes the gradual deterioration of cognitive, physical, and psychological

Figure 10.4   **Possible Effects of Pediatric AIDS**

- chronic, recurring childhood illnesses (e.g., diarrhea)
- life-threatening bacterial and viral infections
- diseases of the lymph nodes
- enlargement of the liver and spleen
- damage to central nervous system
- impaired brain growth
- failure to thrive
- abnormal motor functioning, including spasticity
- sensory impairments, including hearing and visual impairments
- impairment of perceptual and visual integration
- ADHD
- loss of affect, including depression
- severe withdrawal that resembles autism
- psychotic behavior
- negative self-esteem
- cognitive delays, which may include loss of skills

functioning (New York State Department of Health, 1990). A parent's dementia, chronic illness, and death from AIDS usually are very frightening experiences for children. Children who are affected need intervention services that address their emotional and social needs as they attempt to cope with the illness and then death of their parent.

Impact on the Families of Children with HIV.   The social environment of children affected by the AIDS epidemic is of special concern. Children most often contract the virus from their mothers. Mothers may have contracted it from the children's fathers. Additionally, more than one child in a family may be infected. The social and emotional costs to a family affected by AIDS are immeasurable.

The psychological impact of pediatric HIV infection, superimposed on a family's existing problems such as drug addiction, may be devastating. Psychological issues confronting infected families include the stress involved in coping with the chronic illness of mothers and children, grief and mourning as children's levels of function deteriorate, and feelings of guilt on the part of mothers who transmitted the virus to their children.

Family members may experience feelings of isolation if they do not tell people in their family and social networks about the child's health status because they fear stigmatization. Denial is a common coping strategy for dealing with pervasive problems. As families attempt to cope with anxiety, guilt, and grief over the impending loss of a beloved child, family members may withdraw from one another.

To date, most pediatric HIV cases have occurred in families suffering from poverty, chronic unemployment, racial discrimination, homelessness, and welfare dependency (Task Force on Pediatric AIDS, 1989). Such circumstances often lead to confrontational relationships with various agencies and mistrust of authority figures. This may make it difficult for these families to follow the advice of educators or medical personnel.

The magnitude of problems, physical and psychological, confronting families who have children with HIV may be overwhelming. Other existing problems will be compounded if a parent develops AIDS-related dementia. Parents may be too sick or dysfunctional to take care of a chronically ill child. If a child is removed from the home to live elsewhere, they may experience an overwhelming sense of loss.

Normal interactions between parents and their children focus on the future. This focus includes urging children to eat their vegetables, do their schoolwork, and behave in ways that prepare them for adulthood. In contrast, children with HIV may be unlikely to survive to their adult years, and this reality affects the foundation of many family relationships (Lipson, 1993). Adults may be reluctant to discuss their child's fatal infection because this brings to mind the prospect of the child's premature death.

In most cases, children with HIV are precious to their families. Family members need to feel that the professionals caring for the child share their hopes. Special training can help providers work more effectively with families that are experiencing extreme emotional stress.

Impact of HIV on Society.   Costs to society from the pediatric AIDS epidemic include the direct costs of medical care and hospitalization, foster care services, and early intervention services, as well as the enormous indirect cost of the loss of children. Children with AIDS often spend longer periods of time in hospitals, need a greater number of services, and contribute to greater financial losses for hospitals than do adult patients with AIDS (Tokarski, 1990).

Pediatric AIDS has primarily been a disease of the urban poor. Public general hospitals in major cities have provided most of the medical care for these children. Many of these hospitals were already underfinanced before being besieged by the cocaine and AIDS epidemics. From 1981 to 1987 one New York City hospital spent $34 million caring for 37 abandoned infants who tested positive for HIV at birth (Dokecki et al., 1989).

A shortage of foster parents and understaffed child welfare agencies contribute to babies remaining in expensive hospital environments even after they are medically ready to be discharged (Groze et al., 1992). Uncertainties surrounding the HIV status of infants exposed to drugs contribute to the problem of finding foster care for them. About 75% of children born to mothers with HIV do not contract the virus, but these children are placed at developmental risk when abandoned to institutional care (Childhood AIDS, 1991).

Annually, several thousand children, including 25 to 33% of all children with HIV, will enter the child welfare system as a result of the AIDS epidemic (Groze et al., 1992). Only a few of these children will be placed in adoptive homes. The financial burden, including medical costs, of caring for children with AIDS falls heavily on the adoptive parents. Most state Medicaid programs do not cover treatments considered experimental, as are many current treatments for pediatric HIV/AIDS. Adoptive parents often report being provided with too little information about how to deal with children's developmental delays.

Another cost of this epidemic is its impact on people in the helping professions, including social workers, doctors, nurses, and educators. One study found that decisions by medical staff to withhold treatment from infants were influenced not only by the infant's HIV status but also by the mother's HIV status. Staff members justified withholding life-saving medical treatment from infants born to women with HIV on the grounds that the mother was going to die and the infant would have a poor social environment (Levin et al., 1991).

The stress experienced by professionals who work with children who have HIV may be reduced if intervention efforts are focused on maximizing the children's quality of life rather than on their impending death. Programs have been developed for nurses who work with children suffering from other fatal illnesses and should be used as models for working with children who have HIV (Rushton et al., 1993).

It may also be helpful to adopt the perspective that everyone ultimately dies. People find value in their own lives in spite of this truth, and they should find value in the lives of children with HIV/AIDS, however brief.

Families affected by cocaine, alcohol, or AIDS are often concerned about confidentiality. For example, children with HIV may need medication administered during the day. The nature of the medication indicated on an individualized family service plan or individualized education program may identify the child as HIV-infected. Therefore, it is important to use appropriate measures to protect the family's privacy.

Children with AIDS are particularly vulnerable to environmental conditions. Although society tends to be sympathetic toward these children, some people argue that children with fatal illnesses should receive only the care needed to make their lives comfortable (Rushton et al., 1993). Viewing early intervention services solely or primarily as an investment in the future may lead to the denial of such services in the case of terminally ill children. It is important to remember that experiences that are generally valuable to children also are valuable to children born with severe disabilities or life-threatening illnesses. When this is forgotten, early intervention services are unlikely to succeed.

Some children with HIV are taken into state custody and put into foster care before diagnosis of infection because of child abuse or neglect. Professionals working with foster families of these children need to afford the families the same degree of respect they would extend to biological parents. Failure to accept and interact with the adults in a child's life, whether or not they are legal guardians, may leave the child feeling alone and resentful.

Often, parents who have children with AIDS view their children as fragile and in need of close protection. Their efforts to protect their children may create an emotional isolation chamber. Children benefit from normal social interactions. Therefore, families need guidance regarding safe and unsafe child care practices. This information may encourage them to let their children experience most social interactions.

Building a sense of competency may help family members cope with the responsibility of caring for a chronically ill child. For example, family members may need help in discovering their own strengths and their child's strengths. These discoveries may then be used to help plan and implement developmentally appropriate and safe activities for the children.

Simple modifications of the environment may reduce children's exposure to environmental pathogens, thus improving quality of life. Reduction of environmental pathogens includes ensuring that children with HIV do not take part in cleaning animal cages, tanks, or litter boxes because these contain bacteria (New York State Department of Health, 1990). The children are also vulnerable to microorganisms living in the soil. Therefore, children should always wash their hands after playing outside. Staying clean is an imperative preventive health measure for these children. They should shower or bathe frequently and always wash their hands carefully after using the bathroom.

Molds and fungi may also endanger children with compromised immune systems. Because kitchens and bathrooms are environments in which these organisms readily grow, these areas need to be well ventilated. Garbage containers should be covered, and bleach solution should be used as a disinfectant (New York State Department of Health, 1990).

It is important not to expose children with HIV to uncooked food that may harbor microorganisms. Unpasteurized dairy products carry a risk of salmonella infection, and undercooked meats carry the risk of toxoplasmosis. Children with HIV should not be served raw eggs in any form, including homemade mayonnaise, hollandaise, mousse, or ice cream. Vegetables always should be served cooked or peeled. Children with HIV often fail to thrive and may need special high-calorie diets. Nutritionists, nurses, or physicians should be contacted for information on appropriate dietary plans (New York State Department of Health, 1990).

In many cases, parents and guardians are unaware of their child's HIV status. Early childhood educators should be alert to hearing or visual impairments, unexplained gaps in development, repeated bouts of infection that precede a change in a child's developmental status, and developmental delays that may signal HIV infection of the brain.

Children at risk of HIV infection should have developmental screenings similar to those for other children who are at risk for other developmental delays. They should be referred for a comprehensive assessment if delays are detected. Early identification of HIV may directly benefit children by affording them the opportunity to receive aggressive medical intervention (Coleman, 1991; Crocker, 1989; Mayers & Spiegel, 1992).

The fluctuating course of HIV infection means that children require frequent reassessments of their developmental and neurological status. Educators should not assume that skills displayed during an earlier assessment still remain in the child's repertoire of functional skills (Bisiacchi, Suppiej, & Laverda, 2000). Reassessments at 3- to 6-month intervals have been suggested for toddlers and preschoolers with HIV (Byers, 1989). Assessments may help determine how effective medical treatments are for these children and may be used to chart the progression of the illness. For example, assessment results may be used to evaluate how AZT treatment influences a child's cognitive development.

Children change as they develop, and the effects of HIV interact with this process. Instruments sensitive to developmental changes may provide significant information for monitoring interventions with these children. Developmental models that depict typical growth curves may be used to estimate the course of development for a child. Comparing the results of frequent assessments to projected development highlights how a child is changing.

Often, raw scores rather than standardized scores should be used for children with HIV. Using standardized scores may indicate that the child is declining in intelligence between assessments, whereas using raw scores may indicate improvement is occurring but at a delayed rate. Assessment instruments need to be carefully selected and used consistently. This may help avoid the appearance of sudden changes in development that might occur when using a variety of assessment instruments. Tests that are either too difficult or too easy may also create a false picture of a child's development. An instrument's range of measurement should be carefully considered before it is used to track developmental changes in children with HIV (Levenson, Kairam, Bartnett, & Mellins, 1991).

The extended family is an often-overlooked support system for children with developmental delays and their families. A significant proportion of the African American community, hit especially hard by cocaine abuse and the HIV epidemic, lives in extended families (Mayes, 1992; Mayes et al., 1992; Mayes, Grillon, Granger, & Schottenfeld, 1998; Wilson, 1989). This type of household may come into existence as one family absorbs another, often because of inadequate resources in a single-parent household. Extended family members should be encouraged to help with child care, household tasks, and transportation. They may also be able to provide emotional support or instruction. Service providers must understand the resources available within extended families.

Growing up in families headed by grandmothers may provide children with resources, and material and emotional support, that may be in short supply in single-parent, impoverished households (Wilson, 1989). Such families may buffer even the detrimental influences of a parent's AIDS-related dementia, chronic illnesses, or addictions. Unfortunately, grandmothers may be exhausted from spending months or years caring for their adult children with AIDS before they take on the additional responsibility of a chronically ill grandchild (Roberts, Severinsen, Kuehn, Straker, & Fritz, 1992).

Service providers must also carefully consider the ethnic and cultural environments of individual families to ensure that treatment plans are appropriate and meaningful for the families. Whenever possible, normal experiences consistent with their cultural backgrounds need to be provided for all children.

The potentially isolating effects of HIV infection make it especially important to create an environment in which children with HIV and their families may playfully interact. A child with HIV is, first and foremost, a child. Opportunities for play, creative arts, recreation, and field trips appropriate to the child's age and developmental level are important parts of an intervention program. Given the variable nature of the child's medical condition, flexible alternatives easily accessible to the child and family are essential.

The Developmental and Family Services Unit (DFSU) of the Children's Evaluation and Rehabilitation Center at the Rose F. Kennedy Center (Bronx, New York) developed a model program for improving the quality of life of children infected with HIV and their families. This program provides therapy, referrals for education and preschool placements, home-based instruction, individualized occupational and physical therapy, feeding therapy, supportive counseling to help parents care for and cope with a chronically ill child, and advocacy in obtaining other services (Rudigier et al., 1990).

Researchers at a federally funded, university-affiliated program developed another model program: Opportunities for Parents and Children Together. The O-PACT model of intervention focuses on parent–child interactions and is family-centered and family-driven (Forest and Libscomb, 1994). O-PACT provides services for parents accused of child abuse and neglect, parents with developmental delays and mental illness, teen parents, low-income families, and children who have developmental delays or are at risk of delays. Parents who engage in behaviors that have harmed their child need to develop a sense of competence if they are to successfully care for the child. The O-PACT model offers a means of providing early intervention services while reducing the need for out-of-home placements, improving parenting skills, decreasing the family's social isolation, and monitoring child and family development. Methods of intervention provided in the DFSU and O-PACT model programs, and similar programs, may be useful for early childhood service providers.

Children who are infected or orphaned by HIV, who are prenatally exposed to drugs, or who grow up in families in which parents abuse drugs must be provided with appropriate intervention services. These children should be viewed as the innocent victims of their environments. Children do not choose the family into which they are born. To avoid further victimization, prejudices about these children must be discarded. The environmental influences described in this chapter and recently referred to as "the new morbidities" are leaving in their wake a multitude of children in need of human affection.

Conclusions

A small percentage of children are classified with OHI. Many of these children suffer from health needs caused by controllable environmental factors (e.g., prenatal cocaine, alcohol, or HIV/AIDS exposure or lead poisoning). Fortunately, the number of pediatric HIV/AIDS cases has decreased over the last decade. However, the number of children prenatally exposed to drugs continues to rise. Knowledge about causes and symptoms of various health impairments helps service providers best meet the needs of children and their families.

In addition, a small number of young children have multiple disabilities, which typically lead to the need for a variety of early intervention services. These services often require the expertise of a wide variety of professionals for an extended period.

CHAPTER SUMMARY

- Knowledge about the variety of OHI young children may have is crucial for providing optimal early intervention services.

- Prenatal and postnatal exposure to alcohol, cocaine, and HIV are likely to affect children's development in a negative way.

- Pregnant women who use intravenous drugs risk exposing their unborn children to HIV and to the effects of the drugs they use.

- Federal laws require that early intervention services be made available to children with health impairments, and these services appear to be effective.

- Society bears many costs as a result of FAS/FAE, cocaine use, and pediatric HIV/AIDS, but affected children bear the greatest burden.

CHAPTER KEY TERMS

pediatric human immunodeficiency virus (HIV)
acquired immunodeficiency syndrome (AIDS)
other health impairments (OHI)
chronic health problems
acute health problems
asthma
allergies
attention deficit hyperactivity disorder (ADHD)
diabetes
epilepsy
cystic fibrosis
heart condition
hemophilia
lead poisoning
leukemia
cancer
nephritis
rheumatic fever
sickle cell anemia
tuberculosis (TB)
prenatal drug exposure
cytomegalovirus (CMV)
nurse

licensed practical nurse (LPN)
registered nurse (RN)
nurse-educator
pediatrician
nutritionist
grand mal seizure
petit mal seizure
anemia
congenital heart defect
insulin reaction
diabetic coma
methamphetamine
fetal alcohol spectrum disorders (FASD)
fetal alcohol syndrome (FAS)
alcohol-related neurodevelopmental disorder (ARND)
fetal alcohol effects (FAE)
alcohol-related birth defect (ARBD)
cocaine
crack
zidovudine/azidothymidine (AZT)
opportunistic infection

R E V I E W   Q U E S T I O N S

1. Why is it important for service providers to understand OHI?

2. How have the abuse of alcohol and cocaine and the HIV epidemic affected children?

3. What clinical symptoms are associated with intrauterine exposure to cocaine, HIV, and alcohol?

4. Why are early intervention services important for children with AIDS, FAS, and prenatal exposure to cocaine?

S U G G E S T E D   S T U D E N T   A C T I V I T I E S

1. Conduct in-depth research on a health impairment and the services that young children with this health impairment may require.

2. Collect local data on the number of children infected with HIV/AIDS and prenatally exposed to cocaine and alcohol.

3. Compile a list of local organizations that provide services to children with HIV/AIDS or

FAS or who suffer from the effects of exposure to cocaine.

4. Visit an early intervention program that provides services for children prenatally exposed to cocaine or classified as having FAS or FAE.

5. Volunteer to work for a community organization that serves families affected by HIV.

Adaptive Abilities

CHAPTER KEY POINTS

- Adaptive skills are required for day-to-day functioning.

- A variety of behaviors fall under the category of adaptive skills.

- A variety of formal and informal assessments are appropriate for evaluating the level of adaptive skills development.

- Several disabilities characteristically include delays in adaptive skills.

- Many factors contribute to adaptive-skills delays.

- Use of task analysis often aids in helping children acquire adaptive skills.

Early childhood intervention is often thought of as focusing on helping children acquire pre-academic skills. With regard to very young children with disabilities and those with multiple, severe disabilities, the acquisition of **adaptive skills** is often a primary focus. Adaptive skills include conceptual, social, and practical skills that are required for daily functioning and that affect the ability to effectively respond to various situations. Adaptive skills are one of the five major skills areas addressed in special education laws: communication, cognitive, motor, social-emotional, and adaptive (Frieman, 2002).

Adaptive abilities include being able to do things on one's own without getting into trouble and being able to adjust to and manage one's surroundings. These skills are learned and involve proper development and implementation to effectively function and meet social expectations. Acquiring adaptive behaviors helps promote independence at home, at school, and in the community (Ladd, 2003; Lowenthal, 1996).

In contrast, undesirable or socially unacceptable behaviors that interfere with the acquisition of desired skills and performance of everyday activities are **maladaptive behaviors.** Maladaptive behaviors interfere with children's achievement of independence.

Children with delays in adaptive-skills development have difficulty learning or acquiring skills necessary to meet personal needs, be socially responsible, and participate in developmentally appropriate situations. Adaptive behavior areas include **activities of daily living (ADLs)** such as toileting, eating, dressing, and personal hygiene. Problems in acquiring age-appropriate adaptive skills may occur in children at any age. Most adaptive behaviors are related to other areas of development, including communication, cognitive, social-emotional, and physical skills. Those not previously discussed in earlier chapters will be discussed in this chapter.

Assessment of Adaptive Skills

Standardized tests are often used as part of the assessment of adaptive behaviors (Matson et al., 2003). Many of these tests are designed to evaluate general development, including adaptive skills. In addition, several other standardized assessments focus primarily on adaptive skills.

Parental input about children's level of adaptive skills is particularly crucial because parents are typically most familiar with their child's behavior. Parents' personal accounts may be the most accurate indicator of the child's developmental status, rather than information obtained during limited observation in an unfamiliar testing setting. In addition, because behavior is socially defined, a child's abilities are most accurately evaluated within the context of cultural and social expectations.

A variety of adaptive behavior scales are appropriate for young children. Several scales discussed in Chapters 6 and 7 are also useful for evaluating adaptive skills. Tests that specifically focus on adaptive skills are briefly described below.

Developmental Profile II

The **Developmental Profile II (DP-II)** behavior scale is used to screen for developmental delays from infancy to age 9. This scale is a checklist of 186 skills. A parent or therapist who knows the child well indicates whether the child has mastered specific skills. The DP-II assesses physical, self-help, social, academic, and communication development. It is particularly useful for children with severe handicaps (Matson, Mayville, & Laud, 2003).

Early Coping Inventory

The **Early Coping Inventory (ECI)** is based on observation and is used to assess the coping-related behaviors that infants and toddlers use during daily activities. Scores provide information about level of effectiveness, coping style, and specific coping strengths and weaknesses. These data are useful for planning educational and therapeutic interventions. It is appropriate for infants 4–36 months old and for older children with disabilities. The ECI has 48 items divided into three coping clusters.

The first cluster assesses sensorimotor organization, including visual attention, reaction to touch, self-regulation of basic body functions, tolerance for various body positions, and activity level depending on various situations. The second cluster focuses on reactive behavior, which includes a child's capacity to accept emotional warmth and support from other people, reactions to the feelings and moods of others, tolerance of frustration, ability to cope with stressful events, and capacity to adapt to changes in the environment. The third cluster examines self-initiated behavior, including the child's ability to communicate needs, attempt new behaviors, achieve a goal, problem-solve, and persist in activities (Zeitlin, Williamson, & Szczepanski, 1988). Test results can be used to plan educational and therapeutic interventions (Zeitlin et al., 1988).

Vineland Adaptive Behavior Scales

The **Vineland Adaptive Behavior Scales-II (VABS-II)** is designed to assess the personal and social independence of individuals from birth to 18 years old. The VABS uses a checklist to evaluate a wide range of disabilities, including mental retardation, developmental delays, functional-skills impairment, and speech/language impairment. The VABS evaluates interpersonal relationships, play and leisure-time activities, interpersonal coping skills, and gross- and fine-motor skills. It is available in three editions: Interview Edition, Survey Form, and Expanded Form. The Survey Form provides standard scores for five areas as well as a total score. The Expanded Form adds detailed information that can be used in developing intervention programs for children 3–13 years old and includes a teacher questionnaire with scores for four adaptive areas as well as a total adaptive score (Fenton et al., 2003; Sparrow, Balla, & Cicchetti, 1998). Table 11.1 lists the domains and subdomains of the VABS.

AAMD Adaptive Behavior Scales

The **American Association on Mental Deficiency (AAMD) Adaptive Behavior Scales (ABS)** are designed to measure social skills and personal independence in children age 3 years through 18 years, 11 months who are classified as mentally retarded or emotionally maladjusted (Vandergriff, Hester, & Mandra, 1987).

Table 11.1	Domains and Subdomains of the Vineland Adaptive Behavior Scales (VABS)
Domains	**Subdomains**
Communication	Receptive
	Expressive
	Written
Daily living skills	Personal
	Domestic
	Community
Socialization	Interpersonal relationships
	Play and leisure time
	Coping skills
Motor skills	Gross
	Fine

Scales of Independent Behavior, Revised

The **Scales of Independent Behavior, Revised (SIB-R)** assess adaptive and maladaptive behavior to determine the type and amount of special assistance that children with disabilities may need. It can be completed by a psychologist, teacher, or social worker through observation or use of interview materials that involve parents. The SIB-R adaptive behavior items include 14 subscales grouped into four clusters: motor skills, social interaction and communication skills, personal living skills, and community living skills. The examiner rates the child on each task using a scale from zero to three. The ratings are 0 (never or rarely performs the task, even if asked), 1 (does the task but not well, or about 25% of the time, and may need to be asked), 2 (does the task fairly well, or about 75% of the time, but may need to be asked), and 3 (always or almost always does the task very well without being asked) (Frieman, 2002).

Hawaii Early Learning Profile

The **Hawaii Early Learning Profile (HELP)** is appropriate for children birth through 3 years old. It is a nonstandardized curriculum-based assessment used to identify child and family needs, track growth and development, and determine target objectives. HELP covers 685 developmental sequenced skills in six domains (cognitive, language, gross-motor, fine-motor, social, and self-help). It provides suggestions for play-based activities and intervention strategies for each skill (Parks, 1999).

Elements of Adaptive Ability

Young children who have delays in adaptive skills typically have delays in other areas of development. Children with mental retardation, pervasive developmental disorder (PDD), visual impairments, orthopedic impairments, traumatic brain injuries, or fetal alcohol syndrome commonly have delays in adaptive skills. Most disabilities that frequently include significant delays in adaptive skills have been discussed in previous chapters.

Adaptive skills for young children include communication skills (discussed in Chapter 5), self-direction, interpersonal skills, self-esteem (discussed in Chapter 14), following rules, and practical skills (e.g., eating, dressing, toileting, and grooming) (Lowenthal, 1996). Several of the skills not discussed in other chapters are discussed below.

Movement toward Autonomy

Most preschoolers can express their thoughts, feelings, and needs and are ready to be more **autonomous** (independent). To appropriately adapt to increasingly diverse social situations, children must develop independence. From an early age, children's search for independence is based on the desire to feel competent. Children benefit from being allowed to satisfy their curiosity by freely exploring safe environments. Most preschoolers can express their independence by taking responsibility for putting their clothes and toys in the proper locations. They are also capable of participating in family chores such as setting the table, sorting socks, and helping to prepare meals. Completing such activities enhances a sense of competence and allows children to learn to be helpful (Baker et al., 2004).

When children participate in **self-care** activities and attempt to help others, it is often difficult for adults to find the right balance between providing too little and providing too much guidance. Ideally, children receive only the minimal amount of aid necessary for them to complete tasks. Initially, giving minimal assistance is likely to require more time than providing more help or simply doing things for children, even when the children are capable of completing the actions themselves. Too little help often leads children to feel defeated whereas too much frustrates them.

Breaking tasks into smaller parts often makes the tasks seem less overwhelming and provides children with more opportunities to succeed. Successful experiences enhance confidence and lead children to be willing to attempt more-complex tasks. This willingness is needed in school and throughout life. Adults should positively acknowledge children's efforts to complete tasks rather than focus on the outcome of those efforts.

Children should be encouraged to try new activities and attempt increasingly challenging tasks. They should be provided with developmentally appropriate tasks, ones that can be accomplished. Adults should choose tasks that children are likely to complete. When children are not successful or as successful as they would like to be, adults should help them learn to deal with disappointment.

Children need to be taught how to make appropriate choices and should be given ample time to do so. Initially, choices should be kept simple. For example, allowing children to choose an activity from two possibilities or select a snack from two choices is developmentally appropriate for most toddlers. Being required to select from more than two choices may result in frustration. As children mature, they should be encouraged to make more-complex decisions.

When children face problems, they should be encouraged to try to solve them on their own. Problem-solving is a learned skill, and adults need to provide children with problem-solving strategies. When children solve their own problems, they develop confidence and independence. Play time without any structured activities gives children the freedom to play what they want and to learn how to self-entertain. This also allows them to take responsibility by deciding how they will use their time.

Adults promote autonomy and self-regulation (self-monitoring) by modeling such behaviors (Bronson, 2000; Nolen, 1988; Thompson, 1990). They must have the skills needed to direct children's behaviors and overcome challenges. Self-regulation skills are enhanced when children are supported in developing intrinsic motivation (the desire to do something because the behavior itself is enjoyable). The following methods have been demonstrated to be useful for encouraging children's self-regulation in school and other settings.

- Creating orderliness and predictability—Children are better prepared to make appropriate choices when they have structure and relatively stable schedules to guide them.
- Providing age-appropriate opportunities for independence—Some level of guidance is useful, but too much unnecessary assistance inhibits learning and growth. Children need guidance in making good choices; they need to have their behaviors monitored and supported.
- Providing help when needed—Absolute independence in all areas is rarely appropriate. Adults should serve as resources but only when truly needed.
- Providing guidance by making suggestions, giving explanations, and avoiding commands—Children more readily internalize suggestions for accomplishing desired goals when they are told the rationale behind the suggestions.
- Teaching self-management skills—Children benefit from a variety of specific guidelines for controlling and evaluating their own behavior through such techniques as self-monitoring, self-instruction, and self-evaluation.
- Ensuring a safe-environment—Children benefit when adults create safe environments and community settings in which children can comfortably make appropriate decisions. Adults must be caring, respectful, and supportive; solicit children's ideas; emphasize positive behaviors; and develop cooperative learning activities.

Kindergarten teachers indicate that children whom they encourage to explore and take personal responsibility are more successful when they enter elementary school. Children who are confident of their abilities are more willing to try new things (e.g., interact in groups with children and teachers they do not know, introduce themselves to others, attempt to learn new skills, and work independently), display appropriate emotions when dealing with change, and be able to deal with conflicts (Maxwell & Clifford, 2004).

Motivation

Motivation energizes, sustains, and directs behavior. Highly motivated children are more likely to experience high levels of achievement in a variety of areas. Motivation can be **extrinsic** or **intrinsic** (Harter, 1978).

Engaging in an activity as a means to an end involves extrinsic motivation. For example, a student might work on a project for a long time to get a good grade. Engaging in an activity for its own sake involves intrinsic motivation (Covington, 1992). An intrinsically motivated student might work on a project for the sheer enjoyment of learning about new things.

Many children have a natural need to control their environment. The need for control is a form of intrinsic motivation. Children benefit when teachers allow them to have input in classroom decisions, such as developing classroom rules and choosing learning activities. Intrinsic motivation in an academic setting is often referred to as *need for achievement, achievement motivation, motivation to learn,* or *mastery orientation.* Intrinsic motivation often includes one or more of the qualities described below (Covington, 1992; Kuhl, 1984).

- Curiosity—Children naturally seek out information to help them make sense of their environment.
- Need for equilibrium—Children seek consistency between what they believe and what they experience.
- Interest—Children are affected by situation interests (interests evoked by the environment), which tend to be more variable, involve personal interests, and be relatively stable.
- Competence—Children need to deal effectively with their environment. Their belief about their level of competence, often referred to as "self-efficacy," influences their choices of activities and their persistence with challenging tasks.

As children develop, they tend to view their capabilities less positively. Through age 6, children typically are confident and sometimes overly confident about their abilities. Older children better incorporate their past successes and failures and are more aware of how their abilities compare to others' (Lepper, Sthi, Dialdin, & Drake, 1997; Lepper & Hodell, 1989).

Older children tend to have more-stable interests than younger children, who are readily attracted to novel, attention-gaining stimuli. Typically, children show the most interest in activities in which they have experienced success and which they believe are gender-appropriate. Over time, their choices of activities tend to be based less on personal interest and more on their perceived value with regard to achieving long-term goals (Gottfried, 1985; Lepper & Malone, 1987).

Research focusing on the effects of praise indicates that praise has both positive and negative effects on development. Praise is more likely to enhance children's development when it is specific rather than general and when it is related to children's efforts rather than their abilities. Focusing on effort allows children to feel some level of control over their performance. This leads to students' focusing on learning and personal accomplishments rather than performance primarily for the sake of doing better than others (Addison & Tosti, 1979).

Some children display emotions, including indicators of motivation, more readily than others. They are more exuberant and display more positive energy during activities. They are considered to have higher levels of motivation than children who are more introverted and do not tend to show signs of motivation (Ames, 1990; Graham & Weiner, 1996).

Some children love coming to school and enjoy most things they are asked to do during the course of the day. These children also tend to display higher levels of motivation, regardless of level of praise received. Other children have lackadaisical or negative attitudes toward school. They are more likely to be positively motivated by praise. Thus, the degree of motivation displayed following praise must be interpreted in light of the degree of motivation displayed prior to praise. Whether praise enhances motivation or not is likely related to students' current level of enthusiasm about attending school (Ames, 1990).

The method of delivery of praise also has an effect. Adults often use different tones of voice when praising students. These tones affect children's interpretation of the praise received. Children are not merely affected by receiving rewards; they also assess adults' motives for administering rewards, judge how consistently rewards are administered, and evaluate what the rewards suggest about their ability (Abramson, Seligman, & Teasdale, 1978; Harari & Covington, 1981).

Additionally, children often interpret praise from their teacher differently than praise from other adults and peers. Liberally providing general praise to students appears to have limited and sometimes negative effects on student motivation (Harter, 1981, 1990).

Research indicates that receiving extrinsic rewards may decrease children's intrinsic motivation. Offering rewards for engaging in intrinsically motivating tasks often decreases the level of interest in those tasks. Rewarding children for simply completing a task, rather than for specific aspects of their behavior or the quality of the task, is likely to reduce motivation. Focusing simply on the completion of a task may suggest that any level of performance is acceptable and minimal effort is sufficient (Kohn, 1993). Rewards also tend to distract some children by focusing them on rewards rather than the task.

Using rewards to motivate children takes time and energy away from instruction. It is often difficult to determine what will be rewarding for various individuals. Often, what one child finds rewarding is not viewed as desirable by another. When rewards are given to some children and not others, children who do not receive rewards may feel resentment toward those who do or toward the adults administering the rewards. Liberal administration of rewards may lead to dependency on receiving rewards in order to complete required tasks.

Sense of Order

Children benefit when adults seek age- and developmentally appropriate structure. Younger children find comfort in stable environments, schedules, and daily contacts. Tolerance of deviation from daily schedules/expectations develops over time. Even older children (and adults) find comfort in routine, particularly during periods of stress (Fiese, 2002; Kubicek, 2002).

Adults create a sense of order and stability by establishing relatively stable routines. Children find comfort when adults provide meals and snacks at approximately the same time each day, encourage children to wake up and go to sleep around the same time daily, and develop routines for waking up and going to bed. For example, bedtime routines might include viewing an age-appropriate television show together as a family, taking a bath, brushing teeth, or reading a bedtime story.

Children often benefit when day care providers and teachers create daily routines. They find comfort in knowing what will happen next and what is expected of them. Adults should remain open to deviating from set routines to deal with or benefit from unexpected events. Special events often provide unique opportunities for authentic (highly related to life) learning experiences. Rigid adherence to schedules may limit learning opportunities (Emmer, Evertson, & Anderson, 1980). For example, if a hot air balloon lands in a field close by, breaking from routine to look out of the window or go outside to get a better look is appropriate.

Most children find it disconcerting to arrive at a school building and find their classroom has been moved or changed. Ideally, when changes occur, children are informed prior to the changes and allowed to participate in decision making and help make the changes.

Often children find it even more disturbing to learn that school personnel have unexpectedly changed. Any change in child care providers or teachers is uncomfortable for most children. Unexpected changes in other personnel, including bus drivers, food service workers, maintenance individuals, and clerical and administrative staff may also negatively affect children (Evertson, 1998).

When changes occur within children's lives, they benefit not only from advanced warning but also from explanations as to why the changes are going to occur or have occurred. Ideally, children are given ample opportunity to express their feelings about the changes (Evertson et al., 1989).

Modeling how to organize school materials and providing ample, clearly marked storage spaces may enhance learning (Emmer et al., 1980; Evertson et al., 1989). Organization allows for a focus on instructional time because less time is consumed searching for materials to conduct activities. Organization also helps prevent loss of student work, teachers' plans, and materials. Modeling of various organizational methods can be particularly useful for children who tend to be disorganized (Evertson, 1998).

Establishing Goals

Children benefit from being encouraged to set goals and imagine the wide variety of opportunities and possible outcomes in their lives. Initially, their behaviors are naturally purposeful. Children usually choose appropriate goals for themselves and use age-appropriate strategies to reach these goals. Goals can be short- or long-term, although very young children are more likely to focus on short-term goals (Wayson & Lasley, 1984).

Children's goals often influence their engagement in school and other activities and their selection of strategies. Goals can be classified as either mastery, sometimes referred to as "learning" (based on a desire to acquire skills), or performance (based on a desire to receive favorable feedback from others).

Children often find it difficult to achieve multiple goals at the same time or to make decisions about which goals they should prioritize. They benefit from guidance regarding how to choose activities and how to go about accomplishing more than one goal at a time.

Being taught to set personal goals enhances achievement. When children set their own goals, they are more likely to be committed to achieving them. When goals are imposed on them, some students resist them. Effective goals tend to be specific, relatively immediate, and moderately difficult. Children benefit when encouraged to set concrete, challenging, achievable goals.

Self-Care

Like other developmental milestones for young children, the ability to independently accomplish self-care skills is age-related. Understanding the normal sequence for developing self-help skills, providing children with many opportunities to practice these skills, modeling step-by-step methods of completing tasks, and allowing children time to complete tasks will enhance success. Young children learn self-help skills step by step. They learn better from being shown how to complete a task (e.g., by using both hands) than from being told what not to do (e.g., "Don't spill the juice"). Open-ended questions and activities are very important because they stimulate problem-solving and self-help skills.

Self-Feeding.   Children should be encouraged to be as independent as possible while learning how to eat. When they are first learning to feed themselves, they are likely to be very messy, but as they practice self-feeding, they gradually become less messy.

Initially, they use their hands to eat finger food. Over time they learn to use a spoon and then a fork. Child-sized utensils allow children to be more successful during attempts to self-feed because they can better grasp and maneuver small tableware. Infants often attempt to grab the spoon as they are being fed. Letting children hold the spoon while an adult guides it will help them learn to feed themselves. While children are learning to use a spoon and fork, offering them finger foods at each meal gives them a chance to finger-feed themselves part of the meal. This is likely to increase a sense of independence and decrease frustration associated with learning to use utensils. In addition, toddlers may benefit from having access to their own utensils (a spoon and a fork) so that they can practice using them at each meal while an adult helps them by using another spoon or fork. Figure 11.1 lists steps involved in learning to eat with a spoon.

Some young children need assistance while eating.

Figure 11.1   **Steps in Learning to Eat with a Spoon**

The child

1. understands it is time to eat
2. sits upright in chair
3. reaches for and grasps spoon
4. scoops food from bowl
5. brings food to mouth
6. gets some food into mouth (amount increases over trials)
7. removes spoon from mouth with little or no spillage

Most children enjoy learning to pour liquids. Initially, they need practice pouring from a small pitcher. They need to be shown how to pour, which can be accomplished when adults describe what they are doing as they pour. When first learning to pour, children benefit from being reminded to stop pouring before the liquid reaches the top of the cup.

Young children can learn a variety of other skills at mealtime. For example, when children refine their mealtime skills, they also learn to seat themselves at a table. They learn they must pull the chair out from the table, sit in it, slide it close to the table, put on a bib or place a napkin in their lap, keep food on the plate, hold the spoon in a mature way, serve themselves without spilling anything, chew with their mouths closed, appropriately ask for seconds, and ask to leave the table once they are done eating. Mealtime provides excellent opportunities to strengthen the skills needed for fine-motor activities such as drawing and, later, writing. Table 11.2 lists self-feeding milestones.

Some children have **oral-motor delays.** Assessments of oral-motor delays are conducted by a speech–language pathologist, primary health care provider, developmental pediatrician, gastroenterologist, otolaryngologist, occupational therapist, nutritionist, or psychologist. Not all feeding disorders are due to sensory integration difficulties (discussed in Chapter 9). Some feeding problems are due to medical factors, motor deficits, or emotional disorders. Sign of possible oral-motor delays are listed in Figure 11.2.

Children with and without disabilities go through a stage during which they get messy when they eat. It is important for care providers of children with disabilities to allow them to do as much as possible independently, even though they will get messy. Care providers of children with disabilities often focus on helping children to avoid getting messy. Doing this may discourage children from learning to do as much for themselves as possible. Although self-feeding may take longer and is likely to result in children's getting messy, it should be encouraged, provided that it is appropriate to the child's level of impairment and does not adversely affect the number of

Table 11.2	Self-Feeding Milestones
Age	**Behavior**
12 months	Eats table food and finger-feeds self.
10–14 months	Drinks from a cup.
12–18 months	Requests to use spoon and fork independently. Uses double-handled cup with minimal spilling.
15 months	Scoops food and brings spoon to mouth without turning the spoon over.
18–24 months	Eats with spoon, closed fisted, palm down. Drinks from small cup, holding it with one hand. Drinks through a straw.
24–36 months	Begins to properly hold spoon, use a fork, and spread with butter knife. Develops preferences for certain foods and may reject all others.
31–36 months	Brings dishes and eating utensils to the table. Pours milk from a small pitcher. Carries dishes to sink. Eats relatively independently. Needs help cutting food.
36–48 months	Uses a fork more frequently for soft food. Learns how to use a napkin.
4 years	Holds eating utensils like an adult (with three fingers). Cuts soft food with the edge of a fork.

calories consumed and the meal's nutritional content or create a safety risk (e.g., choking).

Speech and language pathologists are trained in various techniques that help children to chew with their mouths closed. Some children with cerebral palsy (CP) have difficulty keeping their mouths closed or have a habit of thrusting out their tongue

Figure 11.2   Symptoms Associated with Oral-Motor Delays in Young Children

Limited weight gain	Undifferentiated cries
Prolonged feeding time	Poor volume or quality of crying
Weak sucking	Lack of reciprocal babbling
Gagging	Reduced vocal play
Excessive drooling	Failure to thrive
Hyper/hyposensitivity	

when they try to eat. These children require support in moving from the mouth movements associated with sucking from the breast or bottle to the rounded mouth movement required for chewing solid food. To help children who have difficulties with this transition, it may be necessary to very gradually increase the density of the food's texture.

In addition, some children with CP have difficulty with their gag reflex. They find it hard to cough up bits of food that go down the wrong way. There is an increased risk of infections and pneumonia when food or fluid gets into the lungs. Some children with CP are hypersensitive to touch in and around their mouth, whereas others have very little sensitivity. Those who over- or underreact to touch can learn self-feeding through a program of controlled oral-motor input. This type of program is designed to gradually desensitize or sensitize them to touch in and around the mouth. If children are oversensitive to touch, it is often best to accustom them to touch by bringing a care provider's hand or a toy closer and closer to their mouth. In addition, firm pressure is often more comfortable for these children than light touch. After children accept the feel of the care provider's hand or toy, the next step is to guide their hands to do the stimulation. When children are underresponsive to touch, it is often useful to provide a wide variety of stimulation from different types of touch and textures.

To most effectively encourage self-feeding in children with oral-motor sensitivity, care providers should schedule feedings when adults and children are relaxed, children are alert and responsive, and the environment is as calm as possible. It is also helpful to have a predictable routine associated with the beginning and end of mealtimes.

Because the face is the most sensitive area of the body and touching in or around the mouth can be very threatening, it is helpful to minimize nonessential touch. For example, it may be necessary to avoid frequent wiping of the mouth during feeding. When the children need to have their mouths wiped, it is often best to use a firm pat instead of a light swipe across the mouth. It is best to allow children to wipe their own faces. Children also need time to close their mouths on the spoon and remove food rather than have an adult scrape food off their upper lip or teeth.

Changes in food texture and temperature must be introduced very gradually. In addition, children benefit from being seated in a stable, supportive chair during eating. Such a chair provides postural stability and minimizes extraneous sensory stimulation (Crump, 1987). Putting a mirror in front of a child during meals may also enhance the child's awareness of the process.

With help and encouragement children with cognitive delays, such as those with Down syndrome, can learn to eat by themselves. Various disorders affect the muscles in the mouth, causing the tongue to stick out. This interferes with feeding, including breast-feeding, bottle-feeding, and eating solid food. Children with motor delays often benefit from initially being encouraged to dip their fingers into food and bring their fingers to their mouth. Initially an adult may need to guide the child's arm and hand to the food and then to the mouth. Using the child's favorite foods will likely best motivate the child to learn this behavior. Once the child masters the finger-to-mouth behavior, it is appropriate to introduce finger foods, followed by spoon-feeding. Again, an adult may initially need to move the child's arm and hand through the motions of eating with a spoon. To help children with cognitive delays to drink from a lidless cup, it is best to use thick liquids. Young children are more likely to try to eat independently when they are with others and can observe others eating.

Dressing. Learning to dress and undress is a major step toward independence. Children should be encouraged to dress and undress themselves, even if it takes them a long time.

When children cannot independently remove their clothes, they should be involved in the process as much as possible while being assisted. Typically, undressing is easier than dressing; therefore, promoting the efforts that children make to help with undressing is the first step toward their learning to dress. Practice with a doll or an activity book that allows children to zip, snap, button, and take clothes off and on often helps children acquire the skills necessary for self-dressing.

Many children find taking off socks to be relatively easy. Initially an adult may need to help children learn to do so by pulling the sock almost off, then letting them tug their socks the rest of the way off.

When helping children learn to undress and dress themselves, adults should position themselves behind the children when undressing or dressing them. Using this position allows children to learn how to undress and dress from their own perspectives. Children benefit when adults describe, step by step, what they are doing as they dress or undress them. This same sequence to slowly dress and undress children should be used repetitively. All care providers should use the same process during the dressing routine. Children benefit from being provided with simple, consistent, and easy-to-complete motions while learning how to dress and undress. In addition, they need ample time to practice undressing and dressing.

It is often useful to allow children to complete the last step of the sequence (e.g., button the last button). Over time they should be encouraged to complete more and more steps in the sequence. For example, children can help pull on shoes once their toes are placed in the shoes, pull up socks once they are placed on their toes, and so on. Over time, adults should reduce their amount of help (i.e., we "backward chaining").

Children are often more motivated to learn dressing skills when they are allowed to make choices regarding what they will wear. Table 11.3 lists children's self-dressing milestones.

As is the case with regard to most activities engaged in by individuals with CP, proper position is crucial for success during dressing. Depending on the type of CP, children's sense of balance (or lack thereof) and their ability to stand steadily may make it difficult to get undressed or dress from a standing position. Children with CP usually find dressing easier when they are seated on a low bench or chair. When a child does not have adequate head and trunk control, an adult may need to seat the child on their lap during dressing. Even when children with CP have very limited ability to control their movements, they can participate in undressing/dressing by looking, when asked, "What comes next?" toward the next item to be removed or put on. When they cannot independently remove their clothes, they should be encouraged to help in any way they can. For example, they can be asked to raise their arms as shirts are removed or to shift their weight so that their pants can be removed.

Table 11.3	Self-Dressing Milestones
Age	**Behavior**
13–18 months	Pulls off loose pants, hats, and socks.
24 months	Completely undresses, assists with dressing, unzips large zippers, puts shoes on with help, pulls down pants on request, unbuttons large buttons.
36 months	Puts clothes on, attempts to close Velcro®, buttons large buttons.
48 months	Dresses and undresses independently except for zippers, snaps, and buttons; distinguishes between front and back of clothing; buckles belts; zips front-opening clothes.
60 months	Laces shoes.
66 months	Ties shoes.

Many children with CP can learn to help dress themselves by being provided with clothes that are easy to put on and take off, such as those that zip or button in the front (not the back) or have large buttons, ties, or Velcro® fasteners. In addition, they can be fitted with easy-to-fasten, comfortable shoes, such as slip-on shoes or shoes with Velcro® closures (Hotte, 1979).

The time during which children are getting dressed and undressed is a good time to encourage them to practice using their hands and fingers, as well as their arms and legs. Extra time for dressing and undressing should be provided so that children can practice. Figure 11.3 lists the steps required to tie shoes.

Toileting. Successful training of toddlers or preschool-age children in using a toilet involves parents and service providers working together. Parents should determine when training begins and decide on the method used (Hussey-Gardner, 1992). Staff members should support the ongoing efforts to train children once they begin to use the toilet at home.

Sending children to preschool or day care not wearing diapers before they are trained is not the best practice. Teachers reasonably cannot be expected to spend large portions of the day cleaning up and changing children after toilet accidents. These activities take time away from programming and can create health issues.

Most parents do not attempt training until the child is at least 2 years old. Most children are fully toilet-trained by 5 years of age. Typically they are daytime-trained before they are nighttime-trained. Toilet-training success depends primarily on the child's level of neurological development. It is also affected by cognitive, speech, and language skills (Seligman & Darling, 1989).

Frequently, parents are pressured to begin toilet-training. They hear comments such as "He's 3 years old. He should already be toilet-trained." Children should be

Figure 11.3   **Steps Required to Tie Shoes**

- Pinch the shoelaces.
- Pull the laces.
- Hang the ends of the laces from the corresponding sides of the shoe.
- Pick up the laces in the corresponding hands.
- Lift the laces above the shoe.
- Cross the right lace over the left one to form a tepee.
- Bring the left lace toward you.
- Pull the left lace through the tepee.
- Pull the laces away from each other.
- Bend the left lace to form a loop.
- Pinch the loop with your left hand.
- Bring the right lace over your fingers and around the loop.
- Push the right lace through the hole.
- Pull the loops away from each other.

toilet-trained when they display readiness signs. Just as some children learn to walk earlier or later than others, children vary in the age at which they are ready to learn to use the toilet. Most children show signs of physical readiness to begin using the toilet between 18 months and 3 years of age. However, some children do not have the intellectual and/or psychological readiness to be trained at this age (Christopherson, 1982).

It is important to focus on each child's developmental level rather than chronological age when determining the time to begin toilet-training. Signs of readiness include being able to follow simple instructions, being cooperative, asking to have soiled diapers changed, asking to use the potty chair, and asking to wear underwear.

Typically, toilet-training is easier when children can dress or partially dress and undress themselves. Children with physical disabilities may have difficulty with toilet-training because they have difficulty undressing and maintaining balance while sitting on a toilet or potty chair. A special child-size chair, special clothing, and other adaptations may be needed to help these children learn to use the toilet.

Toilet-training should not be first attempted during stressful times or periods of change (moving, the presence of a new baby, etc.). When accidents occur, they should be calmly cleaned up. Toileting successes should be praised.

Girls usually gain physical control over their bowel and bladder muscles before boys. Most girls are toilet-trained by 2 years old, whereas most boys are trained by 3 years old. Many 3-year-olds who are considered to display typical rates of

Figure 11.4   **Indicators of Readiness for Toilet-Training**

The child

- knows body parts
- knows words or signs related to using the toilet
- indicates awareness of urges
- announces or otherwise acknowledges elimination
- cooperates
- can follow multi-step instructions
- demonstrates coordination and dexterity
- demonstrates bowel and bladder control
- does not have fears related to using the toilet

development display no interest in learning to use the toilet. These children often appear to be more interested in other activities (e.g., climbing, jumping, running, and talking). A toddler who initially resists toilet-training is likely to be ready to learn within a few months. Figure 11.4 lists the most common indicators of readiness for training. Figure 11.5 lists guidelines that may be useful when attempting to train children.

Children with PDD often have difficulty learning to use the toilet. A wide variety of techniques may need to be used because not all children respond positively to the

Figure 11.5   **Guidelines for Toilet-Training**

- Pick a starting date during a less hectic week.
- Talk about the beginning of toilet-training a few days in advance.
- Obtain child-size toilet equipment.
- Have a set of rewards available (e.g., small toys, stickers).
- Reward success; do not punish accidents (expect them).
- Reward dryness and cleanliness.
- Chart progress.
- Do not have the child stay on the toilet too long (5 minutes maximum).
- Make the child try to use the toilet no more than once an hour.
- Slowly phase out rewards for successfully using the toilet.

same methods. Children with PDD characteristically do not understand and enjoy reciprocal social relationships. This interferes with their willingness to toilet-train. Whereas other 2- and 3-year-olds are proud to wear big-boy/girl pants and strive to please adults, such motivations are less common among children with PDD.

Because children with PDD often have difficulty understanding and using language or imitating models, they may not understand what is expected of them during toilet-training. They may have difficulty organizing and sequencing information and consistently attending to the information needed to successfully toilet-train. Their difficulty in accepting changes in routines also contributes to toilet-training difficulties. Because the routine of wearing a diaper has been firmly established, it is often difficult for them to understand the need to change to using a toilet.

Children with PDD often have difficulty integrating sensory information and establishing the relationship between body sensations and everyday functional activities. This includes difficulty sensing body cues that tell them they need to use the toilet. They may also be overwhelmed by the sensory environment of the toilet (e.g., loud flushing, echoes, rushing water, a chair with a big hole in it, removing their clothes, a change in temperature, the tactile sensation of sitting on the toilet seat).

When attempting to toilet-train children with PDD, it is important to acknowledge each step in the process as a goal. It is useful to determine each child's readiness by keeping a frequent record (e.g., every 30 minutes) of wetness and dryness. In addition, it will be necessary to ensure that each child learns the steps associated with toilet-training, including entering the bathroom, pulling their pants down, sitting on the toilet, getting toilet paper, wiping with the paper, standing up, throwing the toilet paper into the toilet, pulling their pants up, flushing the toilet, and washing and drying their hands. It is often helpful to create a visual communication system to help children understand the sequence of steps needed to complete the goal.

Toilet-training children requires that they understand that elimination is associated with the toilet. Therefore, before attempting to toilet-train children with PDD, it is often useful to move all diapering, cleaning, and dressing associated with elimination to the bathroom, to help children realize this room's purpose. During toilet-training, the bathroom should be as free of distractions as possible.

Additionally, an object associated with toileting (e.g., a picture or drawing of the toilet) may be needed to signal that the toilet routine is beginning. Children need to learn each step in the sequence, when the sequence will be finished, and what will happen when the sequence is finished. This information can be communicated using objects, picture sequences, or a written list. Using a timer indicating how long the child is expected to remain on the toilet is often helpful.

If children resist sitting on the toilet, they may benefit from being allowed to sit on the toilet without removing their clothes or with the toilet covered (e.g., the adult can place cardboard under the seat, gradually enlarge the hole, or place a towel under the seat and gradually remove it), or sit on a potty seat on the floor rather than up high. Children may be put more at ease if an adult or peer demonstrates being comfortable sitting on a toilet or uses a doll as a model. Some children benefit by having added physical support, such as rails.

Children often have one of two reactions to the toilet's flushing. Either they are fascinated by it (and would be willing to flush for hours), or they are fearful.

Many children are not only fearful of the noise and swirling water but also think that they may be flushed away. They need reassurance that only body wastes and toilet paper will be flushed away.

If children are afraid of flushing, it may be helpful to initially not flush until the child is away from the toilet, and then to flush as the child gradually moves closer to the toilet. It may be helpful to provide advance warning of flushing. In contrast, some children are very interested in flushing and want to repeatedly flush the toilet. When this is the case, it may be necessary to physically cover the toilet handle so that it cannot be seen. Some children more readily resist flushing when they are given something special to hold.

When children play with the toilet paper or are distracted by it, it should be kept out of sight until it is needed. Marking toilet paper at the appropriate place helps children learn to use an appropriate amount.

Some children resist being wiped. If this occurs, demonstrating wiping using a doll may help ease their discomfort. Using different materials such as wet wipes, a cloth, or a sponge (make sure the temperature is not too cold) rather than toilet paper may be comfortable for the child.

When children soil their diapers or training pants, it may be useful to empty dirty diapers into the toilet to help demonstrate what they should do when sitting on the toilet. An important part of potty training children is to request that they frequently attempt to use the toilet. Ideally, sitting on the toilet occurs once or twice an hour, even when children indicate that they do not need to use the toilet. However, children should not be asked to remain on the toilet for more than a few minutes.

For children with CP, who have difficulty sitting upright, trying to sit on a toilet seat can be very frightening. A wide variety of child-sized seats are available for children who need special support. Bowel training can be especially challenging for children with CP because they frequently suffer from constipation due to lack of exercise, insufficient fiber and liquid in their diet, and side effects of medications.

Grooming.   Once children learn to help with their own grooming needs, adults can spend time focusing on other children or other learning activities. Table 11.4 shows the ages at which most children can independently accomplish basic grooming skills.

Table 11.4   *Children's Independent Grooming Skills*

Age	Behavior
12–24 months	Like brushing teeth and washing and drying hands but need help.
24–36 months	Have increased success brushing teeth. Independently wash and dry hands.
36 months	Blow and wipe nose with minimal help. Brush teeth independently.
48 months	Blow nose without help.

Washing and Drying Hands.   For children to independently wash their hands, they must be able to reach the water, soap, and a towel. If they are too short to reach these items, they should be provided with a sturdy step stool on which to stand. Children need to learn how to turn the water on so it is not too hot. Learning to turn on cold water and add small amounts of hot water is a good way for children to avoid overly hot water. Children need to be shown and told this process. They should watch an adult turn on the cold water and then the hot water. Next they should be shown how to test the water temperature to make sure it is not too hot. Children should be taught that steam indicates that water is too hot to touch safely; when they see steam, they should not put their hands into water. After several opportunities to observe an adult turning on water, children should be asked to turn the water on while the adult watches to make sure that they are safely adding hot water to cold. This step should be followed by showing the child how to use soap and water to wash their hands and how to dry their hands.

Brushing Teeth.   One-year-olds can begin to help brush their teeth, although most children cannot thoroughly and independently brush their teeth until around 4 years old. One of the most effective ways to teach children how to brush their teeth is to have them watch adults brushing their teeth and then ask them to imitate the adult. Because many children cannot purposely spit until they are 3 or 4, spitting out toothpaste may be one of the most difficult tasks to teach. Asking children to rinse their mouth out with water may help them learn to spit. Adults need to make brushing teeth as enjoyable as possible while helping children to understand why it is important to carefully brush their teeth. Figure 11.6 shows the steps involved in brushing teeth.

Blowing Nose.   Because young children learn by watching and imitating, they benefit from watching others appropriately blow and wipe their noses and properly dispose of used tissues. When a child has a runny nose, they benefit from being asked to look at a mirror while they are helped to blow their nose. This helps them to see why they need to blow their nose and how to go about the process. This observation should be followed by giving them a tissue and having them wipe their nose while they watch themselves in the mirror. After a child can independently accomplish this sequence, they should be taught to get their own tissue, blow and wipe their nose, and throw the tissue into the wastebasket.

Social Skills

Social cognition refers to how children think about others' behaviors, motives, feelings, and intentions (Gnepp, 1983). Social skills allow children to distinguish between accidental and intentional behavior. Many children younger than 5 years old cannot do this, whereas many 5-year-olds can make friends and resolve conflicts. Emotional development directly affects social skills (Kaltman, 2006).

Emotional Development

Emotions help humans adapt to their environment. For example, when infants smile, they are more approachable, so smiling facilitates social relationships. When a baby

Figure 11.6   **Task Sequence for Brushing Teeth**

- Pick up the tooth brush.
- Wet the brush.
- Take the cap off the toothpaste tube.
- Put toothpaste on the brush.
- Put the cap on the toothpaste tube.
- Brush the outside of the bottom teeth.
- Brush the outside of the top teeth.
- Brush the biting surface of the top teeth.
- Brush the biting surface of the bottom teeth.
- Brush the inside surface of the bottom teeth.
- Brush the inside surface of the top teeth.
- Spit toothpaste from mouth into the sink.
- Rinse the toothbrush.
- Put the toothbrush away.
- Grasp cup.
- Fill cup with water.
- Rinse teeth with water.
- Spit rinse water into the sink.
- Replace cup in holder.
- Wipe mouth.

cries, the crying prompts others to try to meet their needs (Graham, Doubleday, & Guarino, 1984). Several **basic emotions** (e.g., fear, joy, anger) appear to be inborn and universal. **Complex emotions** (e.g., pride, guilt, embarrassment), sometimes referred to as **"self-conscious emotions,"** develop over time and are not common to all cultures (Gowen & Nebrig, 2002).

Emotional competence is the ability to express, regulate, and understand emotions (Denham, 1998). These skills must work together in an integrated way. **Emotional expressiveness** is the ability to express and experience emotions. **Emotional regulation** is the ability to recognize and control emotional responses. **Emotional understanding** or **knowledge** is the ability to identify and understand others' emotions (Denham, 1998; Denham et al., 2003).

Initially, infants cannot use words to express their needs, but soon after birth they are capable of indicating their needs through crying, facial expressions, and body movements. They rely on adults to help them regulate their emotional states. When they are wet and uncomfortable, they communicate this by crying. Between

2 and 3 months of age, most infants display a social smile when they see a human face. During this time they display sadness. Between 4 and 6 months, they begin to express anger. They also have the ability to distinguish others' facial expressions, shown by their responding differently to joy and fear. In addition, they use social referencing, using others for cues about unfamiliar situations.

Infants 4–6 months old will look away or close their eyes when they are frightened, in an attempt to control their emotional response. At 6 months, many infants begin to display fear in the form of **stranger anxiety** (wariness) when they are approached by unfamiliar individuals. At approximately 7–8 months old, **social referencing** occurs. Infants begin to recognize others' emotions by using the reactions of those around them. They most frequently use social referencing when confronted by novel situations and individuals.

Between 15 and 18 months old, toddlers demonstrate an understanding of self (i.e., self-recognition), which is necessary for children to develop complex emotion between 18 and 24 months of age. Two-year-olds frown to gain adults' attention. Over time the number of complex emotions expands and is directly linked to children's cultural environments. For example, some cultures encourage display of pride whereas others consider embarrassment or even shame appropriate responses to being acknowledged for accomplishments.

Researchers have reported that between 2 and 4 years old, children learn to accurately label emotions and begin to understand that various situations are linked to particular emotions (Denham, 1998; Harris, 1989). At this age, children typically begin to use adjectives that describe emotions, understand those terms, and express their feelings in order to have their needs met. Most preschoolers can control the display of their emotions to some extent. That is, they have some self-control. As children's language expands, they learn to verbally express their feelings. Articulating emotions often has a self-regulatory effect (e.g., allows children to communicate their feelings to others who will help them control their emotions). At this age children also begin using soothing language to talk themselves through difficult situations.

Older children may use self-talk to help them cope with their emotions. For example, during a thunderstorm a child might chant, "Thunder cannot hurt me; it is just a really loud noise." Four-year-olds often know they will get into trouble if they get mad and then hit their younger sibling. Therefore, they can decide to leave the room rather than display anger. By 5 years old, most children understand what events cause others to be angry, happy, sad, and so on. Additionally, they abide by **display rules,** culturally specific standards regarding the appropriateness of displaying various emotions.

Children are likely to imitate adult models. Adults can help children develop their emotional repertoires by naming emotions for them. In doing so, they enrich children's cognitive development by providing words for experiences they will have again. This also aids children's understanding of human feelings.

Self-Regulation

Self-regulation is actively maintaining a behavior to achieve a goal, without external instruction or motivation. Self-regulation is necessary for a person to have self-control, the ability to inhibit their actions. It involves stepping back to think about the situation instead of just focusing on the goal. Self-regulation is a person's self-control of behavior, emotions, and thoughts (McCabe, Hernandez, Lara, & Brooks-Gunn, 2000).

A preschooler's emerging self-regulation reflects their transition from feelings of helplessness to those of competence. The development of self-regulation is related to a child's experiences. Teaching self-regulation is different than punishing a child. Self-regulation, not forced compliance, is the aim.

Children are not born with self-control. Between 1 and 2 years, children begin to start, stop, change, or maintain motor acts and emotional reactions. They become aware of demands placed on them. Communication skills allow them to understand others' instructions. By the age of 2 years, most children begin to display some self-control. At times they seem to have considerable self-control, and at other times they appear to totally lack control. They need to practice self-control. More-complex control requires development of cognitive, perceptual, and linguistic abilities.

Being able to self-regulate requires the ability to delay gratification. Preschool children vary widely in their ability to delay gratification or inhibit a behavior. The ability to delay gratification is a behavior that begins to emerge around the age of 3½ and is slowly learned. Many preschoolers are not able to devise strategies to distract themselves, and distraction is often required to delay gratification. Adults can help a child learn to delay gratification by setting limits while allowing some flexibility within boundaries. They also can provide problem-solving guidance, such as planning and organizing activities. When adults model self-regulation by stating their thoughts, this also helps children acquire these skills. For example, an adult might say, "I want to read the newspaper, but first I need to clean up the table." This type of self-talk helps children learn this self-regulation strategy. In addition, when adults have appropriate expectations regarding the display of self-control, children are more likely to demonstrate control. Asking an infant to wait 30 minutes to eat may not be appropriate, whereas it may be appropriate to ask a 4-year-old to do so.

Benefits of learning to self-regulate continue throughout life. Children who acquire self-regulatory skills typically are more popular with peers, have greater self-confidence and positive self-esteem, are more independent, have more-mature social skills, perform better academically, and handle stress and frustration more effectively throughout life (Cooper & McEvoy, 1996).

Adults can help children deal with negative emotional states by direct teaching and modeling of verbal reasoning and explanation. For example, they can say, "I know you are sad that it is time to put your toys away. However, we need to clean up now, so we can eat lunch. What can I do to help you feel better?" This type of preparation enables children to develop the skills necessary to regulate their own negative emotional states throughout life. Children who have difficulty acquiring these coping skills are more likely to display disruptive behavior or withdraw during fear- or anxiety-provoking situations.

Empathy

Empathy, a complex emotional response, is the ability to put oneself in another person's place and understand what they are feeling. Empathy is demonstrated in a rudimentary way during infancy (e.g., infants cry when other infants do). The development of empathy requires being able to interpret others' emotional cues, understand that other people have distinct feelings, and assume others' perspectives (put oneself in their position). These skills begin to appear after children's first birthday.

Children first display empathy when they attempt to diminish others' distress. Toddlers often use comforting language such as "I'm sorry" or "It's okay" when speaking to someone who is distressed. They also may seek the help of an adult (often their mother). They may pat or hug another person or look concerned. They may offer a favorite toy to comfort another person or seek an adult to console a crying friend. Toddlers also begin to name feelings.

Egocentric empathy is seen in toddlers (1 to 2 years old) who imitate another's distress. For example, a child may pretend to bump their head and then begin crying when they have observed this scenario. Between 2 and 3 years old, children become empathetic with regard to emotions other than distress (e.g., disappointment, fear, surprise, sadness, anger, and enjoyment).

Children who have developed secure attachments are more likely to be empathetic. Warm, caring, empathetic adults help children perceive the world as a kind, safe place. Adults who value sharing, caring, and helping others are more likely to foster those traits in children. Children are more likely to be empathetic if adults note empathetic behavior when it occurs and explain why such behavior is valued.

Perspective Taking

The ability to understand how others feel is referred to as **perspective taking**. Robert Selman (1980) suggested that children younger than school age are at one of two stages of perspective taking. They may take an undifferentiated perspective (typical of children 3–6 years old), in which case they know that others may not feel the same way they do but they cannot explain why this is so and are often confused. Or, if they are at the next stage and have a social-informational perspective (typical of children 5–9 years old), they know that others have different perspectives because they have access to different information.

Around 4 or 5 years old, most children develop a more complex understanding of others' emotional states. Through repeated experiences, children gradually develop theories regarding the causes and consequences of others' emotional states. They display increased sensitivity to others' behavioral cues that indicate emotional distress. At this age, children also begin to make predictions about others' behavior based on their emotions (e.g., they might predict that a happy child will share their toys, whereas an unhappy one will not).

Although children are increasingly able to assume another person's perspective, most children continue to experience conflict with regard to sharing. Telling children that they must share often is not effective. It is often best for adults to provide duplicates of toys and other objects that they know will be in great demand. Adults also need to monitor children's interactions and model methods of successfully sharing. When conflicts occur, they can be used as opportunities to teach and model problem-solving skills. In addition, after conflicts occur most children benefit from being provided with self-calming strategies (e.g., counting to 10, taking deep breaths, or going to a designated "Calm down" location).

To learn to resolve conflicts, children need to learn to define the problem. Guiding children to put problems into words helps them calm down. For example, saying, "I see we have a problem. Tell me about it," allows children to express their view of the situation. When adults restate what each child says, it helps children to evaluate the conflict.

Children benefit from being encouraged to propose possible solutions to conflicts while adults also offer suggestions. Children should then agree on a solution and be told that if the solution does not work, they will be allowed to try a different solution. It is useful to hear an adult state the agreed-on solution or, better, ask each child to restate it. Over time children begin to resolve conflicts without the teacher's help. Teaching children to resolve conflicts not only is important for their social development; it also promotes cognitive skills.

Moral Development

Moral development entails conduct and attitude toward others and how well one follows societal norms, rules, and laws. Moral development follows a pattern as children age. Initially they behave with the goal of staying out of trouble. Then they behave in ways that are likely to be rewarded. Next they behave according to what they have learned is moral even when doing so may not gain rewards. (Largely, they behave as their cultural community expects them to.)

The first step to moral development is the ability to display **self-control**. This ability begins during infancy and continues developing throughout the preschool years. Most 1-year-olds recognize that others place demands on them. For example, they know that being told "No!" means that they are to stop engaging in a particular behavior. Most 2-year-olds begin to internalize control. For example, if they have been told not to touch something, they may self-talk by saying, "No, don't touch." Most 3-year-olds can adapt to quickly changing situations. For example, they learn that some rules apply in certain settings but not in others (e.g., "Mommy does not let me eat candy, but Grandma does). Disciplinary methods and children's temperaments affect children's ability to control their behavior.

Most 3-year-olds believe that adults always are right simply because they are bigger than children. Preschoolers often think that being strong is equivalent to being right because they observe that adults, who are larger than they are, wield authority through discipline and set the rules that govern behavior. Preschoolers are likely to say that fighting is a good way to win an argument, particularly if they have observed this to be true.

Because preschoolers lack the cognitive skills required to make moral distinctions, adults' warnings against certain behaviors, (e.g., throwing toys or hitting) may be viewed as a challenge of wills. Children around 6 years old begin to respond in particular ways simply because they are the right ways to behave. Initially, an effective way to encourage young children to develop the habit of doing the right thing (what you want them to do), rather than the wrong thing (whatever is contrary to your wishes) is to discuss the consequences of their actions. Telling a child to put their toys away because that is what good children do is unlikely to have much effect on their behavior. Saying "If you put your toys away, we'll have time to go outside for a walk" is more likely to elicit compliance.

Children initially view adults as representatives of what is right. Therefore, adults' behavior plays a crucial role in the child's initial understanding of moral issues. By observing adults' interactions, young children learn appropriate (or inappropriate) behaviors. Children are likely to do what they see rather than what they are told is correct. By the time children are 6 years old, most understand that some things are right and wrong.

The moral development of young children focuses on their ability to distinguish right from wrong. Two well-known theorists, **Jean Piaget** and **Lawrence Kohlberg,** studied children's moral development.

According to Piaget (1965), preschoolers often cannot make moral judgments or determine what is right or wrong based on their own concepts of fairness and justice. In contrast, 7-year-olds are capable of stating that a child who intentionally pushed a friend off the merry-go-round is naughtier than a child who did so accidentally.

Young children (3, 4, and 5 years old) are less likely than older children to make a judgment based on intentions. Instead, young children focus on the amount of damage done rather than the intent in determining who is naughty. This type of moral reasoning is called **external morality, objective morality, heteronomous morality,** or **moral realism.**

During this stage, Piaget reported, children view rules as fixed, permanent, and controlled by authority. They believe that rules are created by adults who know more than they do. Children believe that these rules must be followed and cannot be changed. They also believe in **immanent justice** (breaking a rule always leads to punishment).

Beginning at around 7 or 8 years of age, children consider intent. Piaget referred to this more advanced form of moral reasoning as **subjective morality, moral relativism,** or **autonomous morality,** which is not fully achieved before the ages of 12 or 13. Piaget believed that children 7 years old and older recognize that adults may respond differently to violations of moral rules (such as "Be nice to others") than to violations of social conventions (such as saying "Please" and "Thank you"). For example, parents are more likely to discipline a child for grabbing a toy than for not saying "Please."

At the stage of subjective morality, children can grasp the fact that people create rules to help them get along with one another. This is a more advanced stage of moral reasoning that is brought about by advances in cognitive development. Children now understand that there are reasons for rules. This stage incorporates a more rational concept of fairness; justice is viewed as a process of give and take. At this stage, children begin to rely on themselves, rather than others, to regulate their own moral behavior.

Piaget's work influenced Kohlberg (1984). Similar to Piaget, Kohlberg told children and adults stories of moral dilemmas and then asked them what they thought would be the right thing to do. Based on their responses, Kohlberg proposed three major levels of moral development, each with two stages. The three major levels are preconventional, conventional, and postconventional. Each level is qualitatively different from and more advanced than the previous one.

At the **preconventional level,** children are primarily concerned with avoiding punishment (Stage 1: Punishment-Obedience) and having their own needs met (Stage 2: Individualism). This level includes the **ethic of egocentrism,** a primary focus on meeting one's own needs. This focus typifies children until about age 10.

Children at the preconventional stage do not fully understand the rules set by others. Consequences of actions help children determine whether the actions are good or bad. Children typically make moral decisions without considering others' needs or feelings (Turiel, 1983). Children also obey rules and exchange favors by considering, "What's in it for me?" At this level, children decide what is right or wrong based on external, physical events rather than society's standards. When faced with a moral dilemma, children at this level do not ask themselves whether something is right according to society's standards but instead focus on the consequences. They are likely to ask themselves, "Will I get into trouble?" rather than "What is the right thing to do?" Before elementary school age, children have not had adequate experience to learn societal rules, nor are they cognitively mature enough to process a complex set of rules and information.

Although preschoolers do not reason at a conventional or postconventional level, understanding these stages allows for comparisons among young children's, adolescents', and adults' levels of reasoning. Moral reasoning at the **conventional level** focuses on conformity to social rules. Moral reasoning at the **postconventional level** focuses on abstract principles and values related to social justice. Often, adults appear to expect young children to respond at conventional or postconventional levels of moral reasoning—an unreasonable expectation given children's level of cognitive development.

Prosocial Behavior

Prosocial behaviors are positive and helpful to others. They include acts of kindness (e.g., sharing and helping). Some prosocial behaviors occur due to a desire to have others reciprocate (i.e., do something nice in return). Other prosocial behaviors are **altruistic** (engaged in without the hope of receiving something positive in return). The number and quality of prosocial behaviors increase as children age (Eisenberg, 1992).

Nancy Eisenberg (1982) theorized that most preschoolers have a **hedonistic orientation** (pursue their own pleasures) whereas some preschoolers and many school-age children have a **need-oriented approach** (are concerned about others' needs and want to help).

To behave prosocially, children must have perspective-taking skills, empathy, and moral reasoning. When children feel responsible (e.g., they know someone well), they are more likely to want to help others. When they feel they are competent (i.e., have the skills to help), they are more likely to behave prosocially. When they are in a good mood and believe there is a low cost to behaving prosocially or altruistically (such behavior will not require much energy or time, and their efforts are likely to be effective), they are more likely to do so. In addition, children are more likely to

The child shows prosocial behavior as she attempts to help a friend tie his shoes.

behave prosocially if they have seen others doing so; have frequently experienced warm, supportive environments; and have frequent opportunities to behave prosocially (Allsopp, Santos, & Linn, 2000).

Preschoolers display more prosocial behavior when they have frequently experienced positive interactions (fun ones without conflict). Young children often imitate the behavior of others they observe in everyday activities. For example, if they see others being honest and helpful, they are more likely to be so (Zahn-Waxler, Radke-Yarrow, & King, 1979). When a reinforcer, such as praise, follows children's prosocial behavior, they are more likely to repeat prosocial behavior in the future.

Adults can encourage children to behave prosocially by helping them acknowledge their effect on others and by encourage role-taking and perspective taking. Simply telling children that they hurt others' feelings does little to help them learn to care about others' feelings, whereas role-play allows children to attempt to step into others' shoes and take others' points of view and feelings into account.

Doing Chores

Independence is encouraged when children take responsibility by doing chores. Many toddlers are eager to help with chores. Between the ages of 18 months and 4 years, most children are ready to participate in household jobs. This age is characterized by children's focusing on imitating others and being liked by those they care about.

Initially, children learn to successfully participate in chores by working side by side with an adult while being provided with child-size, safe tools. Doing chores together also encourages children to learn a variety of important concepts. For example, a child could be asked to pick up all blue toys first, then all red ones, and so on. Or a child could be asked to pick up 10 toys while counting aloud as the task is completed. When adults take the time to complete chores with preschoolers, children gain a sense of importance and worth. When working with children, it is important to make the task as enjoyable as possible. Even when children need help to satisfactorily complete chores, their efforts should be acknowledged.

It is appropriate to encourage young children to take their responsibilities seriously, but it is not appropriate to expect perfection. Allowing children to select chores they would like to complete provides them with a sense of control. Table 11.5 lists appropriate chores by age.

Table 11.5	Appropriate Chores by Age
Age	**Appropriate Chores**
2–3 years old	Help make the bed, pick up toys and books, take laundry to the laundry basket/room, help feed pets, help clean up messes, dust, mop with help, use child-size cleaning tools, match socks
4–5 years old	Set the table, take dishes to the sink, help with some simple food preparation, get own snacks from small containers, help weed the garden, fold towels, wash plastic dishes and cups, dust and use a handheld vacuum, clean up many of one's own spills and messes, help put away groceries and clothes

Good Manners

Children do not automatically acquire good manners (socially correct ways of acting; etiquette). Good manners must be modeled and acknowledged. Good manners help give children lifelong social skills and incorporate customs, consideration, and common sense. A custom is a habit considered socially appropriate (e.g., shaking hands or holding doors open). Consideration includes being well-mannered and taking others' needs and feelings into account. Most good manners include common sense. For example, if someone drops their books in front of you, it is common sense to help them pick up the books rather than stepping on them or kicking them from your path.

Children who lack good manners have less positive relationships with peers, family, teachers, and other adults. Others notice and value good manners. Being polite, kind, and honest helps children develop good character. Most children 2 to 5 years old are receptive to learning rules about polite behavior.

Teaching children to respect others is one of the basic good manners. *Respect* has different meanings for different people. It includes displaying regard for others' rights, values, beliefs, and property; demonstrating courteous behavior; attempting to please others; and showing others positive regard, esteem, consideration, and appreciation. To learn respect, children must be respected. They should be treated in the same ways they are expected to behave. Children need well-developed self-respect, referred to as "positive self-esteem" (discussed in depth in Chapter 14), to respect others.

For children to learn the value of apologizing when they do something wrong, they need to see others apologize, including to *them*. When adults apologize to children, this communicates to children that they are respected and that it is okay to make mistakes.

Children learn the value of making requests in polite ways when they include the word "please" in their request. They are most likely to learn to regularly use this word, when they often hear it used. Children as young as 2 years old can learn to consistently say "please" when they make requests. Most children who do not or cannot speak can be taught to sign such words. With these children, it is often helpful for adults to sign the word as they say it. This process reinforces the sign and the verbal word while providing preverbal or nonverbal children with methods of communication.

In addition, when requests are honored, saying "Thank you" demonstrates respect for the person to whom it is being said. When children learn to say "Excuse me," they show awareness of others' needs and feelings. Children also need to learn to respect others' privacy. They most readily learn the value of privacy when *their* privacy needs are met.

Children should also be taught about indoor and outdoor voices. They need to learn when it is and is not appropriate to run, jump, throw balls, and so on. They benefit from learning the importance of appropriate use of napkins and eating utensils, chewing with their mouths closed, keeping their elbows off the table, remaining at the meal table until they have been excused, covering their nose when they sneeze and their mouth when they cough, and answering the telephone politely. Over time, children grow to understand that various settings require different behavior and that different individuals have different rules regarding what they consider acceptable behavior.

Children need to be allowed to display respectful assertiveness to let others know what they think and feel. For their safety, children should learn to respond appropriately to bullying. Being taught to say things such as "Please stop" or "You're hurting (scaring) me" are examples of respectful assertiveness. Children benefit from learning to state their needs without threatening or name-calling. They further benefit from being taught the difference between being mean and assertively expressing their own needs.

By the age of 3, most children can be taught to consistently acknowledge others when they enter their space, by saying "Hello" or "Hi." Over time this can be expanded to longer greetings, such as "Hi, Mr. Smith," or "Hello, I'm so glad you're here." Children should also learn to pause and say "Goodbye" to those leaving their space or when they leave others.

To increase the likelihood of good manners and respectful behaviors in general, it is helpful to regularly and specifically praise children when they display these behaviors. For example, saying "I liked it so much when you said 'thank you' to your friend" reinforces children's respectful behaviors.

When warranted, adults should tell children that their behavior is disrespectful and why it is inappropriate. Children often need guidance on being honest and tactful at the same time. They gradually learn which actions and words are appropriate and which are hurtful.

When children are disrespectful, it is often appropriate to let them know that an apology is appropriate and ask them if they are willing to apologize. Forcing children to apologize when they are not ready to do so does not teach the intended lesson. A forced apology may cause resentment and embarrass or discomfort the person to whom it is made.

Friendships

Children's peer relationships build on the relationships they have with their parents and other adults. Children who have not had the benefit of nurturing adults early in life often have difficulty forming friendships and dealing with the conflicts that occur in nearly all relationships (Brazelton & Greenspan, 2000; Brown, Odom & Conroy, 2001; Kranowitz, 1998).

In most cases the ability to develop and maintain friendships grows as children grow. Humans are social beings preprogrammed to respond and relate to others (Landy, 2002). For example, infants naturally turn their heads in response to a human voice (Ross & Roberts-Pacchione, 2007).

Friendships help children develop emotionally and socially. They allow children to practice methods of relating to others. These experiences help them understand that different people and situations often require different responses. Through interacting with friends, children learn to give and take, create rules, and weigh alternatives and make decisions when faced with dilemmas. Friends provide companionship and stimulation. They help children learn they are both similar to and different from others (English, Goldstein, Shafer, & Kaczmarek, 1996).

As children develop friendships, they gradually develop less egocentric viewpoints. Regular opportunities to play enhance friendships. As children become increasingly independent from their parents, they increasingly need to relate to peers. Additionally, having friends eases the separation process and helps children feel more comfortable away from family members.

Developing friendships includes learning to deal with conflicts. During interactions, children sometimes experience meanness, betrayal, and teasing. They will display bad judgment and hurt others. Most children naturally recognize that good friendship is reciprocal, affectionate, and reliable.

As soon as children can crawl, they begin choosing friends. Children as young as 12 months move into the space of certain peers (e.g., sit or play beside them) more often than they move into the space of other peers. During the early toddler years (1–2 years old), social interactions are characterized by some complementary and reciprocal play, in which children demonstrate the ability to exchange roles (e.g., running and chasing one another or receiving toys from one another). Between 2 and 3 years old, children often begin to engage in cooperative social pretend play (e.g., one plays the mother and the other plays the baby).

For children 3 to 5 years old, social interaction is characterized by knowledge of their peer group and each member's unique behavioral characteristics (e.g., a child will ask another child who likes to ride bikes to go for a bike ride). This knowledge allows children access to a wider range of potential playmates, play activities, and pretend play themes.

Between 4 and 7 years old, reciprocal play becomes the basis of friendship. At this time, children are increasingly able to generate complex fantasy games, taking on roles, giving one another directions, and sharing leadership roles. Table 11.6 summarizes young children's friendship patterns.

Although children greatly vary in how they make friends and the number of friends they have, children with quite a few friends tend to have a greater sense of well-being, more positive self-esteem, and fewer social problems as adults than children who have few or no friends. Children who have difficulty developing or maintaining friendships are more likely to feel lonely, be victimized, have problems adjusting to school, and engage in negative behaviors. Children who get along well with adults tend to have more-positive peer relationships.

Table 11.6	Relationship of Age to Children's Social Interactions with Peers	
Age	**Social Interaction with Peers**	**Friendship Formation**
Early Toddler (13–24 months)	Complementary and reciprocal play	Stable friendships
Late Toddler (25–36 months)	Communication of meaning or cooperative pretend play	Flexible friendships
Preschool (3–5 years)	Social knowledge of the peer group	Differentiation of friends from playmates

Children are likely to maintain friendships with those who have common interests. Those who have difficulty getting along with peers often benefit from more-direct adult supervision and opportunities to talk about how to play successfully with others. Most children also benefit from learning how to deal with conflict with peers.

Intervention Strategies for Enhancing Adaptive Skills

Children with disabilities are at risk for delays in learning various adaptive skills. This may be due to attributes associated with their disabilities or to having developed a sense of **learned helplessness** (a tendency to be a passive learner who depends on others for decisions and guidance). Children who experience learned helplessness are likely to wait for others to initiate interactions. For some children, particularly those who have medical problems that include significant movement and/or learning difficulties, the risk of developing learned helplessness is increased because they often cannot freely explore and interact with their environment.

Although the strategy is more characteristic of school-age children, some preschoolers develop a **self-handicapping strategy,** a tendency to seek out obstacles to their own success in order to avoid seeing their own performance as a cause of failure. Use of this strategy includes looking for an external attribution (excuse) for expected poor performance in the future, as opposed to an internal attribution (e.g., "I did not try" or "I am not strong or smart enough, so I could not do it"). Self-handicapping occurs when a person limits their own ability to succeed, deliberately impairing themselves by avoiding risk in order to maintain control and protect self-esteem. Individuals who use self-handicapping strategies often make less effort, choose easy tasks, have lower expectations, hinder their own performance in order to have an excuse for failing, and offer excuses for a poor performance before attempting tasks.

Often, simple modifications in how others interact with them or to the environment (e.g., use of assistive devices) promote children's independent exploration of their environment. Children accustomed to having adults direct most activities may hesitate to initiate activities. These children are more likely to initiate activities when adults modify their interactive patterns by following children's leads during play while being positive and fun when responding and interacting. Some children learn not to attempt to do things for themselves because they know someone else will do things for them.

When attempting to help children acquire adaptive skills, it is typically most effective to make use of naturally occurring opportunities to learn these skills. Adults need to constantly look for and seize teachable movements, opportunities to naturally integrate adaptive skills. Doing so helps provide children with logical connections and reasons for learning these skills. Taking out several pairs of shoes and spending several minutes practicing learning to tie shoes will likely be less motivating and more frustrating than taking the time to help children learn to tie their shoes while they are dressing. Also, useful, meaningful activities with real objects help children generalize what they have learned.

Children often enjoy learning skills when engaging in pretend play. For example, they can practice setting the table and eating while playing house. They can also learn dressing skills by dressing and undressing dolls.

Adults perform many day-to-day activities without thinking about how complex these activities are. As discussed previously, to help children acquire new skills, it is often useful to complete a **task analysis** (break a task into its component parts). This process is based on the assumption that learning involves prerequisite skills and proper sequencing of instruction. It requires identifying specific tasks to be taught and conducting a detailed analysis of each of those tasks. Task analysis information can be used in developing instructional objectives, identifying and selecting instructional strategies, sequencing instructional content, identifying and selecting appropriate instructional media, and designing evaluation tools.

Once the desired behavior is determined, the adult can define the required behaviors that the child has not mastered yet. The focus should be on teaching essential skills required to perform daily activities. For example, for children to learn to eat using a spoon, they need to be able to scan an object and determine its function, note its position in space, extend their arm, coordinate eye–hand movement, flex their joints, and grasp.

Once the steps required to complete a task have been identified and development of necessary essential skills has occurred, various physical and verbal prompts can be used with backward or forward chaining to help develop target skills. When **backward chaining** is used, children are provided with support as they move through all steps of the task except the last one, which the child performs independently. Adult support is removed one step at a time until children perform the entire task unassisted. With **forward chaining** children complete the first step, followed by assistance with the remaining steps. Over time the child completes more and more steps independently until they are able to complete the entire task without assistance. Forward chaining is most appropriate and useful when children know some of the later steps.

Graduated physical guidance is often useful. This method requires adults to comfortably position themselves in front, on the side, or in back of the child. Depending on the task and the individual child's needs, one position may be more beneficial than another. Graduated physical guidance involves showing children how to complete various tasks using hand-over-hand guidance. In some cases it may be possible to guide from the shoulders or elbows.

During graduated physical guidance, adults should describe what they are doing as they provide support. Movements should not be forced. When children attempt to complete any portion of the task independently, the adult should loosen their hold (provide less direct physical support). If a child does not continue movement toward completing the task, the adult should gently reestablish physical support and continue guidance until the child tries again. This cycle should be continued until children can complete tasks with little or no hand-over-hand support. As children are able to independently complete additional steps of a task, adults should move their grasp to slightly above children's wrists, then move guidance to the elbow, then to the shoulders, and so on.

Graduated physical guidance requires high levels of consistency and patience. Adults must use the same cues, gestures, words, prompts, and procedures across many learning trials. As children become increasingly independent, they benefit from enhanced feedback and encouragement for their efforts. Once children can independently complete skills, they should be provided ample time to do so, even when this approach takes much longer. When children are reluctant to perform tasks independently, they may wait a long time for adults to do for them what they can do for themselves.

A primary consideration in determining appropriate adaptive living goals is to help develop age-appropriate independence within daily activities, which will allow children to more frequently participate within the larger social community. For example, children who are not toilet-trained are unlikely to have access to classrooms with normally developing peers, and parents of children who present safety risks are less likely to take them on community outings. Expectations must remain reasonable. Each child's temperament, experiences, learning style, and developmental delays must be considered. Goals appropriate for one child often are inappropriate for another.

Children often benefit from working together in groups of three to five, because they can learn by imitating other children and are often motivated to learn activities that their friends can perform. Cooperative learning also enhances social skills, including greater understanding and acceptance of children with disabilities.

Conclusions

Although many people assume that the major purpose of early childhood intervention services is to develop pre-academic skills, the acquisition of adaptive skills is particularly crucial for young children. Before it is feasible to focus on the development of skills needed for school success, children need to acquire skills necessary for daily living. When adaptive skills are not acquired, children are less able to meet their personal needs, take social responsibility, or participate in social groups. Children benefit from acquisition of skills that will allow them to cope with the social demands of their environment.

When providing intervention for adaptive-skills delays, it is crucial to consider family history, cultural factors, family expectations, and opportunities to develop self-help skills. In addition, it is important to determine the basic cognitive and motor skills necessary to successfully acquire adaptive skills. It is difficult for children to be fully integrated into various community settings without the development of various adaptive skills.

CHAPTER SUMMARY

- Adaptive skills are one of the five major areas of disabilities addressed by various special education laws. They are necessary for day-to-day functioning and include conceptual, social, and practical skills. They affect the ability to effectively respond to various situations.

- A variety of formal and informal assessments are appropriate for evaluating level of adaptive-skills development.

- Several disabilities characteristically include delays in adaptive skills, including Down syndrome, attention deficit hyperactivity disorder, autism spectrum disorders, and Rett syndrome.

- A variety of behaviors fall under the category "adaptive skills," including autonomy, self-care skills, social cognition, emotional regulation, empathy, moral and prosocial actions, manners, and developing and maintaining friendships.

- Often, learned helplessness and self-fulfilling prophecies contribute to adaptive-skills delays, and these orientations must be modified to enhance adaptive-skills acquisition.

- Use of task analysis involving backward and forward chaining can help children acquire adaptive skills through the use of graduated physical guidance.

CHAPTER KEY TERMS

adaptive skills
maladaptive behaviors
activities of daily living (ADLs)
Developmental Profile II (DP-II)
Early Coping Inventory (ECI)
Vineland Adaptive Behavior Scales-II (VABS-II)
American Association on Mental Deficiency
    (AAMD) Adaptive Behavior Scales (ABS)
Scales of Independent Behavior, Revised (SIB-R)
Hawaii Early Learning Profile (HELP)
autonomous
self-care
extrinsic motivation

intrinsic motivation
oral-motor delays
social cognition
basic emotion
complex emotion
self-conscious emotion
emotional competence
emotional expressiveness
emotional regulation
emotional understanding
emotional knowledge
stranger anxiety
social referencing

display rules
self-regulation
empathy
perspective taking
moral development
self-control
Jean Piaget
Lawrence Kohlberg
external morality
objective morality
heteronomous morality
moral realism
immanent justice
subjective morality
moral relativism
autonomous morality

preconventional level
ethic of egocentrism
conventional level
postconventional level
prosocial
altruistic
Nancy Eisenberg
hedonistic orientation
need-oriented approach
learned helplessness
self-handicapping strategy
task analysis
backward chaining
forward chaining
graduated physical guidance

REVIEW QUESTIONS

1. In what ways do delays in adaptive skills affect other areas of development?

2. In what ways might adaptive-skills delays lead to the development of learned helplessness and self-fulfilling prophecies?

3. How might a preschool special education teacher best motivate young children to develop self-help skills?

4. Describe methods that help young children develop and display prosocial and altruistic behaviors?

SUGGESTED STUDENT ACTIVITIES

1. Attempt to dress yourself using only one hand. Then think about types of clothing or other assistive devices that might help you dress if you had the use of only one hand.

2. Imagine that you are a parent of a 3-year-old child with multiple disabilities. List, in order of priority, adaptive skills that you would want your child to acquire. Why did you rank some skills as more important than others?

3. Visit a preschool classroom with one or more children with developmental delays. What adaptive skills do you see being taught during the day? How are they integrated into the daily routine?

4. Research a specific developmental delay affecting infants, toddlers, or preschool children. Analyze which types of adaptive skills typically are delayed in children with this disability.

The Importance of Play 12

- Play affects all major areas of development.

- Play skills develop in six major stages.

- There should be several play areas in preschool classrooms.

- Children with developmental delays often benefit from specific modifications to play activities and the play environment.

- Play, art, and music therapy are used to help children deal with life experiences.

Previous chapters have discussed major areas of developmental delays and specific therapy services available to help meet the needs of young children with developmental delays. Several chapters have mentioned the importance of play time as a way to integrate a portion of the therapy services. This chapter focuses on the importance of play. It elaborates on the developmental stages of play, major areas in the classroom where children may play, types of play in which children with specific disabilities engage, and special play modifications that may benefit children with disabilities.

Research suggests that the play skills of children with disabilities frequently are qualitatively and quantitatively different from those of children without developmental delays. The play skills of children who have developmental delays tend to be less organized and less complex, and there may be a ritualistic use of toys and other objects (Rubin, 1977; Vickerius & Sandberg, 2006). Children with disabilities tend to engage in less group play (Odom, McConnell, & McEvoy, 1992). Because play skills enhance the young child's overall development, the play characteristics of children with disabilities may negatively affect other areas of development. Therefore, enhancing play skills of children with disabilities may enhance growth. Because most children see play as an enjoyable activity, it may be one of the most intrinsically motivating forms of intervention for children with disabilities (Bowman, Donovan, & Burns, 2000; Lowenfeld, 1971; Samuelsson & Johansson, 2006).

Development through Play

Adequate play time is crucial for young children (Bettelheim, 1987). Play is what young children do. They are driven to play (Bodrova, Leong, Norford, & Paynter, 2006).

According to **Jean Piaget** (1971), play is the work of childhood. Through play, young children learn about themselves and the world around them. During play, children experiment and have the freedom to fully express themselves, hopefully without fearing criticism or rejection. Play allows them to cope with past and present events while imagining future possibilities (Casey, 2005).

Children discover how things work during play and develop a sense of competency. Adults involved in the lives of young children should encourage and support children's play. Play time prepares young children for life (Haller, 1987).

Although the importance of play time is often recognized during the preschool years, the importance of play begins during infancy. For most infants, feeding is one of the earliest play times. Adults and infants trade smiles and imitate each other by making sounds or facial expressions. Through such playful interactions, babies learn that their actions affect the people around them. This allows babies to begin to develop a sense of competency (Allen & Marotz, 1989).

Changing diapers, bathing, dressing, and undressing also can include play between babies and their care providers. Initially, play is limited to looking at objects in the immediate environment. Babies smile at mobiles and stuffed toys within the first few weeks of life. They coo, babble, and laugh when adults shake a rattle. Babies begin reaching for toys as soon as they develop eye–hand coordination. Once they coordinate seeing, grasping, and bringing objects to their mouths, they typically begin to explore objects visually, orally, and tactilely (Marino, 1991; Smilansky & Shefatya, 1990). Play allows young children to work through their anxieties. Frequently, children are frightened of a new toy such as a jack-in-the-box or when a constant in their environment changes, as when an adult dresses in a costume. They appear to be pleased when they overcome their fears and can enjoy new toys and experiences (Einon, 1985).

When adults take time to play with infants and older children, children experience a sense of their own worth (Markun, 1974). Adults' taking the time to pause during their busy schedules to notice children or, better, play with them sends children the important message that they are valued and loved.

During the preschool years, play enhances all areas of development. Children learn new concepts such as "up" and "down." Physical development is enhanced as they learn to coordinate large (gross) and small (fine) muscle movements needed in play as well as in other aspects of life (Curtis, 1982). Children learn that their actions have consequences. They learn how to use their creativity and imagination (Lowenfeld & Brittain, 1969). Play enhances emotional development as they learn how to express feelings and emotions. During play, children have opportunities to practice social skills needed for sharing, taking turns, and cooperating within a group. These varied learning experiences help young children develop a sense of self within the group, as well as positive self-esteem (Hendrick, 1975).

Speech and Language Development

During play activities, children typically use speech and language abilities to communicate with others. The ability to communicate successfully is critical. As discussed in Chapter 5, communication begins at birth with crying, gazing, and cooing. It progresses to babbling and using gestures and isolated words as children begin to grow. During the toddler and preschool years, children use words to express wants, needs, and emotions, and to communicate with peers and adults. Typically, during this time children learn the names of familiar people and objects in their environment and begin to ask questions. It is important for parents and teachers to talk with children about play and daily routines. For example, talking about the bathwater's being warm or talking about the color of a toy with which the child is playing may enhance speech and language development (Kanungo & Soares, 2005; Kennedy, 1991). Talking about the color of a toy and the way it moves also enhances communication skills.

Cognitive Development

Some people seem surprised to learn that young children learn many academic skills through play. Children discover colors, textures, quantities, locations, descriptions, cause and effect, same and different, and relationships between objects as well as a multitude of words that help them make sense of the world (Isaacs, 1972). They learn how to think and solve problems. The number and variety of cognitive concepts that children potentially acquire through play is endless (Gmitrova & Gmitrova, 2003). However, children learn at various rates, when they are developmentally ready to learn (Caplan & Caplan, 1973). For example, most 2-year-olds are not developmentally ready to name the colors of a rainbow, but many 4-year-olds can point to and name colors (Roskos & Christie, 2000).

As discussed throughout this book, some children have delays in their abilities to acquire academic skills and information. Delays range from mild (a lag of several months) to severe (a lag of more than a year). Delays in acquiring academic skills necessitate implementing play activities that modify the presentation of information. Modifications vary depending on the needs of the individual child. Modifications may include presenting material at a slower rate or multiple times (Roskos & Christie, 2000).

The severity of the delay also helps determine the type of information that will be introduced. It is important that children with developmental delays be presented with information appropriate for their developmental age rather than information based on their chronological age. This approach increases the chances that a child will benefit from learning experiences and provides the child with a foundation from which more-complex information may be learned. Individuals working with young children with disabilities must recognize each child's needs and provide a variety of toys, activities, and learning experiences that stimulate each child's desire to learn (Kirk & Gallagher, 1979).

Motor Development

Young children need to be given space and freedom to move. Running, climbing, riding, jumping, and swinging are favorite activities of most children during the preschool years. As discussed in Chapter 7, these activities help develop the body's large muscles and are called gross-motor skills.

Children also develop coordination and balance through play (Howes & Matheson, 1992). Sometimes children trip over people or objects in their path, have difficulty maneuvering around objects, fall down frequently, or fall off toys. Severe gross-motor delays result in safety concerns. Gross-motor delays may also interfere with the ability to play with peers due to an inability to keep up or fully participate in various group activities. As discussed earlier in this book, parents and other care providers may notice the delay in gross-motor skills development; if so, they should discuss their concerns with the child's pediatrician.

Play also aids in the development of fine-motor skills such as finger dexterity and eye–hand coordination. Preschool children usually enjoy playing with blocks, toy tools, puzzles, safety scissors, large beads, crayons, paint, and clay. When doing so, they use their fingers and hands to grasp, pinch, squeeze, stack, draw, and cut.

Evidence of delays in the ability to coordinate movements needed for such tasks may be apparent when a child avoids playing with toys or participating in activities that require fine-motor control (Eliason & Jenkins, 1977). Such avoidance may result in the hindrance of social interactions and opportunities to strengthen fine-motor skills.

Social Development

A child's mind acts like a sponge; it absorbs many aspects of the surrounding environment. Children do not follow the adage "Do as I say, not as I do." They tend to imitate what they see and hear, without considering the consequences. When children observe sharing, caring, manners, cooperation, and conflict resolution (for example, solving a disagreement by talking instead of using mean words, yelling, or hitting), they are likely to imitate such behavior. Acquiring social skills helps children establish and maintain relationships in school, which in turn may lead to positive self-esteem. Chapter 14 discusses the importance of helping children develop positive self-esteem.

Social skills also develop through learning to pay attention to tasks and the people performing them. If a child cannot attend to tasks or wanders from one area to another, these tendencies are likely to interfere with gaining new information and skills. Sometimes it is necessary to set time limits for activities or play choices (e.g., require that children stay in one place for a minimal amount of time), especially when the attention required for the task is more than several minutes. For example, the teacher might ask a child to pick a place to play and remind the child to stay there until a timer rings (e.g., a kitchen timer with a bell). This type of guidance provides children with a better chance to assimilate available information, thus facilitating learning (Anderson, Moore, Godfrey, & Fletcher-Flinn, 2004).

Time limits also provide children with the opportunity to finish projects and games, as well as minimize the chances of distracting their peers. This is especially important for children with disabilities who participate in inclusion programs. It is helpful for children to learn to interact effectively with their peers to help diminish negative attention directed toward them, such as other children's making fun of them. Negative attention often makes it difficult for children to form new friendships and may lead to negative self-esteem.

Self-Help Skills Development

As discussed in Chapter 11, self-help skills allow children to care for their basic needs as independently as possible. Playing dress-up is a favorite play activity of many young children. During this activity, children learn many skills, such as folding, zipping, buttoning, locating the front and back of their clothes, and dressing and undressing themselves. Playing house allows children to practice holding eating utensils.

Arts and crafts and sensory activities often make children's hands dirty. Children involved in these activities have the opportunity to wash their hands (a self-help skill) several times a day. They may also learn to use combs and brushes while caring for a doll's hair. Given the chance, most young children will develop a multitude of necessary self-help skills through play. See Chapter 11 for a discussion of adaptive and self-help skills.

Stages of Play

Play skills develop in sequence. Each stage builds on the skills and knowledge previously obtained and takes children's play to a more complex level. The play skills of children with disabilities are often delayed in direct relation to the degree of the disability. However, the order of the stages of play is the same whether children do or do not have developmental delays (Sawyers & Rogers, 1988).

In the course of play development, it is important to focus on developmental age rather than chronological age. This allows adults to generate appropriate activities, which are likely to enhance the development of play skills. Sometimes two stages of play overlap or occur simultaneously. In fact, even children at the most complex stage of play engage in play characteristic of earlier stages.

The six major stages of play are **exploratory, pretend, solitary, parallel, associative,** and **cooperative.** Understanding the stages of play is crucial when selecting toys and creating developmentally appropriate play opportunities for children with disabilities (Sawyers & Rogers, 1988).

Exploratory Play

Exploratory play (sometimes referred to as **"sensorimotor play"**) dominates children's active waking time from birth to 12 months. Initially, exploration is random, but it soon becomes purposive. During exploratory play, infants explore the world with their senses. Initially they primarily use their eyes and ears to explore their world. As they mature, the other senses become a more important part of exploration (Gordon, 1970). Once children can grasp small objects, the primary mode of exploration is putting objects into their mouth to taste and feel. It is, therefore, essential that the environment of these crawling explorers be clean and safe.

At approximately 6 months old, children have developed simple but consistent ways to make interesting things happen through trial and error. An infant may push a ball again and again, simply to see it go. As children grow older and gain motor skills, these simple actions are coordinated into more complicated play schemes. By 9 months, an infant understands that a ball rolls away as a result of a push.

Children continue to explore the environment throughout childhood. As children mature and gain more knowledge of the world around them, their way of exploring also matures (Barber & Williams, 1981). For example, preschool children begin to notice and label colors and textures.

Pretend Play

Pretend play occurs once children have acquired the knowledge and developed the ability to act out or imitate simple behaviors they have either engaged in themselves or observed someone else engage in, such as sleeping or eating. For example, a child who sees an adult drink from a cup and then pretends to drink from an empty toy tea cup is engaging in pretend play. This is also referred to as "symbolic play." Toward the latter part of this stage, children begin to perform the simple actions of pretend play with others. For example, a child might offer their mother, their teacher, or another child some juice from an empty cup.

During this stage children also begin to use one object to represent another. For example, an orange block may become a carrot. Children also give nonexistent properties to objects. They may pretend that toy dishes are wet and pretend to dry them (Jarrold, Boucher, & Smith, 1993). The knowledge needed for pretend play is based on children's abilities to use real objects in an appropriate manner, such as using a real telephone to call their grandmother (Lewis, Boucher, & Astell, 1992).

By observing adults and older children, young children acquire necessary information for pretend play. It is important for all children to have opportunities to interact with parents, other adults, older siblings, and other children in a non-school setting in order to observe their actions and their use of objects. Pretend play continues to develop in complexity through the solitary and parallel stages of play, described below (Bergen, 2002; Rescorla & Goossens, 1992).

Solitary Play

Children engage in solitary play by playing independently with toys differing from those used by other children within the immediate play area. For example, solitary play occurs when one child plays with a truck while another plays with blocks in the same corner of the room. During solitary play, children make no attempt to interact with one another, although they may walk around or step over other children (Rogers & Sawyers, 1988). Solitary play allows a child time to gain an understanding of objects and toys within their environment before they have to demonstrate that understanding in a group. This stage helps create a sense of security because children do not have to perform for anyone but themselves.

Although solitary play in young children reflects their inability to participate in more-mature forms of play, there are times when older children want or need to engage in solitary play. Some children have a dispositional preference for engaging in extended periods of solitary play. It is important to respect each child's unique play preferences. Some children enjoy more time alone. After stressful periods children may benefit from extended periods of solitary play.

Without assistance, however, children with disabilities may not be able to adaptively play with toys. If this occurs, children often benefit from adults' modeling how to use various toys. In some cases adults may need to physically guide children through the movements required to use various toys. Several repetitions of modeling or guidance may be necessary to help children. As discussed in Chapter 7, children with motor disabilities may need special toys adapted for their use.

Parallel Play

Imagine the double yellow lines on the road. They run side by side but never touch. Such is the case with parallel play. During parallel play, two or more children engage in an activity, or play with similar toys, while playing alongside each other. Typically they do not speak to each other but are comfortable with the proximity of their peers (Gordon, 1972).

Children with disabilities may engage in parallel play, rather than more-complex forms of play, because they do not have the ability or skills to play at the same level as their peers. They often desire to interact in more-social ways but lack the skills to do so. Teaching staff and parents should recognize this desire and provide support to these children, which will allow them to feel comfortable interacting with their peers.

For example, a teacher might show a child with a developmental delay a new toy that is designed to be used simultaneously by several children. The teacher could then demonstrate how the toy works. Next the teacher could encourage the child to practice skills required to interact effectively with the toy and with others using the toy. Next the teacher could ask the child to help them demonstrate to the other children how to use the new toy. This method of introduction is likely to raise the confidence and comfort level of the child with the developmental delay, who otherwise would be likely to remain uncomfortable with the idea of joining in a group activity involving playing with the new toy.

A substage of play occurring during the latter half of the parallel stage is the **onlooker stage.** This substage involves children's watching other children play and, often, talking to them about their play. Children engaged in onlooker play might ask questions about play activities occurring around them without entering into the activities. It is almost as if the children are preparing to enter the play of their peers. Continued observation by the child, paired with their asking questions, helps the child gain an understanding of the rules governing group play.

Associative Play

The associative play stage is characterized by group play that varies in numbers of children and gender. Children play with similar toys or are engaged in a similar activity. They trade toys and comment on one another's behavior but do not play or work together for a shared goal; they are together but separate (Rogers & Sawyers, 1988).

Due to varying levels of ability within the classroom, it is sometimes necessary for teachers to create situations that encourage children to engage in associative play. For example, the teacher might have four children sit at a table, each with some blocks and toy cars on a tray. This would encourage children to play together with the same toys and give them an opportunity to observe and comment on one another's play. This would help set the stage for cooperative play.

Cooperative Play

Children engaged in cooperative play have a shared goal. The goal may be to build a city made of blocks or act out a dramatic play scene (e.g., playing house or school or acting out a story from a book). Typically, cooperative play includes one or two leaders in the group. During cooperative play, meaningful communication among peers occurs to help ensure movement toward a common goal (Rogers & Sawyers, 1988).

Adults often can elicit higher levels of play by encouraging turn-taking games and modeling turn-taking skills. Adults should also help children orient and maintain attention. When children engage in more-complex play, they are more likely to continue to do so when adults respond positively to this behavior. Play activities made available should encourage integration of several or all developmental areas, with a special emphasis on social communication skills. See Table 12.1 for an overview of the six stages of play.

Using Play to Assess Developmental Levels

Formal, standardized tests for young children often take 30 minutes or more to administer. It is not realistic to expect children with suspected developmental disabilities to sit at a table for 30 minutes answering questions and performing tasks that have little or no meaning to them (Chazan, 2002).

Table 12.1	The Six Stages of Play	
Stage	**Age (Months)**	**Characteristics**
Exploratory	0–12	Children use their senses to explore the environment.
Pretend	9–18	Children use objects to represent other objects.
Solitary	18–24	Children are with other children, but they play alone.
Parallel	24–36	Children play next to each other but do not talk or engage in the same activity.
Associative	36–48	Children participate in the same or similar activities but do not work together.
Cooperative	48–60	Children work together toward a common goal.

Typically, standardized tests do not allow examiners to observe how children use information and abilities that the children have acquired through daily activities. Formal tests do not allow adjustments for children who shut down in the face of structured testing situations (Kennedy, 1991). Formal testing is often stressful for young children because they frequently do not understand what is expected and have limited, if any, ways to communicate frustration and confusion (Lewis, 1993).

If the purpose of an assessment is to determine the level at which children function, an ideal way to obtain this information is to observe children playing (Linder, 1990). During play, children spontaneously and authentically demonstrate knowledge and skills. However, not all children or types of skills may be assessed using a less structured play-based form of assessment. One problem with play assessment is that specific tasks, such as putting puzzles together, may not be spontaneously chosen by children during the evaluation and, therefore, must be set up by the examiner. Doing so is appropriate and does not minimize the effectiveness of **play-based assessment.** It is important for the assessor to follow a child's lead, which reveals strengths and possibly weaknesses. Play-based assessment is a nonthreatening, reliable way of obtaining an accurate indication of children's current levels of development (Kirk & Gallagher, 1979).

Play Skills of Children with Disabilities

As discussed earlier, the stages of play development follow a specific sequence. Play is developmental, and children with disabilities usually follow the typical sequence although often at a slower rate. Children with disabilities also tend to differ in the quality of their play, or how they play (Westby, 1988).

In a special education setting, teachers set up the room to encourage and enhance different types of play with toys appropriate for children at various levels

of development (Lieber & Beckman, 1991). The teacher allows children to participate at their own level rather than expecting all of them to play in the same way
(Rogers & Sawyers, 1988). Peer models and tutors may be used even at this early
age to guide children who have difficulty coping or participating. For example, a
teacher might say to a child who does not seem to know how to play with blocks,
"Look at the tall block tower that Chris is building."

The play-skills development of children with disabilities is affected by the other
areas of development discussed earlier in this chapter. For example, a 4-year-old with
the cognitive level of the average 2-year-old probably cannot construct an elaborate
tunnel of blocks through which to drive toy cars. Most 2-year-olds do not play with
blocks in this complex way.

Additionally, children with communication delays may have difficulty speaking,
expressing thoughts, or understanding other children during play. It is the responsibility
of the teaching staff to establish an effective communication system for these children.
For example, a teacher might develop a picture or communication board (a communication aid that allows children to touch or point to a symbol, photograph, drawing, or
words to indicate a desired activity). If the child wants a car but cannot say "car," they
can point to a picture of a car on the communication board (Gowen, 1992).

Children benefit from being allowed to play inside and outside with toys and
real objects such as pots and pans. Most children independently find things to play
with that they enjoy. The need for adequate play time is especially important for children with disabilities (Kennedy, 1991).

Some children who have developmental delays may require play opportunities
that include adult-directed activities because it may be difficult for them to plan and
organize their own play. Special education teachers and therapists should provide
parents and day care providers with information and suggestions for appropriate
games and activities, as well as ideas for stimulating language, which is often used
during play activities. Family members should be encouraged to allow children to be
independent and creative while playing, without the children's fearing criticism or
rejection. Special ways to use play to aid children with specific developmental disabilities are discussed below.

Speech and Language Delays

Children with speech and language delays often exhibit delays in cognitive development as well. Play development is frequently delayed as well because the children do
not have the prerequisite knowledge or familiarity with toys and objects in their play
environment. The play of toddlers who are language-impaired is often limited and
repetitive. Rescorla and Goossens (1992) state, "Previous research indicates that
language development and symbolic play tend to proceed in parallel. Additionally,
existing studies with language-delayed children suggest that symbolic play is delayed
relative to play of age-mates but may be more advanced than the play of younger
children matched on expressive language, at least in some respects" (p. 1294). This
does not imply that these children cannot catch up with their peers. If there are no
other significant delays and a structured early intervention program is in place, it is
possible for these children to progress along the normal continuum.

Children acquire much of their language through play. Play often takes them from what is familiar to new activities. This helps develop and expand language and cognition in young children. Many children with language delays show an inability to spontaneously use the language they have acquired. For example, they might be able to name the items on the dinner table but cannot ask for a napkin or say that they need a cup at mealtime. Similarly, during play they may be able to name toys but have difficulty clearly communicating which toy they desire. They often have difficulty using their knowledge to obtain or receive information or to participate in interactions with peers and adults (Bloom & Lahey, 1978).

It is often necessary to provide verbal cues during play so that these children can use their knowledge base to expand their play scenes. For example, a teacher might cue, "I need a plate to put my food on," and then ask the child, "What do you need to put your food on?" Without the cue, children who have a speech or language delay may be unable to correctly answer the question.

Cognitive Delays

Children with cognitive delays tend to prefer toys that are manipulative in nature, such as push-pull toys, pounding toys, and toys with switches and knobs, rather than toys that require them to be more imaginative, such as small figures of people or nonhuman animals or building blocks (Hellendoorn & Hoekman, 1992). They generally require great repetition to master object play, such as building with blocks, and social play (interacting with peers).

Preschoolers with cognitive delays often exhibit speech and language delays as well. The severity of these delays influences play behavior and abilities. Their use of materials for play is often limited, as are their repertoire and sophistication of play skills. They appear to lack the creativity, imagination, and knowledge needed to combine toys and other props for more-complex play scenes, as well as for the later stages of play development. In addition, they often lack cognitive and language skills necessary for rule-governed play and the communication skills necessary for social interactions and dialogue. Children with cognitive delays may have motor delays, which may further delay their play skills (Gowen, 1992).

Pervasive Developmental Disorder

Children with pervasive developmental disorder (PDD) often engage in solitary play. They appear to be in a world of their own. They are often involved in activities such as spinning wheels on a toy vehicle while making odd noises (Anderson, Moore, Godfrey, & Fletcher-Flinn, 2004; Fay & Schuler, 1980). Such behaviors are self-stimulatory and ritualistic in nature rather than purposeful. Children may line up objects or hold an object in front of their eyes while moving it back and forth. If the children use speech during play, it is usually noncommunicative, such as counting objects or repeating dialogue from a movie.

Children with PDD respond most positively when routines are stable; they often become upset when routines are changed or ritualistic play is interrupted. Working with children who have PDD requires patience, respect, awareness, and persistence on the part of parents and teachers, to help move these children into the play world of their peers (Kirk & Gallagher, 1979).

The deficient language skills of children with PDD often result in significant delays in pretend and symbolic play. In addition to helping children learn to play with toys and interact with peers, staff should provide individual language and play sessions aimed at developing attention and communication skills, prerequisites for certain stages of play. It is unusual for children with PDD to initiate purposeful play unless they have previously observed it. Frequent modeling of appropriate play with toys and interactions with peers maximizes the probability that those skills and behaviors will become part of their spontaneous play (Pushaw, 1976).

Auditory Disabilities

Children who are deaf or hearing-impaired observe, imitate, and explore during play just as their non-hearing-impaired peers do (Brown, Rickards, & Bortoli, 2001). An inability to hear is likely to interfere with the normal development of play. It leads to communication barriers and breakdowns with peers as play becomes more social and cooperative and incorporates more rules. Children with varying degrees of hearing loss rely heavily on sight during solitary play and often notice things that children who do not have hearing loss do not appear to notice, such as the intricacies of how a toy functions or the fact that a wheel on a toy car is cracked. In addition to paying more attention to details, they often are more physical during play—for example, more likely to grab and push to obtain desired toys. However, aggressive physical behavior usually diminishes once they learn how to communicate and negotiate more effectively (Schwartz, 1987).

In the case of children who are deaf or hearing-impaired, the development of symbolic play skills is directly related to the development of communication abilities. This fact supports the need for early intervention (Rescorla & Goossens, 1992). Children who are hearing-impaired typically develop speech, whereas most deaf children do not develop intelligible speech. Language delays of these children often are not obvious until speech and language skills are needed for social components of associative and cooperative play. Reciprocal games, including taking turns and back-and-forth games such as catch, are ideal activities for children who are deaf or hearing-impaired because they require eye contact among all participants. See Chapter 9 for further discussion of the needs of children with hearing impairments.

Physical Disabilities

Children with motor delays often require adaptive equipment or modifications to their environment to most effectively benefit from play experiences. For example, children who are in wheelchairs or use crutches or walkers often require more space to move about. Tables must be at a height that allows them to sit and play with objects such as puzzles. They may benefit from blocks' being placed on tabletops rather than the floor.

As discussed in Chapter 7, children with fine- or gross-motor delays may need adaptive switches or special knobs to play with certain toys. Some equipment may be too challenging or unsafe for children with motor delays. Adults must ensure the safety of play materials. Teachers, parents, and peers may be tempted to assume that children with motor delays cannot participate in certain activities and exclude them from these experiences. Children and adults may need instruction on how to include the children in classroom activities.

Visual Impairment

Children with visual impairments (partial sight or blindness) often exhibit delays in the early stages of play because they cannot see, or cannot clearly see, toys and other objects in the play environment. In addition, they may be unable to observe peers and subsequently be unable to imitate their actions. As discussed in Chapter 9, initially they may be unable to move around the room successfully or safely without assistance.

Exploratory play is essential for children who are visually impaired. Children engaged in exploratory play use senses other than sight; they discover the shapes, sizes, and functions of toys and other objects. Therefore, children who are visually impaired benefit when the play environment includes a wide variety of toys and other materials designed to stimulate senses other than sight.

Children who are visually impaired tend to keep objects close to their body during exploration. When they do so, they are better able to retrieve the object if they drop it. Very young children who are visually impaired often bite and mouth objects as well as rub them on their faces. As children mature, such discovery behaviors become less socially appropriate, and children who are visually impaired learn new ways to explore toys and objects.

Classroom Play Areas

The general program philosophy behind serving young children with disabilities is to provide an environment that encourages and facilitates learning through play experiences. This is the same philosophy behind most regular-education preschools. Most special-needs preschools have staff members trained in special education, and the number of students in each class is lower than in most regular-education preschool classes.

Several key factors affect the ability to learn, including intellectual function, desire to learn, readiness for learning, and attention span. It is important to provide children the freedom and support they need to make choices in their daily routine. This promotes self-initiated (i.e., self-motivated) activity (Hohmann, Banet, & Weikart, 1979). Children with disabilities frequently do not initiate play without some suggestions from a teacher or parent. It is important for adults to be aware of children's interests and developmental levels to provide toys and activities that children find most interesting. Attention to task is most easily achieved when children have a reason to engage in the activity, and learning is most likely to occur when children are motivated to attend to the activity for more than just a few minutes.

It is important that the classroom include a variety of toys and materials that allow for a wide variety of individual differences and needs. Children should have ready access to toys. Teachers should not put items in play areas if they are not for the children to use. Items such as scissors, glue, and paint that require teacher

Children's motor and social skills are being developed as they play.

supervision should be accessible to the children on a regular basis but often are not appropriate for children to access independently.

Children with more-severe delays often spend less time in purposeful play and more time in nonpurposeful play. Attention span is often a factor because children who have difficulty focusing for more than a minute or two often wander around the room until they find something of interest. It is the teacher's responsibility to assist these children in becoming active play participants who are engaged in activities that will enhance their development.

Parents are sometimes dismayed at the thought that their children play at school. Parents want to know that their children are learning and what concepts they are learning in preparation for primary school. Play allows children to learn at their own rate and acquire concepts that might escape them if they were forced to sit at a table and listen to a teacher talk, as often occurs in classrooms not designed for children with disabilities. Parents who question whether learning takes place during play should be encouraged to spend time with their child at school to see how productive play time is. Table 12.2 lists many of the concepts and skills that children learn through play activities, including cleaning up play materials.

The classroom should have well-defined physical areas, including block, house and dramatic play, sensory, art, quiet, music and movement, and science areas (Hohmann et al., 1979). These areas are consistently found in regular- and special-education classrooms.

The items found in each area should be organized, labeled with pictures or words, and stored in plain view so that the children have easy access to them. In addition, storage shelves should be labeled with pictures and words so that when it is time to clean up, the children know where items belong. Area boundaries should

Table 12.2 Concepts and Skills Learned through Play	
Area of Development	**Concepts and Skills**
Cognitive and Language	Concepts: color, shape, size, number, location, weight, distance
	Skills: following directions, understanding cause and effect, categorizing, sequencing, classifying, basic logic, sense of time, reading, theme-related vocabulary, sorting and matching
Social (including attention to task)	Skills: perseverance, taking turns, negotiation, manners, patience, empathy, sharing, role playing, resolving conflict, conversational skills, building relationships, expressing feelings, nonverbal communication
Self-Help	Skills: dressing, buttoning, zipping, eating, washing, folding, snapping (fasteners), drinking
Sensory and Motor	Skills: mixing, pouring, pinching, pulling, strength, maintaining balance, eye–hand coordination, touching, smelling, hearing, tasting, seeing, awareness of one's spatial relation to the environment, stretching, dexterity, writing and drawing

be easy to redefine so that two areas, such as dramatic play and sensory play, can be combined to enhance creativity and learning.

Labeling and organizing toys and materials encourages independence and responsibility when children put away the toys and supplies. In addition, classroom organization gives children a sense of order and security because it allows for a consistent routine in beginning and ending play. Organization also saves time because everything has a specific location, making it is easy to find a particular item. If teachers notice that an area of the room is seldom used, that area should be modified or combined with another area, or other areas should temporarily be closed off to encourage play in an underused area. Teachers should encourage play in this area by familiarizing children with the items found within it.

The classroom environment must be adapted to accommodate the special needs of children with motor delays and visual disabilities. For example, children in wheelchairs need space to move about and access toys and tables. Children with motor delays may need to lean against shelves to move about; therefore, shelves must be very stable.

Block Area

The **block area** is often one of the largest in a classroom. The amount of shelf and play space affects the number of toys that can be made available in this area. This area may also be used for large-group activities, such as during circle time, when teachers and children meet to plan the day's events, sing songs, and dance or exercise. Figure 12.1 shows items that may be found in this area.

Figure 12.1   **Types of Toys Typically Found in the Block Area**

wooden blocks of various sizes and colors	snap-together blocks
cardboard or styrofoam blocks	building sets
a dollhouse	train tracks
toy garages, farm buildings, and other buildings	road maps
cars and trucks of various sizes	traffic signs
toy trains	cardboard
boards	building tiles
carpet squares	puppets
toy people, action figures, or other characters	toy nonhuman animals

At home or in school, as adults observe and play with children, they should be particularly aware of how children play with blocks. According to Hirsch (1984), there are six major stages of building with blocks (outlined in Figure 12.2).

Adults should interact and play with children at each child's developmental level. In preschool, teachers often take a child's play one step beyond the child's abilities and add to what the child has done. That is, the teacher might build a slightly more complex structure to provide a child with ideas without forcing them to build the same thing. Modeling slightly more advanced play skills exposes children to different ways of using blocks, to expand their repertoire of skills.

Figure 12.2   **Hirsch's Six Stages of Block Play**

1. Walk around carrying blocks, or pile them up.
2. Build towers, or lay blocks side by side in rows.
3. Bridge space with blocks, using two blocks parallel to each other and a third across the top.
4. Build enclosures.
5. Build structures that have a particular pattern.
6. Use blocks to build and represent buildings, or other structures with which the child is familiar, and use these structures as props for toy cars and actual people.

Source: Adapted from Hirsch (1984).

House and Dramatic Play Area

In the **house and dramatic play area,** one child might pretend to be a mother cooking dinner for Mickey Mouse (a different child pretending) while Batman (another child pretending) irons his cape. Given an adequate selection of props, young children may become whoever or whatever they wish. Figure 12.3 lists some of the items included in a classroom's dramatic play area.

Most young children love to dress up and act out scenes from their daily lives. Typically, boys and girls wear clothes for men and women during role play and may switch roles several times during a play scene. Sometimes parents feel uncomfortable allowing their sons to wear dresses during play. Parents can rest assured: dress-up is a normal part of play even if boys wear girls' clothing.

Not all children are at the same level of imaginative play or enjoy playing in this area. Teachers should be aware of each child's level of ability and comfort. The teacher's role in this area might be to participate in a play scene—for example, be a patient to whom the doctor applies a bandage or a passenger on a train—or to observe and provide dialogue or suggestions as needed. Teachers might read a familiar story during the day and then put the book in the dramatic play area to give children ideas for dramatic play.

Figure 12.3 **Items Commonly Found in a Dramatic Play Area**

- toy stove or oven, sink, refrigerator
- toy or real (unbreakable) dishes, utensils, pots, and pans
- iron, broom, dustpan
- toy or real telephone
- dress-up clothes and costumes, including aprons, scarves, mittens, hats, old plastic eyeglass frames
- suitcases, wallets, pocketbooks
- baby dolls
- baby bed
- stuffed toy nonhuman animals
- pillows and blankets
- old jewelry
- keys on a ring
- pretend food, and real food containers and boxes
- baskets and small grocery carts
- fake money
- brown paper bags

Sensory Area

Many classrooms have a **sensory area**, which may be combined with other areas. Often the sensory area contains a sensory table, where children can use their senses to learn. This is a mainstay in most preschool classrooms. A **sensory table** is large enough for six to eight children to stand around and has an insert tray about 6 inches deep. The height of the sensory table may need to be adapted for children with motor delays, including children in wheelchairs or whose muscle development does not allow them to stand for extended periods.

A sensory table can accommodate a variety of media (substances or materials) that can be put inside the tray for children to smell, taste, touch, see, and listen to during their play. Sensory tables promote tactile exploration. Materials put into a sensory table must correspond with the children's developmental level. For example, small objects may be a choking hazard if placed in a child's mouth and, therefore, would not be appropriate for children who are still mouthing objects. The sensory table is often used for containing messy substances or for encouraging a group of children to be in one area and play together. Storage shelves containing items that may be used in the sensory table are often close to the table. Figure 12.4 lists items that may be used in the sensory table.

Figure 12.4   **Examples of Sensory Table Materials**

- cups
- funnels
- sponges
- shovels and other containers for dumping and pouring
- sand
- rice and oatmeal (dry and wet)
- dry beans
- shaving cream
- water
- goop (made from corn starch and water)
- snow
- dirt
- cooked macaroni or spaghetti
- dough or clay

As discussed in Chapter 10, some children do not like to play with messy materials, get dirty, or explore new sensations. This may be due to the presence of a sensory integration disorder or disposition tendency. These children should be encouraged to participate at their own comfort level. The teacher should carefully increase their exposure to a substance until they tolerate it more. Often children feel uncomfortable interacting with certain items because they have not been previously exposed to them (Gowen, 1992). Frequent exposure to varying types of materials at school helps children become familiar with them. This often results in children's returning to the sensory area for play, creating new possibilities for learning at home and school.

Sensory activities can also occur at child-size tables, especially when precision or cutting is involved. These tables are often located in a central area or in the dramatic play area to encourage children to explore activities such as cooking. Using the utensils in the play kitchen area, children can slice different foods.

Art Area

Art is a creative form of play. The art area is often close to or part of the sensory area (Anderson, 1978; Atack, 1986; Nixon, 1969). Children who avoid the **art area** need teachers' or parents' support in developing imagination and creativity in the other play areas, such as blocks or dramatic play (Alkema, 1971; Beittel, 1974; Crawford, 1962; Kellogg, 1969).

Toddlers' and preschoolers' scribbles gradually become meaningful pictures as their mental abilities expand and they begin to symbolize objects through pictures and other art forms. Children's drawings reveal their thoughts (Anderson, 1986; Coles, 1992; Harris, 1963; Uhlin, 1972). For example, a 3-year-old may draw a circle with apparently random marks inside it and call it a pizza. See Figure 12.5 for examples of 4- and 5-year-olds' drawings.

Children's artistic abilities progress from making random marks to mastering simple shapes, such as circles and rectangles, to making complex drawings that combine several shapes. Children then combine shapes to form figures such as stick

Figure 12.5 **Young Child's Drawing**

people with circle heads and rectangle bodies (Goodnow, 1977). They might label these figures "Mom" and "Dad." Shapes are also combined to form objects, as when a child uses a circle and rectangle to depict a tree and a square and triangle to depict a house (Gardner, 1973). (See Figure 12.6.)

It is important to honor individuality during art activities (Grozinger, 1955). Adults should allow and encourage children to conceive their own projects rather than only be allowed to work on projects designed by the teacher. Allowing children to design their own creations encourages development of independence and imagination (Moon, 1990). Some children enjoy coloring books and pages that require them to stay within the lines, but those drawing activities do not encourage creativity and individuality. Such activities may be appropriate as free play choices but should not be considered art activities.

During art activities, children often experiment with different materials and use their imaginations to tell stories about their creations. They often seek approval or recognition regarding their creations. It is important for adults not to compare the quality or complexity of one child's work to another child's (Coles, 1992).

Art activities for young children with disabilities should be relatively simple. Room furnishings should not require elaborate protection from messy art materials such as paint and glue. Children and teachers should not have to worry about making a mess or ruining furnishings. An extended amount of time should be allocated to art

Figure 12.6 **Four-Year-Old and Five-Year-Old Children's Drawings**

activities. Children are likely to become frustrated when not given ample time to complete art activities. Art time should be considered an important part of the curriculum rather than something to do when there is nothing else to do (Brittain, 1979).

Whenever possible, the art area should be located near windows because natural light enhances many art creations. If an area of a classroom cannot be set aside for art activities, almost any area in a classroom can be transformed into an art area. Ideally, the classroom contains a sink for use during clean-up. If there is no sink, large buckets with soapy water and rinse water may be placed on drop cloths for children and teachers to use for washing hands and art tools (Brittain, 1979).

The art area should be located away from areas of the classroom that cannot be easily cleaned after messy activities. For example, books, dolls, and stuffed toys should not be adjacent to the art area. The art area should be in a location that allows projects to dry without interfering with other activities. Ideally, the art area is in a spot where teachers may monitor who comes and goes, to help prevent children from damaging other children's artwork or accidentally getting into messy art materials.

Furniture useful for art activities includes movable tables, chairs, blackboards, easels, storage cabinets, closets, racks, and shelves. It is often helpful to use individual trays to allow children a defined work space or to store unfinished projects.

Preschool classroom art supplies can include an endless variety of materials. Many things can be used as protective coverings for floors and furniture, including newspapers, old plastic tablecloths, plastic drop cloths, and old sheets. Ideally, flooring in an art area is a hard surface (e.g., tile or wood) that is easy to clean rather than carpeting. If necessary, carpeting may be protected with the items listed above. Old, discarded adult-size shirts make ideal smocks if plastic children's smocks are unavailable. Figure 12.7 lists methods that may encourage a hesitant child to participate in art activities. Table 12.3 summarizes the relationship between art activities and developmental areas.

Figure 12.7   **Methods That May Encourage a Hesitant Child to Participate in Art Activities**

- Have the child watch the teacher take out and prepare the material for an activity (e.g., mix paints).

- Let the child help take out and prepare the materials (e.g., help mix paint) while the teacher supervises.

- Allow the child to help prepare the art area (e.g., cover the table with old newspapers) while the teacher talks about the upcoming art activity.

- Allow the child to observe the activity without actively participating. While the child is observing, encourage them to ask questions and make suggestions about other children's work on the activity.

- Encourage the child to participate in the activity for a short amount of time while reassuring them that they may quit at any time.

Table 12.3	The Relationship of Art Activities to Developmental Areas
Developmental Area	**Art Activities**
Cognitive	Experimenting with various colors, shapes, and sizes. Learning particular relationships such as above, below, on, over, and next to. Responding to visual and tactile stimuli. Experiencing textures such as smooth, scratchy, bumpy, rough, soft, wet, dry, slippery, and sticky. Learning names of objects. Following instructions, planning, and sequencing.
Language	Asking for supplies. Describing art projects. Responding to questions. Developing conversational skills.
Motor	Enhancing prewriting skills. Squeezing and gripping. Enhancing muscle development and coordination.
Self-help	Opening and closing containers. Putting on and taking off a smock. Organizing supplies. Washing one's hands.
Social-emotional	Expressing emotions. Demonstrating creativity and individuality. Developing cooperation skills.

Table 12.4 lists items that may be used for art activities. The list of potential art supplies is limited only by a child's, parent's, or teacher's imagination. Children should be encouraged to collect art materials such as rocks, shells, leaves, pine cones, twigs, and seed pods. Most children enjoy collecting items that can be used during art activities. Parents often are more than willing to collect the objects listed for use in art activities. Figure 12.8 lists items, found in most homes, that can be used in art activities. Again, the list of items that children and parents may collect is endless. Many items would be thrown away if they were not used in art activities.

In some cases, it may be desirable to compile a **portable art kit.** This type of kit includes easily manipulated materials requiring little preparation or clean-up (Lindsay, 1968). Supplies in the kit can include crayons, water-based markers, colored pencils, glue sticks, scissors, paper, pieces of scrap paper, modeling clay, chalk boards, colored chalk, a plastic covering, and disposable smocks. These materials may be organized on an open, shelved cart or placed in a toolbox type of container. A portable art kit makes materials readily accessible and visible to teachers, therapists, and

Table 12.4   Items Needed for the Art Area

Furniture	Materials
Large, portable, child-height table; easels; drying racks; portable cart; storage cabinets and shelves; trays	Finger-paint paper, construction paper, tissue paper, large rolls of paper, large and small sheets of paper, string and yarn, washable paints and containers, painting tools (e.g., brushes, cotton swabs, sponges, straws, string, and cork), washable markers, colored pencils, regular pencils, crayons, indoor and outdoor chalk, nontoxic glue, glue containers, glue brushes, glue sticks, tape, staplers, children's scissors, plastic cookie cutters, modeling clay, glitter, pipe cleaners, smocks, table coverings

children to encourage spontaneous art activities. It also allows the teacher to use art materials outdoors or in a different area of the classroom or building.

When deciding which choices will be made available for art activities, safety issues must be considered. Art supplies should be easily replaceable and nontoxic because young children explore materials by putting things into their mouths. Breakable containers or sharp objects should not be used.

Although it is important to allow flexibility within the art area, children should also be made aware of the boundaries regarding the appropriate use of art materials. Art activities should encourage children to be creative and stretch their imagination

Figure 12.8   Common Household Items That Can Be Used in Art Projects

popsicle sticks	seed pods
rubber bands	food items (e.g., macaroni, beans)
cotton balls	old jewelry
cork	buttons
spools from thread	fabric scraps
string, yarn, or ribbon	foam padding
metal clothes hangers	wood scraps
cardboard tubing	paper bags
small stones and sticks	paper scraps
pinecones	wallpaper scraps
leaves	

but within limits (Brittain, 1979). Rules may include wearing smocks when painting, sharing, keeping art supplies in the art area, and helping with clean-up. For example, children may be required to wear smocks when they paint or do other messy activities. If wearing a smock is a classroom rule but a child chooses not to wear a smock, the child should not be allowed to paint. If they are told they must keep glue, paint, and glitter in the art area yet they leave the area and take these materials with them, it may be necessary to exclude them from the art area.

Amount of time, size of the classroom, number of children in the class, and number of staff in each classroom are likely to play a role in how art activities are presented. Art activities may be presented to individual children or to small and large groups (Cohen, 1969).

One way of including art activities is to work individually with a child. Interacting one-to-one with a child during an art activity is often very rewarding for the child and adult. The child and teacher may talk to each other, creating a language-rich environment during an activity designed to meet the child's specific needs and interests.

While working individually with children, teachers can introduce concepts such as color or shape, or work hand-over-hand (the teacher guides the child's hands) to help the child develop scissor skills or a mature pencil grip. One-to-one time also allows the teacher to use art time to assess the child's developmental level. Realistically, however, most classroom settings cannot afford the luxury of individual art time on a regular basis. Art activities most often occur in small or large groups (Cohen, 1969).

Small groups are the most common method of providing art activities. A staff member should be assigned to monitor each small group. All of the children in the classroom may work at the same time but in groups of three to five, or one teacher or therapist may work with three to five children while children not in the group engage in other activities. Plans for small-group art activities should include consideration of the materials to be used, space, time, and the needs of each child in the small group (Gaitskell & Gaitskell, 1953).

Participating in art activities allows for observation of a variety of children's cognitive and fine-motor skills. Table 12.5 provides guidelines for using art activities as part of the assessment process.

Quiet Area

Classrooms should have an area where the activity and noise levels are less than those in other areas. This should be cozy and comfortable and may contain books. Most children enjoy looking at books alone but are also likely to pretend to read to one another. Books should be readily accessible and clearly displayed so that they are inviting to children who pass by the area. Books should be sturdy.

The **quiet area** may also include small toys (manipulatives) that aid in the development of fine-motor skills. These items may include pegs for pegboards, stringing beads, puzzles, nesting cups, and stacking rings. Children should be allowed to independently and quietly use toys located in the quiet area. Including these items in the quiet area may help limit the distractions that children experience in other

Table 12.5   *Guidelines for Assessment during Art Activities*

Developmental Area	Age (Years)	Skills
Cognitive	2	Sorts objects by color.
	2½	Sorts four shapes.
	3	Points to bigger, smaller, longer, shorter, and taller; sorts objects by two or three colors; tells whether objects are the same or different.
	4	Names four colors.
	5	Knows basic colors and shapes.
Fine-Motor	1½	Holds crayon with whole hand (palm grasp) and scribbles; crumples and tears paper.
	2	Holds pencil with whole hand; imitates vertical and circular strokes after the teacher models them; attempts to fold paper.
	2½	Holds pencil with fingers rather than in palm; imitates vertical and circular scribble; can roll, pound, squeeze, and pull clay.
	3	Inaccurately uses scissors to nip; copies a circle; imitates a horizontal line, vertical line, V-strokes, and a cross (+); spontaneously scribbles in circular motions; displays a dominant hand.
	4	Copies a cross, square, *V, H,* and *T*; folds and creases paper three times after demonstration; cuts with scissors; makes simple line drawings; cuts along a straight line.
	4½	Threads a lacing card with running string; copies a square; connects dots; cuts circles.
	5	Shows refinement in use of tools such as pencils and scissors; uses a crayon or pencil with more precision in small areas; copies a triangle; traces a diamond.
	5½	Knows left and right; prints some letters and numbers; cuts out pictures with scissors.
	6	Copies a diamond; accurately uses scissors to cut along straight lines, curves, and angles; shows clearly established hand preference (left or right); copies printing from left to right.
Social-Emotional	2	Helps clean up; prefers to be near but not with other children.
	2½	Works side by side with other children during an art activity; makes simple choices during art activities; seeks approval from adults.
	3	Tells about art activity/project.
	4	Completes art activities; understands taking turns; recognizes when peers need help.
	4½	Works with other children in the art area by sharing and taking turns.

parts of the classroom during play time. Figure 12.9 lists items frequently included in this area.

Depending on the developmental levels of the children in the class, there may be a combined reading and writing area. This area might include paper, individual journals, pencils, markers, tape, staplers, and stencils. Many older preschoolers ask to be taught how to write their names and other words. They like to tell stories and have their teachers record these stories to be read at a future time. They often request help in writing notes home (the teacher writes while the child dictates) or ask to address art work to send to others.

Movement and Music Areas

It is essential to give young children time to be physically active during the day. This is especially true for children with disabilities, particularly those who have delays in gross-motor development. During movement activities, motors skills are developed and enhanced through play.

Movement may be as subtle as blinking or as obvious as jumping up and down. Young children need space to run, jump, climb, and skip. They benefit from opportunities to swing and go down slides. The playground or the classroom's gross-motor area is usually a favorite area in preschool because it allows freedom of movement.

Songs are often used in preschool during transition times. Repetitive tunes are relatively easy for most children to learn and may be used to remind them what time it is (e.g., clean-up time). Songs are often sung during circle time. Classical music may be used as background sound or as a soothing agent in an otherwise loud or boisterous room.

Preschool classrooms often have cassette and CD players. Time for singing or listening to familiar songs, with or without accompanying actions, enhances young children's development. Toy musical instruments often are used during music time. Most preschool children are not self-conscious about their voices and are, therefore, eager to sing whether or not they know the words. Children learn new vocabulary and concepts through music, even when they do not grasp the meanings of the same words when those words are used in conversation. Teachers and parents should take advantage of this enjoyable way (through music and movement) to promote learning. Table 12.6 lists examples of items to include in the music and movement area.

Music therapists have been trained in an approved music therapy program at the undergraduate or graduate level. They completed a clinical internship as well as required course work. Music therapists have skills in piano, voice, or guitar and are knowledgeable

Figure 12.9   **Examples of Quiet Area Materials**

- books and magazines
- mats
- pillows
- blankets
- carpet squares
- stuffed toy nonhuman animals
- a small table with chairs around it
- rocking chairs

Table 12.6	Examples of Music and Movement Area Materials
Musical Supplies	**Movement Supplies**
tape recorder and CD player	tricycles
tapes and CDs	balls
drums	swings
bells	slide
sticks to hit together	climbing apparatus
cymbals	
triangles	

in music composition, theory, and history. Music therapy is provided in groups or individually. Although the value of music has long been recognized, only recently has music therapy been recognized as particularly useful in educating children with disabilities (Boxill & Chase, 2007).

Music therapy typically includes musical activities such as listening, singing, clapping, tapping, dancing, walking, moving, and playing various instruments. Music therapists choose songs that are age- and developmentally appropriate and adapt their use to children's specific needs. At the preschool level, folk songs for children, standard nursery rhymes, and adaptations of contemporary songs are often selected that support classroom themes. For example, if children are learning about animals on old-fashioned farms, "Old McDonald" and "Bingo" might be selected to support the theme.

Music therapy may be especially useful for children with disabilities. Songs facilitate vocalization and increase the number and spontaneous use of vocabulary words. Music therapy may be used to increase social, attending, and turn-taking skills and may help to develop fine- and gross-motor skills. Music therapy is often useful for children with behavioral problems. For example, children who have difficulty keeping their attention on large-group activities often are motivated to attend and wait their turn by being allowed to play a drum.

Most children perceive music therapy activities as nonthreatening. Such activities are an enjoyable way for children to receive instruction. During music activities, children are often unaware that certain skills are being worked on because they are having so much fun. Even when children are unwilling to participate in other activities, they are likely to participate in music activities. Music therapy provides children with positive experiences within a school setting. This helps create a positive orientation toward school (Lepper, 1981).

Science Area

Another area that is often a part of preschool or day care settings is the **science area.** Most children enjoy helping with the care of plants and nonhuman animals. Children learn about the needs of other living things and beings by helping to care for plants or nonhuman animals. Some children may have allergies that preclude having plants and nonhuman animals in the classroom. For example, children who are HIV-positive should not help care for classroom animals.

It is not necessary to have a separate designated science area within a classroom. A windowsill or sturdy table or shelves, which cannot be knocked over, make

Table 12.7	*Animals and Objects Often Found in Science Areas*	
Animals	**Natural Objects**	**Science Equipment**
Mice, gerbils, guinea pigs, turtles, lizards, parakeets, hermit crabs, fish, rabbits	Leaves, acorns, seeds, pinecones, shells, rocks, sticks, dried flowers, bones, feathers, snake skins, insect ectoskeletons	Magnifying glass, telescope, binoculars, tweezers, magnets, microscope, clear plastic containers with lids, butterfly nets, small digging tools, child-size work gloves

excellent locations for most plants or animals. The science area should also include objects found in nature and other science equipment. Table 12.7 lists animals and objects often found in this area.

Play Time at Home

Children with disabilities enrolled in preschool or day care programs need additional time for play at home. Parents should be encouraged to allow most of their child's day to be play time and to allow the child opportunities for regular play with other children at or close to their developmental level. Play partners are important because they provide an opportunity for taking turns, sharing, cooperating, and stimulating dramatic play. Parents should avoid comparing children's abilities and should understand and accept developmental needs.

In addition to providing their child with peer play partners, parents should gladly play with their child. Children should know that the adults in their lives want to spend time with them doing what children want to do. Preschoolers enjoy imitating their parents, and imitation is one way that children learn. When parents play with their child, they should get down to the child's level. If the child is on the floor, the parents should be on the floor.

When children do not want to play with their parents, they often let them know by ignoring them, leaving the activity, or telling the parents to leave. Parents should not be offended or upset when children do not want them as play partners. Instead, parents should respect the child's wishes but remain available if the child later invites them to play or needs them to help resolve a problem or conflict.

It is also important for parents to allow their child to be in their space while they perform daily chores or are relaxing, such as when they are reading. Children often imitate their parents' actions in play by recreating them. This allows them to gradually become more advanced and competent in their play skills (Marzollo & Harper, 1972). As discussed in Chapter 11, parents should encourage their children to help them with chores. This enables children to observe what their parents are doing and learn how to manipulate the tools necessary to complete tasks. However, parents must use good judgment and make sure that children always are safe.

These young boys are enjoying playing together in the block area.

Sometimes adults do not approve of the way children play. In such cases they may tell children how to use a toy the right way or what to draw with the crayons and paper. When adults find themselves responding in this way, they should try to find ways to interact with their children that are less judgmental and more supportive of independent play. In choosing play items, children learn about making decisions at an early age. This helps to build positive self-esteem.

It is very important to provide children enough time to play. Most preschools have a daily routine that allows ample time for indoor play. Although it is also important for parents to give their children ample time to play, play time does not have to be a single span of time. Parents should encourage their children to play throughout the day. Interruptions are inevitable, but parents should try to give their children blocks of time reserved for play. Parents should understand that time for play is needed, just as there must be time for eating and resting. Children with disabilities often take longer to become involved in their play and therefore need more time to actually play.

Clean-Up Time

Children should be actively involved in cleaning up their play materials at home and school. Whenever possible, children should receive at least one warning or reminder that play time is ending soon before they are expected to clean up. Telling a 5-year-old that clean-up time is in 5 minutes generally has limited meaning because most 5-year-olds cannot tell time. A timer might be set so that children can see how much time is left. This allows children to finish what they started and lets them know that soon they will need to clean up. If there is no timer or children do not find a timer helpful, putting on the radio or a favorite tape or CD, and telling children that when the song or recording is finished it will be time to put the toys away, often helps children prepare for clean-up time.

Clean-up time may result in conflicts regarding how and where to put toys away. When children have a specific place for toys, this often reduces conflicts. Toy boxes have been popular for years but often become so crowded that it is difficult to find desired toys. If possible, teachers and parents should reserve shelves or a cabinet for toys so that they may be organized and readily found. Parents may want to label shelves as is done within a preschool setting. Labeling helps ensure that the toys have a specific location and are easier to find the next time children want to play.

Sometimes parents and teachers find themselves putting toys away because children resist doing so. If that is the case, they should try to find ways to make clean-up time fun. If items need to go into a bucket or bin, clean-up can turn into a basketball game by asking children to drop items into the basket. Most children enjoy pretending to score points by making a basket and having someone clap after they score a basket. Children are often more inclined to be helpful during clean-up when they are given choices about what to put away first. If children continually take out many toys and then refuse to help clean up, adults should consider limiting the number of toys available for play time. Adults also should teach children that they need to clean up one set of toys or one area of play before they move on to play with a different set of toys or in another area. It is important not to let clean-up time become a battle that eventually discourages children from wanting to take out and play with toys.

Developmentally Appropriate Toys

Many different types of developmentally appropriate toys are available. The packaging of most toys indicates the age range for which the toy is intended. Adults too often focus on this chronological age rather than consider the child's developmental level. Developmentally inappropriate toys often are not interesting to children and can be a safety hazard, even when the child's age corresponds to the age printed on the label (Kaban, 1979). For example, a child who is 4 years old but developmentally only 2 may try to taste, and accidentally swallow, a piece from a toy with many small parts.

To help determine which toys would be developmentally appropriate, children should be observed during play. Children play with objects and toys that interest them. Toys too difficult for them to interact with may frustrate them. For example, a 100-piece jigsaw puzzle would not be appropriate for most 4-year-olds.

Educational toys are designed to stimulate children's natural curiosity and teach certain concepts or skills. Although it is appropriate to provide children with such toys, it is not necessary to demand that children play with these toys only in the way the manufacturer intended. For example, children may use a toy pot as a drum. Children should be allowed to play with toys in the way that most suits or pleases them as long as they are doing so safely. Children should be encouraged to play for the enjoyment of play.

Toys do not always need to be purchased to be enjoyable. Many toddlers love to play with cardboard boxes. They climb in and on them, stack them, and put other items in them to push or pull around the room. Preschool teachers frequently request that parents save and send in items they would otherwise throw away, including paper towel tubes and egg cartons. Many projects and toys can be made from items that would otherwise be tossed into the garbage or recycling bin.

Parents should be encouraged to ask their child's preschool teacher what types of toys are most appropriate for their child. It is often helpful for parents to spend time in the classroom to watch their child play. Parents may benefit from inviting the child's day care provider to spend time in the preschool class to become more familiar with the child's play style. Table 12.8 lists appropriate toys for children birth through preschool as well as appropriate play activities for children 2–5 years old.

Play Therapy

Verbally communicating with young children is often difficult, especially children with disabilities. To children, actions during play are much as verbalizations are to adults. Play can serve as a medium for expressing feelings, exploring relationships, describing experiences, and disclosing needs and desires. **Play therapy** often is a way to access this information in a natural mode (Axline, 1947).

Play therapy is a well-thought-out, philosophically conceived, developmentally based, and research-supported approach to helping children cope with and overcome problems. Play therapists typically have a master's degree in counseling, psychology, or social work. Training typically incorporates knowledge about child development and is extensive in the area of play therapy.

The Rationale for Play Therapy

Most children's language development lags behind their cognitive development. Therefore, they often most effectively communicate their awareness of what is happening in their world through their play. During play therapy, toys are viewed as the child's words.

Play as a form of psychotherapy originated in the 1920s. It is used with children when counseling or other forms of psychotherapy are not developmentally appropriate. Play therapy provides children with a means of expressing their inner world and safely expressing emotionally significant experiences. The use of toys allows children to transfer anxieties, fears, fantasies, or guilt to objects. During play therapy children are less likely to be overwhelmed by their own actions. By role playing during play therapy, children can express frightening or traumatic experiences symbolically. This may allow them to cope with or adjust to problems. Play therapy allows children to consider new possibilities by outwardly expressing what has occurred inwardly. A major function of play therapy is to allow children to manage reality and provide opportunities for learning to cope.

Play therapy has been shown to be useful for guiding the development of school-readiness skills and promoting positive transitions. It also provides a method by which

Table *12.8*	Toys and Play Activities Appropriate for Various Ages	
Age	**Toys**	**Play Activities**
Birth to 6 months	Mobiles (suspended so that the child can see the objects), music boxes, stuffed toys (bright colors or black-and-white), rattles, unbreakable mirror hung where the child can look into it, crib play-gym	
6–12 months	Stacking rings, stacking cubes and other "nesting" toys, puppets, activity box, balls, soft blocks, vinyl books	
12 months to 2 years	Push and pull toys, surprise box, bath toys, toy telephone, bubbles, tape recorder, puzzles, toy figures, toy buildings (e.g., houses, garages, farm buildings)	
2–3 years	Large, brightly colored beads to string on a sturdy cord or pipe cleaner; push and pull toys; blocks with rounded corners; foam blocks (they float and are fun in the tub); picture books and books with minimal dialogue; realistic toys/props for pretend play; dolls; toy vehicles; large pegs and pegboards; toy nonhuman animals; large crayons; nesting cups or other items (kitchen pots will do); wagon; riding toys that move when the child moves; puzzles with pieces that insert into specific spaces; toy lawn mower or vacuum; containers with lids; plastic food; toy dishes and utensils; pots and pans; sponges; broom; play dough; nontoxic paint and fingerpaint	Movement games; riding on toys; using puzzles and pegboards; using scissors to make snips (in modeling clay or paper); chanting familiar songs; using musical instruments; using hands to explore art and sensory media; filling and dumping containers; piling blocks, then stacking and knocking them down; using realistic props for dramatic play; running; climbing; jumping; being messy
3–5 years	Those listed above; building blocks with more shapes; toy action figures or characters to use with blocks and cars; tricycles; simple matching games (e.g., shape or bingo-type games);	Those listed above; evolving sequences during dramatic play; making friends; sharing or taking turns; using tools to fix things; climbing; riding a tricycle; playing group games such as Duck, Duck, Goose;

continued

Age	Toys	Play Activities
	balls of various sizes to throw, catch, and kick; puzzles whose pieces fit together to make a picture; simple tools; dress-up clothes, aprons, and costumes; props for dramatic play (e.g., simple cameras and phones that no longer work)	throwing and catching balls; coloring and painting; cutting and gluing; stringing beads; assembling toys that fit together (e.g., plastic bricks); using puppets in play; learning how to roll out dough; using cookie cutters; using blocks to make a road; simple cooperative or board games; building three-dimensional block structures and acting out scenes with toy people and vehicles; making structures with other toys that fit together; creating a project or picture without adult supervision in the art area (can assemble the needed items and knows how to ask for desired items that are out of sight; can cut out a simple picture); seeking adult approval of a completed project; expanded dramatic play, including scenes from familiar stories and places visited; moving and dancing; playing games with small pieces or moving parts; performing simple experiments

Table 12.8   *Continued*

to familiarize children with school routines through play. Play therapy can occur in individual or group settings. It is also a useful mean of obtaining assessment data.

The Process of Play Therapy

Children spontaneously act out their feelings through play. Often, when adults attempt to encourage children to express their emotions, children have difficulty telling others how they feel or providing information about their experiences. During play therapy, children are more likely to reveal inner feelings by acting out their experiences through the toys and materials they choose. The process allows the therapist to experience, in a personal and interactive way, the inner dimensions of the child's world. During play therapy the therapist attempts to enter the child's world, to better understand the child's experiences and feelings. The child is not restricted to discussing what happened; rather, the child enacts experiences and feelings through play. Play therapy has been demonstrated to be an effective approach with regard to a variety of children's problems including, but not limited to, those listed in Figure 12.10.

Figure **12.10**   **Topics That May Be Appropriate for Play Therapy**

- abuse and neglect
- aggression and acting out
- attachment difficulties
- autism
- burn victims
- chronic illness
- deaf and physically challenged children
- dissociation and schizophrenia
- emotionally disturbed children
- enuresis and encopresis problems
- fear and anxiety

- grief
- hospitalization
- learning disabilities
- mentally challenged children
- reading difficulties
- selective mutism
- self-concept and self-esteem
- social adjustment problems
- speech difficulties
- traumatization
- withdrawn children

Toys and Materials

Although a fully equipped therapy playroom is ideal for allowing children to express themselves, it is not necessary. Play therapy can effectively occur in any relatively private area. During play therapy it is essential for children to have ready access to play materials selected for the purpose of encouraging expression. Toys should be selected that are likely to encourage children to explore real-life experiences. Therefore, mechanical or complex toys are generally not appropriate for effective play therapy. Appropriate play materials do not require the therapist's assistance to manipulate. During therapy, children should be allowed to be messy because open exploration should be encouraged. Figure 12.11 lists toys commonly available during play therapy sessions.

Figure **12.11**   **Play Therapy Toys**

- blocks
- paper and crayons
- clay
- puppets
- dollhouses
- dolls
- cars
- other manipulatives

Art Therapy

Art therapy can be considered a form of play therapy. It is most often used with children older than preschool age but may be useful for children as young as 3 to 4 years old who have social and emotional difficulties or have been battered or sexually abused (Di Leo, 1974). Art therapy encourages children to express their thoughts and experiences through pictures or other creative modes. It is often useful for children who have delayed communication skills and are too emotionally withdrawn to talk about their experiences. Art activities often provide a safe way of expressing feelings (Dalley et al., 1987).

Art therapists who work with children may have degrees in counseling, psychiatry, psychology, social work, teaching, nursing, child care, or art. Art therapists usually have a master's in art therapy or in education or psychology with a concentration in art. The American Art Therapy Association has created education and training guidelines for a master's in art therapy. Recommended course work for art therapists includes studio art, human growth and development, psychopathology, clinical methods, group and family dynamics, and the history of art therapy. To be certified by the American Art Therapy Association, a person must accumulate 1,000 hours of art therapy experience.

Art therapists often work with other professionals, including physicians, nurses, psychologists, social workers, educators, and occupational, physical, and recreational therapists. Art therapy is based on the philosophy that all children need a variety of modes of expression that will allow them to grow in a healthy way. That is, children have a right to become themselves and to deal with any conflicts they carry inside (Rubin, 1984; Salant, 1975; Wohl & Kaufman, 1985).

Recreational Therapy

Recreational therapy may also be used as a form of play therapy. Recreational therapists (therapeutic recreation specialists) provide treatment services and recreational activities for children with disabilities. They use arts and crafts, animals, sports, games, dance and movement, drama, music, field trips, and other activities during therapy. They maintain the physical, mental, and emotional well-being of those to whom they provide services.

Conclusions

The importance of play in the lives of young children, especially young children with disabilities, cannot be overemphasized. Young children live to play; play is their work. Play helps develop a positive self-concept. It allows and supports learning at a rate that is developmentally appropriate.

Play is natural and requires minimal props to interest children. Toys may be bought or homemade but should always be developmentally appropriate, to avoid frustrating or endangering the children using them. Whenever and wherever possible, it is helpful to display available toys so that children know their choices for play. Toys haphazardly thrown into a toy chest may be difficult to locate and parts may become separated, which may lead to frustration.

Although the word *play* implies fun, it also translates into learning and sometimes hard work within a special needs preschool program. Using structured and unstructured settings, the teaching staff may support, enhance, and expand each child's learning endeavors. Through these play experiences, the information presented and skills practiced become the learned behaviors necessary to appropriate development.

CHAPTER SUMMARY

- Play provides opportunities for children to develop speech and language, cognitive, motor, social-emotional, and self-help skills.

- Play skills develop in five major stages: solitary, onlooker, parallel, associative, and cooperative play.

- Children with disabilities often progress through stages of play at a slower rate than children without developmental delays.

- Classroom arrangement, types of play materials, and time available for play affect children's play.

- The classroom's major play spaces are block, house-dramatic, sensory, art, quiet, and music-movement.

- Children need ample play time, at school and home, that involves adults and other children.

- Children with developmental delays may benefit from specific modifications to play activities and the play environment.

- Adults may learn a great deal about children's abilities by observing their play and playing with them.

CHAPTER KEY TERMS

Jean Piaget
exploratory play
pretend play
solitary play
parallel play
associative play
cooperative play
sensorimotor play
onlooker stage
play-based assessment
block area
house and dramatic play area

sensory area
sensory table
art area
portable art kit
quiet area
music therapist
music therapy
science area
play therapy
art therapy
art therapist
recreational therapy

REVIEW QUESTIONS

1. How does play enhance each major area of development?

2. What are the major characteristics of the five major stages of play?

3. How may play be used to assess the developmental levels of preschool-age children?

4. What are the major areas of the classroom, and why is each important?

5. Why is play therapy potentially useful?

SUGGESTED STUDENT ACTIVITIES

1. Plan a sensory table activity. What materials did you choose for the table? How will this activity enhance development?

2. Develop a strategy for ending play time and beginning clean-up time. Will you use a song, timer, or game? Explain why your strategy would succeed and how it would help engage children in positive clean-up experiences.

3. Visit a regular and a special-needs preschool classroom. Observe similarities and differences in the children's play activities.

4. Look through a toy catalogue, go to a store, or search the Web, and select three toys for children ages 1 through 5 years. Explain why you selected each toy based on how it would enhance development.

5. Design a classroom layout that would be effective for young children with disabilities. Justify why you believe you design would be appropriate. Be sure you include a description of the system you could use to organize classroom materials.

6. Design an art activity for a child with fine-motor delays. What problems might this child encounter with art projects in general? How is your activity tailored to the child's needs? Include all the steps of the project and the needed supplies.

7. Imagine that this week's theme for your classroom is the season of spring. Use the Internet to find a spring-related project already designed for preschool children, and evaluate it. Is it clearly designed? Is it age-appropriate? Is it for individual, small, or large-group activities? How would you change it to make it appropriate for special-needs children if it is not already?

8. Draw floor plans for both the art area of a typical classroom and the art area of a classroom for children with special needs. List what has been modified and why. What have you added or removed? How will your design be an effective learning space for children with special needs?

9. Visit a preschool classroom during art time, and do a mock formal assessment log as if you were the teacher. You can either pick one child or make categories of general observations and assess different children across them. What did you notice overall?

Behavior Management 13

- Behavior management involves developing desirable behavior and eliminating undesirable behavior.

- The ultimate goal of behavior management is to help children develop strategies to manage their own behavior.

- A variety of effective behavior management techniques are appropriate for young children.

- When establishing reasonable expectations for children's behavior, adults must consider each child's developmental level.

- Children with developmental delays respond to behavior management techniques that are also appropriate for children without delays.

When children display challenging behaviors, it is a concern in most homes and class-rooms. When children with disabilities display challenging behaviors, dealing with these behaviors often becomes very complex. Earlier chapters discussed the special therapeutic needs of children with developmental delays. Willingness to participate in therapy and the ability to comply with requests from adults affect whether therapy interventions are effective. This chapter focuses on the importance of learning how to effectively manage children's behavior to help maximize their development (Bilmes, 2004; Crary, 1979).

Children with developmental delays have many of the same needs as most children at a particular developmental level. They often respond well to behavior management techniques that are useful for children without developmental delays. It is particularly important for those who work with children with disabilities to be slow to negatively judge children's behaviors. Their behaviors are often an expression of their uniqueness and attributes associated with a particular disability.

The Importance of Developing Desired Behavior

Chapter 12 emphasized the importance of play for enhancing all areas of children's development. During play situations, young children (with and without developmental delays) often have conflicts while interacting with other children (Guralnick, 1990; Sameroff, Seifer, & Zax, 1982). Usually the conflicts are mild and quickly resolved with minimal adult intervention. In some cases children routinely have difficulty getting along with peers, even with adult supervision and intervention.

Lack of ability to successfully interact with others limits learning opportunities and social interactions. For example, children who frequently act aggressively toward other children typically have fewer friends (Brandenburg, Friedman, & Silver, 1990; Mah, 2007; McEvoy, Odom, & McConnell, 1992). This results in children's being less likely to have the opportunity to engage in social interactions.

Inappropriate social interactions often result in children's being removed from the learning environment (Strain et al., 1992). For example, a teacher may tell a child who is bothering other children, "You are not ready for this activity." The child may be asked to leave or be led away from the group. When this occurs, the child is no longer benefiting from the learning experience. Clearly, this is not a positive outcome.

The ecological perspective emphasizes the need to create environments that enhance the likelihood of positive behaviors and healthy emotional development rather than focus on correcting negative behaviors (Bressanutti, Mahoney, & Sachs, 1992). A positive environment is designed to prevent the occurrence of problems as well as help resolve conflicts when they occur. In this type of environment the teacher's role is to provide support for the child who has had difficulty interacting successfully with other children during group activities, which allows the child to successfully participate in group activities.

Parents and teachers too frequently focus exclusively on developing intellectual skills and fail to acknowledge that social skills also are extremely important

(Butz et al., 2001; Guralnick, 1993). During the preschool years, acknowledging the importance of supporting social skills development is often more important than focusing on the development of specific intellectual skills.

Research indicates that children who fail to achieve a minimal level of social competency by age 6 years are more likely to have social interaction difficulties as adults. These difficulties include a greater likelihood of future mental health problems, marital adjustment difficulties, parenting competence problems, and even occupational adjustment difficulties (Baker, Brightman, Heifetz, & Murphy, 1990). Social competency includes the capacity to initiate, develop, and maintain satisfying relationships with others. During the early years, a child's social skills frequently do not appear to be under the child's conscious control (Blechman, 1985). Research results indicate that children who are not socially accepted because of aggressiveness are more likely to drop out of school and become delinquent (Cordisco & Laus, 1993).

Adults need to provide instruction, coaching, and modeling with regard to appropriate ways to interact with others. Young children frequently need help to break negative cycles of interaction patterns (Kaplan, 1991). Adults can help by making specific suggestions about ways to interact. For example, if a child is grabbing toys, the adult might say, "You should ask Jason to share. He does not like it when you grab toys from him." Or the adult might model sharing a toy with a child after seeing a child attempting to grab a toy from another child.

Most preschool environments focus on enhancing social interaction and desirable behavior while encouraging active exploration and interaction with adults, other children, and materials (Smith & Rivera, 1993). Teachers in such environments typically avoid highly structured, **teacher-directed activities**. They provide children with opportunities to select their own activities from a variety of opportunities. Teachers also avoid telling children what they must do and when they must do it. Within these environments, children are physically and mentally active and should not be expected to simply sit, watch, and be quiet for long periods (Cook, Tessier, & Klein, 1992).

Children often benefit from opportunities to work individually or in small, informal groups rather than in large groups in which teacher-directed instruction is often used. Children benefit from direct or hands-on exposure to objects relevant to their lives rather than primarily indirect exposure through workbooks, photocopied sheets, or flash cards (Zirpoli & Melloy, 1993). When children's needs are adequately met, they are less likely to misbehave.

Teachers should move among the children to facilitate their involvement with materials and one another. As they do so, teachers can offer suggestions, ask questions, or add more-complex material. They should not dominate the environment by telling children what to do; rather they should allow children to discover for themselves that there is more than one way to do things (Allen, 1992; Sainato & Carta, 1992).

Children learn best when they are involved in self-directed problem solving and experimentation and when they are elaborating on their own topics rather than topics predetermined by an adult (Kazdin, 1995). Rote memorization and drills should be avoided. Also, parents should be encouraged to follow these principles at home. When children are learning, they are more likely to choose appropriate rather than inappropriate behavior.

Modeling and encouraging desired behavior, redirecting to acceptable behavior, and setting clear limits often enhance children's self-control (Dinkmeyer, McKay, & Dinkmeyer, 1993). Teachers must adjust their expectations for children's behavior to match each child's developmental level. Teachers who spend much of the day enforcing rules, dealing with unacceptable behavior, requiring children to sit and be quiet, or intervening during disagreements likely need to modify classroom activities and rethink their expectations (Campbell, 1990; Kagan, Reznick, & Snidman, 1990).

It is often useful to provide children with opportunities to develop social skills, including cooperating, helping, sharing, showing affection, negotiating, and talking with others to solve interpersonal problems (Landau & Moore, 1991; Porter, 2003). Adults should talk about, model, and provide activities that encourage these behavior patterns. As prosocial behavior increases, negative behavior, including aggression, tends to decrease (Landau & Milich, 1990). Children who play alone or spend most of their time participating in teacher-directed activities likely will not have sufficient opportunities to acquire social skills (Ratcliff, 2001).

Teachers often need to help parents learn appropriate behavior management techniques. The way children act at home often directly relates to how they behave in other settings. In addition, parents who become overly frustrated with their children's behavior do not create an optimal environment for them (Schaefer & Millman, 1981). Adults need to clearly and consistently communicate behavioral expectations to children. Children easily become confused and frustrated when rules or expectations are not clear or are applied inconsistently.

When attempting to determine how to deal most effectively with children's challenging behaviors, adults should first ask several key questions:

1. Are we paying more attention to inappropriate than appropriate behaviors?
2. Are we being consistent with our expectations and reactions to children's challenging behaviors?
3. Are our behavioral expectations and the activities provided to children developmentally appropriate?

Clearly, it is most appropriate to pay more attention to children while they are behaving. It is crucial for adults to be consistent when dealing with behaviors, and all expectations must be developmentally appropriate (Lawry, Danko, & Strain, 1999; Zirpoli, 2004).

General Principles for Behavior Management

Nearly all children demonstrate behavioral problems from time to time. Although these problems may be relatively common, they are disruptive. However, teachers and parents should avoid attempting to control children's behavior (Crary, 1984). Control implies that someone else takes over and determines what occurs. Adults need to learn how to respect children and their ability to control their own behavior. When children are in control of their behavior, it may make them more receptive to learning experiences, whether at home or at school (Eisenberg, Lennon, & Roth, 1983; Sandall & Ostrosky, 1999; Zirpoli, 2004).

Respect for others is demonstrated through language and actions (Honig, 1985). Adults should tell children what they like about them. They should show children they are valued by giving them many smiles and hugs. Showing respect also includes taking the time to listen to what children have to say. When children feel respected, they are more likely to stay in control. However, even when children do not behave rationally or stay in control, they must be respected and loved.

Children respond more positively to being told what they should do than what they should not do. An adult would be bewildered if their boss said, "I don't want you to be lazy today." Adults not only prefer, but expect, to be told what needs to be done rather than warned what not to do. A statement such as "Today we should work together and complete this project" demonstrates positive expectations.

Whenever possible, children should be given choices rather than be told precisely what to do. However, adults must be careful not to overwhelm children by providing too many choices or giving them choices that are developmentally inappropriate (Factor & Schilmoeller, 1983). Saying, "If you want a snack, please come sit at the table," or "Would you like an apple or an orange?" is more appropriate than saying, "Sit down and eat your apple."

Children are likely to respond more positively to a comment such as "Today we are going to have fun sharing with our friends" than "Today we are not going to grab toys from our friends." Adults should avoid overloading children with negatives such as *No, Don't, Stop it, Quit that, Cut it out,* and *You can't.* Children gradually stop listening when there are too many No's in their lives. "No" messages discourage children; they may begin to feel negatively about themselves. Telling children what *not* to do also does not give them information about what they *should* be doing.

Children benefit from being reassured that they are worth loving and are capable of learning how to do new things. When children sense that other people value them, they are more likely to approach and persevere at tasks they find difficult (McGinnis & Goldstein, 1990). When children sense adults do not like them or think they cannot succeed, children are more likely to resist participating, misbehave, or fail when they try.

When children are unsuccessful, they may come to fear comments such as "That was too hard for you" or "Can't you do anything right?" These messages tell children that they are not expected to succeed. Messages such as "This is a really hard puzzle. Let's work on it together" encourage children to attempt challenging tasks (Wyckoff & Unell, 1984).

Adults should never attack children's personal worth by making statements such as "I should have known you'd misbehave." Comments that condemn or compare, such as "You can't do that; it's too hard for you" and "Why can't you be more like your sister?" damage children's self-esteem (Wagonseller & McDowell, 1979).

When children misbehave, adults often assume their behavior must be managed or changed. This may be true in some cases, but in many cases it may be necessary to change the environment rather than the children (Crary, 1979).

For example, children may be misbehaving because they are not developmentally ready to be left to play independently and need more adult guidance. Or they may be misbehaving because the toys they are playing with are developmentally inappropriate or there are too few play materials. In these cases the environment needs to be modified.

Adults may modify their own expectations. Some children intentionally misbehave to get attention. Different children need different levels of attention. Frequently, children with disabilities require extra attention because they find it more difficult to succeed (Baumrind, 1977). They are likely to respond in ways, positive or negative, that help ensure that people will acknowledge them. It is important for adults to ensure they provide children with the optimal level of attention each needs to thrive.

Too often, adults leave children in situations in which the children have difficulty due to inadequate adult supervision. Adults often expect more self-control and mature behavior from children than they can independently achieve. For example, if a child is constantly taking cookies from a cookie jar, the cookie jar should be put out of sight and reach. If children fight over a toy day after day, the toy should be removed. Although attempting to reason with children is admirable, doing so is likely to have limited effect on children younger than 4 years old.

When adults acknowledge each child's unique needs, they work with, rather than against, each child. For example, a child who has difficulty sitting for long periods should not be expected to sit quietly for a 10-minute story. Standing back, observing children, and planning acceptable ways to accomplish certain goals is generally more successful than using a predetermined formula that states how to interact with children (Izard & Malatesta, 1987). Consistency among care providers is also crucial. When care providers respond in different ways or respond inconsistently, children cannot learn what is and is not acceptable for efficiently accomplishing goals.

Teachers must establish appropriate behavioral expectations for each individual child. They need to be certain that they are not requiring children to engage in activities they are not mature enough to handle. Teachers should carefully analyze the classroom activities schedule, room layout, and developmental levels of activities to determine whether these factors are contributing to management problems (Linder, 1983). For example, an overcrowded classroom, too few toys, or tasks that are too difficult or easy may lead to frustration, which may then result in aggression.

Teachers must consistently deal with behavior problems. They must take responsibility for supervising children, anticipating problems, and, whenever possible, preventing them from occurring (Bailey & Wolery, 1984). Teachers may benefit from help from a consultant (e.g., a social worker or psychologist), who is less emotionally involved, in solving behavior problems. Figure 13.1 lists suggestions that may facilitate positive classroom interactions.

At times, adults attempt to modify, limit, or control children's behavior to help ensure their safety. Behavioral expectations should be communicated clearly, calmly, and consistently. It is important for adults to realize that children see the world differently than they do. Things that adults view as obviously unsafe often do not appear unsafe to children (Berkeley & Ludlow, 1989).

For example, adults frequently assume that because children are taught not to run inside one building, they know the rule and they know better than to run indoors anywhere. Children, however, often do not know what adults expect of them. They frequently do not generalize from one situation to another (Bredekamp,

Figure **13.1**   **Strategies for Encouraging Positive Classroom Interactions**

- Keep classrooms neat and organized.
- Create attractive and colorful classrooms.
- Create play centers.
- Establish a special area for disruptive children.
- Begin activities promptly.
- Plan ahead, and develop routines.
- Use positive interaction styles.
- Learn from experience, and be willing to change.
- Ignore undesirable behavior whenever possible.
- Reinforce desirable behavior.
- Use nonverbal signals to indicate that inappropriate behavior must stop.
- Move close to the child who is misbehaving.
- Remove tempting objects that children fight over.
- Follow through on your warnings.
- Discipline privately whenever possible.
- Use time out but not excessively.
- Tell children, "Stop."

1987). In addition, adults often inconsistently respond to children's behavior. For example, they may allow children to run down hallways some days but not others. In fact, some adults allow running in their homes, and others do not.

Rules can help children control impulsive behavior. However, too many rules lead to their being forgotten and broken (Carta, Schwartz, Atwater, & McConnell, 1991). Rules should be reasonable, enforceable, and appropriate for children's age, health, and developmental level. It is unreasonable to tell a child to sit on a chair until they apologize; the child may never apologize. Rather than saying, "Don't throw the blocks," an adult can tell a child, "Build something with the blocks, or it will be time to put them away." If the child throws a block after being told this, the blocks should be put away.

Adults should not overload children with many rules. Ideally, there should be no more than four or five classroom rules. These rules should be easy to understand and focus on what children should do rather than on what they should not do (Dunst, 1985). For example, a rule should be stated as "Walk in the building" rather than "No running in the building."

When children misbehave, it is generally best to focus on teaching them desired behavior rather than on punishment (applying a negative consequence or penalty), which focuses on negative behavior (Dunst, 1986). There are times when punishment may be necessary, but punishing children does not teach them proper behavior. Punishment should not model aggressive behavior, such as yelling, or put the child at physical or emotional risk (Wicks-Nelson & Israel, 1991). When used, punishment should be a logical consequence. For example, if a child throws a block, the child should be told that they must leave the block area for the remainder of free play. It is unethical and illegal (in most cases) for teachers to use aversive behavior management techniques (e.g., spanking, hitting).

Behavior management includes what is modeled to the child. Adults need to make sure they are modeling appropriate behavior (Garwood, 1983). Adults should ask themselves whether they would want a child to repeat their own actions and language.

It is best to manage the classroom by creating a positive learning environment that encourages desirable behavior. One major goal of most preschool and day care programs is to help children acquire socially appropriate behavior (Parker & Asher, 1987). Development of highly effective behavior management takes considerable time and reflection. In fact, it initially takes more time to manage behavior than to discipline or punish children. Punishment indicates only types of behavior that adults find unacceptable. Behavior control also tends to emphasize negative aspects of behavior and is generally used after an undesirable behavior has occurred. It typically includes use of negative comments or punishments and does little to support or encourage desired behavior (Fisher, Hand, Watson, VanParys, & Tucker, 1984). When controlling behavior, adults often attempt to change many different types of negative behavior at once. Doing so is unreasonable.

However, it may be difficult to agree on which types of behavior warrant intervention. The first step to effective behavior management is to determine which behavior should be focused on first. Not all behaviors can be managed at one time.

Determining Which Behavior to Attempt to Modify

Even though it is inappropriate to "go to war" with children, the analogy of "picking battles worth fighting" is useful. Adults should avoid trying to fit children into an ideal mold. It will not work, and a child's individuality may be lost. There are several issues to consider when determining which behavior should be the focus of behavior management. First, it is necessary to collect information as to how often the behavior occurs and evaluate its intensity and duration (Rosenberg, Wilson, Maheady, & Sindelar, 1992). If children easily become angry, and with such intensity that they injure themselves or others, then either the behavior or the environment needs modification. See Figure 13.2 for guidelines for determining which behavior may need modification.

Adults should avoid deciding which behavior must be changed when they are tired or angry (Becker, 1990). A particular behavior may be "the straw that broke the camel's back" rather than a major or consistent concern. Also, behavior should not be modified merely because adults are concerned about what others may think.

Figure 13.2   **Behavior That Warrants Intervention**

Behavior that

- demands a disproportionate amount of time and attention,
- disrupts other children and prevents learning from occurring,
- becomes more severe,
- is more typical of much younger children,
- leads to a negative self-image,
- is negatively perceived by classmates, or
- endangers that child or others.

For instance, a teacher should not decide that all children should be made to sit in a chair during circle time (when children are together in a large group activity) simply because it is expected in another teacher's classroom (Anderson, Hodson, & Jones, 1975). Adults often must be willing to change their own behavior while attempting to modify a child's behavior. For example, if adults tell children that yelling is not allowed, then the adults must also not yell. Once an adult has decided which behavior to attempt to manage, there are several steps that should be taken.

Behavior Management Techniques

To successfully manage behavior, it is first necessary to state specifically what the child should be doing (Christopherson, 1982). For example, saying to children, "Be nice," is too vague. Children need to be told what "nice" means and be given specific directions such as, "You must share the blocks with Chris." At the same time such statements should be modeled.

Several specific techniques are used to manage behavior. Several of the most common are discussed below, including reinforcement, redirection, time out, extinction, and punishment. Reinforcement and redirection should be used whenever possible and may reduce the need to use the other techniques (Miller, 1980).

Reinforcement

One goal of most teachers and parents is to help children acquire the behaviors they need to function effectively day to day. Use of **rewards** (**reinforcers**) often helps to increase appropriate behavior (Miller, 1980). Reinforcers should be given after children behave in desired ways. For example, when children remember to put away their toys, they earn stickers. Adults often praise (reinforce) children for sharing their toys. Children usually enjoy receiving **reinforcements** in the form of a reward such as money, gold stars, blue ribbons, or trophies. A reward is something considered nice or valuable (Patterson, 1990).

Not all rewards reinforce all behavior. A reinforcer is a consequence that follows a behavior and increases the chances of that behavior's recurring (Anderson et al., 1975). For example, if children are given a small snack for spending 5 minutes putting away their toys, they are likely to help put away their toys in the future. The snack is a reinforcer. If, however, children are given a small snack only if they spend an hour cleaning, they may not be willing to help in the future. The reward was the same in both cases. Whereas the snack was a sufficient reinforcer for the 5 minutes of picking up toys, it was not a sufficient reinforcer for working an entire hour.

Reinforcers are usually thought of as nice things, but a reinforcer may be any consequence, such as an event or object, that increases the behavior it follows (Harter, 1978). A reinforcer does not need to be something pleasant, healthy, or valuable (although most are). It is something that increases the number of times a behavior occurs. For example, researchers have found that nagging children for not doing their work actually increases (reinforces) the chances of their not working in the future (Harter & Zigler, 1974). In this case nagging, certainly considered unpleasant, is a reinforcer for not working.

Just as children are different, different things reinforce them. Also, for any one person what reinforces one behavior may not reinforce another behavior (Ickes & Kidd, 1976). When selecting useful reinforcers, it is helpful to consider the wide array of rewards that could be used, choose one, and then find out if the reward really reinforces a specific behavior of a specific child. Table 13.1 lists rewards that teachers and parents often use.

Table 13.1   *Commonly Used Rewards*

Verbal Approval and Praise	Nonverbal Approval	Physical Contact	Pleasurable Activities	Material Objects	Tokens
"Thanks so much for helping me."	Smiling	Hugging	Watching a video	Toys	Stars or points on a chart
"That's right!"	Nodding	Touching	Free time	Trinkets	Marks on an index card
"I really like the way you did that."	Clapping hands	Shaking hands	Helping the teacher	Art materials	Play money
"That's a good job of painting."	Looking interested	Holding Patting	Listening to tapes or CDs	Pennies	Poker chips
"You're such a hard worker."	Laughing	Sitting on lap	Hearing a special story	Snacks Books	
"Wow, you've got a good memory!"	Winking		Being first in line	Games	
"You're playing so nicely together."	Looking surprised		Show and tell	Stickers	
"Tell me about your picture."			Sensory play		

If teachers or parents are considering using material rewards (things rather than praise or hugs), it is often helpful to ask children what they want for a reward. If children cannot clearly communicate their preferences, observing them often provides clues about the types of objects they prefer (Heshusius, 1986). For example, if a child is constantly asking for stickers, it is likely that using stickers as rewards will reinforce that child's behavior.

However, before attempting to modify behavior using reinforcement, it is necessary to determine the number of times the behavior selected to be modified occurs over several days (Lepper, 1981). After the number of times that the behavior occurs has been recorded, rewarding the desired behavior may begin. Rewards should be given immediately after each occurrence of the desired behavior. The adult should keep a record of the number of times a behavior occurs while reinforcements are given. If the frequency of the desired behavior increases after reward, the reward is a reinforcer (Lovaas, 1987). Box 13.1 provides an example of the use of rewards.

Adults need to determine whether **primary** or **secondary reinforcers** are most appropriate (Miyake, Campos, Kagan, & Bradshaw, 1986). Primary reinforcers are

Box 13.1 Jesse

Four-year-old Jesse is having difficulty stacking blocks. For 14 days, Jesse's teacher recorded the number of times that Jesse stacked blocks during free play. She discovered that Jesse rarely played with blocks and never attempted to stack them. Because she wanted Jesse to learn how to stack blocks, the teacher looked for possible reinforcers. Knowing that Jesse loves stickers, she asked him if he wanted a chance to earn some stickers. Jesse nodded. The teacher then told him that if he played in the block area, he could select a sticker to take home. Jesse immediately went to the block area, sat down to play, and asked for a sticker.

The next day the teacher reminded Jesse about the stickers, and he immediately went to play in the block area. Even though Jesse was now playing in the block area, he was not stacking blocks. He made roads with the blocks and played with cars on the "roads." The teacher modified the plan and told Jesse, "I'll give you two stickers if you stack blocks." She demonstrated putting one block on top of another.

The following day, Jesse began lining up blocks. The teacher sat down beside him and modeled stacking blocks. She reminded Jesse about earning stickers for stacking blocks. She walked to her desk, took the table of stickers, returned, and sat beside Jesse. He looked at the stickers and began to stack blocks. The teacher held out the table and Jesse chose two stickers. The teacher said, "I knew you could do it!" Over the next few days, Jesse's teacher continued to reward his stacking blocks. Three weeks after the start of behavior modification, Jesse no longer requested stickers for this type of play.

In Jesse's case, it appears that stickers were reinforcing. However, the stickers alone did not increase block stacking: the teacher also modeled the desired behavior. It is possible that praise or attention would have adequately reinforced Jesse and he would not have needed the primary reinforcer of stickers.

things that people need to live and grow physically and emotionally. Food, air, shelter, sleep, food, water, and physical contact are primary reinforcers. It is generally unethical to fail to provide children with the things they need to remain physically and emotionally healthy. For example, keeping children hungry so that food can be used as a reinforcer is unethical.

Secondary reinforcers, sometimes called conditioned reinforcers, have been paired with primary reinforcers to acquire their reinforcing value. Praise, tokens, and stickers are secondary reinforcers. Praise is a very useful secondary reinforcer because it is easy to give, and the supply is endless. Some children do not initially find praise reinforcing, but if it is initially paired with a primary reinforcer, it may become reinforcing, and the primary reinforcer may gradually be reduced (Peters, Neisworth, & Yawkey, 1985). Box 13.2 illustrates the use of primary and secondary reinforcers.

Nearly anything may become a secondary reinforcer (Whitman, 1990). For instance, tokens or money may be exchanged for other forms of reinforcement. For example, a child may earn enough tokens to be allowed to watch a video. A token system may be used almost anywhere. Stickers, points, or plastic chips may be earned when children engage in a specified behavior. These tokens may then be traded for a variety of things or activities that reinforce a child's behavior. See Figure 13.3 for an example of a token reward system.

The relationship between a reward and behavior is called a contingency. Reinforcers are given to increase the likelihood of the desired behavior (Whitman, 1990). For example, a teacher wanted to increase the time that a child spent cutting with scissors. For every 60 seconds of cutting, the teacher gave the child a sticker. The teacher also gave the child a sticker when the teacher thought the child was about to start cutting because the teacher hoped that the sticker would encourage the child to try harder. The amount of time that the child spent cutting did not increase. Although the teacher was consistent about reinforcing the cutting, the teacher also gave the

Box 13.2 *Aaron*

During story time, 4-year-old Aaron never sat quietly for more than a few seconds. After keeping a record of Aaron's behavior during story time for one week, his teacher found that Aaron sat quietly, on average, 30 seconds at a time. The teacher decided to give Aaron his favorite snack, raisins. She gave him one raisin every 30 seconds that he sat quietly. After two weeks of this consistent reinforcement, Aaron could sit quietly throughout story time, which lasted about 10 minutes.

Next week the teacher gave Aaron a raisin only every minute but patted him on the shoulder and smiled at him every 30 seconds that he sat quietly. The number of raisins was gradually reduced while the patting and smiling continued. Aaron continued to be able to sit quietly for circle time. The patting and smiling had become secondary reinforcers, replacing the need for raisins (a primary reinforcer). Over time the patting and smiling also were reduced, as Aaron continued to be more attentive during an ever-wider variety of activities.

Figure **13.3**   **Tokens and Rewards**

child reinforcement when they were *not* cutting. This provided the child with inconsistent reinforcement. To make the reinforcement effective, the teacher must reinforce only the cutting.

Before implementing a reinforcement program, it should be explained to the child. The child should be told which behavior is desired and the behavior's consequences (Lovaas, 1987). At the beginning of each day, or perhaps more frequently, the child should be reminded of the contingencies. Then each time the behavior is reinforced, the contingency should be stated. For example, every time Steven hangs up his jacket, he receives a sticker. As the teacher gives him a sticker, the teacher says, "I am giving you this sticker because you remembered to hang up your coat." The teacher might also add, "It makes me happy when you remember to hang up your coat." Children should be told about the reinforcement plan, even when adults do not believe they fully understand what they are being told. Often children understand more than adults realize. Figure 13.4 lists actions that help ensure reinforcements will be effective.

Adults should avoid power struggles with children. Using an if-then technique may help avoid them. For example, saying, "If you finish putting the blocks away, then we will have a snack," may help modify a certain type of behavior by establishing a reinforcement contingency. This method requires children to behave appropriately before another activity (reinforcement) may begin. It provides logical and positive consequences rather than negative ones. Figure 13.5 illustrates use of a contingency statement.

Figure 13.4 **Effective Use of Reinforcement**

- Give the reinforcer immediately after the desired behavior.
- Be consistent; reinforce the behavior every time it occurs.
- Be pleasant when presenting the reinforcer.
- Clearly tell the child why the reinforcement is being given.
- Do not try to reinforce and reprimand at the same time; do not provide a reinforcement while stating how the behavior might be improved.

Although using reinforcement is generally preferred to other behavior management techniques, other methods may be necessary. Reinforcements are used only to develop desired behavior. At times the goal of behavior management is to eliminate undesirable behavior. Redirection, time out, extinction, and punishment may be useful techniques when children misbehave (Cordisco & Laus, 1993).

Redirection

Redirection involves orienting children to appropriate, rather than inappropriate, behavior (Rogers & DeLalla, 1991). The focus is on ignoring undesirable behavior while directing children toward more-desirable behavior. For example, a child who

Figure 13.5 **Use of a Contingency Statement**

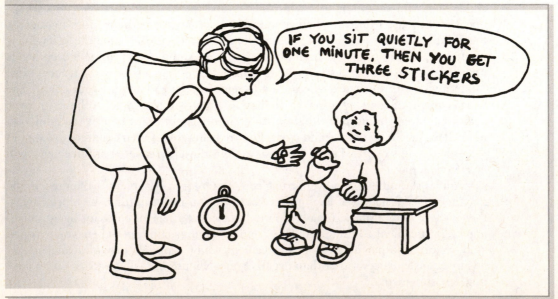

begins to throw sand out of a sand table should be encouraged to play somewhere else or to play with the sand in a more appropriate way. During redirection the teacher does *not* reprimand the child but asks or tells the child to find a new place to play or a new way to play by saying something such as "You've played a long time in the sand box. Please go play on the slide."

Time Out

Time out is similar to redirection. It involves removing children from situations in which they are having difficulty controlling themselves. It is designed to provide children with an opportunity to regain control as well as to help prevent them from disrupting others. It temporarily removes them from interactions with others.

Time out restricts activities and contacts for a short time. It is undesirable because children are removed from playing with toys, engaging in activities, and interacting with others. Adults must avoid interacting with children when they are in time out, because adult attention may be rewarding.

Time out should be used as a calming device rather than as punishment (Strain, Kohler, Storey, & Danko, 1994). For children younger than 6 years old, about a minute for each year of age is generally a reasonable duration for time out. For example, time out should last a maximum of 4 minutes for most 4-year-olds. For children who are very young or who have attention deficit hyperactivity disorder (ADHD), are autistic, or have other developmental delays, using a minute or less may be more appropriate (Betz, 1994; Olson, 1989).

The time-out spot should be located in an uninteresting place where the child cannot interact with others. A chair facing a blank wall is appropriate for a time-out location. Whenever possible, a consistent location should be used for time out. When adults place children in time out, they should limit discussion of the event and avoid emotional reactions (Kaplan, 1991). Children should be told why they are being sent to time out (contingency statement). For example, a teacher might say, "Beth, you need to go sit in the time-out area for 2 minutes because you hit John." Once time out is over (the time has passed), there should be limited discussion about the incident. The teacher in the example might state, "Remember you were in time out for hitting John. Now it is time to go play. I know you can play nicely. Go have fun." It is important not to overuse the time out.

A teacher assists a young child who is in time out after breaking a classroom rule.

Extinction

Extinction is a nonactive way of discouraging undesirable behavior. Children have a tremendous desire to demonstrate their power, ability, and influence. When an adult becomes upset with a child's actions (e.g., begins to cry), the child's goal of gaining control is accomplished. For example, when a child cries for a snack, it is generally most appropriate to ignore the child. Ignoring undesirable behavior is referred to as "extinction" (Kaplan, 1991). Once the child has calmed down (in this case, stopped crying), it is appropriate to attend to the child. If it is a reasonable time to have a snack, the child can be prompted to appropriately ask for a snack (without crying). Once this occurs, it is appropriate to give the child a snack. Giving children a snack when they are crying would reinforce the negative behavior (Polloway & Patton, 1993).

Using extinction involves ignoring undesirable behavior when it occurs. Extinction may be useful when trying to eliminate behavior such as whining. For example, the child who whines should be told that whining is unacceptable and that in the future it will be ignored. At the beginning of each day, the child should be reminded that whining will be ignored. Then if the child whines, this behavior should be ignored. It would not be appropriate to tell the child to stop whining. This type of negative attention likely would reinforce whining. When the child does not whine, they should be told something such as, "I like it when you ask for things in such a nice way."

It is not always easy or safe to ignore undesirable behavior. Unfortunately, some behaviors cannot be successfully managed using reinforcement, redirection, time out, or extinction. In some cases it is necessary to use punishment.

Punishment

Dangerous behavior may require **punishment.** Punishment is a negative consequence that follows undesirable behavior (Alberto & Troutman, 1990). Punishment involves adding something negative to a child's environment, such as requiring the child to clean up after throwing a cup filled with juice. In this case the type of punishment is a logical consequence. Punishment may also involve a penalty, taking something positive away. For example, removing a toy that a child used to injure another child would be a penalty.

When punishment is necessary, a penalty is generally the preferred form (Rosenberg, O'Shea, & O'Shea, 1991). An example of a time to use a penalty would be when Sally grabs another toy from a child. A logical penalty is that Sally not be allowed to play with the toy she took from the other child. This penalty would be more effective than scolding or yelling. Use of penalties does not model angry or aggressive behavior (Wyckoff, & Unell, 1984).

Project SUCCEED

Project SUCCEED (Supporting and Understanding Challenging Children's Educational and Emotional Development) is a model research project funded by a U.S. Department of Education, Office of Special Education Programs grant. The project was developed to help family members and Head Start staff deal with children's

Figure 13.6 **Project SUCCEED Goals**

- Increase family members' and teachers' skills and confidence in helping children with challenging behaviors.
- Reduce family members' and teachers' stress caused by children's challenging behaviors.
- Improve the home and classroom environments.
- Reduce children's problem behaviors while increasing their social, cognitive, and emotional competencies.
- Decrease the incidence of kindergarten failure.
- Increase families' sense of empowerment and ability to advocate for their children.
- Increase community partners' involvement in addressing children's mental health needs.

behavior problems. SUCCEED is based on four key principles: 1) family members and teachers need to be actively involved in developing programs, and family values need to be considered when determining ways to most effectively work with children, 2) children's unique characteristics and challenging behaviors should be holistically assessed and evaluated within each child's environmental context, 3) children with behavioral problems need to receive support to help them modify these behaviors so that they can remain within inclusion settings, and 4) both families and staff must receive support and work collaboratively to help children succeed.

Project SUCCEED provides training focusing on methods to deal with children's challenging behaviors in a 12-session parent and teacher training program. It also provides coaching of family members and teachers. Outcome data indicate that children whose parents and teachers participated in SUCCEED are more likely to experience positive transition to kindergarten. Figure 13.6 lists the primary goals of Project SUCCEED.

Parents' and teachers' evaluations of the program were very positive. They reported that after taking the course they were well or very well prepared to deal with children's challenging behaviors. Based on the outcomes of this model program, it appears that investing in more such programs is warranted.

Dealing with Common Childhood Problems

Young children display a wide variety of behavior problems. Several of the most common are discussed below.

Temper Tantrums

A **temper tantrum** is a child's way of expressing anger or gaining attention. Behavior displayed during tantrums includes crying, yelling, biting, hitting, and kicking. Young children display a tantrum because they cannot verbally express their feelings. Young children with language delays are more prone to throwing tantrums, likely due to their limited ability to communicate (Wagonseller & McDowell, 1979). Children with motor delays are likely to have tantrums because they have difficulty performing tasks they would like to do or observe other children doing (Goodman, 1992).

Tantrums are often responses to frustrating situations, including adult-imposed limits, lack of time to complete tasks, or another child's upsetting actions (e.g., taking away a toy) (Bagnato & Neisworth, 1991). Tantrums are not considered abnormal unless they frequently occur or last for extended periods. Adults should avoid over-reacting to temper tantrums. When a tantrum appears likely, redirection may prevent it or lessen its intensity (Crary, 1979). Methods used to reduce the likelihood of tantrums include avoiding saying "No."

Removing objects that contribute to tantrums and placing them out of a child's sight and reach also help reduce tantrums. Allowing children to make choices and providing them with advanced warning for impending transitions also are helpful (Blechman, 1985). For example, a child who often throws a tantrum when asked to help clean up could be told, "It will be time to put away the toys in 5 minutes. Let's set the timer. After we clean up, we'll have a snack." In this case providing advance warning that it will soon be time to end play helps prepare the child, and the anticipation of having a snack means that the child has something to look forward to after clean-up.

Once a tantrum has begun, it is best to ignore it (use extinction). During tantrums, children may need to be moved to a safe spot. This reduces their chances of being hurt. When children appear to be out of control, it may be necessary to firmly hold them for a few minutes to help them regain control and to prevent them from hurting themselves or someone else (Dreikurs & Cassel, 1972).

Adults should not yield to the unmet demands that lead to a tantrum. For example, if a child's tantrum started because they were not allowed to have another cookie, they should not be given a cookie during or after the tantrum. Giving the child a cookie would likely reinforce their tantrums—that is, result in more tantrums in the future. After the tantrum is over, the child often needs to be comforted because the loss of control may be frightening or embarrassing. Once the tantrum is over, adults should not focus on the tantrum (Blechman, 1985). An adult might say, "You were very upset. I'm glad that you're feeling better," and then continue with the regular activities.

Most children do not have frequent or very intense tantrums, or tantrums that result in aggression toward self or others. In the case of children who do have such tantrums, seeking professional intervention is warranted (Thurman & Widerstrom, 1990).

Aggression

Aggression refers to behavior that results in injury or discomfort to another person and includes hitting, name calling, yelling, and damage to property (Saarni & Crowley, 1990). Dealing with aggression at home or school is one of the most difficult challenges adults encounter. It is difficult not to feel anger toward children who hurt others. It is also difficult not to worry that others will reject a child who behaves aggressively (Barkley et al., 2000; Greenberg, Speltz, DeKlyen, & Jones, 2001).

Acts that result in injury but are unintentional are not classified as aggression (Shelton et al., 2000; Sherburne, Utley, McConnell, & Gannon, 1988). Children playing closely together are likely to experience situations in which a child accidentally gets hurt. Unfortunately, most young children often have difficulty distinguishing between intentional and unintentional acts. For example, a child who is accidentally hit by a ball thrown by another child may respond by hitting that child. Adults should help children learn to interpret these situations by saying something such as, "Joey didn't mean to hit you with the ball. He was playing catch, and the ball hit you." When frequent accidents occur, adults likely need to supervise children more carefully and find ways to modify the environment to minimize unintentional injuries.

Sometimes children are aggressive (Sherburne et al., 1988). For example, a child may push another child aside to be the next to go up the steps on the slide. Adults often need to help children develop more-appropriate methods to obtain their goals. For example, an adult could respond to the slide scenario by saying, "You need to wait your turn to use the slide." This could be followed by the adult's imposing a logical consequence and saying, "Pushing can hurt someone. Since you did not wait your turn, you may not use the slide."

Aggression is more likely to occur when children are frustrated. Frustration occurs for many reasons, including children's being unable to obtain a desired goal, inadequately supervised, involved in activities that are too difficult for them, asked to wait for extended periods of time, or not allowed to participate in activities; play areas' being overcrowded; and there being insufficient toys, materials, or equipment (Strain et al., 1992).

Frustrated children react in various ways. Some act aggressively, have temper tantrums, or cry; others become very sad, withdrawn, or shy. A child who acts aggressively needs reassurance that although adults do not approve of aggressive behavior, they still like the child (Miller & Sperry, 1987).

When confronted with a frustrating situation, children often find comfort in adults' comments that address their feelings. For example, an adult might say, "I can tell you're feeling sad or angry because Shelly is playing with the toy that you wanted to play with. Sometimes when I feel sad or angry, I take a walk. Would you like to take a walk with me?" In this example the adult acknowledges the child's feelings and suggests a positive response (a form of redirection) rather than hitting or having a tantrum.

Most aggression is in immediate response to some event. For example, Katie hit Jenny because Jenny grabbed her ball. Sometimes children behave aggressively when there seems to be no logical reason for the aggression (Saarni, 1984). For example, Katie hit Jenny during circle time because Jenny grabbed a toy car from Katie during free play time.

Children who are frequently aggressive should be encouraged to tell people what they need by saying something like "Don't take my car!" Adults need to allow children to say "No." Saying "No" is a much better response than physical aggression. Some adults interpret saying "No" as being defiant, bossy, or unreasonable. When adults hear a child say, "No," to another child, they should intervene and say something like "Claire, I know you really like this car. You have been playing with it for a long time. In 5 minutes you will let Beth have a turn. Let's set the timer together."

When aggressive acts occur, adults should not expect young children to accurately explain what happened or who was at fault. When children are asked things like "Did you hurt Jill?" they are unlikely to readily admit that they were at fault or that they hurt another child (Saarni, 1985). When adults do not directly observe events that result in children's being upset, they need to resist the temptation to guess what happened because frequently children who have behaved aggressively in the past are automatically blamed for causing conflicts (Saarni & Crowley, 1990).

When adults do not see aggression, it is best that they remind all children involved that they should not hurt one another. Children might also be told, "If you're not happy playing together, it may be better if you don't play together." After this comment, children may indicate that they will try to get along so that they can continue to play together, or they may say that they no longer wish to play together. It is an adult's responsibility to monitor children closely. If conflicts continue, the children may need to be separated, or the environment may need to be changed (e.g., it may be necessary to remove the object that the children were fighting over) (Brown, 2003; Strayer, 1986).

Whining

Whining poses no immediate threat to anyone but quickly becomes intolerable to most people. There are many reasons why children whine. They whine to gain attention, when they are overtired, or in response to a stressful event, such as the birth of a sibling or going to a new school (Baker et al., 1990). With time, most children stop whining without systematic behavior modification (Lee & Axelrod, 2005; Becker, 1990).

Generally, the best way to help children learn not to whine is to avoid reinforcing whining (i.e., use extinction) and teach (usually model) more-pleasant ways to communicate (Baker et al., 1990). When children come to believe that the only way to gain attention or get what they want is to whine, they are more likely to continue whining. Sometimes adults become so busy that they do not pay attention to children unless they whine. The quickest and easiest way to reduce a child's tendency to whine is to pay attention to things the child says without whining.

Children who frequently whine likely have developed a habit of doing so (Kauffman, 1989). Habits are difficult to break. If children have developed the habit of whining, it will need to be replaced with the new habit of *not* whining. Adults should not make comments such as "Whining is for babies." Rather, to modify this habit, an adult might say, "Whining makes me sad. When you whine, I'm not going to listen. But when you don't whine, I'll listen to you." Children should be expected to talk without whining. If whining continues, it should be ignored (i.e., extinction should be used) and non-whining speech should be reinforced. Children should not be held, cuddled, touched, or looked at while they are whining. At times it may be necessary for adults to walk away from a whining child (i.e., impose a form of time out by leaving the child's space) (Campbell, 1990).

Overdependency

Overdependency involves intensely seeking help, affection, or attention from another person, which interferes with the ability to learn. Some level of dependency is normal. In contrast, overdependency prevents children from doing things they are capable of doing for themselves. Overdependency may result in children's being unable to function without adult support (Pader, 1981). Overdependent children often whine and cry and may refuse to do things they are capable of doing. They constantly seek an adult's assistance and physical proximity (nearness) to the adult and say things such as "Watch me," "Talk to me," and "Look at what I made."

Some children attempt to control their environment by acting overdependent or baby-like because this behavior gains adults' attention (Gargiulo, 1985). Many adults feel a sense of sadness as children grow up and unintentionally reinforce immature, overdependent behavior. They may overprotect children to keep them from harm. At times adults reinforce overdependence because they feel guilty for not paying enough attention to children (Blechman, 1985).

Adults can help prevent overdependence by allowing and encouraging children to make choices, such as what to eat, wear, and play. Adults should avoid dominating children by imposing too many rules or by nagging. These actions may result in children's being obedient but overdependent. As emphasized in Chapter 11, adults also should avoid doing things for children that they can do for themselves (Seligman & Darling, 1989).

Once an adult has made a reasonable request such as "Go get your coat and put it on," adults should not help children if they are capable of independently performing the task. Whenever children act overdependent, adults should encourage them to practice their independence by saying, "You can do this yourself." Adults should remind children how good it feels when tasks are completed independently by making comments like "Wow! You did it yourself!" When adults gradually increase expectations for more-independent behavior, most children adjust to the expectations (Hussey-Gardner, 1992).

Intense separation anxiety is a form of overly dependent behavior. This occurs when children become very upset during separation from their parents or other significant people such as teachers, siblings, and friends. It is normal for children to act nervous, be clingy, or regress to more infantile behavior when adjusting to new school settings, new homes, new babies, or other stressful events (Hussey-Gardner, 1992).

It is not normal for children to cry for an excessively long time after separation. To help reduce separation anxiety, adults may comfort children by allowing them to bring something special, such as a favorite toy to hold on to, during the separation process. Children often are less anxious about separation when teachers greet them as they arrive at school or day care and help them select what to do from a variety of potentially enjoyable activities (Blechman, 1985).

Fears

There are a number of common childhood fears, most of which are *not* of major concern. However, strong and consistent fears may result in children's being unable to function normally (Wachs & Gruen, 1982). For example, a child who is extremely afraid of dogs may refuse to leave the house. Extreme fears often result in children's exhibiting nervous mannerisms such as stuttering, biting nails, and sucking thumbs. Deep-rooted fears may lead to shyness, withdrawal, or unexpected acts of aggression (Blechman, 1985). Aggression may also result from prolonged fear. For example, a child who was previously very afraid of a bully may turn into a bully.

Most fears are based on experiences that children cannot readily understand and that they find threatening. Children who lack confidence, are clumsy, or have developmental delays are likely to have more fears. In addition, the lack of communication skills that prevents children from asking questions or understanding explanations contributes to fears. Children with motor delays more frequently fall, bump into things, or have things hit them. This may contribute to their being afraid (Miller, 1980).

Children also acquire fears modeled by other people (Becker, 1990). For example, if a child's father is afraid of heights, the child may develop such a fear. However, children find it comforting to learn that adults are sometimes afraid and that they learn to overcome their fears. The subject matter of television shows and books should be monitored because fears often develop from watching or hearing a scary story (Sherburne et al., 1988). Children have very vivid imaginations and sometimes believe things are real when they are not. Talking with an adult often helps children separate fantasy from reality.

Family tensions, including fighting, separation, divorce, and drug abuse, often contribute to fears and insecurities (Strain et al., 1992). Also, overly anxious adults constantly warning children to be careful contribute to fears. However, appropriate levels of fear are useful because they suggest the need to be cautious and help keep children from being hurt. Children with a pervasive developmental disorder (PDD) frequently develop intense, unfounded fears yet may not develop fears of real danger. For example, they might jump into a pool of water or walk along a narrow ledge. Special precautions must be taken to protect children who do not develop appropriate fears.

Although each child is unique, each age tends to bring particular fears. To help children overcome their fears, adults should encourage them to gradually approach

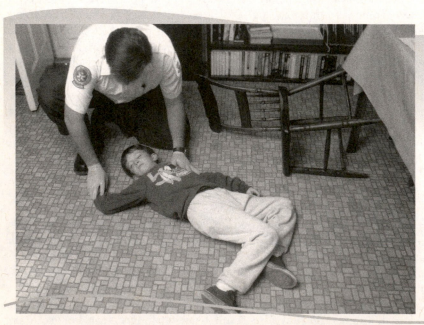

A young child who reacts to a fearful event often needs to be comforted by an adult.

new things while adults provide emotional reassurance. For example, if a child is afraid of the dark, adults should gradually encourage them to sleep in the dark rather than shut the door and make the room completely dark all at once. When children are about to experience something they are likely to fear, such as going to the doctor or hospital, they should be provided with information about what they are likely to experience. Reducing uncertainty often reduces fear (Kaplan, 1991).

Extremely debilitating fears, called phobias, are intense irrational fears. Children rarely exhibit phobic behavior. Those who do should be referred to a professional counselor (Westling & Koorland, 1989). Children should not be ridiculed, scolded, or punished for any type of fear. They should be encouraged to talk about their fears. Requiring children to act as if they are not afraid when they have fears is likely to enhance fears (Kaplan, 1991).

Finicky Eating

As discussed in Chapter 11, parents and teachers frequently worry when young children eat very little or are very **finicky eaters,** such as those willing to eat only two or three favorite foods. One goal of early childhood education is to provide children with new experiences (Smith & Rivera, 1993). Giving them opportunities to try new foods is frequently part of this goal. One method to encourage finicky eaters to try new foods is to involve them in preparing and serving the food. Children should be allowed to explore food through touch and smell. Adults should avoid requiring children to be overly neat when they eat because doing so may discourage them from trying new foods (Johnson, Pugach, & Devlin, 1990).

When children initially resist trying new foods, this does not mean that they never will enjoy them. New food items should be introduced and reintroduced on a regular basis. A food item that a child initially does not like may later become a favorite. Adults should avoid saying things such as "Don't give him that. He won't eat it" or "He doesn't like it." It is often helpful to ask children to sample new foods by taking a spoonful (sometimes referred to as a "no thank you helping") rather than require them to eat a full serving. Adults' and other children's reactions to certain foods often affect children's food preferences. Children are likely to imitate others' reactions to new foods (Deiner, 1993).

Because children's stomachs are smaller than adults', they likely need smaller portions of food provided several times a day. Children can have more frequent snacks, but they should be nutritious. Ideally, children are provided with choices of food to encourage them to eat, but too many choices are likely to be overwhelming (Westling & Koorland, 1989).

Meal and snack times should be pleasant and relaxed and not include a discussion of stressful events. Children should be allowed to eat at their own pace. If children do not eat within a reasonable amount of time, the food should be unemotionally removed. An adult might comment, "I guess you weren't hungry." Children are likely to be hungry the next time food is offered and will probably eat at that time (Kauffman, 1989).

As discussed in Chapters 7 and 11, children who have motor delays may have difficulty controlling the muscles required for chewing. This may make it difficult for them to learn how to eat lumpy foods. They may refuse to try new types of food and become agitated when they are presented to them. In this case new foods should be slowly introduced.

Limited Attention Span

Attention span refers to the length of time an activity is pursued. A child's ability to focus attention often is reduced by distracting noises, sights, or personal feelings. Children with limited attention spans often quickly move from one activity to another and are easily distracted. Some children, such as those diagnosed with ADHD, lack adequate screening or filtering mechanisms, which aid in efficiently attending to relevant tasks or events (McGee & Share, 1988).

Attention span generally increases as developmental age increases. The average attention span is approximately 7 minutes for 2-year-olds, 9 minutes for 3-year-olds, 12 minutes for 4-year-olds, and 14 minutes for 5-year-olds (Siegel, 1999). It is important to remember that a 4-year-old performing tasks typical of a 2-year-old is also likely to have the attention span of a 2-year-old.

Children who are easily distracted may lose belongings, misplace items, not finish tasks, and be drawn from one activity to another. The length of children's attention span often varies, depending on the type of activity presented to them. If a toy is very interesting, even very young children who are easily distracted may play with it for an extended time (Douglas, 1983). Children who have difficulty focusing attention may watch an engaging videotape for an extended time. This misleads some teachers and parents into thinking that children should be able to attend to other tasks for as long as they attend to the videotape.

An unusually short attention span may be due to delayed neurological development; impaired perceptual skills, including hearing or sight impairments; or cognitive delays. Children who feel anxious or insecure may also have a short attention span. Lacking self-confidence may lead children to choose not to attend to tasks because they fear they will not succeed even if they try (Richman, Stevenson, & Graham, 1982).

Children are unlikely to stay with a task if they are frequently criticized or are unsuccessful. They are likely to move to other tasks that are less anxiety-producing. Unfortunately, children quickly learn they cannot fail if they do not try. Tasks that are too difficult or too easy do not promote a feeling of adequacy or competency (McGee & Share, 1988). Children who believe "I can do it" are more likely to pay attention and withstand distractions. Children should be praised for attending to tasks for extended periods of time. It is particularly important to acknowledge children who try to attend.

Children who are easily distracted, such as those with ADHD, often respond positively to environments designed to minimize distractions and maximize the attractiveness of stimuli to which they must attend (Jacob, O'Leary, & Rosenbald, 1978). That is, they are likely to benefit when cabinets and tables are organized and uncluttered and when materials are put away after activities are completed. Children who are easily distracted need to be frequently provided with a variety of short, developmentally appropriate tasks.

An adult's expectation regarding how long a child should remain focused on a task should be gradually increased. Children who have difficulty attending to a task often benefit from a timer that helps them remember to stay on task. In addition, to help children focus their attention, task instructions should be as clear and specific as possible (Jacob et al., 1978). Children should be asked to look directly at adults who provide task instructions. Adults can gain children's attention by modeling reflective thought (thinking aloud). For example, they might say, "I wonder how we can solve this puzzle. First I'll turn all the pieces right side up. Then I'll do the easy pieces first. I can do this." This could be followed by the adult's asking children to show them how they solve the puzzle.

Self-Stimulating Behavior

Self-stimulating behaviors such as rocking back and forth, head-banging, flapping arms, twirling objects in the sunlight, hitting ears, and banging objects together are disruptive and prevent children from engaging in learning experiences. Some children use self-stimulating behaviors to withdraw from the constantly changing demands of the outside world. Children with PDD or ADHD are likely to engage in self-stimulating behavior. Children with PDD appear to deal with environmental demands by moving into their own private world (Lovaas, 1977).

Self-stimulating behavior provides physical sensations that are reinforcing and predictable and provide children with a sense of control. Children may self-stimulate because they lack the play skills that allow them to interact in more-meaningful ways (Cohen & Donnellen, 1987). Encouraging alternative behaviors (using redirection) that are incompatible with self-stimulation may reduce self-stimulation. For example, a child who constantly rocks back and forth could be allowed to hold a favorite toy during circle time only when they are *not* engaging in self-stimulation (in this case, rocking back and forth). Adults must avoid reinforcing self-stimulating behavior by focusing attention on a child. Children should be reinforced only when they are not self-stimulating (Kauffman, 1989).

Genital self-stimulation, called masturbation, is a common form of self-stimulation. It is normal in children aged 2–5 but should be discouraged when it occurs in the presence of others (Kauffman, 1989). Adults should not overreact or humiliate or punish children who masturbate. Teaching children that certain parts of the body are private provides an important safety lesson. When an adult observes a child masturbating, it is appropriate to say something like "Touching yourself in front of other people makes them uncomfortable. Please stop." It may be helpful for adults to use a signal, such as a hand signal for "Stop," to remind a child to stop a self-stimulating behavior (Dreikurs & Cassel, 1972).

Self-stimulation in the form of self-abuse, including hitting, pinching, scratching, or biting oneself, is of particular concern. Children with PDD are more likely to engage in self-abuse. It is important to learn the warning signs that precede this type of behavior and attempt to prevent it. When a child begins to engage in self-abuse, saying "No," redirecting them, placing them in time out, or firmly holding them until they are calm to eliminate or reduce the behavior. If children frequently engage in self-abuse, professional intervention is warranted (Hussey-Gardner, 1992).

Conclusions

Teachers and parents need to remember that creating a positive learning environment is generally more productive than attempting to control children's behaviors. Adults must remember that it is normal for children to misbehave. From time to time all children need guidance in developing positive methods of interacting with others.

A variety of techniques are useful for helping children learn to control their behavior. Children who learn to manage their own behavior are more likely to benefit from learning opportunities. When it is necessary to manage children's behavior, most are more receptive to having their behavior managed when they feel loved and valued.

CHAPTER SUMMARY

- Behavior management includes encouraging desirable and discouraging undesirable behavior.

- Undesirable behavior often interferes with development.

- Typically, children are most cooperative when they are told what they may do rather than only told what they may not do.

- Behavioral expectations must be based on each child's unique needs.

- Reinforcement, redirection, time out, extinction, and punishment are common behavior management techniques.

- Children are more likely to be aggressive when they are frustrated. Adults may reduce a child's frustration by providing them with alternative ways to express frustration.

- A variety of common behavior problems occur in young children, including temper tantrums, aggression, whining, overdependency, fears, short attention span, and self-stimulation.

CHAPTER KEY TERMS

teacher-directed activity
reward
reinforcer
reinforcement
primary reinforcer
secondary reinforcer
redirection
time out
extinction

punishment
Project SUCCEED
temper tantrum
aggression
overdependency
finicky eater
attention span
self-stimulating behavior

REVIEW QUESTIONS

1. What criteria must be met for a behavior to be deemed inappropriate? What are useful ways to deal with such behaviors?

2. What are seven different reasons why a child might misbehave? Select three, and suggest solutions for each problem.

3. Explain why a child might misbehave for that reason, citing examples of the underlying cause and the expected behavior that would result.

4. What are three positive and three negative aspects of punishment as a means of controlling behavior? What is your own opinion about using punishment? Which attributes of punishment methods do you consider acceptable and unacceptable?

5. How could a teacher modify a classroom to ensure that students with various disabilities are able to focus and engage in on-task behaviors?

6. What are the major components of effective behavior management?

7. Why is information about a child's behavior at home useful to others?

8. What are some common fears that children may develop? Why do they develop, and how might adults help children deal with them?

9. Why do children engage in self-stimulating behavior, and how should adults react?

10. What methods of behavior management facilitate positive classroom interactions?

SUGGESTED STUDENT ACTIVITIES

1. Visit an early childhood special education classroom and a regular preschool classroom, and compare behavior management problems and techniques found in each setting. Interview teachers, asking them to describe effective and ineffective management techniques.

2. Visit a playground, an arcade, or a toy store, and look for a child engaging in two of the following three behaviors: doing something they should not be doing, throwing a temper tantrum, being physically aggressive (e.g., hitting, kicking, or pulling another child, themselves, or an object). What were the circumstances in each scenario? How did the parent or guardian deal with them? Was this effective? What would you have done differently and why?

3. Imagine that you just began a job as a teacher in an early childhood special education classroom. Develop a written plan for behavior management in your classroom. What will you be sure to do and not do when dealing with behavior management issues? What behaviors will not be allowed, and what will happen if they occur? How will you encourage proper social interaction? What positive reinforcements will you implement and when?

4. Observe parents in public settings, and notice how they respond to their children's temper tantrums. What guidance would you give them regarding the most effective methods for dealing with tantrums?

5. Design a token economy plan, for a preschool classroom, that includes rewards for appropriate behavior and consequences for inappropriate behavior. Discuss use of primary and secondary reinforcers.

6. Imagine that you are a preschool teacher who has just begun a finger-painting activity. One child insists on painting directly on the table top rather than on paper. Describe how you will deal with this situation. Explain your reasoning.

Transitions: Preparing for the Next Step

14

One hundred years from now, it will not matter
What kind of car I drove,
What kind of house I lived in,
How much money I had in my bank account,
What my clothes looked like.
But the world may be a little better
Because I was important in the life of a child.
—Adapted from a statement by Forest E. Whitcraft

CHAPTER KEY POINTS

- Young children with disabilities and their parents benefit from services focusing on transitions.

- Federal law mandates transition plans for children who receive early childhood intervention services.

- All individuals involved in transition must work together to help reduce the stress for children and their families.

- Several methods are useful for easing transitions.

- Helping children develop positive self-esteem enhances their ability to grow and learn.

- Changes in early childhood intervention services will be required to help ensure that young children with disabilities receive optimal services in the future.

Early childhood intervention services reportedly have many positive effects on the development of young children and their families (Guralnick & Bennett, 1987; Mitchell & Brown, 1991). During the time children receive early intervention services, they must often move from one program to the next or from services provided at their homes to early childhood or elementary school settings. This chapter discusses methods to help children cope with such **transitions**. In addition, it provides a look at the value of enhancing children's self-esteem. It concludes with a discussion of likely future trends in early childhood intervention services.

Dealing with Transitions

For the purpose of this chapter's discussion *transition* is defined as a time of change. All young children experience a variety of transitions in their lives. Transition occurs when a newborn is taken home from the hospital. Transitions include moving from one program to another or from one type of program to another, as well as from one service provider to another (Kagan, 1991b; Quigney & Struder, 1999).

Children with disabilities often experience more transitions than children who do not receive early childhood intervention services. Not only do they experience more transitions, but these transitions are challenging (stressful) for them and their families. Transitions include transition from home to an infant or toddler intervention program and from there to a preschool intervention program. These transitions also involve shifting from a home-based, family-centered program to a center-based, child-centered program. From there, children may attend prekindergarten before entering kindergarten, followed by pre-first (for children developmentally unprepared for first grade) to first grade. Clearly, a child may experience major transitions during the first 5–6 years of life (Marshall, 2003).

Transitions from one program or type of service delivery to another (such as home- or site-based to a clinic) are often stressful for children and their parents, teachers, therapists, and other service providers (Hanline & Knowlton, 1988; Olsen, 1999). Figure 14.1 lists transitions that may occur.

Transitions often involve major changes in routines. Federal laws (in particular, the Individuals with Disabilities Education Act [IDEA]) mandate transition planning. Part B of IDEA focuses on transition planning for children 3 years and older; Part C presents guidelines for transition plans for children younger than 3 (Hanson & Bruder,

Figure 14.1 **Types of Transitions**

- Intensive care unit to home care
- Home care to infant–toddler program
- Infant–toddler to preschool program
- Preschool to primary-school program
- Home-based to clinic- or site-based (classroom at a preschool site)
- Public to private program or vice versa
- Segregated (self-contained) to integrated (mainstream or inclusion) program

2001). Transition plans must be included in individualized family service plans (IFSPs) and individualized education programs (IEPs) and must include a statement of the services. These plans are needed to help children and their families adjust to, and function most effectively with, the new placement (e.g., move from home to clinic, clinic to preschool, or preschool to kindergarten). Figure 14.2 lists IDEA transition guidelines.

A 1992 IDEA amendment (P.L. 102-119) mandates that the agency a child leaves and the new agency that will provide services work together and meet with the child's parents 90 days before the child's third birthday to formally begin the transition process (McGonigel, Kaufmann, & Johnson, 1991). Part H of a 1986 IDEA amendment (P.L. 99-457) dictates the content of procedures that the child's IFSP transition plan must include (Hurley, 1991; Kagan, 1991a). Many states voluntarily use the guidelines for other transitions and these guidelines are included in an IEP (Rosenkoetter & Shotts, 1992) Figure 14.3 (on p. 420) lists requirements for a transition plan for 3-year-olds.

Transition planning includes giving parents information about all potential placement options. Generally, there are more service delivery options for children younger than 3 years old; these include family child care (care provided by an individual), child care provided in a preschool or day care setting, preschool programs (special or regular), play groups, private therapists or programs, public programs, prekindergarten classes, respite care (care of a child while the parents take a break), and recreational programs (Bricker, Peck, & Odom, 1993; Fowler & Titus, 1996; Ramey, Ramey, & Lanzi, 2004).

Transitions must be carefully planned and individualized for each child based on the child's and family members' unique characteristics. Transition information must be openly provided to all members of the service team. Parents must be helped to feel comfortable advocating for their child during the transition process (Conn-Powers & Ross-Allen, 1991; Wehmeyer, Morningstar, & Husted, 1999). Figure 14.4 (on p. 420) lists components of a high-quality transition plan.

Parents of infants and toddlers who have developmental delays often ask, "Will my child be able to attend a day care or preschool program?" Most parents hope

Each application must include a description of the policies and procedures to be used to ensure a smooth transition for children receiving early intervention services under this part to preschool or other appropriate services, including—

(a) A description of how the families will be included in the transition plans;

(b) A description of how the lead agency under this part will—

(1) Notify the local educational agency for the area in which the child resides that the child will shortly reach the age of eligibility for preschool services under Part B of the Act, as determined in accordance with State law;

(2) (i) In the case of a child who may be eligible for preschool services under Part B of the Act, with the approval of the family of the child, convene a conference among the lead agency, the family, and the local educational agency at least 90 days, and at the discretion of the parties, up to 6 months, before the child is eligible for the preschool services, to discuss any services that the child may receive; or

(ii) In the case of a child who may not be eligible for preschool services under Part B of the Act, with the approval of the family, make reasonable efforts to convene a conference among the lead agency, the family, and providers of other appropriate services for children who are not eligible for preschool services under Part B, to discuss the appropriate services that the child may receive;

(3) Review the child's program options for the period from the child's third birthday through the remainder of the school year; and

(4) Establish a transition plan; and

(c) If the State educational agency, which is responsible for administering preschool programs under part B of the Act, is not the lead agency under this part, an interagency agreement between the two agencies to ensure coordination on transition matters.

(Approved by the Office of Management and Budget under control number 1820-0550) (Authority: 20 U.S.C. 1437(a)(8))

Note: Among the matters that should be considered in developing policies and procedures to ensure a smooth transition of children from one program to the other are the following:

The financial responsibilities of all appropriate agencies.

The responsibility for performing evaluations of children.

The development and implementation of an individualized education program ("IEP") or an individualized family service plan ("IFSP") for each child, consistent with the requirements of law (see Sec. 303.344(h) and sections 612(a)(9) of the Act).

The coordination of communication between agencies and the child's family.

The mechanisms to ensure the uninterrupted provision of appropriate services to the child.

[58 FR 40959, July 30, 1993, as amended at 63 FR 18294, Apr. 14, 1998]

Figure 14.3   **Key Components of a Transition Plan for 3-Year-Olds**

- Who is responsible for coordinating the transition process?
- Which agency is responsible for costs associated with the transition?
- Who are members of the transition team?
- Who is responsible for providing access to needed services not provided by the program that the child will attend?

that their child can do this prior to school age. One of the questions most frequently asked by parents of preschoolers with developmental delays is "Will my child be ready for kindergarten?" Most parents hope their children will be by school age (Fowler, Schwartz, & Atwater, 1991).

Children must be provided with opportunities to experience a successful transition into whatever program they are developmentally ready to enter. Parents must be prepared to accept optimal educational placement. In some cases toddlers are unprepared to enter a site-based program. They may most benefit from receiving services at home or a clinic. Some preschoolers are not ready to enter regular kindergarten when they reach school age. They may need to delay entrance, or their needs may be best met in a special education classroom rather than a regular kindergarten classroom (Beckoff & Bender, 1989; Hawley, 2000).

The ultimate goal for most parents and early childhood teachers is to best prepare children for the next step on the educational ladder. Most children have a natural desire to learn. However, this desire is likely to be reduced if they are expected to perform tasks that are not developmentally appropriate. In such cases, children are likely to believe that learning is boring or hard work or that they are destined to fail (Diener & Dweck, 1978).

In most cases children should not be forced to participate in activities such as counting, practicing writing the alphabet, or responding to flash cards. Such activities often have negative side effects, including children's disliking learning, school, teachers, and their parents (Barbour & Seefeldt, 1993). Forcing children to engage

Figure 14.4   **Components of an Effective Transition Plan**

- Carefully planned
- Outcome-oriented process
- Initiated by the primary service provider, who then ensures the development of a written multidisciplinary service plan for each child moving to a new program

Figure 14.5   **Methods to Help Ensure Successful Transitions**

- Ensure service continuity and interagency coordination—for example, by clarifying responsibilities regarding referrals, assessments, and eligibility.
- Reduce family disruptions; keep the family informed.
- Prepare children for program placements—learning new program rules or self-management skills.
- Meet legal requirements.
- Ensure collaboration between professionals and family members.
- Ensure collaboration between sending and receiving program personnel, including training of staff and preparation of materials (e.g., a staff member may need to learn sign language, and equipment may need to be adapted to accommodate a wheelchair).

in tasks for which they are developmentally unprepared results in limited, if any, success. When children are expected to perform tasks too difficult for them, they begin to perceive themselves as failures. They then develop a strategy of not trying rather than trying and risking failure. This process is frequently referred to as "learned helplessness" (Dweck, 1975). Figure 14.5 lists methods that help ensure successful transitions.

Transitions to New Programs

Whether children enter a new classroom, program, or school, the transition often is stressful (Bennett, Raab, & Nelson, 1991). Transitions involve leaving a familiar, safe environment and moving to a place with new adults and children. The change typically involves making new friends, adjusting to new teachers, and learning new rules and skills. Many children approach these changes with enthusiasm whereas others find them very stressful (Caldwell, 1991; Feldman, 2000). Children may be timid; have tantrums, toilet accidents, or difficulty sleeping; complain of stomach aches; or regress to behavior typical of younger children, such as sucking their thumb or using baby talk.

Children often display separation anxiety during the process of separating from their parents when they change to a new classroom environment. Old behavior problems may resurface or new ones emerge. For example, when children experience transitions, they may display old patterns of temper tantrums or become aggressive toward others for the first time. Skills that a child demonstrated in their old school may not be demonstrated in the new school (Balaban, 1985; Bender, 1992). For example, a child could zip their coat at their old school but appears unable to do so at their new school. This may indicate insecurity or lack of generalization of the skill.

Figure 14.6 **Methods That Help Ensure Successful Transitions**

- Meet children's individual needs.
- Respond to children nonconfrontationally.
- Advocate for families.
- Avoid duplication of assessments and services.
- Avoid undue stress for children, families, and service providers.

When a child's behavior regresses, new teachers or parents often assume that the child is not ready for the demands of the new classroom. Many children need an extended period to adjust to a transition. Ideally, preschool staff or a therapist from the program the child is leaving, along with the parents, work with the new classroom teacher to create a positive transition. Children should be provided with opportunities, well in advance of a transition, to gain the skills needed for the new classroom (Bricker et al., 1993). Figure 14.6 lists methods that help ensure successful transitions.

The Role of Staff Members in the Child's Current Program

It is important for teachers and therapists of a current program to evaluate differences between that program and the new one. Teachers and therapists who provide services at the old and new programs should talk with one another. Ideally, the teachers visit one another's classrooms. These visits help children, parents, and new teachers understand the parents' and present teachers' expectations. It is also helpful for parents to visit the new classroom with and without the child to observe the class activities (Epps, 1992).

If major differences between the two settings are noted, children benefit from being taught routines and skills needed in the new classroom. Children should be forewarned about differences they are likely to encounter when entering a new program (e.g., a larger building or fewer teachers and more classmates). Ideally, children are allowed to visit the new school building, see the classroom, and meet the new teacher(s) or therapist(s) before the first day of attending the new program (Dockett & Perry, 2005).

It is also useful for teachers to note similarities between the programs and discuss these with children and their parents. Children, as well as parents, often find comfort in knowing there will be similarities (Conn-Powers & Ross-Allen, 1991).

Typically, as children age and move from one program to another, the number of children in each setting or class increases. For instance, there are typically more children and fewer teachers per child in a kindergarten classroom than in a preschool programs. A larger ratio of children to teachers generally results in less attention being given to each child. Children benefit from being gradually prepared to work and play more independently and expect less one-on-one time with a teacher. They need to learn to function effectively with fewer instructions and prompts and less praise and attention.

Preschool teachers help ease the transition into a new program by gradually reducing teacher guidance during activities. In addition, children benefit when teachers avoid focusing on disruptive behavior, unless it puts someone in physical danger. Ignoring undesirable behaviors through use of extinction should be used more and more frequently. For example, if a child is whining for another snack, it would be best to ignore the child until the child asks for more snacks without whining. Teachers should also gradually reduce the number of secondary reinforcers designed to develop appropriate behavior. For example, if a child is used to being complimented every time he puts his coat on independently, gradually reducing this praise is appropriate (Fowler, Hains, & Rosenkoetter, 1990).

It is often difficult for children to adjust to a classroom with many children when they are accustomed to a classroom with just a few children. To help children adjust, it is often helpful to give them opportunities to get to know the other children who will be in their new classroom. It is also helpful when schools create opportunities for children and families to meet one another before the children enter school (Hanline & Knowlton, 1988). For example, rather than having only one visiting day for entering preschoolers or kindergartners, the transition program could be extended to include a movie night, story time, game night, or ice-cream social.

Children benefit from learning such things as sitting at assigned seats, raising their hands before talking, and walking in line. They benefit from being exposed to similar classroom activities they will experience at their new school while at the old school or at home (Graue, 1993). Preparing children for something simple, such as using a bathroom only for boys or girls, can help prevent them from becoming upset or embarrassed when they attend a new program. Having children learn to take care of their own personal needs, such as washing their hands and dressing, helps prepare them for experiences in a new classroom. A teacher of 25 children cannot readily provide each of them with as much help getting ready to go home as they received in a preschool classroom with 12 children and several staff members. Therefore, preschool teachers should encourage children to develop a wide array of self-help (adaptive) skills as soon as each child is capable of doing so (Hains & Rosenkoetter, 1991).

Children who are accustomed to receiving a star when they hang up their coat are often bewildered to discover that coat hanging does not warrant stars in a new classroom. Children with a history of behavior management problems may be accustomed to receiving frequent, consistent praise for a desired behavior. If the new program does not acknowledge behavior in the same way, children are more likely to have difficulty maintaining self-control. Children often benefit if preschool teachers reduce praise for behaviors that other teachers are likely to expect to occur without rewards or reminders. However, teachers in new programs or classes should also consider increasing the amount of individual attention and praise when children first enter the program (Hains & Rosenkoetter, 1991).

Most preschool children experience free play as a major school activity. Free play is not a major part of the day in most kindergarten schedules. Children in kindergarten classes typically spend most of the time in teacher-directed, large-group activities such as singing songs or story time. Therefore, introducing more structure and rules toward the end of the preschool experience, as well as increasing the level of teacher-directed, large-group time, may help children prepare for the transition to kindergarten (Graue, 1993).

Determining the best placement for a preschooler with special needs is a complex task. School districts providing free kindergarten programs are required to provide appropriate educational experiences for all children of kindergarten age, even if they are not prepared for the standard kindergarten curriculum (Stipek, 2002). If the school district cannot provide a developmentally appropriate program, the district must pay for the costs associated with sending children to an appropriate program. These programs may include a kindergarten class, a self-contained class (class for children with disabilities), or an inclusion class that includes children who do and do not have special needs (Hains, Fowler, Schwartz, Kottwitz, & Rosenkoetter, 1989).

In inclusion classes children with and without special needs often are in the same class for most of the day. However, in some cases a child's needs are best met in a self-contained classroom. Children initially placed in such a classroom often do not remain in special educational classes in later years (Kagan, 1991a).

Some parents hesitate to allow school districts to receive information regarding their child's enrollment in early intervention programs. Parents are often concerned that their child will be labeled for life. In most cases, local school districts have provided approval and partial funding for children to receive early intervention services. Therefore, school districts already have information regarding who has been receiving special education services. Generally, it is helpful for parents to give permission for all records to be released to the new school. Some parents need support for them to fully understand the potential advantages of providing teachers and therapists who work at the new program with as much information as possible (Conn-Powers & Ross-Allen, 1991).

If parents do not give permission for information to be transmitted from one program to another, agencies cannot legally share that information. When this occurs, it is generally very unfortunate because new teachers and therapists typically gain important insights from prior assessments and information from the child's previous preschool teachers or therapists. In addition, valuable time is spent collecting data about the child that may already be available in the child's records (Hains & Rosenkoetter, 1991; Hains, Rosenkoetter, & Fowler, 1991).

Although there are often major differences between preschool and kindergarten programs, most children adjust well to the changes. In fact, most children adjust more quickly to program changes than their parents do (Golant & Golant, 1990). Parents accustomed to writing daily notes, receiving daily communications, or calling the teacher whenever they have a question often find it difficult to adjust to the approach of most kindergarten programs, which involve less communication between parents and teachers and less parental involvement (Kagan, 1991b).

Initially, helping parents adjust to the transition often is as important as directly helping the child adjust. Parents anxious about a transition are likely to display this anxiety when the child is present. The parents' anxiety is ultimately transferred to the child. When this occurs, the child is less likely to maximally benefit from educational experiences (Kilgo, Richard, & Noonan, 1989; Pianta, Rimm-Kaufman, & Cox, 1999).

When transitions occur, parents typically lose relationships with teachers and therapists they have grown to trust and value. Initially, most parents believe that no one else can care for their child as well as the child's current teachers or therapists. Parents are often concerned that new teachers will not like their child, the child will not like the new teachers, or other children in the new class will not like their child. Parents are particularly concerned about these issues when the transition involves their child's moving from a segregated classroom to an inclusion setting (O'Brien, 1991).

When children change programs or classes, the parents must develop new relationships and adjust to new ways of doing things. Parents often report feeling a sense of abandonment. In fact, sometimes when parents are told that their child no longer has significant developmental delays, they are *not* overjoyed by the news because it means that their child will no longer receive special services and the parents' support from the caring professionals will not continue (Sainato & Strain, 1993).

Parents often feel a sense of loss when children move from infant and toddler programs to preschool or primary programs because the level of family services typically diminishes. Reduction of services occurs because mandated family services are for children younger than 3 years. However, federal laws allow for IFSPs to stay in effect until a child enters primary school if the state, school district, and parents agree (Peterson, 1991). When the variety of services diminishes, parents are often dismayed not only for themselves but also for their child. Typically, a wider variety of programs (e.g., more home- and clinic-based programs) is available for infants and toddlers than for preschool and school-age children.

When a child receives services outside the home, this also affects all family members (Stephens & Rous, 1992). Moving from home-based to center-based programs requires special scheduling, coordination of travel, and arrangement of child care during the time parents visit their child's center-based program or meet with teachers or therapists. It is not always appropriate for a child with a disability or their siblings to accompany parents on these visits, which may make it difficult for parents to meet with professionals.

Parents are often concerned that their child cannot deal with the expectations found in the new classroom. Parents may be faced with changes in classification terminology when children move from one program to another or when the family moves to a new school district, particularly when the new school district is located in a different state (Sainato & Strain, 1993).

For example, children are often classified as "cognitively delayed" prior to age 6 and "mentally retarded" after age 6. Hearing someone say, "Your child is classified as mentally retarded" is likely to be more unsettling than hearing "Your child has a cognitive delay." The term *developmentally delayed* implies that a child has fallen behind in skills development, whereas the label *mentally retarded* suggests that a child has a permanent disability. Figure 14.7 lists several common concerns that parents frequently find overwhelming.

Teachers at the program from which the child is transitioning can help alleviate some of the parents' concerns by developing and using a comprehensive transition plan tailored to the individual child's and family's needs and by sharing this plan with all the people involved in the transition (Peterson, 1991). Teachers at the child's

Figure 14.7   **Common Parental Concerns**

- what their child should wear to school
- what supplies the child needs
- what type of food is served at school
- what safety precautions the bus driver and school administrators take
- whether there are appropriate before- and after-school programs
- whether the program staff is qualified to deal with the child's special needs
- whether there are parent support groups
- who will be the parents' advocate or contact at the new program

current placement should obtain information about potential receiving programs and identify the contact people at these programs. When there are choices of possible programs, current program staff should help guide parents in selecting the most appropriate program. Staff should recommend goals and objectives for the child during and after the transition. They should also participate in the child's placement by consulting with the parents on a regular basis before, during, and after placement in the new program (Peterson, 1991).

Whenever possible, teachers, therapists, and parents should include the child in the transition process (Noonan & Ratokolau, 1991). Initially, parents should visit the classroom. If a staff member from the present program can accompany the parents, this is often helpful. Parents should be encouraged to visit the classroom with the child to see the new classroom and meet the teachers. After the visit, parents and teachers should talk about the upcoming change and emphasize how much the child will enjoy the new school. Children facing transitions should be reminded of the things they have already learned and be reassured that there are many more fun things to be learned at the new school. They should also be reminded of features of the programs that are the same and told about changes they are likely to experience.

The New Program's Role in Transitions

The program to which the child is moving can help ease the stress of the transition by openly receiving the child, parents, and staff members from the other programs when they visit the classroom (Stephens & Rous, 1992). With the parents' permission, teachers and therapists at the new program should carefully review the child's records. They should also help parents arrange transportation and make sure that all special assistive equipment that the child needs is available prior to the transition (Early, Pianta, Taylor, & Cox, 2001; Kraft-Sayre & Pianta, 2000; Rimm-Kaufman, Pianta & Cox, 2000).

The new classroom teachers should also become knowledgeable about the philosophy and procedures of the program the child is leaving. They also must make sure they have been properly trained regarding how to best meet the child's special needs. For example, if the child wears arm splints, the teacher must learn when they should and should not be worn. For example, staff will need to know whether they should be worn during water play. If they must be removed, the teacher must learn how to remove the splints and put them on properly after water play (Rimm-Kaufmann, Pianta, & Cox, 2000).

Children and parents are likely to find comfort in new program staff's accentuating similarities between the new and old programs. For example, both programs are likely to have a block area and provide art activities. When methods vary between the two programs, teachers and therapists must avoid implying that one program's methods are more appropriate than the other's.

The new program should prioritize frequent communication with parents during the first few days of the child's transition into the program. Over time the level of required communication typically decreases as children and parents become familiar with the new program. New program staff should assist parents in locating services that the child or parents require and that are not provided through the new program (Kraft-Sayre & Pianta, 2000).

Children and their families benefit from participating in activities designed to ease the transition process. All too often, transition activities are too limited. Effective transitions help create continuity and maintain gains acquired in the present program. When transitions are not smooth, children often respond by demonstrating diminished abilities (Ramey & Ramey, 1999; Shore, 1998).

It is important to remember that no single method of transition is most effective for all children, their parents, or school districts (Education Commission of the States, 2000). That is, what works for one program or for one type of family may not work in another setting. Programs that involve families prior to the beginning of school are crucial and must be maintained once school begins (Child Trends, 2000; Education Commission of the States, 2000; Kraft-Sayre & Pianta, 2000; Pianta, Cox, Taylor, & Early, 1999; Pianta, Rimm-Kaufman, & Cox, 1999). Figure 14.8 lists effective transition activities.

Determining Whether a Child Is Ready for Kindergarten

Although parents and teachers strive to ensure that children are ready to enter a regular kindergarten program, some children are not developmentally prepared to deal with the curriculum demands found in typical kindergarten classrooms. Children must be accepted and educated at their current level of development (Benner, 1992; Murphey & Burns, 2002). When children are pressured to learn things they are not ready to learn, their natural love of learning diminishes. Children must have many opportunities to experience success. This success is achieved when they are provided with developmentally appropriate activities and materials. Readiness is affected by maturation but can be enhanced through effective preschool education (Currie, 2005). Preparing children for transitions into new types of educational

Figure 14.8 **Effective Transition Activities**

- Maintaining regular contact with children
- Maintaining regular contact with family members
- Visiting kindergarten classrooms
- Providing home-learning activities
- Providing open-house activities
- Conducting parent–teacher meetings
- Encouraging involvement in parent–teacher associations
- Providing frequent communication regarding school activities and events
- Conducting home visits
- Developing support groups
- Providing early registration
- Providing necessary support personnel, including interpreters

experiences is also crucial for success (Lee & Burkam, 2002; Peck, Carlson, & Helmstetter, 1992; Saluja, Scott-Little, & Clifford, 2000).

There are several theoretical orientations regarding school readiness. Nativists believe that readiness is based on children's maturity levels. They are likely to support the idea of delaying entrance into kindergarten and repeating grade levels. Environmentalists view readiness primarily in terms of children's skills, such as knowing how to write one's name, the alphabet, and color names. A social view of readiness focuses on how the community defines readiness. Interactionists emphasize the need for children to be ready for school and schools to be ready for children, regardless of the entry-level skills children have (Pianta & Kraft-Sayre, 2003).

The National Association for the Education of Young Children (NAEYC, 2005) emphasizes the importance of considering several factors when evaluating a child's readiness to enter school. The NAEYC states, "School readiness requires (1) addressing the inequities in early life experiences so that all children have access to the opportunities that promote school success, (2) recognizing and supporting individual differences among children, including linguistic and cultural differences, and (3) establishing reasonable and appropriate expectations of children's capacities upon entering school" (p. 424).

It should also be noted that readiness for school is not the same as readiness to learn. Children are conceptually ready to learn during most of their waking hours, but this does not mean they are ready for kindergarten. In contrast, some children are ready for school in terms of their skills but may not ready to learn in terms of their social-emotional development, health, and so on (NAEYC, 2005). Clearly, many factors affect school readiness (e.g., socioeconomic status, pre- and postnatal parental drug abuse, domestic violence, home atmosphere, and parental rearing styles). Table 14.1 lists skills that help prepare young children for kindergarten.

Table 14.1	*Factors That Help Prepare Children for School*
Personal skills	Uses the toilet; washes hands; puts on and takes off jacket/coat; ties shoes; snaps, buttons, zips, and belts clothing; uses silverware; eats unassisted; puts toys away.
Social skills	Follows two-step directions, cooperates with others, plays nonaggressively, attends to task for at least 10 minutes, follows rules.
Intellectual skills	Holds books upright and turns pages front to back, sits and listens to a story, states first and last name and own age, recites some songs and rhymes, tells and retells familiar stories.
Health needs	Has required immunizations, has dental check-ups, eats at regular times each day, runs, jumps, skips, climbs, swings, uses balls.

NAEYC (1990) states:

> Every child, except in the most severe instances of abuse, neglect, or disability, enters school ready to learn school content. However, all children do not acquire the competence needed in the school setting. The absence of basic health care and economic security places many children at risk for academic failure before they enter school. Families who lack emotional resources and support services are likewise not always able to prepare their children to meet school expectations. It is a public responsibility to ensure that all families have access to services and support needed to provide the strong relationships and rich experiences that provide children with a foundation for all future learning. At a minimum, such services include basic health care, including prenatal care and child immunizations; economic security; basic nutrition; adequate housing; family support services; and high-quality early childhood programs. (p. 1)

Various risk factors affect school readiness, including families' poverty status, parents' educational level and ethnic background, and children's health and living environment. Clearly, living in impoverished or unsafe environments negatively affects children's kindergarten readiness. Therefore, providing services prior to kindergarten to children affected by these and other risk factors increases the probability of kindergarten success (Currie, 2005; Meisels, 1999; Perroncel, 2000; West, Denton, & Germino-Hausken, 2000).

Assessing school readiness helps determine children's current developmental levels (Zill & West, 2001). Assessment results can be used to guide classroom and individual kindergarten programming. Five key dimensions of early development and learning are typically the focus of school readiness assessment: physical well-being and motor development, social-emotional development, learning approaches, language development, and cognition/general knowledge (Knitzer, 2001).

In addition, the U.S. Congress defined three key elements of school readiness in their Goals 2000: Educate America Act, which addresses readiness of children and schools as well as family and community supports. Readiness of children depends on the five key dimensions typically assessed in readiness tests. School readiness includes smooth transitions from children's homes or programs. Family and community readiness relates to access to high-quality programs, supportive families, and training and support of parents (West, Denton, & Germino-Hausken, 2000).

Readiness tests are typically skill-oriented (e.g., paper-and-pencil standardized tests such as the Metropolitan Readiness Test), assessments of development (e.g., the Gesell School Readiness Screening Test), behavior screens (e.g., the Brigance K & 1 Screen for Kindergarten and First Grade), or performance-based assessments (e.g., portfolios of work samples).

The **Brigance Comprehensive Inventory of Basic Skills, Revised (CIBS-R)** is a standardized test used for children preschool age through 9 years old. A primary use of this test is to determine school readiness. Figure 14.9 lists readiness skills assessed on the CIBS-R.

Many other standardized assessments may be used to assess kindergarten readiness. Table 14.2 lists some of these tests.

Figure 14.9   **Readiness Skills Assessed on the Brigance Comprehensive Inventory of Basic Skills, Revised (CIBS-R)**

- color naming
- visual discrimination of shapes
- visual discrimination of letters
- visual discrimination of short words
- copying designs
- drawing shapes from memory
- drawing a person
- gross-motor coordination
- recognition of body parts
- following directions/verbal instructions
- self-help skills
- verbal fluency
- sound articulation
- personal knowledge
- memory of sentences
- counting
- alphabet recitation
- number naming and comprehension
- letter naming
- writing own name, numbers, and letters

| Table 14.2 | Tests That Assess School Readiness |

Area Being Assessed	Tests
Child's language and literacy skills	Bracken School Readiness Assessment
	Social Skills Rating System (SSRS)
	Early Screening Inventory (ESI)
	Project Construct Literacy Assessment
	Reynell Language Development Scales
Child's social-emotional development	Social Behavior Ratings
	Social Skills Rating System (SSRS)
	Howes Peer Interaction
	Personal Maturity Scale
Child's numeracy skills	Woodcock-Johnson, Revised (WJ-R)
	Project Construct "Flip" Math Assessment
Child's overall development	Basic School Skills Inventory, Third Edition (BSSI-3)
	Child Assessment Profile (Chicago Longitudinal Study)
	DABERNON-2
	Developmental Test for Kindergarten Readiness, Second Edition (DTKR-II)
	Kindergarten Assessment (Chicago Longitudinal Study)
	Kindergarten Readiness Test (KRT)
	Bracken School Readiness Assessment
	IRT Assessment
	Project Construct "Pretend Party" Conventional
	Test of Kindergarten/First Grade Readiness Skills (TKFGRS)
Readiness of Teachers/Classrooms	Arnett Caregiver Interaction Scale
	School Readiness Rating Scale
	Head Start Teacher Survey
	Kindergarten Teacher Survey
	Early Childhood Environment Rating Scale (ECERS)
	Home Observation for Measurement of the Environment (HOME)
	Observational Record of Caregiving Environment (ORCE)

School readiness assessments are useful guides for classroom and individual kindergarten programming. They should not be used to prevent children from entering school or to track them into ability-level classrooms. Developmental screening tools are used to screen children for developmental delays and, when indicated, referral for a full developmental evaluation. They should not be used as the sole measure of school readiness.

Children who have low scores on readiness tests are likely to benefit from individualized attention and education plans. Low scores may suggest the need for smaller class size or additional teacher aids.

Preparing Children for Kindergarten

Many kindergarten programs are like the first or second grade of the past. Not all children, whether or not they have special needs, are ready for kindergarten when they are 5 years old (Datar, 2003; Stipek, 2002). Although age requirements for entering kindergarten vary across school districts, 5 years old is the typical age requirement. This was not always the case. Thirty years ago, approximately half of all school districts enrolled children who did not turn 5 until December or January of the kindergarten year. Currently, although age of entry to kindergarten ranges from July 1 to January 1, the typical date falls in September. Because young kindergarteners tend to be less able to listen to directions and comply with teacher requests, increasing the age of entrance may help children experience more success in kindergarten (Datar, 2003; De Cos, 1997; Graue & DePerna, 2000; Vecchiotti, 2001).

Figure 14.10 lists goals typical of kindergarten programs. This list does not include higher-level academic goals found in some kindergarten programs, such as learning to read and solving simple addition and subtraction problems. Clearly, such goals are beyond the abilities of many 5-year-olds (Barbour & Seefeldt, 1993; Kilgo, Richard, & Noonon, 1989; Maxwell & Clifford, 2004; Stipek & Byler, 2001).

Typical kindergarten programs require young children to focus on teacher-directed activities for extended periods of time.

Figure 14.10   **Typical Goals for Kindergarten Programs**

Children should be able to

- recognize and print their names.
- state the names of colors and letters.
- distinguish among sounds.
- tell a picture story in sequence.
- name six shapes.
- name and count objects 1–10.
- sequence the numerals 1 through 10.
- match numerals with objects 1–10.
- color within boundaries.
- know personal facts (e.g., name, telephone number, address).
- independently dress and undress.
- use scissors with ease.
- express ideas during group discussions.
- listen attentively for up to 30 minutes.
- recognize similarities and differences.
- work and play cooperatively.
- practice self-control.
- complete projects promptly, independently, and neatly.
- follow directions and obey rules.
- practice good health habits (e.g., wash hands).

More than 85% of U.S. kindergarten programs focus on academic activities; 70% attempt to teach the children how to read (Golant & Golant, 1990). A kindergarten teacher may teach as many as 20 to 35 children in one class. This requires that children be prepared to function successfully in kindergarten with limited assistance from an adult.

Because most children attend preschool programs before entering elementary school, many kindergarten programs do not emphasize social skills, as kindergarten programs did in the past. In many school districts, waiting in line, sharing, and playing cooperatively are considered skills that children should have acquired before entering kindergarten (Graue, 1993; McClelland, Morrison, & Holmes, 2000; National Education Goals Panel, 1997; Pulsifer, Radonovich, Belcher, & Butz, 2004).

Clearly, school readiness encompasses more than academic skills—including physical, social, and emotional development. It is not the children's responsibility to be school-ready but the responsibility of the adults who care for them and the systems that support them to be child-ready (Carlton & Winsler, 1999; Maxwell & Clifford, 2004; Prakash, West, & Denton, 2003).

Various research studies have asked teachers what factors they believe help ensure children's success in kindergarten. In a 1990 Carnegie Foundation study, teachers believed that 35% of students were not ready for kindergarten upon entrance to kindergarten. Teachers often disagree as to which skills children need to bring to kindergarten. When asked to rate the importance of various factors, teachers selected being able to identify colors, identify body parts, respond to one's own name, and respond to "No" and "Stop" as skills that children should have before entering kindergarten (La Paro & Pianta, 2000).

In a 1993 study, teachers reported that the top three attributes for kindergarten success were for children to be (1) physically healthy, rested, and well nourished; (2) able to communicate their thoughts and needs in words; and (3) curious and enthusiastic in their approach to new activities. These teachers also reported that children who can communicate their needs and thoughts, are enthusiastic and curious, can follow directions, and are sensitive to others' feelings are far more likely to succeed than children who know how to properly use a pencil, know several letters of the alphabet, or can count but are relatively weak in the other skills (Ladd, Birch, & Bluhs, 1999; McClelland, Morrison, & Holmes, 2000; Reynolds & Temple, 1998; Rimm-Kaufman, Pianta, & Cox, 2000).

In other studies, teachers reported that children highly motivated to achieve in school and highly self-regulating (autonomous/independent) are likely to succeed in kindergarten (Kuhl, 2000; Pintrich, 2000; Rimm-Kaufman et al., 2002). Other factors that predict success in kindergarten include being less distractible and having moderate levels of emotionality (Rothbart & Jones, 1998; Shore, 1998).

Kindergarten teachers in urban settings are more likely to emphasize the importance of academic skills than teachers in nonurban settings. Urban teachers reported that recognizing numbers and letters predicts kindergarten success better than social skills do. Opinions as to whether social skills are crucial varied based on teachers' ethnicity as well. African American and Hispanic teachers tended to view both academic and social skills as crucial to readiness. White, non-Hispanic teachers more frequently reported social skills to be more crucial for success than academic skills (Datar, 2003).

Kindergarten teachers report that children enter their classrooms unprepared to learn because they lack experiences that help prepare them for kindergarten. Approximately half of all kindergarten teachers indicate that they believe that about half of their students are unprepared to learn when they begin kindergarten due to lack of attentiveness or ability to appropriately interact with materials and classmates (Clifford, 1999; Early et al., 2001; Emig, Moore, & Scarupa, 2001; Pianta, Cox, Taylor, & Early, 1999; Pianta, Rimm-Kaufman, & Cox, 1999; Shepard & Smith, 1989).

In many learning activities found in kindergarten classrooms, teachers present information in a large-group format or children sit quietly at their desks working independently on work sheets. Such tasks require longer attention spans and well-developed listening skills (Mogg & Bradley, 1999). When these tasks are too long or too difficult and instruction techniques are primarily teacher-directed, they are incompatible with the developmental levels, learning styles, or social maturity of children 4–6 years old (Barbour & Seefeldt, 1993; Kuhn, 1999; Luciana & Nelson, 1998).

Most parents believe that their children will succeed in kindergarten if they have positive feelings about attending school and have acquired certain specific preacademic skills. Parents' views about the importance of academic skills often do not match teachers'. In one study, fewer than 10% of teachers felt that counting to 20 and knowing the alphabet is necessary for kindergarten success. In contrast, more than 58% of preschool parents reported that these skills are critical (Piotrkowski, Botsko, & Matthews, 2000).

Parents' views regarding the skills necessary for kindergarten success vary based on their socioeconomic and educational backgrounds. In one study, approximately 75% of parents who did not graduate from high school reported that they believed that counting to 20 and reciting the alphabet was essential or very important for kindergarten success. In contrast, fewer than 50% of parents with college degrees felt that those skills were necessary for their children's success in kindergarten. Approximately 79% of lower-socioeconomic parents felt that counting to 10 and knowing letters and colors were necessary for kindergarten success. Approximately 70% also believed that children needed to know their addresses and telephone numbers (Diamond, Reagan, & Bandyk, 2000).

Children also have perceptions regarding what is required to succeed in kindergarten. In one study, they reported believing that knowing and following teachers' rules, knowing where things are and what to do, and knowing how to make friends were most necessary for kindergarten success (Valeski & Stipek, 2001).

The Role of Early Intervention Programs

Early childhood special education programs meet a variety of needs. As then Arkansas Governor Mike Huckabee stated, "The best way to ensure children get a good education is to give them a strong foundation in their early years" (National Governors Association Task Force on School Readiness, 2005 p. 1). Federal and state leaders must continue to support collaboration among all professionals and paraprofessionals who provide services for children and their families from birth through school age. This will result in increased early identification and referrals of children with disabilities, which will lead them to services that will help ensure that their needs are adequately met (Barnett & Yarosz, 2004; Wesley & Buysse, 2003).

The National Education Goals Panel discussed what it means to be a "Ready School." The panel stated that ready schools focus on determining what supports children need to succeed. First, ready schools recognize cultural, linguistic, and contextual variations in children's needs. These factors also affect how children adjust to the transition to kindergarten. Ready schools also create links between children's previous preschool experiences and kindergarten, which help the school appropriately adjust its instructional approaches. Additionally, they help ensure that service providers are highly qualified and create environments that are highly conducive to learning. Highly qualified professional staff recognize that all children can learn regardless of their past life experiences (Gonzalez, 2002).

Ready schools also support professional development of all staff. They use and monitor educational methods that focus on individual students' specific needs. Ready schools also facilitate parental involvement. Specific strategies for involving parents include teaching parents specific methods to support literacy and numeracy skills (Gonzalez, 2002).

Finally, ready schools acknowledge the need for outside-of-school support. Because schools cannot provide all useful services, effective schools facilitate collaboration with other programs and services for children and their families (Gonzalez, 2002). High-quality early intervention programs play a critical role in meeting a variety of young children's needs. Providing support for children and their families through investment in early intervention programs can alter children's educational paths during the school years and beyond.

Effective intervention programs are likely to have lifelong benefits for children who participate and economic benefits for society (Espinosa, 2002). Early learning success predicts future learning success, and lack of early learning success, such as entering kindergarten unprepared to learn, tends to predict later lack of success (Boethel, 2004).

Ideally, one major focus of early intervention programs for children, with or without special needs, is on opportunities to develop social skills. Research indicates that a lack of social maturity is the major reason some children are unsuccessful in preschool and kindergarten programs (Campbell, Helms, Sparling, & Ramey, 1998; Rule, Fiechtl, & Innocenti, 1990). Effective preschool programs provide children with opportunities to work cooperatively with adults and other children. Research indicates that children who have developed satisfying relationships with peers are most likely to adjust well to new programs (Chandler, 1992; Vincent et al., 1980). Interaction with peers provides opportunities to learn social skills such as taking turns, compromising, and interacting with unfamiliar children.

Academic readiness is important for kindergarten success (Christian, Morrison, & Bryant, 1998). The single most important academic readiness skill is communication skills. Parents and teachers who provide children with activities that expose them to many types of books, storytelling, songs, and other language experiences help prepare children for academic activities. Most preschool programs provide many opportunities for conversation and cooperative play activities, which also help prepare children for academic activities (Gormley, Gayer, Phillips, & Dawson, 2004; Murphey, 2003; Wolery, 1989). Parents should be encouraged to extend these opportunities at home as well.

In addition, most preschool programs provide many opportunities to use pencils, paper, crayons, and markers, which help children develop prewriting skills. Teachers also provide access to books and other print materials that enhance prereading skills. Preschools consistently, although often informally, help children learn many important concepts, such as color, number, and season, and classifications. They also provide opportunities that enhance fine- and gross-motor abilities, attending skills, and independence (Espinosa, 2002; Magnuson, Meyers, Ruhm, & Waldfogel, 2004; O'Brien, 1991; Peisner-Feinberg et al., 2001).

Children benefit from learning methods of organization and the importance of being on time and prepared. For example, they should have opportunities to learn that putting things away where they belong saves time and later frustration. Children benefit from practice organizing things that they take to school, remembering to take them, finding them at school to bring home, and remembering to bring them home. They also learn what things do and do not belong to them and that they may not take home items that belong to others or the school without permission (Rule et al., 1990).

Early childhood special education programs provide children with encouragement and opportunities to practice newly acquired skills. Teachers also strive to help children develop a sense of accomplishment, which often provides excellent motivation to continue to learn (Rimm-Kaufman, Voorhees, Snell, & La Paro, 2003).

Research clearly suggests that high-quality, center-based early childhood education programs increase the likelihood of children's success in kindergarten. Although high-quality programs aid all children, they have the most pronounced impact on disadvantaged children. Positive effects include performing better on reading and math tests and greater increases in vocabulary, phonemic awareness, and preliteracy skills (Snow & Páez, 2004). School readiness is a critical issue for middle-income families. Many of these families do not have access to high-quality programs provided at no cost to low-income families, yet they cannot afford high-quality programs available to the wealthy (Child Trends, 2002; Loeb, Fuller, Kagan, Carrol, & Carroll, 2004; Piotrkowski, 2004; Rouse, Brooks-Gunn, & McLanahan, 2005).

Preschool programs that provide for smooth transitions to kindergarten for children and their families also help ensure kindergarten success. This critical process takes planning and collaboration between programs and parents (Rimm-Kaufman & Pianta, 2005; LaParo, Kraft-Sayre, & Pianta, 2003; Rimm-Kaufman & Pianta, 2000; Cox, 2004).

The Parents' Role

Parents must be encouraged to guide rather than push their preschool-age children. They should encourage their children to respond cooperatively to requests that adults make. Parents often need to be reminded of the value of providing children with many opportunities to follow directions (Kagan, 1991a). Parents should gradually increase the number of steps in the directions to which they expect children to respond. For example, parents should initially give one-step directions such as "Go get your socks" and later add another step: "Go get your shoes and socks" or "Go get your socks, and put them on."

Children benefit from learning to respond to an adult's request at the time that the adult makes it. For example, when a parent calls a child to dinner, the child should respond promptly. Parents need to be encouraged to avoid repeating the request or waiting an unreasonable length of time for the child to respond. Prompt responses are important; when a teacher announces to 25 students that it is time to clean up or perform some other activity, it is unreasonable for the 25 to dictate their own preferred schedules. Many kindergarten teachers expect children to follow relatively rigid classroom schedules (Wasserman, 1990).

Parents also need to be encouraged to teach children to take responsibilities by giving them small jobs to complete that help the entire family, such as setting the table and collecting the trash. Whenever possible, children should be encouraged to complete these jobs without supervision. Although young children may need reminders to ensure that they carry out these jobs, directions, prompts, and assistance should gradually be reduced. It is also useful for parents to expect children to engage in activities without expecting to be rewarded. Children should take responsibility for self-help skills such as washing their hands and dressing and undressing without adult help or supervision or expectation of receiving rewards for completing these tasks (Caldwell, 1991; Conn-Powers, Ross-Allen, & Holburn, 1990; Ross-Allen & Conn-Powers, 1991).

Reading books to children helps develop language skills and strengthens attending skills. Parents should be encouraged to read books that have increasing numbers of words. After reading to the child, parents should ask them to retell the story or recall specific details from it. Parents should be reminded of the value of reading books, appropriate for preschool-age children with disabilities, about going to school or moving to a new place. These stories provide excellent opportunities to discuss any upcoming transitions and fears or anxieties associated with them.

Providing opportunities for children to play with children their own age helps children learn how to get along with others. Over time, children should be expected to resolve minor arguments with their peers and to successfully play with minimal adult supervision. Young children need adult supervision that ensures their safety. However, adults frequently intervene too quickly and attempt to fix problems without allowing children to attempt to resolve them.

Parents often give children attention when they whine or cry. Most kindergarten teachers consider whining or crying immature and inappropriate. Children benefit from learning acceptable ways to gain attention and ask for help. Parents should be guided toward creating situations in which children ask for help without crying, whining, or having tantrums. Children must learn how to solve problems and effectively seek help when they cannot do so independently (Graue, 1993).

Parents help children develop academic readiness skills while helping to ensure children's safety by teaching them personal information. Children's safety and school-readiness skills are enhanced when they learn their first and last names, parents' first and last names, street address, city, and telephone number. Children should be taught how to use a telephone to call home or for emergency help. They should learn to recognize their printed name. Some children are also ready to learn to print their own name, but they should not be pressured to do so (Graue, 1993).

Parents must avoid last-minute cramming sessions designed to force children to acquire new skills. Cramming does not result in learning and presents learning as a negative experience (Fowler, Schwartz, & Atwater, 1991). Parents should be guided to take advantage of everyday activities that promote concept development. Folding laundry can include a discussion of such things as colors, ownership, size, shape, number, one-to-one correspondence while pairing socks, and organizational skills while putting clothes away. Cooking activities can incorporate measuring, counting, estimating, and time concepts. Taking walks can include conversations about changes in the environment and discussions about what will be seen next. Countless daily

Figure 14.11   **Transition to Kindergarten for Children with Disabilities**

- Parents gather information about kindergarten programs within their school district.
- If children are in a preschool program or receiving intervention services, the program refers them to the school district's Committee on Special Education (CSE).
- The program meets with parents to explain the transition process and discuss educational options.
- A school psychologist or other professional(s) may observe the child and conduct evaluations.
- Parent meets with the CSE chairperson, the principal, or some other designated person to discuss educational options.
- The Committee on Preschool Special Education (CPSE) completes an annual review and makes recommendations for placement and services.
- The CSE meets to make a placement decision and develop the IEP (this may immediately follow the CPSE annual review).
- Kindergarten orientation activities occur, including registration and school visitations.

activities can provide learning opportunities. Teachers and parents should take advantage of these real-life, natural learning experiences. Figure 14.11 lists transition activities for children with disabilities.

Helping Children Believe in Themselves

This book has discussed the attributes and needs of children with developmental delays and the types of services available to them. Throughout, the importance of valuing each child as a unique individual has been emphasized. The next section further discusses the importance of total acceptance of the child. Children who feel accepted are more likely to develop positive self-esteem. Children benefit when adults help them develop positive self-esteem.

Unconditional Positive Regard

Children benefit from knowing they are valued as they are. Children must not think they are broken and need to be fixed. All children inherit different characteristics—among them, learning aptitudes and physical attributes. Children must be assured that teachers, therapists, parents, and day care providers value them as individuals, even though certain aspects of their development are delayed (Mahoney, Robinson, & Powell, 1992).

Acceptance and approval must be unconditional ("no strings attached"). A person shows **unconditional positive regard** when they completely accept another person and show this acceptance through actions and words. Children should not have to be well-behaved or able to do things well in order to know that they are loved and accepted. Adults should separate the deed from the doer; they may dislike the child's actions without rejecting the child (Barrett & Campos, 1987). It is relatively easy for adults to accept children when they behave in appropriate ways. The kind of acceptance children most benefit from is acceptance that continues when they do undesirable things. Adults can indicate displeasure regarding undesirable behaviors while assuring children that they are loved. This requires loving and liking children even when their behavior is not likeable. It means sending children the message "We like you just the way you are." In addition, children must be helped to learn to like themselves. At times some children find it difficult to feel positive about themselves.

Positive Self-Esteem

Self-concept (**self-image**) consists of the perceptions, feelings, and attitudes that one has about one's self (Bullock & Lütkenhaus, 1990; Lewis & Brooks-Gunn, 1979; Pruett, 1999; Strain et al., 1992). **Self-esteem** is one dimension of self-concept. It is self-evaluation, or judgment of one's own worth. Positive self-esteem includes knowing and accepting one's self without feeling ashamed of limitations or differences (Tabassam & Grainger, 2002).

This young child is developing a sense of self through self-observation.

Children benefit when the adults in their lives have positive self-esteem. It is very difficult for children to believe that they are valued and can succeed when the adults in their lives lack confidence. Therefore, it is often necessary for early intervention service staff to help parents realize that they are essential to their children's success and feel confident in their abilities to support their children's growth.

Parents' early interactions with their children set the stage for the development of self-esteem. When parents help their children feel that they are good rather than bad, and accepted rather than rejected, children have a greater chance of developing positive self-esteem. Adults who label children as bad or unworthy often find that children live up to those expectations. That is, children often fulfill adults' expectations. When adults expect success, children are more likely to succeed. Likewise, low expectations often result in negative outcomes.

Listening to children, getting down to their eye level, and praising them even when they are less than perfect help them develop positive self-esteem. They also help reduce a child's anxiety, allowing for easier transitions into new situations and a greater willingness to approach new tasks (Lewis, Sullivan, Stanger, & Weiss, 1989). Simply paying attention to children raises their self-esteem. Showing interest in their daily activities and effort provides children with a sense that they are important. When adults attend to children—really stop and listen—children are less likely to behave in ways aimed at gaining attention. If disruptive behavior is the only behavior that will gain them attention, they are likely to be disruptive.

Children with positive self-esteem are more likely to try new tasks with enthusiasm and approach peers and adults with confidence. They are more likely to explore the environment and assume some control over events in their lives. They believe "I can." This makes them more open to new ideas, willing to face challenges, enjoy success, and cope with disappointment. Children with positive self-esteem also tend to have greater creativity, be more assertive and vigorous in social interactions (participants rather than listeners), and have more friends (Marsh, 1989).

Additionally, adults must avoid being overprotective. Adults often shelter children with disabilities in an attempt to ensure they will not get hurt, but children benefit from being allowed to experience as many normal daily activities as possible. Adults must help children build on their strengths while helping them accommodate for their weaknesses. Even very young children develop defeatist attitudes and give up when things appear too difficult or puzzling (Mahoney et al., 1992b).

Children benefit when they are taught that all people should be valued and treated with respect, including themselves. In addition to supporting the development of positive self-esteem, acknowledging the value of all people reduces prejudice.

By having reasonable behavior expectations, adults contribute to children's self-esteem. To help ensure that children are cooperative and responsible, adults need to set standards for acceptable behaviors. Setting limits helps children learn how others may judge their behavior. It guides children toward behaviors others will find acceptable. When children's behavior is acceptable, others are more likely to acknowledge them in positive ways and seek their companionship. When children successfully meet adults' expectations, they come to view the world as a predictable place and gain confidence that they can successfully interact in the world. Expectations must be age-appropriate and reasonable. When no demands are placed on children, they miss the opportunity to demonstrate that they are competent. They may assume demands are not made of them because others do not believe they can meet those demands (Altermatt, Pomerantz, Ruble, Frey, & Greulich, 2002; Mantzicopoulos, 2006).

Children with negative self-esteem often react as if they believe they are incapable of succeeding in most situations. Negative self-esteem is related to impaired mental health and lower academic achievement. Children with negative self-esteem are more likely to make comments such as "I can't." This orientation often interferes with the ability to learn. Feelings of inadequacy are likely to result in children's being bossy and aggressive or submissive and unsure. Children with negative self-esteem often appear withdrawn or self-conscious and tend to focus on themselves (Loomans & Loomans, 2003). Figure 14.12 lists some principles that help children feel they are valued and develop positive self-esteem.

Figure 14.12　**Procedures That May Help Children Develop Positive Self-Esteem**

- Listen attentively to children, and ask them for suggestions.
- Help children learn to identify their own positive attributes.
- Provide many experiences in which children are likely to feel successful.
- Allow children to carry out and complete tasks independently.
- Help children learn to evaluate their own accomplishments and work for improvement rather than perfection.
- Give children responsibilities, such as jobs around the house or school.
- Avoid comparisons and competition among children.
- Create an atmosphere of trust and love.
- Be available to children (make time for them).
- Stimulate and lead, but do not push.
- Make sure that children know they are unique and special.

Every child has a right to know that they are unique and special. Children feel unique, special, and valued depending on what others say about them and how others act toward them. Children who are told, "I'm glad you're here," are likely to feel valued. When adults take the time to stop and listen or give them a hug, children sense that they are valued (Nottelmann, 1987). Children need a great deal of affirmation. They need to hear, "I know you can do it." When children are treated with concern and approval, they are more likely to develop positive self-esteem. Children who are rejected or frequently criticized are likely to develop negative self-esteem. Figure 14.13 lists statements of affirmation.

When children finish tasks, such as buttoning their coat unassisted, they have a reason to feel good about themselves. Adults must make certain that children have many such experiences. Too often, when adults are in a rush, they do things for children that they are capable of doing themselves. This approach denies children opportunities to feel good about their accomplishments.

Self-esteem develops through positive interactions with others. It is strengthened by undertaking challenging tasks, overcoming obstacles, and helping others. If a task is too easy, it will not help boost self-esteem. If a task is too difficult, it is likely to lead to a sense of failure and have a negative effect on a child's self-esteem (Marsh, 1986). When children receive appropriate levels of help in acquiring skills, their self-esteem is often enhanced. Developing skills provides children with a sense of competency, which generally translates into esteem building.

When children are taught new skills, there must be ample opportunity for them to feel successful. Positive feedback must be provided at different points in the process

Figure 14.13   **Statements of Affirmation**

A child's self-esteem may be enhanced by statements of affirmation
such as these:

- I am glad you are you.
- You may grow at your own pace.
- I value you just the way you are.
- You may make mistakes; I will see them as mistakes, not failures.
- When I feel I must discipline you, I will try to do so in private.
- I will teach you what I want you to do as well as what I don't want you to do.
- You may express your feelings.
- You may explore and experiment while I support you.
- I like to watch you initiate activities and grow and learn.
- I love and willingly care for you.
- I love you whether you are active or quiet.
- Even when you are not with me, I love you.

of learning a task. For example, a teacher could say, "I really like how hard you are working on your picture. You are using so many colors." In this example the adult does not say, "It's a beautiful picture" or "You made the best picture." Often, children's pictures are not particularly beautiful, and only one child draws the "best" picture. Stating facts about their pictures such as "You used many colors" is not judgmental or comparative but tells children that their work is important and someone took the time to notice their picture's uniqueness. Children benefit when adults acknowledge the completion of tasks, whatever they are. Saying things such as "Wow! You're done. You worked for a very long time" avoids comparative evaluation but acknowledges perseverance.

False or comparative praise such as "You are the best" is misleading, and children ultimately realize this when the same compliments are used for other children. Adults too frequently repeat the same praise to all children. When adults uniformly respond using general comments, children learn that praise is not directed at them but is just something adults say and perhaps do not really mean. Such praise also does not provide specific information to the child regarding why they are receiving praise. For example, "Good job" is not as informative as "I really like your tall tower."

Just as a plant needs sun and water, children need encouragement. Far too often, the children who most need encouragement receive the least. This may result in their behaving in ways that contribute to adults' negative reactions and make the children feel discouraged or even rebellious.

Realistic Expectations

Children with developmental delays are particularly vulnerable to adults' unrealistic expectations. Comments such as "Isn't he ready for regular kindergarten?" or "I hope my child will outgrow this delay by the time he is school age" may indicate to children that they are not good enough the way they are. Such messages certainly do not convey unconditional positive regard. Such comments place pressure on children to succeed at unrealistic goals or be unsatisfied with their accomplishments. Attempting to reach developmentally inappropriate goals leads children to a sense of failure (Stipek, Gralinski, & Kopp, 1990). Lack of success often results in negative self-esteem, which results in children's avoiding certain tasks. Avoiding tasks is likely to increase developmental delay. Failures create a vicious cycle of more inappropriate expectations, frustrations, and failures.

Children with developmental delays may feel guilty about the inconvenience they perceive they have caused others. They may hear comments such as "All these doctor bills prevent us from taking a vacation" or "She requires all of my time." Even children who cannot fully process the meaning of these statements are likely to sense their meaning. Children with developmental delays also become aware of their siblings' feelings of frustration because they overhear remarks such as "Mom, it isn't fair that you spend all your time with Billy."

At times, individuals involved with children with developmental delays become frustrated, overwhelmed, or angry when dealing with the children's needs is especially challenging or their dreams for the child do not come true. Although this is logical, they should avoid showing these feelings when the children are present.

Children with disabilities can sense others' frustrations, anger, and depression, which lead to their developing the same feelings (Mahoney et al., 1992a). When children sense that others feel good about them, they are more likely to feel good and succeed. When they sense that others do not feel good about them, they are unlikely to attempt tasks or to succeed (Bullock & Lütkenhaus, 1988). When adults indicate confidence in children, children are more likely to attempt increasingly difficult tasks.

Perhaps no area of development is more important than children's self-esteem. Because self-esteem depends on successes in relation to expectations, adults must help children develop appropriate expectations. Children must be taught to value differences in themselves and other people (Marsh, 1986). If appropriate expectations have been established, children are more likely to succeed. When children succeed, adults should acknowledge the success (e.g., say, "Good job."). Gradually, children must be helped to learn to acknowledge their own accomplishments as well.

The Future of Early Childhood Special Education

As discussed in Chapter 1, education in general, early childhood education, and early childhood special education have changed a great deal over the past 2 decades. Changes will continue and are necessary to help ensure that young children with disabilities receive optimal intervention services.

Funding and Research

Additional federal and state research and money are needed to ensure adequate and frequent screenings for possible developmental delays. Ideally, pediatric health service settings will increasingly prioritize incorporating early screenings into well-child care and will guarantee high-quality health services.

Funding for the development and distribution of assistive technology for children with disabilities must continue. More emphasis should be placed on the use of assistive technology in early childhood intervention services. Such technology increases children's options and independence. Staff will need continued support in how to most effectively use this technology.

To enhance early childhood intervention services, adults must ensure that children have access to environments that provide developmentally appropriate experiences. Research continues to support the need to identify and use everyday activities to enhance children's development.

Staff Training

The type of pre-service training available in various disciplines to individuals who will work with children who have disabilities and their families has been criticized. For example, there is no guarantee that graduates in these fields have been trained specifically to work with young children and their families. All staff working with young children should be trained regarding the unique developmental needs of young children. More higher education programs must be developed to help ensure that increased staffing needs are adequately met. These programs should require students to develop skills specifically related to infancy, early childhood development, and families. Students need to develop in-depth knowledge of child development theory, identification and assessment strategies, intervention methods, family attributes, communication methods, and ways to develop highly effective team relationships.

Students must be adequately trained to work with other disciplines as well as a wide variety of agencies. It is crucial that all professionals develop knowledge about effective interagency coordination and service integration strategies, as required by Part H of IDEA. In addition, enhanced in-service training is needed to help ensure that staff remain current in their understanding of the most effective early intervention services.

Evaluation

As discussed in Chapter 2, highly accurate and efficient evaluation is crucial to providing young children with high-quality intervention services. Evaluation of screenings, full assessment, and programs must be ongoing. Increased focus on assessment practices and use of data to improve developmentally appropriate practices, instruction, and outcomes for young children are crucial.

Professionals working with young children with disabilities and their families must address an ever-increasing number of issues as they develop and revise intervention plans based on assessment data. This process is complex, due to the increasing heterogeneity of children and their families. A limited number of standardized assessment devices are currently available that meet the diverse developmental needs. To help remedy inherent assessment problems, evaluation must increasingly be multi-dimensional. Professionals will be expected to assess the outcomes of increasingly diverse family issues and other variables. Assessment will need to be both formative (occurring during service delivery) and summative (occurring at the conclusion of services).

Family and Community Involvement

As required by the 1986 amendments to the Education of the Handicapped Act (P.L. 99-457), inclusive, coordinated, comprehensive, family-centered services require continued reshaping of early intervention specialists from nearly exclusively direct service providers to increasingly indirect service providers capable of assuming multiple roles. Additionally, the focus on family-centered services requires service providers to increase focus on the importance of family involvement in all aspects of decision making regarding planning, implementation, and evaluation of services for children.

The effectiveness of family involvement must be evaluated. The assessments must result in families' being treated with dignity and respect and be culturally and socioeconomically sensitive. Families must be provided with service choices that focus on their priorities and concerns. They must have full, easy access to all information about the services being provided. This allows families to be more directly involved in decisions about service plans.

As children are provided services, they have a large number and variety of learning experiences within programs and family and community activities. The relationships among all these experiences must continually be researched, evaluated, and modified.

Transitions

State and federal legislation, federal funding initiatives, and the professional literature have addressed the importance of transition planning. As discussed in this chapter, successful transitions require carefully planned steps, which guide child and family into future settings. Successful transitions must remain a priority of early childhood intervention programs. More-intensive research about methods to reduce the number of transitions and to help ensure smooth transitions is needed. Enhanced assessment of parents' satisfaction with the transition process is crucial.

Collaborative Service Models

Early childhood intervention requires that agencies develop collaborative service models. A logical extension of this requirement for services for young children with disabilities is to create collaborative service models that include the early care and education needs of all young children. The goal should be to ensure seamless service delivery that focuses on children's and families' needs instead of on funding constraints and other potential program limitations. Evaluation of collaboration's efficiency, reduction of service duplication, and cost savings should be further investigated.

Conclusions

High-quality early intervention programs are crucial for children with disabilities. The quality of interaction is important, but children also need ample amounts of time interacting with caring adults. Parents usually are children's long-term teachers. They must be encouraged and allowed to work with professionals on behalf of their children. As children move from one program or service delivery method to another, it is crucial that transition plans be created. These plans must be collaboratively developed and must consider each child's and family member's specific needs.

Adults must provide children with unconditional positive regard by using kind words, smiling, and always greeting children as if they are valued, special, and welcome. Children need help in developing positive self-esteem.

Increased and more effective advocacy for all young children, including those with disabilities, must remain a priority (Gargiulo, 2003). Development of high-quality guaranteed health care would help ensure the well-being of children with disabilities. Enhanced family involvement will require increased provisions for family leave, flex-work schedules, and parent training and support. Federal standards regarding the meaning of "quality" early childhood intervention and educators are needed. Ideally, these standards will include a comprehensive plan for personnel preparation and ongoing professional development. Continued integration of early childhood special education services with federal and state at-risk programs and regular preschool and day care settings will help ensure that local school districts routinely prioritize providing services within the least restrictive environments.

CHAPTER SUMMARY

- Transitions to new programs are often stressful for children, parents, teachers, and therapists.

- Transition plans must be included in the child's IFSP and should also be part of the IEP. They must include a timetable and procedures for the transition and be developed cooperatively by parents and all professionals who are a part of the transition team.

- The staff of children's current and new programs can help ease the transition for the child and their family.

- Some children are unprepared to enter kindergarten programs when they are 5 years old because many programs expect high levels of social maturity and cognitive skills.

- There are several readiness activities that preschool teachers and parents should provide for children to help prepare them for kindergarten.

- Children must receive unconditional positive regard, which promotes positive self-esteem.

- Children with positive self-esteem are likely to try new things and have the confidence to interact with peers and adults in new situations.

- The future of early childhood special education is likely to include additional health care services, research, funding, and staff training; enhanced family and community involvement; refined assessment methods; and greater focus on collaboration.

CHAPTER KEY TERMS

transition
Brigance Comprehensive Inventory of Basic Skills,
    Revised (CIBS-R)
unconditional positive regard

self-concept
self-image
self-esteem

REVIEW QUESTIONS

1. How important is it to have a transition plan for each child with a disability? How might teachers and therapists help ease the stress of transition for children and their families?

2. What are the federal requirements with regard to transition planning in early childhood education?

3. What skills are key to children's success in kindergarten? How might teachers and parents help children develop kindergarten readiness skills?

4. What is meant by providing unconditional positive regard? How does it affect self-esteem?

5. Why are children with disabilities at risk of developing negative self-esteem? What can parents and teachers do to help them develop positive self-esteem?

6. Imagine you are on staff in a kindergarten special education classroom in which a new student has just arrived for their first day of school. What steps would you take to ensure an easy transition for the child from the time they are dropped off in the morning to the time they are picked up at the end of the day? What would you do differently when engaging with a special-needs child?

7. Review the federal laws for transitioning in early childhood education. What law would you amend and why? Is the law a positive law, or does it have inherent problems? How would you rewrite the law to better meet the needs of a transitioning child?

8. How can a transition plan help reduce parental stress? What are the benefits to both the child and the parent of making sure that the child is ready to transition?

9. What skills are important for a child to develop before they transition to a school environment? How can children work to develop these skills at home?

SUGGESTED STUDENT ACTIVITIES

1. Develop a transition plan for a child with a specific disability who is moving from a center-based program for children with disabilities to an inclusion kindergarten program.

2. Interview two teachers, one in a regular preschool and the other in a special education preschool. Ask how they prepare chil-

dren for kindergarten and which skills they believe are most crucial for children's kindergarten success.

3. Ask a kindergarten teacher how they prepare for the inclusion of a child with a disability. Also ask them to tell you about transition problems they have encountered.

4. Assume the role of a professional who has been asked to give a parent–teacher workshop on developing positive self-esteem in children. Describe what you will include in your workshop presentation.

5. Observe a regular preschool classroom and a preschool special education classroom on the first days of school. Pick one child and make notes on their day, including how their parent interacts with them when they are dropped off and picked up. Return to the classroom a few weeks later, and observe the same child. Has anything changed? Has the child transitioned well?

6. Describe how you would plan a day in which your child and a friend of theirs would play, to help pretransition the child for an academic setting. What activities would you plan and what would be their purpose? How would you make sure they were fun and engaging, yet meaningful?

7. Assume the role of teacher, and design an organization system for your early childhood classroom. It can be for toy storage, coats and shoes, art supplies, or something else. Include a description of each part of your proposed organization system and how each part can help children develop useful methods of organization. Be sure to include how the system could be modified for a child with special needs.

REFERENCES

Abel, E. L. (1999). What really causes FAS? *Teratology, 59,* 4–6.

Able-Boone, H., Sandall, S., Stevens, E., & Frederick, L. L. (1992). Family support resources and needs: How early intervention can make a difference. *Infant-Toddler Intervention, 2*(2), 93–102.

Abramson, L. Y., Seligman, M. E. P., & Teasdale, J. D. (1978). Learned helplessness in humans: Critique and reformulation. *Journal of Abnormal Psychology, 87,* 49–74.

Accardo, P. J., O'Connor-Leppert, M. L., Lipkin, P. H., & Rogers, B. T. (2005). *Early intervention: Biomedical and social perspectives.* Austin, TX: Pro-Ed.

Acredolo, L. P., Goodwyn, S. W., Horobin, K. D., & Emmons, Y. D. (1999). The signs and sounds of early language development. In C. Tamis-LeMonda & L. Balter (Eds.), *Child psychology: A handbook of contemporary issues* (pp. 116–142). New York: Psychology Press.

Addison, R., & Tosti, D. T. (1979). Taxonomy of educational reinforcement. *Educational Technology, 19,* 24–45.

Adelson, E., & Fraiberg, S. (1974). Gross motor development in infants blind from birth. *Child Development, 45,* 114–126.

Aiello, B. (1976). Especially for special educators: A sense of our own history. *Exceptional Children, 42,* 244–252.

Aiello, J. (1987). Human spatial behavior. In D. Stokols & I. Altman (Eds.), *Handbook of environmental psychology.* New York: Wiley.

Ainsworth, M. D. S., Blehar, M. C., Waters, E., & Wall, S. (1978). *Patterns of attachment: A psychological study of the strange situation.* Hillsdale, NJ: Lawrence Erlbaum Associates.

Alberto, P. A., & Troutman, A. C. (1990). *Applied behavior analysis for teachers: Influencing student performance* (3rd ed.). New York: Macmillan.

Alexander, K., & Alexander, M. D. (2001). *American public school law* (5th ed.). Belmont, CA: Wadsworth/Thomson Learning.

Alexander, R., & Tompkins-McGill, P. (1981). Notes to the experts from the parent of a handicapped child. *Social Work, 32,* 361–264.

Alkema, C. J. (1971). *Art for the exceptional child.* Boulder, CO: Pruett.

Allen, K. E. (1992). *The exceptional child: Mainstreaming in early childhood education* (2nd ed.). Albany, NY: Delmar.

Allen, K. E., & Marotz, L. (1989). *Developmental profiles: Birth to six.* Albany, NY: Delmar.

Allen, K. E., & Schwartz, I. S. (2001). *The exceptional child: Inclusion in early childhood education.* Albany, NY: Thomson/Delmar Learning.

Allsopp, D. H., Santos, K. E., & Linn, R. (2000). Collaborating to teach pro-social skills. *Intervention in Schools and Clinics, 33,* 142–147.

Altermatt, E. R., Pomerantz, E. M., Ruble, D. N., Frey, K. S., & Greulich, F. K. (2002). Predicting changes in children's self-perceptions of academic competence: A naturalistic examination of evaluative discourse among classmates. *Developmental Psychology, 38,* 903–917.

American Academy of Allergy, Asthma, and Immunology. (2004). *Allergy and Asthma Advocate.* Retrieved January 16, 2008, from www.aaaai .org/patients/advocate/2004/fall/costs.stm

American Academy of Child and Adolescent Psychiatry. (2008). The depressed child. *Facts for families fact sheet series.* Retrieved January 4, 2008, from www.aacap.org/publications/facts fam/depressd.htm.

American Academy of Pediatrics (1999). Newborn and infant hearing loss: Detection and intervention. *Pediatrics, 103,* 537–630.

American Academy of Pediatrics. (2000). Clinical practice guidelines for the diagnosis and evalation of children with ADHD. *Pediatrics, 105,* 1158–1170.

American Academy of Pediatrics. (2002a). *The classification of child and adolescent mental diagnoses in primary care: Diagnostic and statistical manual for primary care (DSM-PC), child and adolescent version.* Oak Park, IL: Author.

American Academy of Pediatrics (2002b). Supervision for children with sickle cell disease. *Pediatrics, 109,* 69–74.

American Academy of Pediatrics. Committee on Substance Abuse and Committee on Children with Disabilities. (1993). Fetal alcohol syndrome and fetal alcohol effects. *Pediatrics, 91,* 10004–10006.

American Association on Mental Retardation. (2002). *Mental retardation: Definition, classification, and systems of supports* (10th ed.). Washington, DC: Author.

American Association on Mental Retardation. (2006). *Definition of mental retardation.* Retrieved January 17, 2008, from www.aamr.org/

American Educational Research Association (AERA), American Psychological Association, & National Council on Measurement in Education. Joint Committee on Standards for Educational and Psychological Testing. (1999). *Standards for educational and psychological testing.* Washington, DC: AERA.

American Foundation for the Blind. (1998*). AFB directory of services for blind and visually impaired persons in the United States and Canada* (27th ed.). New York: Author.

American Occupational Therapy Association. (2000). *Occupational therapy services for children and youth under the Individuals with Disabilities Education Act.* Bethesda, MD: Author.

American Physical Therapy Association. (1996). *Evaluative criteria for accreditation of education programs for the preparation of physical therapists.* Alexandria, VA: Author.

American Psychiatric Association (2000). *Diagnostic and statistical manual of mental disorders* (4th ed.). Washington, DC: Author.

American Speech-Language-Hearing Association. (2001). *Roles and responsibilities of speech-language pathologists with respect to reading and writing in children and adolescents* (guidelines). Rockville, MD: Author.

Amerson, M. J. (1999). Helping children with visual and motor impairments make the most of their visual abilities. *Review, 31,* 17–20.

Ames, C. (1990). Motivation: What teachers need to know. *Teachers College Record, 91,* 409–421.

Anderson, A., Moore, D. W., Godfrey, R., & Fletcher-Flinn, C. M. (2004). Social skills assessment of children with autism in free-play situations. *Autism, 8,* 369–385.

Anderson, D. R., Hodson, G. D., & Jones, W. G. (1975). *Instructional programming for the handicapped student.* Springfield, IL: Charles C. Thomas.

Anderson, F. (1978). *Art for all the children.* Springfield, IL: Charles C. Thomas.

Anderson, J. P. (1986). Humanism, art educational philosophy in transition. *Art Education, 25*(7), 18–19.

Anderson, R. D., Bale, J. F., Blackman, J. A., & Murphy, J. R. (1986). *Infections in children: A source book for educators and child care providers.* Rockville, MD: Aspen.

Anderson, R. M. (1982). The possible role of paternal alcohol consumption in the etiology of the fetal alcohol syndrome. In E. Abel (Ed.), *Fetal alcohol syndrome* (Vol. 3: *Animal studies,* pp. 152–189). Boca Raton, FL: CRC Press.

Anderson, R. M., & May, R. M. (1992, May). Understanding the AIDS pandemic. *Scientific American,* 58–66.

Anita, S. D., & Kreimeyer, K. H. (1992). Social competence intervention for young children with hearing impairments. In S. L. Odom, S. R. McConnell, & M. A. McEvoy (Eds.), *Social competence of young children with disabilities* (pp. 113–134). Baltimore: Paul H. Brookes.

Annie E. Casey Foundation. (1998). *1998 kids count data book: Overview.* Baltimore: Author.

Apel, K., & Masterson, J. J. (2001). *Beyond baby talk.* Roseville, CA: Prima Publishing.

Apgar, V. (1953). A proposal for a new method of evaluation of the newborn infant. *Current Research Anesthesia and Analgesia, 32*(4), 260–267.

Apple, W., & Hecht, K. (1982). Speaking emotionally: The relationship between verbal and vocal communication of affect. *Journal of Personality and Social Psychology, 37,* 715–727.

Appleby, E. T. (1994). *The relationship between self-advocacy and self-concept.* Ann Arbor, MI: University Microfilms International. No. 9411230.

Appleton, R., Nicolson, A., Smith, D., Chadwick, D., & Mackenzie, J. (2006). *Atlas of epilepsy* (2nd ed.). New York: Taylor & Francis.

Arc. (2002). Introduction to mental retardation. Retrieved January 2, 2008, from www.thearc.org.

Armstrong, F. D., Seidel, J. F., & Swales, T. P. (1993). Pediatric HIV infection: A neuropsychological and educational challenge. *Journal of Learning Disabilities, 26(2),* 92–103.

Arnos, K. S., Israel, J., Devlin, L., & Wilson, M. P. (1996). Genetic aspects of hearing loss in childhood. In F. N. Martin & J. G. Clark (Eds.), *Hearing care for children* (pp. 20–44). Boston: Allyn & Bacon.

Aslin, R. N. (1987a). Motor aspects of visual development in infancy. In P. Salapatek & L. Cohen (Eds.), *Handbook of infant perception* (Vol. 1: *From sensation to perception,* pp. 43–113). Orlando, FL: Academic Press.

Aslin, R. N. (1987b). Visual and auditory development in infancy. In J. D. Osofsky (Ed.), *Handbook of infant development* (2nd ed., pp. 5–97). New York: Wiley-Interscience.

Aslin, R. N., & Smith L. B. (1988). Perceptual development. *Annual Review of Psychology, 39,* 435–473.

Association for the Care of Children's Health. (1984). *Home care for children: An annotated bibliography.* Washington, DC: Author.

Association of Teacher Educators & National Association for the Education of Young Children. (1991). Early childhood teacher certification: A position statement. *Young Children, 47(1),* 16–27.

Astley, S. J., & Clarren, S. K. (2005). Diagnosing the full spectrum of fetal alcohol-exposed individuals: Introducing the 4-digit diagnostic code. *Alcohol 2000, 35,* 400–410.

Atack, S. M. (1986). *Art activities for the handicapped.* Englewood Cliffs, NJ: Prentice-Hall.

Axline, V. M. (1947). *Play therapy.* New York: Ballantine Books.

Ayres, J. (1972). *Sensory integration and learning disorders.* Los Angeles: Western Psychological Services.

Ayres, J. (2005). *Sensory integration and the child: Understanding hidden sensory challenges* (25th anniversary ed.). Austin, TX: Pro-Ed.

Azuma, S. D., & Chasnoff, I. J. (1993). Outcome of children prenatally exposed to cocaine and other drugs: A path analysis of three-year data. *Pediatrics, 92(3),* 396–402.

Bagnato, S. J., & Neisworth, J. T. (1981). *Linking developmental assessment and curricula: Prescriptions for early intervention.* Rockville, MD: Aspen.

Bagnato, S. J., & Neisworth, J. T. (1991). *Assessment for early intervention: Best practices for professionals.* New York: Guilford.

Bagnato, S. J., & Neisworth, J. T. (1999). Collaboration and teamwork in assessment for early intervention. *Comprehensive Psychiatric Assessment of Young Children, 8(2),* 347–363.

Bagnato, S. J., Neisworth, J. T., & Munson, S. M. (1997). *LINKing assessment and early intervention: An authentic curriculum-based approach.* Baltimore: Paul H. Brookes.

Bagnato, S. J., Neisworth, J. T., Salvia, J., & Hunt, J. (1999). *Temperament and Atypical Behavior Scale (TABS): Early childhood indicators of developmental dysfunction.* Baltimore: Paul H. Brookes.

Bailey, D. B. (1987). Collaborative goal-setting with families: Resolving differences in values and priorities for services. *Topics in Early Childhood Special Education, 7,* 59–71.

Bailey, D. B. (1996). Assessing family resources, priorities, and concerns. In M. McLearn, D. B. Bailey, & M. Wolery (Eds.), *Assessing infants and preschoolers with special needs* (2nd ed., pp. 202–233). Columbus, OH: Merrill.

Bailey, D. B. (2001). Evaluating parent involvement and family support in early intervention and preschool programs. *Journal of Early Intervention, 24,* 1–14.

Bailey, D. B., Hebbeler, K., Scarborough, A., Spiker, D., & Mallik, S. (2004). First experiences with early intervention. *Pediatrics, 11(4),* 887–896.

Bailey, D. B., & McWilliams, R. (1990). Normalizing early intervention. *Topics in Early Childhood Special Education, 10(2),* 33–47.

Bailey, D. B., McWilliams, P., & Simeonsson, R. J. (1991). *Implementing family-centered services in early intervention: A team-based model for change.* Chapel Hill, NC: Carolina Institute for Research on Infant Personnel Preparation, University of North Carolina.

Bailey, D. B., Palsha, S. A., & Simeonsson, R. J. (1991). Professional skills concerns and perceived importance of work with families in early intervention. *Exceptional Children, 58(2),* 156–165.

Baily, D. B., Scarborough, A., & Hebbeler, K. (2003). *Families' first experiences with early intervention.* Menlo Park, CA: SRI International.

Bailey, D. B., & Simeonsson, R. J. (1988a). Assessing the needs of families with handicapped infants. *Journal of Special Education, 22*(1), 117–126.

Bailey, D. B., & Simeonsson, R. J. (1988b). *Family assessment in early intervention.* Columbus, OH: Merrill.

Bailey, D. B., Skinner, D., Hatton, D., & Roberts, J. (2000). Family experiences and factors associated with the diagnosis of fragile X syndrome. *Developmental and Behavioral Pediatrics, 21,* 315–321.

Bailey, D. B., & Wolery, M. (1984). *Teaching infants and preschoolers with handicaps.* Columbus, OH: Merrill.

Baker, B. L., & Brightman, A. J. (with Blacher, J., Heifetz, L., Hinshaw, S., & Murphy, D.). (1997). *Steps to independence: Teaching everyday skills to children with special needs* (4th ed.). Baltimore: Paul H. Brookes.

Baker, B. L., Brightman, A. J., Heifetz, L. J., & Murphy, D. M. (1990). *Behavior Problems.* Champaign, IL: Research Press.

Baker, E. T., Wang, M. C., & Walberg, H. J. (1995). Synthesis of research: The effects of inclusion on Learning, *Educational Leadership, 52*(4), 33–34.

Baker, M. J., Banfield, C. S., Killburn, D., & Shuflebarger, K. J. (1991). *Controlling movement: A therapeutic approach to early intervention.* Gaithersburg, MD: Aspen.

Balaban, N. (1985). *Starting school: From separation to independence.* New York: Teachers College Press.

Ballard, J., Ramirez, B. A., & Weintraub, F. J. (1982). *Special education in America: Its legal and governmental foundations.* Reston, VA: Council for Exceptional Children.

Bambring, M., & Troster, H. (1992). On the stability of stereotyped behaviors in blind infants and preschoolers. *Journal of Visual Impairments and Blindness, 86*(2), 105–110.

Barber, L. W., & Williams, H. (1981). *Your baby's first 30 months.* Tucson, AZ: Fisher.

Barbour, N. H., & Seefeldt, C. A. (1993). *Developmental continuity across preschool and primary grades: Implications for teachers.* Wheaton, MD: Association for Childhood Education International.

Barkley, R., Shelton, T., Crosswait, C., Moorehouse, M., Fletcher, K., Barrett, S., Jenkins, L., & Metevia, L. (2000). Multimethod psycho-education for preschool children with disruptive behavior: Preliminary result at post-treatment. *Journal of Child Psychology and Psychiatry and Allied Disciplines, 41*(3), 319–332.

Barnett, W. S. (1993). Benefit-cost analysis of preschool education: Findings from a 25-year follow-up. *American Journal of Orthopsychiatry, 63,* 500–508.

Barnett, W. S., & Yarosz, D. J. (2004). *Who goes to preschool and why does it matter?* New Brunswick, NJ: National Institute for Early Education Research.

Barraga, N. C., & Erin, J. N. (1992). *Visual handicaps and learning* (3rd ed.). Austin, TX: Pro-Ed.

Barrett, K., & Campos, J. (1987). Perspectives on emotional development: A functionalist approach to emotions. In J. Osofsky (Ed.), *Handbook of infant development* (2nd ed., pp. 555–578). New York: Wiley.

Bartel, N. R., & Guskin, S. L. (1980). A handicap as a social phenomenon. In W. M. Cruickshank (Ed.), *Psychology of exceptional children and youth* (4th ed.). Englewood Cliffs, NJ: Prentice-Hall.

Barth, R. P. (2001). Research outcomes of prenatal substance exposure and the need to review policies and procedures regarding child abuse reporting. *Child Welfare, 80*(2), 275–296.

Bates, E. (1993). Commentary: Comprehension and production in early language development. *Monographs of the Society for Research in Child Development, 58* (Nos. 3–4, Serial No. 233), 222–242.

Bates, E., Bretherton, I., & Snyder, L. (1988). *From first words to grammar: Individual differences and dissociable mechanisms.* Cambridge: Cambridge University Press.

Bates, E., O'Connell, B., & Shore, C. M. (1987). Language and communication in infancy. In J. D. Osofsky (Ed.), *Handbook of infant development* (2nd ed., pp. 149–203). New York: Wiley-Interscience.

Batshaw, M. L. (1991). *When your child has a disability: The complete sourcebook of daily and medical care.* Boston: Little, Brown.

Batshaw, M. L., & Perret, Y. M. (1986). *Children with handicaps: A medical primer* (2nd ed.). Baltimore: Paul H. Brookes.

Baumrind, D. (1977). Some thoughts about child rearing. In S. Cohen & T. J. Comiskey (Eds.),

Child development: Contemporary perspectives. Itasca, IL: F. E. Peacock.

Bayley, N. (1935). The development of motor abilities during the first three years. *Monographs of the Society for Research in Child Development, 1*(1), 1–26.

Becker, W. C. (1990). *Parents are teachers: A child management program.* Champaign, IL: Research Press.

Beckoff, A. G., & Bender, W. N. (1989). Programming for mainstream kindergarten success in preschool: Teachers' perceptions of necessary prerequisite skills. *Journal of Early Intervention, 13*(3), 269–280.

Beckwith, L., Crawford, S., Moore, J. A., & Howard, J. (1995). Attentional and social functioning of preschool-age children exposed to PCP and cocaine in utero. In M. Lewis & M. Bendersky (Eds.), *Mother, babies and cocaine: The role of toxins in development* (pp. 287–303). Hillsdale, NJ: Lawrence Erlbaum Associates.

Behren, D. (1988). Overextensions in early language comprehension: Evidence from a signal detection approach. *Journal of Child Language, 15,* 63–75.

Beirne-Smith, M., Patton, J. R., & Ittenbach, R. (1994). *Mental retardation* (4th ed.). Columbus, OH: Merrill.

Beirne-Smith, M., Patton, J. R., & Kim, S. H. (2006). *Mental Retardation: An introduction to intellectual disability* (7th ed.). Upper Saddle River, NJ: Prentice-Hall.

Beittel, K. E. (1974). *Alternatives for art education research.* Dubuque, IA: William C. Brown.

Beller, E. K. (1979). Early intervention programs. In J. D. Osofsky (Ed.), *Handbook of infancy research.* New York: Wiley.

Bender, W. N. (1992). *Learning disabilities: Characteristics, identification, and teaching strategies.* Needham Heights, MA: Allyn & Bacon.

Benner, S. M. (1992). *Assessing young children with disabilities: An ecological perspective.* White Plains, NY: Longman.

Benner, S. M. (1998). *Special education issues within the context of American society.* Belmont, CA: Wadsworth.

Bennett, T., Raab, M., & Nelson, D. C. (1991). The transition process for toddlers with special needs and their families. *Zero to Three, 11*(3), 17–21.

Bergen, A. F. (1990). *Positioning for function.* Valhalla, NY: Valhalla Rehabilitation Publications.

Bergen, D. (2002). The role of pretend play in children's cognitive development. *Early Childhood Research Practice,* [Electronic version] Retrieved June 2, 2007, from http://ecrp.uiuc.edu/v4n2/bergen.html.

Berger, L., & Waldfogel, J. (2000). Prenatal cocaine exposure: Long-run effects and policy implications. *Social Science Review, 74*(1), 28–54.

Berger, M., & Fowlkes, M. A. (1980). Family intervention project: A family network model for serving young handicapped children. *Young Children, 35,* 22–32.

Bergland, M., & Hoffbauer, D. (1996). New opportunities for students with traumatic brain injury: Transition to postsecondary education. *Teaching Exceptional Children, 28,* 54–57.

Berk, L. E. (1992). Children's private speech: An overview of theory and the status of research. In R. M. Diaz & L. E. Berk (Eds.), *Private speech: From social interaction to self-regulation* (pp. 17–53). Hillsdale, NJ: Lawrence Erlbaum Associates.

Berk, L. E. (1994). *Child development* (3rd ed.). Boston: Allyn & Bacon.

Berk, L. E. (2005). *Child development* (7th ed.). Boston: Allyn & Bacon.

Berkeley, T. R., & Ludlow, B. L. (1989). Toward a reconceptualization of the developmental model. *Topics in Early Childhood Special Education, 9,* 51–66.

Berko, G. J. (1989). Studying language development. In J. Berko Gleason (Ed.), *The development of language* (pp. 1–34). Columbus, OH: Merrill.

Berman, C., & Shaw, E. (1996). Family-directed child evaluation and assessment under the Individual with Disabilities Education Act (IDEA). In S. J. Meisels & E. Fenichel (Eds.), *New vision for the developmental assessment of infants and young children* (pp. 361–390). Washington, DC: Zero to Three.

Bernstein, D. K., & Tiegerman, E. (1989). Language and communication disorders in children (2nd ed.). Columbus, OH: Merrill.

Bertenthal, B. I., & Campos, J. J. (1987). New directions in the study of early experience. *Child Development, 58,* 560–567.

Bess, F. H. (Ed.). (1988). *Hearing impairment in children.* York, PA: York Press.

Bettelheim, B. (1987, March). The importance of play. *The Atlantic, 35.*

Betz, C. (1994). Beyond time-out: Tips for a teacher. *Young Children, 49*(3), 10–14.

Beukelman, D. R., & Mirenda, P. (1998). *Augmentative and alternative communication* (2nd ed.). Baltimore: Paul H. Brookes.

Biale, R. (1989). Counseling families of disabled twins. *Social Work, 34,* 531–535.

Bigge, J. L. (1991). *Teaching individuals with physical and multiple disabilities* (3rd ed.). Columbus, OH: Merrill/Macmillan.

Bigge, R. A., & Burton, E. C. (1989). *The dynamic infant.* St. Paul, MN: Toys 'n Things.

Biklen, D. (1992). Typing to talk: Facilitated communication. *American Journal of Speech-Language Pathology, 1*(2), 15–17.

Biklen, D., Morton, M., Gold, D., Berrigan, C., & Swaminathan, S. (1992). Facilitated communication: Implications for people with autism and other developmental disabilities. *Topics in Language Disorders, 12,* 1–28.

Bilmes, J. (2004). *Beyond behavior management: The six life skills children need to thrive in today's world.* St. Paul, MN: Redleaf.

Bishop, K. K., Rounds, K., & Weil, M. (1993). P.L. 99-457: Preparation for social work practice with infants and toddlers with disabilities and their families. *Journal of Social Work Education, 29,* 36–45.

Bisiacchi, P. S., Suppiej, A., & Laverda, A. (2000). Neuropsychological evaluation of neurologically asymptomatic HIV-infected children. *Brain Cognition, 43*(1–3), 49–52.

Black, B. (1992). Negotiating social pretend play: Communication differences related to social status and sex. *Merrill-Palmer Quarterly, 38,* 212–232.

Blackman, J. A. (Ed.). (1984). *Medical aspects of developmental disabilities in children birth to three* (Rev. ed.). Rockville, MD: Aspen.

Blackman, J. A. (2002). Early intervention: A global perspective. *Infants and Young Children, 15*(2), 11–19.

Blanc, A., & Wardlaw, T. (2005). Monitoring low birth weight: An evaluation of international estimates and an updated estimate procedure. *Bulletin of the World Health Organization, 83*(3), 178–185.

Blank, M. S., Rose, S., & Berlin, L. (1978). *The language of learning: The preschool years.* Orlando, FL: Grune & Stratton.

Blechman, E. A. (1985). *Solving child behavior problems at home and at school.* Champaign, IL: Research Press.

Bleck, E. (1987). *Orthopedic management in cerebral palsy.* Philadelphia: J. B. Lippincott.

Bleck, E., & Nagel, D. A. (1982). *Physically handicapped children: A medical atlas for teachers* (2nd ed.). New York: Grune & Stratton.

Bloom, L., & Lahey, M. (1978). *Language Development and Language Disorders.* New York: Wiley.

Bloom, T. (1996). Assistive listening devices. *Hearing Journal, 49,* 20–23.

Blumberg, H. M., Leonard, M. K., Jr., & Jasmer, R. M. (2005). Update on the treatment of tuberculosis and latent tuberculosis infection. *Journal of the American Medical Association, 8*(22), 2776–2784.

Bobath, B., & Bobath, K. (1975). *Motor development in the different types of cerebral palsy.* London: Heinemann.

Bodrova, E., & Leong, D. J. (2001). *The Tolls of the Mind Project: A case study of implementing the Vygotskian approach in American early childhood and primary classrooms.* Geneva, Switzerland: International Bureau of Education, UNESCO.

Bodrova, E., Leong, D., Norford, J., & Paynter, D. (2006). It only looks like child's play. *Journal of Staff Development, 2*(24), 15–19.

Bodrova, E., Leong, D. J., Paynter, D. E., & Hensen, R. (2002). *Scaffolding literacy development in a kindergarten classroom.* Aurora, CO: Mid-continent Research for Education and Learning.

Boethel, M. (2004). *Readiness: School, family, & community connections: Annual synthesis 2004.* Austin, TX: National Center for Family and Community Connections with Schools.

Bono, K. E., Bolzani-Dinehart, L. H., Claussen, A. H., Scott, K. G., Mundy, P. C., & Katz, L. F. (2005). Early intervention with children prenatally exposed to cocaine: Expansion with multiple cohorts. *Journal of Early Intervention, 27*(4), 268–284.

Boone, D. R. (1987). *Human communication and its disorders.* Englewood Cliffs, NJ: Prentice-Hall.

Boothroyd, A. (1978). Speech perception and severe hearing loss. In M. Ross & T. G. Giolas (Eds.), *Auditory management of hearing-impaired children* (pp. 117–144). Baltimore: University Park Press.

Bornstein, M. H. (1992). Perception across the life span. In M. H. & M. E. Lamb (Eds.), *Developmental psychology: An advanced textbook* (3rd ed., pp. 155–210). Hillsdale, NJ: Lawrence Erlbaum Associates.

Bower, T. J. P. (1977). Blind babies see with their ears. *New Scientist, 73,* 255–257.

Bowerman, M. (1985). Beyond communicative adequacy: From piecemeal knowledge to an integrated system in the child's acquisition of language. In K. E. Nelson (Ed.), *Children's language* (Vol. 5, pp. 369–398). Hillsdale, NJ: Lawrence Erlbaum Associates.

Bowlby, J. (1969). *Attachment* (2nd ed.), *Attachment and Loss* (Vol. 1), New York: Basic Books.

Bowlby, J. (1980). *Attachment and loss.* (Vol. 3: *Loss*). New York: Basic Books.

Bowlby, J. (1990). A secure base: Parent–child attachment and healthy human development. New York: Basic Books.

Bowman, B., Donovan, M. S., & Burns, M. S. (2000). *Eager to learn: Educating our preschoolers.* Washington, DC: National Academies Press.

Boxill, E. H., & Chase, K. M. (2007). *Music therapy for developmental disabilities* (2nd ed.). Austin, TX: Pro-Ed.

Bracken, B. A. (2000). *The psychoeducational assessment of preschool children* (2nd ed.). Boston: Allyn & Bacon.

Brandenburg, N. A., Friedman, R. M., & Silver, S. E. (1990). The epidemiology of childhood psychiatric disorders: Prevalence findings from recent studies. *Journal of the American Association of Child and Adolescent Psychiatry, 29,* 76–83.

Brazelton, T. B., & Greenspan, S. I. (2000). *The irreducible needs of children: What every child must have to grow, learn, and flourish.* Cambridge, MA: Perseus.

Bredekamp, S. (Ed.). (1987). *Developmentally appropriate practice in early childhood programs serving children from birth through age 8* (Expanded ed.). Washington, DC: National Association for the Education of Young Children.

Bredekamp, S., & Copple, C. (Eds.). (1997). *Developmentally appropriate practice in early childhood programs.* (Rev. ed.). Washington, DC: National Association for the Education of Young Children.

Bressanutti, E., Mahoney, G., & Sachs, J. (1992). Predictors of young children's compliance to maternal requests. *International Journal of Cognitive Education and Mediated Learning, 2,* 198–209.

Bricker, D. D. (2002). *Assessment, evaluation and programming system for infants and young children* (2nd ed.). Baltimore: Paul H. Brookes.

Bricker, D. D., Peck, C. B., & Odom, S. L. (1993). Integration: Campaign for the new century. In C. B. Peck, S. L. Odom, & D. D. Bricker (Eds.), *Integrating young children with disabilities into community programs* (pp. 271–276). Baltimore: Paul H. Brookes.

Bricker, D. D., & Squires J. (1989). The effectiveness of parental screening of at-risk infants: The infant monitoring questionnaires. *Topics in Early Childhood Special Education, 9,* 67–85.

Bricker, W. A., & Bricker, D. D. (1976). The infant, toddler, and preschool research and intervention project. In T. D. Tjossem (Ed.), *Intervention strategies for high risk infants and young children.* Baltimore: University Park Press.

Brill, N. I. (1976). *Teamwork: Working together in human services.* Philadelphia: J. B. Lippincott.

Brinkerhoff, J., & Vincent, L. (1987). Increasing parental decision-making at the individualized program meeting. *Journal of the Division of Early Childhood, 11,* 46–58.

Brittain, W. L. (1979). *Creativity, art, and the young child.* New York: Macmillan.

Bronfenbrenner, U. (1979). *The ecology of human development: Experiments by nature and design.* Cambridge, MA: Harvard University Press.

Bronson, M. P. (2000). *Self-regulation in early childhood: nature and nurture.* New York: Guilford Press.

Brooke, M. H. (1991). *A clinician's view of neuromuscular disease* (2nd ed.). Baltimore: Williams & Wilkins.

Brown v. Board of Education, 347 U.S. 483 (1954).

Brown, J. F. (Ed.). (1982). *Curriculum planning for young children.* Washington, DC: National Association for the Education of Young Children.

Brown, P. M., Rickards, F. W., & Bortoli, A. (2001). Structures underpinning pretend play and word production in young hearing children and children with hearing loss. *Journal of Deaf Studies and Deaf Education, 6*(1), 15–31.

Brown, R. T. (1993). An introduction to the special series: Pediatric chronic illness. *Journal of Learning Disabilities, 26,* 4–6.

Brown, W. H., Odom, S. L., & Conroy, M. A. (2001). An intervention hierarchy for promoting preschool children's peer interactions in natural environments. *Topics in Early Childhood Special Education, 21,* 90–134.

Brown, W. N. (2003). *Relational discipline: Strategies for in-your-face kids.* Boston: Allyn & Bacon.

Brownell, C. A., & Brown, E. 1992). Peers and play in infants and toddlers. In V. B. V. Hasselt & M. Hersen (Eds.), *Handbook of social development: A lifespan perspective* (pp. 183–200). New York: Plenum.

Bruder, M. B. (1993). The provision of early intervention and early childhood special education within community early childhood programs: Characteristics of effective service delivery. *Topics in Early Childhood Special Education, 13*(1), 19–37.

Bruder, M. B., Klosowski, S., & Daguio, K. (1989). *Personnel standards for ten professional disciplines serving children under P. L. 99-457: Results from a national survey.* Farmington, CT: Division of Child and Family Studies, Department of Pediatrics, University of Connecticut Health Center.

Brudoff, M., & Orenstein, A. (1984). *Due process in special education: On going to a hearing.* Cambridge, MA: Brookline Books.

Bruer, J. T. (1999). *The myth of the first three years: A new understanding of early brain development and lifelong learning.* New York: Free Press.

Buck, G. H., Polloway, E. A., Patton, J. R., & McConnell, K. (2002). *The pre-referral guide.* Austin, TX: Pro-Ed.

Buckley, J. J. (1983). Roles of the professionals. In R. K. Mulliken & J. J. Buckley (Eds.), *Assessment of multihandicapped and developmentally disabled children* (pp. 63–73). Rockville, MD: Aspen.

Bullock, M., & Lütkenhaus, P. (1988). The development of volitional behavior in the toddler years. *Child Development, 59,* 664–674.

Bullock, M., & Lütkenhaus, P. (1990). Who am I? The development of self-understanding in toddlers. *Merrill-Palmer Quarterly, 36,* 217–238.

Bundy, A. C. (1991). Play theory and sensory integration. In A. G. Fisher, E. A. Murray, & A. C. Bundy (Eds.), *Sensory integration: Theory and practice.* Philadelphia: F. A. Davis.

Bundy, A. C., Lane, S. J., & Murray, E. A. (2002). *Sensory integration: Theory and practice.* Philadelphia: F. A. Davis.

Burack, J. S., Hodapp, R. M., & Zigler, E. (Eds.) (1998). *Handbook of mental retardation and development.* New York: Cambridge University Press.

Burry, C. L., & Noble, L. S. (2001). The STAFF project: Support and training for adoptive and foster families of infants with prenatal substance exposure. *Journal of Social Work Practice in the Addictions, 1*(4), 71–82.

Burton, C. B., Hains, A., Hanline, M. F., McLean, M., & McCormick, K. (1992). Early education policy, practice, and personnel preparation: The urgency of professional unification. *Topics in Early Childhood Special Education, 11*(4), 53–69.

Buscaglia, L. (1975). *The disabled and their parents: A counseling challenge.* Thorofare, NJ: Charles B. Slack.

Butera, G., & Haywood, H. C. (1992). A cognitive approach to the education of young children with autism. *Focus on Autistic Behavior, 6*(6), 1–14.

Butler, K. G. (Ed.). (1991). *Communicating for learning.* Gaithersburg, MD: Aspen.

Butz, A. M., Lears, M. K., & O'Neil, S. (1998). Home intervention for in utero drug-exposed infants. *Public Health Nursing, 15*(5), 307–318.

Butz, A. M., Pulsifer, M., Marano, N., Belcher, H., Lears, M. K., & Royall, R. (2001). Effectiveness of a home intervention for perceived child behavioral problems and parenting stress in children with in utero drug exposure. *Archives of Pediatric and Adolescent Medicine, 9,* 1029–1037.

Byers, J. (1989). AIDS in children: Effects on neurological development and implications for the future. *Journal of Special Education, 23*(1), 5–15.

Cahan, E. (1989). *Past caring: A history of U.S. preschool care and education for the poor, 1820–1965.* New York: National Center for Children in Poverty.

Caldwell, B. M. (1991). Continuity in the early years: Transitions between grades and systems.

In S. L. Kagan (Ed.), *The care and education of America's young children: Obstacles and opportunities: Nineteenth yearbook of the National Society for the Study of Education* (pp. 69–89). Chicago: University of Chicago Press.

Calvert, D. (1984). *Parents' guide to speech and deafness*. Washington, DC: Alexander Graham Bell Association.

Campbell, F. A., Helms, R., Sparling, J. J., & Ramey, C. T. (1998). Early-childhood programs and success in school: The Abecedarian Study. In W. S. Barnette & S. S. Boocock (Eds.), *Early care and education for children in poverty: Promises, programs, and long term effects* (pp. 145–166). Albany, NY: SUNY Press.

Campbell, P. H. (1987a). Physical management and handling procedures with students with movement dysfunction. In M. E. Snell (Ed.), *Systematic instruction of persons with severe handicaps* (3rd ed., pp. 174–187). Columbus, OH: Merrill.

Campbell, P. H. (1987b). Programming for students with dysfunction in posture and movement. In M. E. Snell (Ed.), *Systematic instruction of persons with severe handicaps* (3rd ed., pp. 188–211). Columbus, OH: Merrill.

Campbell, P. H., Green, K. M., & Carlson, L. M. (1977). Approximating the norm through environmental and child-centered prosthetic and adaptive equipment. In E. Sontag (Ed.), *Educational programming for the severely and profoundly handicapped*. Washington, DC: Council for Exceptional Children, Division of Mental Retardation.

Campbell, S. B. (1990). *Behavioral problems in preschool children: Clinical and developmental issues*. New York: Guilford.

Cannings, T. R., & Finkel, L. (1993). *The technology age classroom*. Wilsonville, OR: Franklin, Beedle & Associates.

Cantwell, D. P., & Baker, L. (1987). *Developmental speech and language disorders*. New York: Guilford.

Caplan, F., & Caplan, T. (1973). *The power of play*. Garden City, NJ: Anchor Press/Doubleday.

Carlton, M. P., & Winsler, A. (1999). School readiness: The need for a paradigm shift. *School Psychology Review, 28,* 338–352.

Carney, I. H. (1983). Services for families of severely handicapped preschool students: Assumptions and implications. *Journal of the Division for Early Childhood, 7,* 78–85.

Carr, M., & Schneider, W. (1991). Long-term maintenance of organizational strategies in kindergarten children. *Contemporary Educational Psychology, 16,* 61–75.

Carroll, D. W. (1986). *Psychology of language.* Monterey, CA: Brooks/Cole.

Carroll, J. (2003). The Blackwell handbook of childhood cognitive development. *Journal of Child Psychology and Psychiatry, 44*(6), 928–929.

Carta, J. J. (1994). Developmentally appropriate practices: Shifting the emphasis to individual appropriateness. *Journal of Early Intervention, 18*(4), 242–243.

Carta, J. J., Schwartz, I. S., Atwater, J. B., & McConnell, S. R. (1991). Developmentally appropriate practice: Appraising its usefulness for young children with disabilities. *Topics in Early Childhood Special Education, 11,* 1–20.

Cartwright, C. A. (1981). Effective programs for parents of young handicapped children. *Topics in Early Childhood Special Education, 1,* 1–9.

Casey, T. (2005). *Inclusive play: Practical strategies for working with children ages 3 to 8.* Austin, TX: Pro-Ed.

Casto, G., & Mastropieri, M. A. (1986). The efficacy of early intervention programs: A meta-analysis. *Exceptional Children, 52,* 417–424.

Cavallaro, C. C., & Haney, M. (1999). *Preschool inclusion.* Baltimore: Paul H. Brookes.

Chakrabarti, S., & Fombonne, E. (2001). Pervasive developmental disorders in preschool children. *Journal of the American Medical Association, 285,* 3093–3099.

Chambers, J. G., Parrish, T. B., Lieberman, J. C., & Woman, J. M. (1999). *What are we spending on special education in the U.S.? CSEF brief.* Palo Alto, CA: Center for Special Education Finance.

Chandler, L. K. (1992). Promoting children's social/survival skills as a strategy for transition to mainstreamed kindergarten programs. In S. L. Odom, S. R. McConnell, & M. A. McEvoy (Eds.), *Social competence of young children with disabilities: Issues and strategies for intervention* (pp. 245–267). Baltimore: Paul H. Brookes.

Chase, P. A., Hall, J. W., & Werkhaven, J. A. (1996). Sensorineural hearing loss in children:

Etiology and pathology. In F. N. Marin & J. G. Clark (Eds.), *Hearing care for children* (pp. 78–88). Boston: Allyn & Bacon.

Chasnoff, I. J. (1988). Drug use in pregnancy: Parameters of risk. *Pediatric Clinical Neurology of America, 35,* 1403–1412.

Chasnoff, I. J., Bussey, M. E., Savich, R., & Stack, C. M. (1986). Perinatal cerebral infarction and maternal cocaine use. *Journal of Pediatrics, 108,* 456–459.

Chasnoff, I. J., Landress, H., & Barrett, M. (Eds.) (1990). The prevalence of illicit drug or alcohol use during pregnancy and discrepancies in mandatory reporting in Pinellas County, Florida. *New England Journal of Medicine, 322,* 1202–1206.

Chavkin, W. I., & Kandall, S. R. (1990). Between a "rock" and a hard place: Perinatal drug abuse. *Pediatrics, 85,* 223–225.

Chazan, S. E. (2002). *Profiles of play: Assessing and observing structure and process in play therapy.* Philadelphia: Jessica Kingsley Publishers.

Chen, J., Krechevsky, M., & Viens, J. (1998). *Building on children's strengths: The Project Spectrum experience.* New York: Teachers College Press.

Chen, J., & McNamee, D. (2007). *Assessing for teaching and learning in early childhood classrooms.* Thousand Oaks, CA: Corwin Press.

Cheng, L. L. (1989). Intervention strategies: A multidisciplinary approach. *Topics in Language Disorders, 9*(3), 84–91.

Chess, S., & Thomas, A. (1986). *Temperament in clinical practice.* New York: Guilford.

Child Trends. (2000). *School readiness: Helping communities get children ready for school and schools ready for children.* Washington, DC: Author.

Child Trends. (2002). *Children in working poor families: Updates and extensions.* Washington, DC: Author.

Childhood AIDS. (1991). *Pediatric Clinical Neurology of America, 38*(1), 1–16.

Children's Hospital of St. Paul. (1984). *CMV: Diagnosis, prevention and treatment.* St. Paul, MN: Author.

Christian, K., Morrison, F. J., & Bryant, F. B. (1998). Predicting kindergarten academic skills: Interactions among child care, maternal education, and family literacy environments. *Early Childhood Research Quarterly, 13,* 501–521.

Christopherson, E. R. (1982). *Little people: Guidelines for common sense child rearing* (2nd ed.). Austin, TX: Pro-Ed.

Clark, E. V. (2006). *Language acquisition.* West Nyack, NY: Cambridge University Press.

Clark, S. G. (2000). The IEP process as a tool for collaboration. *Teaching Exceptional Children, 33,* 56–66.

Clarren, S. K., & Smith, D. W. (1978). The fetal alcohol syndrome. *New England Journal of Medicine, 298*(19), 1063–1067.

Claussen, A. H., Scott, K. G., Mundy, P. C., & Katz, L. F. (2004). Effects of three levels of early intervention services on children prenatally exposed to cocaine. *Journal of Early Intervention, 26*(3), 204–220.

Clifford, R. M. (1999). Personnel preparation and the transition to kindergarten. In R. C. Pianta & M. J. Cox (Eds.), *The transition to kindergarten* (pp. 317–324). Baltimore, MD: Paul H. Brookes.

Cohen, A. J. (1996). A brief history of federal financing for child care in the United States. *The Future of Children, 6,* 26–40.

Cohen, D. J., & Donnellen, A. M. (Eds.). (1987). *Handbook of autism and pervasive developmental disorders.* Silver Spring, MD: Winston.

Cohen, H. J. (1969). Learning stimulation. In D. L. Barclay (Ed.), *Art education for the disadvantaged child* (pp. 20–25). Washington, DC: National Art Education Association.

Cohen, H. J. (1992). Pediatric AIDS vaccine trials set. *Science, 258,* 1568–1570.

Coleman, M. (1991). Pediatric AIDS: The professional responsibilities of child caregivers to children and families. *Early Childhood Development Care, 67,* 129–137.

Coleman, M. C., & Webber, J. (2002). *Emotional and behavioral disorders: Theory and practice* (4th ed.). Boston: Allyn & Bacon.

Coles, R. (1992). *Their eyes meeting the world: The drawings and painting of children.* Boston: Houghton Mifflin.

Coles, R. (2001). *The Erik Erikson reader.* New York: Norton.

Collins, B., & Collins, T. (1990). Parent-professional relationships in the treatment of seriously emotionally disturbed children and adolescents. *Social Work, 35,* 522–527.

Condition of Education. (1990). Washington, DC: Office of Educational Research and Improvement.

Cone, J. D., Delawyer, D. D., & Wolfe, V. V. (1985). Assessing parent participation: The parent/family involvement index. *Exceptional Children, 51,* 417–424.

Conners, C. K. (1989). *Manual for Conners' Rating Scales.* N. Tonawanda, NY: Multi-Health Systems.

Connolly, B., & Russell, F. (1978). Interdisciplinary early intervention programs. *Physical Therapy, 56,* 155–158.

Connolly, J. A., Doyle, A. B., & Reznick, E. (1988). Social pretend play and social interactions in preschoolers. *Developmental Psychology, 9,* 301–313.

Connor, D. (2002). Preschool attention deficit hyperactivity disorder: A review of prevalence, diagnosis, neurobiology, and stimulant treatment. *Journal of Developmental and Behavioral Pediatrics, 23*(Suppl. 1), 1–9.

Connor, E. M., Sperling, R. S., Gelber, R., Kiselev, P., Scott, G., O'Sullivan, M. J., et al. (1994). Reduction of maternal-infant transmission of human immunodeficiency virus type 1 with zidovudine treatment. *New England Journal of Medicine, 331*(18), 1173–1225.

Connor, F., Williamson, G. G., & Siepp, J. (1978). *Program guide for infants and toddlers with neuro-motor and other developmental disabilities.* New York: Teachers College Press.

Conn-Powers, M. C., & Ross-Allen, J. (1991). *TEEM: A manual to support the transition of young children with disabilities and their families from preschool into kindergarten and other regular education environments.* Burlington: Center for Developmental Disabilities, University of Vermont.

Conn-Powers, M. C., Ross-Allen, J., & Holburn, S. (1990). Transition of young children into the elementary mainstreamed kindergarten programs. *Topics in Early Childhood Special Education, 9*(4), 91–105.

Conti-Ramsden, G., & Botting, N. (2001). Psycholinguistic markers for specific language impairment. *Journal of Child Psychology and Psychiatry, 42*(6), 741–748.

Cook, R. E., Tessier, A., & Klein, M. D. (1992). *Adapting early childhood curricula for children with special needs.* New York: Merrill.

Cooper, S. (1987). The fetal alcohol syndrome. *Journal of Child Psychology and Psychiatry, 28*(2), 223–227.

Cooper, S., & McEvoy, M. A. (1996). Group friendship activities: An easy way to develop the social skills of young children. *Exceptional Children, 28*(3), 67–69.

Copeland, M. E. (1982). Development of motor skills and the management of common problems. In K. E. Allen & E. M. Goetz (Eds.), *Early childhood education: Special problems, special solutions.* Rockville, MD: Aspen.

Cordisco, L. K., & Laus, M. K. (1993). Individualized training in behavioral strategies for parents of preschool children with disabilities. *Teaching Exceptional Children, 25*(2), 43–47.

Council for Exceptional Children. (1993). *CEC policy manual.* Reston, VA: Author.

Council for Exceptional Children. (2003). *What every special educator should know: Ethics, standards, and guidelines for special educators* (5th ed.). Arlington, VA: Council for Exceptional Children.

Covington, M. (1992). Making the grade: A self-worth perspective on motivation and school reform. Cambridge, MA: Harvard University Press.

Cox, M. J. (2004) School transitions/school readiness: An outcome of early childhood development: Commentary on Ladd and Stipek. In R. E. Tremblay, R. G. Barr, & R. D. Peters (Eds.), *Encyclopedia on Early Childhood Development* [Electronic version]. Retrieved January 17, 2008, from www.child-encyclopedia.com/documents/CoxANGxp.pdf.

Craig, A. (1993, September 6). Cocaine: Thrill carries high price tag. *Poughkeepsie Journal,* p. 3B.

Craig, B. (1992, Fall). Wendy's cochlear implant. *Our kid's magazine,* p. 3.

Crane, L. (2002). *Mental retardation: A community integration approach.* Belmont, CA: Thomson Publishing.

Crary, E. (1979). *Without spanking or spoiling: A practical approach to toddler and preschool guidance.* Seattle: Parenting Press.

Crary, E. (1984). *Kids can cooperate: A practical guide to teaching problem solving.* Seattle: Parenting Press.

Cravioto, J., & DeLicardie, E. R. (1975). Environmental and nutritional deprivation in children with learning disabilities. In W. M. Cruickshank & D. P. Hallahan (Eds.), *Perceptual and learning disabilities in children.* (Vol. 2: *Research and theory*), pp. 3–102. Syracuse, NY: Syracuse University Press.

Crawford, J. W. (1962). Art for the mentally retarded. *Bulletin of Art Therapy, 2*(2), 67–72.

Creaghead, N. A., Newman, P. W., & Secord, W. A. (1989). *Assessment and remediation of articulatory and phonological disorders* (2nd ed.). Columbus, OH: Merrill/Macmillan.

Crocker, A. C. (1989). Developmental services for children with HIV infection. *Mental Retardation, 27,* 223–225.

Cromer, R. F. (1991). *Language and thought in normal and handicapped children.* Oxford: Basil Blackwell.

Crump. I. (Ed.). (1987). *Nutrition and feeding of the handicapped child.* Boston: College-Hill/Little, Brown.

Cunningham, J. C., & Taussig, L. M. (2003). *An introduction to cystic fibrosis for patients and families.* Bethesda, MD: Cystic Fibrosis Foundation.

Currie, J. (1998). The effects of welfare on child outcomes: What we know and what we need to know. In Robert Moffitt (Ed.), *Welfare, the family, and reproductive behavior: Research perspectives.* Washington, DC: National Academy Press.

Currie, J. (2005). Health disparities and gaps in school readiness. *The Future of Children–School Readiness: Closing Racial and Ethnic Gaps, 15*(1), 117–138.

Curtis, S. (1982). *The joy of movement in early childhood.* New York: Teachers College Press.

Czarniecki, L., & Dillman, P. (1992). Pediatric HIV/AIDS. *Critical Care Nursing Clinics of North America, 4*(3), 447–456.

Dalley, T., Case, C., Schaverien, J., Weir, F., Halliday, D., Hall, P., & Waller, D. (1987). *Images of art therapy: New developments in therapy and practice.* New York: Tavistock.

Dane, E. (1985). Professional and lay advocacy in the education of handicapped children. *Social Work, 30,* 505–510.

Danesco, E. R. (1997). Parental beliefs on childhood disability: Insights on culture, child development, and intervention. *International Journal of Disability, Development, and Education, 44*(1), 41–52.

Daniels, S. M. (1982, August). From parent-advocacy to self-advocacy: A problem of transition. *Exceptional Education Quarterly, 3,* 25–32.

Darling, R. B. (1983). *Families against society: A study of reactions to children with birth defects.* Beverly Hills, CA: Sage.

Datar, A. (2003). *The impact of changes in kindergarten entrance age policies on children's academic achievement and the child care needs of families.* Santa Monica, CA: RAND.

Davidson, R. J., Jackson, D. C., & Kalin, N. H. (2000). Emotion, plasticity, context, and regulation: Perspectives from affective neuroscience. *Psychological Bulletin, 126,* 890–909.

Davie, R., Butler, N., & Goldstein, N. (1972). *From birth to seven: A report of the National Child Development Study.* Highlands, NJ: Humanities Press.

Davis, B. H. (1987). Disability and grief. *Social Casework, 68,* 352–357.

Davis, H., Stroud, A., & Green, L. (1988). Maternal language environment of children with mental retardation. *American Journal of Mental Deficiency, 93,* 144–153.

Davis, W. E., & Broadhead, G. D. (2007). *Ecological task analysis perspectives on movement.* Champaign, IL: Human Kinetics.

Dawson, G., Ashman, S. B., & Carver, L. J. (2000). The role of early experience in shaping behavioral and brain development and its implication for social policy. *Developmental Psychopathology, 12,* 695–712.

Dawson, G., & Osterling, J. (1997). Early intervention in autism: Effectiveness and common elements of current approaches. In M. J. Guralnick (Ed.), *The effectiveness of early intervention: Second generation research* (pp. 307–326). Baltimore: Paul H. Brookes.

DeAngelis, M. D., & Zylke, M. D. (2006). Theme issue on chronic diseases in infants, children, and young adults: Call for papers. *Journal of the American Medical Association, 296,* 1780.

Decker, L. E., & Decker, V. A. (2003). *Home, school, and community partnerships.* Lanham, MD: Scarecrow Press.

De Cos, P. L. (1997). *Readiness for kindergarten: What does it mean?* Sacramento, CA: California Research Bureau.

DeGangi, G. (2000). *Pediatric disorders of regulation in affect and behavior: A therapist's guide to assessment and treatment.* New York: Academic Press.

De Gruttola, V., Ming Tu, X., & Pagano, M. (1992). Pediatric AIDS in New York City: Estimating the distributions of infection, latency, and reporting delay and projecting future incidence. *Journal of the American Statistician Association, 87(419),* 633–640.

Deiner, P. L. (1993). *Resources for teaching children with diverse abilities.* Ft. Worth, TX: Harcourt Brace Jovanovich.

DeLoache, J. S., & Todd, C. M. (1988). Young children's use of spatial categorization as a mnemonic strategy. *Journal of Experimental Psychology, 46,* 1–20.

DeMers, S. T., & Fiorello, C. (1999). Legal and ethical issues in preschool assessment and screening. In E. V. Nuttall, I. Romero, & J. Kalesnik (Eds.), *Assessing and screening preschoolers: Psychological and educational dimensions* (pp. 50–58). Boston: Allyn & Bacon.

DeMyer, M. K. (1979). *Parents and children in autism.* New York: Wiley.

Denham, S. A. (1998). *Emotional development in young children.* New York: Guilford.

Denham, S. A., Blair, K. A., DeMulder, E., Levita, J., Sawyer, K., Auerbach-Major, S., & Queenan, P. (2003). Preschool emotional competence: Pathway to social competence? *Child Development, 74(1),* 238–256.

Denning, C. B., Chamberlain, J. A., & Polloway, E. A. (2000). An evaluation of state guidelines for mental retardation: Focus on definition and classification practices. *Education and Training in Mental Retardation and Developmental Disabilities, 25,* 135–144.

Dennis, R. E., Williams, W., Giangreco, M. F., & Cloninger, C. J. (1993). Quality of life as context for planning and evaluation of services for poeple with disabilities. *Exceptional Children, 59(6),* 499–512.

DePaulo, B. M., Rosenthal, R., Green, C. R., & Rosenkrantz, J. (1982). Diagnosing deceptive and mixed messages from verbal and nonverbal cues. *Journal of Personality and Social Psychology, 18,* 433–446.

Desrochers, J. (1999). Vision problems—How teachers can help. *Young Children, 54,* 36–38.

Dettmer, P. (2002). *Consultation, collaboration, and teamwork for students with special needs.* Boston: Allyn & Bacon.

Deutch, M. (1973). *The resolution of conflict: Constructive and destructive processes.* New Haven, CT: Yale University Press.

de Villiers, P. A., & de Villiers, J. G. (1992). Language development. In M. H. Bornstein & M. E. Lamb (Eds.), *Developmental psychology: An advanced textbook* (3rd ed., pp. 337–418). Hillsdale, NJ: Lawrence Erlbaum Associates.

Diamond, G. W. (1989). Developmental problems in children with HIV infection. *Mental Retardation, 27(4),* 213–217.

Diamond, K. E. (1993). The role of parents' observations and concerns in screening for developmental delays in young children. *Topics in Early Childhood Special Education, 9,* 67–85.

Diamond, K. E., Reagan, A. J., & Bandyk, J. E. (2000). Parents' conceptions of kindergarten readiness: Relationships with race, ethnicity, and development. *The Journal of Educational Research, 94,* 93–100.

Diefendorf, A. O. (1996). Hearing loss and its effects. In F. N. Martin & J. G. Clark (Eds.), *Hearing care for children* (pp. 3–18). Boston: Allyn & Bacon.

Diener, C., & Dweck, C. (1978). An analysis of learned helplessness: Continuous changes in performance, strategy, and achievement cognitions following failure. *Journal of Personality and Social Psychology, 36,* 451–462.

Di Leo, J. H. (1974). *Children's drawings as diagnostic aids.* New York: Brunner/Mazel.

DiMatteo, M. R., Friedman, H. S., & Taranta, A. (1979). Sensitivity to bodily nonverbal communications as a factor in practitioner-patient rapport. *Journal of Nonverbal Behavior, 4,* 18–26.

DiMichele, L. (1993). The role of the school social worker in early childhood special education. *School Social Work Journal, 18,* 9–16.

Dinkmeyer, P., McKay, G. D., & Dinkmeyer, J. S. (1993). *Early childhood STEP.* Pines, MN: AGS.

Dockett, S., & Perry, B. (2005). Researching with children: Insights from the Starting School Research Project. *Early Childhood Development and Care, 175(6),* 507–521.

Dokecki, P. R., Baumeister, A. A., & Kupstas, A. (1989). Biomedical and social aspects of pediatric AIDS. *Journal of Early Intervention, 13(2),* 99–113.

Donovan, C. L. (1991). Factors predisposing, enabling, and reinforcing routine screening of patients for preventing fetal alcohol syndrome: A survey of New Jersey physicians. *Journal of Drug Education, 21*(1), 35–42.

Douglas, V. I. (1983). Attentional and cognitive problems. In M. Rutter (Ed.), *Developmental neuropsychiatry* (pp. 280–329). New York: Guilford.

Drasgow, E., Yell, M. L., & Robinson, T. (2001). Developing legally correct and educationally appropriate IEPs. *Remedial and Special Education, 22,* 359–373.

Dreikurs, R., & Cassel, P. (1972). *Discipline without tears: What to do with children who misbehave.* New York: Hawthorn/Dutton.

DuBois, B., & Miley, K. K. (1992). *Social work: An empowering profession.* Boston: Allyn & Bacon.

Dubowitz, H. (1990). Costs and effectiveness of interventions in child maltreatment. *Child Abuse and Neglect, 14,* 177–186.

Dubowitz, V. (1978). *Muscle disorders in childhood.* Philadelphia: W. B. Saunders.

Duckworth, S. V., & Norton, T. L. (2000). Fetal alcohol syndrome and fetal alcohol effects: Support for teachers and families. *Dimensions of Early Childhood, 28*(3), 19–23.

Dudley, J. R. (1987). Speaking for themselves: People who are labeled as mentally retarded. *Social Work, 32,* 80–82.

Dunn, W. (1999). *Sensory Profile.* San Antonio, TX: Psychological Coorporation.

Dunst, C. J. (1985). Rethinking early intervention. *Analysis and Intervention in Developmental Disabilities, 5,* 165–201.

Dunst, C. J. (1986). Overview of the efficacy of early intervention programs. In L. Bickman & D. L. Weatherford (Eds.), *Handbook of special education: Research and practice* (Vol. 3, pp. 259–293). New York: Elmsford.

Dunst, C. J. (2002). Family-centered practices: Birth through high school. *Journal of Special Education, 36,* 139–147.

Dunst, C. J., Snyder, S. W., & Mankinen, M. (1989). Efficacy of early intervention. In M. C. Wang, M. C. Reynolds, & H. J. Walberg (Eds.), *Handbook of special education* (Vol. 3, pp. 146–168). Oxford: Pergamon.

Dunst, C. J., Trivette, C. M., & Deal, A. (1988). *Enabling and empowering families.* Cambridge, MA: Brookline Books.

Duwa, S. M., Wells, C., & Lalinde, P. (1993). Creating family-centered programs and policies. In D. M. Bryant & M. A. Graham (Eds.), *Implementing early intervention* (pp. 92–123). New York: Guilford.

Dweck, C. (1975). The role of expectations and attribution in the alleviation of learned helplessness. *Journal of Personality and Social Psychology, 31,* 674–685.

Dworkin, P. H. (1992). Developmental screening: Still expecting the impossible? *Pediatrics, 89,* 1253–1255.

Early, D. M., Pianta, R. C., Taylor, L. C., & Cox, M. J. (2001). Transition practices: Findings from a national survey of kindergarten teachers. *Early Childhood Education Journal, 28*(3), 199–206.

Early, T. J., & Poertner, J. (1993). Families with children with emotional disorders: A review of the literature. *Social Work, 38,* 743–764.

Eastman, M. K., & Safron, J. S. (1986). Activities to develop your students' motor skills. *Teaching Exceptional Children, 19,* 24–27.

Ebrahim, S., Diekman, S., Decoufle, P., Tully, M., & Floyd, R. (1999). Pregnancy-related alcohol use among women in the United States, 1988–1995. *Prenatal and Neonatal Medicine, 4,* 39–46.

Education Commission of the States. (2000). *Easing the transition to kindergarten.* Denver, CO: Author.

Edyburn, D., Higgins, K., & Boone, R. (2005). *Handbook of special education technology research and practice.* Austin, TX: Pro-Ed.

Einon, D. (1985). *Play with a purpose: Learning games for children 6 weeks to 2–3 years old.* New York: St. Martin's.

Eisenberg, N. (1982). The development of reasoning regarding prosocial behavior. In N. Eisenberg (Ed.), *The development of prosocial behavior.* New York: Academic Press.

Eisenberg, N. (1992). *The caring child.* Cambridge, MA; Harvard University Press.

Eisenberg, N., Lennon, R., & Roth, K. (1983). Prosocial development: A longitudinal study. *Developmental Psychology, 19,* 846–855.

Eisenberg, N., & Miller, P. A. (1987). The relation of empathy to prosocial and related behaviors. *Psychological Bulletin, 101,* 91–119.

Elbers, L., & Ton, J. (1985). Play pen monologues: The interplay of words and babbles in the first word period. *Journal of Child Language, 12,* 551–565.

Eliason, C. F., & Jenkins, T. L. (1977). *A preschool guide to early childhood curriculum.* St. Louis: C. V. Mosby.

Emig, C., Moore, A., & Scarupa, H. J. (2001). *School readiness: Helping communities get children ready for school and school ready for children.* Washington, DC: Child Trends.

Emmer, E., Evertson, C., & Anderson, L. (1980). Effective classroom management at the beginning of the school year. *Elementary School Journal, 80,* 219–231.

English, K., Goldstein, H., Shafer, K., & Kaczmarek, L. (1996). "Buddy skills" for preschoolers. *Exceptional Children, 28*(3), 62–66.

Epps, W. J. (1992). Program coordination and other real-world issues in strengthening linkages. In U.S. Department of Education, *Sticking together: Strengthening linkages and the transition between early childhood education and early elementary school—Summary of a national policy forum* (pp. 9–30). Washington, DC: Office of Educational Research and Improvement.

Erikson, E. (1950). *Childhood and society.* New York: Norton.

Espenschade, A., & Eckert, H. (1980). *Motor development.* Columbus, OH: Merrill.

Espinosa, L. (2002, November). High-quality preschool: Why we need it and what it looks like. *Preschool Policy Matters,* pp. 2–11.

Esposito, L., & Campbell, P. H. (1993). Computers and individuals with severe and physical disabilities. In J. Lindsey (Ed.), *Computers and exceptional individuals* (Rev. ed., pp. 105–124). Columbus, OH: Merrill/Macmillan.

Evans, A. D., & Falk, W. W. (1986). *Learning to be deaf.* New York: Moutan de Gruyter.

Evertson, C. M. (1998). Classroom rules and routines. In L. W. Anderson (Ed.), *International encyclopedia of teaching and teacher education* (2nd ed., pp. 215–219). Tarrytown, NY: Elsevier Science.

Evertson, C. M., Emmer, E. T., Clements, B. S., Sanford, J. P., & Worsham, M. E. (1989). *Classroom management for elementary teachers* (2nd ed.). Englewood Cliffs, NJ: Prentice Hall.

Ewing Marion Kauffman Foundation. (2002). *Set for success: Building a strong foundation for school readiness based on the social-emotional development of young children.* Kansas City, MO: Author.

Eyler, F. D., Behnke, M., Conlon, M., Woos, N. S., & Wobie, K. (1998). Birth outcome from a prospective, matched study of crack/cocaine use: II. Interactive and dose effects on neurobehavioral assessment. *Pediatrics, 101*(2), 237–241.

Factor, D., & Schilmoeller, G. L. (1983). Social skill training of preschool children. *Child Study Journal, 13*(1), 41–56.

Fahey, K. B., & Reid, D. K. (2000). *Language development, difference, and disorders.* Austin, TX: Pro-Ed.

Farber, H., & Boyette, M. (2001). *Control your child's asthma: A breakthrough program for the treatment and management of childhood asthma.* Bellingham, WA: Owl Books.

Farran, D. C. (1990). Effects of interventions with disadvantaged and disabled children: A decade review. In: S. J. Meisels and J. P. Shonkoff (Eds.), *Handbook of early childhood intervention* (pp. 428–444). Cambridge, MA: Cambridge University Press.

Favazza, P. C., Phillipsen, L., & Kumar, P. (2000). Measuring and promoting acceptance of young children with disabilities. *Exceptional Children, 66,* 491–508.

Fay, W. H., & Schuler, A. L. (1980). *Emerging language in autistic children.* University Park, MD: University Park Press.

Featherstone, H. (1981). *A difference in the family.* New York: Penguin.

Feil, E. G., Severson, H., & Walker, H. (1998). Screening for emotional and behavioral delays: The Early Screening Project. *Journal of Early Intervention, 21*(3), 252–266.

Feil, E. G., Walker, H., Severson, H., & Ball, A. (2000). Proactive screening for emotional/behavioral concerns in Head Start preschools: Promising practices and challenges in applied research. *Behavioral Disorders, 26*(1), 13–25.

Feldman, J. (2000). *Transition tips and tricks: For teachers.* Beltsville, CA: Gryphon House.

Fenton, G., D'ardia, C., Valerte, D., Del Vecchio, I., Fabrizi, A., & Bernabei, P. (2003). Vineland adaptive behavior profiles in children with autism and moderate to severe developmental delay. *Autism, 7*(3), 269–87.

Ferris, P. A., & Marshall, C. A. (1987). A model project for families of the chronically mentally ill. *Social Work, 32,* 110–114.

Fey, M. E. (1986). *Language intervention with young children.* San Diego: College-Hill Press.

Fiene, J. I., & Taylor, P. A. (1991). Serving rural families of developmentally disabled children: A case management model. *Social Work, 36,* 323–327.

Fiese, B. H. (2002). Routines of daily living and rituals in family life: A glimpse at stability and change during the early child-raising years. *Zero to Three, 22,* 10–13.

Filer, J. D., & Mahoney, G. J. (1996). Collaboration between families and early intervention service providers. *Infants and Young Children, 9*(2), 22–30.

Final regulations for IDEA. (1999). Washington, DC: U.S. Government Printing Office.

Finnie, N. R. (1975). *Handling the young cerebral palsied child at home* (2nd ed.). New York: Dutton.

Fiorentino, M. (1972). *Normal and abnormal development: The influence of primitive reflexes on motor development.* Springfield, IL: Charles C. Thomas.

Fisher, K. W., Hand, H. H., Watson, M. W., Van-Parys, M. M., & Tucker, J. L. (1984). Putting the child into socialization: The development of social categories in preschool children. In L. G. Katz, P. J. Wagemaker, & K. Steiner (Eds.), *Current topics in early childhood* (Vol. 5, pp. 27–72). Norwood, NJ: Ablex.

Fitzgerald, M. (2004). *Autism and creativity: Is there a link between autism in men and exceptional ability?* London: Brunner-Routledge.

Flavell, J. H. (1992). Cognitive development: Past, present, and future. *Developmental Psychology, 28,* 997–1005.

Flavell, J., Miller, I. H., & Miller, S. A. (2001). *Cognitive development* (4th ed.). Upper Saddle Ridge, NJ: Prentice-Hall.

Fletcher, J. M., Francis, D. J., Pequegnat, W., Raudenbush, S. W., Bornstein, M. C., Schmitt, F., et al. (1991). Neurobehavioral outcomes in diseases of childhood: Individual change models for pediatric human immunodeficiency viruses. *American Psychologist, 46*(12), 1267–1277.

Forest, S., & Libscomb, S. (1994). *Opportunities for parents and children together (O-PACT): A dynamic model of intervention for at-risk infants and toddlers.* Missoula: University of Montana.

Forness, S. R. (2001). Special education and related services: What have we learned from meta-analysis? *Exceptionality, 9,* 185–197.

Forness, S., Serna, L., Nielsen, E., Lambros, K., Hale, M., & Kavaie, K. (2000). A model for early detection and primary prevention of emotional or behavioral disorders. *Education and Treatment of Children, 23*(3), 325–345.

Fowler, S. A., Hains, A. H., & Rosenkoetter, S. E. (1990). The transition between early intervention services and preschool services: Administrative and policy issues. *Topics in Early Childhood Special Education, 9*(4), 55–65.

Fowler, S. A., Schwartz, I. S., & Atwater, J. B. (1991). Perspectives on the transition from preschool to kindergarten for children with disabilities and their families. *Exceptional Children, 58*(2), 136–145.

Fowler, S. A., & Titus, P. E. (1996). Managing transitions. In P. Beckman & G. B. Boyce (Eds.), *Deciphering the system: A guide for families of young children with disabilities.* Boston: Brookline Books.

Fraiberg, S. (1977). *Insight from the blind.* New York: Basic Books.

Fraser, B. A., & Hensinger, R. N. (1983). *Managing physical handicaps.* Baltimore: Paul H. Brookes.

Fredrick, J., & Fletcher, D. (1985). Facilitating children's adjustment to orthotic and prosthetic appliances. *Teaching Exceptional Children, 17,* 228–230.

Freedman, S. A., & Clarke, L. L. (1991). Financing care for medically complex children. In N. J. Hochstadt & D. M. Yost (Eds.), *The medically complex child: The transition to home care* (3rd ed., pp. 259–286). Boston: Allyn & Bacon.

Frieman, J. L. (2002). *Learning and Adaptive Behavior.* Florence, KY: Wadsworth.

Friend, M. (2000). Myths and misunderstandings about professional collaboration. *Remedial and Special Education, 21,* 131–132.

Friesen, B. J. (1989). National study of parents whose children have serious emotional disorders. In A. Algarin, R. Friedman, A. Duchnowski, K. Kutash, S. Silver, & M. Johnson (Eds.), *Second annual research conference* proceedings: *Children's mental health services and policy: Building a research base* (pp. 36–52). Tampa, FL: Research and Training Center for Children's Mental Health, University of South Florida.

Frieze, I. H. (1980). Beliefs about success and failure in the classroom. In H. H. McMillan (Ed.), *The social psychology of school learning* (pp. 39–78). New York: Academic Press.

Frolov, Y. P. (1937). *Pavlov and his school.* New York: Oxford University Press.

Frostig, M., & Maslow, P. (1970). *Movement education: Theory and practice.* Chicago: Follett.

Fry, A. F., & Hale, S. (1996). Processing speed, working memory, and fluid intelligence: Evidence for a developmental cascade. *Psychological Science, 7,* 237–241.

Fuchs, D., & Fuchs, L. (1994–1995). Sometimes separate is better. *Educational Leadership, 52(4),* 22–26.

Gaitskell, C. D., & Gaitskell, M. R. (1953). *Art education for slow learners.* Peoria, IL: Charles A. Bennett.

Gallagher, J. J. (1989). A new policy initiative: Infants and toddlers with handicapping conditions. *American Psychologist, 44(2),* 387–391.

Garcia Coll, C. T. (1990). Developmental outcome of minority infants: A process-oriented look into our beginnings. *Child Development, 61(2),* 270–289.

Gardner, H. (1973). *The arts and human development.* New York: Wiley.

Gardner, H. (1999): *Intelligence reframed: Multiple intelligences for the 21st century.* New York: Basic Books.

Gargiulo, R. M. (1985). *Working with parents of exceptional children: A guide for professionals.* Boston: Houghton Mifflin.

Gargiulo, R. M. (2003). *Special education in contemporary society.* Belmont, CA: Wadsworth.

Gartin, B. C., & Murdick, N. L. (2001). A new IDEA mandate: The use of functional assessment of behavior and positive behavior supports. *Remedial and Special Education, 22,* 344–349.

Garwood, S. G. (1983). Special education and child development: A new perspective. In S. G. Garwood (Ed.), *Educating young handicapped children: A developmental approach* (pp. 3–37). Rockville, MD: Aspen.

Gatty, C. G. (1996). Early intervention and management of hearing in infants and toddlers. *Infants and Young Children, 9(1),* 1–13.

Gatty, J. C. (1992). Teaching speech to hearing-impaired children. *Volta Review, 94,* 49–61.

Geers, A. E., & Tobey, E. (1992). Effects of cochlear implants and tactile aids on the development of speech production skills in children with profound hearing impairment. *Volta Review, 94,* 135–163.

Gelman, R. (1972). Logical capacity of very young children: Number invariance rules. *Child Development, 43,* 75–90.

Gibb, G. S., & Dykes, T. T. (2000). *Guide to writing quality individualized educational programs.* Boston: Allyn & Bacon.

Gibbs, E. D., & Teti, D. M. (1990). *Interdisciplinary assessment of infants: A guide for early intervention professionals.* Baltimore: Paul H. Brookes.

Gibson, E. J., & Walk, R. D. (1960). The "visual cliff." *Scientific American, 202,* 64–71.

Gibson, E. S., & Spelke, E. S. (1983). The development of perception. In J. H. Flavell & E. M. Markman (Eds.), *Handbook of child psychology* (Vol. 3: *Cognitive development*) (4th ed., pp. 1–76). New York: Wiley.

Gillberg, C., & Coleman, M. (2000). *The biology of the autistic syndromes* (3rd ed.). London: MacKeith Press.

Gilliam, W., & Zigler, E. (2001). A critical meta-analysis of all evaluations of state-funded preschools from 1977 to 1998: Implications for policy, service delivery and program evaluation. *Early Childhood Research Quarterly, 15,* 551–73.

Ginsburg, H. P., & Opper, S. (1988). *Piaget's theory of intellectual development* (3rd ed.). Englewood Cliffs, NJ: Prentice-Hall.

Girolametto, L. E. (1988). Developing dialogue skills: The effects of a conversational model of language intervention. In K. Marfo (Ed.), *Parent-child interaction and developmental disabilities* (pp. 145–162). New York: Praeger.

Glascoe, F. P. (1996). Developmental screening. In M. Wolraich (Ed.), *Disorders of development and learning: A practical guide to 20* (2nd ed., pp. 89–128). St. Louis: C. V. Mosby.

Glascoe, F. P., Altemeier, W. A., & McLean, W. E. (1989). The importance of parents' concerns about their child's development. *American Journal of Disabled Children, 143,* 955–958.

Glidden, L. M. (1993). What we do not know about families with children who have developmental disabilities: Questionnaire on resources and stress as a case study. *American Journal of Mental Retardation, 97,* 315–332.

Gmitrova, V., & Gmitrova, J. (2003). The impact of teacher-directed and child-directed pretend play on cognitive competence in kindergarten children. *Early Childhood Education Journal, 30*(4), 241–246.

Gnepp, J. (1983). Children's social sensitivity: Inferring emotions from conflicting cues. *Developmental Psychology, 19,* 805–814.

Golant, S., & Golant, M. (1990). *Kindergarten: It isn't what it used to be.* Los Angeles: Lowell House.

Gold, M. W. (1976). Task analysis of a complex assembly task by the retarded child. *Exceptional Children, 43,* 78–84.

Goldberg, B. (1993). Universal hearing screening of newborns: An idea whose time has come. *ASHA, 35,* 63–64.

Goldberg, S. (1997). *Parent involvement begins at birth: Collaboration between parents and teachers of children in the early years.* Boston: Allyn & Bacon.

Goldfarb, L. A., Brotherson, M. J., Summers, J. A., & Turnbull, A. P. (1986). *Meeting the challenge of disability or chronic illness: A family guide.* Baltimore: Paul H. Brookes.

Goldfield, B. A., & Reznick, J. S. (1990). Early lexical acquisition: Rate, content, and the vocabulary spurt. *Journal of Child Language, 17,* 171–183.

Goldin-Meadow, S. (1998). The development of gesture and speech as an integrated system. In J. Iverson & S. Goldin-Meadow (Eds.), *The balance between gesture and speech in childhood* (pp. 29–44). San Francisco: Jossey-Bass.

Goldstein, H. (1993). Use of peers as communication intervention agents. *Teaching Exceptional Children, 25*(2), 37–40.

Gomby, D. P., Culross, P., & Behrman, R. (1999). Home visiting: Recent program evaluations—analysis and recommendations. *Future of Children, 9*(1), 4–26.

Gomby, D. S., & Shiono, P. H. (1991). Estimating the number of substance-exposed infants. *Future of Children 1*(1), 17–25.

Gonzales, R. (2002). Ready schools: Practices to support the development and educational success of young children. *First 5 California Implementation Tools for School Readiness Series.* Los Angeles, CA: UCLA Center for Healthier Children, Families, and Communities.

Gonzalez-Mena, J. (1998). *Foundations: Early childhood education in a diverse society.* Mountain View, CA: Mayfield.

Goodman, J. F. (1992). *When slow is fast enough: Educating the delayed preschool child.* New York: Guilford.

Goodnow, J. (1977). *Children drawing.* Cambridge, MA: Harvard University Press.

Goodwyn, S. W., & Acredolo, L. P. (1998). Encouraging symbolic gestures: A new perspective on the relationship between gesture and speech. In J. Iverson & S. Goldin-Meadow (Eds.), *The balance between gesture and speech in childhood* (pp. 61–73). San Francisco: Jossey-Bass.

Goodwyn, S. W., Acredolo, L. P., & Brown, C. A. (2000). Impact of symbolic gesturing on early language development. *Journal of Nonverbal Behavior, 24,* 81–103.

Gopnik, A. A., & Meltzoff, A. N. (1986). Relations between semantic and cognitive development in the one-word stage: The specificity hypothesis. *Child Development, 57,* 1040–1053.

Gopnik, A., Meltzoff, A. N., & Kuhl, P. (1999). *The scientist in the crib: Minds, brains, and how children learn.* New York: William Morris.

Gordon, J. I. (1970). *Baby learning through baby play.* New York: St. Martin's.

Gordon, J. I. (1972). *Child learning through child play: Learning activities for 2–3 year olds.* New York: St. Martin's.

Gormley, W., Gayer, T., Phillips, D., & Dawson, B. (2004). *The effects of universal pre-K on cognitive development.* Washington, DC: Georgetown University, Center for Research on Children in the United States.

Gottfied, A. (1985). Academic intrinsic motivation in elementary and junior high students. *Journal of Educational Psychology, 82,* 525–538.

Gowen, J. W. (1992). Object play and exploration in children with and without disabilities: A longitudinal study. *American Journal on Mental Retardation, 97*(1), 21–37.

Gowen, J. W., & Nebrig, J. B. (2002). *Enhancing early emotional development: Guiding parents of young children.* Baltimore: Paul H. Brookes.

Graham, M. A., & Bryant, D. M. (1993). Developmentally appropriate activities for children with special needs. *Infants and Young Children, 5*(3), 31–42.

Graham, S., Doubleday, C., & Guarino, P. A. (1984). The development of relations between perceived controllability and the emotions of pity, anger, and guilt. *Child Development, 55,* 561–565.

Graham, S., & Weiner, B. (1996). Theories and principles of motivation. In D. Berliner & R. Calfee (Eds.), *Handbook of Educational Psychology* (pp. 63–84). New York: Macmillan.

Graue, M. E. (1993). *Ready for what? Constructing meanings of readiness for kindergarten.* Albany, NY: State University of New York Press.

Graue, M. E., & DiPerna, J. (2000). Redshirting and early retention: Who gets the "gift of time" and what are its outcomes? *American Educational Research Journal, 37,* 509–534.

Graves, M., & Strubank, R. (1991). Helping children manage themselves. In M. Brickman & L. Taylor (Eds.), *Supporting young learners: Ideas for preschool and day care providers.* Ypsilanti, MI: High Scope Press.

Green, D. M. (1976). *An introduction to hearing.* Hillsdale, NJ: Erlbaum.

Greenberg, A. (2004). *Primer on kidney diseases.* Philadelphia: Saunders.

Greenberg, M., Speltz, M., DeKlyen, M., & Jones, K. (2001). Correlates of clinic referral for early conduct problems: Variable- and person-oriented approaches. *Development and Psychopathology, 13*(2), 255–276.

Greene, J. (1975). *Thinking and language.* London: Methuen.

Greenough, W. T. (1991). Experience as a component of normal development: Evolutionary considerations. *Developmental Psychology, 27,* 11–27.

Greenspan, S. (1999). *Building healthy minds: The six experiences that create intelligence and emotional growth in babies and young children.* New York: Perseus Publishing.

Greenspan, S., & Weider, S. (1999). A functional developmental approach to autism spectrum disorders. *Journal of the Association for Persons with Severe Handicaps, 24*(3), 147–161.

Greenwood, C. R., Luze, G. J., & Carta, J. J. (2002). Best practices in assessment of intervention results with infants and toddlers. In A. Thomas & J. Grimes (Eds.), *Best practices in school psychology* (Vol. 4, pp. 1219–1230). Bethesda, MD: National Association of School Psychologists.

Griswold, D. E., Barnhill, G. P., & Myles, B. S. (2002). Asperger's syndrome and academic achievement. *Focus on Autism and Other Developmental Disabilities, 17,* 94–102.

Groark, C. J., Mehaffie, K. E., McCall, R. B., & Greenberg, M. T. (2007). *Evidence-based practices for early childhood care and education.* Thousand Oaks, CA: Corwin Press.

Gronlund, N. (2006). *Assessment of student achievement* (8th ed.). Boston: Pearson.

Gross, R. T., Spiker, D., & Haynes, C. W. (Eds.). (1997). *Helping low birth weight, premature babies: The infant health and development program.* Stanford, CA: Stanford University Press.

Groze, V., Haines-Simeon, M., & Barth, R. P. (1994). Barriers in permanency planning for medically fragile children: Drug affected children and HIV infected children. *Child and Adolescent Social Work Journal, 11*(1), 63–84.

Groze, V., Haines-Simeon, M., & McMillen, J. C. (1992). Families adopting children with or at risk of HIV infection. *Child and Adolescent Social Work Journal, 9*(5), 402–426.

Grozinger, W. (1955). *Scribbling, drawing, painting: The early forms of the child's pictorial creativeness.* New York: Humanities Press.

Grusec, J. E. (1988). *Social development: History, theory, and research.* New York: Springer-Verlag.

Grusec, J. E. (1992). Social learning theory and developmental psychology: The legacies of Robert Sears and Albert Bandura. *Developmental Psychology, 49,* 920–923.

Gunnar, M. R. (1990). The psychobiology of infant temperament. In J. Colombo & J. Fagen (Eds.), *Individual differences in infancy: Reliability, stability, prediction* (pp. 387–410). Hillsdale, NJ: Erlbaum.

Gunnar, M. R., Brodersen, L., Nachmias, M., Buss, K., & Rigatuso, J. (1996). Stress reactivity and attachment security. *Developmental Psychobiology, 29*(3), 191–204.

Guralnick, M. J. (1990). Social competence and early intervention. *Journal of Early Intervention, 14,* 3–14.

Guralnick, M. J. (1993). Developmentally appropriate practice in the assessment and intervention of children's peer relations. *Topics in Early Childhood Special Education, 13*(2), 344–371.

Guralnick, M. J. (Ed.). (1997). *Effectiveness of early intervention.* Baltimore: Paul H. Brookes.

Guralnick, M. J. (Ed.). (2001). *Early childhood inclusion.* Baltimore: Paul H. Brookes.

Guralnick, M. J., & Bennett, F. C. (1987). *The effectiveness of early intervention for at-risk and handicapped children.* New York: Academic Press.

Hagerman, R. J. (1999) *Neurodevelopmental disorders: Diagnosis and treatment.* New York: Oxford University Press.

Hagood, L. (1997) *Communication: A guide for teaching students with visual and multiple impairments.* Austin, TX: Texas School for the Blind and Visually Impaired.

Hains, A. H., Fowler, S. A., Schwartz, I. S., Kottwitz, E., & Rosenkoetter, S. E. (1989). A comparison of preschool and kindergarten teacher expectations for school readiness. *Early Childhood Research Quarterly, 4,* 75–88.

Hains, A. H., & Rosenkoetter, S. E. (1991). *Planning transitions for young children with disabilities and their families: Wisconsin manual.* McPherson, KS: Associated Colleges of Central Kansas, Bridging Early Services Transition Project.

Hains, A. H., Rosenkoetter, S. E., & Fowler, S. A. (1991). Transition planning with families in early intervention programs. *Infants and Young Children, 3,* 38–47.

Hale, G. (1979). *The source book for the disabled.* London: Imprint Books.

Hall, B. J., Oyer, H. J., & Haas, W. H. (2001). *Speech, language and hearing disorders: A guide for the teacher* (3rd ed.). Boston: Allyn & Bacon.

Haller, I. (1987). *How children play.* Edinburg, UK: William Collins Sons.

Hamlin, S. (1988). *How to talk so people listen.* New York: Harper & Row.

Hanline, M. F., & Knowlton, A. (1988). A collaborative model for providing support to parents during their child's transition from infant intervention to preschool special education public school programs *Journal of the Division for Early Childhood, 12*(2), 116–125.

Hanson, J. J., & Hanline, M. F. (1990). Parenting a child with a disability: A longitudinal study of parental stress and adaption. *Journal of Early Intervention, 14,* 234–248.

Hanson, J. J., Lynch, E. W., & Wayman, K. I. (1990). Honoring the cultural diversity of families when gathering data. *Topics in Early Childhood Special Education, 10*(1), 112–131.

Hanson, M. J. (1984). *Atypical infant development.* Baltimore: University Park Press.

Hanson, M. J., & Bruder, M. E. (2001). Early intervention: Promises to keep. *Infants and Young Children, 13*(3), 47–58.

Hanson, M. J., & Hanline, M. F. (1985). An analysis of response contingent learning experiences for young children with severe handicaps. *The Journal of the Association for Persons with Severe Handicaps, 10,* 31–40.

Hanson, M. J., & Lynch, E. W. (1992). Family diversity: Implications for policy and practice. *Topics in Early Childhood Special Education, 12*(3), 283–306.

Harari, O., & Covington, M. V. (1981). Reactions to achievement behavior from a teacher and student perspective: A development analysis. *American Educational Research Journal, 18,* 15–28.

Harris, D. B. (1963). *Children's drawings as measures of intellectual maturity.* New York: Harcourt, Brace and World.

Harris, M. (1998). Can connectionism model developmental change? *Mind & Language, 13,* 442–447.

Harris, P. L. (1989). *Children and emotion: The development of psychological understanding.* Oxford: Basil Blackwell.

Harris, S. L. (1983). *Families of the developmentally disabled: A guide to behavioral intervention.* New York: Pergamon.

Harrison, H., & Kositsky, A. (1983). *The premature baby book: A parent's guide to coping and caring in the first years.* New York: St. Martin's.

Harry, B. (1992). *Cultural diversity, families, and the special education system: Communication and empowerment.* New York: Teachers College Press.

Harter, S. (1978). Effectance motivation reconsidered: Toward a developmental model, *Human Development, 21,* 34–64.

Harter, S. (1981). Models of mastery motivation in children: Individual differences and developmental change. In W. A. Collins (Ed.), *Aspects on the development of competence: The Minnesota symposia on child psychology* (Vol. 3, pp. 219–250). Greenwich, CT: JAI Press.

Harter, S. (1990). Causes, correlates, and the functional role of global self-worth: A life-span perspective. In J. Kooigan & R. Sternberg (Eds.), *Competence considered: Perceptions of competence* (pp. 44–82). New Haven, CT: Yale University Press.

Harter, S., & Zigler, E. (1974). The assessment of effectance motivation in normal and retarded children. *Developmental Psychology, 10,* 169–180.

Harvey, B. (1975). Why are they blind? *Sight Saving Review, 45*(1), 3–22.

Harwood, M., & Kleinfeld, J. S. (2002). Up front, in hope: The value of early intervention for children with fetal alcohol syndrome. *Young Children, 57*(4), 86–90.

Haslam, R. H. A., & Valletutti, P. J. (2004). *Medical problems in the classroom: The teacher's role in diagnosis and management* (4th ed.). Austin, TX: Pro-Ed.

Hawley, T. (2000). *Starting smart: How early experiences affect brain development.* Chicago: Ounce of Prevention Fund.

Hayes, D., & Northern, J. L. (1996). *Infants and hearing.* San Diego: Singular Publishing Group.

Haywood, H. C., Brooks, P., & Burns, S. (1990). *Cognitive curriculum for young children* (Experimental version). Watertown, MA: Charlesbridge Publishing.

Heagarty, M. C. (1993). Day care for the child with acquired immunodeficiency syndrome and the child of the drug-abusing mother. *Pediatrics, 3,* 199–201.

Hebbeler, K., Wagner, M., Spiker, D., Scarborough, A., Simeonsson, R., & Collier, M. (2001). *A first look at the characteristics of children and families entering early intervention services.* Menlo Park, CA: SRI International.

Heckman, J. J., & Masterov, D. V. (2004). *The productivity argument for investing in young children.* Invest in Kids Working Group, Working Paper 5. Washington, DC: Committee for Economic Development.

Heffron, M. C. (2000). Clarifying concepts of infant mental health: Promotion, relationship-based preventive intervention and treatment. *Infants and Young Children, 12,* 14–21.

Heisler, V. (1972). *A handicapped child in the family: A guide for parents.* New York: Grune & Stratton.

Hellendoorn, J., & Hoekman, J. (1992). Imaginative play in children with mental retardation. *Mental Retardation, 30*(5), 256.

Hendrick, J. (1975). *The whole child: New trends in early education.* St. Louis: C. V. Mosby.

Herer, G., & Reilly, M. (1999). Pediatric audiology: Poised for the future. *ASHA, 13,* 24–30.

Heshusius, L. (1986). Pedagogy, special education, and the lives of young children: A critical and futuristic perspective. *Journal of Education, 186,* 25–38.

Hirsch, E. S. (Ed.). (1984). *The block book.* Washington, DC: National Association for the Education of Young Children.

Hirst, M. (1989). Patterns of impairment and disability related to social handicaps in young people with cerebral palsy and spina bifida. *Journal of Biosocial Science, 21,* 1–12.

Hoagwood, K., Kelleher, K. J., Feil, M., & Comer, D. M. (2000). Treatment services for children with ADHD: A national perspective. *Journal of the American Academy of Child and Adolescent Psychiatry, 39*(2), 198–206.

Hoffang, A. S. (1989). The nature of language. In P. J. Valletutti, M. McKnight-Taylor, & A. S. Hoffang (Eds.), *Facilitating communication in young children with handicapping conditions: A guide for special education* (pp. 33–62). Boston: Little, Brown.

Hohmann, M., Banet, B., & Weikart, D. P. (1979). *Young children in action.* Ypsilanti, MI: High Scope Press.

Holbrook, M. C. (Ed.). (1996). *Children with visual impairments: A parents' guide.* Bethesda, MD: Woodbine.

Holmes, J. (1993). *John Bowlby and attachment theory.* New York: Routledge.

Honig, A. S. (1985). Research in review: Compliance, control, and discipline. Part 1. *Young Children, 40*(2), 50–58.

Hopkins, H., & Smith, H. (Eds.). (1991). *Willard and Spackman's occupational therapy.* Philadelphia: Lippincott.

Hopkins, K. D. (1998). *Educational and psychological measurement and evaluation* (8th ed.). Boston: Allyn & Bacon.

Horowitz, F. D. (1990). Developmental model of individual differences. In J. Colombo & J. Fagen (Eds.), *Individual differences in infancy: Reliability, stability, prediction* (pp. 3–18). Hillsdale, NJ: Lawrence Erlbaum Associates.

Horowitz, F. D. (1992). John B. Watson's legacy: Learning and environment. *Developmental Psychology, 28,* 360–367.

Hotte, E. B. (1979). *Self-help clothing for children who have physical disabilities.* Chicago: National Easter Seals Society for Crippled Children and Adults.

Howes, C., & Matheson, C. C. (1992). Sequences in the development of competent play with peers: Social and pretend play. *Developmental Psychology, 28,* 961–974.

Hoyme, H. E., May, P. A., Kalberg, W. O., Kodituwakku, P., Gossage, J. P., Trujillo, P. M., et al. (2005). A practical clinical approach to diagnosis of fetal alcohol spectrum disorders: Clarification of the 1996 Institute of Medicine criteria. *Pediatrics, 115,* 39–47.

Huebner, K., Merk-Adams, B., Stryker, D., & Wolffe, K. (2004). *The national agenda for the education of children and youth, including those with multiple disabilities, revised.* New York: American Foundation for the Blind.

Hughes, R. C., & Rycus, J. S. (1983). *Child welfare services for children with developmental disabilities.* New York: Child Welfare League of America.

Huitt, W. (2003). The information processing approach to cognition. *Educational Psychology Interactive.* [Electronic version] Valdosta, GA: Valdosta State University. Retrieved July 29, 2007, from http://chiron.valdosta.edu/whuitt/col/intro/research.html.

Huitt, W., & Hummel, J. (2006). An overview of the behavioral perspective. *Educational Psychology Interactive.* [Electronic version] Valdosta, GA: Valdosta State University. Retrieved July 29, 2007, from http://chiron.valdosta.edu/whuitt/col/behsys/operant.html.

Hurley, O. L. (1991). Implications of P. L. 99-457 for preparation of preschool personnel. In J. J. Gallagher, P. L. Trohanis, & R. M. Clifford (Eds.), *Policy implementation and P. L. 99-457: Planning for young children with disabilities* (pp. 133–146). Baltimore: Paul H. Brookes.

Hussey-Gardner, B. (1992). *Parenting to make a difference: Your one- to four-year-old child.* Palo Alto, CA: Vort Corporation.

Ickes, W. J., & Kidd, R. F. (1976). An attributional analysis of helping behavior. In J. H. Harvey, W. J. Ickes, & R. F. Kidd (Eds.), *New directions in attribution research* (Vol. 1, pp. 311–334). Hillsdale, NJ: Erlbaum.

Illingworth, R. S. (1987). *The development of the infant and young child: Normal and abnormal.* New York: Churchill Livingstone.

Individuals with Disabilities Education Act. (1997). Washington, DC: U.S. Government Printing Office.

Individuals with Disabilities Education Act. (2002). *Data note for IDEA, Part B.* Retrieved February 1, 2007, from www.ideadata.org/docs/bdatanotes2002.doc.

Inman, S., Buck, M., & Burke, H. (Eds.) (1998). *Assessing personal and social development: Measuring the unmeasurable?* Bristol, PA: Falmer Press.

Irvine, J. J. (2003). *Education teachers for diversity: Seeing with a cultural eye.* New York: Teachers College Press.

Isaacs, S. (1972). *Intellectual growth in young children.* New York: Schocken Books.

Izard, C. E., & Malatesta, C. A. (1987). Perspectives on emotional development, I: Differential emotions theory of early emotional development. In J. D. Osofsky (Ed.), *Handbook of infant development* (2nd ed., pp. 494–554). New York: Wiley.

Jacob, R. B., O'Leary, K. D., & Rosenbald, C. (1978). Formal and informal classroom settings: Effects on hyperactivity. *Journal of Abnormal Child Psychology, 6*(1), 47–59.

Jaeger, D. L. (1987). *Home program instruction sheets for infants and young children.* Tucson, AZ: Communication and Therapy Skill Builders.

Jaeger, D. L. (1989). *Transferring and lifting children and adolescents: Home instruction sheets.* Tucson, AZ: Therapy Skill Builders.

Jansson, L. M., & Velez, M. (1999). Understanding and treating substance abusers and their infants. *Infants and Young Children, 11*(4), 79–89.

Jarrold, C., Boucher, J., & Smith, P. (1993). Symbolic play in autism: A review. *Journal of Autism and Developmental Disorders, 23*(2).

Jensen, E. (2000). *Learning with the body in mine: The scientific basis for energizers, movement, play, games, and physical education.* Austin, TX: Pro-Ed.

Jipson, J. (1991). Developmentally appropriate practice: Culture, curriculum, connections. *Early Education and Development, 2*(2), 120–136.

Johnson, L. J., Pugach, M. C., & Devlin, S. (1990). Professional collaboration. *Teaching Exceptional Children, 22,* 9–11.

Johnson-Martin, N., Jens, K., & Attermeier, S. (1986). *The Carolina curriculum for handicapped infants and infants at risk.* Baltimore: Paul H. Brookes.

Johnson-Martin, N., Jens, K. G., Attermeier, S. M., & Hacker, B. J. (1991). *The Carolina curriculum for preschoolers with special needs* (2nd ed.). Baltimore: Paul H. Brookes.

Johnston, R. B., & Magrab, P. R. (1976). *Developmental disorders: Assessment, treatment, education.* Baltimore: University Park Press.

Jones, E. (1981). *The life and work of Sigmund Freud.* New York: Basic Books.

Jones, L. J., Smith, D. W., Ulleland, C. N., & Streissguth, A. P. (1973). Patterns of malformation in offspring of chronic alcoholic mothers. *Lancet, 1,* 1267–1271.

Kaban, B. (1979). *Choosing toys for children from birth to five.* New York: Schocken Books.

Kaderavek, J. N., & Pakulski, L. A. (2002). Minimal hearing loss is not minimal. *Teaching Exceptional Children, 34,* 14–18.

Kaesler, N. (2006). *The tactful teacher: Effective communication with parents, colleagues, and administrators.* White River Junction, VT: Nomad Press.

Kagan, J. J., Reznick, J. S., & Snidman, N. (1990). The temperamental qualities of inhibition and lack of inhibition. In M. Lewis & S. M. Miller (Eds.), *Handbook of developmental psychopathology* (pp. 219–226). New York: Plenum.

Kagan, S. L. (1991a). The strategic importance of linkages and the transition between early childhood programs and early elementary school.

In U.S. Department of Education, *Sticking together: Strengthening linkages and the transition between early childhood education and early elementary school—Summary of a national policy forum.* Washington, DC: Office of Educational Research and Improvement.

Kagan, S. L. (1991b). Moving from here to there: Rethinking continuity and transitions in early care and education. In B. Spodek & O. N. Saracho (Eds.), *Yearbook in early childhood education of America's young children: Obstacles and opportunities* (pp. 50–68). Chicago: University of Chicago Press.

Kagitcibasi, C. (1996). *Family and development across cultures: A view from the other side.* Mahwah, NJ: Lawrence Erlbaum Associates.

Kaiser, A. P., & Warren, S. F. (1988). Pragmatics and generalization. In R. L. Schiefelbusch & L. L. Lloyd (Eds.), *Language perspectives II: Acquisition, assessment, and intervention* (pp. 397–442). Austin, TX: Pro-Ed.

Kalat, J. W. (1995) *Biological psychology.* New York: Brooks/Cole.

Kaltman, G. S. (2006). *Help! For teachers of young children.* Austin, TX: Pro-Ed.

Kalyanpur, M., & Harry, B. (1999). *Culture in special education: Building reciprocal family-professional relationships.* Baltimore: Paul H. Brookes.

Kamii, C., & DeVries, R. (1997). *Physical knowledge in preschool education: Implications of Piaget's theory.* New York: Teachers College Press.

Kamphaus, R. W., Petosky, M. D., & Rowe, E. W. (2000). Current trends in psychological testing of children. *Professional Psychology: Research and Practice, 31,* 155–164.

Kanungo, S., & Soares, N. (2005). The New Language of Toys—Teaching Communication Skills to Children with Special Needs. *Journal of Developmental and Behavioral Pediatrics, 26,* 332.

Kaplan, J. S. (1991). *Beyond behavior modification: A cognitive-behavior approach to behavior management in the school.* Austin, TX: Pro-Ed.

Karnes, M. B., & Stayton, V. (1988). Model programs for infants and toddlers with handicaps. In J. Jordan, J. Gallagher, P. Hutinger, & M. Karnes (Eds.), *Early childhood special education: Birth to three* (pp. 67–108). Reston, VA: Council for Exceptional Children.

Karoly, L. A., Greenwood, P. W., Everingham, S. S., Hoube, J., Kilburn, M. R., Rydell, C. P., et al. (1998). *Investing in our children: What we know and don't know about the costs and benefits of early childhood interventions.* Santa Monica, CA: RAND.

Katsiyannis, A., Yell, M. L., & Bradley, R. (2001). Reflections on the 25th anniversary of the Individuals with Disabilities Education Act. *Remedial and Special Education, 22,* 234–334.

Katz, K. (1997). *A developmental approach to assessment of young children.* Champaign, IL: ERIC Clearinghouse on Elementary and Early Childhood Education. Retrieved May 15, 2007, from http://ceep.crc.uiuc.edu/eecearchi dle/digest/1997/Katz97.html.

Kauffman, J. M. (1989). *Characteristics of behavior disorders of children and youth* (4th ed.). Columbus, OH: Merrill.

Kaufman, J. M. (1993). *Characteristics of emotional and behavioral disorders of children and youth* (5th ed.). Columbus, OH: Merrill.

Kaufman, S. (1999). *Retarded isn't stupid, Mom!* (Rev. ed.). Baltimore: Paul H. Brookes.

Kazdin, A. E. (1995). *Conduct disorders in childhood and adolescence.* Thousand Oaks, CA: Sage.

Kellogg, R. (1969). *Analyzing children's art.* Palo Alto, CA: National Press Books.

Kennedy, M. D. (1991). Play-language relationships in young children with developmental delays: Implications for assessment. *Journal of Speech and Hearing Research, 34,* 112–122.

Keogh, J., & Sugden, D. (1985). *Movement skill development.* New York: Macmillan.

Kerr, A. M., & Ravine, D. (2003). Breaking new ground with Rett syndrome. *Journal of Intellectual Disabilities Resources, 47*(8), 580–587.

Kerrin, R. G. (1996). Collaboration: Working with the speech-language pathologist. *Intervention in School and Clinic, 32,* 56–59.

Kilbride, H., Castor, C., Hoffman, E., & Fuger, K. L. (2000). Thirty-six month outcome of prenatal cocaine exposure for term or near-term infants: Impact of early case management. *Journal of Developmental and Behavioral Pediatrics, 21*(1), 19–26.

Kilgo, J. L., Richard, N., & Noonan, M. J. (1989). Teaming for the future: Integrating transition planning with early intervention services for young children with disabilities and their families. *Infants and Young Children, 2,* 37–48.

Killen, M., & Turiel, E. (1991). Conflict resolution in preschool social interactions. *Early Education and Development, 2,* 240–255.

Kim, Y. M., Sugai, G. M., & Kim, G. (1999). Early intervention needs of children at risk due to prenatal drug exposure: A survey of early childhood educators. *Journal of Research in Childhood Education, 13*(2), 207–215.

Kinnison, L. R., Cates, D., & Baker, C. (1999). Day care givers: The front line force in combating the effects of prenatal drug exposure. *Preventing School Failure, 43*(2), 52–56.

Kirk, S. (1962). *Educating exceptional children.* Boston: Houghton Mifflin.

Kirk, S. A., & Gallagher, J. J. (1979). *Educating exceptional children* (3rd ed.). Boston: Houghton Mifflin.

Kirk, S. A., Gallagher, J. J., & Anastasiow, N. J. (2003). *Educating exceptional children* (10th ed.). Boston: Houghton Mifflin.

Kirst-Ashman, K. K., & Hull, G. H., Jr. (1993). Brokering and case management. In K. K. Kirst-Ashman & G. H. Hull, *Understanding Generalist Practice* (pp. 492–520). Chicago: Nelson-Hall.

Klein, M. D., & Chen, D. (2000). *Working with children from culturally diverse backgrounds.* Clifton Park, NY: Thomson Delmar Learning.

Klein, N. K. (1988). Children who were very low birth weight: Cognitive abilities and classroom behavior at five years of age. *Journal of Special Education, 22*(1), 41–49.

Klimes-Dougan, B., & Kistner, J. (1990). Physically abused preschoolers' responses to peers' distress. *Developmental Psychology, 26,* 599–602.

Knitzer, J. (2000). Early childhood mental health services: A policy and systems development perspective. In J. P. Shonkoff & S. J. Meisels (Eds.), *Handbook of early childhood intervention* (2nd ed., pp. 416–438). Cambridge: Cambridge University Press.

Knitzer, J. (2001). *Using mental health strategies to move the early childhood agenda and promote school readiness.* New York: Carnegie

Corporation of New York & National Center for Children in Poverty.

Koenig, A., & Holbrook, M. C. (2000). Professional practice. In M. Cay Holbrook & A. Koenig (Eds.), *Foundations of Education* (Vol. 1: *History and theory of teaching children and youths with visual impairments*, 2nd ed., pp. 260–276). Baltimore, MD: American Foundation for the Blind.

Kohlberg, L. (1969). Stage and sequence: The cognitive-developmental approach to socialization. In D. A. Goslin (Ed.), *Handbook of socialization theory and research* (pp. 347–480). Chicago: Rand McNally.

Kohlberg, L. (1984). *Essays on moral development: Vol. 2. The psychology of moral development.* New York: Harper & Row.

Kohler, F., & Strain, P. S. (1993). The early childhood social skills program. *Teaching Exceptional Children 25*(2), 41–42.

Kohn, A. (1993). *Punished by rewards.* Boston: Houghton Mifflin.

Kohn, A. (1997). How not to teach values. *Phi Delta Kappan, 78*(6), 429–439.

Koniditsiotis, C. Y., & Hunter, T. L. (1993). Speech-pathology-based language intervention within an early childhood education environment. *Enhancing young children's lives.* [Special issue] *Early Childhood Development and Care, 96,* 93–99.

Korfmacher, J., & Spicer, P. (2002). Toward an understanding of the child's experience in a Montessori early Head Start program. *Infant Mental Health Journal, 23,* 197–212.

Kostelnick, M. J. (1992). Myths associated with developmentally appropriate practice. *Young Children, 47*(4), 17–23.

Kraft-Sayre, M. E., & Pianta, R. C. (2000). *Enhancing the transition to kindergarten: Linking children, families, and schools.* Charlottesville: University of Virginia, National Center for Early Development & Learning.

Kranowitz, C. S. (1998). *The out of sync child.* New York: Berkley Publishing Group.

Kratochvil, M. S., & Devereux, S. A. (1988). Counseling needs of parents of handicapped children. *Social Casework, 69,* 420–426.

Krauss, M. W. (1997). Two generations of family research in early intervention. In M. Guralnick (Ed.), *The effectiveness of early intervention* (pp. 611–624). Baltimore: Paul H. Brookes.

Krauss, M. W., & Selzer, M. M. (1998). Life course perspectives in mental retardation research: The case of family caregiving. In J. A. Burack, R. M. Hodapp, & E. Zigler (Eds.), *Handbook of mental retardation and development* (pp. 553–603). Cambridge, UK: Cambridge University Press.

Krauss, R. B., Thurman, S. K., Brodsky, N., Betancourt, L., Giannetta, J., & Hurt, H. (2000). Caregiver interaction behavior with prenatally cocaine-exposed and nonexposed preschoolers. *Journal of Early Intervention, 23*(1), 62–73.

Kripke, Clarissa. (2004). Therapy for speech and language delay. *American Family Physician, 69*(12), 282–392.

Kubicek, L. F. (2002). Fresh perspectives on young children and family routine. *Zero to Three, 22,* 4–9.

Kubiszyn, T. & Borich, G. (1993). *Educational testing and measurement: Classroom application and practice.* New York: Harper Collins.

Kuczak, S. A. (1986). Thoughts on the intentional basis of early object word extension: Evidence from comprehension and production. In S. Kuczak, II, & M. D. Barrett (Eds.), *The development of word meaning* (pp. 99–120). New York: Springer-Verlag.

Kuhl, J. (1984). Volitional aspects of achievement motivation and learned helplessness: Toward a comprehensive theory of action control. In B. A. Maher (Ed.), *Progress in experimental personality research* (Vol. 13, pp. 99–171). San Diego: Academic Press.

Kuhl, J. (2000). A functional-design approach to motivation and self-regulation: The dynamics of personality systems and interactions. In M. Boekaerts & P. R. Pintrich (Eds.), *Handbook of self regulation* (pp. 44–87). San Diego, CA: Academic Press.

Kuhn, D. (1992). Cognitive development. In M. H. Bornstein & M. E. Lamb (Eds.), *Developmental psychology: An advanced textbook* (3rd ed., pp. 211–272). Hillsdale, NJ: Erlbaum.

Kuhn, D. (1999). Metacognitive development. In L. Balter & C. Tamis-LeMonda (Eds.), *Child psychology: A handbook of contemporary issues* (pp. 259–286). New York: Psychology Press.

Ladd, G. W. (2003). Probing the adaptive significance of children's behavior and relationships in the school context: A child by environment perspective. *Advances in Child Development Behavior, 31,* 43–104.

Ladd, G. W., Birch, S. H., & Buhs, E. S. (1999). Children's social and scholastic lives in kindergarten: Related spheres of influence? *Child Development, 70*(6), 1373–1400.

Lahey, M. (1988). *Language disorders and language development.* New York: Macmillan.

Laing, S. P., & Kamhi, A. (2003). Alternative assessment of language and literacy in culturally and linguistically diverse populations. *Language, Speech, and Hearing Services in Schools, 34*(1), 44–54.

Landau, S., & Milich, R. (1990). Assessment of children's social status and peer relations. In A. M. LaGreca (Ed.), *Through the eyes of the child* (pp. 259–291). Boston: Allyn & Bacon.

Landau, S., & Moore, L. (1991) Social skill deficits in children with attention-deficit hyperactivity disorder. *School Psychology Review, 20*(2), 235–251.

Landecker, A. W. (1980). Lifting and carrying. In J. Unbreit & P. J. Cardullias (Eds.), *Educating the severely physically handicapped: Basic principles and techniques.* Columbus, OH: Special Press.

Landy, S. (2002). *Pathways to competence: Encouraging healthy social and emotional development in young children.* Baltimore: Paul H. Brookes.

Lane, H. (1988). Is there a "Psychology of the Deaf"? *Exceptional Children, 55,* 7–19.

Lane, S. J., Miller, L. J., & Hanft, B. E. (2000). Towards a consensus in terminology in sensory integration theory and practice, Part 2: Sensory integration patterns of function and dysfunction. *Sensory Integration Special Interest Section, 23*(2), 1–3.

Langdon, H. W. (1989). Language disorders or difference? Assessing the language skill of Hispanic students. *Exceptional Children, 56,* 160–167.

Lange, G., & Pierce, S. H. (1992). Memory-strategy learning and maintenance in preschool children. *Developmental Psychology, 28,* 453–462.

LaParo, K. M., & Pianta, R. C. (2000). Teachers' reported transition practices for children transitioning into kindergarten and first grade. *Exceptional Children, 67*(1), 7–20.

LaParo, K., Kraft-Sayre, M., & Pianta, R. (2003). Preschool to kindergarten transition activities: Involvement and satisfaction of families and teachers. *Journal of Research in Childhood Education, 17*(2), 147–158.

Larsen, S., & Hammill, D. (1975). The relationship of selected visual perceptual skills to academic abilities. *Journal of Special Education, 9,* 281–291.

Lavigne, J. V., Cicchetti, C., Gibbons, R. D., Binns, H. J., Larsen, L., & DeVito, C. (2001). Oppositional defiant disorder with onset in preschool years: Longitudinal stability and pathways to other disorders. *Journal of the American Academy of Child and Adolescent Psychiatry, 40,* 1393–1400.

Law, J., Boyle, J., Harris, F., Harkness, A., & Nye, C. (1998). Screening for primary speech and language delay: A systematic review of the literature. *International Journal of Language and Communication Disorders, 33*(Suppl.), 21–3.

Lawry, J., Danko, C., & Strain, P. (1999). Examining the role of the classroom environment in the prevention of problem behaviors. In S. Sandall & M. Ostrosky (Eds.), *Young exceptional children: Practical ideas for addressing challenging behaviors* (pp. 49–62).

Lazzaro, J. J. (1993). Adaptive technologies for learning and work environment. Chicago: The American Library Association.

Lee, D., & Antia, S. (1992). A sociological approach to the social integration of hearing-impaired and normally hearing students. *Volta Review, 95,* 425–434.

Lee, D. L., & Axelrod, S. (2005). *Behavior modification: Basic principles* (2nd ed.). Austin, TX: Pro-Ed.

Lee, J., O'Shea, L. J., & Dykes, M. K. (1987). Teacher wait-time: Performance of developmentally delayed and non-delayed young children. *Education and Training in Mental Retardation, 22,* 176–184.

Lee, V. E., & Burkam, D. (2002). Inequality at the starting gate: Social background differences in achievement as children begin school. Washington, DC: Economic Policy Institute.

Leeper, L. H., & Gotthoffer, D. (2000). *Quick guide to the Internet for speech-language pathology and audiology.* Boston: Allyn & Bacon.

Leonard, L. (1986). Early language development and language disorders. In G. H. Shames & E. H. Wiig (Eds.), *Human communication disorders* (2nd ed., pp. 291–330). Columbus, OH: Merrill/Macmillan.

Lepper, M., & Hodell, M. (1989). Intrinsic motivation in the classroom. In C. Ames & R. Ames (Eds.), *Research on motivation in education* (Vol. 3, pp. 73–105). San Diego, CA: Academic Press.

Lepper, M. R. (1981). Intrinsic and extrinsic motivation in children: Detrimental effects of superfluous social controls. In W. A. Collins (Ed.), *Aspects of the development of competence* (pp. 155–214). Hillsdale, NJ: Lawrence Erlbaum Associates.

Lepper, M. R., & Malone, T. W. (1987). Intrinsic motivation and instructional effectiveness in computer-based education. In R. E. Snow & M. J. Farr (Eds.), *Aptitude, learning, and instruction: Cognitive and affective process analysis* (Vol. 3, pp. 255–286). Hillsdale, NJ: Lawrence Erlbaum Associates.

Lepper, M. R., Sthi, S., Dialdin, D., & Drake, M. (1997). Intrinsic and extrinsic motivation: A developmental perspective. In S. S. Luthar, J. A. Burack, D. Cicchetti, & J. R. Weisz (Eds.), *Developmental psychopathology: Perspectives on adjustment, risk, and disorder* (pp. 23–50). New York: Cambridge University Press.

Lerner, J. W. (2000). *Learning disabilities: Theories, diagnosis, and teaching strategies.* Boston: Houghton Mifflin.

Lerner, J. W., Mardell-Czudnowski, C., & Goldenberg, D. (1987). *Special education for the early childhood years.* Englewood Cliffs, NJ: Prentice-Hall.

Lesare, S., Trivette, C. M., & Dunst, C. J. (1995). Families of children and adolescents with special needs across the life-span. *Exceptional children, 62*(3), 224–236.

Lester, B. M., LaGasse, L. L., & Seifer, R. (1998). Cocaine exposure and children: the meaning of subtle effects. *Science, 282,* 633–634.

Levenson, R. L., Kairam, R., Bartnett, M., & Mellins, C. A. (1991). Equivalence of Peabody Picture Vocabulary Test, Revised, Forms L and M for children with acquired immune deficiency syndrome (AIDS). *Perceptual and Motor Skills, 72,* 99–102.

Levenson, R. L., & Mellins, C. A. (1992). Pediatric HIV disease: What psychologists need to know. *Professional Psychologist: Research and Practice, 23*(5), 410–415.

Levin, B. W., Driscoll, J. M., & Fleischman, A. R. (1991). Treatment choice for infants in neonatal intensive care unit at risk for AIDS. *Journal of the American Medical Association, 265*(22), 2976–2981.

Levine, A. J. (1992). *Viruses.* New York: Scientific American Library.

Levine, C., & Dubler, N. N. (1990). HIV and child bearing: Uncertain risks and bitter realities: The reproductive choices of HIV-infected women. *Milbank Quarterly, 68*(3), 321–349.

Leviton, A., Mueller, M., & Kauffman, C. (1992). The family-centered consultation model: Practical applications for professionals. *Infants and Young Children, 4*(3), 1–8.

Levy, J. (1974). *The baby exercise book.* New York: Pantheon.

Lewis, J. M. (1993). Childhood play in normality, pathology and therapy. *American Journal of Orthopsychiatry, 63*(1), 6–15.

Lewis, J. M., & Miller, S. M. (Ed.). (1990). *Handbook of developmental psychopathlogy.* New York: Plenum.

Lewis, J. M., Sullivan, M. W., Stanger, C., & Weiss, M. (1989). Self-development and self-conscious emotions. *Child Development, 60,* 146–156.

Lewis, M., & Brooks-Gunn, J. (1979). *Social cognition and the acquisition of self.* New York: Plenum Press.

Lewis, S., & Allman, C. B. (2000). *Seeing eye to eye: An administrator's guide to students with low vision.* New York: American Foundation for the Blind.

Lewis, V., Boucher, J., & Astell, A. (1992). The assessment of symbolic play in young children: A prototype test. *European Journal of Disorders of Communication, 27,* 232–236.

Lieber, J., & Beckman, P. J. (1991). The role of toys in individual and dyadic play among young children with handicaps. *Journal of Applied Developmental Psychology, 22,* 691–700.

Lifchez, R., & Winslow, B. (1979). *Design for independent living: The environment and physically disabled people.* Berkeley: University of California Press.

Lindenberg, C. S., Alexander, E. M., Gendrop, S. C., Nencioli, M., & Williams, D. G. (1991). A review of the literature on cocaine abuse in pregnancy. *Nursing Research, 40*(2), 69–75.

Linder, T. W. (1983). *Early childhood special education: Program development and administration.* Baltimore: Paul H. Brookes.

Linder, T. W. (1990). *Transdisciplinary play-based assessment.* Baltimore: Paul H. Brookes.

Lindfors, J. W. (1987). *Children's language and learning* (2nd ed.). Englewood Cliffs, NJ: Prentice-Hall.

Lindsay, Z. (1968). *Art is for all: Arts and crafts for less able children.* New York: Taplinger.

Ling, D. (1984). *Early intervention for hearing-impaired children: Oral options.* San Diego: College Hill.

Ling, D. (1989). *Foundations of spoken language for hearing-impaired children.* Washington, DC: Alexander Graham Bell Association for the Deaf.

Lipsitt, L. P. (1990). Learning and memory in infants. *Merrill-Palmer Quarterly, 36,* 53–66.

Lipson, M. (1993). What do you say to a child with AIDS? *Hastings Center Report, 23,* 6–12.

Litt, J., & McNeil, M. (1997). Biological markers and social differentiation: Crack babies and the construction of the dangerous mother. *Health Care Women International, 18,* 31–41.

Lockhart, L. L., & Wodarski, J. S. (1989). Facing the unknown: Children and adolescents with AIDS. *Social Work, 2,* 2215–2221.

Loeb, S., Fuller, B., Kagan, S. L., Carrol, B., & Carroll, J. (2004). Child care in poor communities: Early learning effects of type, quality, and stability. *Child Development, 75*(1), 47–65.

Loehlin, J. C. (1992). *Genes and environment in personality development.* Newbury Park, CA: Sage.

Loomans, D., & Loomans, J. (2003) *100 ways to build self-esteem and teach values.* Tiburon, CA: H. J. Kramer.

Loraas, O. I. (2002). *Teaching Individuals with Developmental Delays: Basics.* Austin, TX: Pro-Ed.

Losardo, A., & Notari-Syverson, A. (2001). *Alternative approaches to assessing young children.* Baltimore: Paul H. Brookes.

Lovaas, O. I. (1987). Behavioral treatment and normal educational and intellectual functioning in young autistic children. *Journal of Consulting and Clinical Psychology, 55,* 3–9.

Love, R. J. (1992). *Childhood motor speech disability.* New York: Macmillan.

Lowenbraun, S. (1988). Hearing-impaired. In E. L. Meyen & T. M. Skotric (Eds.), *Exceptional children and youth: An introduction* (3rd ed., pp. 321–350). Denver: Love Publishing.

Lowenfeld, M. (1971). *Play in childhood* (2nd ed.). New York: Wiley.

Lowenfeld, M., & Brittain, W. L. (1969). *Creative and mental growth* (6th ed.). New York: Macmillan.

Lowenthal, B. (1992). Interagency collaboration in early intervention: Rationale, barriers, and implementation. *Infant-Toddler Intervention, 2*(2), 103–111.

Lowenthal, B. (1996). Teaching basic adaptive skills to young children with disabilities. *Early Child Development and Care, 111,* 77–84.

Luciana, M., & Nelson, C. A. (1998). The functional emergence of prefontally guided working memory systems in four- to eight-year-old children. *Neuropsychologia, 36,* 273–393.

Luckasson, R. (2002). *Mental retardation: Definition, classification and system of supports.* Washington, DC: American Association on Mental Retardation.

Lue, M. S. (2001). *A survey of communication disorders for the classroom teacher.* Boston: Allyn & Bacon.

Lueck, H. A., Chen, D., & Kekelis, L. (1997). *Developmental guidelines for infants with visual impairment: A manual for early intervention.* Louisville, KY: American Printing House for the Blind.

Luterman, D. (1970). *Counseling parents of hearing-impaired children.* Boston: Little, Brown.

Lutkenhoff, M. (Ed.). (1999). *Children with spina bifida: A parents' guide.* Bethesda, MD: Woodbine House.

Lynch, E. W., & Hanson, M. J. (1992). *Developing cross-cultural competence.* Baltimore, MD: Paul H. Brookes.

Lynch, E. W., & Hanson, M. J. (1996). Ensuring cultural competence in assessment. In M. McLean, D. B. Bailey, & M. Wolery (Eds.), *Assessing infants and preschoolers with special needs* (2nd ed., pp. 27–52). Columbus, OH: Merrill.

Lyon, G. R., Fletcher, J. M., Shaywitz, S. E., Shaywitz, B. A., Torgesen, J. K., Wood, F. B., et al.

(2001). Rethinking learning disabilities. In C. E. Finn, A. J. Rotherham, & C. R. Hokanson, Jr. (Eds.), *Rethinking special education for a new century* (pp. 259–287). Washington, DC: Thomas B. Fordham Foundation.

MacDonald, J. (1985). Language through conversation: A model for intervention with language-delayed persons. In S. Warren & A. Rogers-Warren (Eds.), *Teaching functional language: Generalization and maintenance of language skills* (pp. 89–122). Baltimore: University Park Press.

Maddox, S. (Ed.). (1987). *Spinal networks: The total resource for the wheelchair community.* Boulder, CO: Author.

Maddox, T. (2003). *Tests: A comprehensive reference for assessments in psychology, education, and business.* Austin, TX: Pro–Ed.

Magnuson, K. A., Meyers, M. K., Ruhm, C. J., & Waldfogel, J. (2004). Inequality in preschool education and school readiness. *American Educational Research Journal, 41*(1), 115–157.

Mah, D. (2007). *Difficult behavior in early childhood: Positive discipline for PreK–3 classrooms and beyond.* Austin, TX: Pro-Ed.

Mahoney, G. J., & Filer, J. (1996). How responsive is early intervention to the priorities and needs of families? *Topics in Early Childhood Special Education, 16,* 437–457.

Mahoney, G., O'Sullivan, P., & Fors, S. (1989). Service provider practices with young handicapped children. *Journal of Early Intervention, 13,* 261–268.

Mahoney, G. J., Robinson, C., & Powell, A. (1992a). Modifying parent-child interaction: Enhancing the development of handicapped children. *Journal of Special Education, 22,* 82–96.

Mahoney, G. J., Robinson, C., & Powell, A. (1992b). Focusing on parent-child interactions: The bridge to developmentally appropriate practices. *Topics in Early Childhood Education, 12*(1), 105–120.

Male, M. (1994). *Technology for inclusion: Meeting the special needs of all students.* Boston: Allyn & Bacon.

Malina, R. M. (1980). Biological correlates of motor development during infancy and early childhood. In L. S. Green & F. E. Johnstone (Eds.), *Social and biological predictors of nutritional status, physical growth and neurological development.* New York: Academic Press.

Malone, D. M., & Stonemen, Z. (1990). Cognitive play of mentally retarded preschoolers: Observations in the home and school. *American Journal on Mental Retardation, 94*(5), 475–487.

Mangione, P. L. (Ed.) (1995). *A guide to culturally sensitive care.* Sacramento, CA: California Department of Education.

Mannix, D. (1987). *Oral language activities for special children.* West Nyack, NY: Center for Applied Research in Education.

Mantzicopoulos, P. (2006). Young children's changing self-concepts: Boys and girls from preschool through second grade. *The Journal of Genetic Psychology, 167*(3), 289–308.

March of Dimes. (1992). *Spinal bifida: Public health education sheet.* White Plains, NY: Author.

Marcus, G. F., Pinker, S., Ullman, M., Hollander, M., Rosen, T. J., & Fei, X. (1992). Overregularization in language acquisition. *Monographs of the Society for Research in Child Development, 57*(4, Serial No. 228).

Marino, B. L. (1991). Studying infant and toddler play. *Journal of Pediatric Nursing, 6*(1), 16–20.

Markun, P. M. (1974). *Play: Children's business.* Washington, DC: Association for Childhood Education International.

Marsh, H. (1986). Global self-esteem: Its relation to specific facets of self-concept and their importance. *Journal of Personality and Social Psychology, 51,* 1224–1236.

Marsh, H. (1989). Age and sex effects in multiple dimensions of self-concept: Pre-adolescence to early adulthood. *Journal of Educational Psychology, 81,* 417–430.

Marshall, G., & Herbert, M. (1981). *Recorded telephone messages: A way to link teacher and parents.* An evaluation report prepared for CEMREL, Washington, DC: Department of Education.

Marshall, H. (2003). Research in review: Opportunity deferred or opportunity taken? An updated look at delaying kindergarten entry. *Young Children 58*(5), 84–93.

Martin, E. W., Martin, R., & Terman, D. L. (1996). The legislative and litigation history of special education. *Future of Children, 6*(1), 25–39.

Martin, F. M. (Ed.). (1987a). *Hearing disorders in children*. Austin, TX: Pro-Ed.

Martin, F. M. (Ed.). (1987b). *Hearing disorders in children: Pediatric audiology*. Boston: Allyn & Bacon.

Martin, J. A., Hamilton, B. E., Sutton, P. D., Ventura, S. J., Menacker, F., & Kirmeyer, S. (2006). Births: Final data for 2004. *National Vital Statistics Reports, 55*(1). Hyattsville, MD: National Center for Health Statistics.

Marzollo, J., & Harper, J. L. (1972). *Learning through play*. New York: Harper & Row.

Massey, G. N., & Wheeler, J. J. (2000). Acquisition and generalization of activity schedules and their effects on task engagement in a young child with autism in an inclusive pre-school classroom. *Education and Training in Mental Retardation and Developmental Disabilities, 35*, 326–335.

Masterson, J., Swirbul, T., & Noble, D. (1990). Computer generated information packets for parents. *Language, Speech, and Hearing Services in Schools, 21*, 114–115.

Mathew, A., & Cook, M. (1990). The control of reaching movements by young infants. *Child Development, 61*, 1238–1257.

Matson, J. L., Mayville, S. B., & Laud, R. B. (2003). A system of assessment for adaptive behavior, social skills, behavioral function, medication side-effects, and psychiatric disorders. *Research in Developmental Disabilities, 24*(1), 75–81.

Maxwell, K., & Clifford, R. M. (2004). Research in review: School readiness assessment. *Young Children, 59*(1), 42–46.

Mayers, A., & Spiegel, L. (1992). A parental support group in a pediatric AIDS clinic: Its usefulness and limitations. *Health Social Work, 17*(3), 183–191.

Mayes, L. C. (1992). The effects of prenatal cocaine exposure on young children's development. *Analysis of the American Academy of Political and Social Science, 521,* 11–27.

Mayes, L. C., & Bornstein, M. H. (1995). Developmental dilemmas for cocaine-abusing parents and their children. In M. Lewis & M. Bendersky (Eds.), *Mothers, babies, and cocaine: The role of toxins in development* (pp. 251–272). Hillsdale, NJ: Erlbaum.

Mayes, L. C., Granger, R. H., Bornstein, M. C., & Zuckerman, B. (1992). The problem of prenatal cocaine exposure: A rush to judgement. *Journal of the American Medical Association, 267*(3), 406–408.

Mayes, L. C., Grillon, C., Granger, R., & Schottenfeld, R. (1998). Regulation of arousal and attention in preschool children exposed to cocaine prenatally. *Annals of the New York Academy of Sciences, 846*, 126–143.

Mayfield, P. K., & Chapman, J. K. (1998). Children's prenatal exposure to drugs: Implications for early childhood educators. *Dimensions of Early Childhood, 26*(3–4), 38–42.

McArthur, S. H. (1982). *Raising your hearing-impaired child: Guidelines for parents*. Washington, DC: Alexander Graham Bell Association.

McCabe, L. A., Hernandez, M., Lara, S. L., & Brooks-Gunn, J. (2000). Assessing preschoolers' self-regulation in homes and classrooms: Lessons from the field. *Behavioral Disorders, 26*(1), 53–69.

McClelland, M. M., Morrison, F. J., & Holmes, D. L. (2000). Children at risk for early academic problems: The role of learning-related social skills. *Early Childhood Research Quarterly, 15*(3), 307–329.

McConkey, R. (1985). *Working with parents: A practical guide to teachers and therapists*. Cambridge, MA: Brookline Books.

McConnell, K., & Ryser, G. R. (2006). *Early start for young children with autism/PDD: Practical interventions*. Austin, TX: Pro-Ed.

McConnell, S. R., McEvoy, M., Carta, J. J., Greenwood, C. R., Kminski, R., Good, R. H., & Shinn, M. (1998). *Family outcomes in a growth and developmental model*. Minneapolis: Early Childhood Research Institute on Measuring Growth and Development, University of Minnesota.

McConnell, S. R., Priest, J. S., Davis, S. D., & McEvoy, M. A. (2002). Best practices in measuring growth and development for preschool children. In A. Thomas & J. Grimes (Eds.), *Best practices in school psychology* (Vol. 4, pp. 1231–1246). Bethesda, MD: National Association of School Psychologists.

McConnell, S. R., Rush, K. L., McEvoy, M. A., Carta, J., Atwater, J., & Williams, R. (2002). Descriptive and experimental analysis of child-caregiver interactions that promote development of young children exposed prenatally to drugs and alcohol. *Journal of Behavioral Education, 11*(3), 131–161.

McCormick, L., & Schiefelbusch, R. L. (1990). *Early language intervention* (2nd ed.). Columbus, OH: Merrill/Macmillan.

McDermott, R. P., & Varenne, H. (1996). Culture, development, disability. In R. Jessor, A. Colby, & R. A. Shweder (Eds.), *Ethnography and human development*. Chicago: University of Chicago Press.

McEvoy, M. A., Odom, S. L., & McConnell, S. R. (1992). Peer social competence intervention for young children with disabilities. In S. L. Odom, S. R. McConnell, & M. A. McEvoy (Eds.), *Social competence of young children with disabilities: Issues and strategies for intervention* (pp. 113–133). Baltimore: Paul H. Brookes.

McEwen, I. (Ed.). (2000). *Individual education program: Providing physical therapy services under Parts B and C of the Individuals with Disabilities Education Act*. Alexandria, VA: American Physical Therapy Association.

McGee, R., & Share, D. L. (1988). Attention deficit disorder-hyperactivity and academic failure: Which comes first and what should be treated? *Journal of the American Academy of Child and Adolescent Psychiatry, 27,* 318–325.

McGinnis, E., & Goldstein, A. (1990). *Skillstreaming in early childhood: Teaching prosocial skills to the preschool and kindergarten child*. Champaign, IL: Research Press.

McGoey, K., Eckert, T., & Dupaul, G. (2002). Early intervention for preschool children with ADHD: A literature review. *Journal of Emotional and Behavioral Disorders, 10*(1), 14–28.

McGonigel, M. J., Kaufmann, R. K., & Johnson, B. H. (Eds.). (1991). *Guidelines and recommended practices for the individualized family service plan* (2nd ed.). Bethesda, MD: Association for the Care of Children's Health.

McHale, S. M., & Lerner, R. M. (1990). Stages of human development. In R. M. Thomas (Ed.), *The encyclopedia of human development and education* (pp. 163–166). Oxford: Pergamon.

McKnight-Taylor, M. (1989). Stimulating speech and language development of infants and young children. In P. J. Valletutti, M. McKnight-Taylor, & A. S. Hoffnung (Eds.), *Facilitating communication in young children with handi-capping conditions: A guide for special educators* (pp. 68–92). Boston: Little, Brown.

McLean, L. K., & Cripe, J. W. (1997). The effectiveness of early intervention for children with communication disorders. In M. J. Guralnick (Ed.), *The effectiveness of early intervention* (pp. 133–165). Baltimore: Paul H. Brookes.

McLoughlin, J. A., & Lewis, R. B. (1999). *Assessing special students* (3rd ed.). Columbus, OH: Merrill.

McMorrow, M. J., Foxx, R. M., Faw, G. D., & Bittle, R. G. (1986). *Looking for the words: Teaching functional language strategies*. Champaign, IL: Research Press.

McMurray, G. L. (1986). Easing everyday living: Technology for the physically disabled. In A. Gatner & T. Joe (Eds.), *Images of disabled/disabling images*. New York: Praeger.

McReynolds, L. V. (1986). Functional articulation disorders. In G. H. Shames & E. H. Wiig (Eds.), *Human communication disorders* (2nd ed., pp. 139–182). Columbus, OH: Merrill/Macmillan.

McWilliam, R. A., Snyder, P., Harbin, G. L., Porter, P., & Munn, D. (2000). Professionals' and families' perceptions of family-centered practices in infant-toddler service. *Early Education and Development, 11,* 519–538.

McWilliams, R. A., & Sekerak, D. (1995). Integrated practices in center-based early intervention: perceptions of physical therapists. *Pediatric Physical Therapy, 7,* 51–58.

Meisels, S. J. (1996). Charting the continuum of assessment and intervention. In S. J. Meisels & E. Fenichel (Eds.), *New visions for the developmental assessment of infants and young children* (pp. 27–52). Washington, DC: Zero to Three.

Meisels, S. J. (1999). Assessing readiness. In R. C. Pianta & M. J. Cox (Eds.), *The transition to kindergarten* (pp. 39–66). Baltimore: Paul H. Brookes.

Meisels, S. J., & Atkins-Burnett, S. (2000). The elements of early childhood assessment. In J. P. Shonkoff & S. J. Meisels (Eds.), *Handbook of early childhood intervention* (2nd ed., pp. 231–257). New York: Cambridge University Press.

Meisels, S. J., & Fenichel, E. (1996). *New visions for the developmental assessment of infants and young children.* Washington, DC: Zero to Three.

Meisels, S. J., & Provence, S. (1989). *Screening and assessment: Guidelines for identifying young disabled and developmentally vulnerable children and their families.* Washington, DC: Zero to Three.

Meisels, S., & Shonkoff, J. P. (Eds.). (1990). *Handbook of early intervention.* New York: Cambridge University Press.

Merrell, K. W. (1999). *Behavioral, social, and emotional assessment of children and adolescents.* Mahwah, NJ: Lawrence Erlbaum Associates.

Messinger, D. S., Bauer, C. R., Das, A., Seifer, R., & Lester, B. M. (2004). The maternal lifestyle study: Cognitive, motor, and behavioral outcomes of cocaine-exposed and opiate-exposed infants through three years of age. *Pediatrics, 113*(6), 1677–1685.

Messinger, D. S., & Fogel, A. (1998). Give and take: The development of conventional infant gestures. *Merrill-Palmer Quarterly, 44,* 566–590.

Michaud, L. J. (2004). Prescribing therapy services for children with motor disabilities. *Pediatrics, 113*(6), 1836–1838.

Miller, L. J., & Lane, S. J. (2000). Towards a consensus in terminology in sensory integration theory and practice, part 1: Taxonomy of neurophysiological processes. *Sensory Integration Special Interest Section, 23*(1), 1–4.

Miller, L. K. (1980). *Principles of everyday behavior analysis* (2nd ed.). Monterey, CA: Brooks-Cole.

Miller, P. A., & Sperry, L. L. (1987). The socialization of anger and aggression. *Merrill-Palmer Quarterly, 33*(1), 1–31.

Miller-Wood, D. J., Efron, M., & Wood, T. A. (1990). Use of close-circuit television with a severely visually impaired young child. *Journal of Visual Impairment and Blindness, 84*(12), 559–564.

Minnes, P. (1998). Mental retardation: The impact upon the family. In J. A. Burack, R. M. Hodapp, & E. Zigler (Eds.), *Handbook of mental retardation and development* (pp. 693–712). Cambridge, UK: Cambridge University Press.

Mistrett, S. G., Raimondi, S. L., & Barnett, M. P. (1990). *The use of technology with preschoolers with handicaps.* Buffalo, NY: Preschool Integration through Technology Systems.

Mitchell, D., & Brown, R. I. (Eds.). (1991). *Early intervention studies for young children with disabilities.* New York: Chapman & Hall.

Miyake, K., Campos, J. J., Kagan, J., & Bradshaw, D. L. (1986). Issues in socioemotional development. In H. Stevenson, H. Azuma, & K. Kakuta (Eds.), *Child development and education in Japan* (pp. 239–261). New York: Freeman.

Mogg, K., & Bradley, B. P. (1998). A cognitive-motivational analysis of anxiety. *Behavior Research and Therapy, 36,* 809–848.

Montie, J. E., Xiang, Z., & Schweinhart, L. J. (2006). Preschool experience in 10 countries: Cognitive and language performance at age 7. *Early Childhood Research Quarterly, 21,* 313–331.

Moon, B. L. (1990). *Existential art therapy: The Mayvas mirror.* Springfield, IL: Charles C. Thomas.

Moore, P. (1986). Voice disorders. In G. H. Shames & E. H. Wiig (Eds.), *Human communication disorders* (2nd ed., pp. 183–229). Columbus, OH: Merrill/Macmillan.

Moore, S. T. (1990). A social work practice model of case management: A case management grid. *Social Work, 35,* 444–448.

Moores, D. F. (1985). Early intervention programs for hearing-impaired children: A longitudinal assessment. In D. Nelson (Ed.), *Children's language* (Vol. 5, pp. 199–232). Hillsdale, NJ: Lawrence Erlbaum Associates.

Moores, D. F. (2001). *Educating the deaf: Psychology, principles, and practices.* Boston: Allyn & Bacon.

Morales, A. T., & Sheafor, B. W. (1992). *Social work: A profession of many faces.* Boston, MA: Allyn & Bacon.

Morris, S. E. (1977). *Program guidelines for children with feeding problems.* Edison, NJ: Childcraft Education.

Moss, P. (1994). Defining quality: Values, stakeholders, and process. In P. Moss & A. Pence (Eds.), *Valuing quality in early childhood services: New approaches to defining quality* (pp. 1–9). New York: Teachers College Press.

Moxley, R. (1989). *The practice of case management.* Newbury Park, CA: Sage.

Mulligan, G. M., & Flanagan, K. D. (2006). *Findings from the 2-year-old early childhood longitudinal study, birth cohort (ECLS-B).* Retrieved February 1, 2007, from http://nces.ed.gove/ecls

Mulligan-Ault, M., Guess, P., Smith, L., & Thompson, B. (1988). The implementation of health-related procedures in classrooms for students with severe multiple impairments. *Journal of the Association for Persons with Severe Handicaps, 13,* 100–109.

Mulliken, R. K. (1983). The child in the environment. In R. K. Mulliken & J. J. Buckley (Eds.) *Assessment of multihandicapped and developmentally disabled children.* (pp. 37–62). Rockville, MD: Aspen.

Murphey, D. A. (2003). Discriminant validity of a community-level measure of children's readiness for school. *Early Childhood Research and Practice, 5*(2) [Electronic version]. Retrieved January 17, 2008, from http://ecrp.uiuc.edu/v5n2/murphey.html.

Murphey, D. A., & Burns, C. E. (2002). Development of a comprehensive community assessment of school readiness. *Early Childhood Research & Practice, 4*(2) [Electronic verions]. Retrieved January 17, 2008, from http://ecrp.uiuc.edu/v4n2/murphey.html

Myles, B. S., & Simpson, R. L. (2003). *Asperger syndrome: A guide for educators and parents* (2nd ed.). Austin, TX: Pro-Ed.

Nagle, R. J. (2000). Issues in preschool assessment. In B. A. Bracken (Ed.), *The psychoeducational assessment of preschool children* (3rd ed., pp. 19–32). Boston: Allyn & Bacon.

Naiman, D., & Schein, J. (1978). *For parents of deaf children.* Silver Spring, MD: National Association for the Deaf.

National Association for the Education of Young Children. (1990). *School readiness: A position statement of the National Association for the Education of Young Children.* Washington, DC: Author.

National Association for the Education of Young Children. (1995). *Promoting appropriate early childhood intervention practices.* Washington, DC: National Association for the Education of Young Children.

National Association for the Education of Young Children. (2005). *Code of ethical conduct and statement of commitment* [Electronic verion]. Retrieved January 2, 2008, from www.naeyc.org/about/postings/PSETH05.asp.

National Council on Disability. (1993). *Meeting the unique needs of minorities with disabilities: A report to the President and the Congress.* Washington, DC: Author.

National Early Intervention Longitudinal Study (NEILS). (2003). *Families' first experiences with early intervention.* Menlo Park, CA: SRI International.

National Education Goals Panel, Goal 1. (1997). *Getting a good start in school.* Retrieved February 1, 2007, from http://ofcn.org/cyber.serv/academy/negp/1997/negp106.html

National Governors Association Task Force on School Readiness. (January 2005). *Building the foundation for bright futures: Final report of the National Governors Association Task Force on School Readiness.* Washington, DC: Author.

National Institute of Child Health and Human Development, National Institutes of Health. (1990). *The new face of AIDS: A material and pediatric epidemic.* Atlantic Information Services.

National Institute on Drug Abuse. (1990). *National household survey on drug abuse: 1990 findings.* DHHS Pub. No. (ADM) 91–1732. Washington, DC: Author.

National Institutes of Health. (2000). National Institutes of Health consensus development conference statement: Diagnosis and treatment of attention-deficit/hyperactivity disorder. *Journal of the American Academy of Child and Adolescent Psychiatry, 39,* 182–193.

Neisworth, J. T., & Bagnato, S. J. (2000). Recommended practices in assessment. In S. Sandall, M. E. McLearn, & B. J. Smith (Eds.), *DEC recommended practices in early intervention/early childhood special education* (pp. 17–27). Longmont, CO: Sopris West.

Neisworth, J. T., Bagnato, S. J., Salvia, J., & Hunt, F. M. (1999). *Temperament and atypical behavior scales: Early childhood indicators of developmental dysfunction.* Baltimore: Paul H. Brookes.

Nelson, D. C. (1991). *Practical procedures for children with language disorders: Preschool–adolescence.* Austin, TX: Pro-Ed.

Nelson , K. E. (1973). Structure and strategy in learning to talk. *Monographs of the Society for Research in Child Development, 38* (1–2, Serial No. 149).

Nelson, K. E. (1989). Strategies for first language teaching. In M. L. Rice & R. L. Schiefelbusch

(Eds.), *The teachability of language* (pp. 263–310). Baltimore: Paul H. Brookes.

Nelson, N. W. (1993). *Childhood language disorders in context: Infancy through adolescence.* Columbus, OH: Merrill/Macmillan.

Nelson, N. W. (1998). *Childhood language disorders in context: Infancy through adolescence* (2nd ed.). Boston: Allyn & Bacon.

New picture of who will get AIDS is crammed with addicts. (1995, February 28). *The New York Times*, 4.

New York State Department of Health (1990). *Prehospital care provider's guide to AIDS.* Albany, NY: Author.

New York State Department of Health. (2002). *Report of the recommendation clinical practice guideline communication disorders: Assessment and intervention of young children (age 0–3 years).* Albany, NY: Author.

Nicoladis, E., Mayberry, R., & Genesee, F. (1999). Gesture and early bilingual development, *Developmental Psychology, 35*, 514–526.

Nielson, S., & McEvoy, M. A. (2003). Functional behavioral assessment in early education settings. *Journal of Early Intervention, 26*(2), 115–131.

Nilsson, L. (1990). *A child is born.* New York: Delacorte.

Nixon, A. (1969). A child's right to expressive arts. *Chilhood Education, 2*, 299–310.

Nolen, S. B. (1988). Reasons for studying: Motivational orientations and study strategies. *Cognition and Instruction, 5*(4), 269–287.

Noonan, M. J., & Ratokolau, N. B. (1991). Project profile—PPT: The Preschool Preparation and Transition Project. *Journal of Early Intervention, 15*(4), 390–398.

Norman, M. J., & McCormick, L. (1993). *Early intervention in natural environments.* Pacific Grove, CA: Brooks/Cole.

Norris, J. A. (1991). Providing developmentally appropriate intervention to infants and young children with handicaps. *Topics in Early Childhood Special Education, 11*(1), 21–35.

Northern, J., & Downs, M. (1984). *Hearing in children* (3rd ed.). Baltimore: Williams & Wilkins.

Nottelmann, E. (1987). Competence and self-esteem during transition from childhood to adolescence. *Developmental Psychology, 23*, 441–450.

O'Brien, M. (1991). *Promoting successful transition into school: A review of current intervention practices.* Lawrence: Kansas Early Childhood Research Institute, University of Kansas.

Odom, S. L. (1994). Developmentally appropriate practices, policy and use for young children with disabilities and their families. *Journal of Early Intervention, 18*(4), 346–348.

Odom, S. L. (2002). *Widening the circle: Including children with disabilities in preschool programs.* New York: Teachers College Press.

Odom, S. L., McConnell, S. R., & McEvoy, M. A. (1992). Social competence of young children with disabilities: Issues and strategies for intervention. Baltimore, MD: Paul H. Brookes.

Odom, S. L., & McEvoy, M. (1988). Integration of young children with handicaps and normally developing children. In S. Odom and M. Karnes (Eds.), *Early intervention for infants and children with handicaps: An empirical base* (pp. 241–248). Baltimore, MD: Paul H. Brookes.

Odom, S. L., & McEvoy, M. A. (1990). Mainstreaming at the preschool level: Potential barriers and tasks for the field. *Topics in Early Childhood Special Education, 10*(2), 48–61.

Oller, D. K., & Eiler, R. E. (1988). The role of coordination in infant babbling. *Child Development, 59*, 441–449.

Olsen, D. A. (1999). *Universal preschool is no golden ticket.* Washington, DC: Cato Institute.

Olson, S. L. (1989). Assessment of impulsivity in preschoolers: Cross-measure convergence, longitudinal stability, and relevance to social competence. *Journal of Clinical Child Psychology, 8*(2), 176–183.

Ondersma, S., Simpson, S., Brestan, E., & Ward, M. (2000). Prenatal drug exposure and social policy: The search for an appropriate response. *Maltreatment, 5*(2), 93–108.

O'Neil, J. (1994–1995). Can inclusion work? A conversation with Jim Kauffman and Mara Sapon-Shevin. *Educational Leadership, 52*(4), 7–11.

Ordover, E. K., & Boundy, K. B. (1991). *Educational Rights of Children With Disabilities: A Primer for Advocates.* Cambridge, MA: Center for Law and Education.

Orelove, F. P., & Sosbey, D. C. (1987). *Educating children with multiple disabilities.* Baltimore: Paul H. Brookes.

Oro, A. S., & Dixon, S. D. (1987). Perinatal cocaine and methamphetamine exposure: Maternal and neonatal correlates. *Journal of Pediatrics, 111,* 571–578.

Overholser, J. C. (1990). Fetal alcohol syndrome: A review of the disorder. *Journal of Contemporary Psychotherapy, 20*(3), 163–175.

Owens, R. E. (1982). *Program for acquisition of language with the severely impaired.* Washington, DC: Psychological Corporation & Harcourt Brace Jovanovich.

Owens, R. E. (1991). *Language disorders: A functional approach to assessment and intervention.* New York: Merrill/Macmillan.

Owens, R. E., Metz, D. E., & Haas, A. (2000). *Introduction to communication disorders.* Boston: Allyn & Bacon.

Oyler, H. J., Crowe, B. J., & Haas, W. H. (1987). *Speech, language, and hearing disorders: A guide for the teacher.* Boston: Little, Brown.

Paasche, C. L., Gorrill, L., & Strom, B. (2003). *Children with special needs in early childhood settings.* Florence, KY: Thomsen Delmar.

Pader, O. F. (1981). *A guide and handbook for parents of mentally retarded children.* Springfield, IL: Charles C. Thomas.

Palazesi, M. A. (1986). The need for motor development programs for visually impaired preschoolers. *Journal of Visual Impairment and Blindness, 80,* 573–576.

Pappas, D. (1985). *Diagnosis and treatment of hearing impairment in children.* San Diego: College Hill.

Paradis, J. (2005). Grammatical morphology in children learning English as a second language: Implication of similarities with specific language impairments. *Language, Speech, and Hearing Services in Schools, 36*(3), 172–187.

Parker, J. G., & Asher, S. R. (1987). Peer relations and later personal adjustment: Are low-accepted children at risk? *Psychological Bulletin, 102,* 357–389.

Parks, S. (1999). *Inside HELP: Administration and reference manual.* Palo Alto, CA: VORT Corporation.

Parr, J. R., Ward, A., & Inman, S. (2003). Current practice in the management of attention deficit disorder with hyperactivity. *Child Care, Health and Development, 29*(3), 215–218.

Patterson, C. J., Kupersmidt, J. B., & Griesler, P. C. (1990). Children's perception of self and of relationships with others as a function of sociometric status. *Child Development, 61,* 1335–1349.

Patterson, G. R. (1990). *Families: Application of social learning to family life.* Champaign, IL: Research Press.

Paul-Brown, D., & Caperton, C. J. (2001). Inclusive practices for preschool-age children with specific language impairment. In M. J. Guralnick (Ed.), *Early childhood inclusion: Focus on change* (pp. 433–463). Baltimore: Paul H. Brookes.

Pauls, J. A., & Reed, K. L. (2003). *Quick reference to physical therapy* (2nd ed.). Austin, TX: Pro-Ed.

Pavri, S. (2001). Developmental delay or cultural difference? Developing effective child find practices for young children from culturally and linguistically diverse families. *Young Children, 4*(4), 2–9.

Peccei, J. S. (1994). *Child language.* New York: Routledge.

Peck, C. B., Carlson, P., & Helmstetter, E. (1992). Parent and teacher perceptions of outcome for typically developing children enrolled in integrated early childhood programs: A statewide survey. *Journal of Early Intervention, 16*(1), 53–63.

Peck, C. B., Odom, S. L., & Bricker, D. D. (1993). *Integrating young children with disabilities into community programs: Ecological perspectives on research and implementation.* Baltimore: Paul H. Brookes.

Pedlow, R., Sanson, A., Prior, M., & Oberklaid, F. (1993). Stability of maternally reported temperament from infancy to 8 years. *Developmental Psychology, 29*(6), 998–1007.

Peisner-Feinberg, E. S., Burchinal, M., Clifford, R. M., Culkin, M., Howes, C., Kagan, S. L., & Yazejian, N. (2001). The relation of preschool child care quality to children's cognitive and social developmental trajectories through second grade. *Child Development, 72*(5), 1534–1553.

Pellegrino, L. (2002). Cerebral palsy. In M. Batshaw (Ed.), *Children with Disabilities* (5th ed., pp. 443–466). Baltimore: Paul H. Brookes.

Pengra, L. M. (2000). *Your values, my values.* Baltimore: Paul H. Brookes.

Perroncel, C. B. (2000). *Getting kids ready for school in rural America* [Electronic version].

Charleston, WV: Appalachia Regional Educational Laboratory. Retrieved April 28, 2006, from www.ael.org/rel/rural/abstract/perroncel.htm.

Perske, R., Clifton, A., McClean, B. M., & Stein, J. I. (Eds.). (1986). *Mealtimes for persons with severe handicaps*. Baltimore: Paul H. Brookes.

Peters, D., Neisworth, J. T., & Yawkey, T. D. (1985). Early childhood education: From theory to practice. Monterey, CA: Brooks/Cole.

Peterson, N. L. (1991). Interagency collaboration under Part H: The key to comprehensive multidisciplinary, coordinated infant/toddler intervention services. *Journal of Early Intervention, 15,* 89–105.

Petr, C. G., & Barney, D. D. (1993). Reasonable efforts for children with disabilities: The parents' perspective. *Social Work, 38,* 247–254.

Piaget, J. (1950). *The psychology of intelligence.* New York: International Universities Press.

Piaget, J. (1952). *The origins of intelligence in children.* New York: International Universities Press.

Piaget, J. (1965). *The moral judgment of the child.* New York: Free Press.

Piaget, J. (1971). *Biology and knowledge: An essay on the relation between organic regulation and cognitive process.* Chicago: University of Chicago Press.

Piaget, J. (1980). *Adaptation and intelligence.* London: University of Chicago Press.

Pianta, R. C., Cox, M. J., Taylor, L., & Early, D. (1999). Kindergarten teachers' practices related to the transition to school: Results of a national survey. *The Elementary School Journal, 100*(1), 71–86.

Pianta, R. C., & Kraft-Sayre, M. (2003). *Successful kindergarten transition: Your guide to connecting children, families, and schools.* Baltimore: Paul H. Brookes.

Pianta, R. C., Rimm-Kaufman, S., & Cox, M. J. (1999). An ecological approach to conceptualizing the transition to kindergarten. In R. Pianta & M. J. Cox (Eds.), *The transition to kindergarten* (pp. 3–12). New York: Brooks/Cole.

Pickett, A. L., & Gerlach, K. (2003). *Supervising paraeducators in education settings: A team approach* (2nd ed.). Austin, TX: Pro-Ed.

Pickett, A. L., Gerlach, K., Morgan, R. L., Likens, M., & Wallace, T. L. (2007). *Paraeducators in schools: Strengthening the education team.* Austin, TX: Pro-Ed.

Pickstone, C., Hannon, P., & Fox, L. (2002). Surveying and screening preschool language development in community-focused intervention programs: A review of instruments. *Child Care, Health and Development, 28*(3), 251–264.

Pintrich, P. R. (2000). The role of goal orientation in self-regulated learning. In M. Boekaerts, P. R. Pintrich, & M. Zeidner (Eds.), *Handbook of self-regulation.* San Diego: Academic Press.

Piotrkowski, C. S. (2004). A community-based approach to school readiness in Head Start. In E. Zigler & S. Styfcoe (Eds.), *The Head Start debates* (pp. 129–142). New Haven, CT: Yale University Press.

Piotrokowski, C. S., Botsko, M., & Matthews, E. (2000). Parents' and teachers' beliefs about children's school readiness in a high-need community. *Early Childhood Research Quarterly, 15*(4), 537–558.

Plomin, R. (1989). Environment and genes: Determinants of behavior. *American Psychologist, 44,* 105–111.

Plomin, R., & McClearn, G. E. (Eds.). (1993). *Nature, nurture and psychology.* Washington, DC: American Psychological Association.

Polloway, E. A. (1997). Developmental principles of the Luckasson et al. AAMR definition: A retrospective. *Education and Training in Mental Retardation and Developmental Disabilities, 32,* 174–178.

Polloway, E. A., & Patton, J. R. (1993). *Strategies for teaching learners with special needs* (5th ed.). New York: Merrill.

Polloway, E. A., & Smith, J. D. (2001). Biological sources of mental retardation and efforts for prevention. In M. Beirne-Smith, R. F. Ittenbach, & J. R. Patton (Eds.), *Mental retardation* (6th ed., pp. 150–195). Upper Saddle River, NJ: Merrill/Prentice-Hall.

Popple, P. R., & Leighninger, L. (1993). *Social work, social welfare, and American society* (2nd ed.). Boston: Allyn & Bacon.

Porter, L. (2003). *Young children's behavior: Practical approaches for caregivers and teachers* (2nd ed.). Baltimore: Paul H. Brookes.

Powell, A. (1991). Be responsive. In Brickman, M., & Taylor, L. (Eds.), *Supporting young learners:*

Ideas for preschool and day care providers. Ypsilanti, MI: High Scope Press.

Powers, M. D. (2000). What is autism? In M. D. Powers (Ed.), *Children with autism: A parents' guide* (2nd ed., pp. 1–44). Bethesda, MD: Woodbine House.

Prakash, N., West, J., & Denton, K. (2003). *Schools' Use of Assessments for Kindergarten Entrance and Placement: 1998–99* (NCES 2003–2004). U.S. Department of Education. Washington, DC: National Center for Education Statistics.

Pratt, P. N., & Allen, A. S. (1989). *Occupational therapy for children* (2nd ed.). St. Louis: C. V. Mosby.

Progrund, R. L., Frazzi, D. I., & Schreier, F. M. (1993). Development of a preschool "kiddy lane." *Journal of Visual Impairment and Blindness, 86,* 52–54.

Pruett, K. D. (1999). *Me, myself and I: How children build their sense of self.* New York: Goddard.

Pueschel, S. M. (Ed.). (2001). *A parent's guide to Down syndrome: Toward a brighter future* (2nd ed.). Baltimore: Paul H. Brookes.

Pulliam, J. D., & Patten, J. J. (2006). *History of education in America* (9th ed.). Upper Saddle River, NJ: Prentice-Hall.

Pulsifer, M. B., Radonovich, K., Belcher, H. M. E., & Butz, A. M. (2004). Intelligence and school readiness in preschool children with prenatal drug exposure. *Child Neuropsychology, 10*(2), 89–101.

Pushaw, D. (1976). *Teach your child to talk.* New York: CEBCO Standard Publishing.

Quay, H. C., & Werry, J. S. (1986). Conduct disorders. In H. C. Quay & J. S. Werry (Eds.), *Psychopathological disorders of childhood* (pp. 89–115). New York: John Wiley.

Quigley, S. P., & Paul, P. V. (1990). *Language and deafness.* San Diego: Singular Publishing.

Quigney, T., & Struder, J. (1999). Transition, students with special needs, and the professional school counselor. *Guidance and Counseling, 15*(1), 8–12.

Ramey, C., Campbell, F., & Blair, C. (1998). Enhancing the life course for high-risk children. In J. Crane (Ed.), *Social programs that work* (pp. 184–199). New York: Russell Sage Foundation.

Ramey, C. T., & Ramey, S. L. (1999). Beginning school for children at risk. In *The Transition to Kindergarten.* Baltimore, MD: Paul H. Brookes.

Ramey, S. L., Ramey, C. T., & Lanzi, R. G. (2004). The transition to school: Building on preschool foundations and preparing for lifelong learning. In E. Zigler & S. J. Styfco (Eds.), *The Head Start debates* (pp. 397–413). Baltimore, MD: Paul H. Brookes.

Ratcliff, N. (2001). Use the environment to prevent discipline problems and support learning. *Young Children, 56*(5), 84–87.

Rescorla, L., & Goossens, M. (1992). Symbolic play development in toddlers with expressive specific language impairment (SLI-E). *Journal of Speech and Hearing Research, 12,* 1292–1298.

Resnick, R. J. (2000). *The hidden disorder: A clinician's guide to attention deficit hyperactivity disorder in adults.* Washington, DC: American Psychological Association.

Reynolds, A. (1998a). Extended early childhood intervention and school achievement: Age thirteen findings from the Chicago longitudinal study. *Child Development, 69*(1), 231–246.

Reynolds, A. (1998b). Developing early childhood programs for children and families at risk: Research based principles to promote long-term effectiveness. *Children and Youth Services Review, 20*(6), 503–523.

Reynolds, A. (2000). *Success in early intervention: The Chicago Child-Parent Centers.* Lincoln: University of Nebraska.

Reynolds, A., Chang, H., & Temple, J. A. (1998). Early educational intervention and juvenile delinquency: An exploratory analysis. *Evaluation Review, 22,* 341–372.

Reynolds, A. J., & Temple, J. A. (1998). Extended early childhood intervention and school achievement: Age 13 findings from the Chicago Longitudinal Study. *Child Development, 69,* 231–246.

Reznick, J. S., & Goldfield, B. A. (1992). Rapid change in lexical development in comprehension and production. *Developmental Psychology, 28,* 406–413.

Richardson, G. A. (1998). Prenatal cocaine exposure: A longitudinal study of development. *Annals of the New York Academy of Sciences, 846,* 144–152.

Richman, N., Stevenson, J., & Graham, J. J. (1982). *Preschool to school: A behavioral study.* London: Academic Press.

Ries, L. A. G., Smith, M. A., Gurney, J. G., Linet, M., Tamra, T., Young, J. L., & Bunin, G. R. (Eds.). (1999). *Cancer incidence and survival among children and adolescents: United States SEER program 1975–1995,* Bethesda, MD: SEER Program, National Cancer Institute.

Rimm-Kaufman, S. E., Early, D., Cox, M., Saluja, G., Pianta, R., Bradley, R., & Payne, C. C. (2002). Early behavioral attributes and teachers' sensitivity as predictors of competent behavior in the kindergarten classroom. *Journal of Applied Developmental Psychology, 23,* 451–470.

Rimm-Kaufman, S. E., & Pianta, R. C. (2000). An ecological perspective on children's transition to kindergarten: A theoretical framework to guide empirical research. *Journal of Applied Developmental Psychology, 21,* 491–511.

Rimm-Kaufman, S. E., & Pianta, R. C. (2005). Family–school communication in preschool and kindergarten in the context of a relationship-enhancing intervention. *Early Education and Development, 16*(3), 287–316.

Rimm-Kaufman, S. E., Pianta, R. C., & Cox, M. (2000). Teachers' judgments of problems in the transition to school. *Early Childhood Research Quarterly, 15,* 147–166.

Rimm-Kauffman, S. E., Voorhees, M. D., Snell, M. E., & LaParo, K. M. (2003). Improving preservice teachers' sensitivity and responsivity toward young children with disabilities. *Topics in Early Childhood Special Education, 23,* 151–163.

Roberts, C. S., Severinsen, C., Kuehn, C., Straker, D., & Fritz, C. J. (1992). Obstacles to effective case management with AIDS patients: The clinician's perspective. *Social Work Health Care, 17*(2), 27–40.

Roberts, J. E., Babinowitch, S., Bryant, P. M., Burchinal, M. R., Koch, M. A., & Ramey, C. T. (1989). Language skills of children with different preschool experiences. *Journal of Speech and Hearing Research, 32,* 773–786.

Robinson, R. O. (1973). The frequency of other handicaps in children with cerebral palsy. *Developmental Medicine and Child Neurology, 15,* 305–312.

Rogers, A. (1991). Settings for active learning. In M. Brickman & L. Taylor (Eds.), *Supporting young learners: Ideas for preschool and daycare providers.* Ypsilanti, MI: High Scope Press.

Rogers, C. S., & Sawyers, J. K. (1988). *Play in the lives of children.* Washington, DC: National Association for the Education of Young Children.

Rogers, S. J. (1982). Assessment considerations with the motor-handicapped child. In G. Ulrey & S. Rogers (Eds.), *Psychological assessment of handicapped infants and young children.* New York: Thieme-Stratton.

Rogers, S. J., & DeLalla, D. (1991). A comparative study of the effects of a developmentally based instructional model on young children with autism and young children with other disorders of behavior and development. *Topics in Early Childhood Special Education, 11*(2), 29–47.

Rogoff, B., & Morelli, G. (1989). Perspectives on children's development from cultural psychology. *American Psychologist, 44*(2), 334–348.

Rolland, J. S. (1994). *Families, illness, and disability.* New York: Basic Books.

Root, R. W., & Resnick, R. J. (2003). An update on the diagnosis and treatment of attention-deficit/hyperactivity disorder in children. *Professional Psychology: Research and Practice, 34*(1), 34–41.

Roseberry-McKibbin, C., & Hegde, M. N. (2000). *An advanced review of speech-language pathology.* Austin, TX: Pro-Ed.

Rosenberg, M. S., O'Shea, L. J., & O'Shea, D. J. (1991). *Student teacher to master teacher: A handbook of preservice and beginning teachers of students with mild and moderate handicaps.* New York: Macmillan,

Rosenberg, M. S., Wilson, R., Maheady, L., & Sindelar, P. (1992). *Educating students with behavior disorders.* Boston: Allyn & Bacon.

Rosenkoetter, S. E., & Shotts, C. (1992). *Bridging early services: Interagency transition planning.* McPherson, KS: Bridging Early Services Transition Project, Associated Colleges of Central Kansas.

Rosetti, L. (1990). *The Rosetti infant-toddler language scale.* East Moline, IL: LinguiSystems.

Roskos, K., & Christie, J. F. (Eds.). (2000). *Play and literacy in early childhood: Research from multiple perspectives.* Mahwah, NJ: Lawrence Erlbaum Associates.

Ross, M. (1981). Classroom amplification. In W. R. Hodgson & R. H. Skinna (Eds.), *Hearing aid assessment and use in audiologic habilitation* (2nd ed., pp. 234–257). Baltimore: Williams & Wilkins.

Ross, M. (1982). *Hard of hearing children in regular schools.* Englewood Cliffs, NJ: Prentice-Hall.

Ross, R. H., & Roberts-Pacchione, B. (2007). *Wanna play: Friendship skills for preschool and elementary grades.* Thousand Oaks, CA: Corwin.

Ross-Allen, J., & Conn-Powers, M. (1991). *TEEM: A manual to support the transition of young children with disabilities and their families from preschool into kindergarten and other regular education environments.* Burlington: Center for Developmental Disabilities, University of Vermont.

Roth, E. F. (1992). The nature of AIDS and babies. *Child and Adolescent Social Work Journal, 9*(5), 373–379.

Rothbart, M. K., & Jones, L. B. (1998). Temperament, self-regulation, and education. *School Psychology Review, 27,* 479–491.

Roulstone, S., Peters, T. J., Glogowska, M., & Enderby, P. A. (2003). Twelve-month follow-up of preschool children investigating the natural history of speech and language delay. *Child: Care, Health & Development, 29*(4), 245–255.

Rouse, C., Brooks-Gunn, J., & McLanahan, S. (Eds.). School readiness: Closing racial and ethnic gaps. *Future of Children, 15*(1). Washington DC: Brookings Press.

Rubin, J. A. (1984). *Child art therapy* (2nd ed.). New York: Van Nostrand Reinhold.

Rubin, K. H. (1977). Play behaviors of young children. *Young Children, 32,* 16–24.

Rubinstein, A. (1986). Pediatric AIDS. *Current Problems in Pediatrics, 16,* 363–409.

Rudigier, A., Crocker, A. C., & Cohen, H. J. (1990). The dilemmas of childhood HIV infection. *Child Today, 19*(4), 26–29.

Rule, S., Fiechtl, B. J., & Innocenti, M. S. (1990). Preparation for transition to mainstreamed post-preschool environments: Development of a survival skills curriculum. *Topics in Early Childhood Education, 9,* 78–90.

Rury, J. R. (2002). *Education and social change: Themes in the history of American schooling.* Mahwah, NJ: Lawrence Erlbaum Associates.

Rushton, C. H., Chapman, K., Hogue, E. E., Greenberg-Friedman, D., Billett, C. A., Joyner, M., & Park, C. D. (1993). End of life care for infants with AIDS: Ethical and legal issues. *Pediatric Nursing, 19*(1), 79–83.

Russman, B. S., & Gage, J. R. (1989). Cerebral palsy. *Current Problems in Pediatrics, 19,* 65–111.

Saarni, C. (1984). An observational study of children's attempts to monitor their expressive behavior. *Child Development, 55*(4), 1504–1513.

Saarni, C. (1985). Indirect processes in affect socialization. In M. Lewis & C. Saarni (Eds.), *The socialization of emotions* (pp. 187–209). New York: Plenum.

Saarni, C., & Crowley, M. (1990). The development of emotion regulation: Effects on emotional state and expression. In E. A. Blechman (Ed.), *Emotions and the family: For better or for worse* (pp. 53–73). Hillsdale, NJ: Lawrence Erlbaum Associates.

Sackes, S. Z., & Silberman, R. K. (1998). *Educating students who have visual impairments with other disabilities.* Baltimore: Paul H. Brookes.

Safford, P. L., & Safford, E. J. (Eds.) (2005). *Children with disabilities in America: A historical handbook and guide.* Westport, CT: Greenwood.

Safran, S. P., & Safran, J. S. (1996). Intervention assessment program and pre-referrential teams: Directions for the twenty-first century. *Remedial and Special Education, 17,* 363–369.

Sainato, D. M., & Carta, J. J. (1992). Classroom influences on the development of social competence in young children with disabilities. In S. L. Odom, S. R. McConnell, & M. A. McEvoy (Eds.), *Social competence of young children with disabilities: Issues and strategies for intervention* (pp. 93–109). Baltimore: Paul H. Brookes.

Sainato, D. M., & Strain, P. S. (1993). Increasing integration success for preschoolers with disabilities. *Teaching Exceptional Children, 25*(2), 36–37.

Salant, E. G. (1975). Preventive art therapy with a preschool child. *American Journal of Art Therapy, 14*(3), 67–74.

Salisbury, C. L., & Vincent, L. J. (1990). Criterion of the next environment and best practice: Mainstreaming and integration 10 years later.

Topics in Early Childhood Special Education, 10(2), 78–89.

Saluja, G., Scott-Little, C., & Clifford, R. M. (2000). Readiness for school: A survey of state policies and definitions. *Early Childhood Research and Practice, 2*(2) [Electronic version]. Retrieved November 11, 2006, from http://ecrp.uiuc.edu/v2n2/Saluja.html.

Salvia, J., & Ysseldyke, J. E. (1998). *Assessment* (8th ed.). Boston: Houghton Mifflin.

Sameroff, A. J., Seifer, R., & Zax, M. (1982). Early development of children at risk for emotional disorders. *Monographs of the Society for Research in Child Development, 47*(199), 64–79.

Samuelsson, I. P., & Johansson, E. (2006). Play and learning—inseparable dimensions in preschool practice. *Early Child Development and Care, 176,* 47–65.

Sandall, S., & Ostrosky, M. (Eds.). (1999). *Practical ideas for addressing challenging behaviors.* Longmont, CO: Sopris West.

Sander, S. W. (2002). *Active for life: Developmentally appropriate movement programs for young children.* Washington, DC: National Association for the Education of Young Children.

Saranson, S. B. (1990). *The predictable failure of educational reform: Can we change course before it's too late?* San Francisco, CA: Jossey-Bass.

Sattler, J. M. (2001). *Assessment of children: Behavioral and clinical applications* (4th ed.). Lutz, FL: Psychological Assessment Resources.

Sattler, J. M., & Hoge, R. D. (2006). *Assessment of children: Behavioral, social, and clinical foundations* (5th ed.). Austin, TX: Pro-Ed.

Savage, R. C., & Wolcott, G. F. (Eds.). (1994). *Educational dimensions of acquired brain injury.* Austin, TX: Pro-Ed.

Sawyers, J. K., & Rogers, C. S. (1988). *Helping young children develop through play.* Washington, DC: National Association for the Education of Young Children.

Scarr, S., & Kidd, K. K. (1983). Developmental behavior genetics. In M. M. Haith & J. J. Campos (Eds.), *Handbook of Child Psychology* (Vol. 2: *Infancy and developmental psychobiology*) (5th ed., pp. 345–433). New York: Wiley.

Scarr-Salapatek, S., & Williams, M. L. (1993). The effects of early stimulation on low birthweight infants. *Child Development, 33,* 94–101.

Schaefer, C. E., & Millman, H. L. (1981). *How to help children with common problems.* New York: Van Nostrand Reinhold.

Scherer, P. (1991). How AIDS attacks the brain. *American Journal of Nursing, 4,* 44–53.

Scherling, D. (1994). Prenatal cocaine exposure and childhood psychopathology. *American Journal of Orthopsychiatry, 64,* 9–19.

Schildroth, A. N., & Hotto, S. A. (1991). Hearing-impaired children under age 6: Data from the annual survey of hearing-impaired children and youth. *American Annals of the Deaf, 137*(7), 168–175.

Schildroth, A. N., Rawlings, B. W., & Allen, T. E. (1989). Hearing-impaired children under age 6: A demographic analysis. *American Annals of the Deaf, 134*(2), 63–69.

Schleickorn, J. (1993). *Coping with cerebral palsy: Answers to questions parents often ask* (3rd ed.). Austin, TX: Pro-Ed.

Schlosser, R. W., & Lloyd, L. L. (1991). Augmentative and alternative communication: An evolving field. *Augmentative and Alternative Communication, 7,* 154–160.

Schneider, W., & Pressley, M. (1989). *Memory development between 2 and 20.* New York: Springer-Verlag.

Schorr, L., & Yankelovich, D. (2000, February 16). What works to better society can't be easily measured. *Los Angeles Times,* p. B7.

Schwartz, S. (Ed.). (1987). *Choices in deafness: A parents' guide.* Kensington, MD: Woodbine House.

Schweinhart, L. J., Montie, J., Xiang, Z., Barnett, W. S., Belfield, C. R., & Nores, M. (2005). *Lifetime effects: The High/Scope Perry Preschool study through age 40.* Ypsilanti, MI: High/Scope Press.

Schweinhart, L. J., & Weikart, D. P. (1980). *Young children grow up: The effects of the Perry Preschool Program on youths through age 19.* Ypsilanti, MI: High/Scope Educational Research Foundation.

Scott, K. G., Hollomon, H. A., Claussen, A. H., & Katz, L. F. (1998). Conceptualizing early intervention from a public health perspective. *Infants and Young Children, 11*(1), 37–48.

Scott-Little, C., Kagan, S. L., & Clifford, R. M. (2003). *Assessing the state of state assessments: Perspectives on assessing young children.* Greensboro, NC: SERVE.

Seaman, J. A., & Depauw, K. P. (1989). *The new adapted physical education: A developmental approach*. Mountain View, CA: Mayfield.

Seligman, M., & Darling, R. B. (1989). *Ordinary families, special children: A systems approach to childhood disabilities*. New York: Guilford.

Selman, R. L. (1980). *The growth of interpersonal understanding*. New York: Academic Press.

Serna, L., Nielsen, E., Lambros, K., & Forness, S. (2000). Primary prevention with children at risk for emotional or behavioral disorders: Data on a universal intervention for Head Start classrooms. *Behavioral Disorders, 26*(1), 70–84.

Shackelford, J. (1998). *State and jurisdictional eligibility definitions for infants and toddlers with disabilities under IDEA*. Chapel Hill, NC: Frank Porter Graham Child Development Institute, University of North Carolina at Chapel Hill.

Shames, G. H., Wiig, E. H., & Secord, W. A. (1994). *Human communication disorders: An introduction* (4th ed.). New York: Merrill.

Shanker, A. (1994). Full inclusion is neither free nor appropriate. *Educational Leadership, 52*(4), 18–21.

Shapiro, E. S., & Kratochwill, T. R. (Eds.) (2000). *Conducting school-based assessments of child and adolescent behavior*. New York: Guilford.

Shapiro, J., Blacher, J., & Lopez, S. R. (1998). Maternal reactions to children with mental retardation. In J. A. Burack, R. M. Hodapp, & E. Zigler (Eds.), *Handbook of mental retardation and development* (pp. 606–636). Cambridge: Cambridge University Press.

Shaw, D., Bell, R., & Gilliom, M. (2000). A truly early start model of antisocial behavior revisited. *Clinical Child and Family Psychology Review, 3*(3), 155–172.

Shea, T. M., & Bauer, A. M. (1991). *Parents and teachers of children with exceptionalities: A handbook for collaboration* (2nd ed.). Boston: Allyn & Bacon.

Sheehan, R. (1988). Involvement of parents in early childhood assessment. In R. D. Wachs & R. Sheehan (Eds.), *Assessment of young developmentally disabled children*. (pp. 75–90). New York: Plenum.

Shelton, T., Barkley, R., Crosswait, C., Moorehouse, M., Fletcher, K., Barrett, S., et al. (2000).

Multimethod psychoeducational intervention for preschool children with disruptive behavior: Two-year post-treatment follow-up. *Journal of Abnormal Child Psychology, 28*(3), 253–266.

Shepard, L., Kagan, S. L., & Wurtz, E. (1998). *Principles and recommendations for early childhood assessments*. Washington, DC: National Archives.

Shepard, L. A., & Smith, M. L. (1988). Flunking kindergarten: Escalating curriculum leaves many behind. *American Educator, 2*(3), 33–38.

Sherburne, S., Utley, B., McConnell, S. R., & Gannon, J. (1988). Decreasing violent and aggressive theme play among preschool children with behavior disorders. *Exceptional Children, 55,* 166–172.

Shields, C. V. (1987). *Strategies: A practical guide for dealing with professionals and human service systems*. Baltimore: Paul H. Brookes.

Shonkoff, J., & Phillips, D. (2000). *From neurons to neighborhoods: The science of early childhood development*. Washington, DC: National Academy Press.

Shore, R. 1998. *Ready schools resource group*. Washington, DC: National Education Goals Panel.

Siegel, D. J. (1999). *The developing mind*. New York: Guilford Press.

Siegel, L. M. (2004). *The complete IEP guide: How to advocate for your special education child* (3rd ed.). Berkeley, CA: NOLO.

Simeonsson, R. J., Huntington, G. S., McMillen, J. S., Dodds, A. H., Halperin, D., Zipper, I. N., et al. (1996). Evaluating services for young children and families: Documenting intervention cycles. *Infants and Young Children, 9,* 1–13.

Singer, L. T., Arendt, R., Minnes, S., Farkas, K., Salvator, A., Kirchner, H. L., & Kliegman, R. (2002). Cognitive and motor outcomes of cocaine-exposed infants. *Journal of the American Medical Association, 287*(15), 1952–1960.

Skeels, H. M., & Dye, H. B. (1939). *A study of the effects of differential stimulation on mentally retarded children*. Proceedings: American Association on Mental Deficiency, 44, 114–136.

Skinner, B. F. (1957). *Syntactic structures*. The Hague: Monton.

Slentz, K. L., & Bricker, D. (1992). Family-guided assessment for IFSP development: Jumping off the family assessment bandwagon. *Journal of Early Intervention, 16,* 11–19.

Smilansky, S., & Shefatya, L. (1990). *Facilitating play: A medium for promoting cognitive, social-emotional, and academic development in young children.* Gaithersburg, MD: Psychological and Educational Publications.

Smith, B. J. (1988). *Does early intervention help?* ERIC Digest #455. Retrieved February 1, 2007, from www.ericdigests.org/pre-928/help.htm

Smith, D. D., & Luckasson, R. (1995). *Introduction to special education: Teaching in an age of challenge* (2nd ed.). Boston: Allyn & Bacon.

Smith, D. D., & Rivera, D. (1993). *Effective discipline* (2nd ed.). Austin, TX: Pro-Ed.

Smith, J. C. (1992). Parenting seriously disturbed children. *Social Work, 37,* 293–294.

Smith, T., Finn, D., & Dowdy, C. (1993). *Teaching students with mild disabilities.* Fort Worth, TX: Harcourt Brace Jovanovich.

Snell, M. E. (Ed.). (1987). *Systematic instruction of persons with severe handicaps* (3rd ed.). Columbus, OH: Merrill.

Snow, C. E., & Páez, M. (2004). The Head Start Classroom as an oral language environment: What should the performance standards be? In E. Zigler & S. Styfco (Eds.), *The Head Start debates: Friendly and otherwise* (pp. 215–244). Baltimore, MD: Paul H. Brookes.

Snow, J. H., & Hooper, S. R. (1994). *Pediatric traumatic brain injury.* Thousand Oaks, CA: Sage.

Sokol, R. J., Delaney-Black, V., & Nordstrom B. (2003). Fetal alcohol spectrum disorder. *Journal of the American Medical Association, 290,* 2996–2999.

Sood, B., Delaney-Black, V., Covington, C., Nordstrom-Klee, B., Ager, J., Templin, T., et al. (2001). Prenatal alcohol exposure and childhood behavior at age 6 to 7 years, I: Dose-response effect. *Pediatrics, 108*(2), 34–38.

Sparrow, S. S., Balla, D. A., & Cicchetti, D. V. (1998). *Vineland social-emotional early childhood scale.* Circle Pines, MN: American Guidance Service.

Speltz, M., DeKlyen, M., & Greenberg, M. (1999). Attachment in boys with early onset conduct problems. *Development and Psychopathology, 11*(2), 269–285.

Spinelli, C. G. (2004). Dealing with cancer in the classroom: The teacher's role and responsibilities. *Teaching Exceptional Children, 36,* 14–21.

Spitz, R. A. (1965). *The first year of life.* New York: International University Press.

Squires, J. K. (2000). Identifying social/emotional and behavioral problems in infants and toddlers. *Infant-Toddler Intervention, 10*(2), 107–119.

Stephens, P., & Rous, B. (1992). *Facilitation packet for the development of a system for the transition of young children and families.* Lexington, KY: Child Development Centers of the Bluegrass.

Stern, F. M., & Gorga, D. G. (1990). Neurodevelopmental treatment (NDT): Therapeutic intervention and it efficacy. *Infants and Young Children, 1*(1), 22–32.

Stewart, D. A. (1990). Rationale and strategies for American Sign Language intervention. *American Annals of the Deaf, 135*(3), 205–210.

Stewart, D. A., & Kluwin, T. N. (2001). *Teaching deaf and hard of hearing students.* Boston: Allyn & Bacon.

Stipek, D. (2002). At what age should children enter kindergarten? A question for policy makers and parents. *Society for Research in Child Development Social Policy Report, 16*(2), 3–16.

Stipek, D., & Byler, P. (2001). Academic achievement and social behaviors associated with age of entry into kindergarten. *Journal of Applied Developmental Psychology, 22,* 175–189.

Stipek, D., Gralinski, H., & Kopp, C. B. (1990). Self-concept development in the toddler years. *Developmental Psychology, 26,* 972–977.

Stock, J. R., Wnek, L. L., Newborg, J. A., Schenck, E. A., Gabel, J. R., Spurgeon, M. S., & Ray, H. W. (1976). *Evaluation of the handicapped children's early education program.* Columbus, OH: Battelle Memorial Institute.

Stodolsky, S. S. (1974). How children find something to do in preschools. *Genetic Psychology Monographs, 90,* 245–303.

Stoel-Gammon, C. (1991). Issues in phonological development and disorders. In J. F. Miller (Ed.), *Research on child language disorders: A decade of progress* (pp. 255–265). Austin, TX: Pro-Ed.

Stoel-Gammon, C., & Otomo, K. (1986). Babbling development of hearing-impaired and normally hearing subjects. *Journal of Speech and Hearing Disorders, 51,* 33–41.

Stoler, J. M., & Holmes, L. B. (2004). Recognition of facial features of fetal alcohol syndrome in the newborn. *American Journal of Medical Genetics, 127,* 21–27.

Strain, P. S., Kohler, F. W., Storey, K., & Danko, C. D. (1994). Teaching preschoolers with autism to self-monitor their social interactions: An analysis of results in home and school settings. *Journal of Emotional & Behavioral Disorders, 2,* 78–88.

Strain, P. S., McConnell, S. R., Carta, J. J., Fowler, S. A., Neisworth, J. T., & Wolery, M. (1992). Behaviorism in early intervention. *Topics in Early Childhood Special Education, 12*(1), 121–141.

Strayer, J. (1986). Children's attributions regarding the situational determinants of emotion in self and others. *Developmental Psychology, 22*(5), 649–654.

Streissguth, A. P., Clarren, S. K., & Jones, K. (1985). Natural history of the fetal alcohol syndrome: A 10-year follow-up of eleven patients. *Lancet, 2,* 85–91.

Summers, J. A., Dell'Oliver, C., Turnbull, A. P., Benson, H. A., Santelli, E., Campbell, M., & Siegel-Causey, E. (1990). Examining the individualized family service plan process: What are family and practitioner preferences? *Topics in Early Childhood Education, 10*(1), 78–99.

Swanson, J. (2000). *Infant & toddler health sourcebook: Basic consumer health information about the physical and mental development of newborns, infants, and toddlers.* San Diego: Omnigraphics.

Tabassam, W., & Grainger, J. (2002). Self-concept, attributional style, and self-efficacy beliefs of students with learning disabilities with and without ADHD. *Learning Disabilities Quarterly, 25,* 141–151.

Tabors, P. (1997). *One child, two languages: A guide for early childhood educators of children learning English as a second language.* Baltimore: Paul H. Brookes.

Tannock, R., & Girolametto, L. E. (1992). Reassessing parent-focused language intervention programs. In S. Warren & J. Reichle (Eds.), *Communication and language intervention: Vol. 1. Causes and effects in communication and language intervention* (pp. 49–79). Baltimore: Paul H. Brookes.

Tansley, A. E. (1986). *Motor education.* Tucson, AZ: Communication and Therapy Skill Builders.

Task Force on Newborn and Infant Hearing. (1999). Newborn and infant hearing loss: Detection and intervention. *Pediatrics, 103*(2), 527–530.

Task Force on Pediatric AIDS, American Psychological Association (1989). Pediatric AIDS and human immunodeficiency virus infections. *American Psychologist, 5,* 258–264.

Teplin, S. W. (1995). Visual impairment in infants and young children. *Infants and Young Children, 8*(1), 18–51.

Thelen, E. (1989). The (re)discovery of motor development: Learning new things from an old field. *Developmental Psychology, 25,* 946–949.

Thelen, E., & Adolph, K. E. (1992). Arnold L. Gesell: The paradox of nature and nurture. *Developmental Psychology, 28,* 368–380.

Theler, E., & Ulrich, B. D. (1991). Hidden skills. *Monograph of the Society for Research in Child Development, 56*(1, Serial No. 223).

Thiele, J., & Hamilton, J. (1991). Implementing the early childhood formula: Programs under P.L. 99–457. *Journal of Early Intervention, 15*(1), 5–12.

Thomas, D. G., Whitaker, E., Crow, C. D., Little, V., Love, L., Lykins, M. S., & Letterman, M. (1997). Event-related potential variability as a measure of information storage in infant development. *Developmental Neuropsychology, 13,* 205–232.

Thomas, J., & Clark, R. (1998). Disruptive behavior in the very young child: *Diagnostic classification: 0–3* guides identification of risk factors and relational intervention. *Infant Mental Health Journal, 19*(2), 229–244.

Thomas, R. M. (1990). Basic concepts and applications of Piagetian cognitive development theory. In R. M. Thomas (Ed.), *The encyclopedia of human development and education: Theory, research, and studies* (pp. 53–55). Oxford, UK: Pergamon.

Thompson, A. (1990). On emotion and self-regulation. In R. A. Thompson (Ed.), *Nebraska Symposia on Motivation* (Vol. 26, pp. 383–483). Lincoln: University of Nebraska Press.

Thompson, G. H., Rubin, I. L., & Bilenker, R. M. (1983). *Comprehensive management of cerebral palsy.* Orlando, FL: Grune & Stratton.

Thompson, L., & Kaufman, L. M. (2003). The visually impaired child. *Pediatric Clinics North America, 50*(1), 225–239.

Thurman, S. K., & Widerstrom, A. H. (1990). *Infants and young children with special needs.* Baltimore: Paul H. Brookes.

Tincani, M. (2004). Comparing the picture exchange communication system and sign language training for children with autism. *Focus on Autism and Other Developmental Disabilities, 19*(3), 152–163.

Tingey-Michaelis, C. (1983). *Handicapped infants and children: A handbook for parents and professionals.* Baltimore: University Park Press.

Tizard, B., Mortimore, J., & Burchell, B. (1988). *Involving parents in nursery and infant school.* Ypsilanti, MI: High Scope.

Tokarski, C. (1990, April). Higher costs of pediatric AIDS care documented. *Modern Health Care, 20*(16), 18.

Tomlin, A. M., & Viehweg, S. A. (2003). Infant mental health: Making a difference. *Professional Psychology: Research and Practice, 34*(6), 617–625.

Toppelberg, C. O., & Shapiro, T. (2000). Language disorders: A 10-year research update review. *Journal of the American Academy of Child and Adolescent Psychiatry, 39,* 143–152.

Treanor, R. B. (1993). *We overcame: The story of civil rights for disabled people.* Falls Church, VA: Regal Direct Publishing.

Trombly, C. A. (Ed.). (1983). *Occupational therapy for physical dysfunction* (2nd ed.). Baltimore: Williams & Wilkins.

Tronick, E. Z. (1989). Emotions and emotional communication in infants. *American Psychologist, 44*(2), 112–119.

Turiel, E. (1983). *The development of social knowledge: Morality and convention.* New York: Cambridge University Press.

Turnbull, A. P. (1983). Parental participation in the IEP process. In J. A. Mulick & S. M. Pueschel (Eds.), *Parent-professional partnerships in developmental disability services* (pp. 107–122). Cambridge, MA: Ware Press.

Turnbull, A. P., & Turnbull, H. R. (1990). *Families, professionals, and exceptionality: A special partnership* (2nd ed.). Columbus, OH: Merrill.

Turnbull, A. P., Turbiville, V., & Turnbull, H. R. (2000). Evolution of family-professional partnerships: Collective empowerment as the model for the early 21st century. In S. J. Meisels & J. P. Shonkoff (Eds.), *Handbook of early intervention* (2nd ed., pp. 630–650). Cambridge, MA: Cambridge University Press.

Turnbull, H. R., & Turnbull, A. P. (2000). *Free appropriate public education* (6th ed.). Denver: Love Publishing.

Tyler, J. S., & Mira, M. P. (1993). Educational modifications for students with head injuries. *Teaching Exceptional Children, 25,* 24–27.

Uhlin, D. M. (1972). *Art for exceptional children.* Dubuque, IA: William C. Brown.

UNICEF. (2005a). *The state of the world's children 2006: Excluded and invisible.* New York: UNICEF Publications.

UNICEF. (2005b). *A call to action: Children of the missing faces of AIDS.* New York: UNICEF Publications.

U.S. Census Bureau. (2000). Retrieved January 20, 2007, from www.census.gov/main/www/cen2000.html.

U.S. Department of Education. (1997). Nineteenth annual report to Congress on the implementation of the Individuals with Disabilities Education Act. Washington, DC: Author.

U.S. Department of Education. (2000). *Twenty-second annual report to Congress on the implementation of the Individuals with Disabilities Education Act.* Washington, DC: U.S. Government Printing Office.

U.S. Department of Education, National Center for Educational Statistics. (1995). *Digest of education statistics, 1995.* Washington, DC: U.S. Government Printing Office.

U.S. Department of Education, National Center for Educational Statistics. (2002). *Digest of education statistics, 2001.* Washington, DC: U.S. Government Printing Office.

U.S. Department of Education. (2002). *Twenty-fourth annual report to Congress on the implementation of the Individuals with Disabilities Education Act.* Washington, DC: Author.

U.S. Department of Education. (2006). *Twenty-eighth annual report to Congress on the implementation of the Individuals with Disabilities Education Act.* Washington, DC: Author.

U.S. Department of Education, National Center for Education Statistics. (2001). *The Condition of Education, 2001* (NCES 2001–072). Washington, DC: U.S. Government Printing Office.

U.S. Department of Education, National Center for Education Statistics (2003a). *Digest of education statistics, 2002.* (NCES 2003-060). Washington, DC: Author.

U.S. Department of Education, National Center for Education Statistics (2003b). *The condition of education, 2003.* (NCES 2003-067). Washington, DC: Author.

U.S. Department of Labor. (2002). *Demographic characteristics of early childhood teachers and structural elements of early care and education in the United States.* Retrieved January 20, 2007, from http://ecrp.uiuc.edu/v4n1/saluja.html

U.S. Public Health Service. (2000). *Report of the Surgeon General's Conference on Children's Mental Health: A national action agenda.* Washington, DC: Department of Health and Human Services.

Valeski, T. N., & Stipek, D. J. (2001). Young children's feelings about school. *Child Development, 72*(4), 1198–1213.

Vandergriff, D. V., Hester, J. R., & Mandra, D. A. (1987). Composite ratings on the AAMD Adaptive Behavior Scales. *American Journal of Mental Deficiency, 92*(2), 203–206.

van Dyck, P. C., Kogan, M. D., McPherson, M. G., Weissman, G. R., & Newacheck, P. W. (2004). Prevalence and characteristics of children with special health care needs. *Archives of Pediatric and Adolescent Medicine, 158,* 884–890.

VanTasell, D. J., Mallinger, C. A., & Crump, E. S. (1986). Functional gain and speech recognition with two types of FM amplification. *Language, Speech and Hearing Services in Schools, 17,* 28–37.

Vaughn, S., Bos, C., Harrell, J., & Lasky, B. (1988). Parent participation in the initial placement/IEP conference ten years after mandated involvement. *Journal of Learning Disabilities, 21*(2), 82–84.

Vecchiotti, S. (2001). *Kindergarten: The overlooked school year.* (Working Paper Series). New York: Foundation for Child Development.

Vickerius, M., & Sandberg, A. (2006). The significance of play and the environment around play. *Early Child Development and Care, 176,* 207–217.

Vincent, L. J. (1992). Families and early intervention: Diversity and competence. *Journal of Early Intervention, 16,* 166–172.

Vincent, L. J., Salisbury, C. L., Walter, G., Brown, P., Gruenwald, L., & Powers, M. (1980). Program evaluation and curricular development in early childhood/special education: Criteria for the next environment. In W. Sailor, B. Wilcox, & L. Brown (Eds.), *Methods of instruction for severely handicapped students* (pp. 303–328). Baltimore: Paul H. Brookes.

Vondra, J., Shaw, D., Swearingen, L., Cohen, M., & Owens, E. (2001). Attachment stability and emotional and behavioral regulation from infancy to preschool age. *Development and Psychopathology, 13*(1), 13–33.

Vygotsky, L. (1978). *Mind in society: The development of higher psychological processes.* Cambridge, MA: Harvard University Press.

Wachs, T. D. (2000). Nutritional deficits and behavioural development. *International Journal of Behavioral Development, 24,* 435–441.

Wachs, T. D., & Gruen, G. E. (1982). *Early experiences and human development.* New York: Plenum.

Wagonseller, B. R., & McDowell, R. L. (1979). *You and your child: A common sense approach to successful parenting.* Champaign, IL: Research Press.

Walker, H., Kavanaugh, K., Stiller, B., Golly, A., Severson, H., & Feil, E. (1998). First step to success: An early intervention approach for preventing school antisocial behavior. *Journal of Emotional and Behavioral Disorders, 6*(2), 66–80.

Walker, K. F., & Ludwig, F. M. (Eds.). (2004). *Perspectives on theory for the practice of occupational therapy* (3rd ed.). Austin, TX: Pro-Ed.

Waller, M. B. (1993). Helping crack-affected children succeed. *Educational Leadership, 50*(4), 63–66.

Walsh, D. J. (1991). Extending the discourse on developmental appropriateness: A developmental perspective. *Early Education and Development, 2*(2), 109–119.

Walzer, S. (1985). X chromosome abnormalities and cognitive development: Implications for understanding normal human development. *Journal of Child Psychology and Psychiatry, 26*(2), 177–184.

Warren, A. R., & Kaiser, A. P. (1988). Research on early language intervention. In S. L. Odom & M. B. Karnes (Eds.), *Early intervention for infants and children with handicaps* (pp. 80–108). Baltimore: Paul H. Brookes.

Warren, S. F., & Reichle, J. (1992). The emerging field of communication and language intervention. In S. Warren & J. Reichle (Eds.), *Communication and language intervention: Vol. 1: Causes and effects in communication and language intervention* (pp. 1–8). Baltimore: Paul H. Brookes.

Wasik, B. H., Ramey, C. T., Bryant, D. M., & Sparling, J. J. (1990). A longitudinal study of two early intervention strategies: Project CARE. *Child Development, 61*(6), 1682–1696.

Wasserman, S. (1990). *Serious players in the primary grades: Empowering children through active learning experiences.* New York: Teachers College Press.

Watkins, P. J. (2002). *ABC of diabetes.* London: BMJ Publishing Group.

Wayson, W., & Lasley, T. (1984). Climates for excellence: Schools that foster self-discipline. *Phi Delta Kappan, 65,* 419–421.

Wehman, P., McLaughlin, P. J., & Wehman, T. (Eds.). (2005). *Intellectual and developmental disabilities: Toward full community inclusion* (3rd ed.). Austin, TX: Pro-Ed.

Wehmeyer, M. L., Morningstar, M., & Husted, D. (1999). *Family involvement in transition planning and implementation.* Austin, TX: Pro-Ed.

Wehmeyer, M. L., & Patton, J. R. (2000). *Mental retardation in the 21st century.* Austin, TX: Pro-Ed.

Wellman, H. M., Somerville, S. C., & Haake, R. J. (1979). Development of search procedures in real-life spatial environments. *Developmental Psychology, 15,* 530–542.

Wentworth, R. A. L. (1998). *Montessori for the new millennium.* Mahwah, NJ: Lawrence Erlbaum Associates.

Wermer, D. (1987). *Disabled village children: A guide for community health workers, rehabilitation workers, and families.* Palo Alto, CA: Hesperian Foundation.

Wesley, P., & Buysse, V. (2003). Making meaning of school readiness in schools and communities. *Early Childhood Research Quarterly, 18,* 351–175.

Wesson, M. D., & Maino, D. M. (1995). Oculovisual findings in children with Down syndrome, cerebral palsy, and mental retardation without specific etiology. In D. M. Maino (Ed.), *Diagnosis and management of special populations* (pp. 17–54). St. Louis: Mosby Year Book.

West, J., Denton, K., & Germino-Hausken, E. (2000). *America's kindergartners:* (NCES No. 2000-070). Washington, DC: U.S. Department of Education.

West, J., Denton, K., & Germino-Hausken, E. (2000). *America's kindergartners: Findings from the Early Childhood Longitudinal Study, Kindergarten Class of 1998–99, Fall 1998.* Washington, DC: National Center for Education Statistics, U.S. Department of Education.

Westby, C. E. (1980). Language abilities through play. *Language, Speech, and Hearing Services in Schools, 11,* 154–168.

Westby, C. E. (1988). Children's play: Reflections of social competence. *Seminars in Speech and Language, 9*(1), 2–12.

Westling, D. L., & Koorland, M. A. (1989). *The special educator's handbook.* Boston: Allyn & Bacon.

Wetherby, A. M., Allen, L., Cleary, J., Kublin, K., & Goldstein, H. (2002). *Communication and Symbolic Behavior Scales: Developmental profile.* Baltimore: Paul H. Brookes.

Whalen, C. K. (2001). ADHD treatment in the 21st century: Pushing the envelope. *Journal of Clinical Child Psychology, 30,* 136–140.

White, K. R. (1991). *Longitudinal studies of the effects and costs of early intervention for handicapped children. Final report, October 1, 1985– December 31, 1990.* Logan, UT: Utah State University, Early Intervention Research Institute.

Whitman, T. L. (1990). Self-regulation and mental retardation. *American Journal of Mental Deficiency, 94,* 347–362.

Wicks-Nelson, R., & Israel, A. C. (1991). *Behavior disorders of childhood.* Englewood Cliffs, NJ: Prentice-Hall.

Wiener, L., Moss, H., Davidson, R., & Fair, C. (1993). Pediatrics: The emerging psychosocial challenge of the AIDS epidemic. *Child and Adolescent Social Work Journal, 9*(5), 381–407.

Wikler, L., Wasow, M., & Hatfield, E. (1983). Seeking strengths in families of developmentally disabled children. *Exceptional Children, 51*(5), 417–424.

Wilcox, M. J. (1989). Delivering communication-based services to infants, toddlers, and their families: Approaches and models. *Topics in Language Disorders, 10*(1), 68–79.

Wilcox, M. J., Kouri, T. A., & Caswell, S. B. (1991). Early language intervention: A comparison of classroom and individual treatment. *American Journal of Speech-Language Pathology, 1,* 49–62.

Wilfert, A. (Ed.) (1994). *Pediatric AIDS: The challenge of HIV infection in infants, children, and adolescents.* Baltimore: Williams & Wilkins.

Willett, E. (2001). *Hemophilia.* Berkeley Heights, NJ: Enslow Publishers.

Williamson, G. G. (1987). *Children with spina bifida: Early intervention and preschool programming.* Baltimore: Paul H. Brookes.

Willoughby, M., Kupersmidt, J., & Bryant, D. (2001). Overt and covert dimensions of antisocial behavior in early childhood. *Journal of Abnormal Child Psychology, 29*(3), 177–187.

Wilson, M. N. (1989). Child development in the context of the Black extended family. *American Psychologist, 44*(2), 380–385.

Wing, L., & Potter, D. (2002). The epidemiology of autistic spectrum disorders: Is the prevalence rising? *Mental Retardation and Developmental Disabilities Research Reviews, 8,* 151–162.

Wohl, A., & Kaufman, B. (1985). *Silent screams and hidden cries.* New York: Brunner/Mazel.

Wolery, M. (1989). Transitions in early childhood special education: Issues and procedures. *Focus on Exceptional Children, 22,* 1–16.

Wolery, M., & Bredekamp, S. (1994). Developmentally appropriate practices and young children with disabilities: Contextual issues in discussion. *Journal of Early Intervention, 18*(4), 331–341.

Wolery, M., Doyle, P. M., Gast, D. L., Ault, M. J., & Simpson, S. L. (1993). Comparison of progressive time delay and transition-based teaching with preschoolers who have developmental delays. *Journal of Early Intervention, 17*(2), 160–176.

Wolery, M., Holcombe, A., Venn, M., Brookfield, J., Huffman, K., Schroeder, C., et al. (1993). Mainstreaming in early childhood programs: Current status and relevant issues. *Young Children, 49*(1), 78–84.

Wolery, M., Strain, P. S., & Bailey, D. B. (1992). Reaching potentials of children with special needs. In S. Bredekamp & T. Rosegrant (Eds.). *Reaching potentials: Appropriate curricula and assessment for young children* (Vol. 1, pp. 92–111). Washington, DC: National Association for the Education of Young Children.

Wolff, P. (1979). Theoretical issues in the development of motor skills. In L. Taft & M. Lewis (Eds.), *Developmental disabilities in the preschool child.* Symposium presented by Rutgers Medical School, Educational Testing Service, and Johnson & Johnson Baby Products, Chicago.

Wolock, E. (1990). *The relationship of teacher interaction style to the engagement of developmentally delayed preschoolers.* Unpublished doctoral dissertation, University of Michigan, Ann Arbor.

Wood, B. S. (1981). *Children and communication: Verbal and nonverbal language development* (2nd ed.). Englewood Cliffs, NJ: Prentice-Hall.

Wood, D. J., Bruner, J., & Ross, G. (1976). The role of tutoring in problem solving. *Journal of Child Psychology and Psychiatry, 17*(2), 89–100.

Wood, M. E. (1981). Costs of intervention programs. In C. Garland (Ed.), *Early intervention for children with special needs and their families: Findings and recommendations* (Westar Series Paper No. 11). Seattle: University of Washington.

Woody, R. H., Woody, J. D., & Greenberg, D. B. (1991). Case management for the individualized family service plan under Public Law 99–457. *American Journal of Family Therapy, 19,* 67–76.

Wooley, J. D., & Wellman, H. M. (1990). Young children's understanding of realities, nonrealities, and appearances. *Child Development, 61,* 946–961.

Wyckoff, J., & Unell, B. C. (1984). *Discipline without shouting or spanking: Practical solutions to the most common preschool behavior problems.* New York: Meadowbrook Books.

Yoder, P. J., & Warren, S. F. (1993). Can developmentally delayed children's language be enhanced through prelinguistic intervention? In A. P. Kaiser & D. B. Gray (Eds.), *Enhancing children's communication: Research foundations for intervention* (pp. 5–62). Baltimore: Paul H. Brookes.

Ysseldyke, J. E., Algozzine, B., & Thurlow, M. L. (2000). *Critical issues in special education* (3rd ed.). Boston: Houghton Mifflin.

Zahn-Waxler, C., Radke-Yarrow, M., & King, R. M. (1979). Child-rearing and children's prosocial initiations toward victims of distress. *Child Development, 50,* 319–330.

Zaichkowsky, L. D., Zaichkowsky, L. B., & Martinek, T. J. (1980). *Growth and development: The child and physical activity.* St. Louis: C. V. Mosby.

Zeitlin, S. G., Williamson, G., & Szczepanski, M. (1988). *Early Coping Inventory: A measure of adaptive behavior.* Bensenville, IL: Scholastic Testing Service.

Zero to Three. (2005). *Diagnostic classification of mental health and developmental disorders of infancy and early childhood* (Rev. ed.). Washington, DC: Author.

Zevin, D. (1998). *Assessing and fostering the development of a first and a second language in early childhood: Training manual.* Sacramento: California Department of Education.

Zhang, C., & Bennett, T. (2000). The IFSP/IEP process: Do recommended practices address culturally and linguistically diverse families? (CLAS Technical Report #10). Champaign, IL: Early Childhood Research Institute on Culturally and Linguistically Appropriate Services, University of Illinois at Urbana-Champaign.

Zill, N., & West, J. (2001). *Entering kindergarten: A portrait of American children when they begin school: Findings from* The Condition of Education, 2000 (NCES 2001-035). Washington, DC: National Center for Education Statistics, U.S. Department of Education.

Zirpoli, T. J. (2004). *Behavior Management: Applications for teachers* (4th ed.). Upper Saddle River, NJ: Prentice Hall.

Zirpoli, T. J., & Melloy, B. (1993). *Behavior management: Applications for teachers and parents.* Columbus, OH: Merrill.

Zito, J., Safer, D., dosReis, S., Gardner, J., Boles, M., & Lynch, F. (2000). Trends in the prescribing of psychotropic medications to preschoolers. *Journal of the American Medical Association, 283*(8), 1025–1030.

Zuckerman, B., & Bresnahan, K. (1991). Developmental and behavioral consequences of prenatal drug and alcohol exposure. *Pediatric Clinics of North America, 38*(6), 1387–1406.

Zuckerman, B., & Frank, D. A. (1992). Prenatal cocaine and marijuana exposure: Research and clinical implications. In I. S. Zagon & T. A. Slotkin (Eds.), *Maternal substance abuse and the developing nervous system* (pp. 125–154). Boston: Academic Press.

INDEX